0.60

Holiday Which?
Good Walks Guide

D0169825

Holiday Which?
Good
Walks Guide

Edited by Tim Locke

Published by Consumers' Association
and Hodder & Stoughton

Which? Books are commissioned and researched by
The Association for Consumer Research
and published by Consumers' Association,
14 Buckingham Street, London WC2N 6DS and
Hodder & Stoughton,
47 Bedford Square, London WC1B 3DP

Some of the walks in *Holiday Which! Good Walks Guide* were collated and distributed, in the autumn of 1985, to *Holiday Which!* readers who were involved in the early stages of the book's preparation.

Typographic design by Paul Saunders
Cover design by Mon Mohan
Cover photograph, from Fotobank, of Martindale in the Lake District,
close to Walks 131 and 132
Walk maps by Tim Locke. Key maps (pages 543 to 547) by David Perrott Cartographics

British Library Cataloguing in Publication Data
    Holiday which? good walks guide.
    1. Great Britain —— Description and
    travel —— 1971 —— Guide-books
    I. Locke, Tim II. Consumers' Association
    914.1'04858   DA650

    ISBN 0-340-40453-1

Typeset by Gee Graphics Ltd, London and Crayford
Printed and bound in Great Britain by
Hazell, Watson & Viney Limited
Member of the BPCC Group,
Aylesbury, Bucks

CONTENTS

INTRODUCTION

This is a book of good walks. Far from being arbitrary strolls in acceptably pleasant countryside, they are all designed to help the walker get the best out of an area, and they are all walks we would do again. Many routes are, we believe, making their debut in print.

In 1984 we dipped a tentative toe in the mud and asked *Holiday Which?* readers to send in details of their favourite walks – a rough sketch map, a summary of the attractions of the walk and some directions, if possible. Over the next two years we received about two hundred ideas, ranging from very short ambles to full-day mountain expeditions. We then sent draft copies of walks to interested *Holiday Which?* readers, who tried them out. Hundreds of completed questionnaires came back, detailing, in particular, what people thought of the route; suggestions for improvement; obstructed paths; points of interest along the way; problems following the directions. This information was enormously helpful; it gave a good idea of what people expected from a walk and what level of detail to aim for in the directions. It helped us to improve the routes and to shortlist the best.

There were still some large blanks on the map of walks, notably in Scotland, Wales and the South-West of England. And while some readers had been meticulous in checking directions, the prospect of spending a Sunday afternoon taking detailed notes throughout a walk could hardly be appealing to many. So we took the precaution of checking just about all the walks ourselves, and then went on to work out new ones where we needed them. Our thanks to everyone who helped check walks or contributed ideas for new ones. Special thanks go to Stephen Locke for his advice throughout, especially for his walk suggestions, and for checking some of the routes.

What makes a good walk?

When we asked *Holiday Which?* readers to send details of their favourite walks, we set out the following criteria:
All walks must

- be between three and fifteen miles long

- form a sensible round trip, if not on foot then completing it by public transport
- follow recognised public rights of way, permissive paths, or roads.

We've stuck rigorously to these throughout, but we've also found ourselves developing – with the help of checkers from the *Holiday Which?* readership – a kind of philosophy.

The starting-point should be easy to find
We assume readers will have a standard road atlas but not necessarily an Ordnance Survey map and have given road directions where appropriate. We have avoided starting walks on anonymous roadside verges, for instance.

The walk should be organised so that it follows a good sequence
Ideally, a walk should get you into the spirit of things immediately. One example is Walk 50, which starts from the platform at Cowden Station in Kent. When we took the train out of London one bright spring morning, the effect of stepping from the station footbridge straight into a wood full of bluebells was magical.

There should be enough features (natural features, views, interesting buildings and so on) to sustain interest
In particular, one of the climaxes should be near the end – the walk shouldn't play all its trump cards right at the start. Examples are Walk 93, of which the last two miles are gently downhill on springy turf along Hergest Ridge, with marvellous views on three sides; and Walk 181 on the Isle of Kerrera, which keeps for the final stages a dramatic ruined castle followed by the best of the coastal views.

There should be a pub or tea-room on the way
On a long walk, there should, ideally, be a pub or tea-room about a third to half way round.

The end of the walk should be easily managed
In the final stage, the route should be quite easy to find and not too physically demanding.

The terrain should be varied
A particular aspect of the British landscape is its rich variety, often over a comparatively small area, due, mainly, to its complicated geology. Wherever possible, walks have been compiled to take advantage of this, to get a good mix of steep-sided valleys, grassy pasture, woodland, moorland and exhilarating ridge. Short walks with a lot of variety are rare, which is why we haven't included routes

under three miles (except for one or two short versions of longer walks). Elongated, sausage-shape routes have only been included where the topography gives the two halves of the walk quite different character. There-and-back routes are usually rather unsatisfactory for the same reason.

Obvious walks are not included

We haven't put in straightforward there-and-back mountain ascents, linear walks based entirely on the Countryside Commission's Long-Distance Paths, Forestry Commission waymarked circuits and organised trails (though we have incorporated parts of these). Some of our more straightforward walks, like the linear Walk 81, along the coast east of Edinburgh, have been included because they are easily missed and well worth seeking out.

Road-walking is generally to be avoided

Road-walking should not be for long, especially if the road is busy. Also, it should not come too near the start of the walk, though usually a stretch at the very end is tolerable. Occasionally a road is enjoyable in its own right, for instance, the one running along the spectacular Winnat's Pass in Derbyshire (Walk 81). It may also be more pleasant to take a quiet lane for half a mile than to crunch through a series of ploughed fields or find one's way through a maze of forest tracks.

The walk must be legal

It should follow public rights of way, permissive paths and tracks, or roads (see page 17).

The walk must be reasonably safe

Many of the upland routes we have included can be quite perilous in bad weather conditions if you're not properly equipped, and some of the cliff paths should be taken slowly, but there should be no problems for anyone exercising a reasonable standard of care.

The walk shouldn't require great navigational skills

Though it is essential to take a compass with you, in case of mist, on all hill and mountain expeditions (and prudent in some complicated lowland areas, too), there are no walks in the book demanding compass-reading as a matter of course.

Checking the walks

This confirmed what an extraordinary diversity of walking Britain has to offer. It is impossible to single out a favourite walk from all those we researched but we can nominate some favourite areas. For mountain walking (and we know this isn't a very original choice) we found the Lake District very hard to beat, because it offers such remarkable variety: round walks; low-level ones against the back-drop of the fells; high-level ridge walks which require a steady ascent to begin with but then reward the walker with marvellous views. Less wild but immensely appealing, with their limestone features and pretty stone villages, are the Yorkshire Dales, which give an abundance of good circuits. The Welsh border seems to be less known than it deserves to be, and the remoteness and splendid scenery of some of its central sections prompted us to include some walks here. Scotland presented us with some problems: we had comparatively few suggestions from readers, and couldn't glean much from reading between the contours on OS maps. We are pleased with the batch of walks we managed to find, however, and would recommend all of them to anyone considering making a grand Scottish tour by car. For coastal scenery, we particularly liked Exmoor and Pembrokeshire. Cornwall has some terrific cliff scenery but is a bit messed up inland, partly by development and partly by what has happened to its public rights of way. Choosing our routes carefully, we have come up with a selection that most people should find highly worthwhile. Other sections of coast we particularly liked were Dorset (good for anyone interested in for geology), and North Norfolk, though it's hard to find good round walks in the latter. Inland, lowland areas are often plagued by the prairie-like appearance of hedgeless arable fields, but there are many exceptions, especially where agricultural improvements have been limited; such 'traditional' landscapes can make for the most English type of scenery – small fields, deciduous woods, attractive farmsteads and pretty villages. Though close to London, much of the countryside in West Kent, Surrey and Sussex gives good examples of these.

Though we have tried to get a wide geographical spread, we would like to offer our special apologies for the areas which are not featured in the *Guide*: Bedfordshire, Northamptonshire, Lancashire, Durham, Dumfries and Galloway, Shetland, and Northern Ireland.

Help wanted

Please let us know if you find that a walk's directions are no longer accurate. In particular, field boundaries, signposts, stiles, woodlands and buildings, can change. Also, if you have a walk to suggest for any subsequent edition of the *Holiday Which? Good Walks Guide*, send it to us. We need a rough sketch map and a brief summary of the walk's attractions: directions are not necessary. All walks must be in Great Britain, Northern Ireland, the Isle of Man or the Channel Islands and should fit the criteria given in this Introduction.

Write to: *Holiday Which? Good Walks Guide*,
Consumers' Association, 14 Buckingham Street, London WC2N 6DS.

How the walks are presented

The contributor of a walk is given first (if there was one), or an acknowledgement that the walk was based on a contribution from someone, where we have altered the suggested route to get it in line with our concept of a good walk. Under 'recommended by' are the names of checkers who returned questionnaires and said they would recommend the walk for inclusion in the *Guide*. There is then a summary of what to expect from the walk, including what the terrain is like, the ascent (if relevant), any problems of access, and how easy the route is to find.

Next, some basic information. **Length** and **time** (at an average walking pace, excluding stops) is given for the full walk and any variants. **Difficulty** is graded from 1 to 5; for an explanation see the inside front cover. For the **start**, we assume readers have a standard road atlas and give further directions where needed. We have inserted a grid reference where helpful; the key on all Ordnance Survey maps explains how to use a grid reference, which will locate a point within 100 metres. Railway stations are given, where relevant, but because of the uncertainties following the deregulation of bus services, it hasn't been possible to say what bus to take (enquire at the relevant bus station or Tourist Information Centre). **Ordnance Survey (OS) map numbers** are given, for those who want them, at 1:50,000 (*Landranger* maps, about 1¼in to the mile) and 1:25,000 (*Pathfinder* maps, about 2½in to a mile) scales; some of the latter are covered by Outdoor Leisure sheets which cover a larger area than the Pathfinder sheets. At the time of writing some areas are only covered by First Series 1:25,000 maps, which cover only half the area of Pathfinder ones, by which they will soon be replaced; in each case we list the Pathfinder number. For instance, sheet SO 25 is currently available as a First Series map, but will soon be amalgamated with sheet SO 35 to form a Pathfinder sheet described as SO 25/35 (the number we give). **Refreshments** lists pubs, cafés, restaurants and tea-rooms on the route, though it is possible that one or two have slipped through the net (please tell us if you find any more, or if any of those listed have closed). As it hasn't been possible to make inspections, we do not make specific recommendations. You may like to refer to our sister publications, *The Good Pub Guide* and *Budget Good Food Guide*. Where no refreshments are listed, we found none.

The feedback we have had from checkers encouraged us to make the **walk directions** very detailed. We have broken up the text into numbered sections which refer to the map; if you feel confident of finding the way for one section, skip the text for a bit and pick it up later. As well as telling you where to turn right, left, etc., we have peppered the text with 'confirmers' – features confirming that you're on the right path or helping you identify certain points on the route. Though we've always tried to use the most obvious confirmer, often the only way of identifying the route is by the tedious use of distances: this typically happens in woodland criss-crossed by paths and tracks, with few or no landmarks. We've paced these out carefully, and they should be followed carefully; the number of yards given is based on paces. Some otherwise useful 'confirmers' we felt might disappear quite soon: we've avoided the less permanent features like dead trees, paths across arable fields and colours of houses. Particularly susceptible to disappearance are signposts, waymarks, gates and stiles and field boundaries: sometimes we mention several confirmers in one breath, for instance 'after 100 yards, immediately after shed, cross stile on right (signposted Exton), and proceed along left edge of field making for prominent barn.' If you come across a landmark whose disappearance or change makes the directions hard to follow, *please* tell us about it (the address to write to is on page 10). **What to look out for** lists points of interest and occasionally references to other paths we tried, including unsuccessful ones, so that readers don't waste time. Though the directions don't include compass bearings, a compass can be useful to pick out landmarks from viewpoints.

Clothing

Footwear Comfortable walking boots are essential for walks graded 3 or 4 and higher, and make the going noticeably easier on less demanding routes. Even if you only plan to walk three or four times a year, it might be worthwhile to invest in a pair of walking boots. Some advantages are:

Ankle support. Rough ground isn't confined to scree and boulders; it is quite possible to turn an ankle walking across a ploughed field.

Grip. Boots with a composition-type sole get a good grip on rock and some other potentially slippery surfaces.

Durability. Providing they are cleaned after use, and treated with dubbin, they should last for years.

Protection. If they're well-dubbined, they should keep much of the water out; boots also protect you against mud, branches, scree, wire and rough terrain.

Comfort. Boots which fit you properly and are well broken in will make walking far less tiring than ordinary shoes will. Wellington boots are quite good for wet but level walks up to about four miles, but thereafter can begin to be uncomfortable. Stout shoes are generally fine for short lowland strolls, though the suction effect of mud can prise off shoes completely.

Socks Wear a thin pair next to the skin, then a thicker woollen pair (ideally, knee-length loopstitch type) over the top. Take a spare pair of each in case the others get soaked.

Trousers Corduroy or woollen trousers (or, even better, breeches) are the best; jeans restrict knee movement too much when wet and are not advisable. Overtrousers keep out the wind effectively; some brands are waterproof and don't force you to sweat. They are also a good means for keeping the mud off your trousers. Skirts are not ideal for walking: they can be a hindrance in wind, and are particularly prone to getting caught on barbed-wire fences.

Jackets There is a wide range of anoraks, cagoules (nylon or 'breathable' man-made materials), and waxed cotton jackets on the market, and which you use is largely a matter of taste. For hill-walks take two woollen sweaters – one thick and one thin – to help you maintain your body heat in case the weather changes rapidly.

Gloves Take a pair that won't get soaked through in the rain; waxed wool or leather is the best.

Hat A substantial amount of body heat is lost through the head: a woollen hat or balaclava, coupled with the hood of your jacket (in case of rain) should prove effective.

Other equipment
Essential for hill and mountain expeditions (can be useful on less ambitious outings, too):

Compass. Many of the upland routes in this book are easy to find in reasonably clear weather, but in thick mist all the landmarks can vanish and if you have no compass, you will have to rely on your sense of direction. This can quickly fail even experienced walkers.

Whistle. For emergency use only; the distress signal is six blasts, repeated every minute.

Torch. Useful for all types of walks in case you are benighted; can also be used for signalling. Take spare batteries.

Food and drink (water purifying tablets enable you to drink spring water in safety). Emergency rations should include chocolate, mint cake or anything with plenty of sugar which gives you quick energy. Take some food with you for long lowland walks too (especially those where no pubs or tea-rooms are listed in the text).

Survival bag. To get into to avoid exposure.

Rucksack. Even the cheapest day sack will be much more satisfactory (and safer, as it's easier to balance yourself) than a bag slung over your shoulder or carried in your hand.

OS maps. Our sketch-maps and painstaking directions should (we hope) make it difficult for you to get lost on lowland routes, but in accordance with what we have said about the need to take a compass, an OS map for hill and mountain walks is essential in case of mist, or if you have to stray off the route (for example in an emergency).

First-aid kit. Include plasters and a needle (which can be sterilised by passing it through a flame) for blisters; antiseptic cream; massage cream for cramp or other muscular discomfort.

Optional extras
Map-cases protect your map or this book from the elements. Available at outdoor shops and map shops, though it is quite possible to make one of your own with some thick, clear plastic and zip, stud or velcro fastening. A *folding pocket lens* (about 8x or 10x magnification; available at some optical shops) can add greatly to the enjoyment of wild flowers. Useful for bird-watching is a pair of *lightweight binoculars.* The contents of a *vacuum flask* can warm you up on a cold hill-top.

Sense and safety on foot

Although we haven't included walks in this guide which require great
feats of navigation or unacceptably high degrees of physical danger,
some of the hill and mountain walks could cause problems for anyone
who isn't sensibly prepared. Even on the most innocuous-looking day,
the weather on high ground can surprise you with a sudden change for
the worse – mist, gale-force winds, blizzards, or driving rain, for
instance. Also, while serious risks on a lowland walk are fairly
minimal, suitable clothing will make the outing more comfortable
and you should be able to cover greater distances without getting tired
as a result. Occasionally, we refer in the text of the walks to areas of
possible danger: disused mine-shafts, or an eroded cliff path, for
example. In researching the walks, we do not claim to have
pinpointed every possible hazard, so you should generally take care.

Walking safely on the hills

Allow plenty of time and attempt only walks well within your ability.
The grading system for standard of difficulty and rough timings are
designed to help you choose the walk that suits you.

Time yourself carefully

The timings are rough ones, based on an average rate; you will need to
add on estimated stoppage time for refreshments and to look at
features of interest. Generally, two miles per hour is an average speed
for lowland walking; quite a lot of time is spent crossing stiles and
reading directions. Quicker types of terrain to cross include downland
tracks, gentle descending mountain tracks, firm sandy beaches and
old railway lines, where it is easy to average three miles per hour.
Much slower are shingle beaches, mountain ascents, steep mountain
descents, scree, boulders and boggy moorland, where you should
reckon on an average speed of one mile per hour.

Slow and steady wins the mountain race

A useful rule for mountain ascents is to walk at a slow but rhythmic
plod, a rate so gentle that you won't need to stop too often on the way
and so can gain some momentum. A brisk pace can be exhausting, and
except for the fittest and most experienced fell-walkers, is nearly
always slower than the rhythmic plod over a long distance.

It is safest to walk in a group of at least four: if one member gets
injured or ill, one can stay with him or her while the other two go off
to find help. Learn some elementary first-aid. If sudden dire weather
falls, huddle against a wall, boulder or anything else at hand, put on all
the clothes in your rucksack and improvise a shelter with a survival

bag or whatever is available. Do not rub to keep warm, nor take alcohol, as both encourage blood to the surface of the body, which reduces the body core temperature.

Look after your feet
If your boot is rubbing unpleasantly, take it off immediately and put a plaster over the sore part before it develops into a blister. Blisters should be lanced with a sterilised needle, squeezed with a tissue and then covered with a cushioned plaster trimmed of its medicated gauze surround, which can otherwise aggravate the blister further.

Check the weather
Before setting out, check the local weather forecast. In National Parks, information centres should be able to help you; otherwise there are pre-recorded weather forecasts given by weather centres over the telephone. One way of telling what the weather will do in the next few hours is to stand with your back to the surface wind: if the clouds come from the right-hand side, it will probably improve; if the clouds come from the left-hand side, it will probably deteriorate; and if the clouds are moving in parallel, then there is unlikely to be a change.

Leave messages
Leave a note of where you are going – with a hotel, youth hostel, tourist office or on a car windscreen. Be sure to tell them when you get back. Otherwise a search party may be sent out.

Take the right equipment
See page 13.

Walking in the countryside: law and practice

To the best of our knowledge, none of the walks in this book involve trespassing or following obstructed footpaths. But if you're walking in the countryside it's useful to have an understanding of the rights and duties of visitors to it. The countryside isn't an open playground through which we can wander at will, but the law in England and Wales (see below for Scotland) gives you specific rights of access to parts of it. And even where there are no such rights many landowners are happy to allow you on part of their property.

Paths for the walker

Public rights of way On these, you have a legal right of passage, and no one can stop you using it. Most rights of way are marked on Ordnance Survey (OS) maps. You can walk along a public right of way whether it's a public footpath, a public bridleway (where you can also ride or cycle) or a byway (or 'road used as a public path'; this you can often drive along). They should, by law, be signposted where they leave a road, but in practice, signs may be missing. On the way, a landowner, local authority, local footpath group or private individual may have waymarked the route; there is no legal requirement to do this, however, and waymarkings are far from universal. The conventional symbols are yellow arrows for public rights of way, blue ones for bridleways and acorn motifs for Countryside Commission Long-Distance Paths. Blobs of paint and other signs are sometimes used.

Forestry Commission tracks and paths, ie those which are not public rights of way. You have permissive access – which means you're generally welcome, but you can't insist on any legal rights of access, so that tracks can be closed off, notably during tree-felling.

Canal towpaths Unless there is a sign to the contrary, you can usually use them.

Other paths and tracks If you find a well-trodden path or track but an OS map doesn't show it as a right of way, it isn't safe to assume you can use it. However, some landowners, including some private ones as well as, for example, local councils and water authorities, give permissive access to parts of their land (signposts or waymarks will confirm if this is so), and occasionally a new public right of way may have been created.

Land you are allowed on

Some commons A common is simply an area of land over which local people have a series of rights, for example, to graze cattle; there isn't necessarily any legal right for the public to walk or picnic. But some privately owned common land is open to the public, and any local authority-owned common will have been set aside for public use.

Areas where 'access agreements' have been made Occasionally, a local authority will have made a formal agreement with a landowner to allow public access (except in some cases in the lambing or shooting seasons). These have occurred in some National Parks, but otherwise are rather uncommon. Notices will usually be displayed.

Moorland Much moorland is owned privately, for the purposes of raising game birds, and you shouldn't assume you have access to it. But out of the shooting season the public is permitted access to many moorland paths and tracks.

Country parks and picnic sites If they are owned by a local authority.

Beaches If owned by a local authority, and usually if privately owned, too.

National Trust land Including open land, coast, beaches and woodland; often marked by signs and shown on OS maps. You are allowed access unless there are notices to the contrary.

How to complain

If you want to complain about missing or broken stiles, ploughed-out paths, impenetrable vegetation, bulls, fierce dogs, missing signposts or other problems hindering your use of a public right of way, contact the rights of way section of the County Council, which may refer you to the District Council. The District Council holds the *County Definitive Map*, a record of rights of way, including the latest footpath diversions, closures and creations. It also has a legal duty to see that public rights of way are usable: it should provide signposts where a public right of way leaves a public road and is responsible for maintaining the surface of the right of way. Where necessary, it has a duty to put pressure on landowners to erect stiles and remove obstructions. Do report problems (we do), because otherwise the path may deteriorate further and fall into disuse. Local authorities will welcome reports (and may even rely on them) and though they may not have the resources to act immediately, should look into it in due course. A quick telephone call should be enough.

Some questions answered

The path I want to use has a sign saying 'Trespassers will be prosecuted' and there's an irate landowner pacing towards me.
If you are on a public right of way, legally there is nothing he can do to stop you. But if you are somewhere you have no right to be, then he's entitled to feel irate: you are trespassing and he can order you off his land by showing you to the nearest public right of way or road. If necessary, he can use reasonable force to evict you. He can sue you for trespass, but he only has a case if he can prove you had caused damage – for example to his livestock, crops or fences. Whatever the notice might say, you can't normally be *prosecuted* for trespassing on private land because this isn't a criminal offence, except on land owned by the Ministry of Defence or British Rail, or as a public order offence. (Despite this however we have seen this meaningless sign time and time again in our researches for this book.)

The Ordnance Survey map shows a public path crossing a field, but I can see no trace of it. Am I entitled to follow the route?
Usually yes – but make sure you follow the precise route. By walking the route you are quite within your rights, are doing a service to others by marking the line of the path, and making the landowner aware that people want to use it. A path might be obscured by crops: you have a right to follow the route through them, but if they are really impenetrable you are entitled to skirt the field. There's a chance that the path may have been closed or diverted; if so, you could expect signs to that effect. By law, within two weeks of ploughing, farmers must make good the surface of a public path which crosses a field; and mustn't plough paths which skirt fields. Unfortunately this law is often flouted.

I can see where the path goes, but I can't get to it. What should I do?
It's all too common for a path to be obstructed by rubbish, thick vegetation, fallen trees or barbed wire. You can remove just enough of an obstruction to allow you to pass, but don't cause any unnecessary damage, and ensure that no livestock can stray as a result. It may be more practical to find a way round it, but if this takes you on to someone else's land, you are trespassing. By law a landowner must not keep a fierce dog which deters people from using a right of way. On the other hand, a farmer can quite legally put a bull in a field crossed by a right of way, provided the bull is either of a non-dairy breed and is accompanied by cows or heifers, or is less than 10 months old. If such a bull charges you, the farmer is unlikely to be prosecuted, although you may be entitled to damages.

Can the dog come with us wherever we go?
Generally yes, and certainly on rights of way, provided you keep it under close control at all times. It's best to put the dog on a lead if you

are crossing a field with livestock in it. A farmer is quite within his rights to shoot a dog that is worrying livestock – and the dog-owner could face prosecution. A dog can do untold damage to birds during the nesting season, and to other wildlife, even if it is doing no more than hunting along a hedgerow. It may also be unwelcome on moorland: some moorland areas display notices expressly prohibiting dogs.

There's an unfenced field with a pretty view – can we have a picnic there?
Don't assume that an unfenced field is intended as an open invitation, but provided you take your litter with you, you can normally picnic anywhere to which you're allowed access (see above). But you don't have any legal rights to do so, and you may have to move on if a landowner asks you to.

Can I pick wild flowers and wild fruit?
A a general rule, leave wild flowers well alone. Some species are protected, and picking them is a criminal offence. In many areas it is permissible by consent or custom, although not by legal right, to gather wild fruit (particularly blackberries), provided you do not stray from the public right of way or area to which you are allowed access.

Scotland
The law and practice differs in two main ways. First, you do not have legal rights of access to much of the countryside and along many of its paths. But there is a tradition of relatively free access to moorland and mountain areas (subject to closure at certain times, principally deer-stalking and shooting seasons). And if a path is defined on the ground you can usually assume you can follow it. In fields, keep to the edges. Second, such public rights of way which exist aren't distinguished from other paths on OS maps, although they are normally signposted. Black dashed lines on OS maps can be anything from a right of way to an unfollowable route across moorland, and plenty of clear paths (sometimes even signposted ones) don't appear on OS maps at all. For further information on rights of way, contact the Planning Department of the District or Regional Council.

Based on an article that first appeared in Which? *in May 1986.*

SOUTH-WEST ENGLAND

Avon, Cornwall, Devon, Dorset, Somerset, Wiltshire

A major holiday destination, famous for its two National Parks (Dartmoor and Exmoor) and an outstanding coastline, which is followed by the South-West Peninsula Path, Britains longest official long-distance path – a good basis for round walks as there are rewarding inland paths close to the sea. Cornwall offers some of the most exciting coastal walking in Britain. The switchback coast path is often quite hard going, and you can expect some steep gradients. Parts of the county – notably the western peninsula – are rich in archaeology. Sadly we found a lot of the inland paths in poor condition, and signposting away from the coast path is virtually non-existent. In South Devon, the lush eastern edge of the Dartmoor National Park is an extremely pretty landscape of wooded river valleys, unspoilt farmland and thatched villages – at its best in the Teign Gorge and Lustleigh Cleave. To the west, the moor is famous for its granite tors, many of which make fine viewpoints. Walking on the moor takes you into truly remote scenery (and, regrettably, some big Ministry of Defence training areas). Though there are no great mountain climbs, the moor can become an inhospitable place in foul weather, and the longer walks across the heart of the wilderness are beyond the scope of this book.

Somerset and Exmoor (part of which lies in Devon) offer some of the most varied walking in the country, especially on the coast, where the cliffs are degraded into steep grassy slopes, covered in places by ancient oak woods. Inland Exmoor is very deserted and makes for good walking where there are sufficient focal points. Further into Somerset the Quantocks command splendid views and provide easy walking on their moorland top. In Avon the Mendips have superb limestone features, such as the gorge of Burrington Combe, less well known than Cheddar Gorge, but very nearly as spectacular. Wiltshire has large areas of chalk downland, at its best in its natural state, as at Ashcombe Bottom and Pewsey Down. The county's ancient chalk trackways along the tops of ridges can make very easy walking. Dorset has an exceptionally fine coastline, especially interesting for its geology and for fossils. However, the slitheriness of the chalk mud together with many sheer, unfenced drops means that the coast path should be treated with respect.

AVON

Burrington Combe and Dolebury Warren

Route is along a wooded valley, over moorland, along the road at the bottom of a spectacular limestone gorge, then climbs gently through woodland and pasture to reach one of the best viewpoints in the Mendips, before the final descent. Paths are reasonably well defined; route-finding a little involved, but not difficult.

Length 6½ miles (10.5km), 3½ hours
Difficulty 2
Start Small car park at foot of Dolebury Warren. From Churchill Gate (junction of A38 and A368) continue S on A38 towards Cheddar for 600 yards, then take first left (cul-de-sac called Dolberrow), just after terrace of brick cottages. Immediately keep right (parallel to main road) and follow lane to end; parking space by gate. Grid reference SY 446588
OS maps 1:50,000 172 or 182; 1:25,000 ST 45/55
Refreshments Crown Inn, Churchill, near start; Burrington Inn (bar, café and restaurant) just before 8 .

WALK DIRECTIONS

1 Pass through gate and follow level track along bottom of wooded combe. 2 After ½ mile, 100 yards after passing NT sign for Dolebury Warren on your left, fork left. 3 ¾ mile later keep straight on at crossing of tracks (avoiding turnings half right to forest gate and sharp left). 4 Where open moorland (a) appears on right, continue on track alongside woodland on left for ¼ mile.

5 Turn right (across moorland) on broad track, opposite gate with private footpath sign, in front of large wooden cabin among the trees. Turn left at crossing of tracks after 200 yards;

track now makes towards Burrington Combe, a deep rocky valley ahead. Fork right after 50 yards, and 50 yards later fork left. Track leads down to small combe, across stream, then left up other side.

6 At next (even smaller) combe, track descends to bottom – waterfall where stream disappears underground can be heard away to right – then bends left up other side. 30 yards later turn left on steep path descending along edge of bracken, then soon along right side of stream. Step across stream just as it disappears into cavern, then continue down bottom of combe to road 7 .

Left on road, along bottom of Burrington Combe (b). 8 150 yards after Burrington Inn, turn left at crossroads. Road ascends, soon bending sharp left, and 30 yards after hedge on your right ends, fork right on to track between hedges, soon entering woods. Ignore any turnings to the

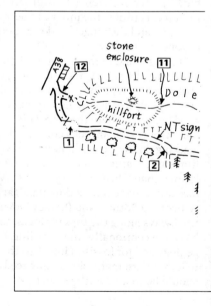

left and follow ¾ mile. **9** Pass ruins of Mendip Lodge on your left and 30 yards later fork left up track. Turn right on path at junction after 100 yards, then 20 yards later turn left up sunken track, soon between walls.

10 After ¼ mile turn right through gate into field by NT sign for Dole-bury Warren. Proceed alongside fence on left to its corner, then maintain direction along line of hedgerow trees to reach fence. Here, take gate/stile on right to enter scrubby woodland; bear half left to gain top of ridge, keeping right at first fork. At top of ridge, make for grassy summit ahead **(c) 11**.

Summit itself is encircled by large grassy bank (ramparts of hillfort). Continue forward on track, keeping just to left of/below small stone enclosure. On passing between grassy banks turn left on track to descend to lane **12**. Left on lane, and keep left at next junction to return to start.

WHAT TO LOOK OUT FOR

(a) Carpets of **bluebells** on this moorland in spring indicate that it was once covered with forest.

(b) Burrington Combe Deep lime-stone gorge honeycombed with caves and underground streams. Like its more famous neighbour, Cheddar Gorge, the combe was cut in the Ice Age by the action of streams that could not sink through the permeable rock while it was frozen. As you round the corner along the bottom of the combe you pass a large outcrop, immortalised in 1792 by the Revd Augustus Toplady of Blagdon, who wrote the words for the hymn *Rock of Ages* while sheltering from a storm in a crevice in the rock. Opposite is Aveline's Hole, a cave in which human skeletal remains dating back 10,000 years were found. **Flora** By the roadside, occasional tway-blade orchids.

(c) Dolebury Warren Grassy ridge with some planted forestry and the ramparts of a 20-acre prehistoric hillfort at the far end. Views NE to Dundry Hill; NW over the Severn Estuary towards S Wales; S over the Mendips; E across Chew Valley Lake, and towards Bath.

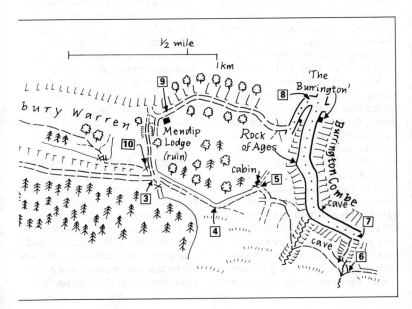

CORNWALL

Land's End and Nanjizal

Recommended by William Niven

Approaches cliffs of Land's End along a dramatic coast path that continues over cliff-tops to the remote bay of Nanjizal, before climbing steeply over gorsy hillside to return via field paths. Take care with route-finding from 3 , as field paths may be undefined.

Length 6 miles (9.5 km), 3½ hours
Difficulty 3
Start Sennen Cove, 3 miles NE of Land's End. Car park by seafront. Grid reference SW 352263
OS maps 1:50,000 203; 1:25,000 SW 32/42
Refreshments Pub and cafés in Sennen Cove; pub at Land's End

WALK DIRECTIONS

1 (**a**) From car park in Sennen Cove turn left past toilets on uphill lane, which divides into two paths almost immediately; fork right on coastal footpath (signposted). After ascending and passing castellated lookout point, Land's End (**b**) comes into view ahead. Follow coastal path past large building (pub) on horizon (signposts to John O'Groats, New York, Brazil etc.).

2 Beyond Land's End continue along cliff edge (or on an alternative path a little inland if you prefer) for 1¼ miles. Path eventually descends into series of tiny enclosures marked by low granite boulders; you are now above Mill Bay (**c**). ¼ mile further on (but 200 yards before isolated house with two bay windows on ground floor) path crosses tumbledown wall.

3 40 yards after wall fork left and 70 yards later turn sharp left on narrow path steeply uphill (not immediately obvious, this path is just before path ahead descends between banks, then past granite wall on your left and over the footbridge).

After path levels off keep right at first fork of paths. Follow path through gorse, joining stone wall on your left after 200 yards, and crossing it by stone steps beside dilapidated gate ¼ mile later, at break in bushes **4**. Emerge into large field (path not defined) and continue forward at 90 degrees to line of wall behind you. Once over brow of hill head straight on to left-hand of two gates in corner of field. Turn right into second field, following right edge alongside wall to gateway. Bear half left across third field and, on reaching opposite wall, turn right along it and follow through farm and then along lane to T-junction **5**.

Keep straight over at T-junction, crossing stone steps. Pass through farmyard and leave by stone steps beside gate. Follow path on right edge of first field, with line of telegraph poles on other side of wall, and cross stone stile at end. Follow left edge of second field towards houses, find gate leading through garden. Emerge on to road at Trevescan, and turn left along it. **6** After 300 yards reach road junction and take a signposted footpath opposite, at first along driveway, then where driveway swings left turn half right (signposted), crossing first field and passing telegraph pole with signposts on it, to pass through kissing-gate ahead, and another gate just beyond.

7. Turn half right in second field aiming for gate in corner. In third field turn half right again, but keep to lower track, keeping below coastguard cottages on your right. Continue forward (quarter right) aiming for left-hand end of gabled houses to find gate leading on to tarmac lane **8**. Turn left on lane and keep on it as it bends right 30 yards later. ¼ mile later turn sharp left downhill on path signposted Sennen Cove, to return to starting-point.

WHAT TO LOOK OUT FOR

(a) **Sennen Cove** Unprepossessing holiday development overlooking the popular Whitesand Bay, with vestiges of its days as a fishing village.

(b) **Land's End** The westernmost point on the English mainland is Dr Syntax's Head, the headland immediately N of the First and Last House. **View** W to Longships Rocks (with huge lighthouse) and beyond to the Isles of Scilly.

(c) **Mill Bay** or **Nanjizal** By footbridge, remains of a mill used for crushing corn and ore. At NW (Land's End) side of bay are remains of a collier steam ship, the *City of Cardiff*, which was wrecked without loss of life.

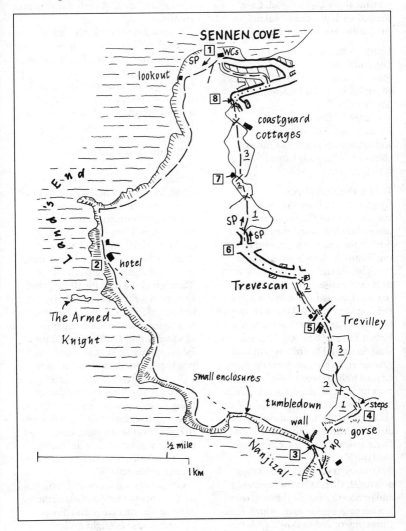

Lamorna Cove and the Merry Maidens

Contributed by Jack Crewe
Recommended by Frances Roxburgh

Crosses arable dry-stone walled fields before descending through a wooded hollow (full of wild daffodils in spring) for the cliff path to Lamorna. Field paths and tracks lead past a fine prehistoric stone circle, with the final section along a quiet road. Care needed with directions inland, as field paths are undefined.

Length 8 miles (13km), 4 hours
Difficulty 3
Start St Buryan, on B3283, 5 miles E of Land's End. Grid reference SW 409257
OS maps 1:50,000 203; 1:25,000 SW 32/42
Refreshments St Buryan Inn and shops in St Buryan; Lamorna Wink Inn, Lamorna

WALK DIRECTIONS

1 (**a**) From St Buryan church make your way past St Buryan Inn and immediately beyond it turn left on Boskennal Lane, which soon becomes unmetalled. ¼ mile later, where track bends right, continue forward over stone stile. Continue across field to gate opposite; continue in next field on well-marked track through farmyard. On other side continue forward through first field, soon with wall on right. Do not pass through gate on right but continue on right edge of field to stone stile. After stile pick up path in same direction, which now follows left edge of field. Cross six more fields, maintaining same direction throughout and crossing stone stiles ahead, and emerge on road (**b**) **2**.

Turn right on road, which dips downhill, then by cattle road-sign and opposite Rôsvale (house), turn left on path beside gate, which leads through wooded hollow. **3** After

¼ mile path turns right (signposted footpath) by gate just before houses, then crosses stream; turn left on other side. 100 yards later turn left over stile on to coastal footpath (signposted). Follow coastal path for 2 miles. First it briefly crosses left edge of beach with boulders, then swings uphill between banks; the path is clearly signposted and easy to follow. **4** Coastal path finally reaches Lamorna Cove (**c**) (beach, car park and small quay).

Follow lane that climbs uphill through village. After ½ mile, shortly after passing Lamorna Wink Inn, look out for village hall and phone box on right. **5** 150 yards after them, fork left uphill on track. Keep straight on at oblique junction after 30 yards, and continue until reaching tarmac lane with hotel entrance on right **6**.

Continue forward for ¼ mile until road junction, at which turn immediately left through gap in hedge to right of hotel sign. Turn half right across field (path undefined), aiming past nearest electricity pole to find stile in hedge opposite. Emerge into next field and bear half right through Merry Maidens stone circle (**d**) to gate leading on to road (**e**) **7**. Turn left along road for 10 yards only, then turn right over stile (partly concealed in hedge; avoid larger and more prominent track to right of electricity pole). *NB This path may be overgrown in summer: use roads if you prefer (see map).* Bear quarter right across first field to stile 50 yards to right of standing stone. In second field, maintain same direction to stile (partly concealed) in hedge 100 yards to right of same standing stone. Pass through thicket, over stile and into third field. Bear half right across it, to reach further stile **8**.

Continue straight on in fourth field for 20 yards to find clear path leading half left through gorse and down towards house in slight hollow

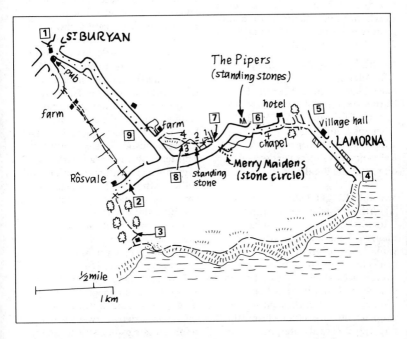

(Choone Farm). Cross further stile 50 yards to left of house; go forward across tarmac driveway, and cross stile opposite. Proceed alongside fence on right for 30 yards and, where it veers to right, bear half left to gate on to road. **9** Turn right on road which leads to St Buryan (**f**).

WHAT TO LOOK OUT FOR
(**a**) **St Buryan church** The 90-ft tower is a landmark for miles around. The church itself is 15th-century, Perpendicular, and one of Cornwall's finest; it has a good rood screen of the same period.
(**b**) By the roadside where you emerge is a **Celtic stone cross**. Many such crosses in Cornwall were erected during visits by missionaries in the Dark Ages and the Middle Ages.

(**c**) **Lamorna Cove** Popular former fishing village, now an artists' colony, with craftshops and a scattering of cottages in the long, steep-sided cove.
(**d**) **Merry Maidens stone circle** There is a legend that girls were turned to stone for dancing on the sabbath; the unromantic explanation is that 'maiden' is probably a corruption of the Cornish for stone; there are 19 of them, and the circle apparently survives intact.
(**e**) As you emerge on to the road, **the Pipers**, two standing stones, are visible in the field opposite and to the right. The pipers provided the music for the maidens' dance, and suffered the same fate.
(**f**) By the first houses reached, there is another **stone cross**.

Carnyorth Common and the Levant tin mines

Follows moorland tracks before taking the cliff path along a rugged coastline with spectacular remains of the tin-mining industry. Paths across pasture fields undefined; follow directions carefully throughout.

Length 8 miles (13km), 4 hours
Difficulty 3
Start Grass triangle at centre of Carnyorth, on B3306 2 miles N of St Just. Grid reference SW 375333.
OS maps 1:50,000 203;
1:25,000 SW 33/43/part 53
Refreshments Pub at Pendeen (just off route) and Botallack

WALK DIRECTIONS

1 With grass triangle in centre of Carnyorth behind you, turn left on main road out of village. After 250 yards, just after group of cottages and just before Carnyorth village sign (which faces other way) turn left on tarmac track uphill. After ¼ mile, just before it enters through gate on to open land, fork left on clear walled track. **2** 200 yards later, track reaches open moorland; turn left to proceed with wall on left (path not very well defined, but after 300 yards it is joined by larger track from right reaching road ½ mile later **3**.

Turn right on road, then left, opposite house, to take track. After 50 yards fork right, and 30 yards later fork left. Track snakes slightly downhill past abandoned mine buildings after ¼ mile; 50 yards beyond them avoid descending further, but turn right to proceed with stone wall on left on edge of common. Follow this wall, passing old quarries, and after ¼ mile reach unmetalled walled cross-track **4**.

Cross track to stone stile opposite and follow left-hand edge of field. Emerge by stile ahead on to another walled track: turn right for 10 yards then left, over stone stile. Continue forward close to left edge of field, aiming for lowest part of wall ahead (20 yards to right of left-hand corner). Climb wall into second (small) field, and continue ahead following right-hand edge to gate. Continue quarter right across third field, aiming for stone stile 50 yards to left of gate. Emerge on to main road **5**.

Left on road, then immediately turn right through gate. Turn left, following left edge of field, to pass through gap into the second field. Half-way along left edge of field make for gap in bushes, by electricity pole. This leads over low wall (path a bit overgrown at time of writing). Follow walled path in front of cottages to emerge on tarmac lane **6**. Turn right, and 50 yards later keep on lane as it bends left in front of cottages and then leads to reach T-junction with main road (Bodjewyan Men's Institute is opposite) **7**.

Turn right on to road and after 30 yards turn left opposite chapel, on small path leading to stile, then continuing briefly between walls before crossing stone stile to emerge into field. Follow left edge of field, to climb gap in wall ahead. Continue forward over next field to reach gap (to left of nearest electricity pole) leading on to tarmac lane. Turn right on lane, passing through Portherras Farm after 600 yards **8**.

In farmyard turn right, around modern house. Path passes first between walls then over stone stile/gate into field: take clear path leading quarter left, and when path reaches corner of wall continue same direction (avoiding path to left). 50 yards further on turn sharp right at top of steep slope on left, and 50 yards further on turn sharp left on clear path along side of valley heading towards sea. After 300 yards turn left on coast path **9**.

Follow coast path (signposted with

acorn motifs, wooden signposts, or concrete bollards) for 3 miles. Coast path proceeds as follows: it joins road after ½ mile, above lighthouse, then ¼ mile later, just after coastguards' cottages on left, turns right on grassy path (signposted on stone bollard). ½ mile later it passes seat at Carn Rôs. ¼ mile further on it passes through ruined Levant tin mine (**a**) (route marked with yellow markers). After ascending from Levant mine fork right away from main track following direction indicated by signpost. This soon brings you to second track where bear half right for 30 yards then turn left just before barrier (entrance to Geevor tin mine). (¾ mile later pass derelict cottage on your left **10**). Keep straight on after derelict cottage (leaving coast path which forks right) on track. Continue

along track ignoring all side turns: after ½ mile it passes through Botallack mine (**b**). **11** Reach junction of lanes (Manor Farm on left) and turn right. 30 yards later, at edge of Botallack village, turn left at next road junction. Follow to main road, turn left and 50 yards later turn left on lane leading between terraces of cottages. Behind cottages proceed across stone stile, and continue across two fields. In third field, bear half right to gate in far corner, which leads into centre of Carnyorth.

WHAT TO LOOK OUT FOR
(**a**) **Levant mine** (ruins) 200ft deep and extending a mile out to sea. Closed in 1930.
(**b**) **Botallack mine** (being restored). Visited by Queen Victoria and Prince Albert in 1846.

29

Morvah Cliff and Chûn Castle

One of the most varied short walks we found in the South-West of England. Takes a dramatic section of coast path before turning inland to follow paths and tracks over moorland, past relics of the old mine workings. A quiet lane precedes the highlight of the walk, Chûn Castle. Route-finding tricky just after ④, where an easily-missed path is not signposted, and field paths are undefined.

Length 6 miles (9.5km), 3 hours
Difficulty 3–4
Start By church at Morvah, on B3306 (St Just to St Ives). Grid reference SW 403355
OS maps 1:50,000 203; 1:25,000 SW 33/43/part 53

WALK DIRECTIONS

1 From road, find stone stile by gate immediately to right of Morvah church, and enter field. Follow left-hand edge of field and in far corner continue forward on walled track, heading for sea. **2** After ½ mile reach coast path. Turn right on it and follow for 1 mile. Coastal scenery becomes increasingly dramatic and eventually path leads up over craggy rocks on skyline, requiring a bit of a scramble. **3** 200 yards later pass old stone wall enclosures on your right and shortly after look out for small (and recently walled) enclosure containing disused mine shafts, on right of path (**a**). Turn right inland immediately beyond this, finding well-defined track, leading half right to gate, across open land then emerging by second gate on to road **4**.

Turn right on road and count out 40 paces. Turn left off road, finding path (not easily visible from road but visible as soon as you cross low grass bank by road). Follow path, ignoring

all left forks, as it zigzags uphill and passes just to left of fenced-in shaft (path looks indistinct by shaft, but keep going). **5** Just beyond shaft reach track at top, and turn right along it, immediately passing between stone posts. After 100 yards, at old mine workings, keep quarter left. Soon this track passes house on your right then becomes stony and descends gently for ¾ mile to reach road **6**.

Left on road for 300 yards, then turn right by phone box on lane (signposted Chûn Castle). After ¾ mile keep straight on at junction, and follow through Trehyllys farmyard **7**. At end of farmyard, just after farmhouse, turn right and proceed with wall on right for 30 yards, then bear half left uphill, aiming for white painted stones in gorse. This path leads up to Chûn Castle, which is just on right of path (**b**) **8**.

After viewing castle, leave between stone posts (the way you came) and continue forward with centre of castle circle behind you) to burial chamber of Chûn Quoit (just visible) (**c**). At Quoit, retrace steps for 10 yards and turn left at track junction. This leads downhill, and is soon joined by wall on left; where wall ends continue forward, avoiding left turn, and descend to reach farm track. Turn left along it and 200 yards later turn right at junction of tracks.

Follow track, which soon becomes tarmacked, for ¼ mile, until reaching farm on left and bungalow (The Cabin) on right **9**. Turn left through farmyard, keeping round to left in it and, just after last barn on right, cross stone stile by cattle-grid on right. Emerge into first field (Morvah church visible ahead), and bear half left to left-hand of two gates. In second field follow left-hand edge to cross stone stile in far left-hand corner. Continue along left hand edge of two more fields, crossing stone stiles, to reach road. Turn left to return to starting-place.

WHAT TO LOOK OUT FOR

(a) The **mine shaft and workings** here and a little further on are some of the hundreds of reminders of copper, tin, arsenic and tungsten mining in the area. Some mines shelter vast bat populations, many of which have in the past inadvertently been trapped by the filling-in of old shafts; re-cently some shafts have been re-walled to prevent this happening again.

(b) **Chûn Castle** Commandingly situated Iron Age hillfort with two ramparts and many of the stones still remaining, encircling a 280ft-diameter site.

(c) **Chûn Quoit** Megalithic cromlech or chambered tomb, with its horizontal covering slab in position. Set in a round barrow 35ft across.

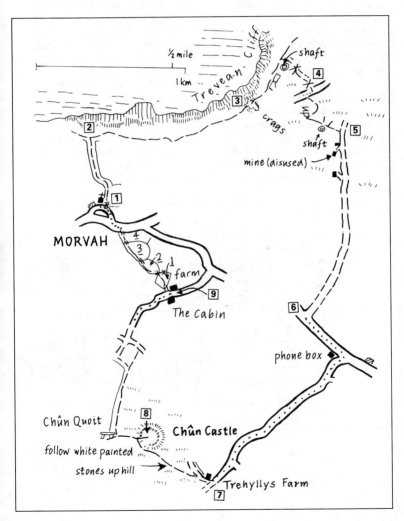

St Ives and the coffin route

After following winding lanes around the most unspoilt parts of St Ives, takes a good section of cliff path for the outward leg, and the 'coffin route' across small, dry-stone walled pasture fields for the return. A gorse and bracken-covered combe links the two halves. Easy route-finding along the coast, but more complex inland; helpful waymarking from [10].

Length 7½ miles (12km), 4 hours
Difficulty 2–3
Start St Ives station
OS maps 1:50,000 203; 1:25,000 SW 33/43/part 53
Refreshments In St Ives only

WALK DIRECTIONS

[1] (a) With railway station behind you, cross car park and go down steps to Beach Road (signposted to the beach). Continue along Beach Road, which later becomes the Warren. At junction turn half right to follow harbour wall. Follow round until wall swings to right; at this point turn sharp left (just past greengrocer), and then turn immediately half right along Bailey's Lane.

[2] Turn left at top (along 'Norway') and immediately right to cross Porthmeor Square. Follow road in far left corner; it soon bends right to reach seafront. Take lower path between road and seafront gardens. [3] After 200 yards fork right on asphalted path which winds round the back of the bowling-green, later passing stone shelter and stone coast-path marker sign for Zennor. Follow coast path for a further 2½ miles, ignoring all paths branching inland.

[4] ¼ mile after passing trig. point coast path descends to cross footbridge and ascends for 150 yards. At top turn sharp left inland on well-defined path leading along right-hand side of valley for ½ mile before reaching track [5]. Left on track, down to Trevail Mill.

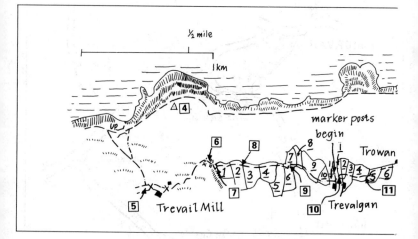

Pass round in front of cottage on your right, and after it bear half left between fence and hedge. 50 yards later continue ahead through gate (shed on left) on path between hedges, soon leading to open land.

Follow path ahead which leads uphill and after ½ mile continues straight across grassy track, past gate on your right. 6 50 yards later emerge between stone posts and cross further track and continue on to narrow path in bushes opposite and slightly to right. This soon leads to stone stile on left; cross it and emerge into field 7. Keep left, to follow left edge of first field, avoiding going into bushes on left, but at left-hand corner leave by stone stile into second field (b). Again follow left edge of field, but find stone stile 30 yards to right of far left-hand corner 8. Cross third, fourth and fifth fields, keeping to left edge and making for stone stiles, then emerge into sixth field, to pass almost immediately through

gate on left into seventh field, containing prominent standing stone 9. Turn right and follow right edge of seventh field, aiming for stone stiles, then emerge into ninth field and aim for left-hand of two gates. Continue quarter left across tenth field by stone stile/gate by black and white marker posts then across eleventh field, keeping just to left of farm buildings.

10 Route back to St Ives across fields after this farm (Trevalgan) is well waymarked by black and white marker posts indicating stiles ahead, but in case there are any problems, the following description may be helpful.

In first three fields after farm, head for stiles ahead (stepping stones at beginning of third field); in fourth field bear quarter left to next stile 11. In fifth and sixth fields, follow left edge. Beyond sixth field, turn left into Trowan farmyard (avoid keeping straight on through gate) and turn

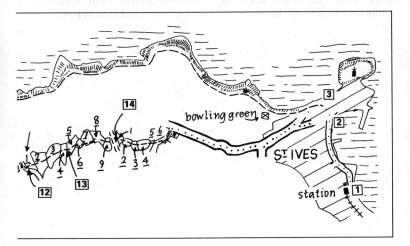

right at back of farmyard to find walled track on other side of farm. **12** Once out of farmyard, immediately after last barn, cross stile on left (avoid continuing on walled track). Cross left edge of first field and maintain same direction (away from farm) across second, third and fourth fields **13**. Follow right edge of fifth field (cutting off small corner) and right edge of sixth and seventh fields.

In next two fields a defined track leads to cross-track with signpost 'Footpath to Zennor' pointing the way you have come **14**. Cross track to stile opposite, and maintain direction across first field on path leading half right. Continue on left edge of next four fields, then path leads downhill (avoid gate on left) along edge of field which soon tapers into a narrow area-cum-track between walls. After 50 yards cross stile on right and follow left edge of field downhill to next stile, then follow narrow path to left of house down to tarmac lane, at edge of St Ives. Turn right on lane and left at T-junction with road. This leads down to St Ives; after 400 yards take turning on right signposted to town centre.

WHAT TO LOOK OUT FOR
(a) **St Ives** Popular seaside resort sited on a hill that narrows into a promontory, with a sandy beach on its N side and a harbour to its S. Grew up after the railway was opened in 1877, with sedate hotels built high up on the hill; at the bottom, the fishing village (of which some of the character has survived in a tidied-up form) attracted an international colony of artists, including Scandinavians, Russians and Americans. Whistler and Sickert joined them; later Nicholson and Hepworth settled here. On the promontory is St Leonard's Chapel, where friars used to bless the fishermen before they sailed out; a plaque inside lists some of those who did not come back.
(b) This route across fields and over ancient stone stiles is an old one, formerly used by coffin-bearers on their way to and from St Ives.

Pentire Point, the Rumps and St Enodoc's church

A figure-of-eight route that can be divided into two walks: the northern loop has good cliff scenery, the southern one is through sand dunes along the Camel Estuary, with woods and farmland for the inland section, well screened from most of the holiday development. Paths are well used and well signposted.

Length *Full walk* 9 miles (14.5km), 4½ hours
Difficulty 3
Short walks from New Polzeath
4½ miles (7km), 2–2½ hours
Difficulty 2–3 (northern loop); 1–2 (southern loop)
Start *Full walk* Car park, Rock, 5 miles NW of Wadebridge, where road ends, next to ferry terminal to Padstow. Grid reference SW 928758 *Short walks* New Polzeath: at 2 for northern loop via the Rumps; at 7 for southern loop via St Enodoc's Grid reference SW 936789
OS maps 1:50,000 200; 1:25,000 SW 87/97
Refreshments Pubs, café and shop in New Polzeath

WALK DIRECTIONS

1 Take path to left of car park toilets, leading up initially half right on to sand dunes. Follow left edge of sand dunes by any of several paths (a) (beach just below on left); after ¾ mile you will be level with bungalow up on right. Very soon after this coast path merges from right. Follow coast path on low cliffs for ½ mile, swinging left over footbridge (keep left on other side) (b), and follow coast path round close to coast, avoiding any tracks inland for another 1 mile, until path leads between houses at sprawling village of New Polzeath, and on to road, on which turn left 2. Turn left immediately beyond petrol station (on seaward side of road) on

track which swings to right between houses. After 150 yards turn left on signposted coastal path (just before Polzeath Beach Holiday Park sign ahead). Follow this as it passes seafront of New Polzeath and rejoins road that swings right inland. 3 50 yards later, where road swings right again (straight ahead is Baby Beach Lane), turn left on coastal path. Follow coastal path for 3 miles (c) before turning inland.

4 The point where you turn inland is not signposted but is 100 yards after crossing stile, descending steeply to reach junction of paths by wooden barrier on left (sheer drop beyond). Path, sharp right, is well trodden and leads through two fields to reach road 5.

Turn right on road and after ½ mile take first road on left with sign to Lundynant caravan site. Road descends, then after 200 yards, just as it is about to ascend, turn right through gate. Pass in front of cottage and through second gate ahead, then follow path ¼ mile along bank which descends to caravan site 6. At caravan site, turn right: this track leads you back to main road in Polzeath. Turn right.

7 From centre of New Polzeath take track just to left of post office, to pass through caravan site. After 200 yards, by 5mph speed restriction sign, fork left 8. Track passes Shilla Mill (cottage) after 300 yards, then over cattle-grid, just after which turn right (yellow waymarks) on narrow path. Path crosses stream by footbridge in woods after 100 yards. 20 yards beyond stream keep half right uphill at junction of paths.

9 Emerge from woods at top, follow right edge of first field, turn right along edge of second field and left along edge of third field (path waymarked with white arrows). 10 Path emerges through gate by houses; turn right to reach road. Left on road

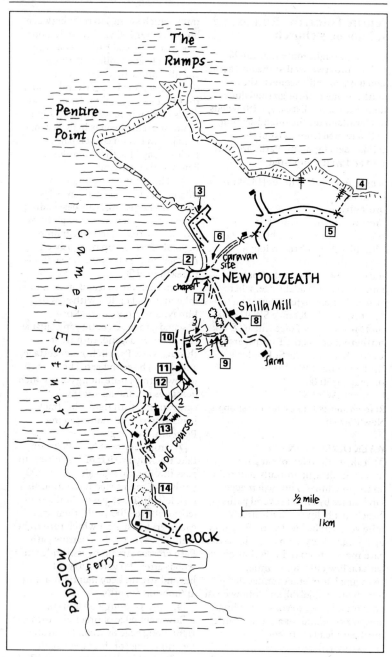

for 300 yards (avoiding three road turnings to right) and just beyond 'road narrows' sign, turn right on track, signposted public footpath, which soon leads to narrow path between fences.

11 Emerge into field at end, cross footbridge and bear quarter right across first field (towards house). In second field keep straight ahead to stile (with top of church steeple just visible ahead) leading into golf course **12**. On golf course turn right then immediately left, following white marker stones to St Enodoc's church (**d**).

Turn half left at church, taking prominent track at foot of hill on right. This again follows white marker stones; avoid first crossing over stream but cross it 50 yards later by footbridge, signposted Rock, over small weir. **13** Turn left on metalled track on other side of bridge and 20 yards later turn half right on grassy track, also again marked by white stones. At fence at edge of golf course (Duchy of Cornwall sign) do not continue into sand dunes, but turn left on path, keeping fence on right. **14** Path passes to other side of fence after ½ mile, at signpost to Rock, and leads to lane at bottom. Turn left on lane, then immediately right at

junction. Turn right at T-junction to reach ferry terminal.

WHAT TO LOOK OUT FOR
(**a**) **View** Over the Camel Estuary towards Padstow, and out to sea. The river is much frequented by various migrating waders, including godwits, plovers, greenshanks and knots.
(**b**) This is **Daymer Bay**, where St Petroc landed from Ireland in the 6th century; he later founded a monastery in Padstow.
(**c**) **Pentire Point** The crag of pillow-lava was not climbed until well into this century. The next headland is the Rumps, a ridge with some striking pinnacles, capped by an Iron Age hillfort.
(**d**) **St Enodoc's church** No road leads to it, and it's curiously situated in the sand dunes. Norman, with later additions, it has from time to time been engulfed by sand. When, in the 18th century, it was actually under the dunes, the vicar cut a hole in the roof for him and the parishioners to crawl through, so that the weekly service could be held that qualified the church to collect tithe dues from local fishermen and farmers. It was dug out properly and restored in 1863. Sir John Betjeman is buried in the churchyard.

The Luxulyan Valley and Treffry Viaduct

Contributed by C M Bristow
Recommended by Maysie Webb,
L K Robinson, Ian and Hope Fry

A wooded valley with waterways built in the last century to serve granite quarries; lush vegetation of ferns, rhododendrons and bluebells; arable fields in the final section. Very wet underfoot; wellingtons are advisable. Route-finding easy up to 6, then rather involved; field path at end is undefined.

Length 4 miles (6.5 km), 2 hours
Difficulty 2
Start Luxulyan parish church, 5 miles NE of St Austell. *By train* Luxulyan. Grid reference SX 052580
OS maps 1:50,000 200; 1:25,000 SX 05/15
Refreshments Pub and shop in Luxulyan

WALK DIRECTIONS

1 (a) With parish church on your left, follow road downhill, out of village. After ¼ mile, just after crossing stream, turn right at road junction. Stream on right becomes feed for a leat (an artificial waterway) which crosses under road to left side. Follow road for ½ mile (b) to road junction 2. Turn left and immediately right to enter woods by two granite posts. Bear left up incline and pick up footpath running on right-hand side of leat. Follow leat, passing under viaduct, for 1 mile until remains of huge water wheel are seen on left (c).

About 100 yards further on is Carmears Incline going obliquely across line of leat, up and down (d) 3. Follow incline down, soon passing under stone bridge. 4 Reach Ponts Mill (e). Retrace your steps for about ½ mile back up incline, and continue on it past lower leat, until you reach the point where the

upper leat discharges into the derelict water wheel 5.

Follow upper leat from fork along line of old railway (some chairs and rails visible) for 1 mile to Treffry Viaduct (f), which now cross over 6. Follow line of railway (quite muddy in places). After 200 yards this crosses small aqueduct (sluices are visible on right). 100 yards later and 20 yards before old railway crosses river, turn left on path leading steeply down to steps. After 80 yards fork right by shed and follow path by river bank, until coming to stile leading to bridge over river. Cross this and 50 yards later (avoid passing between stone posts on left after 20 yards) cross stone steps in wall on left. This follows leat for short distance before entering field 7.

Follow right edge of field and, at the end, enter second field by the gate-posts on right. Bear half left

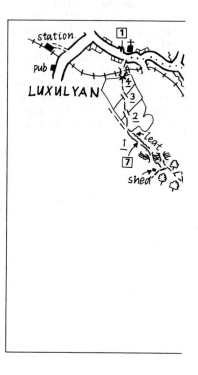

38

across second field, heading for stone stile slightly to left of Luxulyan church in distance. Continue half left to stone stile in third field, and in fourth field head for gate in front of Luxulyan church. Cross railway beyond gate and return to start.

WHAT TO LOOK OUT FOR

(**a**) About 100 yards downhill from Luxulyan post office, on the left, is a **holy well**, in good condition and easily reached from the road. Many Cornish villages used to have one of these, but now they're something of a rarity.

(**b**) Large **granite quarry** on left (in distance) is still active. On opposite side of the valley curious, large, rounded granite boulders are 'core stones' produced by weathering attacking the rock's joints. Many of London's granite kerbstones came from this valley.

(**c**) This **water wheel** provided power for Carmears Incline (see below).

(**d**) **Carmears Incline** Entirely water powered, opened in 1841 to enable trucks to be hauled up from the Ponts Mill area. Early locomotives could not take the slope of the Luxulyan Valley, hence the need for a constructed incline. The railway line up the valley was built at end of the 19th century.

(**e**) **Ponts Mill** Remains of a complex of mills that crushed minerals by means of water power.

(**f**) **Treffry Viaduct** Built to carry the railway conveying granite and china clay over the valley to Par, and also carrying (in a trough under the tracks) the main leat supplying water to the Ponts Mill area. Built by mining prospector John Thomas Austin (who also built Par harbour) in 1837, it is 98ft high, 650ft long.

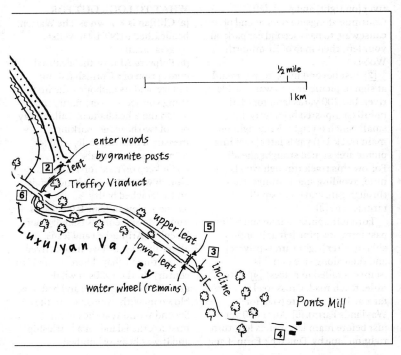

The West Looe River, Talland Bay and Polperro

Leads through woods high above the River Looe, then follows quiet lanes to the sea, where the coast path gives the most scenic approach to Polperro. Easy route-finding.

Length 7½ miles (12km), 3½ hours
Difficulty 2
Start Main car park, Looe, just on W (Polperro) side of road bridge over River Looe. Grid reference SX 253537. *By train* Looe
OS maps 1:50,000 201;
1:25,000 SX 25/35
Refreshments Pubs and tea-rooms in Looe and Polperro; hotel in Talland Bay

WALK DIRECTIONS

1 Start at end of car park nearest Looe itself (by toilets) and go towards river, passing small play area and at end crossing stone causeway between river (on right) and pool (left). Continue alongside river at end of causeway, to pass second car park on your left, then map of Kilminorth Woods.

2 Just beyond map, keep forward at sign to picnic area to walk beside river, but 200 yards later fork left uphill (signposted bridleway) by small bench on right. Keep right on main track 150 yards later (avoiding picnic area signed straight ahead). Follow this track through woods for 1 mile, avoiding side turnings. Pass through gate and on to small tarmac lane **3**.

Turn left uphill on lane and follow past farm, keeping left at junction shortly after (right turn is private), and then along both side of fields (semi-metalled in places) **4** After 1 mile, reach road. Cross road to tarmac lane opposite (sign for Waylands Farm). **5** After 600 yards, just before main lane bends left, turn right on lane by Tencreek Farm. Lane

descends, passing 'unsuitable for motor vehicles' sign, crossing ford/footbridge at bottom, and then becomes track on other side. Ascend to pass through farmyard and reach road **6**.

Left on road towards sea. Keep straight on at junction after ¼ mile to beach at Talland Bay, then follow lane to 'no through road' sign. Keep straight on, and coast path is picked up on left, at signpost 50 yards later. It briefly re-emerges on to lane 100 yards later, but after this it is an easy route all the way into Polperro (**a**), (**b**) **7**.

From Polperro retrace steps to Talland Bay, past beach and up past toilets on your right, turning right immediately after them **8**. Follow road for 300 yards before forking right on to coastal path opposite isolated house (**c**), (**d**). Follow well-trodden path back to Looe (**e**).

WHAT TO LOOK OUT FOR

(**a**) **Clifflands** Known as The Warren, bequeathed to NT by novelist Angela Brazil.
(**b**) **Polperro** Almost the idealised conception of a Cornish fishing village, and its harbour – the first thing you see – is very pretty indeed.
(**c**) On the E headland of Talland Bay, one of two **beacons** marking a measured nautical mile, used for Admiralty speed trials.
(**d**) Or keep on road for **Talland church** which has fine bench-ends and a detached belfry.
(**e**) Soon, view of **Looe Island** (also known as St George's Island) where Joseph of Arimathea and Jesus allegedly stayed. Two monks lived in a now-ruined chapel here in the 12th century. In the 1930s, a whale grounded on the island and had to be blown up with explosives. In the Second World War the enemy mistook the island for a battleship and it was heavily bombed.

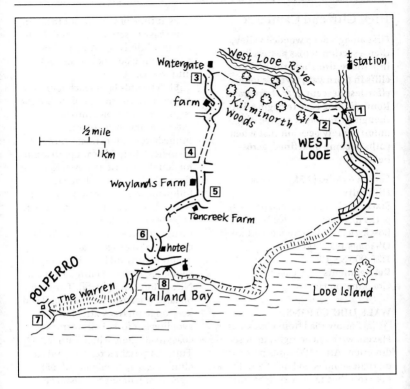

High Cliff and Cambeak

First along a deep wooded valley, then a section across pasture leads into the return along the highest cliffs in Cornwall, giving a long, effortless descent over short grass. Route-finding easy to begin with, though enthusiastic signposting unfortunately pegs out just when paths become undefined, across fields.

Length 6 miles (9.5km), 3 hours
Difficulty 3
Start Crackington Haven (two car parks in village), 6 miles NE of Boscastle. Grid reference SX 143968
OS maps 1:50,000 190;
1:25,000 SX 19
Refreshments Compass Inn, Crackington Haven

WALK DIRECTIONS

1 (**a**) Follow road from Crackington Haven, with sea on right, in Boscastle direction. After 100 yards pass road on right signposted High Cliff. Do not take this, but take next right turn, leading to farm. At farm, keep straight on (avoiding half right turn down to gate and sharp left turn uphill) to gate with yellow marker, and continue on well-trodden path into woods.

2 After 300 yards cross bridge. Beyond bridge keep right by signpost to Woodgates (avoiding straight on to Hallagather) and cross second bridge **3**. Keep left (yellow waymark) after second bridge. **4** After ½ mile reach signpost indicating Woodgate on right, and continue half left on well-trodden path signposted 'Sheepdip' to continue along main valley (path blocked by some fallen

trees at time of writing but these are quite easy to scramble under). Path emerges briefly by stile into field after ¼ mile but soon leads back into woods.

5 300 yards later reach four-way signpost. Keep straight on/half right (signposted Pengold) through gate/stile and over stream. Immediately after stream turn right up to field. In field bear uphill aiming for double electricity posts. Keep to right-hand side of bank ahead, following it until reaching electricity posts, then bear quarter right to gate at brow of hill where a clear track turns left across corner of field then continues to Pengold farm.

Enter farmyard by public footpath signposts, between farm on left and Nissen huts on right. **6**. Turn right on farm track through farmyard and keep on main track after farm, avoiding left fork. Follow track to coast road, along which turn left. **7** Turn sharp right after 100 yards to climb steps up to High Cliff (NT sign). Bear half left to coastal path (not well defined initially) at edge of cliff 50 yards away. Turn right on coastal path and follow for 2 miles back to Crackington Haven (avoid any paths leading inland) (**b**).

WHAT TO LOOK OUT FOR

(**a**) **Crackington Haven** Has a graveyard for shipwrecked sailors who were not allowed to be buried in consecrated ground.
(**b**) The first rise (after 300 yards) is **High Cliff**, the highest cliff in Cornwall. 1¼ miles later is a headland called Cambeak which gives views of High Cliff and the coast N towards Hartland Point.

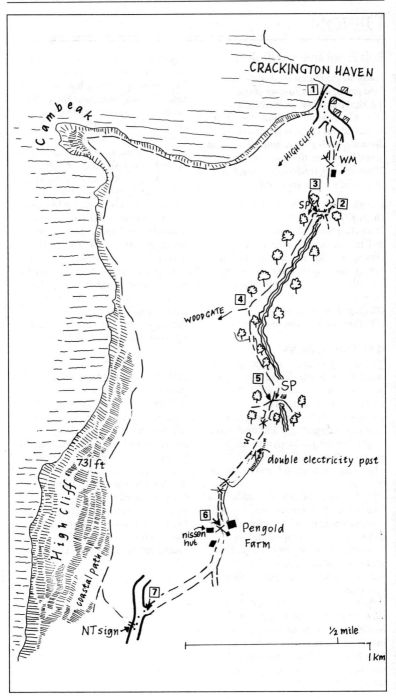

CRACKINGTON HAVEN

1

HIGH CLIFF

WM

3

SP

2

Cambeak

WOODGATE

4

5

SP

UP

double electricity post

731 ft

High Cliff

6

nissen hut

Pengold Farm

Coastal Path

7

NT sign

½ mile

1 km

43

DEVON

Bolt Head and Starehole Bay

Starts off along farmland tracks and field paths, with glimpses of the Salcombe Estuary, then reaches cliff-tops. Beyond Starehole Bay, path is hacked out of the rock for a short distance, with a sheer drop beyond the metal barrier on the seaward side. Route-finding moderately easy, but not all field paths are visible.

Length 4 miles (6.5km), 2 hours
Difficulty 2
Start Overbecks/Sharpitor NT car park (NT museum/gardens at Youth Hostel), 1 mile S of Salcombe (fee; free to members). Well signposted along coastal road from Salcombe. Grid reference SX 728374
OS maps 1:50,000 202; 1:25,000 Outdoor Leisure 20

WALK DIRECTIONS

1 Turn right out of car park, ignoring entrance to Overbecks (**a**). Road soon becomes track, ascending. **2** 200 yards later turn right on track signposted Tor Woods. Track runs between hedges (**b**). **3** 250 yards later, at gate, left into field, signposted Starehole Bottom. Follow right edge of first and second fields (there is no path).

4 Follow right edge of third field as far as stone barn, taking two gates/stiles on right just before it. Bear quarter right (no path) aiming for prominent break in gorse ahead. Here, signpost to Malborough points forward to track through gorse. Follow as far as gate.

5 Do not pass through gate but turn right in front of it, signposted Malborough, on to narrow path leading into field; keep to left edge to reach gate. Maintain direction in second field to pass through gate/stile into farmyard on the left.

6 On far side of farm keep quarter right on to stony track between fences. Ten minutes' walking leads to tarmac lane **7**. Turn left on lane then, 100 yards later, turn right through gate, signposted to cliffs. Grassy track leads to derelict farm ahead; continue forward through gate out of farmyard and forward with hedge on right to next gate **8**. Emerge into grassland (The Warren, NT-owned).

Continue forward (no path) for short distance to reach cliff-top path just beyond gorse. Turn left. Route from here is easy to find. **9** At Bolt Head (**c**) (which is after 1 mile: a promontory with disused look-out approached by grassy hollow with crag on right side) be sure to drop down into hollow (obvious path). At next hollow (Starehole Bottom), keep forward at signpost. Follow back to starting-point.

WHAT TO LOOK OUT FOR

(**a**) **Overbecks Garden and Museum** (NT; open to public; fee) Peaceful six-acre landscaped site of rare plants, shrubs and trees, overlooking Salcombe Estuary, with small natural history museum. Picnicking permitted in garden.
(**b**) **View** Over Salcombe Estuary towards Kingsbridge.
(**c**) These cliffs provided the setting for Masefield's adventure novel *Jim Davis*. **View** E to Prawle Point, the southernmost point in Devon.

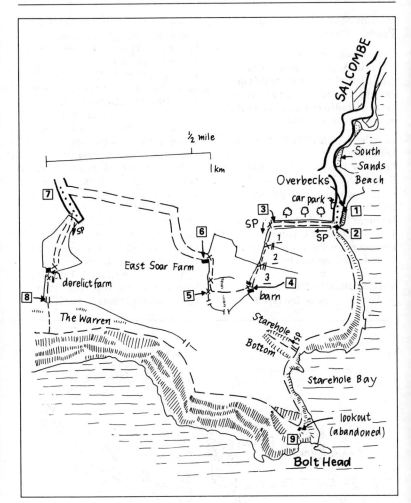

SALCOMBE

South
Sands
Beach

Overbecks

car park

SP

3

SP

1

2

SP

1

2

6

East Soar Farm

3

4

barn

5

7

SP

derelict farm

8

The Warren

Starehole Bottom

SP

Starehole Bay

lookout
(abandoned)

9

Bolt Head

½ mile

1 km

Woodcombe Point and Prawle Point

Takes tracks between hedges to sea, where coast path runs above low sandstone cliffs and at the foot of craggy slopes of gorse and bracken; small secluded beach at foot of cliffs at end. Easy route-finding.

Length 5½ miles (9km), 2½ hours
Difficulty 2
Start East Prawle, 9 miles SE of Kingsbridge. Car parking by village green, opposite Pig's Nose Inn. Grid reference SX 781364
OS maps 1:50,000 202; 1:25,000 Outdoor Leisure 20
Refreshments Pig's Nose Inn and Providence Inn, both in East Prawle.

WALK DIRECTIONS

1 With Pig's Nose Inn on left, follow road down to T-junction, at which turn left then take first right.

2 After 200 yards turn right on lane in front of phone box. Ignore right turn to Maelcombe House after 250 yards and ignore left turn 100 yards later. 100 yards after latter, track narrows to path, at first between hedges, then through bracken with hedge on left, then forward along left edge of field (well waymarked).

3 At end of field emerge on corner of track and turn right, signposted Woodcombe Sand. Track bends left after 100 yards; 100 yards later keep forward on grassy track where main (stony) track turns right. Grassy track itself bends right shortly by marker post and descends towards sea.

4 After ½ mile, reach T-junction with coast path (signposted). Turn right. Path is obvious and well

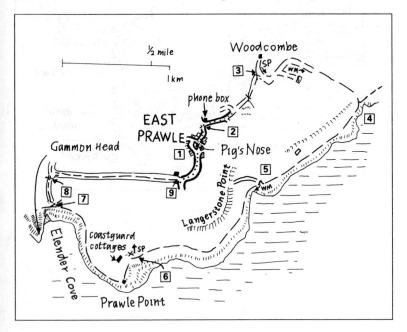

waymarked as it passes farm, then keeps slightly inland, making for craggy headland (Langerstone Point) (**a**). **5** Two fields before Langerstone Point turn sharp left, waymarked on post on left (ahead is a track between hedges which soon ascends). Follow left edge of field to regain cliff-top.

6 Just before coastguard cottages, avoid turning inland, signposted East Prawle, but follow fence below cottages to reach look-out hut at Prawle Point (**b**). Continue to end of next bay, Elender Cove. **7** 75 yards before path ahead reaches NT sign (Gammon Head) (**c**), turn sharp right on path. 75 yards later, sharp left. **8** Cross stile after 400 yards and 100 yards later turn right on to track between hedges. **9** After 1 mile, left on road, and follow back to start.

WHAT TO LOOK OUT FOR
(**a**) The **moorland slope** on your right was once a cliff, but has been eroded, and the eroded material washed down to its base to form a less steep slope, separated from the sea by the present low cliffs.
(**b**) **Prawle Point** The southernmost point in Devon, for centuries an important marker for seamen navigating the English Channel. An 11th-century record refers to vessels stopping here on their way from Denmark to the Holy Land. View W across the mouth of the Salcombe Estuary to Bolt Head; E to Great Sleaden Rock, near Start Point.
(**c**) Steps down on left lead to a **small sandy beach**, a good detour at low tide. Two Spanish galleons were driven ashore here, and doubloons were found in the last century.

Dartmouth Castle and Compass Cove

Ascends road briefly to continue on farm tracks with sea views, then follows coast path back (reaching sea-level at Compass Cove) for a splendid entrance into Dartmouth Harbour. Easy route-finding on clear paths and tracks.

Length 3 miles (5km), 1½ hours (4 miles (6.5km), 2 hours, if starting from Dartmouth)
Difficulty 2
Start Car park at Dartmouth Castle (free), ½ mile S of Dartmouth. *Or, from Dartmouth,* follow road alongside river estuary towards sea. At Warfleet road bends right inland; shortly after, turn left into Castle Road, signposted Dartmouth Castle. Fork right 200 yards later (left leads to castle); car parks are on right of road. Grid reference SX 884503
By train Kingswear (Torbay and Dartmouth Railway); ferry from Kingswear to Dartmouth
OS maps 1:50,000 202; 1:25,000 Outdoor Leisure 20
Refreshments Pubs and cafés in Dartmouth

WALK DIRECTIONS

1 Go uphill on road. ¼ mile later keep to road at sign indicating no through road ahead, but access to Compass Cove (ignoring coast path on left). **2** After 200 yards keep right at cottage, signposted to Little Dartmouth. At coastguard cottages road reaches gate; follow track ahead for ¾ mile to farm **3**. Continue forward at farm, signposted 'NT car park ¼ mile'.

4 Immediately before car park turn left over stile, signposted coast path. Route from here is obvious and waymarked with acorn markers; at next stile coast path turns left, close to sea. **5** ½ mile later cross bridge and keep left, over stile; avoid next stile 100 yards later but keep right, on coast path. Path later descends to stile (right is pleasant diversion down to tiny beach at Compass Cove). Follow back to start (**a**), (**b**).

WHAT TO LOOK OUT FOR

(**a**) **View** Across Dartmouth Harbour to the Day Mark, a hollow tower put up in 1864 as a navigational aid. The excellent natural harbourage has meant that Dartmouth has long been an important maritime town; the second and third crusades sailed from here in 1147 and 1190.
(**b**) **Dartmouth Castle** (English Heritage; open to public; fee). Small, intact 15th-century castle that, with Kingswear Castle on the other side, forms the fortifications of the harbour mouth. There are two floors and a roof, from which there is a good view of the harbour. Adjoining is St Petroc's church, much rebuilt in the 17th century.

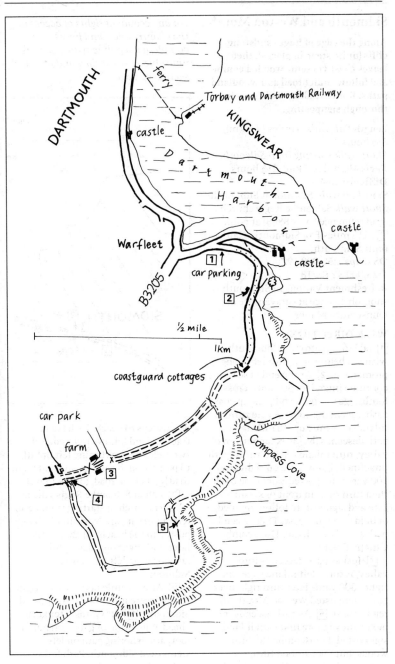

DARTMOUTH

ferry

Torbay and Dartmouth Railway

KINGSWEAR

castle

D a r t m o u t h

H a r b o u r

castle

Warfleet

B3205

castle

1 car parking

2

½ mile

1km

coastguard cottages

car park

farm

Compass Cove

3

4

5

Sidmouth and Weston Mouth

Along the edge of huge sandstone cliffs (quite steep in places), then leaves coast via semi-wooded combe and follows quiet road and woodland paths. Route-finding made easy by thorough signposting.

Length *Full walk* 6 miles (9.5 km), 3½ hours
Short walk starting from Salcombe Regis 4½ miles (7km), 2½ hours
Difficulty 3–4
Start *Full walk* Seafront at Sidmouth
Short walk Salcombe Regis church (grid reference SY 148888) at point 7 , 1½ miles E of Sidmouth. Can omit Sidmouth
OS maps 1:50,000 192; 1:25,000 SY 08/18
Refreshment Various in Sidmouth, shop/off-licence at caravan site at Dunscombe Manor

WALK DIRECTIONS

1 (a) From seafront in Sidmouth, with sea before you, turn left along promenade. 2 At the end of seafront continue inland for 50 yards, cross footbridge on right, and pick up coast path, ascending steps. Avoid turns inland; continue up. ¾ mile later path descends (b). 3 Near bottom of valley, turn inland for 300 yards (path undefined; ignore gate on right after 100 yards signposted Salcombe Bay), then turn right in front of kissing-gate and signpost, to follow right edge of field to rejoin coast. Then ascend path steeply to Higher Dunscombe Cliff (NT sign).

4 Just as path descends into valley, it turns left inland (trees on right). 300 yards later turn right over stile, signposted Weston Mouth, to rejoin coast. 5 As path ascends into next valley ignore first turn inland, signposted 'Dunscombe ⅓', into woods, but take second turn, signposted 'Dunscombe ½', shortly after; first, however, detour ahead

For an account of rights of access in the countryside – and how to complain if a public right of way is unusable – see the 'law and practice' section on page 17.

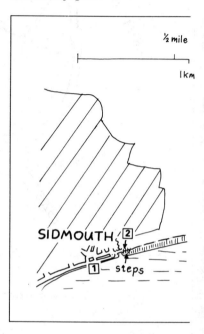

down steps to beach. Path (soon track) inland follows right edge of two fields before turning left uphill, to pass through caravan site and on to road 6 . Left on road, follow ½ mile.

7 Left at Salcombe Regis village (c), past church (if starting from here, left out of car park by church), signposted to the beach. 8 200 yards later, fork right on track uphill by last house on left, signposted Sidmouth.

9 After ¼ mile take path on right through gate into woods, signposted Sidmouth. 10 300 yards later keep ahead at junction of paths, on public footpath, ignoring path on left signposted Sidmouth. Path follows inside edge of woods for 500 yards, with fields on left. 11 Cross track to

If you have a walk to suggest for any subsequent edition of the Holiday
Which? Good Walks Guide, *please send it to us. We need a rough sketch map
and a brief summary of the walk's attractions. Directions are not necessary.
Write to:* Holiday Which? Good Walks Guide, *Consumers' Association,
14 Buckingham Street, London WC2N 6DS.*

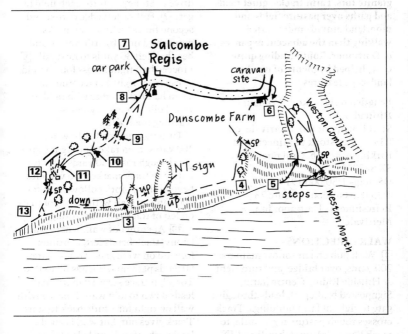

take path opposite/slightly to right.
100 yards later cross driveway, then
immediately left through gate.

⌐12¬ Straight on at signpost 100
yards later; follow any paths ahead to
sea. ⌐13¬ At coast path signpost, right
to return to Sidmouth *or* left to
continue route if starting from
Salcombe Regis; continue to ⌐3¬.

WHAT TO LOOK OUT FOR
(**a**) **Sidmouth** Became fashionable
after the Duke and Duchess of Kent
came here in 1819 with their
daughter, the young Princess
Victoria, and stayed at what is now
the Royal Glen Hotel. Victoria later
returned as Queen and presented the
stained glass window to Sidmouth
church, in memory of her father. The
town contains some of the best
seaside Regency architecture in the
country, with an elegant terrace of
white stucco villas and hotels along
the seafront, and a square further W.
Beyond that are some eye-catching
Victorian hotels in country-house
and rustic styles.
(**b**) The **cliffs** are formed of layers of
red marl, greensand and clay, the
change of rock shown up by
alternating bands of vegetation type.
(**c**) **Salcombe Regis** A handful of
cottages and a church, in a small
hollow. Outside the restored Norman
church is the grave of Sir Norman
Lockyer, Astronomer Royal, founder
of the nearby Salcombe Hill
Observatory and discoverer of helium
in the rays of the sun.

Sampford Spiney and Pew Tor

*Based on a contribution from
Brian Marsden*

**A lush valley with good views from
granite tors. Farm tracks, quiet roads
and paths over pasture fields and
moorland provide more varied
walking than the adjacent expanses
of Dartmoor. Route-finding quite
easy, helped by plenty of nearby
landscape features.**

Length 5 miles (8km), 2½ hours
Difficulty 2
Start Dartmoor Inn, Merrivale, on
B3357 (Tavistock to Princetown).
Parking near pub. Grid reference
SX 548752
OS maps 1:50,000 191 or 201;
1:25,000 Outdoor Leisure 28
Refreshments Dartmoor Inn,
Merrivale

WALK DIRECTIONS

[1] With pub on left follow main road
200 yards, over bridge, and turn right
at Hillside Riding Centre (farm).
Signposted bridlepath leads through a
gate to right of farm buildings. Track
crosses rough pasture for ½ mile, to
reach Longash Farm (abandoned) [2].
Continue forward through farm to
gate (blue waymark) to emerge on
less well-defined path with wall on
right. This crosses stream, then
becomes better defined and arrives at
gate next to rock outcrop, ½ mile
beyond Longash Farm. Follow track
downhill for further ¼ mile to arrive
at tarmac lane, with Daveytown
Farm on left [3].

Continue straight down lane for ¾
mile to reach crossroads. [4] Turn
right on lane, signposted Horrabridge,
going first downhill, then across
river-bridge, up past cottages on your
left to reach cattle-grid ¼ mile from

bridge [5]. Turn right uphill on track
at cattle-grid, after ¼ mile reaching
tarmac lane with large house
(Stoneycroft) on right [6].

Take signposted path to right of
drive to Stoneycroft to reach field by
gate [7]. Follow left edge of first and
second fields (yellow waymarks),
enter third field by stile ahead, and
bear half left 30 yards to next stile [8].
Proceed half right across fourth field,
to gap in far right-hand corner and
again half right across fifth field, to
gate. Follow track beyond, soon
reaching road (**a**) [9].

Turn right on road, following it for
200 yards, then take first right signed
'no through road'. 50 yards later turn
left on to track marked 'no vehicles
beyond this point'. Follow track for
400 yards to wall with screen of trees
on left of track (Pewtor Cottage).

[10] At corner of wall, where main
(stony) track bends left, continue
forward on wide grassy track. After
80 yards path on left leads up to Pew
Tor (**b**); retrace steps from it. Track
leads down to join wall. Proceed with
wall on right for 1 mile back to start.
Track gives out, but wall is good
landmark; after ½ mile ladder- stile
leads over wall to Vixen Tor (optional
detour); just before stile is area of
boggy ground, avoidable by keeping
to left.

WHAT TO LOOK OUT FOR

(**a**) 300 yards to left, below the
church, the former **manor-house**,
now a farmhouse. Dated 1617, but
some parts are older.
(**b**) **View** From Pew Tor S over Tamar
Valley towards Plymouth; W into
Cornwall; N beyond Merrivale
quarry to Great Staple Tor; E across
Walkham Valley to King's Tor and
Leeden Tor.

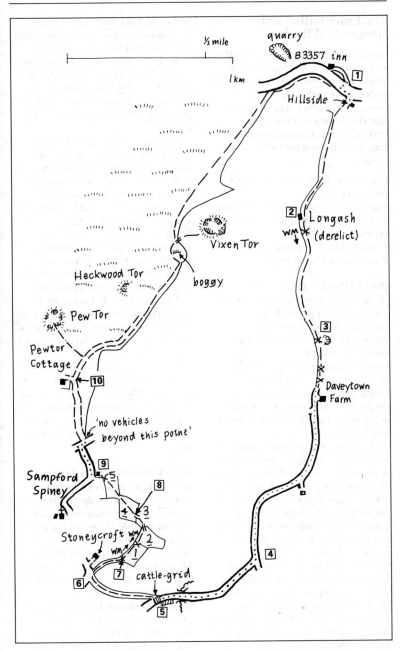

The Erme Valley and Hangershell Rock

Quickly reaches deciduous woodland and pasture overlooking the gentle slopes of the Erme Valley, then much wider views to the south from the moor. Field paths not all defined; moorland route just after 11 is invisible (easy, though, providing Hangershell Rock isn't shrouded in mist).

Length 7 miles (11km), 3½ hours
Difficulty 2–3
Start Ivybridge town centre, at river, by National Westminster Bank
OS maps 1:50,000 202; 1:25,000 Outdoor Leisure 28
Refreshments In Ivybridge

WALK DIRECTIONS

1 (**a**) Follow Erme Road, with river on right, out of town. 2 After ½ mile, just before road passes under railway viaduct, fork right on to track, under viaduct and into woods, soon rejoining river. 3 600 yards later look out for small disused concrete reservoir to left of path. 200 yards after, turn sharp left uphill on stony path opposite boundary stone marked ILB.

4 After 300 yards reach junction with track; turn right along it. Track leads out of woods and bends left just after entrance to farm on right. 5 200 yards after this bend keep ahead through gate at junction of tracks (signposted). Track follows left (top) edge of two fields 6. At end of second field, keep forward (signposted) to farm. Beyond farm keep on walled track; after 80 yards keep left (signposted) to reach field 7. Follow right edge of field (no path). In second field keep forward to reach gate opposite. Follow clear path beyond, through bracken to gate, then through woods.

8 On leaving woods by gate, turn right along edge of first field with woods on right (no path). In second field maintain direction to protruding corner of wall (80 yards to left of stone barn), then forward along wall to gate. Walled track beyond leads to tarmac lane. 9 Turn right on lane. Follow ½ mile to Harford church (**b**) 10. Turn left immediately beyond church.

11 After ½ mile, at end of lane, climb up bank above car park and stand so that lane you have just followed is behind you. Continue same direction as lane and head across moorland (no path) aiming for prominent tor (rock outcrop), Hangershell Rock, ¾ mile away. (Valley below tor is slightly boggy; it is best to skirt round left of bogs.)

12 100 yards before Hangershell Rock, reach stony track and turn right along it (**c**), (**d**). Follow for 1 mile. 13 Fork right on to grassy track just by small section of old stone wall on right and boulders on left of main track. Fork right 30 yards later and follow down to gate 14. Beyond gate, walled track leads to outskirts of Ivybridge. 15 After ½ mile turn right at T-junction and immediately left on road. Keep straight on after crossing railway and follow back to starting-place.

WHAT TO LOOK OUT FOR

(**a**) **Ivybridge** Largely 19th-century town of few charms, despite the loveliness of the countryside that surrounds it. At the top of the town (seen at the end of the walk) is the striking Victorian paper mill that brought about the town's expansion. The old part along the River Erme is passed at the start.
(**b**) **Harford church** Largely restored, but contains a tomb-chest of 1566 with a brass of Thomas Williams, Speaker of the House of Commons.
(**c**) **View** Ahead (S) over the South Hams; to the right (SW), Wembury Bay near Newton Ferrers, and further

round to the right (W) towards Plymouth and into Cornwall.
(**d**) The moor is rich in **antiquities**, including numerous sites of prehistoric hut circles, cairns and enclosures. Crossing the track just N of Hangershell Rock is a long prehistoric stone row, running N to S. The track itself is the bed of an old tramway, built in 1910 to serve the Redlake china-clay works; the rails were taken up in 1932.

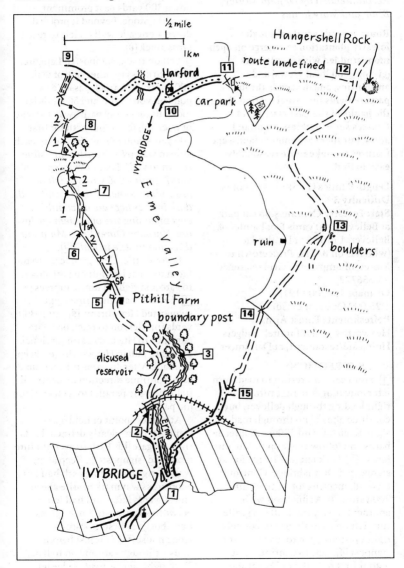

Dartmoor clapper bridges, Bellever Tor and the East Dart River

Based on contributions from Jack Crewe and Brian Marsden Recommended by Dr John Morley, Brian and Mary James

Route ascends gently through forestry plantation to emerge on open moor studded with granite tors (giving good local views) and antiquities, and descends through pasture fields for a final section along the banks of the East Dart River. Crosses some pathless moorland areas, but there are enough landscape features to make route reasonably easy to find.

Length 9 miles (14.5km), 4½ hours
Difficulty 3
Start Forestry Commission car park at Bellever, 100 yards E of hamlet of Bellever, 1 mile S of Postbridge (which is on B3212, Princetown to Moretonhampstead). Grid reference SX 656772
OS maps 1:50,000 191; 1:25,000 Outdoor Leisure 28
Refreshments Forest Arms, Hexworthy (just off route); Badgers Holt (café/restaurant) at Dartsmeet

WALK DIRECTIONS

1 From car park return to road, turn left along it. Ignore first turning on right leading through Bellever, but continue ahead ('no through road' sign). Keep forward 200 yards later at barns and follow track up to gate into forest. **2** Fork left just inside forest, signposted Dunnabridge. Continue forward, meeting forest track after 200 yards. **3** At junction with another forestry track after ½ mile, turn left on to it, then immediately right up stony path to leave forest at signpost **4**. Left to continue (but detour first to Bellever Tor (**a**) ahead, signposted, for view).

At end of forest on left, turn left across wall, signposted Huccaby. Proceed along forest wall on left up to rocky outcrop, Laughter Tor (no path) **5**. Turn right from Laughter Tor (no path), keeping just to right of ruined stone wall enclosure and bearing down 300 yards past prominent standing stone. Beyond it proceed down alongside wall on left to reach cross-track **6**.

Left on track, signposted Laughter Hole, to cross to other side of wall. 100 yards later, track passes dew pond on your right, and 50 yards later look out for grassy path away to right of track (**b**); join it (no path for first 100 yards) and follow ½ mile to reach stile in wall (*NB: If path is invisible return to wall. Bear down slope (no path), aiming 200 yards to left of protruding corner of right-hand wall; dark bushes here are discernible, encompassing site of ancient enclosure, Huccaby Outer Ring. Maintain direction to stile in wall*) **7**.

Beyond stile, clear path leads to tor. From tor bear half left on path down to gate just right of house in trees (**c**) **8**. Left on road, then first right, signposted Hexworthy. **9** After 300 yards turn left on to track opposite entrance to Huccaby Farm (optional detour to pub in Hexworthy (**d**): keep on road). After 40 yards turn left up to gate, continue direction up centre of field, keeping parallel to wall on right (no path).

At highest point of field, pass signpost; path, clearly defined, leads through gate **10**. Path turns right into next field (signposted). Keep along wall on right, avoiding path half left. Soon cross waymarked stile ahead, and 50 yards later turn half left between stone posts down across field (boggy at first) towards grey stone house **11**. Left just before house, through gate and on to lane. Turn right, across road-bridge (**e**), then left on riverside path to join driveway to restaurant **12**.

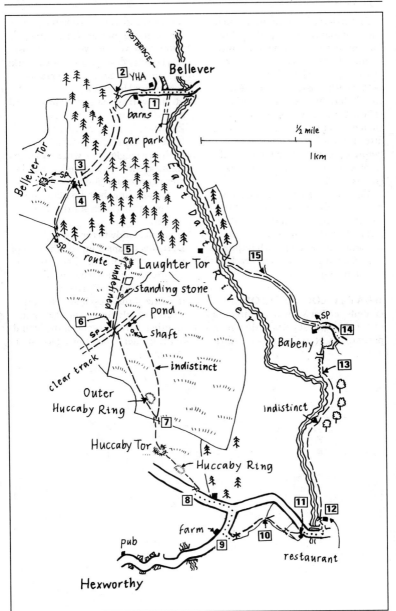

POSTBRIDGE

Bellever

2 YHA

1

barns

car park

½ mile

1 km

Bellever Tor

3 ←SA

4

route

undefined

SP

5

Laughter Tor

standing stone

pond

6

SP

shaft

clear track

indistinct

Outer
Huccaby Ring

7

Huccaby Tor

Huccaby Ring

East Dart River

15

SP

Babeny

14

13

indistinct

8

farm

pub

9

10

11

12

restaurant

Hexworthy

Pass to left of restaurant, through gate and join riverside path. Follow for 1 mile until reaching substantial tributary stream. Turn right along stream. ¼ mile later **13** and 20 yards before path crosses minor stream, turn half right by electricity pole and follow path 100 yards towards wall, then quarter left to reach tarmac lane after 100 yards **14**. Left on lane. Just before farm, right as signposted, then immediately right again up track (signposted).

15 ½ mile later enter open area, proceed with wall on left (heading towards house) down to river. Pick up riverside path running inside forest on same side of river. Path improves, and leads to bridge at Bellever. Left to return to start.

WHAT TO LOOK OUT FOR
(a) **Bellever Tor** View in all directions over the emptiest parts of the moor, particularly N to the army training areas.

(b) Path passes close to **shafts**, part of a tin mine known as North Mine, 156ft deep. Was active in the 1850s.

(c) Half way down, a gorsy area marks the site of **Huccaby Ring**, a prehistoric pound for stock.

(d) **Hexworthy** Scattered hamlet, with a pub by the green. A cottage nearby known as Jolly Lane Cot was the last house on Dartmoor to have been built in a single day – when squatters' rights allowed anyone to enclose an area of open land and claim it as his own, providing the house built on it was put up between sunrise and sunset.

(e) Immediately to the left is **Dartsmeet clapper bridge**, the first of three such bridges on this walk, the granite skeleton of a medieval packhorse bridge. Dartsmeet, the meeting of the West and East Dart rivers (in early times 'the Dart' and 'another Dart') was one of the bounds of the former royal hunting forest of Dartmoor.

Lustleigh Cleave and Hunter's Tor

Based on contributions from Brian Marsden and Jack Crewe

Through mixed forest, passing the Becka Falls and later rising to Lustleigh Cleave ('cleave' meaning cliff), a moorland edge capped by Hunter's Tor. An idyllic thatched village half way (with tea-room to match). Dense network of paths, but route-finding is made easy by thorough signposting.

Length 9 miles (14.5km), 4½ hours
Difficulty 3
Start Manaton, 4 miles S of Moretonhampstead, in car park at crossroads by bus shelter, opposite turning to Leighon. Grid reference SX 750812
OS maps 1:50,000 191; 1:25,000 Outdoor Leisure 28
Refreshments Kestor Inn, Water; café (in season) at Becka Falls; Cleave Inn and Primrose Cottage tea-room, Lustleigh

WALK DIRECTIONS

1 Leave car park at far (church) end, cross first road (which leads to church (**a**)) and turn left on second one 20 yards later, passing village green. Continue past village hall on your left and 30 yards later turn right on track signposted 'Horsham for paths to Lustleigh'.

2 At T-junction of tracks after ½ mile, turn right, signposted 'Water ½ mile'. Track passes through woods for further ½ mile. **3** Just before reaching thatched cottages, turn right, signposted 'Manaton direct'. After 100 yards turn right again on to tarmac lane, following it past cottages (and ignoring first road on right), to reach junction of lanes after 100 yards. Turn right, soon reaching main road **4**.

Left on road for 100 yards, then cross stile on left, signposted Lustleigh via Becka Falls and Bovey Valley. Path skirts right side of playing field, then passes through woods with stream away to right. **5** After ½ mile reach wooden bridge over Becka brook (leading to car park, toilets and café/kiosk). Do not cross bridge but carry straight on for 75 yards. Next right fork leads down to falls (left fork is continuation of route); retrace steps and continue, signposted Lustleigh Cleave.

Path crosses stile after ¼ mile and becomes wider forest track. Follow ¼ mile, to junction **6**. Turn quarter right, downhill, signposted Lustleigh. **7** 300 yards later fork left on track (yellow waymarks) and after 20 yards turn left up narrow path (way-marked). Path immediately reaches wall and bends right, soon descending (**b**). **8** ¼ mile later, sharp right at wall. This and next three turnings signposted Lustleigh. **9** At river, cross bridge. **10** Take right turn ¼ mile later. After 600 yards keep forward at fork.

11 Turn right on to road, then take first road on left 50 yards later. Fork right after 100 yards in front of phone box, follow into Lustleigh village, keeping right at next T-junction, then left up to church (**c**). **12** Follow road with church on left and Primrose Cottage tea-room on right. Avoid left turn immediately after church, but 30 yards later turn left by war memorial and almost immediately left again at rectory (signposted Lustleigh-N. Bovey Road'), to follow track which ends at house directly ahead after 300 yards. Take path to right of house, alongside wall, through gate into field **13**.

Continue forward, keeping to left of huge boulder, to gate. Left in second field, soon on clear path to gate. Follow fenced path ahead for ¼ mile to house **14**. Turn left, past house, then ahead along track between stone posts; fork left 30

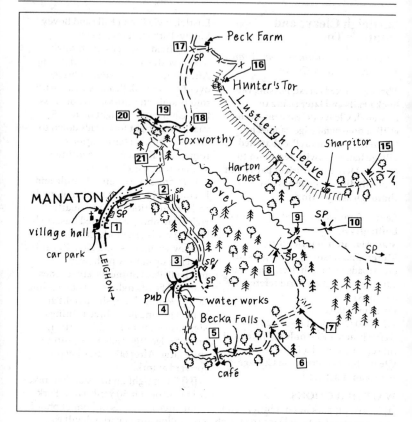

yards later to cross stream by
footbridge, and keep right at junction
100 yards later. Path then twists
uphill through trees for ¼ mile.

15 Turn left on tarmac lane, then
30 yards later right on path
signposted Hunter's Tor 1¼ miles.
After 100 yards pass through gate and
maintain direction, signposted
'Hunter's Tor (ancient camp)', rising
through more trees and, after ¼ mile,
reaching wooded crest of Sharpitor
(**d**). Path continues ahead, at first
with wall on right, and later over
open moorland. Ignore path on left (to
first rock outcrop, Harton Chest).

16 After 1 mile reach Hunter's Tor
(**e**). Pass through gate in wall ahead
and follow 'path' signs, first right
downhill, then left at T-junction with

cart track 300 yards later, and finally
passing left side of Peck Farm to
emerge by gate on track beyond
farm.

17 100 yards later, turn left at
junction, signposted Foxworthy
Bridge, and follow track for ½ mile to
reach farm at Foxworthy **18**. Turn
right on farm road signposted
Manaton to cross Bovey River. Just
after bridge turn left as signposted to
by-pass private residence on road
ahead, and left again (signposted) on
rejoining road.

19 30 yards later ignore path on
left to Manaton, and continue along
the road (marked 'County Road') for
300 yards. **20** Sharp left on to track
signposted 'Horsham or County Road
near Manaton', which leads up to

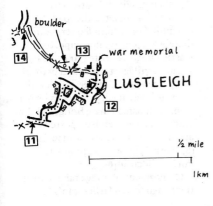

stile and continues as forest track 50
yards beyond stile. Soon fork left
where track divides. **21** After ¼
mile, cross wall on right by signpost
'Manaton ½ mile', turn left to
gate/ladder-stile and proceed half
right across next field, to tarmac lane
by cattle-grid and houses. Follow
lane to T-junction, then turn left to
car park.

WHAT TO LOOK OUT FOR
(a) **Manaton church** 15th-century,
with a fine rood screen.
(b) **Bovey Valley nature reserve**
Wooded valley, predominantly
semi-natural oak and hazel, with
some bogland. **Flora** Rare lichens and
bryophytes, moonwort, adder's
tongue. **Birds** Pied flycatchers,
redstarts, wood warblers, grey
wagtails and dippers.
(c) **Lustleigh** Carefully preserved and
much-visited village of thatched
cottages. The 13th-century church
contains an unusual 16th-century
rood screen bearing the pomegranate
badge of Catherine of Aragon.
(d) **Sharpitor** Group of rocks
overlooking Lustleigh Cleave. Until
pushed over by vandals in 1951, the
Nut Crackers Rock, a rocking stone,
used to be here. The army tried
unsuccessfully to push it back into
position, but it fell down the slope
and was smashed to pieces.
(e) **Hunter's Tor** Tors in the distance,
left to right: Haytor, Rippon Tor,
Great Tor rocks (below the skyline),
Hound Tor.

The Teign Gorge and Castle Drogo

Based on a contribution from Dr G Morley

A wooded gorge, entered from above, then a stretch along the river, followed by a short, easy climb to pick up the Hunter's Path, doubling back on a moorland edge high above the river, past the back entrance to Castle Drogo. Pasture fields and woodland in the final stages. Route-finding quite easy, with well-defined paths and tracks and thorough sign-posting nearly all the way.

Length 5 miles (8km), 2½ hours
Difficulty 1–2
Start Main square at village of Drewsteignton, S of A30 and 16 miles W of Exeter. Grid reference SX 736908. Limited parking: if full, continue down, to start walk at

Fingle Bridge car park at **6**. Grid reference SX 743900
OS maps 1:50,000 191; 1:25,000 Outdoor Leisure 28
Refreshments Drewe Arms, Drewsteignton; pub/restaurant at Fingle Bridge

WALK DIRECTIONS
1 (a) From village centre with church away to left, take road downhill (away from Exeter), immediately keeping right, signposted Castle Drogo. **2** After 100 yards, at end of village, turn left on path signposted Fingle Bridge. **3** ¼ mile later turn left at edge of woods by NT sign, signposted Fingle Bridge. **4** 200 yards later, fork left (signposted again). Follow track to tarmac lane. **5** Turn right on lane, follow to Fingle Bridge (b) **6**.

On near side of bridge take path on right, signposted Fisherman's Path.

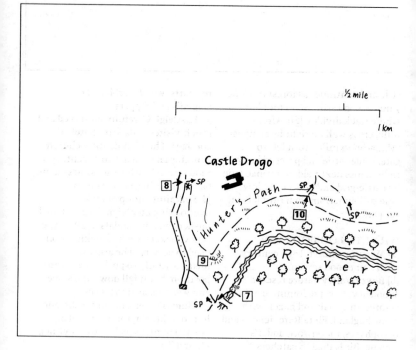

Follow path along bank of River Teign for 1½ miles. **7** Turn right opposite metal footbridge and follow path, signposted Hunter's Path, uphill for 300 yards to join lane (driveway). Continue forward. **8** After 400 yards turn sharp right through gate along path signposted Hunter's Path. **9** After 400 yards keep on main path as it bends left and continue high above Teign Gorge. **10** Optional (small) detour to visit Castle Drogo (**c**) (path on left is signposted).

11 400 yards after second path signposted to Castle Drogo, turn left, signposted Drewsteignton, and pass through gate/stile. Keep forward, following left edge of two fields. **12** Leave second field by gate/stile into woods, 50 yards to right of far left-hand corner of field. Path leads down through woods. **13** Left at junction of paths, signposted Drewsteignton. Turn right at road at top into Drewsteignton.

WHAT TO LOOK OUT FOR
(**a**) **Drewsteignton** Compact village of immaculate thatched cottages (many built of granite) arranged on a rectangle, with a late 15th-century church at one end.
(**b**) **Fingle Bridge** 16th-century granite bridge, previously used by packhorses, now a renowned (but still unspoilt) beauty spot.
(**c**) **Castle Drogo** (NT; open to public; fee) The last stately home to be built in England, Sir Edwin Lutyens' Tudoresque granite masterpiece was completed in 1930 for Julius Drewe, founder of Home and Colonial Stores. Its highly individual style is best appreciated from the inside, where the extraordinary detail extends right down to the sanitary arrangements.

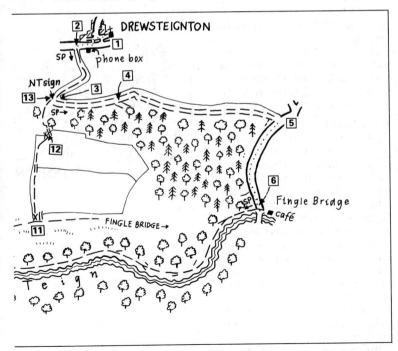

Watersmeet, Lynmouth and the Valley of Rocks

Contributed by A Randall Recommended by Christine and Allan Friar, Geoff Peacock, Dr and Mrs B W Davies

Emerges, after a short climb, high above the oak and whitebeam woodlands of the Lyn Valley, then follows the river along the valley bottom to Lynmouth, where the ascent to Lynton can be made by path or cliff railway. A short and easy (optional) western loop leads along the cliffs, into the Valley of Rocks and back over Hollerday Hill. Paths are well defined; route-finding made easy by thorough signposting.

Length *Full walk* 7 miles (11km), 3½ hours
Two short walks 4½ miles (7km), 2 hours; 2½ miles (4km), 1½ hours
Difficulty 2
Start *All walks* Lynton, on B3234, just off A39 (Minehead to Barnstaple)
OS maps 1:50,000 180; 1:25,000 SS 64/74
Refreshments Plenty in Lynton and Lynmouth. NT café at Watersmeet (closes at 5.30pm); tables are beneath a large Monterey pine

WALK DIRECTIONS

1 Standing with Lynton town hall behind you, turn left and take second right, downhill (Queen Street). After 150 yards fork left uphill past Crown Inn and 100 yards later turn left on tarmac path opposite Alford Terrace. Follow 600 yards to road **2**. Cross road, take path to right of Olde Cottage Inne opposite, cross bridge, then left on path signposted Watersmeet. Path ascends between the trees, soon emerging with views of Lynmouth and Lynton. Path is easy to follow, as it runs along fence/ bank on right, high above Lyn Valley; avoid side turnings.

Path zigzags down after ¾ mile,

crosses stream and zigzags up to rejoin fence on right. **3** 250 yards after fence on right ends, fork left downhill, signposted Watersmeet, to road. Cross road, take path opposite to reach rivers at Watersmeet (**a**). Cross two bridges **4**. Turn left in front of café. Avoid crossing first bridge (signposted Lynmouth) but keep straight on (signposted as alternative path to Lynmouth). Then follow signs to Lynmouth along side of valley. **5** After 1 mile, cross bridge at NT sign to Watersmeet, pointing way you have come. Follow riverside path into Lynmouth (**b**) **6**.

Cross road and follow seafront at Lynmouth as far as funicular railway (**c**), then *either* take path (which avoids Lynton town centre) 20 yards before cliff railway (signposted Lynton), ascending coast path to reach narrow residential road (turn

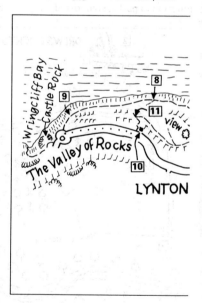

left to finish at Lynton) *or* take cliff railway into centre of Lynton.

7 /**1** *From path route* turn right on residential road, following signs to Valley of Rocks.

7 /**2** *From cliff railway* continue to town centre. Standing with Lynton town hall behind you, turn left and take third turning on left, signposted to coast path.

Both routes lead on to surfaced cliff path (**d**). **8** Ignore left fork where crags begin on left. **9** Turn left where slope ends on left, to reach road and turning-circle. (**e**) Here you can turn right to detour to Wringcliff Bay (path signposted, about 5 minutes). Turn left on road to continue up Valley of Rocks. **10** 400 yards after car park turn left by stone shelter (opposite second entrance to picnic site). Immediately fork right (signposted Lynton). Path zigzags

uphill. **11** Keep right at T-junction (signposted again Lynton) after 200 yards, and follow back to Lynton. (After ¼ mile, sharp left turn signposted to viewpoint only is an optional detour (**f**)).

WHAT TO LOOK OUT FOR

(**a**) **Watersmeet** Junction of the West Lyn and East Lyn Rivers; after the first bridge you can detour ¼ mile to right to view the waterfalls of the right-hand river. The café was built by the Halliday family in 1830 for use as a hunting- and fishing-lodge. Irish spurge, a botanical rarity found only in a few sites on the SW Peninsula, grows in these woods.

(**b**) **Lynmouth** Small, restrained Victorian resort with one or two reminders of its days as a fishing village. It was devastated in the 1952 floods, when 9 inches of rain fell in 24

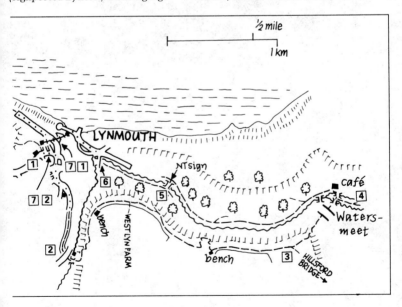

hours on to an already saturated subsoil, and 90 million tons of water surged down the Lyn Valley, carrying houses and some inhabitants right out to sea.

. (**c**) **Cliff railway** (frequent services; small fee) When built by Sir George Newnes in 1890 it was the steepest railway in the world, rising 400ft over just 860ft horizontal distance. It operates on water gravity, the weight of the water-tank in the car at the top providing the haulage for the car at the bottom (the water emptying out of the top car as it descends).

(**d**) **Coast path** Views across to Wales, especially the cliffs at Nash Point in S Glamorgan. **Birds**: Guillemots, razorbills, fulmars. Mammals: feral horned goats (both on coast path and in the Valley of Rocks).

(**e**) **Valley of Rocks** A dry valley – probably the course of the Lyn before it cut through to the sea at Lynmouth – of striking sedimentary Devonian rock formations and open moorland. Immediately ahead, above the coast as you leave the cliff path, is Castle Rock; two of the inhabitants of its cave appear to have been Aggie Norman, a madwoman who became Mother Meldrum in *Lorna Doone*, and a 'white lady' whose ghost returned to haunt the Black Abbot of Lynton, who wronged her. View W to Jennifred's Leap, a folly, prominent on the cliff-top on other side of Wringcliff Bay, and Woody Bay beyond. The valley's romantic charm appealed strongly to Shelley, Coleridge and Wordsworth; now it is somewhat marred by a road and too-prominent car park.

(**f**) **Hollerday Hill** View of the whole walk: Valley of Rocks, the Lyn valleys and Lynton.

Heddon's Mouth and Woody Bay

Based on a contribution from Mr and Mrs A Friar

Views along one of the finest parts of the Exmoor coast, as path follows heather-clad cliffs. About 20 minutes' walking on a quiet lane, with views over the Heddon Valley and beyond. Can detour to Woody Bay, a large cove beneath sandstone cliffs. Easy route-finding.

Length 5 miles (8km), 2½ hours
Difficulty 2
Start Hunter's Inn, 5 miles W of Lynton. Free parking along roadside. Signposted Hunter's Inn from crossroads ½ mile S of Martinhoe. Grid reference SS 655482
OS maps 1:50,000 180; 1:25,000 SS 64/74
Refreshments Hunter's Inn, at starting-point

WALK DIRECTIONS

1 Take track to right of Hunter's Inn, signposted coast path; 50 yards later, just after gate, fork left (straight on is coast path), to Heddon's Mouth and beach (a). 2 Fork left after 250 yards, follow to footbridge (do not cross).

Continue ahead. 3 200 yards later right at fork (or detour to beach ahead), signposted Woody Bay. Path rises (b). 4 Path enters NT oak wood by stile (NT sign). 5 Leave wood by gate.

For detour to Woody Bay (½ mile) fork left downhill. To continue walk fork right (signposted Lee Bay). Path ascends to junction with tarmac lane 6. Turn right on lane and where it bends sharp left continue ahead on narrow path to left of gate (not through gate itself). Ascend to road 7. Turn right on road; past Martinhoe church, road bends left. 8 Turn right by phone box, signposted Hunter's Inn.

WHAT TO LOOK OUT FOR

(a) **Heddon's Mouth** Tiny cove, once a port; a local lime kiln was used for making fertiliser, which was then shipped across the Bristol Channel.
(b) **View** Over the Bristol Channel into Glamorgan; along the coast towards the Valley of Rocks and Foreland Point beyond. Nearer is the prominent tower at Winifred's Leap, a folly named after Jennifred de Wichehalse, who in the 1680s was jilted by Lord Auberley and then threw herself off the cliff.

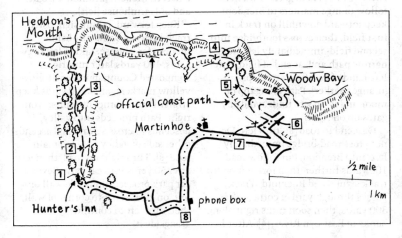

Brendon, Countisbury and the Foreland

Based on a contribution from
G C and R J Clarke
Recommended by J W Taylor,
Christine and Allan Friar

Shows what makes Exmoor special: the combination of wild cliff scenery, moorland and semi-wooded river valley. A short stretch of planted forestry near the end. Route-finding made easy by thorough signposting; all on clear paths and tracks.

Length 11 miles (17.5km), 5½ hours
Difficulty 3–4
Start County Gate, on Devon/Somerset border on A39 (Porlock to Lynmouth).Car park at information centre (free). Grid reference SS 794486
OS maps 1:50,000 180; 1:25,000 SS 64/74
Refreshments Pub and tea-rooms at Brendon; pubs at Rockford and Countisbury

WALK DIRECTIONS

1 (**a**) From end of car park furthest from main road take signposted path for Brendon (middle of three paths starting from view-indicator: this path keeps roughly level at first). **2** After ½ mile reach gate. From here follow orange markers to Brendon: keep forward downhill on track in first field, then across footbridge into second field; immediately left along narrow path and, at end of field, enter left-hand of two fields by steps (orange marker). Path along top of moorland is easy to find: avoid any gates up on right.

Descend to road **3**, turn left. Do not cross road-bridge immediately left, into Brendon, but follow road 100 yards further, then fork left on to track signposted Rockford. Track passes through yard of cottage after 300 yards, then soon turns right along banks of East Lyn River. **4** After 1

mile pass (but do not cross) bridge, opposite hamlet of Rockford (**b**). 100 yards later turn right uphill, signposted Countisbury via Wilsham. **5** Track turns sharp right after 400 yards, through gate, then along left edge of field to next gate and on to track between walls **6**. Left on track, follow into Wilsham Farm **7**. Pass between modern farmhouse (right) and old farmhouse (left).

Keep forward, taking signposted track between walls just below modern farmhouse, taking left of two gates. 100 yards later turn right, signposted Countisbury, and follow yellow markers; after 200 yards keep straight on at corner of wall on your right. Path proceeds into valley, descends to cross stream and ascends other side of valley to reach main road **8**. Turn right on road, then left after 50 yards into car park. Beyond car park proceed alongside wall on left, on clear track to corner of wall, then turn left to continue alongside it.

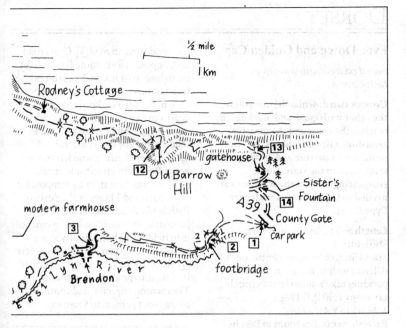

9 Turn right by Countisbury church (c) signposted 'coast path to lighthouse'. **10** Turn right after ½ mile (ahead is 'unmaintained path' leading to lighthouse), signposted coast path. Descend to road **11**. (For detour to lighthouse (d) turn left.) To continue turn right on road, then left after 250 yards as road bends right (signposted coast path). **12** After 1½ miles, path turns slightly inland skirting combe, then soon turns left (signposted coast path, Porlock and County Gate) to return to cliffs (e). **13** 1 mile later emerge on track and turn right, signposted Culbone. After 300 yards, just past gatehouse, track turns right through gate-posts (f): fork left on to coast path immediately after, to pass Sister's Fountain (g), then up steps to track **14**. Turn right on track signposted County Gate, then left after 50 yards, signposted County Gate. Ascend ½ mile to start.

WHAT TO LOOK OUT FOR
(a) **County Gate** Heart of *Lorna Doone* country. In the 1860s, at nearby Oare, R D Blackmore wrote the famous story of the feud between John Ridd and the Doones. Many places in this area feature in the book.
(b) **Rockford** Very little to it, but this inn is pleasantly situated on a lane at the bottom of the wooded East Lyn Valley.
(c) **Countisbury church** Restored, but with fine, early 18th-century rood screen of unusual design.
(d) **Foreland lighthouse** (open to the public (no fee) from 1pm to one hour before sunset). View across to S Wales, notably Nash Point, S Glamorgan.
(e) Up the slope to the right, **Old Barrow Hill**, the site of a Roman signal station; its outer wall is best seen from the road.
(f) **Gate** bears heraldic motif of the Halliday estate.
(g) **Sister's Fountain** Rough cross (probably 19th-century), supposedly where Joseph of Arimathea rested on his way to Glastonbury.

DORSET

Eype Down and Golden Cap

*Based on a contribution from
Jack Crewe*

Crosses two downlands, one grassy, the other with gorse and bracken, then reaches the coast and the massive sandstone cliff of Golden Cap. Short route across pasture and down a farm track back to the start. Good signposting most of the way, but care needed to follow correct path over Eype Down.

Length 5½ miles (9km), 3 hours
Difficulty 3
Start Chideock village centre, on A35 (Charmouth to Bridport). Roadside parking; take road to left of church
OS maps 1:50,000 193;
1:25,000 SY 49/59
Refreshments Tea-room in Beech-worth House Hotel, pubs and shop, in Chideock; Anchor Inn, kiosk and Old Boat House tea-room at Seatown

WALK DIRECTIONS
1 With Chideock church on your left, follow A35 downhill through village. After last house on left take surfaced farm track on left and turn right after 100 yards at T-junction. Track passes barn, then becomes unsurfaced as it turns left to lead up valley. **2** Turn right immediately in front of gate at top of rise, passing through another gate, then follow fence on right side of field. After 50 yards turn half left (waymarked) aiming for gate/stile below right-hand end of hillside **3**.

Beyond gate/stile turn half left on grassy track leading to lowest point of ridge. Continue over brow (track peters out) and bear right where view opens out on other side, to find signposted track leading along top of hill through grassed-over quarry workings. 150 yards later keep to main track (signposted) as it bends left downhill.

Descend to main road **4**. Cross road and, opposite, fork immediately right on to lane, past house. Just after house fork left on to path signposted Eype Down. Path rises; shortly after it ceases to rise take left fork of grassy paths (still leading away from main road); path now heads towards scrub-covered hill. Ignore left turns and follow path up left side of hill.

5 At top, turn right by signpost for coast path and Thorncombe Beacon. Path leads along ridge of hill. Cross gate/stile, by woods on left, to emerge into field. Keep left, initially along woods on left, then with hedge on left.
6 At end of field cross stile and bear half right to prominent bench on Thorncombe Beacon, and continue along coast path (**a**) to Seatown.

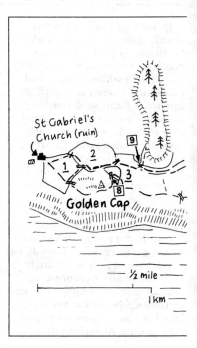

7 Continue on coast path from Seatown, following signs to Golden Cap (the prominent flat-topped, golden-coloured cliff ahead (**b**)); ignore other signposted paths to right. **8** At top, continue on path past trig. point, then descend to stile at edge of scrubby ground. (Below, half right, are remains of St Gabriel's Church (**c**) – optional detour.) Turn right and proceed alongside fence on right, to next stile and signpost. In second field turn right up to top and skirt field with fence on right to stile and signpost in top right-hand corner. Bear half right across third field to gate on right-hand edge of woodland **9**. Follow signs to Chideock, with woods on left. Ignore path into wood, and later another path, on right. After woods end, path widens to track and soon descends. Keep left at fork, still descending, and left on joining road at edge of village.

WHAT TO LOOK OUT FOR

(**a**) Just before descending to Seatown, you may choose to take a very careful look over the cliff edge for a spectacular view of the undercliff.

(**b**) **Golden Cap** Dorset's highest cliff has a strikingly flat top, the result of horizontal bedding of rocks (softer rock has been eroded, leaving the upper greensand cap). **View** E to Isle of Portland, W to Lyme Bay and beyond into Devon. The Cobb at Lyme Regis, which juts out into the sea, is one of the oldest man-made harbours in Britain.

(**c**) **St Gabriel's Church** This meagre ruin, plus the thatched farmhouse nearby, are all that remains of the village of Stanton St Gabriel, which was abandoned in the 18th century when the old Dorchester road was moved from here to its present course.

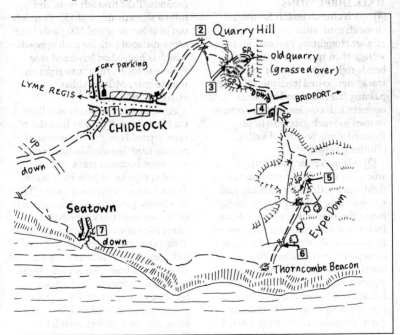

Bulbarrow Hill and Milton Abbas

Contributed by Jack Crewe
Recommended by R Banford,
Malcolm and Anne East

Takes in one of Dorset's grandest views and one of England's most picturesque villages. Grassland, scrub and coppice; one short stretch along a quiet lane. Route-finding quite easy, nearly all on well-defined paths.

Length 8 miles (13km), 4 hours
Difficulty 2–3
Start Winterbourne Houghton, 5 miles W of Blandford Forum. Roadside parking near church and phone box. Grid reference ST 820045
OS maps 1:50,000 194; 1:25,000 ST 60/70 and ST 80/90
Refreshments Tea Clipper tea-room and Hambro Arms in Milton Abbas

WALK DIRECTIONS

1 With church on left follow 'no through road' ahead, signposted Higher Houghton. Proceed out of village then turn right where road bends right at junction of road and track, signposted Ibberton. **2** After passing farm, the road becomes unmetalled; continue past two more houses to reach gate into field. Proceed along bottom of valley, climbing slowly.

3 After ¾ mile track enters woods by gate. At far end emerge into field and continue forward (no path) to small gate in hedgerow up on right. Beyond gate turn left on road. Keep forward at next junction, signposted Bulbarrow. **4** Where road reaches viewpoint on Bulbarrow Hill (**a**) continue forward, taking left turn, signposted Ansty and Hilton. Turn left shortly before mast, on to track immediately to left of Bulbarrow Farm entrance; track is signposted Milton Abbey. Do not enter area of Nissen huts. Where track becomes unsurfaced by farm, continue forward

and descend steadily (**b**).

5 At next barn, track forks; take left-hand fork, through gate, and proceed with hedge on right along top of two large fields. **6** Enter Green Hill Down nature reserve by gate and sign, and continue with hedge on right through scrubby land, ignoring left turns and ignoring gate/stile on right by overhead cable. Proceed to small gate, leaving reserve and continuing on twisty narrow path, through scrub and coppice, which gradually descends to road **7**. Left on road, follow to houses, then fork left slightly uphill, on road.

8 Where road descends, continue sharp right (signposted Milton Abbey car park) but first detour left up steps leading around top of chalk pit to chapel (**c**). Retrace steps (down towards abbey, then first path on right) to road and cross into school grounds. Take first left turn, and follow signs to abbey (**d**) **9**. Turn left out of abbey door and 100 yards later cross surfaced path for path opposite which is hedged on left-hand side. Follow to lodge, then turn right on road to enter Milton Abbas village (**e**) **10**.

Proceed up main street of village, turn left at top. **11** Take first right turn, signed Forestry Commission private road. Ignore side turnings; road soon becomes track and enters wood at sign for Milton Park Wood. Track then curves round to left. **12** Just before gate across track, turn left on to narrower track which rises along edge of woods, then descends to T-junction with forest track. Turn left, then 100 yards later keep forward where main track bends to the right. Ascend to gate, into field, then go forward with fence on left, to road **13**.

Turn right on road and, 250 yards later, left on track between fences. Follow ¼ mile to enter scrubby area by gate, and turn half right on to grassy track leading downhill to

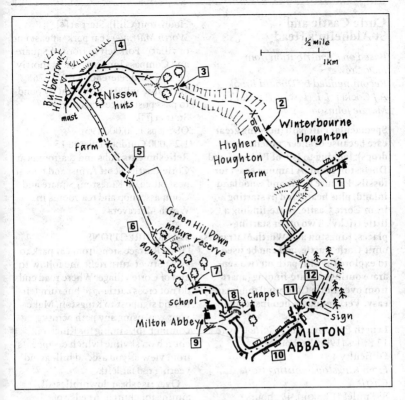

corner of lane. Continue forward to starting-point.

WHAT TO LOOK OUT FOR

(**a**) **Bulbarrow Hill** View WNW to the Quantocks, NW Glastonbury Tor and the Mendips, N White Sheet Hill and NE Salisbury Plain.

(**b**) **View** Right (SE) towards Poole Harbour and Corfe Castle.

(**c**) **Norman chapel** Has some Gothic alterations, but is very simple, set deep in the woods with only a rough path leading to it. Former uses were as a pigeon loft and a labourer's cottage. Just below it, some 100 grass steps enclosed by a yew hedge form a vista of Milton Abbey.

(**d**) **Milton Abbey** Built on the site of a college of canons founded in AD932 by King Athelstan, and later a Bene-

dictine monastery. Only the choir, crossing and the transepts of the 14th/15th-century abbey church were built, as the Dissolution came before the nave could be added. Inside, the effect is of great airiness and height, accentuated by the lightness of the stonework. The school building was erected as a country house in 1771 by Sir William Chambers, for Lord Milton.

(**e**) **Milton Abbas** Lord Milton wanted more privacy around his house, so set about totally rebuilding the village in the late 18th century. The result is all of a piece: identical detached, thatched cottages flank the grass verges on both sides of a broad sloping street. Opposite the church, some handsome brick almshouses (1674; re-erected here in 1779).

Corfe Castle and
St Aldhelm's Head

*Based on a contribution from
Jack Crewe
Recommended by Donald Brook,
A J Cocker, L E Hawke, P B Hall,
Margie Johnson*

**Spectacular cliff path (needing great
care because of sheer, unfenced
drops), looking to Isle of Portland and
Durleston Point. A famous coast for
fossils. Pasture fields and woodland
inland, plus heathland (if starting
from Corfe Castle; route-finding a
little tricky). Two other starting-
places, Kingston and Worth Matravers,
omit Corfe Castle, and can be used
to explore the cliff path on two sep-
arate outings. Route-finding (apart
from over Corfe Common) moderately
easy. Very muddy when inspected.**

Length *Full walk from Corfe Castle*
12 miles (19km), 6 hours
Difficulty 4
*From Kingston, omitting Corfe
Castle*
8½ miles (13.5km), 4½ hours
Difficulty 4
*From Kingston, omitting St
Aldhelm's Head and Corfe Castle*
5 miles (8km), 3 hours
Difficulty 3–4
*From Worth Matravers omitting
Hounstout Cliff and Corfe Castle*
5 miles (8km), 3 hours
Difficulty 3–4
Start *Corfe Castle* car park. Grid
reference SY 959819. Take West
Street from village centre, opposite
Bankes Arms; car park soon
signposted to right.
Kingston. Turn off B3069 into village
by pub. Fork right in front of church
with big tower. ¼ mile later, pass
turnings on your left; car park is 50
yards further on, on left. Grid
reference SY 954795. Start walk by
information board in free car park,
turn right on track (signposted

Hounstout Cliff). Start at 4.
Worth Matravers car park, at east end
of village. Fork left in front of Square
and Compass Inn; car park is shortly
on left. Grid reference SY 974776.
Walk into village, fork right by pond
to pass post office and church.
Start at 11.
OS maps 1:50,000 195;
1:25,000 Outdoor Leisure 15
Refreshments Pubs and tea-rooms at
Corfe Castle; Scott Arms, and teas at
post office, in Kingston; Square and
Compass, shop and tea-rooms in
Worth Matravers

WALK DIRECTIONS

1 (a) Retrace steps from car park to
West Street, turn right and follow to
end of Corfe village. Where road ends
do not cross cattle-grid but turn left
to find signpost to Kingston. Make
your way using any path across
common (b), aiming for Kingston
church on skyline (which disappears
from view as you ascend hill; avoid
veering too far left).

Over rise, bear downhill, still
aiming for church. At edge of
common turn right to cross waymarked footbridge on left, then continue across first field to stile 2.
Continue forward along right edge of
second field, and at end do not pass
into next field but turn left, with
hedgerow on right. After 50 yards
pass through break in hedge on right;
follow right edge of third field to stile
in corner. Enclosed path leads to next
field; follow left edge uphill to reach
farm track, cross it and take stile
opposite.

Head straight on up across field to
church, finding kissing-gate just to
right of electricity post at top 3.
Turn right on track, then left after 50
yards to pass in front of cottages and
30 yards later take steps on right into
Kingston Village (c). Turn right,
taking road leading right of church.
Then turn half left after ¼ mile on

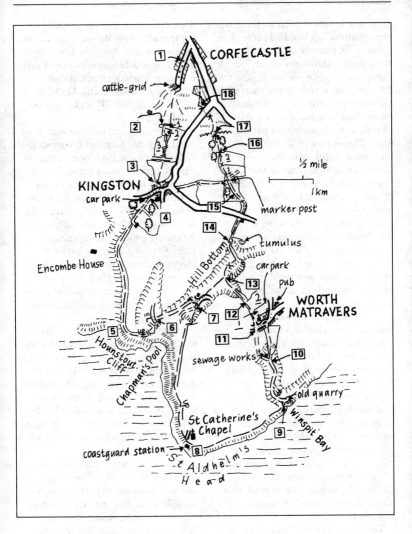

Map labels (clockwise):
[1] CORFE CASTLE
cattle-grid
[18]
[17]
[16]
[2]
½ mile
1 km
marker post
[3]
KINGSTON
car park
[4]
[15]
[14]
tumulus
Encombe House
Hill Bottom
car park
[13]
pub
WORTH MATRAVERS
[5]
[6]
[7]
[12]
[11]
[10]
Hounstout Cliff
Chapman's Pool
sewage works
old quarry
St Catherine's Chapel
[9]
Winspit Bay
coastguard station
[8]
St Aldhelm's Head

to stony track signposted to Hounstout Cliff (but otherwise a private
drive) [4].

Follow track, ignoring first left turn
(marked as private) but forking left 30
yards later, signposted Hounstout
Cliff. Where track bends left into
driveway of private house, continue
forward on unmade track (**d**) to
cliff-top [5]. At cliff-top (**e**), path soon
ascends steeply, then descends by
steps. At bottom, path ahead is signed

as closed, so turn left by coast path
marker stone, over stile, to cross
field, aiming for fence ahead. Turn
left at fence (marker stone), and on
ascending grassy bank (wall on right
ends) turn right (marker stone), to
reach surfaced track (marker stone),
on which turn right.

[6] Where tarmac track ends, by
gate, turn left, signposted coast path,
and follow track inland along side of
valley until cottages, at which turn

right at T-junction with surfaced lane to prominent left bend 50 yards later.

For walk starting at Kingston omitting St Aldhelm's Head and Corfe Castle continue along lane for 200 yards until right bend, then take path on left, signposted Afflington Farm along bottom of valley. After ½ mile reach signpost for Afflington Barn. This is point **13** ; continue forward. *For full walk starting at Corfe Castle* turn right on track, signposted coast path, for 50 yards. **7** Pass through gate and fork left up grassy slope (signposted coast path). Path rises to cross old stone wall, then becomes indistinct; continue up centre of grassy valley. At top turn right, with wall on left, to cliff-top, then left to continue (with great care, as drops are enormous and path often slippery).

Next ascent leads to coastguard station, just to left of which is St Catherine's Chapel (**f**)(**g**) **8**. Continue on cliff path, passing just to left of coastguard station. **9** After 1 mile path descends to old quarries at Winspit Bay (**h**). Turn left by quarry and beach warning notice, to leave coast path for track leading along bottom of valley. **10** Where track divides, fork right to reach stile, then take field path quarter left, aiming for left part of main group of buildings. Cross stile, follow path to road, then forward into Worth Matravers village (**i**).

Turn right at first T-junction, then next left just above village pond, to pass post office and church. **11** At end of village, immediately after playground on right, turn right, signposted Hill Bottom, up driveway. Where driveway ends at house, forward over stile and follow left edge of two fields. **12** At end of second field, cross stone stile; path beyond is enclosed and descends into scrubby combe, reach stile at bottom.

For walk starting at Worth

Matravers turn left, signposted Chapman's Pool. Where tarmac lane appears on left, drop down to it, and continue to where it bends right up to cottages. Leave for track ahead (signposted Coast Path). After 50 yards, reach point **7** and continue to **11**.

To continue full walk or walks from Kingston turn right, signposted Afflington Barn. Path along valley is easy to find: it passes through gate after 300 yards and soon turns left uphill. **14** Take gate on right at end of walled section of path, enter field and proceed uphill with wall on left. At corner, proceed along enclosed track to road. Cross road, take signposted track opposite. Track descends gently (**j**). **15** After ¼ mile, wall on right leaves track: 250 yards later, reach marker post (yellow and blue arrows).

To return to Kingston turn left slightly uphill through scrubby area. Route is not obvious, but avoid losing height and don't bear too far to left. After 80 yards reach edge of scrubby area and turn left uphill until you spot waymarked stile, rather hidden in bushes. Beyond stile, aim straight for Kingston churches, with wall on the right.

To return to Corfe turn half left as indicated by right-hand of yellow arrows, downhill on path through scrubby area. At bottom, cross stone stile by drinking-trough and follow left edge of two fields. **16** Shortly before end of second field, and where trees on left end, take gate on left, follow left edge of strip-shaped field until finding small gate on left. Cross ditch by footbridge, turn right, soon recross ditch by next bridge near house, then left through gate into common **17**. Continue forwards to stream, turn left for 30 yards then cross/step across stream by plank bridge. Keep forward uphill (no obvious path).

At top, Corfe comes into view. You can take the road back, but better: aim to reach left-hand fork of roads just before built-up area begins; here, gate leads on to road. Cross road to gate/NT sign opposite, make towards corner of hedge on right by leftmost house **18**. Proceed into Corfe, with hedge on right; at end, fenced path leads into housing estate. Forward to T-junction; cross to path between fences. Take next entrance on right, and follow right edge of fields to Corfe Castle.

WHAT TO LOOK OUT FOR

(**a**) **Corfe Castle** (NT; open to public; fee) Very pretty Purbeck-stone village, dominated by ruined 12th-to 16th-century castle standing on a detached portion of the Purbeck ridge. In AD978 King Edward the Martyr was murdered here by his stepmother, so that her own son could succeed to the throne. It was besieged by parliamentary forces in 1646. Stones from the castle were used for building much of the village centre.

(**b**) **Corfe Common** (NT) Heathlands like these were once characteristic of the Dorset landscape, but since 1945 the county has lost 75 per cent of them (mostly to agriculture).

(**c**) **Kingston** Has two churches, both 19th-century. The disused 'old' church, on the main road, is undistinguished. The 'new' one, 1880, in Purbeck stone, is considered the best church design of G E Street, the architect of the Strand Law Courts in London.

(**d**) On emerging from trees on your right across the valley, and below the obelisk, remains of **medieval farming strips** covering the hillside. At the bottom of the valley is **Encombe House**, built c.1735.

(**e**) **Hounstout Cliff** Hard limestone caps the softer shales, creating a craggy cliff-top with an undercliff. Chapman's Pool, the next cove, has no protective limestone cap and the sea has cut in to form a bay of great beauty (unhappily, now closed to the public owing to erosion).

(**f**) **St Catherine's Chapel** (formerly 'the Devil's Chapel') Simple 12th-century building whose square plan betrays a different original purpose, probably either a beacon for sailors or an oratory for a priest to pray for lost sailors' souls. No electricity, no organ, and no altar; and just a stone pier for its centre-piece.

(**g**) **St Aldhelm's Head** Site of the first radar station; radar pioneering experiments took place here in the Second World War.

(**h**) Quarries for **Purbeck marble**, a handsome yellow stone much used for public buildings.

(**i**) **Worth Matravers** In the centre, stone cottages are grouped around a pond. One of them is Gulliver's Cottage, the former residence of smuggler Isaac Gulliver, who would form a smuggling-ring in one village and then move on to another. The church has a splendid Norman chancel arch and some Norman work around the door; in the churchyard is an epitaph to a Mr Jesty who vaccinated his family (but not himself) with a live cowpox vaccine, 20 years before the invention by Jenner of human vaccination.

(**j**) View of **Corfe Castle**, standing on a hillock in a break in the main Purbeck ridge. On the coast path, **birds** include guillemots, kittiwakes, razorbills, puffins, shags. **Flora** includes spotted orchid, yellow rattle, black bryony, goatsbeard, speckled wood, lords and ladies. Butterflies include the rare Lulworth Skipper (orange wings edged with brown; flits quickly from plant to plant).

Studland Heath and Ballard Down

Based on contributions from Jack Crewe and Donald Brook Recommended by A J Cocker, L E Hawke

Woodland paths soon reach open heath, followed by a climb on to Ballard Down, a ridge with views on three sides, ending abruptly at chalk cliffs. Route follows cliff-top for final stage. Route-finding moderately easy; all on defined paths and tracks, with short sections of road-walking.

Length 6 miles (9.5km), 3 hours
Difficulty 2
Start Studland village centre, 4 miles N of Swanage. Grid reference SZ 034824
OS maps 1:50,000 195; 1:25,000 Outdoor Leisure 15
Refreshments Bankes Arms and shop at Studland

WALK DIRECTIONS

1 From crossroads at village centre, with Studland Stores on right and village hall on left, follow main street downhill, in Bournemouth direction. Follow beyond speed derestriction signs, then take track on left opposite bus-stop, signed Wadmore Lane. Follow to Wadmore Cottages, then forward on wide path through woods. On crossing footbridge, path turns left and enters open heathland by nature reserve sign (a).

2 50 yards into heathland, take narrow path on left heading for the Agglestone, the unmistakable large stone boulder on hillock (b). Beyond boulder, continue on broad sandy path. **3** Keep left on main path shortly before reaching golf course. 200 yards later, pass marker stone for Studland village on your left and continue 50 yards to T-junction with track. Turn right on track, now with fence on left.

4 At corner of fence, where golf clubhouse comes into view ahead, turn left, on path along fence. **5** At road, cross to stile opposite, into golf course.

Cross to trees ahead, making for derelict shed just visible towards left side of trees. Find path to right of shed, leading through trees to stile, then half right aiming for nearest bend in road; stile and gate give access to road.

6 Left on road for 300 yards, then right through gate at NT sign for Ballard Down (c). Track ascends to obelisk, then continues along top of grassy ridge for 1½ miles, continuing forward at trig. point to edge of cliffs **7**. Path then bends round left, past coastal stacks and headland (Old Harry Rocks (d)), then soon forks right, signposted Studland. Path leads to corner of road in Studland village **8**. Turn left to return to village centre, but there are two further things to see: South Beach (e) (turn right, first gate on right on reaching road); and Studland church (f) (turn left on road, then first road turning on right).

WHAT TO LOOK OUT FOR

(a) Godlingston Heath nature reserve Part of Studland Heath, one of Dorset's most extensive heathlands.
(b) Agglestone Natural sandstone boulder left standing on its own; the weaker rock around it has weathered away. **View** E across Poole Harbour to Bournemouth.
(c) Ballard Down A whaleback chalk ridge, with excellent views. It was ploughed up in wartime for emergency crop production, and only the coarser plants have re-established themselves on it. At its W end is an obelisk, built to commemorate the opening of waterworks and removed in wartime, so as not to aid enemy bombers (though the coastline would have been sufficient

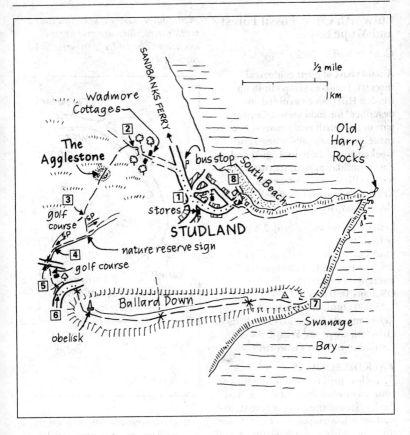

navigational aid). Someone has painstakingly re-erected it. **View** E over Swanage Bay; W over Poole Harbour. The largest island in the harbour is Brownsea, where Baden-Powell took 20 boys on camp to teach them woodcraft and discipline in 1907, so forming the Boy Scout movement.

(**d**) **Old Harry Rocks** A chalk headland, now detached from the mainland by coastal erosion, with a natural arch. This is the western end of the Purbeck ridge, a vast geological fold extending across Europe, thrown up 13 to 15 million years ago in the Alpine Orogeny, in which the Alps themselves were formed.

(**e**) **South Beach** Sands are stained red and yellow by zinc oxide, and are similar to those at Alum Bay, at the western end of the Isle of Wight (the two were once joined). Good views of the low chalk cliffs from which you have just descended.

(**f**) **Studland church** Norman, splendidly intact, and bearing a striking similarity to Romanesque churches on the Cotentin Peninsula in France, 60 miles S.

Lulworth Cove, Fossil Forest and Mupe Bay

Contributed by Jack Crewe

A wild coast of great geological interest. Involves steep climb up Bindon Hill (can be avoided, as described) for good views. Crosses part of Lulworth army ranges, but these are open to public nearly all weekends and daily in August and at Easter holiday period; waymarked with yellow posts and signposted. Keep to the paths; unexploded shells about. Easy route-finding.

Length 3½ miles (5.5km), 2 hours
Difficulty 3
Start Lulworth Cove (large car park; free), 17 miles SE of Dorchester. Grid reference SY 822800
OS maps 1:50,000 194; 1:25,000 Outdoor Leisure 15
Refreshments Café and restaurants in Lulworth Cove and West Lulworth; Castle Inn in West Lulworth

WALK DIRECTIONS

1 Follow road to cove (**a**) and make your way round the pebbly beach to the left side of the cove, where steps lead up to lowest point of cliffs. Continue away from cove at signpost, and follow, ignoring right turn signposted Pepler Point, to enter Lulworth Ranges by gate (**b**) **2**.

Beyond gate turn right, signposted Fossil Forest, down to metal hurdle and descend steps to view Fossil Forest (**c**). You can continue along rocky cleft for a short distance, but there is no way out at far end. Return to cliff-top and follow grassy path marked by yellow posts along edge of cliffs.

3 At Mupe Bay (**d**), steps on right give access to sandy beach. If tired, fork left, signposted Little Bindon, and follow easy track back to cove. Otherwise, keep right along cliff-top: at next stile, coast path climbs Bindon Hill, very steeply – follow yellow marker posts. **4** At top turn sharp

Please let us know if you find that a walk's directions are no longer accurate. The address to write to is on page 10.

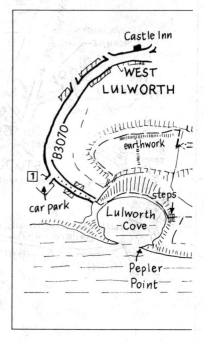

left (**e**), signposted Lulworth, on track along ridge, soon passing flagpole and then reaching radar station.

Continue forward beyond radar station, signposted West Lulworth, on track between fences. 100 yards later pass through gate (track ends) and turn right along fence for 75 yards, then left along grass bank, an ancient earthwork. Follow bank around hill until Lulworth Cove comes into view; cross stile and descend steeply to bottom.

WHAT TO LOOK OUT FOR

(**a**) **Lulworth Cove** The great Alpine earth movement, which crossed Europe and pushed up what are now the Alps, is seen at its westernmost extent here, with the folding of the layers of chalk, sandstone and hard

If you have a walk to suggest for any subsequent edition of the Holiday Which? Good Walks Guide, *please send it to us. We need a rough sketch map and a brief summary of the walk's attractions. Directions are not necessary. The address to write to is on page 10.*

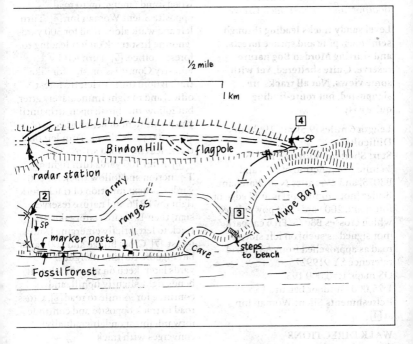

Portland limestone exposed. The circular bay was formed when a 400ft breach in the Portland stone along the coast allowed the sea to cut into the weak rock behind.

(**b**) **Little Bindon** Just on right on entering ranges, the remains of a small chapel and cottage built by monks in the 12th century.

(**c**) **Fossil Forest** Petrified algae that surrounded stumps of trees millions of years ago, exposed just under the edge of the cliff.

(**d**) **Mupe Bay** Huge chalk and sandstone cliffs; excellent sandy beach below. Was one of the biggest centres for smuggling in Dorset; there is a smugglers' cave at the near end of the first (smaller) bay. **Birds** Numerous shags and cormorants. **View** Ahead, Worbarrow Bay. Butterflies on this coast include the rare Lulworth skipper (orange wings, edged with brown).

(**e**) **Bindon Hill** View W to Isle of Portland.

Wareham Forest

Contributed by R W Banford
Recommended by Susan Jeffries,
L E Hawke, A J Cocker, Monte
Booth, Malcolm East, Jack Crewe

**Level sandy tracks leading through
semi-open pine and spruce forests,
and skirting Morden Bog nature
reserve. Quite sheltered, yet with
some views. Not all tracks are
signposted, but route-finding
quite easy.**

Length 6 miles (9.5km), 2½ hours
Difficulty 1
Start Sherford Bridge on B3075
¾ mile S of junction of A35 and
B3075, and 2½ miles N of Wareham.
Bridge (not prominent) is at N edge of
forest and 200 yards S of power line
which crosses B3075. Free car park
(not signed as such) on left side of
road as approached from A35. Grid
reference SY 919927
OS maps 1:50,000 195;
1:25,000 Outdoor Leisure 15
Refreshments Silent Woman Inn
at 4

WALK DIRECTIONS

1 From end of car park furthest from
Sherford Bridge, cross road to gate
marked with fire point and FRP3
signs, and follow gravel track,
signposted Bridleway to Stroud
Bridge, which soon enters forest. 2
After ½ mile pass under power line
and continue for 150 yards to
T-junction. Turn left, again passing
under power line and 200 yards later
passing derelict cottage (Decoy
House), to edge of nature reserve (a).
Follow path as it turns right (ahead is
'No admittance'), through gate after
50 yards. Continue forward on forest
track for ½ mile. 3 Take next major
fork right, by fire-beaters. Continue
along sandy track and turn left at
T-junction at end, after ½ mile.

Continue along edge of forest for
500 yards and where main track turns
left downhill, continue forward on
minor track (still along edge of
woods) and emerge on to road
opposite Silent Woman Inn 4. Turn
left and walk along road for 500 yards
ignoring first track on left leading to
forestry office. 5 Turn left by
Forestry Commission sign for Sika
trail. Ignore turns to left (to forestry
office) and to right immediately after,
but follow this broad open strip until
you are in sight of bench at edge of
slope 100 yards ahead. Turn left on
track, leaving broad strip.

6 After 100 yards turn right at
T-junction and follow track for 200
yards. At next junction of tracks fork
right (by FRP6 and nature reserve
sign) then 100 yards later take first
track to left, briefly emerging from
forest. 7 Cross bridge and 100 yards
later ignore turning to right. 170
yards later, keep on main track as it
bends right, slightly uphill, and
continue for ½ mile to road 8. Cross
road to track opposite and continue
forward; forest on left gradually
converges with track.

9 Where forest on left joins track,
continue forward on main track along
edge of forest, with forest on left. 10
After ¾ mile forest begins on right.
Continue on main track, passing
enclosed pond on your left after ¼
mile, and ¼ mile later keeping on
main track which bends left. Follow
back to starting-place.

WHAT TO LOOK OUT FOR

(a) **Morden Bog nature reserve** 149
hectares of rich heathland, once
characteristic of Dorset. Supports a
variety of insect life and bog plants. A
permit is required to enter the most
important areas of the reserve, but
much of the bogland comes into view
later in the walk.

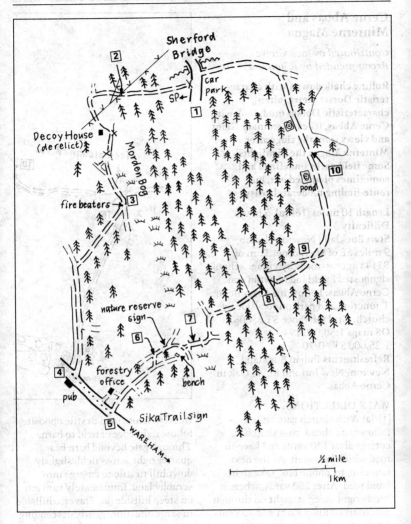

Sherford Bridge

2

car park

SP

1

Decoy House (derelict)

Morden Bog

fire beaters

3

nature reserve sign

6

7

forestry office

bench

4

pub

5

Sika Trail sign

WAREHAM

10

9

8

6

pond

½ mile

1km

Cerne Abbas and Minterne Magna

Contributed by Jack Crewe
Recommended by R Banford

**Rolling chalk downs with charac-
teristic Dorset views (often
characteristic Dorset mud, too), with
Cerne Abbas, its extraordinary Giant
and views from the ridge after
Minterne Magna the highlights.
Some field paths undefined and
sometimes ploughed out, but
route-finding moderately easy.**

Length 10 miles (16km), 5 hours
Difficulty 3
Start Buckland Newton church,
9 miles SE of Sherborne. Turn off
B3143 at crossroads by village school,
signposted Buckland Newton and
Cerne Abbas. Follow road ½ mile to
T-junction and park on roadside by
church. Grid reference ST 686053
OS maps 1:50,000 194;
1:25,000 ST 60/70
Refreshments Pub in Buckland
Newton; New Inn and Royal Oak in
Cerne Abbas

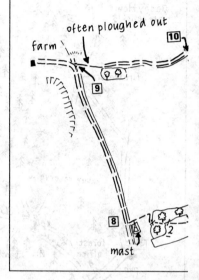

WALK DIRECTIONS

1 (**a**) With church gate on left,
follow road ahead; pass thatched
cottage after 120 yards and keep to
road which bears left. At the next
junction, by phone box, take right-
hand road. After 250 yards, where it
bends right, keep straight on through
gate marked Knap Farm and 30 yards
later turn right on track (soon
between hedges) which leads to left of
farm buildings. Ascend steadily for 1
mile. **2** At barn turn left on to
another track between hedges. Turn
right after 300 yards at T-junction.

3 300 yards later, just by barn on
left, turn left through gate. Bear half
right across field to stile visible in
hedgerow on right (to right of and
above right-hand corner of woods).
Maintain same direction across next
field to stile beyond clump of beech

trees **4**. Cross road to stile opposite;
follow right edge of field to barn.
Through gate beyond barn bear
quarter right across field, slightly
downhill to stile to emerge into
scrubby land. Immediately turn left
on steep hillside (**b**). Traverse hillside
in same direction, gently descending
on to small tracks which continue
along foot of hill, eventually passing
just below Cerne Giant (fenced-off
chalk carving on hillside).

5 Just after Giant, descend
through clump of trees, turn right and
cross left-hand of two stiles to emerge
into field. Bear half right aiming for
church tower, entering graveyard
through archway, then past entrance
of Cerne Abbey House and into Cerne
Abbas (**c**) **6**. In village centre turn
right and right again opposite New

84

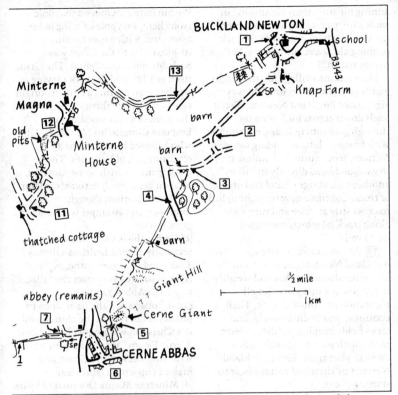

Inn into Duck Street. At A352 road junction (where there is a lay-by from which Cerne Giant is best viewed), turn right along main road for 50 yards, and just before barn take track on left, signposted Buckland Down.

7 Where track turns right pass through small gate on left and follow track which proceeds with hillside on your right. Eventually, radio mast can be seen on skyline. Note its position. Cross two stiles close together and enter first field. After two more gates in quick succession enter second field, bear quarter right and head steadily uphill towards mast, which disappears from view. Pass through gate in recessed corner of woodland and continue uphill through trees.

On emerging into open (with mast ahead), turn right alongside wood,

then at corner of wood, turn left across field to stile in hedge just to right of mast **8**. Turn right on to track and follow for 1½ miles. **9** Just before track curves left around valley head and where line of overhead cables leaves track, turn 90 degrees to right and go through hedge. Head quarter right across field, aiming just to left of nearest clump of trees to join track which runs downhill alongside trees. **10** At T-junction turn right and continue along track for ⅓ mile.

11 Shortly after passing thatched cottage (set back on right) turn left along track which leads uphill through trees. At top, left at T-junction, then 20 yards later turn right through small gate. Turn half left and descend hillside slowly, aiming for stile, then continuing in same direction to bottom corner of next field, where gate leads to track running along avenue of trees. Follow to join road **12**.

Turn left into village (**d**), then right just before church on to bridleway signposted Buckland Newton. Track leads down across ford, then up through gate into field and continues with fence on left, ascending to trees. At trees, fence turns left; follow it up to gate, and head directly uphill to another gate at right-hand end of line of trees. Continue quarter right uphill to cross stile at ridge and turn right along track (**e**) which continues for ½ mile.

13 At road, cross to gate opposite. Buckland Newton can be seen to the left in the distance. Descend steadily to left passing just above small plantation and through gate. Then continue, descending slowly, and cross fields keeping parallel to farm road which passes through valley away to your right. Enter Buckland Newton by thatched cottage near to starting-point.

WHAT TO LOOK OUT FOR
(**a**) **Buckland Newton church** Building itself is unremarkable, but above the door just inside is a fragment of an Anglo-Saxon image of St Peter the Apostle, dug up in a neighbouring garden.
(**b**) **Giant Hill** On top, covered with gorse and scrub, is an ancient rectangular earthwork known both as the Trendle and the Frying Pan.

Within living memory a maypole stood here; maypole dancing being associated with pagan fertility rites, its proximity to the Giant was probably not coincidental. The Giant itself is a 180ft-high chalk carving of a naked man bearing a club. Its origin is uncertain; one theory is that it was the work of a cult worshipping Emperor Commodus (AD180–193), who believed himself to be a reincarnation of Hercules. The carving makes little sense close up, but you get a much better view later on. The Victorians thought it improper, and attempts were made to grass it over.
(**c**) **Cerne Abbas** Large but architecturally almost faultless village of Tudor and Georgian cottages. Turn right as soon as you enter the village to see the Abbey gateway, guest-house and tithe barn (open to public; small fee). In the churchyard is a Christian wishing-well inscribed 'Cerno Deum'; you make your wish with your back to the Giant, and make a cup with a laurel leaf.
(**d**) **Minterne Magna** Dominated by its Edwardian mock-Tudor country house with adjoining wild shrub garden, noted for rhododendrons (open to public; fee). The church has a memorial on the nave floor to a 17th-century Winston Churchill. The hamlet features as Great Hintock in Hardy's Wessex novels.
(**e**) **View** Right to Minterne House and lake; left (N) over Blackmoor Vale; NE towards Whitesheet Hill in Wiltshire (N of Shaftesbury).

SOMERSET

Cow Castle and the Barle Valley

Contributed by Mr and Mrs A Friar

Quiet inland Exmoor. Level farmland for most of the early stages, then distant views from pasture and moorland tracks, followed by a riverside path along the steep-sided Barle Valley. Good waymarking, but field paths are undefined and directions should be followed carefully; often muddy just after ⑫.

Length 9 miles (14.5km), 4½ hours
Difficulty 2–3
Start Car park, Simonsbath, ¼ mile E of junction of B3223 and B3358, 8 miles SSE of Lynton. Grid reference SS 774392
OS maps 1:50,000 180 and 181; 1:25,000 SS 63/73 and SS 83/93
Refreshments Exmoor Forest Hotel, Simonsbath House Hotel, both in Simonsbath (teas)

WALK DIRECTIONS

1 Turn right out of car park approach road, along main road for 200 yards, then turn left opposite Pond Cottage through small gate signposted Landacre (and others). Fork left after 30 yards, signposted Landacre (follow red waymarks until **11**). Follow path up to edge of woods (**a**); path turns left along inside edge of woods for 200 yards.

2 Pass through gate on right, along left edge of first field (no path) to pass through gate in far left corner, then take gate 30 yards ahead **3**. Follow right edge of second field for 200 yards then turn right through gate. Turn left, proceeding with hedge on left through third and fourth fields. **4** Skirt left edge of fifth field by proceeding 30 yards to corner of fence and following it to banked hedgerow (ignore gate on left giving

access to track leading to farm). Then turn right to proceed alongside hedgerow on left.

5 Turn left through gate 300 yards later. Follow left edge of sixth, seventh and eighth fields. In eighth field, route continues past conifer plantation on your left, and then enters open grassland **6**. Continue forward on grassland for 50 yards to waymark post, then turn right on track, which runs just above pronounced slope down on your right. Track descends to stream (**b**), then climbs up. 250 yards after stream, fork right (waymarked). **7** Track is soon joined by fence on right, passes through gate, crosses top of field to next gate **8**.

Beyond gate route is undefined, but continue forward with hedge on left, then turn left through gate after 200 yards, pass through farmyard, and take far road ahead. Road rises to pass through break in hedge after 200 yards. **9** 30 yards after hedge bear half right through waymarked gate and into field. Continue forward (no path) parallel to hedge on right, to reach gate 50 yards to left of far right-hand corner of field **10**. Emerge on to moorland: follow clear path ahead (**c**). **11** Sharp right at junction of tracks after ¾ mile, signposted Cow Castle. Route now waymarked in yellow.

12 Track enters woodland after 1 mile. Follow to river, at which turn right along river bank to footbridge (do not cross), from which bear half right (signposted Cow Castle) to small footbridge over stream. Cross stile on left just beyond footbridge; from here Cow Castle can be seen, the further and larger of two nearby hillocks ahead (**d**). **13** Either ascend Cow Castle or skirt round base on river side. Beyond, take stile beside

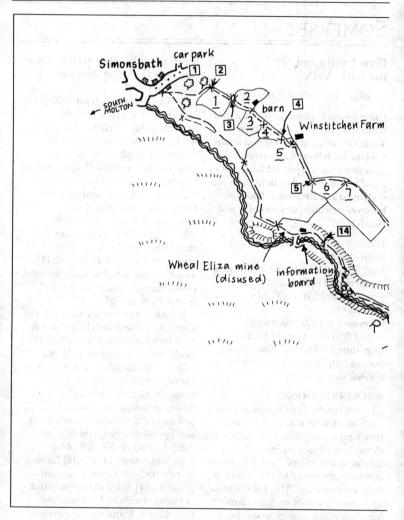

river. Route back is obvious, as path follows close to river most of the way. Path soon reaches line of trees, at which keep right, then rejoins river (soon ascending and descending bank on right; take care here). **14** Just after next gate ruins of mine building are seen ahead (**e**). Path keeps to right of abrupt hillock (old spoil heap) and follows river back into beech woods (keep to upper forks to avoid mud on track). Then follow to Simonsbath, emerging opposite Pond Cottage.

WHAT TO LOOK OUT FOR
(**a**) **Birch Cleavewoods** At over 1,000 ft, Britain's highest beech wood. Planted in 1840, the wood is decaying, and the area is now being managed and partly replanted to ensure the woodland's survival.
(**b**) The **ruined cottage** on the right by the bridge was the home of William Burgess, the 'Wheal Eliza murderer', who was hanged at Taunton. He concealed the body of his seven-year-old daughter at Wheal Eliza mine, which

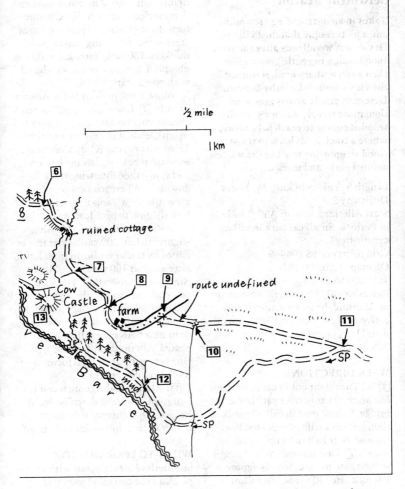

you pass later in this walk.
(**c**) View down the Barle Valley to Withypool and beyond, towards Hawkridge. You are now on the Two Moors Way, a long-distance path connecting Exmoor and Dartmoor.
(**d**) **Cow Castle** Hillock capped by the grassy ramparts of an Iron Age hillfort.
(**e**) **Wheal Eliza** Remains of an iron

and copper mine, where minerals were extracted for 300 years until closure in the last century; features as Uncle Ben's Gold mine in *Lorna Doone*. Cross by the river-bridge and turn left for an information board, where there is a cleverly positioned Victorian photograph of the mine when still working.

Hurlstone Point and Selworthy Beacon

Takes in an outstanding viewpoint and a picturesque thatched village. Deciduous woodlands after the start, soon leading to gentle grassy cliffs, then a steep, sharp haul, rewarded by the views from Selworthy Beacon. Descends gently across grassland, then more steeply down a partially wooded combe to reach Selworthy, where a track leads back to the start. Good signposting most of the way on defined paths and tracks.

Length 5½ miles (9 km), 2½ hours
Difficulty 2-3
Start Allerford, just off A39, 1 mile E of Porlock. Small car park in village centre (free).
Grid reference SS 904469
OS maps 1:50,000 181;
1:25,000 SS 84/94
Refreshments Cross Lane Restaurant in Allerford, by main road; tea and coffee at West Somerset Museum of Rural Life, opposite car park in Allerford.

WALK DIRECTIONS

1 (**a**) Turn right out of car park, then left after 50 yards, over packhorse bridge. Follow road uphill 50 yards, then left over stile (signposted Bossington). Bear half right up to gate by woods **2**. Pass immediately through second gate to enter woods. Ignore left fork after 30 yards, but follow path to next junction **3**. Continue forward on level (signposted Hurlstone Point Lower Path). **4** Ignore left fork after 400 yards. 200 yards later, just beyond gate, keep forward at junction (signposted Hurlstone Point), continue on level to leave woods by gate.

Path continues through open ground close to sea and follows coast round towards Hurlstone Point (**b**) (optional detour). **5** 250 yards before

Hurlstone Point turn right, steeply uphill (path signed by acorn marker denoting coastal path). **6** Continue forward at crossing of paths at top of steep slope, following coastal path markers. 130 yards later keep right at oblique T-junction of tracks (signed with acorn marker).

Follow coast path signs for another ¾ mile. **7** Leave coast path for track ahead (where coast path is signposted to left), leading to prominent cairn on Selworthy Beacon (**c**) **8**. Continue forward from beacon, forking left after 250 yards, then following track downhill. Where road comes into view just a few yards to your right, fork right on to path leading to it **9**.

Cross road, take track opposite, slightly to left. 200 yards later this is joined by track coming in from left; after another 100 yards turn right (signposted Selworthy). Track descends into valley, through woods and into Selworthy village (**d**) **10**. Descend through Selworthy, take first right near bottom of village (signposted 'Allerford, no vehicles'), passing between barns, then forward on track between hedges.

11 After ½ mile ignore forest track half right; continue down between hedges. **12** Continue forward at corner of lane, follow into Allerford.

WHAT TO LOOK OUT FOR

(**a**) **Allerford** Straggly, but with some pleasant old cottages around its picturesque packhorse bridge. West Somerset Museum of Rural Life houses a dairy and a Victorian kitchen, and there are craft displays.
(**b**) **Hurlstone Point** Craggy headland and look-out. View W along coast to Foreland Point near Lynton. The path E of here is signed dangerous (immediately around the corner, before the path ascends, there is a fine view of the cliffs).
(**c**) **Selworthy Beacon** View N across

the Bristol Channel to Cardiff, the Glamorgan uplands, Gwent and the Wye Valley; S to Dunkery Hill, W to Porlock Hill.

(d) **Selworthy** Tiny village. The white-painted church, the first building you see, is famous for its barrel-vaulted ceiling and south aisle. Down the street are a handful of thatched cottages and a handsome tithe barn.

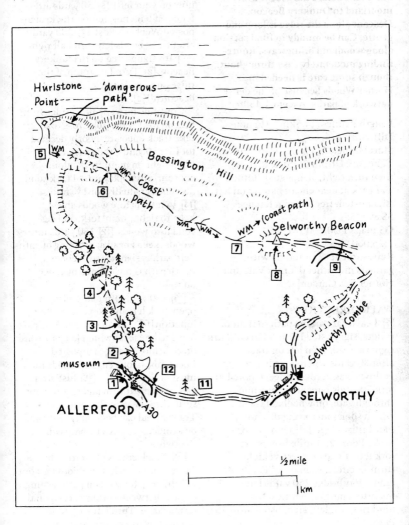

Horner Woods and Dunkery Beacon

A steady ascent through NT-owned Horner Woods, then sea views from a quiet lane before the ascent over moorland to Dunkery Beacon. Descent along the ridge is long and gentle. Can be muddy in final section along woodland bridleways. Route-finding moderately easy throughout, though some care is needed in Horner Woods because of the dense network of paths. Ascent 1,450ft.

Length 9 miles (14.5km), 4½ hours
Difficulty 3–4
Start Horner, 1¼ miles SE of Porlock. Take A39 E from Porlock ¾ mile, then turn right, signposted Horner. Car park at near end of hamlet on left (signposted; free). Grid reference SS 897455
OS maps 1:50,000 181; 1:25,000 SS 84/94
Refreshments Tea-rooms with gardens in Horner (Horner Vale and Horner Tea Garden)

WALK DIRECTIONS

1 Leave car park by path to right of toilets, signposted Horner Green. Turn right on road, then left on track after 80 yards where road bends right. Follow track across bridge, ignore left fork 30 yards later, and continue, through gate, on woodland track which soon joins river (**a**). Ignore foot-bridges, and follow signs for Stoke Pero. **2** 1 mile from start fork left at end of forest-vehicle turning-circle, signposted Poolbridge. Ignore footbridge 250 yards later, but after another ½ mile cross footbridge on left, signposted Stoke Pero.

Path ascends to top of forest (ignore sharp left turn 200 yards from river). **3** Leave forest by gate into field, forward for 30 yards past signpost and continue ahead on grassy track; at end of field it continues between

hedges, through farmyard and on to road **4**. Left on road, past Stoke Pero church (**b**). **5** Turn right at T-junction after ½ mile (**c**), signposted Exford (Dunkery Hill is the ridge now on your left). **6** 50 yards after fence on left ends, left on track, signposted Webber's Post. **7** 300 yards after track bends left turn half right on path signposted up to Dunkery Beacon. **8** Turn left at top of the ridge on to wide track leading to beacon (**d**) **9**.

Continue forward along ridge from beacon for 1 mile. **10** Cross road, take track opposite (poorly defined for first 50 yards, then very clear). Keep right on main track (along contour) after 300 yards. Track soon descends gradually for 1¼ miles. **11** ¼ mile before woods ahead keep to right (main) fork, and descend into woods. **12** 150 yards into woods, keep ahead at crossing of paths (left path is signposted Webber's Post); path is now joined by fence on right.

13 100 yards after emerging into open, fork left and descend to lane junction **14**. Left on lane, follow past drive to house, at which keep forward on rightmost track, signposted Luccombe (along edge of woods for most of rest of walk). **15** Just after gate ignore left turn and ignore right turn, through gate, 30 yards later. Track ahead can be muddy, but can be avoided in places by paths on the right.

16 Track enters plantation by gate. After ½ mile main track goes half left uphill; keep forward on path leading to gate, between cottages, then on to tarmac lane. Turn left to gate, re-entering forest; turn right along fence. **17** At road, descend to cross-roads, turn left, signposted Horner. *Either* follow road back, *or* 50 yards later take gate on left and follow track around edge of woods to emerge on road at Horner.

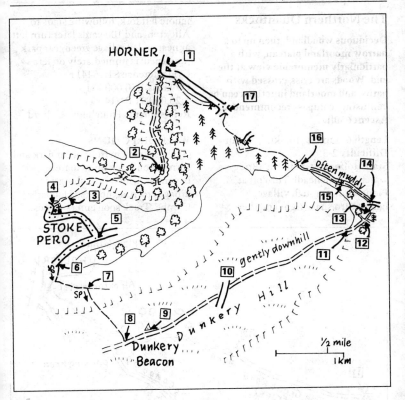

WHAT TO LOOK OUT FOR

(a) **Horner Wood** Ancient woodlands, predominantly oak with rowan, birch, hazel and holly. Some rare lichens. **Birds** Dipper, grey wagtail, wood warbler, redstart and pied flycatcher. **Flora** Cornish moneywort, St John's wort, lesser skullcap, wood spurge, bitter vetch, golden-rod, bell-flower and others. Prolific red deer.

(b) **Stoke Pero church** Interesting only as being the smallest, most remote and, at 1,013ft, highest church in Exmoor; Victorian, apart from a medieval tower. The village which once surrounded it has now all but disappeared.

(c) A public **bridleway** is marked on OS maps straight ahead here, but it was impassable when inspected.

(d) **Dunkery Beacon** At 1,705ft, the highest point in Exmoor. The beacon

is the cairn on top; what you are about to walk along is Dunkery Hill. Helpful view-indicator. **View** can include points up to 150 miles apart: N over the Bristol Channel to Swansea Bay and Cardiff and, beyond, the Black Mountains and Brecon Beacons; in the channel itself, the two islands of Steep Holm and Flat Holm near Weston-super-Mare; NE to the distinctive Sugar Loaf near Abergavenny and beyond to the jagged outline of the Malverns near Ledbury; ESE to the prominent Wellington Monument on the Black-down Hills; SE to the Brendons and Quantocks; SE towards Sidmouth; SSW over Exmoor and beyond to Hay Tor, Yes Tor and Cawsand Beacon (all in SSW Dartmoor); W into the centre of Exmoor.

The Northern Quantocks

Deciduous woodland, then up to a narrow moorland plateau, with a particularly memorable view at the end. Woods are criss-crossed with paths, and moorland junctions can be confusing; compass recommended. Ascent 650ft.

Length 6½ miles (10.5km), 3 hours
Difficulty 2-3
Start Holford, just off A39 (Bridg-water to Minehead). Turn off at Plough Inn, through village, ignore turn sharp right and then

ignore left fork, following signs to Alfoxton, and 100 yards later turn left at near end of village green; car park (unsigned) is immediately on left.
Grid reference ST 154411
OS maps 1:50,000 181;
1:25,000 ST 04/14
Refreshments Plough Inn, Holford

WALK DIRECTIONS

1 Cross track in front of car park and turn left on track immediately beyond it, which runs alongside village green, signposted Hodder's Combe. Track soon enters woods,

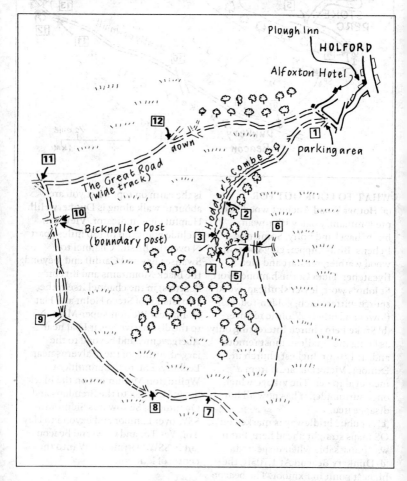

with stream on right; track later narrows to path. **2** After ½ mile, on descending to stream level, where stream bends right, keep forward on path. **3** 200 yards later, ford stream (easy) and fork left beyond. **4** After 120 yards and immediately after recrossing stream, bear left uphill on either of two ascending paths (which soon merge).

5 Fork left as soon as you leave woods. **6** Turn right at crossing of grassy tracks 200 yards later. Track contours round hill (ignore left fork after 200 yards), with views of wooded valley down on right, and narrows to path. **7** After 1 mile join coming in from left; keep forward. **8** As soon as view on left opens out (**a**), take middle (highest) of three tracks ahead. Track rises gently.

9 500 yards after track descends, fork right at fork of wide stony tracks (**b**). **10** Reach complex of tracks by prominent wooden boundary post; follow stony track ahead, just to left of post. Turn right 200 yards later at fork of stony tracks. **11** After 150 yards, turn right at crossing of tracks. Descend steadily (**c**) for ¾ mile, ignoring minor side turns.

12 200 yards before woods ahead, fork right down to corner of woods. At corner, take track half left which runs along edge of woods, with woods on left and moorland on right. Descend to corner of road (**d**) then continue ahead to start.

WHAT TO LOOK OUT FOR

(**a**) **View** Straight ahead, W, over Brendon Hills; SW towards Tiverton.
(**b**) **View** Minehead Bay, with Selworthy Beacon beyond.
(**c**) **View** Severn Estuary, including Steep Holm and Flat Holm, the two islands near Weston-super-Mare; across the estuary, left to right: Nash Point, the Glamorgan uplands, Cardiff, the Sugar Loaf near Abergavenny, and the hills of the Wye Valley.
(**d**) Emerge by an ancient (restored) **stone dog-pound**, decorated with a heraldic motif.

WILTSHIRE

Old Wardour Castle and White Street Hill

Based on a contribution from Jack Crewe

Woodland and parkland on the outward leg to Old Wardour Castle, then a chalk track along a ridge looking over Cranborne Chase on the return. On well-defined tracks with a quiet minor road at the end; easy route-finding.

Length 5 miles (8km), 2½ hours
Difficulty 2
Start Donhead St Andrew, close to Foresters Inn. From A30 (Shaftesbury to Salisbury) take Donheads turning, ignore left turns, and follow signs to Tisbury and Wardour Castle, to reach Foresters Inn. Continue to next fork, by post-box. Roadside parking just past pub. Grid reference ST 250918
OS maps 1:50,000 184; 1:25,000 ST 82/92
Refreshments Foresters Inn, Donhead St Andrew; Maypole, Ansty (detour from route)

WALK DIRECTIONS

1 With post-box on right, fork right, signposted Salisbury. At next crossroads continue forward on 'no through road', which soon becomes track. **2** Track soon enters woods by gate. 250 yards later track bends right; 20 yards later turn sharp left to leave track, then immediately turn right to small gate (**a**). Continue down across field, to gate/stile in front of lake **3**. Follow path around left side of lake, then continue forward on left side of field aiming for left-hand corner of forest, where track continues ahead. Soon ruins of Old Wardour Castle come into view (**b**).

4 Turn right at the car park, immediately on passing castle. Where track bends right into castle

entrance continue up on track running close to castle wall. At corner of wall, track bends right along wall, rises through woods, soon passing through tunnel. Near top of woods, wall on your right ends; ignore left turn and continue to edge of woods and follow fenced track between fields. **5** On reaching woods at end of fields keep forward across first crossing track, and 20 yards later turn right at T-junction with second track.

6 Where track reaches corner of surfaced lane (**c**), continue forward to A30 (**d**), cross to track signposted Harepath slightly to right, soon between hedges. **7** Track bends left at foot of ridge; ignore right turns into chalk pit and proceed on track which

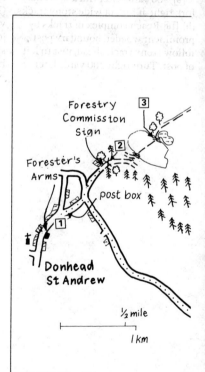

ascends gently. **8** By strip of woodland at top, turn right at T-junction with track. Follow along top of ridge for 1½ miles (**e**). **9** After passing trig. point away to your right (**f**), track descends between grassy banks; avoid left (ascending) fork 100 yards later. Descend to A30 **10**. Cross road to minor road opposite and follow down to crossroads near start of walk, at which turn left to return to Foresters Inn in Donhead St Andrew.

WHAT TO LOOK OUT FOR

(**a**) **New Wardour Castle** Seen half left as you emerge from woods. A Palladian design of 1768 by James Paine; now belonging to Cranborne Chase School. The lake you shortly pass was constructed as a landscape feature in the 18th century.

(**b**) **Old Wardour Castle** (English Heritage; open to public; fee). Former seat of the Arundell family; ruined in a siege in the Civil War. Licence to crenellate (ie to build as a stronghold) was given in 1393.

(**c**) ¾ mile detour left, along lane (see map) to Ansty, with an attractively set pub next to the pond and the tallest **maypole** in England.

(**d**) On the right, a former **tollhouse**. Before the 19th century the road ran along the ridge of Whitesheet Hill.

(**e**) **View** S towards Win Green, the next ridge, and Cranborne Chase beyond; N over the Nadder Valley and towards Salisbury Plain.

(**f**) For evidence of this track being the old highway to London, look out for a well-preserved **milestone**, dated 1736, just inside a field to the left shortly before the track descends.

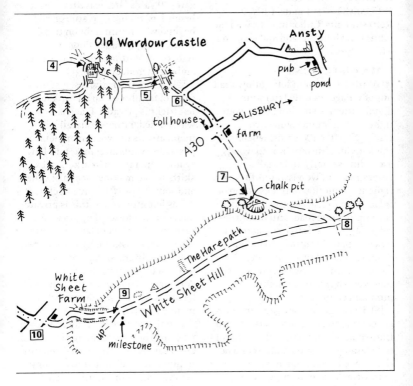

Tollard Royal and Cranborne Chase

Contributed by Jack Crewe

A tour of some of the hunting country of Cranborne Chase, with a long gentle descent over farmland, then a track along the secluded valley of Ashcombe Bottom, and finally a ridge track near Win Green, with a view of the whole area. One very steep ten-minute climb through trees from Ashcombe Bottom, with no defined path; not all field paths visible on the ground, but route-finding moderately easy.

Length 9 miles (14.5km), 4½ hours
Difficulty 3
Start Talbot Inn, Berwick St John, 6 miles E of Shaftesbury. Roadside parking. Grid reference ST 947223
OS maps 1:50,000 184;
1:25,000 ST 81/91 and ST 82/92
Refreshments Talbot Inn, Berwick St John; King John's Hotel and shop in Tollard Royal

WALK DIRECTIONS
1 With pub on your left, follow road out of village. ¼ mile later, immediately after passing houses on your right, turn right on signposted track. **2** After 400 yards, where track divides, turn right into woods, ascending steadily and finally emerging from woods at top. **3** Turn right at T-junction of tracks at top of ridge, soon to reach corner of road; turn right along road, still on top of ridge. **4** Turn left to track between fences, opposite turning to Berwick St John. Where fences end, after 200 yards, continue forward across large field keeping to top of slightly pronounced ridge (**a**).

5 Pass through two gates in quick succession to enter second large field; immediately turn left to skirt edge of field, alongside woodland. At end of field leave by gate and proceed on grassy track down into valley. At bottom, continue forward to join track leading through gate, and continue with fence on left.

6 100 yards later bear half right up slope following overhead cables to small gate on skyline. Beyond gate continue to follow cables, passing through double gate just to left of large grove of beeches. Proceed with fence on right to small gate into wood, then bear half left downhill to next power post; where power lines go uphill, proceed more steeply downhill to find gate on to road. Turn left into Tollard Royal village (**b**) **7**.

From Tollard Royal take road by which you just emerged (ie with war memorial behind you and phone box on left, take road ahead), fork left after 100 yards by last building, and follow track along valley which curves to left. **8** After ¾ mile reach gate; 30 yards later leave track as it bends left, taking gate/stile on right beyond which turn right on track. Track leads up valley floor of Ashcombe Bottom, soon into woods and past derelict cottage (**c**).

9 Where track divides, just in front of farmhouse up on bank, fork left (right is private). Track is waymarked, rather erratically, by metal arrows on wooden or metal posts. 250 yards after fork, fork left again by metal post/marker; track skirts wood, making for end of valley, and soon drops. **10** Leave track as it bends left into woods (this is private) but continue forward up slope, skirting edge of woodland (no path). Rise briefly to skirt edge of field then enter thistly grassland; continue forward to end of valley, passing entrance to large side valley on your left and entering woods at head of main valley **11**.

Climb steep wooded slope (no path) up centre of valley. Emerge into open, cross gate above valley head and turn right on track (**d**) (or left to detour to Win Green; follow until NT sign,

then fork left up to clump of trees and trig. point). Follow to junction at end of road and turn sharp left on road.
12 20 yards later turn left again at T-junction, then immediately take narrow path on right between high banks. Path widens to track.

13 Where track divides, take either fork: they rejoin. Track then follows right edge of field (e). **14** Where hedgerow on right bends right, continue to follow it to road. Left on road, right at next junction and proceed to start.

WHAT TO LOOK OUT FOR

(a) **View** Over Cranborne Chase, an area associated with hunting since at least King John's reign. The Lord of the Chase had the right to hunt over other people's land, even if it meant riding over their crops. Many disputes arose over the centuries, in which attempts were made to restrict the hunting rights to the area bounded by the Inner Chase. The Chase was finally disenfranchised in 1828.

(b) **Tollard Royal** 'Royal' because King John's hunting-lodge was built here – the now largely medieval and Elizabethan house (though some 13th-century parts remain) next to the church.

(c) Shortly after passing the derelict cottage, look out for a small shed just to the right of the track. It is a **tram**, very much on its last wheels (not that it has any). Inside is some Bourne-mouth tramway memorabilia.

(d) **Ox Drove** This prehistoric track formed the northern boundary of the Inner Chase. Good picnic place and viewpoint at Win Green (NT). View N to Whitesheet Hill: S to Dorset and the Needles, Isle of Wight.

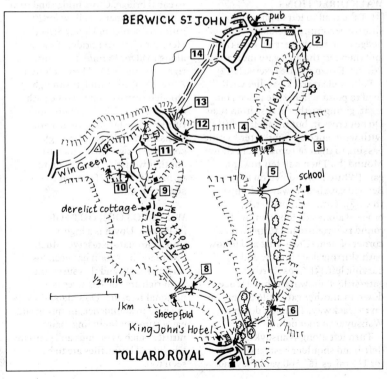

99

Pewsey Down, the Wansdyke and the Kennet and Avon Canal

Contibuted by Geoff Peacock

Chalk downland above the Vale of Pewsey on the outward half, offering fine walking over cropped turf and some of the best views in Wiltshire; return is along the canal at the foot of the down. A short stretch of quiet road; field paths not all defined, but route-finding reasonably easy.

Length 8½ miles (14 km), 4 hours
Difficulty 3
Start Phone box at Alton Priors, 4 miles NW of Pewsey. Grid reference SU 110623. Roadside parking
OS maps 1:50,000 173; 1:25,000 SU 06/16
Refreshments Barge Inn (waterside pub) at Honey Street

WALK DIRECTIONS

1 Take road to left of phone box, shortly becoming track between hedges. On reaching road, turn right and then left through gate indicating Pewsey Down nature reserve (**a**) **2**.

Follow clear track parallel with road to point where stile is seen on right, giving further access from road. Do not cross it, but turn left uphill, with wire fence on right, after ½ mile passing to right of tumulus of Pillow Mound (**b**). Then half left towards gate (White Horse down on left). Beyond gate bear towards clump of trees **3**. Turn right over stile; proceed alongside fence on right round two right-hand turns to reach corner of field. Cross stile and follow path skirting deep hollow and curving left. **4** Cross further gate/stile. Follow right-hand fence down to another gate/stile to emerge on to trackway. Turn left down to Wansdyke at foot of hill.

Turn left along Wansdyke (**c**) (left-hand shoulder best) and follow for 1½ miles. **5** 500 yards beyond

point where Dyke bears right do not go over fence which crosses it, but turn left along fence. Pass trig. point (**d**) (see in adjacent field on right), and continue ahead to reach stile. Cross and continue by path visible beginning slightly to left and curving downhill (**e**). Go over barrier-stile at foot of hill and continue down next field with fence on right-hand side.
6 At metal gate at bottom turn left to skirt field, outside fence, to way-marked stile on right. Cross and turn left on track between hedges to gate/stile. Follow track beyond down to road **7** .

Cross road to farm. Go through gate between farm buildings and cottages, then across field to stile in far right-hand corner. Beyond stile continue along edge of second field, keeping right **8** where fence bends right, to reach broad track leading left to canal bridge. Cross bridge and turn left along towpath. Follow for 2¼ miles to hamlet of Honey Street. Here turn left over bridge. Proceed along road for ¼ mile, then turn right, signposted St Mary's church. After 200 yards turn left through wooden turnstile on to stone path crossing field. Through two more turnstiles on far side where path turns sharp right to church (**g**), continue forward over grass to another turnstile. Emerge on to tarmac driveway. Turn left to starting-point.

WHAT TO LOOK OUT FOR

(**a**) **Pewsey Down** is a highly important nature reserve. Much downland in Britain has been lost under plough, and this surviving herb-rich area of 400 acres is a national treasure. Downland flowers are here in abundance, in spring and early summer including many rarities, such as orchids and gentians. Chalkland butterflies are to be seen too.

(**b**) The short diversion to the top of **Pillow Mound** is recommended.

(**c**) This **rampart** is a surviving section of a 60-mile bank and ditch originally stretching from the Bristol Channel to E of the Savernake Forest. Dating from the 6th or 7th century, it was probably a West Saxon defensive work against the Mercians 'Wansdyke' may be a corruption of 'Woden's Dyke', as though the Saxon god had created it.

(**d**) At 964ft, this is the highest point in Wiltshire.

(**e**) **Rybury Camp** up to the left is an Iron Age hillfort.

(**f**) The **Kennet and Avon Canal** was built originally to provide a link by waterway from Bristol to London. After years of neglect, it is now being restored. **View** of Pewsey White Horse, created in 1812 and re-cut in 1936 to commemorate the coronation of George VI.

(**g**) The tiny church of **Alton Barnes** has a Saxon nave and an 18th-century wall painting. Nearby is Alton Priors church, which has a Perpendicular tower, some Norman work, Jacobean stalls and box pews.

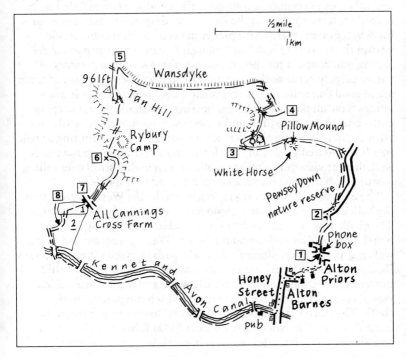

SOUTH-EAST ENGLAND

Hampshire, Isle of Wight, Kent, Surrey, Sussex

It is easier than you might think to escape the crowds in the
South-East, into quiet and rural pockets that offer some of the best
lowland walking in the country. For the walker the keys to the area's
charm are its variety and small scale, which mean you can often cover
several types of scenery in a single walk. London's Green Belt, too, has
helped preserve the best of the landscape: despite enormous pressures
for development, there's still plenty of deep unspoilt countryside
within thirty to forty miles of Trafalgar Square. In many parts of the
region, you're spoilt for choice, because there's a dense network of
paths. Largely because they are used by so many people, many of them
are in good condition: local authorities, landowners and voluntary
groups have all done work in signposting, waymarking and keeping
paths usable. But we still found it necessary to pick routes with care –
with the help of many checkers and contributors – as rerouting a walk
by a few hundred yards can transform a boring trudge over flat fields
with distant views of suburban roads into an idyllic stroll over rolling
pasture with fine distant views over hills and woodlands.

   The eastern part of the area is dominated by the Weald, a great ring
of chalk downs encompassing wooded greensand ridges and pastures.
The chalk downs – crossed by two official long-distance paths, the
North Downs Way and the South Downs Way – give some excellent
walking, particularly along their crests, with sea views from the South
Downs. In their natural state the downs are splendid sites for wild
flowers. More good scenery (typically wood and heath with sudden
views) is found on the greensand ridges which run parallel to the
chalk. The ridge to the south of the North Downs, in particular, has
some fine summits, including the near 1,000-ft heights of Leith Hill
and Black Down, but offers some more intimate scenery, too,
especially south of Westerham and Sevenoaks. The area between the
North and South Downs has mostly escaped agricultural
'improvement' and still has small grassy fields lined with hedgerows,
deciduous woodlands (particularly oak and beech woods), orchards,
oast houses and some patches of rough land, for example Otford
Mount, Older Hill and the Ashdown Forest. There are smart but
pretty villages with half-timbered and pantiled cottages.

   The coast here is heavily developed and, unlike in the South-West or Norfolk, there's no official long-distance coastal path (if there were, it would often follow suburban roads). But there are a handful of unspoilt stretches: the Seven Sisters near Eastbourne, Fairlight Glen near Hastings, and the cliffs near Dover. And on the Isle of Wight, there are some superb coastal walks, offering views of cliffs and downland, together with glimpses across to Hampshire, Dorset and Sussex. Walks have to be carefully planned to avoid the more developed parts, though.

In Hampshire an obvious attraction for walkers is the New Forest, a large and largely unsettled area (it was originally a hunting reserve for William I) with remote-feeling open heathland and superb oak and beech woods. Though it is criss-crossed by a vast number of paths and tracks (all of which are accessible to the public and are pleasant enough to saunter along), finding walks with enough focus and scenic variation to stand out from the rest is quite a challenge. We felt the north-western part of the New Forest had most to offer in this respect. We haven't found any walks we felt merited inclusion in eastern Hampshire, for instance around Petersfield and Alton, and would particularly welcome new suggestions from readers – see page 10.

Because of the intricate nature of the terrain in the South-East, route-finding can be complex, involving successions of small fields and networks of woodland paths and tracks. Accordingly, our directions for some of these walks are among the most elaborate in the *Guide*, and should be followed with care. Mud can also be quite a problem in places. After heavy rain, chalk turns very sticky (especially where it has been churned up by horses) and can prise off shoes completely: walking boots are strongly recommended, even for easy walks, though you could probably manage in wellingtons for the shorter ones.

HAMPSHIRE

Breamore House and the Mizmaze

Contributed by Jack Crewe
Recommended by Reg Kirk,
Gillian Goddard

Takes in much of architectural interest, while leading through quiet green farmland and woods in an unspoilt corner of the county. Easy route-finding; nearly all on clearly defined tracks.

Length 5 miles (8km), 2½ hours
Difficulty 1
Start Village of Whitsbury, 4 miles NW of Fordingbridge. Car parking space by phone box opposite Cartwheel Inn, otherwise park further up street in village. Grid reference SU 129188
OS maps 1:50,000 184; 1:25,000 SU 01/11
Refreshments Cartwheel Inn, Whitsbury; tea-room at Countryside Museum near Breamore House

WALK DIRECTIONS
1 With Cartwheel Inn on right, walk up main street of Whitsbury for ½ mile, ignoring turning on your right to Whitsbury Manor Stud (signed). 30 yards later, where road bends left, take surfaced track on right (not sharp right through gate of Manor House). 50 yards later follow track as it bends to right behind stables, then fork left on to unmetalled track (**a**). Follow downhill for ½ mile. **2** At bottom cross track, take gate ahead and follow grassy track along edge of two fields before it enters woods, then continue forward ignoring cross-tracks **3**. Track soon emerges into the open, following right edge of field to the gate/stile by next group of trees. Beyond gate/stile turn right on track, and proceed, looking carefully for sign to Mizmaze at edge of woods, which soon

appears up on right (Mizmaze itself is hidden in the woods) (**b**).

4 From Mizmaze return to track, which soon bends left and runs between hedges. Shortly, track enters woods; avoid side turns, and proceed to bottom, emerging into parkland and passing just to right of entrance to Breamore House, where driveway is picked up (**c**). **5** Just after passing between gateposts capped by stone lions turn right (**d**), past Countryside Museum (**e**). Keep left 200 yards later and emerge on to road. Turn right on road, through hamlet of Upper Street (**f**), then take next road turning on right, by grassy triangle.

6 Where road ends, continue forward on track between hedges, forking right after 250 yards. **7** Where track reaches gate/stile, continue forward along left side of field to pass through gate, then turn right on track. **8** After ¼ mile, just as track begins to bend right, take track on left leading to farm. Pass through farmyard (avoiding right turn in centre of farmyard), picking up track at far end marked by line of trees on its right-hand side. Track leads up to woods, at far side of which turn right.

9 Where track reaches end of surfaced road by first house, turn left on track between fences (**g**) heading for Whitsbury Church, half-hidden in trees. Turn left at T-junction of tracks, then right through gate to enter churchyard. In front of church, with Whitsbury in view below, *either* take gate and proceed down to gate by thatched building to emerge close to pub; *or*, if you parked further up in village, take gate at far end of church-yard which leads on to fenced path and down into village.

WHAT TO LOOK OUT FOR

(**a**) On the right, the overgrown 16-acre site of **Whitsbury Iron Age camp**, with three lines of ramparts and ditches. Excavation has revealed the outline of a circular timber house.

(**b**) **Mizmaze** Cobweb-like turf maze 87ft across, cut in the grass and surrounded by yew trees. Its origin is uncertain; it may be Anglo-Saxon.

(**c**) **Breamore House** (open to public; fee) Elizabethan mansion, home of the Hulse family since 1748, containing a collection of paintings and furniture. Partially rebuilt after fire damage in 1856.

(**d**) Just to left, **Breamore church**.

Partly Saxon, with some 'long and short' work on the quoins of the tower, alternating horizontal and vertical stones at the corner of the building, typical of the period. Several windows and all of the south transept date from this time; otherwise mostly Norman and 14th century.

(**e**) **Countryside and Carriage Museum** Farm museum with workshops, smithy, carriages, old steam engines.

(**f**) **Upper Street** Particularly well-preserved hamlet of thatched cottages. The next left turn leads to a common, flanked by scattered cottages (probably put up by squatters).

(**g**) **View** Over to edge of New Forest.

Hale House and Godshill Inclosure

Contributed by Anne Sayer
Recommended by Jack Crewe, Reg
Kirk, Gillian Stuart, Sally Johnson

Woods and pasture as the farmland of the Avon Valley meets the western fringes of the New Forest, with a track along the edge of heathland at the end. Not all field paths are defined, and woodland paths in the early stages potentially confusing; follow directions with care.

Length: 6½ miles (10.5km), 3 hours
Difficulty 2
Start Forestry Commission car park at Godshill Inclosure. Take B3078 (Fordingbridge to Cadnam), turn off at Fighting Cocks Inn at Godshill and take minor road signposted Woodgreen. ¾ mile N of Godshill, where road bends sharp left, turn right into Godshill Wood car park (signed). Grid reference SU 176160
OS maps 1:50,000 184; 1:25,000 Outdoor Leisure 22
Refreshments Bat and Ball Inn, Hatchet Green (½ mile off route)

WALK DIRECTIONS

1 From end of car park furthest from road pass through gate number 4 into woods on left. Turn left at first junction of tracks, after 100 yards. After 300 yards cross road and continue opposite through gate. Keep to main track, turning right after 200 yards, and fork left ¼ mile later.

2 Emerge on to road at Castle Hill (viewpoint). Turn right on road for 100 yards to reach T-junction. Continue straight over, following track to left of road signpost, shortly past cemetery on your right. Avoid prominent track swinging away to left. At end of cemetery railings bear half right (no path) to reach wire fence, then turn left downhill on sunken path. Cross stream at bottom of slope and continue uphill to reach

small green, flanked by cottages, and soon pick up gravel track (**a**).

3 After 100 yards, where track swings away left, continue direction across green, making for prominent thatched wooden barn; take gravel track to left of it. After a few yards fork left by footpath sign and descend past houses for ¼ mile to where track bends sharply to right **4**. Cross stile ahead and proceed with fence on left (**b**), crossing two more stiles. At last stile emerge on road at Hale rectory. Turn right, then immediately left, on road signposted to Downton.

5 After 400 yards turn right (**c**) up steep path to Hale church (**d**), after which keep left, avoiding climbing steps on right. Fence and path then swing half right to emerge at end of avenue nearest Hale House (**e**).

Follow fence on left-hand side of avenue, ignoring track on left 300 yards later. **6** At road, turn right, then left at next road junction. After 300 yards, immediately before road fork, take bridleway (signposted) which climbs bank on left and goes through small gate **7**. Cross field heading for second gate in front of barns built on staddle stones (**f**). Path goes between barns, then through small gate, to run alongside edge of wood, at first between fences.

8 Shortly after field on left ends and forest starts, ignore right turn, and 50 yards later turn left at oblique T-junction with gravel track. Follow gate leading on to road at Hatchet Green. (For Bat and Ball Inn, cross green to far end and take road ahead for ½ mile ignoring side turns; pub is on right.) Bear half right on to road and half right down track which passes in front of Hale Village Hall then leads downhill for 100 yards. Turn right along road. **9** After 80 yards turn right on to bridleway (signposted) through woods (**g**). After ½ mile keep straight on at crossing in middle of woods and carry on to

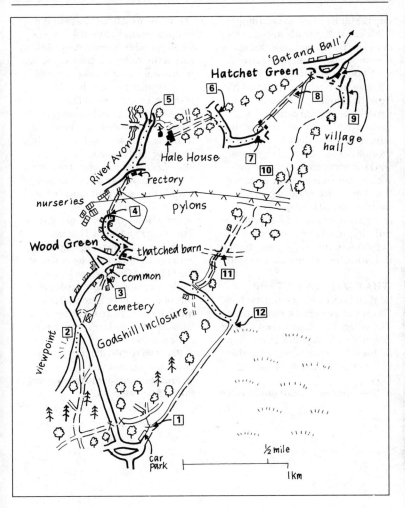

'Bat and Ball'
Hatchet Green
6
5
8
9
River Avon
Hale House
7
village hall
10
rectory
nurseries
4
Pylons
Wood Green
thatched barn
11
common
3
cemetery
2
Godshill Inclosure
12
viewpoint
1
car park
½ mile
1 Km

emerge under pylon in clearing **10**.

Make for diagonally opposite foot of pylon; track continues through woods opposite. Emerge on to path with house opposite. Turn left and walk up the track to T-junction **11**. Turn right and after 20 yards find partially concealed path leading up through hedgerow on your left, over stile then across field. Cross two more stiles and descend into copse, walking between fences. Join drive which continues in same direction. Cross over cattle-grid opposite Godshill Wood Cottage. Turn left along tarmac lane and follow for ¼ mile. **12** Just before lane bends 90 degrees left, turn right (away from it) following forest fence back to start.

WHAT TO LOOK OUT FOR
(a) **Wood Green** Characteristic New Forest village of brick and thatch. The village hall contains a 1930s mural of everyday life of the village.
(b) **View** Over the nurseries to the Elizabethan mansion, Breamore House.
(c) Two-minute detour: on the other side of the road from this path is a footpath leading to prettily set **wooden bridge** over the Avon. In this part of the valley are some of the last traditional water-meadows in the country (now found only in W Hampshire and parts of Dorset and Wiltshire). They are low-lying fields dug with channels to let the silt in from the river, to enrich the grazing. Good for wild flowers.
(d) **Hale church** Predominantly early 18th-century work by Archer (see (e)), with 17th-century masonry in the nave and chancel.
(e) **Hale House** (not open to public) The country house of Thomas Archer, a practitioner of English baroque architecture who designed the N face of Chatsworth House in Derbyshire and probably redesigned this one, though it is uncertain how much he contributed. The house is dominated by its late 18th-century Ionic portico.
(f) **Barns** were raised in this way as a protection against rats.
(g) Proliferations of **rhododendrons**, in flower May/June.

Brockenhurst and Setley Pond

Recommended by Gillian Stuart

By far the best round walk we could find in this part of the New Forest, through a nature reserve of ancient woodland and across pasture fields to the Hobler Inn, then emerging suddenly on to wide, open heathland with belts of woodland in the distance; in the middle of the heath is Setley Pond, used for model-boat sailing (or skating in deep winter). Returns to Brockenhurst station by footpaths; the walk is rural in character until the very end. Paths undefined across fields, and directions need care over the heath.

Length 6½ miles (10km), 3 hours
Difficulty 2
Start Brockenhurst station (S side), on A337 (Lymington to Lyndhurst)
OS maps 1:50,000 195 and 196; 1:25,000 Outdoor Leisure 22
Refreshments Pubs and cafés in Brockenhurst; Hobler Inn at 8

WALK DIRECTIONS

1 From station car park on S side of station, walk to main road, turn right and after 30 yards turn left on road signposted to St Nicholas Parish Church. After church, continue on road half right for 200 yards. 2 Turn left opposite stables through wicket gate and walk between fences through Brockenhurst Park and into Brockenhurst Woods nature reserve. Path is undulating and marked with yellow waymarks at regular intervals. 3 After 1 mile, join large track coming in from right and after 100 yards pass isolated cottage known as The Lodge, keeping straight on at junction of tracks just after. Ignore left turn at bottom of slope, but continue uphill for 200 yards on same track. 4 Look out carefully for yellow marker post indicating small path on right, which leads up through woods then passes through gate 5.

Pass through gate and carry straight on across turf, with fence on left, heading for houses and reach road. Cross road and take path between fences (signposted) directly opposite, soon to reach another road 6.

Again cross road, to path opposite, leading down to cross footbridge. Continue uphill across left edge of two fields to enter left-hand edge of woods by stile. 7 Follow path running on edge of woods and where path emerges into fields follow right edge of field to stile right of rear of pub (Hobler Inn). Cross two further stiles to reach main road 8.

Cross road and turn left on it. After 30 yards, opposite pub sign, turn right over stile on path immediately to right of cottage. Path runs between hedges and after ¼ mile crosses stile and emerges at corner of heathland 9. Make towards red-brick house in front of you, and just beyond it take right track at junction of tracks. After 30 yards cross gravel cross-track and continue direction on path which soon runs alongside Setley Pond.

10 At end of pond continue half right, keeping to left of car park, to reach wooden barrier. Turn left on gravel roadway after 10 yards by Setley Pond sign, and turn half left on path across heath. This soon runs parallel to road and merges with it just before railway bridge. 11 Pass under railway bridge and, 50 yards beyond it, bear half right on path next to height-restriction road-sign (which faces away from you; avoid path immediately after railway bridge which runs parallel to railway). This rises gently, and after ¼ mile crosses railway by footbridge 12.

After bridge, bear quarter left on path (not immediately obvious) making for road-sign showing mileages and destinations. At road, continue opposite on path which bears half right, and follow this, making for

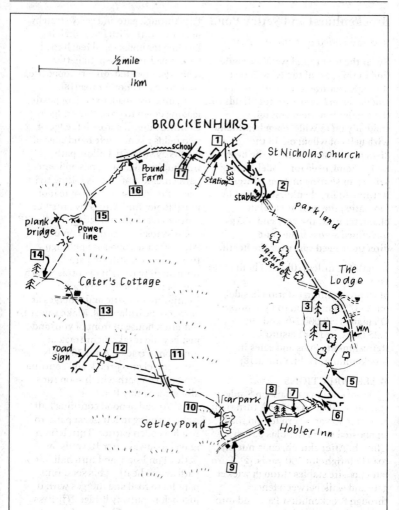

BROCKENHURST

school

1

St Nicholas church

17

station

A337

2

stables

Pound Farm

16

parkland

½ mile

1km

15

plank bridge

Power line

nature reserve

14

The Lodge

Cater's Cottage

3

13

4

WM

road sign

12

11

5

carpark

8

7

10

6

Setley Pond

Hobler Inn

9

white house with shutters and lodge, ¼ mile distant. **13** At house (Caters Cottage) and lodge, pick up gravel track which leads between them to wooden barrier and then narrows to become path leading across open heath.

14 ¼ mile after barrier, immediately before prominent group of trees, turn sharp right on path. This path bends 90 degrees left after ¼ mile and then, after 200 yards, crosses stream by footbridge, after which it briefly becomes indistinct and crosses another stream by plank-bridge. Turn immediately right to power lines, at which turn left to pass gabled house, where direction is continued on gravel track. Follow for 300 yards.

15 Where main track bends left, take track straight on, passing an-other house, and go through kissing-gate. Path at first runs between fences and soon runs alongside stream. Ignore side-turns by bridge and cross final stile to emerge on road **16**. Turn right on road for 100 yards and, just before small road-bridge, turn right on driveway to Pound Farm. Just across stream, before farm, turn left past hurdle and make for distant red-brick buildings (no path), with stream on left. After 100 yards, by footbridge on left, turn half right on path which emerges on road (school on left) **17**.

Turn left and after 30 yards turn right through kissing-gate on path between fences. Cross stile at end of path, and turn left along residential road, near end of which a small gate on right leads down to Brockenhurst station.

Fritham, Cadman's Pool and High Corner Inn

Contributed by Jack Crewe
Recommended by Gillian Stuart

One of the less enclosed parts of the New Forest, where the heathland undulates enough to provide good walking and some views; wild enough to feel genuinely remote. Also mixed woodland of conifers and ancient oaks and beeches. Plenty of opportunities to see New Forest ponies and deer; geese sometimes on Cadman's Pool. Often very wet in places. All on defined paths and tracks, but numerous junctions and few distant landmarks; follow directions with care

Length 9 miles (14.5km), 4½ hours
Difficulty 2
Start Fritham (well signposted) 1 mile S of B3078 (Cadnam to Fording-bridge). Car park signposted beyond Royal Oak. Grid reference SU 230141
OS maps 1:50,000 195;
1:25,000 Outdoor Leisure 22
Refreshments Royal Oak, Fritham; High Corner Inn near **9**

WALK DIRECTIONS

1 Take road opposite Royal Oak, marked 'Forestry Commission no through road, cottages only'. Where road ends, keep straight on as track branches into three. Gravel track then leads down through trees, past more cottages on your left and through barrier on to open land. **2** Cross footbridge after 100 yards and then turn right along banks of small stream. After 80 yards bear half left away from stream through trees (indistinct at first but path soon appears) and after 100 yards emerge at clearing. Continue in same direction, and after 150 yards step across small rivulet. Continue same direction, steadily uphill with fence on right.

3 At top of hill, cross concrete drive (ignore gate on right into wood)

Special interest lists at the back of the book give opening times for castles, houses, gardens and museums passed on the walks.

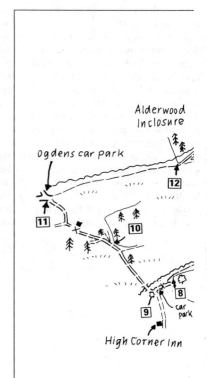

and continue alongside fence for another 200 yards to corner of woodland fence. Turn left for 80 yards to reach corner of driveway (former runway for Stoney Cross aerodrome). Turn 90 degrees right, with driveway now behind you. Follow course of old runway (now grassed over) for ½ mile. Pass through barriers and continue ahead on tarmac forestry track. **4** Reach pond (Cadman's Pool), keep straight on, on concrete path across open heathland. Path ceases to be concrete after ¼ mile, and ½ mile later reaches woodland fence **5**.

For a key to the symbols used on the maps, and for an explanation of the difficulty grading, see the inside front cover.

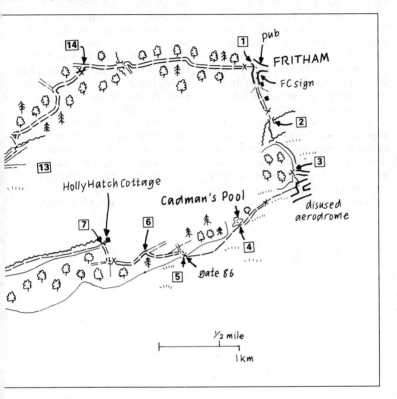

Turn right through gate (number 86) into woods, then left at first crossing of tracks, after 50 yards. Follow track which winds its way downhill (ignoring cross-tracks) and reach gravel track at T-junction **6**. Turn left along it, eventually passing through gate. Turn right at junction immediately beyond and, after 400 yards, emerge from forest just to the left of Holly Hatch Cottage **7**. Turn left along track, which runs parallel to banks of stream (not immediately visible – away to right) and with edge of wood on left.

8 After 1 mile reach corner of wood and turn left for 30 yards to meet gravel track. Turn right along this, passing hurdle and through small car park. Shortly beyond car park reach Y-junction of tracks **9**. (Turn left to get to High Corner Inn; 5 minutes' walk.) Turn right, then immediately right again over wooden footbridge. Take the rough moorland track uphill, passing up to right of clump of isolated pine trees. **10** At top of rise, on reaching left-hand corner of forest, take the leftmost of three tracks by group of trees. After 100 yards fork right on track which soon becomes clearly marked and

113

heads towards houses on distant skyline, soon with enclosed fields and thatched farmstead on right. Keep to the main track by keeping right at oblique T-junction 100 yards beyond farmstead and follow track. Turn right at car park sign and reach Forestry Commission Ogdens car park **11**.

Turn right and follow grassy tracks, keeping alongside stream on left, and pass through open grassland and gorse. Grassy tracks alongside meandering stream soon merge to form path. **12** After 1 mile, western end of Alderhill Inclosure (fenced-off woodland) is reached and is marked by tall pines fenced in on left. Pass to right of these and, after 75 yards, bear left on to wide grassy strip with inclosures of conifers on either side.

13 After ¼ mile, pass through small gate on left (number 41) and immediately cross bridge over stream, entering Alderhill Inclosure. At first path junction continue half right on main track and follow uphill to turn right 100 yards later at oblique T-junction of tracks. Follow track for ¾ mile, ignoring any tracks on left leading uphill, until passing through gate and reaching T-junction **14**.

Turn right along forest track, crossing wooden bridge (Fritham Bridge) after ¼ mile. Keep left on main track beyond bridge. Eventually track passes through barrier; continue ahead (avoiding track on left) to reach car park and Royal Oak at Fritham.

ISLE OF WIGHT

The Needles, Tennyson Down and the Yar

Contributed by Chris John and Jack Crewe
Recommended by Mr and Mrs B H James

Varied coastal section along beach, through woods, for a short stretch along residential roads, then up on to scrub-covered cliffs. Descent to Alum Bay, followed by West High Down and Tennyson Down, is on a long grassy ridge with a variety of chalk-loving plants. Sea views on three sides. Inland, takes a level route on old railway track along River Yar (of botanical interest for its reed and marsh plants). Route-finding made quite easy by thorough signposting; all on clearly defined paths and tracks.

Length 11 miles (17.5km), 5 hours
Difficulty 3
Start Yarmouth ferry terminal (train to Lymington for ferry to Yarmouth). *Or* start at Totland pier (point **7**) and finish at Freshwater Bay, returning to Totland by bus
OS maps 1:50,000 196; 1:25,000 Outdoor Leisure 29
Refreshments Wide range at Yarmouth, Alum Bay and Freshwater Bay; café at S end of Headon Warren (see map)

WALK DIRECTIONS

1 (**a**) From ferry terminal, with sea on right, cross bridge over River Yar. 400 yards later, where road veers left, turn right on path signposted to sea wall. (**b**) **2** Where sea wall ends, after 400 yards, and shortly before jetty, turn left up wooden steps into woods and follow 50 yards to tarmac lane. Turn right along lane and fork left after 100 yards along track signposted to coastal path **3**. Follow track (**c**) 200 yards, then continue on path

ahead where track veers right.
4 After ½ mile path climbs up steps and leaves woods, passing between fences to reach road on fringes of Colwell. Turn left on road, then ¼ mile later turn right at junction, signposted Colwell. **5** After 200 yards road gives out at Brambles Holiday Camp. Continue to left of toilets and just beyond take signposted coastal path on left. After 200 yards emerge from between hedges. Unless it is low tide (in which case you can walk along the shore to pick up the sea wall – see map) do not take path on right signposted coastal path; when walk was checked this was closed, owing to erosion. Instead, continue straight on for ¼ mile to road and turn right **6**.

Follow road ¼ mile and turn right down Colwell Chine Road. Follow to end and turn left along sea wall, ½ mile to pier **7**. From pier continue along sea wall, with sea on right. After 300 yards, and just past Old Totland lifeboat house, take steps up on left (signposted to Cliff Road). Turn right at top, and follow road for 200 yards. **8** Where road veers left take path half right, signposted Alum Bay, to Headon Down. After 400 yards emerge at open gorse heathland; keep straight on uphill at junction of paths.

9 After 150 yards, just beyond where a path comes in sharp left, take right fork and ¼ mile later keep right where left fork leads to summit. Continue past bench on left and follow path on to ridge to descend to Alum Bay. Keep left at bottom in front of bunker, taking track on left for 200 yards. Pass through gate and turn left to reach road **10**. Turn right on road and fork left just after phone box to pass through the Needles Pleasure Park.

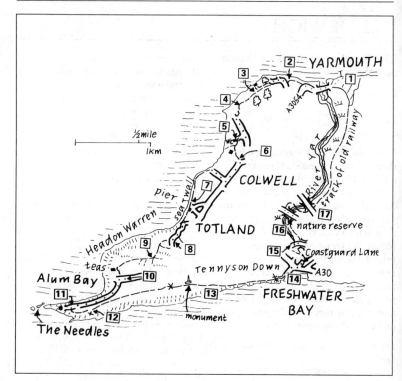

Follow surfaced track 500 yards round edge of cliffs (**d**), (**e**), then **11** take path half left up to West High Down. After 100 yards turn across stile to emerge on road, just below coastguards' cottages. Turn left on road which curves left (or take detour to Needles viewpoint (**f**) via metalled track on right). Between coastguards' cottages (left) and mast (right), head half right to gate **12**.

Proceed along middle of ridge (**g**) (path is undefined) for 1 mile to reach gate. Turn half right up to Tennyson's monument (signposted Freshwater Bay). Beyond monument keep close to cliffs **13**. After ¾ mile leave Tennyson Down by stile and follow fence on left down to track. Turn left on track, ignoring immediate right fork to Fort Redoubt. At road turn right into Freshwater Bay (**h**) **14**. After 75 yards turn left along Coastguard

Lane. At end of lane continue on path straight on. Cross stile and, 100 yards after kissing-gate, fork right and follow path to road **15**.

Turn right along road for 50 yards, then left just before bridge on path into Afton Marsh nature reserve. After 50 yards path crosses to other side of stream and in ½ mile reaches road **16**. Left along road for 50 yards, then turn right on path signposted Yarmouth. After 50 yards path makes right turn. **17** After ½ mile cross road and then follow track of old railway (with River Yar on left) all the way back to Yarmouth (**i**), (**j**). Turn left on road, back to starting-place.

WHAT TO LOOK OUT FOR
(**a**) **Yarmouth** Small, well-heeled port dominated by the yachting on the Yar Estuary. On its sea-front is one of a chain of castles built by Henry VIII as

116

a defence against a French invasion; its design was based on the use of cannon (the first generation of English castles to be so built) and the tower was dispensed with. Nearby is a crenellated house with bogus gun-ports to fool the French.

(**b**) **View** On mainland, Hurst Castle, another of Henry VIII's protective chain.

(**c**) Just off to the right, **Fort Victoria country park**. Two forts, Fort Victoria and Fort Albert, were built in 1840 as part of the defences of the Solent. Fort Albert, which is quite remarkably hideous, has been recently used for torpedo testing. Small museum at Fort Victoria gives the history.

(**d**) View of **Alum Bay**. The cliffs are brilliantly coloured, like those a few miles over to the W, on the mainland at Studland in Dorset (to which the Isle of Wight was once connected). The sands are coloured white by quartz, red by iron oxide, grey by carbonaceous remains and yellow by limonite. On the downs above Alum Bay is a monument to Marconi, who made experimental wireless transmissions from here in 1897.

(**e**) Detour ahead to **the Needles Old Battery** (NT; open to public; fee). Part of the Solent defences, built 1862. Best viewpoint for the Needles (see below).

(**f**) **The Needles** Five chalk pinnacles, gradually being destroyed by the sea. A sixth, Lot's Wife, collapsed in 1764 with a crash that was heard on the mainland. The lighthouse, built 1858, sends out a beam visible for 15 miles.

(**g**) **West High Down** and **Tennyson Down** View E and SE over much of the island, including Bonchurch Down near Ventnor and Brighstone Forest; N over the Solent into Hampshire. On Tennyson Down is a monument to the poet, who lived for 40 years at Farringford House in Freshwater.

(**h**) **Freshwater Bay** Residential and holiday area with a natural rock arch on its sandy beach and some caves on its eastern side. Artist George Morland stayed here in 1799 when the bay had an inn and nothing else; while at Yarmouth he was arrested by the Isle of Wight Defensibles because they thought his pen and ink drawing of a spaniel was a spy map.

(**i**) **Old railway line** Former Freshwater, Yarmouth and Newport railway, the only line to have been built in the western part of the island, although there was a dense network further east.

(**j**) The three-storey brick building on the right at the end of the dyke path is an old **tide mill**.

Appuldurcombe House and Bonchurch Down

Recommended by Mr and Mrs B H James

A crescent of grassy and gorsy chalk ridges just north of Ventnor, giving views over most of the island. Good signposting in the early stages; route-finding a little harder beyond Wroxhall.

Length 6 miles (9.5km), 3 hours
Difficulty 2–3
Start High Street, Ventnor, or by post office above town, just before **2** (grid reference SZ 556776); this avoids part of first ascent
OS maps 1:50,000 196; 1:25,000 Outdoor Leisure 29
Refreshments Pubs and cafés in Ventnor; Worsley Inn and Star Inn, Wroxhall

WALK DIRECTIONS

1 (**a**) Standing in High Street with Midland Bank behind you, turn left up Church Street. After passing church, keep on main road which ascends and bends right then left. 400 yards later turn right on to Zigzag Road, signposted Newport. At next zigzag take Castle Road (ahead), then first right into Gills Cliff Road and after 50 yards turn right up St Albans Steps (signed).

At top continue forward on main road but turn left in front of post office on no through road, signposted Ventnor Golf Club **2**. Follow road uphill and just before it bends right to golf clubhouse take path on left signposted Godshill. Path is well signposted (follow Godshill signs around golf course); after 100 yards ignore path on right but continue forward to signpost, at which turn right downhill **3**.

At T-junction of paths at next signpost again turn right, signposted Godshill, on path which runs with fence on left. Next signpost, to Nettlecombe, indicates path between

fences: this follows top of ridge with wide views on both sides (**b**).

4 Shortly before mast, track merges with surfaced track coming in from right: follow it past mast, heading towards second mast, but leave track at 'no vehicular access beyond this point' sign, taking instead path through gate signposted Godshill. This descends, following right edge of two fields **5**.

At bottom of slope ignore tree-lined path on left, but continue to follow right edge of third (large) field. In fourth field avoid path half left downhill but bear quarter left on path which soon runs closer to wall on right and enters woods. Avoid side turns and leave woods by gate **6**. Path follows right edge of three fields then enters more woodland.

7 Once through woodland, turn right through triumphal arch (part of Appuldurcombe estate). Follow right edge of field beyond (avoid left fork across field after 50 yards) to reach entrance of Appuldurcombe House (**c**). Turn left on tarmac lane in front of entrance and follow into Wroxhall village (if house is closed you can get a good view of it by turning right after 20 yards along estate wall – this is a public footpath).

8 At main road in Wroxhall turn right, then left after 300 yards, just before church, into Castle Road. Ascend, avoiding side turns, then 30 yards after Castle Lane on left, cross stile on right signposted Shanklin and Ventnor **9**. Path follows left edge of field then runs between hedges for 50 yards, and at end crosses stile on left; here keep left in direction of signpost, following left edge of field with slope on left. **10** Path enters scrubby area by gate, and next gate leads into woodland. Leave by stile on right 20 yards before gate on other side of woodland (this stile avoids mud); turn left alongside hedge for 20 yards then turn right on path which makes for gate, beyond which continue direction up on to grassy ridge. Masts are visible away to the right; you will soon be passing close to them.

After 300 yards pass through gate and head straight up to signpost on skyline **11**. Turn right, signposted Ventnor, continuing on ridge towards masts and avoiding side turns. This soon becomes a chalky track (**d**). **12** ½ mile later, and 200 yards before masts, turn left on chalky track signposted Bonchurch and Ventnor. Avoid right turn after 30 yards, and 50 yards later cross large chalky area to find gate on far side. Turn right beyond gate on grassy path which very soon follows perimeter fence of masts.

13 After ½ mile, reach corner of perimeter fence and turn half left on grassy path signposted Ventnor. Avoid stony track which initially runs beside it. 200 yards later, where track bends right, continue forward

across turf, on spur of hill. Shortly, steps appear slightly to left to lead you steeply down to road. Turn left, cross main road and take steps opposite to town centre.

WHAT TO LOOK OUT FOR
(**a**) **Ventnor** 19th-century watering-place with an unusually mild climate due to its sheltered position on the undercliff below St Boniface Down. Victorian villas climb the hillside, then the development gets newer.
(**b**) **View** Left (W), over western Wight, Brighstone Forest to Tennyson Down and towards the Needles beyond.
(**c**) **Appuldurcombe House** (English Heritage; open to public; fee) Shell of a Palladian mansion, built 1710 for Sir Robert Worsley. Became a school in the 19th century and was ruined when a land-mine exploded nearby.
(**d**) **View** E over Shanklin and Sandown to Bembridge Down and Ryde.

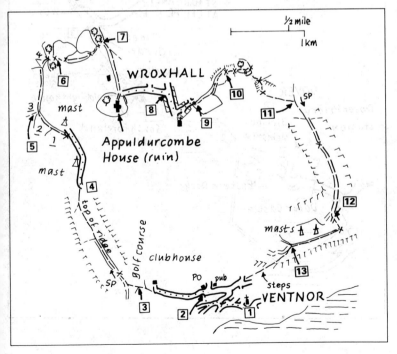

KENT

Dover to Deal

Contributed by Alan Bostock
Recommended by S Johnston,
L and V Sherwood, M Vingoe,
S Empson-Ridler

The high chalk cliffs, better known to cross-Channel travellers than to walkers, make a linear walk of exceptional interest, with views to France on a clear day. Very sheer cliff drops. Beyond Kingsdown, route descends to shingle beach. Occasionally leaves the cliff-edge to follow roads slightly inland. Route-finding fairly easy. Return to Dover by train from Deal (frequent services, daily). Can also finish at St Margaret's at Cliffe (buses to Dover) or Kingsdown (buses to Deal). Check bus times before travelling.

Length *Full walk* 9½ miles (15km), 4½ hours
Difficulty 3
Walk finishing at St Margaret's at Cliffe 4 miles (6.5km), 2 hours
Difficulty 2
Walk finishing at Kingsdown

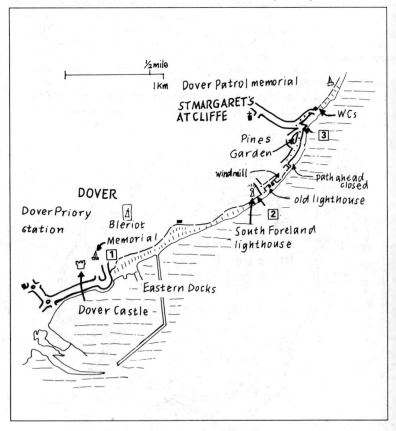

6½ miles (10.5km), 3 hours
Difficulty 2–3
Start Atholl Terrace, Dover (near terminal of Calais car ferry). Parking at multi-storey car park in town centre, also at and around Dover Priory station. (Alternatively, park at Deal and take the train to Dover before the walk.) From these either get a bus to Eastern Docks or walk to the seafront, turn left and walk along promenade until you reach Eastern Docks. Grid reference TR 329416
By train Dover Priory

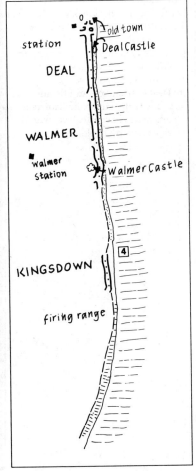

OS maps 1:50,000 179;
1:250,000 TR 24/34 and TR 25/35
Refreshments Full range in Dover, Walmer and Deal; pubs, tea-room and shop, St Margaret's at Cliffe; Zetland Inn, Kingsdown

WALK DIRECTIONS
1 (a) From Atholl Terrace follow path which rises sharply behind ferry terminal and gains cliff-top. Continue along cliff-top (b).

2 Approaching St Margaret's Bay keep to right of lighthouse, then immediately beyond it pick up track leading inland. Turn right at point just beyond lighthouse, on hard track (c), past houses on right. Beyond houses, rejoin cliff-top until end of path (path ahead is closed owing to cliff fall). Turn left and follow hard track for 75 yards and then turn right (d).

3 At T-junction (where gardens on left end), turn right. Next left turn leads to St Margaret's at Cliffe (optional detour) (e). To continue, proceed forward down to St Margaret's Bay, where coast path continues by toilets up steps on to cliff. Follow cliff path, soon past Dover Patrol memorial (f).

1½ miles later, path skirts golf course, and drops down steps to emerge on road. Continue forward, through Kingsdown village 4. From Kingsdown proceed along seafront, and proceed to shingle beach at Walmer (g), then continue to pier at Deal (h).

WHAT TO LOOK OUT FOR
(a) **Dover** Heavily bombed in the Second World War, and not sympathetically redeveloped; at first glance a disappointing place considering it is one of the finest situated towns in Britain. Contains some treasures, however, including the Roman Painted House and the superb Norman castle (English Heritage; open to public; fee), plus Roman lighthouse

and Saxon church.

(**b**) Below and to the left is a **memorial** on the site of Blériot's landing after the first powered flight across the Channel in 1909. Further on, the new coastguard station, where all Channel movement is monitored and rescue operations co-ordinated. Then, to the left, wartime radar chain; it is still used by the Ministry of Defence. Of the same period are concrete emplace-ments, from which there are good views over the Channel. The highest point visible on the French coastline is Cap Gris-Nez in Picardy.

(**c**) On your right, the original **light-house**. Beside it, a scaled-down wind-mill, built as an electrical generator in 1928; ceased working in 1939.

(**d**) On your left, **Pines Garden** (open to the public), containing a lake, floral gardens and sundry objects, including a gypsy caravan, an old shop-front from the City of London and a statue of Sir Winston Churchill.

(**e**) **St Margaret's at Cliffe church** (½ mile off route) Complete and impressive Norman church, rich in ornament, with decorated arches and a fine W door.

(**f**) **Views** Along the coast (N) to Ramsgate on the Isle of Thanet (a prominent headland), and out to sea the Goodwin Sands (at low tide) and the South Goodwin lightship.

(**g**) **Walmer Castle** (English Heritage; open to public; fee). This and Deal Castle (English Heritage; open to public; fee) a little further on were among 20 artillery forts built by Henry VIII, who feared attack from the continent after his break with Rome in 1531. Romney Marsh and the area around Deal were regarded as particularly vulnerable. The plans of Walmer and Deal castles are both in the form of a Tudor rose.

(**h**) **Deal** Retirement-cum-fishing town with a wealth of unspoilt Georgian streets in its old centre (level with the pier); well worth exploring.

Saltwood Castle, Chesterfield Wood and Hythe

Recommended by Anne Hill, James and Vera Sherwood

Approaches Saltwood Castle through a sweep of parkland, then passes through woodland and farmland. Finishes at the picturesque end of Hythe. Paths mainly well defined, some signposted; route-finding quite easy.

Length 4 miles (6.5km), 2 hours
Difficulty 1–2
Start Hythe, on A259 4 miles W of Folkestone, in car park (fee) opposite police station, 300 yards W of A259/B2065 roundabout
OS maps 1:50,000 179 or 189; 1:25,000 TR 13/23
Refreshments Pubs and cafés in Hythe High Street

WALK DIRECTIONS

1 From car park cross road to police station and find Sun Lane to left (signposted to town centre). Reach High Street, turn right along it to end. Turn left along Station Road and immediately right into Mill Road. After 100 yards turn left into Mill Lane (signposted footpath), follow up to road 2. Cross road to take footpath by posts opposite (avoid gate just to left of this). At end turn left on track, leading to stile. After stile, follow right edge of fields; Saltwood Castle soon visible ahead (a).

Avoid right turn under old railway shortly before castle but continue ahead to road 3. Turn left on road; ignore first left turn (Castle Road). After 50 yards take footpath on right (signposted) leading to kissing-gate; from here head to Saltwood church, entering churchyard by next kissing-gate. Pass through churchyard and on to road 4. Turn right on road and fork right after 50 yards, taking 'no through road'. Where road bends right, pick up bridleway (sign-posted on left side of road, initially parallel to road but soon leading uphill, eventually into woodland with old railway down on right (b). After 400 yards cross stile on left (yellow markers) and fork right immediately beyond it.

5 20 yards later (just after 'foot-path only' sign on tree) continue forward at four-way crossing of paths (in direction of yellow markers). This path snakes through woods (avoid any paths on right, up slope). After 400 yards turn left (yellow marker on tree) at T-junction of paths with fence immediately ahead. Follow path to leave wood by stile 6. Cross stile into field, follow right edge to next stile, then path leads between hawthorn trees, across footbridge and on to road. Cross road to gate opposite/slightly to left, picking up clear grassy path ahead.

7 After 400 yards do not continue forward through gate but turn left just before it, on path leading down into Chesterfield Wood. Keep to main path: after further 400 yards leave woods by stile. Beyond it, take faint grassy track leading to group of buildings 8. Emerge on to lane by Pedlinge church, at which turn left then immediately left again – encircling church and passing through gates to re-enter the field that you just left, via different track. Track proceeds with fence on right. Avoid ladder-stile on right after 30 yards, but continue along fence which swings right. After second gate, small wood appears on right of track; where wood and fence ends continue forward on well-trodden path across to gate at corner of wood 9.

Follow path beyond this gate down to footbridge. Cross left-hand of two footbridges, enter Brock Hill Country Park on path marked 'Permissive footpath detour' (this avoids mud) and continue up slope, following markers, parallel to fence on right.

At top of rise bear half right to stile, then left on to path. At end turn right on track which immediately swings left, and follow round to emerge at corner of residential road **10**. Turn right on road and follow for ½ mile, ignoring all side turnings until Hythe churchyard appears on right (**c**). **11** Take steps down, just before churchyard, and at end of it turn left (Oak Lane). From church descend by any means to High Street.

WHAT TO LOOK OUT FOR
(**a**) **Saltwood Castle** Originally 11th-century, with 14th-century gatehouse (now the main residential part), and altered in the 16th century following a minor earthquake; retains a substantial curtain wall. Once belonged to the Archbishop of Canterbury, ironically, for it was here that four knights met to plan the murder of Thomas à Becket. Restored in Victorian times, and in this century became the home

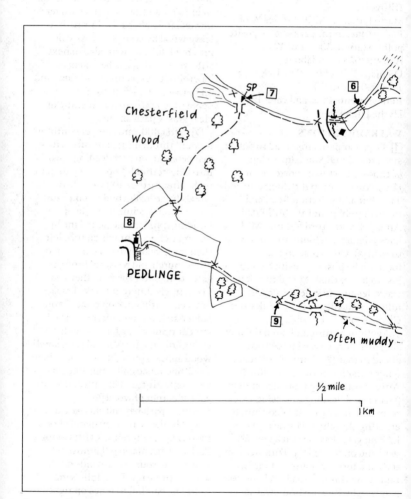

of art historian Sir Kenneth Clark.
(**b**) **Old railway line** Linked Sandling on the main line to Sandgate on the coast. It was to be extended to Folkestone but never made it.
(**c**) **Hythe** The most attractive part of the town is the hillside maze of alleyways and lanes, above the high street. Superb Early English church, with a huge soaring nave; in the crypt is a macabre and mystifying accumulation of 590 human skulls and over 800 thigh bones. The town was one of the Cinque Ports – towns along the

Kent and East Sussex coast which were granted special privileges by the Crown in return for supplying ships for the navy; in 1588 Hythe sent out 11 ships against the Armada. Since then the sea has receded and the town is no longer a port. At the foot of the hill is the Royal Military Canal, built as a defence system against Napoleon. Also in the town is the terminus for the Romney, Hythe and Dymchurch Railway, a 15-inch gauge railway which steams down to the odd shingle landscape at Dungeness.

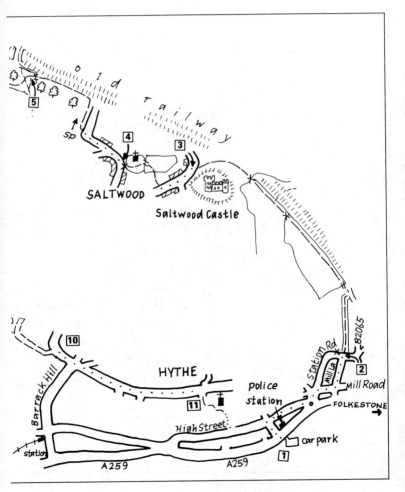

Tolsford Hill and Frogholt

Recommended by J and V Sherwood, Mr and Mrs Dudley, Anne Hill, R J Dunnett, Bryony Coulson

Over scrubby downland, with views of Folkestone and the English Channel; earlier, farmland and a short section along a wooded old railway track. Mostly on long-distance paths; some waymarking and signposting; route-finding is quite easy.

Length 5½ miles (9km), 2½ hours
Difficulty 2
Start Newington, 3 miles WNW of Folkestone, on minor road 200 yards just N of A20. Park in village centre. Grid reference TR 183374
OS maps 1:50,000 179 or 189; 1:25,000 TR 13/23
Refreshments Shop at Newington

WALK DIRECTIONS

1 With Newington church behind you, follow the road past village shop

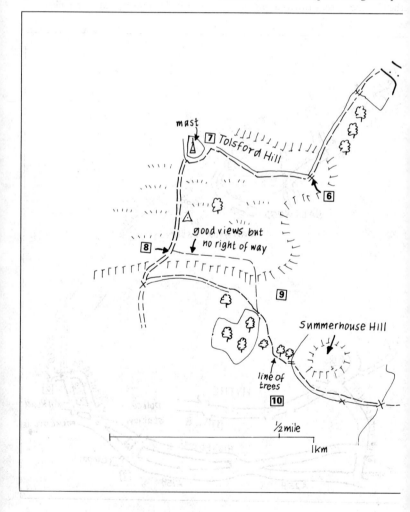

(**a**) and through Newington village, away from A20. 300 yards after end of village cross line of former railway (**b**) (dismantled bridge clearly visible) and 50 yards later turn left over stile signposted Etchinghill. Follow left edge of field, keeping close by old railway, to far end of field, and leave field by small stile in left-hand corner 2 .

Turn right on railway line for 20 yards, then left over stile into field. Head across field 100 yards to woods opposite, then turn right to continue with fence and woods on left for 350 yards, to enter coppice by gate. 3 After 150 yards emerge through gate into field. Turn right to skirt field and leave field by gate in far right-hand corner. 4 Follow path adjacent and parallel to railway for 300 yards, then immediately after passing railway arch (**c**), path leads half left to lead into field. Follow left edge of field (North Downs Way, with acorn markers), and at top find stile 50

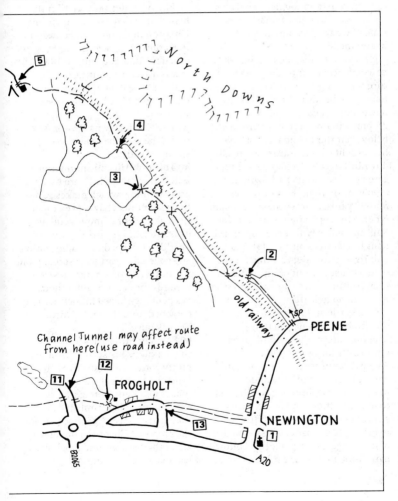

North Downs

5

4

3

2

old railway

PEENE

Channel Tunnel may affect route from here (use road instead)

12

11

FROGHOLT

13

NEWINGTON

1

B2065

A20

yards to right of garden of house **5**. Turn right on driveway beyond stile, and follow to road.

Cross road to continue on North Downs Way opposite. This leads uphill, alongside fence on right. At end of field it continues through wood. **6** At end of wood, cross stile and continue with fence on right, which now makes right turn. **7** After 500 yards turn left on perimeter track by radio mast. After 50 yards, where fence makes 90-degree bend to right, turn left on rough track (Saxon Shore Way but not waymarked at time of writing) leading through heathland (**d**).

8 ½ mile later track begins to descend steeply: it is tempting to turn left along top of ridge, just where main path bends right, then to drop down along spur after 300 yards, dropping to line of trees mentioned below, but there is no right of way here. Right of way continues steeply downhill to gate. Do not pass through gate but turn left on path, with fence alongside on right. Follow this path for 600 yards, past wood on right, and emerge into open field with conical Summerhouse Hill ahead and prominent line of trees on right **9**. Bear half right across field aiming for end of fence just in front of line of trees, then continue same direction to stile, in left-hand field **10**.

Cross stile and continue same direction, with fence on right, keeping Summerhouse Hill on left (or climb over top of hill if you like). Avoid side turns and follow to gate ahead. Pass through gate and maintain same direction to stile just to left of traffic roundabout. Cross stile to emerge on to road **11**. Cross road to stile opposite. Cross left edge of field to gate on far side **12**. Follow path through private garden of house

to tarmac lane. Turn left on lane, passing through Frogholt (**e**).

13 50 yards after last cottage on right and just where lane bends right, take path ahead signposted to Newington (avoid signposted path on left just before this), and follow back to starting-point.

WHAT TO LOOK OUT FOR
(**a**) Opposite the shop are the remains of the **village pound** (used for keeping animals in).
(**b**) **Elham Valley railway** 17-mile branch line that used to run from Cheriton Junction, near Folkestone, to Harbledown, near Canterbury. Its proudest moment came in 1941 when it was used for the siting of Churchill's Boche Buster, Europe's largest railway gun. The line closed six years later.
(**c**) The **North Downs Way** passes under the arch; beyond is a steep-sided dry valley.
(**d**) **Tolsford Hill** and **Summerhouse Hill** Parts of these hills are used for army training, which makes access limited but may have saved them from agricultural 'improvement'. Tolsford Hill is a slightly sinister heathland, capped by a radio station and covered in part with scrub. From its southern slope, a fine view towards the coast. Summerhouse Hill is a pudding-shaped hillock actually detached from the main North Downs ridge.
(**e**) **Frogholt** Still a backwater, this tiny hamlet consists of a handful of pretty cottages flanked by Seabrook Stream. On the right-hand side of the road is Old Kent Cottage, an extremely old half-timbered and thatched cottage. A service road for the proposed Channel Tunnel may affect the route around Frogholt; waymarking is promised.

Wye Down

Recommended by Paul Bilson,
Pat, Roy and Stephen Galbraith

Mixed woodland and open farmland, with the huge view from Wye Down nature reserve as the climax. Nearly all on defined paths; route-finding moderately easy.

Length 8 miles (13km), 3½ hours
Difficulty 3
Start Wye, 1 mile E of A28 (Ashford to Canterbury). *By train* Wye
OS maps 1:50,000 179 or 189; 1:25,000 TR 04/14
Refreshments In Wye only. Three pubs, including The Tickled Trout, which has a garden overlooking the river. Terracotta's, a tea-and-coffee-shop opposite church, also serves food

WALK DIRECTIONS

1 (**a**) Take North Downs Way through Wye churchyard, passing to right of church and out along narrow path to road **2**. Turn right, to cross crossroads, then up Occupation Road, which soon becomes track. **3** Straight across minor road after 600 yards on to path up into woods and out at top on to road **4**. Turn right on road, passing head of valley on your left, for 300 yards to farm where road ends **5**. Left on track, which runs alongside hedge on right for ¼ mile to next farm, at which turn left at electricity post on path between hedges.

6 After 150 yards, where hedges give out at edge of woodland and main path makes half left towards gate, take path half right into woods. **7** Fork right after 30 yards and follow ½ mile to road **8**. Turn right along road for 500 yards. **9** Just before Crundale village sign and where road reaches brow of hill, take path on right leading into woods. Ignore side turns, leave wood and keep straight on 400 yards after the woods end, ignoring right turn.

10 Keep straight on at house on left, follow tarmac track ahead and keep to right of second house, making straight uphill on path through two gates. Make straight up to top of ridge, crossing fence by stile in front of church (**b**) **11**. Turn right on track, through gate. Continue direction along top of ridge for 1¼ miles until track veers left downhill to T-junction with another track **12**. Turn left uphill to hamlet of Hassell Street. 50 yards after track becomes road, turn sharp right opposite bungalow, taking path between fences.

13 After ½ mile bear quarter right at oblique junction of tracks, passing through gate 150 yards later, then continue downhill towards fence **14**. Left at fence, then immediately right through gate, 75 yards to farm road. Turn left along it, and follow 600 yards to T-junction **15**. Cross to stile opposite leading half left into nature reserve (**c**) (North Downs Way). Follow path until leaving woods by stile, then make for left-hand corner of right-hand group of woods ahead, after which bear right on wide grassy track, on to spur to viewpoint, then steeply downhill. (As there have been serious erosion problems here, keep to zigzag path as requested.)

16 Leave reserve by stile at bottom and turn half right to cross next stile. Turn right on road for 30 yards, then left over stile and turn right to follow first field until fence at end, in front of house garden **17**. Turn left, alongside fence on right (still in first field) for 100 yards, then cross stile on right immediately before gate ahead. Follow path on left edge of second field and continue this direction to Wye, passsing through gate at end of second field, crossing over track and changing to other side of fence (fence now on right). Ignore all side turns. Path becomes track and then tarmac lane leading into Wye.

129

WHAT TO LOOK OUT FOR

(a) **Wye** Small town notable for its Georgian buildings. The nave of the church was truncated in 1686 when the central tower collapsed, leaving a curious but pleasing mixture of Gothic and baroque. Wye College was founded as a college of priests in 1432, became a grammar school in the next century and is now the Agricultural Department of the University of London. Most of the original building survives. Above the town is a crown cut in the chalk of the downs by students to commemorate Edward VII's coronation in 1902.

(b) **Crundale church** Tiny church in a beautiful position. 12th- to 14th-century, with Victorian additions. Contains a fine carved slab in memory of a 15th-century rector, and the Royal Arms of Queen Anne.

(c) **Wye Down nature reserve** An area of uncultivated chalk downland and woodlands; an especially good site for orchids, including bee, pyramid, man, fly, fragrant, spider, burnt and musk orchids. **View** S to Romney Marsh and the Channel; W over the Weald; N towards Faversham and the Isle of Sheppey.

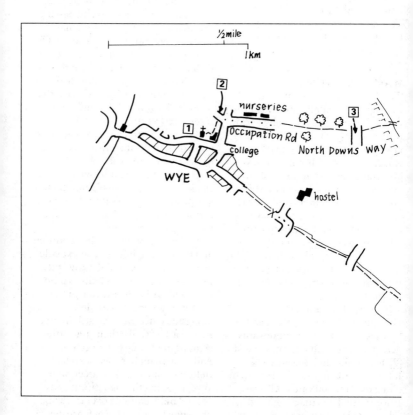

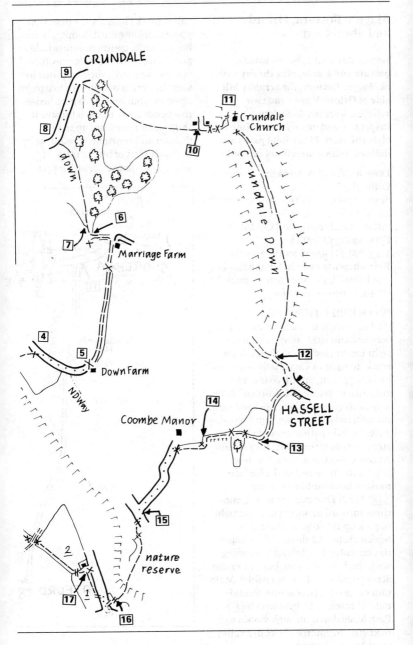

Magpie Bottom, Otford and Shoreham

Gentle downland, beech woods, pasture and arable, plus the dry valley of Magpie Bottom, the scrubby hill-side of Otford Mount and two villages. Very muddy when inspected, and one slithery climb just after the start. Many field paths not defined; follow directions carefully.

Length 6½ miles (10.5km), 3½ hours
Difficulty 3
Start Shoreham station (free car park), on A225 ½ mile E of Shoreham village. Grid reference TQ 526615
OS maps 1:50,000 188;
1:25,000 TQ 45/55 and TQ 46/56
Refreshments Pubs in Shoreham; Fox and Hounds, Romney Street; pubs, shops, tea-room in Otford

WALK DIRECTIONS

1 From station forecourt make your way to main road, along which turn right for 20 yards only, then left on track (to right of Copt Hall), between hedges, leading uphill, past gate entrance to White Hill Cottage. After 200 yards pass concrete post and turn immediately left on path into woods. After ¼ mile path ascends very steeply (take either fork: they rejoin). At top, cross remains of concrete stile, enter field and make for left-most of farm buildings ahead.

2 Enter Dunstall farmyard, continue forward (ignoring farm on right), to pick up track between fences which drops and then rises; at top of rise enter field on left and, standing with track behind you, bear half right across field to stile (just visible). Maintain same direction across second field to reach stile, into woods **3**. Path leads down through woods to next stile to emerge above dry valley (**a**) of Magpie Bottom.

Bear slightly left down through scrubby area to reach wide stile. (The hedgerow rising on other side of

valley marks roughly the direction you will follow until Romney Street. Beyond stile, continue across field to projecting corner of hedgerow, which you cross by stile, then continue in same direction uphill with hedgerow down on your left. **4** Where hedgerow bends away to the left leave it and continue forward up to stile. Cross it and continue forward, keeping just to left of line of trees, at which bear quarter right, up past

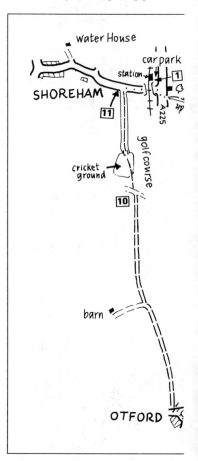

small clump of trees. At top of rise, hamlet of Romney Street comes into view; head for it, taking stile just to right of first house, across paddock, then between fences to emerge by Fox and Hounds **5**.

Take stile opposite pub, and bear half right across field. Keep well to right; soon stile comes into view. Beyond stile turn left to reach second stile, and proceed on track along left-hand edge of long, strip-shaped field

flanked by trees. Leave track where it bends left at end of field, to continue forward over stile, follow right edge of field to next stile and then follow path to road **6**. Turn left on road for 20 yards then right over gate/stile. Proceed with garden fence on your right for 70 yards, and where fence veers right keep forward to reach stile in top right-hand corner of field. Beyond, follow path down through trees, soon to re-emerge at

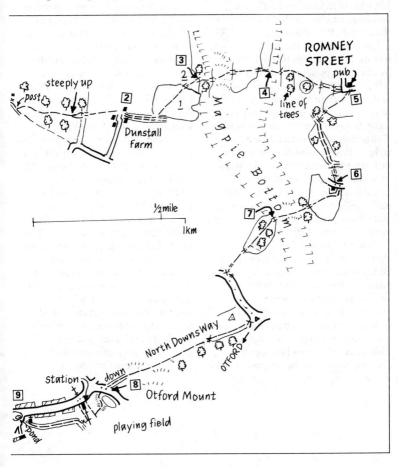

side of valley (Magpie Bottom again).

Continue down to bottom of the valley, then straight on up other side, through scrub to stile **7**. Beyond stile follow woodland path (avoiding any minor side-turns) to stile out of woods, then forward with fence on left to reach road. Left on road, follow 300 yards to road junction. Immediately before reaching road signposted Kemsing/Otford, take gate/stile on right (North Downs Way) and follow left edge of field to next stile, then continue on clear path through woods, then scrub. Path descends to road **8**.

Cross road, turn right along it, then left after 20 yards on woodland path by old chalk pits. Immediately bear left down to bottom of wooded slope and follow right edge of sports field until taking obvious track on your right, between banks. On reaching T-junction with surfaced path turn right, follow to road, then left over railway and immediately take steps down on left past Otford station. Beyond station, on right side of car park, find entrance between railings and follow path away from railway to Otford church (**b**) **9**.

Take road on far side of Otford Pond, turn left on it, past Crown Inn. 50 yards later take track on right (signs to Shoreham and Park Farm). Ignore all side-turns. After ½ mile main track bends left to barn; keep forward on narrower path. **10** Cross track, take path opposite, signposted Shoreham; this runs between fences, then follows right side of cricket field

before again being fenced. **11** At road, station is on right; Shoreham village is a very short distance on left (**c**).

WHAT TO LOOK OUT FOR
(**a**) **View** Dartford paper-mills are glimpsed briefly to N (left).
(**b**) **Otford** Centre retains some rural charm, despite substantial recent development further out. Has some good examples of pantiled Kentish houses, and a splendid half-timbered yeoman's house, Pickmoss, opposite the Horns Inn. Near the pond in the village centre is Otford Palace, a ruin which has been partly incorporated in a terrace of brick cottages, and displaying an unlikely mixture of plain Victorian vernacular and fine Tudor brickwork. Initially it was one of the Archbishop of Canterbury's houses, later acquired by Henry VIII.
(**c**) **Shoreham** More tucked away than Otford and a rural oasis, considering its proximity to London. Turn right just before the bridge over the stream and you will reach the Water House, home of visionary painter Samuel Palmer from 1827 to 1834; William Blake visited him here in 1827. The Kings Arms has what it claims is the last surviving Ostler Box, a sort of horseman's cubby-hole adjacent to the bar but fronting the street. The restored late-Perpendicular church contains the only surviving rood screen in Kent to span the entire width of the church; plus stained glass by Burne-Jones, installed in 1903, after the artist's death.

Toy's Hill, Chartwell and Squerries Park

Contributed by W E Gilbert
Recommended by M G Bruce,
M J Vingoe and J M Empson-Ridler,
Mr and Mrs S Gilmartin,
Mrs M E Kitney

Genuinely rural, belying its proximity to London, with small grassy fields fringed by hedgerows, broad-leaved (predominantly oak and beech) woodland, patches of scrubby heath and parkland. Quite hilly, but all on a small scale. Shorter walk omits Toy's Hill and Fox and Hounds. Criss-crossed with path junctions, so route-finding is rather intricate, though not difficult.

Length *Full walk* 9 miles (14.5km), 4½ hours
Difficulty 3
Shorter walk 6 miles (9.5km), 3 hours
Difficulty 2–3
OS maps 1:50,000 177;
1:25,000 TQ 45/55
Start Westerham, 6 miles W of Sevenoaks. Park at green just W of Market Square
Refreshments Pubs and tea-rooms in Westerham; Fox and Hounds after point **12**; tea-room in Chartwell

WALK DIRECTIONS

1 (a) Leave Westerham along Water Lane, the footpath to left of Westerham Park Gallery, opposite village green. At end, cross small stone stile, emerge into field and go forward uphill to cross stile on skyline **2**. Bear slightly left across second field aiming for stile 100 yards to right of red brick house. Do not cross stile, but follow left edge of field down to stile in bottom left-hand corner. **3** After stile, follow path along edge of woodland, climbing gently (woods soon appear on left of path). **4** After ½ mile cross road to path opposite. After 20 yards avoid right fork, and continue straight over

cross-track 50 yards later.

5 Reach road, turn right along it and after 80 yards turn left by gate signposted to French Street. Follow this path through woodland keeping straight ahead and descending. Path is joined by track coming in from right after 50 yards. 30 yards later ignore left fork and keep straight on at next junction of tracks by water-main sign; presently this track passes to left of cottage at end of tarmac lane.

6 *For shorter walk* proceed along lane 50 yards then turn sharp right opposite water-main (avoiding path half right). At hedge (50 yards on) turn half right, with hedge on left. This is point **16**.

For full walk follow lane past several houses and at T-junction turn sharp right downhill. **7** Just beyond burial ground on left, cross stile on left (signposted Pipers Green, Brasted Chart) and bear steeply downhill alongside fence on your right. At bottom take footbridge half right ahead, then bear straight up to gate to left of farm **8**.

After gate, path crosses track to proceed with hedge on left, and after 150 yards crosses stile. Clear path leads half right to stile leading into woods. In woods proceed with fence on left, ignoring side turns, until reaching road **9**.

Turn right on road, and pass cottages on your right. 50 yards after cottages, turn right by NT sign for horseriders. **10** After 70 yards turn left on prominent track. 200 yards later, keep left by blue marker on tree (NT horsetrack), avoiding yellow-marked path straight on. **11** 150 yards after, turn left at next crossing of tracks (where NT horsetrack goes straight on). This track is marked periodically by posts with green and blue marks; after 200 yards it is joined by wheelchair path (signed) coming in from left.

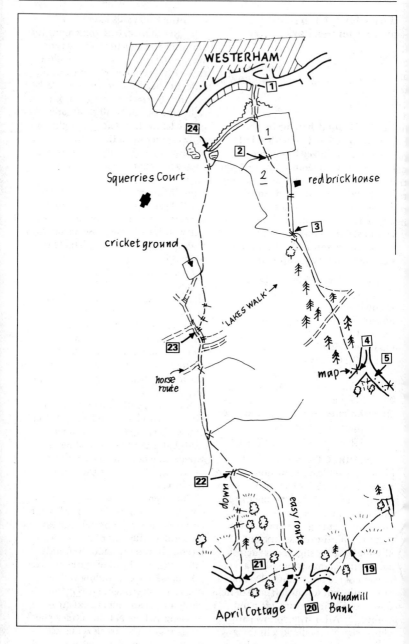

12 Shortly after, emerge by obelisk (left) and benches (right) (**b**). Keep straight on, immediately crossing remains of brick parapets, after which path swings round to left in large loop.

If you do not want to take in Fox and Hounds, turn sharp right at junction of tracks reached where house comes into view ahead. This path leads to point **13**, the NT car park. For Fox and Hounds, follow track straight on to road. Turn left on road: pub soon comes into view. After pub, retrace steps on road until reaching Toy's Hill car park on right of road.

13 From entrance to car park, go through car park and up steps on left. Bear right by marker post at top of them (route now periodically signed French Street by small markers), and then left at next marker post (50 yards on). Woodland path may be obscured by leaves but maintain direction, keeping round slightly to right after 80 yards, and 20 yards later emerge on to well-trodden cross-path **14**. Turn sharp right, following path marked with blue on trees. This descends to edge of woods (¼ mile).

15 When nurseries come into view away to left, fork left on fenced path

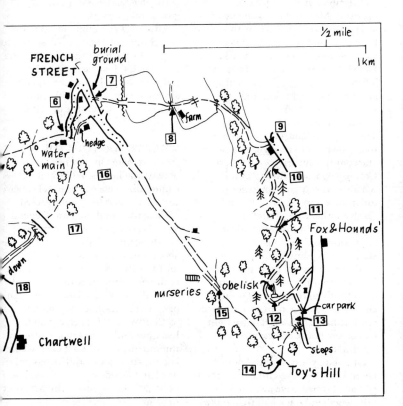

(signposted public bridleway). Follow this until it becomes track and then road leading uphill. In middle of French Street turn left to take tarmac lane, passing entrance signs to Mannings Wood. After 50 yards, continue ahead on grassy track until end of hedge on your left, then bear sharp left along it.

16 Proceed along avenue of beech trees. **17** After ¼ mile cross road and immediately turn left at fork of paths (signed FP365), which after 100 yards turns left between fences and drops steeply downhill. On left is Chartwell (c). **18** At end, cross road and climb steep path up bank opposite. After 150 yards, at end of steep slope, keep on main path which bends left, and 50 yards later (tree 20 yards down to left ahead is marked FP365) turn right across open land. **19** After ¼ mile, path is joined by another sharp right; fork right 50 yards beyond this (FP365 yellow marker on tree) and follow to lane. Turn right on lane (marked private road) downhill to road **20**. Cross road and continue on driveway to April Cottage, opposite. After 50 yards, where driveway goes up to house, fork right on track. After 10 yards reach another fork: if tired, take right fork; avoid right turn after 50 yards but continue along line of trees to stile. This is point **22**.

Alternatively (far more pleasant), fork left uphill, ignoring side turns (avoid path on right after 100 yards and cross-track soon after), until you reach isolated house **21**. Turn right just before house and emerge on turning-circle.

Orientate yourself with house behind you, turning-circle in front of you and tarmac drive away to left; take woodland track half right (take care to avoid track half left). After 200 yards, turn right at T-junction of tracks (fence now on left), and proceed to next stile. Continue across open ground to second stile, then descend to third stile **22**.

Cross stile and take prominent grassy track up to, then along, left edge of two fields, then continue ahead between fences. Ignore track on right 100 yards later; ignore also Lakes Walk sign by stile immediately after. Follow uphill before taking stile on right marked 'All dogs must be kept on a lead' **23**. Continue ahead to next two stiles, then ahead on path between fences, passing cricket ground on your left.

After cricket ground, Westerham comes into view and path descends to cottage by pond. Cross stile here, and turn left. **24** Just past pond, turn right across small bridge to walk alongside stream. After 300 yards pass over low stone stile on left to return to starting-point.

WHAT TO LOOK OUT FOR
(a) **Westerham** On the green, statues of two local heroes, Wolfe and Churchill. Quebec House (NT; open to public; fee), a handsome gabled 17th-century building, was General Wolfe's family house; it contains family portraits and an exhibition about the Battle of Quebec.
(b) **Toy's Hill** (NT) The highest point of the greensand ridge in Kent, here covered with a mixed forest of beech, oak, sweet chestnut and conifers.
(c) **Chartwell** (NT; open to public; fee) Churchill's character is strongly imprinted: his books are everywhere and the study looks as if he has only just left. Outside is a garden wall he built, and the studio in which he used to paint.

Ightham Mote and Knole Park

Recommended by M Vingoe and J M Empson-Ridler, Paul Bilson, John and Rosemary Roberts, Stuart Gilmartin, J A Walton, M G Bruce

Along a greensand edge, with views over the Weald, descending to Ightham Mote; after a short stretch along roads, deciduous woodlands and the landscaped deer park of Knole House. Mostly on defined paths and tracks, often muddy, and hard going after rain. Route-finding rather involved to begin with, then moderately easy.

Length 10 miles (16km), 5 hours
Difficulty 3
Start One Tree Hill NT car park (free), 3 miles E of Sevenoaks and 1 mile S of Godden Green. From A25 Riverhead roundabout follow A25 2½ miles, turn right at centre of Seal village, signposted Wildernesse Golf Club. Follow signpost to Tonbridge and Godden Green: car park is 2½ miles along, on left. Grid reference TQ 558532
By train Sevenoaks station, 1¼ miles off route. Turn right out of station, ignore side turns, then take signposted turn for Knole House on left, just after church. Beyond park gates, fork right and start walk from Knole House (after point 12)
OS maps 1:50,000 188; 1:25,000 TQ 45/55
Refreshments Shop and Plough Inn at Ivy Hatch; Rose and Crown (½ mile off route) at Stone Street; Buck's Head at Godden Green

WALK DIRECTIONS

1 From NT brick pillar (money-box) in car park, standing so that road is to your right, take faint broad path leading quarter left: it becomes well defined beyond wooden railings, and leads to viewpoint (**a**). From stone bench turn your back to view, cross

low grassy ridge, then after 20 yards take second turn on right, which is crossed by wooden barrier. Proceed to T-junction by NT sign, with house visible ahead 2 . Turn right. Path leads along edge of woods, with orchards on right: ignore left turns, keeping close to orchards. Reach tarmac lane, turn left along it, then after 150 yards turn right on to signposted bridleway.

3 After 200 yards, just before fence on right ends, turn left on track, which soon descends to bottom of slope then rises, soon between fences (**b**). 4 After ½ mile keep on main track, which bends left, ignoring gate/stile on right marked GW (denoting Greensand Way). Track eventually leads to farm, where it bends left and descends to tarmac lane 5 .

Turn right on lane, then immediately left through wrought-iron gates, on metalled track passing Ightham Mote (**c**), then rising to reach field, with car park on left. Continue forward on track between fences. 6 After 500 yards, and just before electricity post, take waymarked gate on left, proceed up left edge of field, into woods by gate and follow winding woodland track to road. Left on road, using path just to left and parallel to road. Ignore next road turning on left, but proceed to Ivy Hatch village centre. Keep to left, passing in front of Plough Inn, then take next left, signposted Stone Street.

7 300 yards later turn sharp right into Pine Tree Lane, then 50 yards later take woodland path on left. Ignore all side turns and follow path uphill, along ridge, then down.
8 Turn right on tarmac lane, past school and church. 50 yards after church take second track on left (first track is signed to Cone Hill House) by electricity generator and bridleway signpost. Maintain direction, keeping close to top of slope on left, until next tarmac lane 9 .

Cross to signposted bridleway opposite and follow sunken track that eventually runs between fences to emerge by house on to tarmac driveway. Turn right on driveway, then immediately sharp left on sunken track downhill to road **10**. Left on road, then after 150 yards where road veers left, take gate on right. Track leads towards fence ahead, in front of which it bends right to reach open fairway of golf-course. Turn left along this fairway, and after 50 yards, bear half right (*NB not sharper right, immediately into woods*) on to track which initially runs alongside fairway, then enters woods between yellow marker posts, soon re-emerging on to golf course, where make for marker posts just to

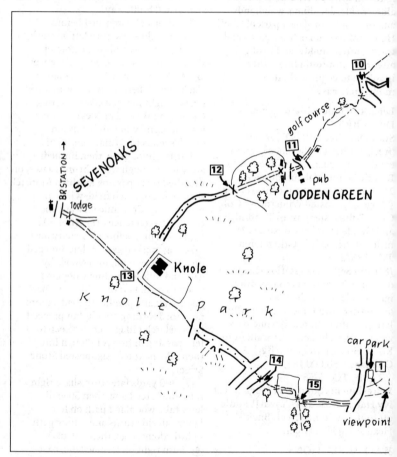

right of nearest house. Proceed between fences to emerge at road at Godden Green **11**.

Cross the road and take track by post-box, then go forward at next cross-track to proceed between two terraces of bungalows. Track enters woods: ignore side turns, and proceed to enter Knole Park by deer-gate **12**.

Continue forward on tarmac track,

and follow to Knole House (**d**), where keep forward, past main entrance gates to house, then alongside wall. **13** At corner, turn left, continuing alongside wall, then at next corner continue forward to leave wall for grassy track. After 200 yards reach T-junction of tarmac tracks and continue forward on track which forms stem of this T-junction. Ignore

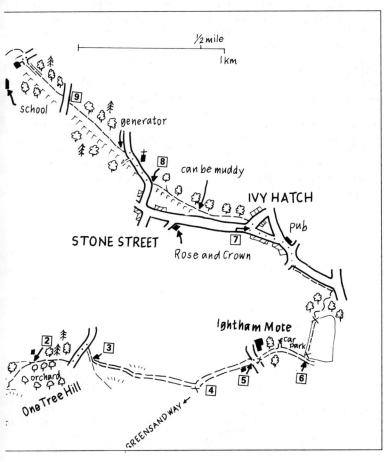

right turns and proceed to next
T-junction, where continue forward
on path to reach deer-gate, then on to
road **14**. Cross road to woodland path
opposite, and follow to stile; your
objective is stile, not yet visible, half
right in corner of field. Reach it by
continuing forward, keeping just to
left of wooden paddock fence, then at
end of field turn right to find stile in
corner. **15** 20 yards after stile, take
stile on left for path between fences,
and follow until road. Left on road,
and follow up to car park.

WHAT TO LOOK OUT FOR

(a) **View** Over much of the Weald,
including Oxted and Limpsfield at
the bottom of the valley.
(b) **View** S towards Ashdown Forest;
SE a prominent spire-like structure
is Hadlow Tower, an enormously tall
folly (170ft), dating from the 1830s.
(c) **Ightham Mote** (NT; open to
public; fee) Moated and timber-
framed medieval manor-house; one
of the best of its kind in the country.
Of various periods; its hall, old chapel
and crypt are *c*.1340. Its perfectly
preserved chapel is Tudor.
(d) **Knole House** (NT; open to public;
fee) Probably the largest house in
England, containing 365 rooms and
52 staircases: childhood home of
novelist Vita Sackville-West, and
described by Virginia Woolf in
Orlando as 'a town rather than a
house'. Its residents have included
the Archbishop of Canterbury, Henry
VIII and Thomas Sackville, who all
played a part in adding to it between
the 15th and 17th centuries. The
last-named co-wrote *Gorboduc*, the
first formal English tragedy; the
Sackvilles still live here. The
collection of 17th-century English
furniture in the house is one of the
finest in the world.

Hever, Hoath Corner and Penshurst

Recommended by Rosemary and John Roberts, Dr J S Staffurth, S Gilmartin

Unspoilt lowland Kent, particularly charming at bluebell time in spring. Deciduous and planted woodlands alternate with grassy fields. Nettly in summer and often muddy. Not all paths defined and route-finding quite intricate, though not difficult.

Length 6 miles (9.5km), 3 hours
With extension to Penshurst 9 miles (14km), 4½ hours
Difficulty 2–3
Start Cowden station, 1 mile NE of Cowden and ½ mile NE of B2026 (Hartfield to Edenbridge). Car park at station. Grid reference TQ 476416
OS maps 1:50,000 188; 1:25,000 TQ 44/45
Refreshments Kentish Horse at Markbeech; Greyhound Inn at Newtown; Leicester Arms at Penshurst; the Rock at Hoath Corner; two tea-rooms and village shop in Penshurst

WALK DIRECTIONS

1 From station car park enter station and cross footbridge to 'up platform'. Leave station by gate leading into woods. After 20 yards turn right on track. Avoid right turn after 400 yards, by wooden gate on left, and 300 yards later avoid left turn shortly before isolated cottage ahead, but follow up to stile into field **2**.

Follow left edge of field, initially with ditch on left, then just before projecting corner of woods ahead, cross to other side of fence (as waymarked) and continue same direction. **3** At corner of fence, continue forward to stile leading into churchyard. Turn left at church to emerge on to road at Markbeech **4**.

Left on road. After 300 yards, just before entrance to Bramsell's Farm on right, turn right through small gate leading to path between fences (can be nettly; avoidable by road – see map). At end of fenced section, path continues forward to next fenced section and soon enters woods. Path passes under railway ½ mile later and leads to road **5**. Turn right along road, then after 100 yards take fenced path on left, on the far side of the Greyhound Inn.

At end of fenced section, cross double stile and continue forward along left edge of field, and after 50 yards cross stile on left (*NB avoid confusing with hurdle on left after only 20 yards*) to continue between fences to end of field, where stiles are on either side of you. **6** Cross left-hand stile to take path on right edge of field: this path (easy to follow) turns right over waymarked stile, snakes in and out of woods and emerges on to road.

7 Left on road, and after 30 yards turn right on to path by 'No horse riding' sign. This leads to Hever village **8**. Turn right on road: route continues through lychgate and into churchyard (**a**), signposted to Chiddingstone (but if you want to see Hever Castle (**b**) and/or the grounds, continue along road to the castle entrance). Leave churchyard by path at bottom right-hand corner. Path soon skirts Hever castle estate (castle not visible) and after ½ mile crosses driveway by bridge. **9** ½ mile later reach gate by houses and fork half right on grassy path (signposted) alongside second house, proceeding with fence on right until reaching road **10**.

Cross road and cross stile opposite: follow right edge of first field, bearing right at end through gateway, then along left edge of second field, soon to cross footbridge on left and then enter woods. **11** After 300 yards reach corner of track, turn right and, 20 yards later, follow track as it bends left uphill (**c**). Reach a junction of tracks 100 yards before cottages ahead (hamlet of Hill Hoath) **12**.

For 6-mile walk turn right uphill on track (avoid very sharp right path which doubles back on way you came). Either of two closely parallel tracks will do. Look out for where field appears on right; 130 yards after end of field (ie where woodland reappears) fork left (yellow marker) on path leading to stile at edge of woods **12**/**1**. Continue in the same direction across field, aiming for right-hand corner of projecting woodland opposite, then follow path down, with scrubby woodland on left, to stile **12**/**2**. Path leads through woods to stile: head up across field keeping along right side of line of trees ahead and aim for right-hand cottage. Once over brow of hill bear quarter right down to stile (just to left of it are giant plaster hands in garden of cottage) **12**/**3**. Head straight up next field to stile just to right of cottage garden to emerge on road.

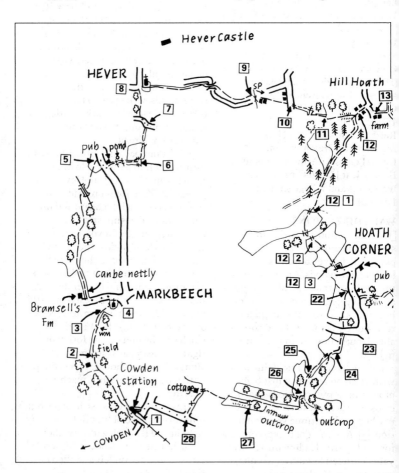

Turn left on road, follow to hamlet of Hoath Corner. At road junction turn right, follow 300 yards to take track on right. This is point **22**.

For 9-mile walk via Penshurst continue straight on from **12** to pass cottages, and at junction of lanes turn right to Hill Hoath Farm **13**. At turning-area in front of farm turn left on track, then right after 200 yards at junction of tracks (avoiding stile ahead). This track soon enters edge of woodland: 200 yards into it avoid right fork but continue ahead to road **14**. Turn right on road, and after 100 yards turn left on driveway to Wat Stock Farm **15**. Keep ahead at farm, ignoring right turn. **16** After ¾ mile,

join lane coming in from right, and continue forward. At road turn right into Penshurst village (**d**).

17 From Penshurst, with the Quaintways tea-rooms on your left, follow road ahead. Just beyond primary school turn right into lane called the Warren **18**. Reach farm, continue forward over stile, following right edge of field to stile at end, shortly after which cross footbridge and proceed to next stile. Cross field to gate/stile ahead **19**. Cross lane and take path up bank opposite, which runs between fence and hedge.

20 At top, continue through wood (avoiding waymarked path on left after 30 yards) and leave wood by

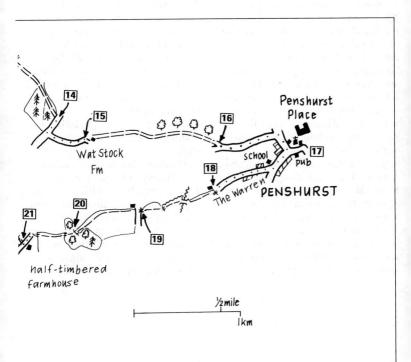

145

gate/stile. Follow right edge of field to stile in right-hand corner, and take path (soon track) beyond it. **21** After 100 yards, opposite half-timbered farmhouse, turn right up steps over stile and follow left edge of field. After 100 yards, cross gate/stile on left, and follow left edge of field, soon past more sandstone outcrops up on your left, to pick up track leading through gate/stile into woods and up to road. Turn right for 50 yards, then take track on left **22**.

Follow track into field for 20 yards then turn left at junction of tracks, to cross field in direction of power lines. Leave field by stile, then bear right to descend through woods, soon alongside wooden railing on your left. **23** Cross road at bottom and take path opposite, which follows left edge of two fields; the second field is entered by a large gap in the field boundary. **24** At end, do not cross stile, but turn right, with hedge on left, soon to cross wooden barrier into woods. After 200 yards, and just before second barrier, cross stile on right, turn left along left edge of field with woods on left.

25 Re-enter woods by stile at end of field and proceed along descending track. **26** After 300 yards turn sharp right at oblique junction of tracks (if you see sandstone outcrop on left, you've come 80 yards too far) to descend to footbridge, then ascend to stile. Bear half right uphill in field, then turn right along the foot of

bank of trees and by rocky outcrop.

27 After 300 yards track (now well-defined) keeps forward, over stile, to enter and pass through coppiced woodland. On leaving it by stile at far end maintain same direction (slightly to right) uphill across large field to find stile in hedgerow, marked 'footpath'. Head down to gate to left of cottages, and follow track to tarmac lane **28**. Turn right on lane, and at T-junction turn left to reach Cowden station.

WHAT TO LOOK OUT FOR

(**a**) **Hever church** Contains the tomb-chest of Sir Thomas Boleyn (or Bullen), father of Anne Boleyn.
(**b**) **Hever Castle** (open to public; fee) Home of Anne Boleyn before it was seized by Henry VIII and given to Anne of Cleves. Largely 15th-century, modified internally by the Astor family in Edwardian times. Gardens best appreciated when the rhododendrons are out (late spring to early summer).
(**c**) Track passes through **sandstone cutting**, one of several exposures seen on the walk.
(**d**) **Penshurst** Much-visited village, with Penshurst Place – a superb Tudor manor-house with an almost perfectly preserved Great Hall (open to public; fee) – tucked behind. Churchyard is entered by an archway by some attractive half-timbered cottages (some of which are in fact good 19th-century imitations).

SURREY

Polesden Lacey and Ranmore Common

Based on a contribution from Roy and Pat Galbraith

A glimpse of the tower blocks of Croydon remind you how close to the edge of London you are; otherwise a rural walk through woods and quiet farmland, with views from the top and foot of the North Downs escarpment. Route intricate, but quite easy to find, though turn-off at 13 needs care.

Length 9½ miles (15km), 4½ hours
Difficulty 3
Start Boxhill and Westhumble station. Westhumble, 1½ miles N of Dorking. Car park at station (fee); some roadside parking. Grid reference TQ 167519
OS maps 1:50,000 187; 1:25,000 TQ 04/14 and TQ 05/15
Refreshments Café/restaurant at Polesden Lacy house (no admission charge if using restaurant only)

WALK DIRECTIONS

1 From station car park turn left on road leading over railway, then immediately fork right into Crabtree Lane. After ½ mile, and 30 yards after lane enters woods, pass through gate on right, keeping forward (left) at bridleway signpost 20 yards later. Follow this tarmac track for ½ mile, then 2 turn left at bridleway signpost (bridleway is often churned up but use the path alongside it). Follow to T-junction of paths, turn right, signposted bridleway, and 200 yards later fork left where main path bends right, taking grassy path over semi-open area. This continues forward at bridleway sign after 100 yards and heads for junction of earthy tracks 100 yards away (bridleway signpost). Continue forward here, until barn on right is seen, then 3

turn left at crossing of tracks. Follow on to farm.

Continue forward at staggered junction of tracks just beyond farm, but at end of field turn sharp right on track following left edge of field. At end of second field turn left at crossing of tracks (a). Follow ½ mile to road 4. Cross road and take tree-lined track opposite, which runs parallel to drive to Polesden Lacey. Beyond NT sign avoid drive which forks left to house and grounds (b), but keep forward on same track.

5 After 100 yards continue forward at crossing of tracks and 20 yards later fork left on fenced track which soon becomes tarmac lane and descends under thatched footbridge. 6 Where lane bends left ('no horses' sign), continue forward on yew-lined track, follow to T-junction of tracks and turn right. Just before entrance to Yewtree Farm keep right on main track and 10 yards later fork right on to another track (c).

7 After 100 yards cross stile on left and bear down to bottom right-hand corner of field. Turn sharp left on track and follow for 1 mile in all, avoiding side turns; where it joins tarmac lane coming in from right keep forward: at next house it becomes an unsurfaced track again and then enters woods of Ranmore Common. 8 30 yards before reaching main road, turn left at junction of tracks. 50 yards later turn right by NT sign. Cross road and take track opposite, on right side of car park.

Keep right 50 yards later and pass through gate (broken at time of checking). Continue forward beyond it, keeping to left of Forestry Commission notice, following broad woodland track and continuing forward at 'riding on bridleway only' sign. Follow for ½ mile (track soon descends steeply). **9** At bottom of slope turn left at T-junction of tracks and keep straight on at first junction, by Forestry Commission sign. 200 yards later reach horseshoe-shaped corner of track and fork left along it. Track passes through small wood after 500 yards.

10 50 yards after track enters second wood, turn left up wooden steps, follow path to stile, then bear half right uphill, alongside fence on right. At top (**d**), continue forward past North Downs Way (ND) sign. Most of route back follows NDW, which crosses road to follow minor road signposted Westhumble and then passes church (**e**).

11 Where road bends left, turn right on track signposted NDW, past old lodge house, then immediately fork left on fenced track. 200 yards later keep left at junction as signposted (**f**). **12** After ¾ mile keep straight on at crossing of woodland tracks, and 50 yards later avoid sharp right fork. 30 yards later, fork right (acorn marker). This descends through woods: some care is needed in finding the path off NDW: after 500 yards **13** look out for and turn left on narrow (but well-trodden) cross-path (on the right it leads away to enter field by gate, just visible from track).

Having thus turned off NDW, follow path to barrier (concealed from NDW), then across field to next barrier. Fenced path leads between

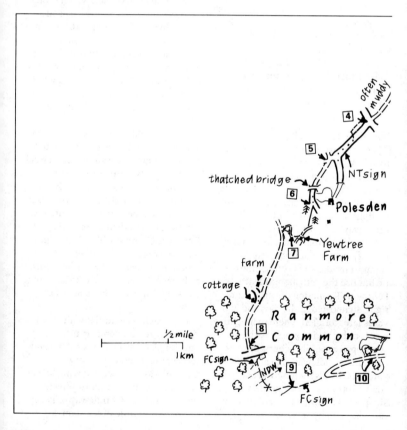

backs of houses to residential lane: continue on (even narrower) fenced path opposite to reach road. Turn right on path along right of road and follow to start.

WHAT TO LOOK OUT FOR

(**a**) **View** Over the London suburbs and WNW towards Windsor.

(**b**) **Polesden Lacey** (NT; open to public; fee) Country house in fine grounds, built by Thomas Cubitt in 1824 and extended and remodelled inside in 1906 by Ambrose Poynter. Into its hall and staircase a reredos from a demolished Wren church (St Matthew, Friday Street in the City

of London) has been incorporated. Of two earlier houses on the site, one was owned by playwright Sheridan from 1796; he also bought Yewtree Farm nearby.

(**c**) **View** On right, Polesden Lacy (the only time it is visible from the walk).

(**d**) **View** Over Dorking and the Greensand ridge, including Leith Hill.

(**e**) **Church of St Bartholomew** Visible for miles around, a cobble-faced building with an octagonal tower; designed by Sir George Gilbert Scott (1859).

(**f**) **View** Towards Box Hill, the continuation of the chalk escarpment which has been broken by the Mole Gap.

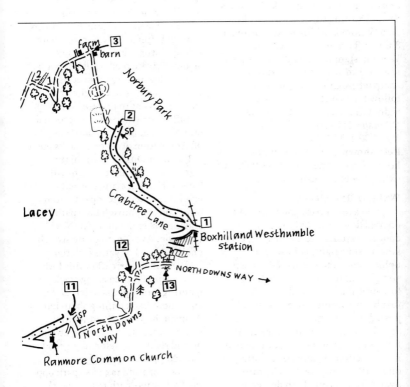

Friday Street and Leith Hill

*Contributed by M Vingoe and
Andrew Bailey*
*Recommended by A B Woodyer,
C and J McCue, G Burton, J C Scholey,
W E Gilbert, Paul Bilson, Roy and Pat
Galbraith, D Dirmikis, B A White*

**Two popular beauty spots linked by a
route through quiet, mainly wooded
hillsides. Not all field paths are
defined, and there are numerous path
junctions, but route-finding
moderately easy.**

Length *Full walk* 6 miles (9.5km),
3 hours. *Short walk omitting Leith
Hill* 4 miles (6.5km), 2 hours
Difficulty 2
Start Friday Street car park (3½ miles
SW of Dorking town centre). Take
A25 W from Dorking town centre for
3 miles. Turn left ½ mile W of
Wotton, signposted Friday Street. Fol-
low for 1 mile and take first turning
sharp left, signposted Friday Street;
follow for ¼ mile to car park on
right. Grid reference TQ 126458.
OS maps 1:50,000 187;
1:25,000 TQ 04/14
Refreshments Stephan Langton Inn at
Friday Street; café at Leith Hill Tower
(when tower is open)

WALK DIRECTIONS

1 (**a**) Leave car park and turn right
on road downhill. At junction
continue straight on along lane, past
lake on your right. Follow lane
uphill; when lane turns right, keep
straight on, turn left over stile following drive to Kempslade Farm.
Just before farmhouse gates, signposted to Wotton.
2 Almost immediately take right
fork, and after 200 yards turn right at
next junction of paths. Carry straight
on to stile. Cross road and continue
over stile opposite. Path descends
steeply through wood, alongside
fence on right, to stile (it is best to
zigzag downhill to stile). Cross stile

and emerge into meadow. Cross lake
and continue over stile to reach track
3 . Turn right on track, follow past
waterfall, ignoring turnings to left.
4 After ½ mile reach corner of road,
which comes in from right, at hamlet
of Broadmoor.
For short walk follow road ahead,
which peters out into track after 300
yards; continue on track. **4**/**1**
When track joins driveway to large
house (Shootlands), turn right and
follow it for 100 yards. Leave it again
when drive turns sharp right. Proceed
on track straight ahead up valley,
ignoring minor paths to left and right.
4/**2** At major junction, where other
tracks join from left and right, turn
sharp right and proceed straight
uphill to road. This is point **9**.
For full walk continue forward on
road and after a few yards, opposite
riding centre, take track on left,
signed 'Private road – public footpath
and bridleway only'. Proceed straight
ahead along this track, ignoring all
turnings to left to private houses. **5**
¼ mile after Warren Farm, proceed
straight on at junction of tracks.
6 At junction of several tracks (near
NT sign for Duke's Warren) turn
right steeply uphill to Leith Hill
Tower (**b**). On leaving tower, be
careful to take correct path. From
direction of approach take path
leaving tower in half right (NW)
direction. Avoid path going straight
on (W). After 120 yards fork right.
7 After another 100 yards fork
right again. Proceed along track,
ignoring minor paths to left and right,
and ignore track joining sharp left. **8**
At major junction (¾ mile from
tower), where tracks go left, straight
on and right, veer left and proceed
straight uphill to road **9** .
Cross road and take footpath opposite. Follow footpath inside right
edge of woods and emerge by stile into
field. Go straight across field maintaining same direction to second

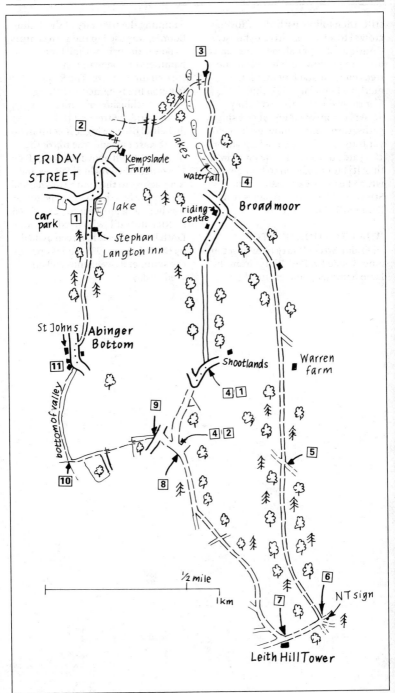

FRIDAY STREET

Kempslade Farm

lakes

waterfall

Broadmoor

lake

Car park

Stephan Langton Inn

riding centre

St Johns

Abinger Bottom

Shootlands

Warren farm

bottom of valley

½ mile

1km

Leith Hill Tower

NT sign

stile, then follow path ahead (over-grown) to an access drive to houses. Continue straight ahead across end of drive and follow path between line of trees on right and fence on left, marking boundary of Foxholt. Continue down into next valley.
10 At bottom of valley, at crossing of paths, turn right. Follow path for 600 yards to road. Follow road ahead for 100 yards until last house (St John's) then **11** fork right on to bridleway which heads back to lake at Friday Street. At T-junction of lanes turn left uphill to car park.

WHAT TO LOOK OUT FOR
(a) **Friday Street** Pretty hamlet set in a pine-wooded valley. Water from the large hammer pond, created by damming the tributary of the Tilling Bourne, was used in the 17th century to power the bellows and forge hammers of iron works in the surrounding forests. The Stephan Langton Inn is named after King John's Archbishop of Canterbury, born at Friday Street c.1150.
(b) **Leith Hill** The highest point in South-east England: the top of the tower is 1,029ft above sea-level. Fine views over the Weald of Sussex and Kent across to the South Downs, and N over the North Downs. The tower was built as a prospect tower in 1766, by Richard Hull, who lived at nearby Leith Hill Place. It has been owned by the NT since 1923, and is open in the summer at weekends and on Wednesdays.

Black Down and Haslemere

Takes farm tracks, driveways and woodland paths over lowland countryside with pantiled and timber-frame cottages and hammer ponds (relics of the iron-smelting industry). Ascends by quiet tarmac lane and tracks to mixed woods of Black Down, the highest point in Sussex at 918ft. Re-enters Haslemere along pleasant side-roads.

Length 9 miles (14.5km), 4½ hours
Difficulty 3
Start Haslemere, by town hall
By train Haslemere; turn left out of station, ignore side turns
OS maps 1:50,000 186;
1:25,000 SU 82/92 and SU 83/93
Refreshments Full range in Haslemere

WALK DIRECTIONS

1 (**a**) From town hall take B2131, signposted Petworth. After 100 yards turn left into Collards Lane (signposted public footpath). This bends right after 200 yards then passes through gate, 20 yards after which turn half left through wooden barrier and proceed down to footbridge leading up steps into woods. Just inside woods, turn right by NT sign (indicating circular route in other direction), on track running inside woods.

2 After 300 yards cross stream by footbridge (which is a few yards to your right) then keep forward (avoiding right fork which leads past Haslemere and NT signs 50 yards away). Soon track is joined by fence on your left. Track soon leaves wood by hurdle; follow left edge of field alongside woods, pass briefly through patch of woodland, then follow left edge of second field, then through gate and pick up track.

Opposite first house turn left by signpost, over stile. Proceed alongside fence on left, then between fences, to road **3**. Cross to tarmac farm track opposite, signposted public footpath and leading to Imbhams Farm. **4** After ½ mile, just after end of lake on your left, where track bends left, turn sharp right through gate into woods. Proceed along track, which after ½ mile joins corner of unsurfaced driveway. Keep forward along it, then forward on joining tarmac driveway (house called Furnace Place is on left).

5 75 yards after driveway crosses stream by bridge, turn right by footpath signpost into drive for Stream Cottage, then immediately left over stile. Bear quarter right, aiming for stile on skyline, beyond which turn right on road. Turn left at B-road, and follow 500 yards to where it bends left at bottom of dip **6**. Turn right on driveway for Anstead Brook Stud. Where driveway bends left to farm, keep forward on track which runs between hedges and which makes small but sudden kink to left after 300 yards; immediately after, turn right by signpost, through small gate, and follow right edge of field to small gate into woods **7**.

Immediately on your right in these woods is slightly raised dyke. Follow it up through woods to small gate at top. Continue forward in field, with woods on left for 20 yards, then at the corner of woods head straight up across field, finding well-defined track along other side. Left on this track, follow to gate then forward in next field with line of hedgerow trees on left, then between fences, past house and on to tarmac lane **8**. Turn right on lane, then after ½ mile, where it bends sharp right, turn left on track into NT car park (**b**), beyond which track bends right where view opens out; immediately fork right (left leads to bench). Ignore next minor right fork and proceed along top of slope to next bench (**c**), beyond which continue on track a little further into woods.

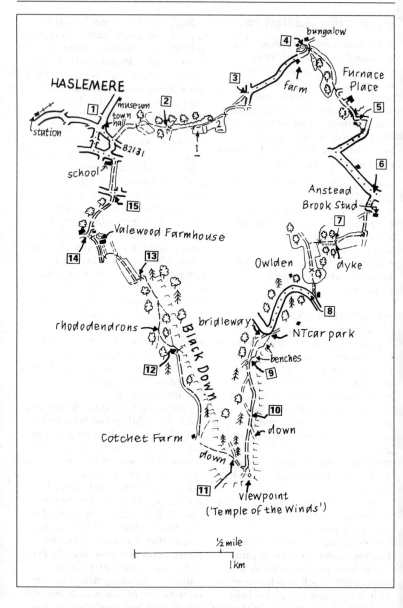

HASLEMERE

station

museum
town
hall

school

B2131

bungalow

farm

Furnace
Place

Anstead
Brook Stud

Valewood Farmhouse

rhododendrons

Black Down

bridleway

Owlden

dyke

NT car park

benches

Cotchet Farm

down

down

viewpoint
('Temple of the Winds')

½ mile

1 km

9 Keep left at fork by bridleway signpost after 50 yards and again 50 yards later. Ignore next right fork (signpost) after 100 yards. **10** ¼ mile later ignore sharp right turn, and 70 yards later fork right. Proceed ¼ mile to next junction, where 30 yards before bridleway signpost left turn is signed to viewpoint (sign is facing other way). Detour to viewpoint (view-indicator (**d**) and stone bench, just beyond wooden hurdles), and proceed to above-mentioned bridleway signpost where ignore left turn.

11 100 yards later, where view opens out by bench, fork left downhill. Turn right by farm at bottom, then ignore signposted right turn after 50 yards. **12** After ½ mile, at next signposted crossing of tracks, turn left. Fork left at signpost 75 yards later, then turn right at signpost at T-junction. **13** ⅓ mile later path bends left at edge of wood and then emerges into open via gate. 30 yards later turn right by signpost and follow grassy track across field, heading in line with distant but prominent brick house on hillside. Leave field by gate in corner, then immediately turn left, descending with fence on left. At bottom, left on track which winds round to T-junction, where turn right. Proceed past Valewood Farm House, then soon through double gates to emerge by next T-junction in front of cottage **14**.

Turn right and fork left after 50 yards at signpost, to follow track uphill to road **15**. Left on road, then immediately turn right through barriers for path between fences. Emerge on road, turn left, keep across at next crossroads, then fork right into College Hill to return to start.

WHAT TO LOOK OUT FOR
(**a**) **Haslemere** A small town with an immaculate centre and many Victorian and Edwardian houses on the attractive wooded hillsides that surround it. A centre of the Arts and Crafts movement at the end of the last century. Arnold Dolmetsch set up his workshop here in 1914 to make and repair musical instruments; other residents have been George Eliot and Sir Arthur Conan Doyle. Small museum with a good natural history collection.
(**b**) Sharper left leads to **Aldworth House** (private), home of Lord Tennyson for the last 23 years of his life; Black Down was one of his favourite walking areas. Haslemere church has a memorial window to him by Burne-Jones.
(**c**) **View** W to the sandstone escarpment of Pitch Hill, Holmbury Hill and Leith Hill.
(**d**) **View** Not everything on the view-indicator is visible, but the long ridge of the South Downs with the prominent knob of Chanctonbury Ring is obvious, and Ashdown Forest is also in view. Occasionally you can see the sun shining on the sea at Shoreham Gap.

St Martha's Hill

*Recommended by Pat and Roy
Galbraith, M Collier, Mike Vingoe
and S Empson-Ridler*

**Short but varied, on a section of
wooded greensand escarpment above
the Tilling Bourne Valley. Views
open out at the summit by St
Martha's Chapel, before descent to
mill ponds. Mostly on defined paths
and tracks, but directions should be
followed carefully; one steep climb,
just after** 4.

Length 5 miles (8km), 2½ hours
Difficulty 2
Start Chilworth station (E end of
Chilworth on A248), 4 miles E of
Guildford. Park by phone box outside
station. Grid reference TQ 031473
OS maps 1:50,000 186;
1:25,000 TQ 04/14
Refreshments Percy Arms,
Chilworth

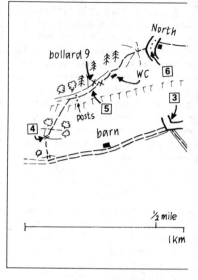

WALK DIRECTIONS

1 (a) From phone box by station
make your way to main road ahead
and turn left along it, passing Percy
Arms and then primary school on
your right. Immediately after primary
school, turn right on path (signed 'no
cycling, no horses') leading to footbridge in woods 2. After footbridge
turn left at junction of paths and
follow to road. Turn right on road, then
left after 100 yards by corner of road on
signposted footpath (next to Halfpenny
Lane sign) leading up between fences.

3 At top, turn left on road and,
after 20 yards, where road bends
right, pass through gate ahead to
follow track along left (bottom) side
of field. After 400 yards it passes
barn; track then rises between banks
and descends. Just before it is about
to ascend again (400 yards after barn),
cross stile on right to follow path
leading to projecting left-hand corner
of wood ahead.

4. Cross stile into wood, and then

climb steeply up, to reach T-junction
of earthy paths after 30 yards. Here
keep straight on up (very steep) on
grassy area between bushes. At top
bear half right to edge of woods, and
turn right (with woods on left) along
grassy track leading between posts.
5 After 100 yards ignore gate by
bollard 9 on left, leading into woods,
but continue forward on track which
enters woods by next gate/stile.
Avoid side turns; proceed to road 6.

Left on road and, after 30 yards (just
after house on right), right on to track
signposted North Downs Way. Avoid
side turns and follow ½ mile uphill
to St Martha's Chapel 7 (b). Pass
through churchyard and leave by gate
on other side to descend on path with
wooden railings. After 400 yards
avoid North Downs Way, which
forks off to left, but continue forward,
soon passing concrete pillbox on left.

8 200 yards after pillbox look out
for notice-board displaying map on
right of path; 10 yards beyond this
fork half right on path leading
downhill. After 50 yards turn right at
T-junction of paths and descend
steeply through woods, with water

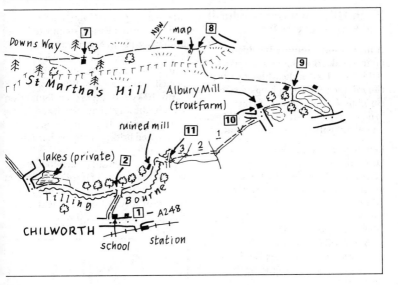

visible away to right in later stages. After ½ mile, pass house at bottom of slope and reach lake ahead (**c**) **9**. Turn right to pass end of lake and turn right at end, by 'SCC no horses' sign on left (or, if you prefer, walk round the lake by continuing forward on path which leads through garden of house, then following drive to road; turn right and immediately right again on signposted path leading on other side of lake).

Follow track through woods past old watermill on your right – now a trout farm – to reach lane in front of watermill **10**. Left on lane and then immediately right on signposted footpath leading alongside fence to stile. Follow left edge of first field to next stile; in second field proceed with stream on left to next stile.

In third field continue forward to stile leading on to track **11**. Turn right on track to cross brook, just after which turn left on path alongside it. Brook is canalised and remains of lock and mill buildings are visible (**d**); after passing these, path forks half right away from brook and shortly footbridge you crossed at beginning

of walk is visible on left. Cross it and follow path back.

WHAT TO LOOK OUT FOR

(**a**) **Chilworth** Banknotes were produced here from the 16th century until recently.

(**b**) **St Martha's Chapel** The solitary parish church of Chilworth, which looks out over much of the best countryside in Surrey. The original 12th-century building was owned by the Prior of Newark from 1262, but it was ruined later by a nearby explosion. It was virtually rebuilt in 1848 in striking Norman style, using the old materials. Its dedication is obscure, either to St Martha, who reputedly came here with Joseph of Arimathea, or as a corruption of St Martyr's – an old legend tells of a massacre of Christians on this hill.

(**c**) The first of two **mill ponds**.

(**d**) The shell of a **gunpowder mill**, standing among the alders and willows on the banks of the Tilling Bourne. In the 17th century this was an important area for manufacturing gunpowder; an ordnance factory existed here in the First World War.

157

Pitch Hill, Ewhurst windmill and Holmbury Hill

A tour of some remote Wealden countryside, the first and last parts on field, woodland and parkland paths, the middle section high up on tracks through the open forest of Hurt Wood. Easy route-finding on field and woodland paths; one steep ascent.

Length 9 miles (14.5km), 4½ hours
Difficulty 3
Start Bull's Head Inn, Ewhurst, at junction of B2127 and Shere road, at NW corner of village. Roadside parking. Grid reference TQ 090408.
OS maps 1:50,000 187;
1:25,000 TQ 04/14
Refreshments Bull's Head and others in Ewhurst; Windmill Inn near Pitch Hill

WALK DIRECTIONS

1 Take minor road to right of petrol station opposite Bull's Head Inn. After 500 yards woods begin on left; 100 yards later turn left on woodland path (signposted public footpath). 2 After path crosses bridge, fork right on path leading to stile (signposted). Follow left edge of field for 50 yards, then at corner of fence continue same direction to next stile, just in front of barn with tiled roof, where path leads to lane.

3 Cross lane to take fenced path opposite, soon into woods. 200 yards into woods turn right on bridleway at signpost. 4 After 600 yards track crosses footbridge; fork right immediately beyond. After leaving woods, reach junction of tracks with field ahead of you; turn right, after 30 yards turn left (just before footpath sign ahead) through gate and cross middle of field to head across field to gate. 300 yards later cross footbridge.
5 100 yards later turn sharp right up bank on track for 5 yards then turn left and follow to road. Turn right on road and after 50 yards turn left on

driveway (signs to Colman's Farm and Winterfold Farm), signposted bridleway. 6 Keep straight on where driveway bears right to Coach House, and shortly after turn left as signposted, by entrance to Winterfold Farm. 100 yards later reach T-junction with bridleway (signposted) and turn right on fenced track, avoiding signposted bridleway up on left 50 yards later.

7 After 500 yards reach foot of wooded slope with house away to left and end of field on right behind you. Continue forward/quarter right steeply uphill. After 30 yards

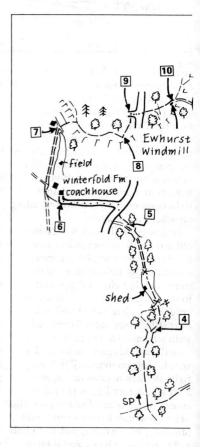

continue forward over cross-track and continue up, taking right-hand fork of two paths. At top of steep slope reach another cross-track and turn right along it, with steep slope immediately on your right. **8** After 300 yards, keep to main path which swings left as fainter path continues forward to open area/viewing-point. Reach road 400 yards later.

9 Turn right on road, then at T-junction continue forward, to take track opposite. After 40 yards keep straight on, avoiding driveway on right to Summerfold, and 30 yards later cross track to continue ahead.

10 Pass Ewhurst windmill and bear right, continuing with fence on right downhill to road (Windmill Inn is visible on right). Cross road to car park, and after 20 yards fork right uphill to Pitch Hill, following edge of slope and follow to trig.point **11**.

Continue past trig. point, soon passing metal bench on your right. 40 yards after bench, fork right downhill to cross-track. Turn left to cross barrier (with Hurt Wood Control sign). Ignore first right turn (and left turn immediately after), but 130 yards later **12** turn right down to reach cross-track after 100 yards and

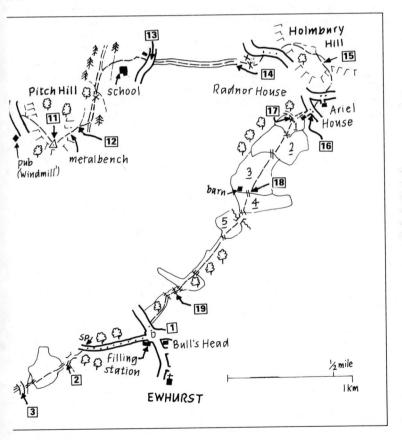

continue down to metal fence. Pass through fence, and continue (school ahead is visible) down to school drive. Continue forward to road **13**.

Turn left, and after 5 yards only turn right (signposted public footpath). After 400 yards, at end of fenced section, continue forward, soon again between fences. **14** 400 yards later emerge from between fences at foot of wooded hillside, turn right for 30 yards to gate, then continue ahead, avoiding track on left beyond gate, and follow to road. Turn right on road and after 50 yards turn left on track opposite house. At top of rise, turn right up steps and follow along edge of escarpment, avoiding all left turns, to viewpoint on Holmbury Hill **15**.

Facing S – with pillar/circular seat behind you and metal bench behind on right – take grassy track ahead, which descends steeply. At road at bottom turn right and after 100 yards turn left on path (between hedges;

can be overgrown) between entrance to Ariel House and Wayfarers. **16** Emerge by steps on to road, turn left for 10 yards, then right into driveway to Radnor House. Keep to right of house on paved path and at lamp-post by pond beyond it keep straight on, avoiding paved path leading up on right. Track follows edge of woods.

17 After 200 yards cross stile on left and head downhill through first field to gate; in second field bear quarter right to stile by tall post. In third field continue to stile 100 yards to left of barn. **18** Continue direction across fourth field to gate/stile (with yellow marker) and cross footbridge into fifth field, where waymarks on trees indicate way ahead (stream on left) to gate, to pass through woods. **19** Emerge into fields, follow path along right edge of fields (later through woods). Left on road into Ewhurst village.

SUSSEX

Kingley Vale

Recommended by D H Ogden

Kingley Vale nature reserve includes an ancient yew forest – a place of almost eerie darkness – though later there are wide views as the downland opens out. Rising farm track at beginning gives no indication of what is to follow. Dense network of paths, but route-finding made easy by nature trail marker points. Full walk takes in nature trail and the most dramatic parts of the forest; leaflet available from stand outside kiosk in reserve just after 3 .

Length 4½ miles (7km), 2 hours
Short walk 3½ miles (5.5km),
1½ hours
Difficulty 1–2

Start *Both walks* Stoughton, 9 miles NW of Chichester. Roadside parking in village. Grid reference SU 802114
OS maps 1:50,000 197;
1:25,000 SU 81/91
Refreshments Hare and Hounds Inn, Stoughton

WALK DIRECTIONS
1 (a) With Hare and Hounds Inn on right, follow road, avoiding right fork to phone box and church, and 100 yards later, turn left on surfaced driveway immediately before Tythe Barn House. Driveway soon becomes track and ascends steadily. Steepest part of ascent is through forest, after which track emerges to follow left edge of field; avoid two grassy forest rides on left, both signposted bridleways, but continue on track to

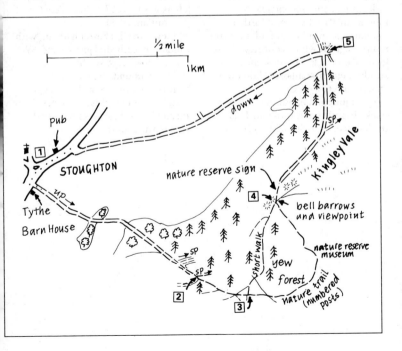

descend to bottom left-hand corner of field **2**.

Keep straight on, taking path into yew forest (**b**) (leaving track which bends right still following perimeter of field). After a few yards avoid turning coming in sharply from right. On emerging from forest continue forward at junction, taking (indistinct) narrow path through scrubby area (avoiding track quarter right alongside fence on right). **3** After 70 yards, at next junction of tracks, continue forward a few paces to post marked '23'. *For short walk* turn sharp left through dense forest to emerge by viewpoint at top; continue from **4**.

For full walk (recommended) turn right to reach nature reserve museum; outside you can buy nature trail leaflet. Follow trail (waymarked) round to viewpoint **4**.

Reach viewpoint (**c**) on ridge by either route, and standing with slope on right and grassy mounds on left, fork left just after second grassy mound (**d**). Path leads past further mounds and over brow of hill to nature reserve sign, at which continue forward on track. This descends steadily; ignore signposted bridleway on right after ¼ mile.

5 At junction of number of forest tracks ¼ mile later, turn left. This track descends to Stoughton, at first between fences, then on edge of fields and finally between fences again.

WHAT TO LOOK OUT FOR
(**a**) **Stoughton** Birthplace of George Brown (1764), a fast bowler of such ferocity that his long-stop padded himself with straw and once even held up a coat to stop the ball. The ball broke through it and killed a dog that happened to be on the other side.
(**b**) **Kingley Vale nature reserve** Yew forest of great antiquity, one of the largest in Europe, and where the trees are thick, nothing else grows, for yew trees blot out all the light. Elsewhere in the reserve there is herb-rich grassland with chalk-loving plants.
Flora Eleven types of orchid, harebells, milkwort, round-headed rampion, heather, and others. Butterfly population, richly varied, includes blues, fritillaries, white admiral and the purple emperors. For further reading about the reserve, see Richard Jefferson's book *The Great Yew Forest* (Macmillan, 1978).
(**c**) **View** S to Chichester harbour, with Chichester cathedral just visible; SW towards the Isle of Wight.
(**d**) These **mounds** are two 'bell barrows' and two 'bowl barrows', the burial places of prehistoric kings. They are among the best specimens of their kind in the country.

Older Hill and Woolbeding Common

Very varied, in a remote corner of the West Sussex Weald, leading out over field and riverside paths to pass through deciduous woodland. Short climb through scrub leads to heathy summit of Older Hill, from where there is a long gentle descent over Woolbeding and Pound Commons, with good views of South Downs. Final section through secluded, woody river valley past an ancient water mill. Easy underfoot, and route-finding mostly straightforward on tracks and field paths, though care needed on Woolbeding and Pound Commons.

Length 8 miles (13km), 4 hours
Difficulty 3
Start Stedham church, at N end of Stedham village; roadside parking 2 miles W of Midhurst. Grid reference SU 864225
OS maps 1:50,000 197; 1:25,000 SU 82/92
Refreshments Hamilton Arms, Stedham (½ mile off route, at start/finish)

WALK DIRECTIONS

1 With gateway to churchyard behind you, follow driveway down to main road, turn right and immediately left on signposted bridleway (just before bridge across river). Follow clear path for ½ mile until row of cottages comes into view on right. Fork right towards them, through gate and left on to tarmac driveway. After passing in front of cottages, continue forward on cobbled track leading steeply downhill.

2 Turn right on road, soon crossing bridge over Rother with fine mansion on left. 100 yards beyond river turn right through wooden gate (footpath signpost) and continue round right-hand edge of two fields,

crossing two stiles. **3** Turn right on road, cross small bridge and then immediately left, taking sunken path gently uphill (avoid steeper path to right). Path passes through woods to join tarmac track merging from right. Continue forward avoiding driveway to large stone house, to reach isolated cottage in valley bottom **4**.

Turn left in front of cottage, past public bridleway sign and, 20 yards further on, fork left on woodland track. Continue on this for 1¼ miles, avoiding all turns to left, and passing further isolated house after about ¾ mile. **5** Track emerges from wood at small village green surrounded by a few houses. Fork right in front of this, and after 20 yards fork right again on signposted path (indistinct at first, but soon improves). Continue on this path for ½ mile, winding through woodland and passing several signposts pointing to indistinct or absent paths (which you avoid).

6 Cross road by Redford post office and general store and continue on tarmac driveway opposite. After 50 yards fork right, following signpost to Bracken Hill. Turn left after 150 yards, still on driveway, again following signpost to Bracken Hill. Avoiding driveway into Bracken Hill House itself, continue to end of driveway which loops in front of cottage. Take left-hand of two paths leading on from this loop, and fork right after 5 yards with short wooden post on left. Path (well-defined despite undergrowth), winds up hillside, to reach seat at top **7**.

From seat, follow path heading just to right of trig. point (marking summit of Older Hill). Path then continues half right across hillside to reach road. Turn right and then immediately left on path that climbs over open heathland. Keep right at T-junction of paths, to emerge on gravel drive just after it emerges from house on left **8**.

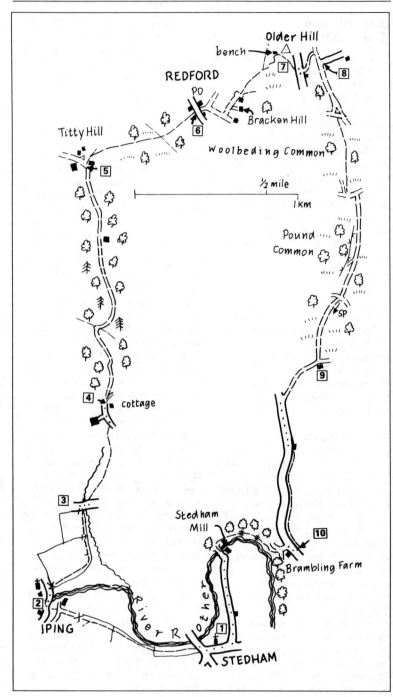

Continue forward on gravel drive for 200 yards, until footpath signpost on right. Continue for another 10 yards beyond this, then turn right on unmade track for 5 yards, then left on smaller path winding out of wood, which diverges gradually from gravel drive. This heads gradually towards power lines: at its closest point to them fork left, heading for wooden public footpath signpost (which marks cross-track). Continue forward past this signpost and head down valley on clear path for ¾ mile, avoiding cross-tracks.

9 On reaching house on edge of common, turn right and follow gravel drive to road. Turn left on road, and soon (after first house on left) turn left into field to follow right-hand side field, parallel to road. **10** Leave field opposite entrance to Brambling Farm, cross road and follow signposted track to right of farm. At grassy clearing after 50 yards turn left then immediately right on narrow path which heads steeply downhill (signpost rather overgrown). At bottom, cross stile and turn right along river bank. Cross two stiles and footbridge, and turn left after second stile to cross narrow footbridge over weir. Turn right in front of Stedham Mill to follow tarmac driveway back to Stedham church.

The Racton Monument and Stansted Park

*Recommended by J F M Haye,
W I and M A Lamont, D J Unwin,
Paul Bilson*

**Memorable for its approach to
Stansted House, along a broad, grassy
avenue flanked by beeches.
Elsewhere crosses farmland by easy
(mostly fenced), level tracks. If
planning to stop at a village half-way,
start at Walderton and aim for
Rowland's Castle. All tracks well
defined (though often very muddy);
easy route-finding.**

Length 7 miles (11km), 3½ hours
Difficulty 1–2
Start Walderton, on B2146 (village
centre is just off it), 7 miles NW of
Chichester. Roadside parking. Grid
reference SU 787105
By train Rowland's Castle. Turn left
out of station, left at T-junction, then
left at next T-junction, taking left
fork under railway arch, past Castle

Inn. Where road bends left at end of
village, pass through gap between
brick pillars (signposted) on right, and
continue to reach tarmac track.
Forward on path up rise. At top,
forward on wide grassy avenue for
1 mile. Pick up directions at ⑧
OS maps 1:50,000 197;
1:25,000 SU 60/70 and SU 61/71
Refreshments Barley Mow, Walderton; shops, two pubs and baker's
shop serving teas at Row-
land's Castle; tea-room at Stansted
House when house is open

WALK DIRECTIONS

① From B2146 in Walderton, with
bus-shelter and turning signposted to
Stoughton on your right, follow
B-road, and take first turning on left
by group of houses. After 50 yards
turn left into first field by signpost,
head 10 yards to right of nearest
electricity post and maintain
direction over brow of hill to reach
signposted stile. Proceed across
second field, heading towards

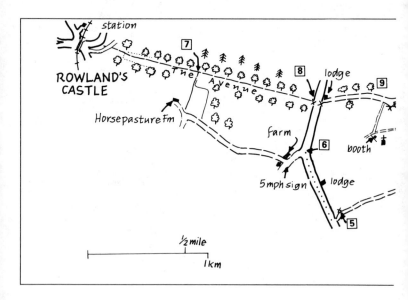

prominent house (**a**), and leave by stile in far (bottom) left corner **2**.

Continue along left side of third field to gate, then proceed alongside pond to driveway. Left on driveway, over bridge, then immediately right through kissing-gate. Bear quarter left across field to gate, then proceed across next field in same direction to stile. Emerge on road, turn right along it. **3** Keep right at next fork, then 50 yards later (immediately after road crosses stream) turn right on to track (**b**). Proceed uphill, past Racton Monument (**c**) after ¼ mile.

4 300 yards later, fork left (right is signed to New Barn Cottage) and keep straight on at the next two junctions (which appear at ¼-mile intervals), then **5** ½ mile later keep left (ignoring sharp right turn through gate signposted as public footpath). Soon, emerge on to road; turn right along it. **6** 500 yards later, by farm buildings and pillar box on left, turn left on farm track, then 150 yards later turn right into farmyard by

signpost with 5 mph restriction sign (referring to track ahead). Follow ½ mile, then at next junction (just before farm) turn 90 degrees right through gap in hedge, aiming for break in woods ahead.

7 Emerge on to open grassy avenue (**d**). *For detour to Rowland's Castle (for refreshments)* turn left; at end of avenue find track in right-hand corner, maintain same direction along it, downhill, then over metalled track to road. Turn left into village.

To continue main walk turn right along avenue, and follow until road **8**. Cross road, and take driveway by lodge ('private' signs refer to vehicles); ignore left fork after 100 yards. Driveway soon leaves woodland, emerges into open (**e**). **9** On entering next wood keep left (ignoring driveway ahead through gates and past entry booth). 200 yards later fork right to pass to right of estate cottages, and follow track ½ mile. **10** At 5-way junction keep forward on track between hedges,

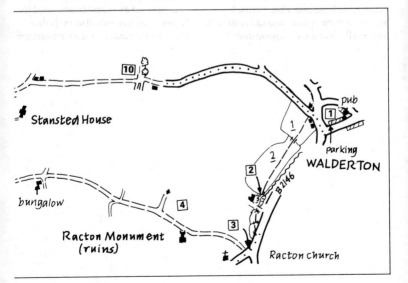

167

which soon becomes tarmac lane.
Follow down to Walderton. (To
continue route, turn right opposite
first house on left, and resume
directions from ⬚1.)

WHAT TO LOOK OUT FOR
(a) **Lordington House** Mostly 18th-
century, but still on the 'L'-plan of
the original Tudor house. The
meadow crossed just below the
house, by the duck pond, is covered
in daffodils in early spring.
(b) Continue on road for a few
hundred yards for **Racton church**.
Simple, 13th-century (restored);
originally the family chapel for
Rampton Court. Has two interesting
(16th- and 17th-century) monuments
to the Gounter family, and an 18th-
century royal coat of arms on its tie-
beam. Next to the church is King
Charles Cottage, a half-timbered
building where the king allegedly
once stopped off (a royal coat of arms
inside confirms the story).
(c) **Racton Tower** Built by Theodosius
Keene in 1772 as a folly; consists of a
triangular base and a tall central
tower. It now stands as a sad ruin, but
originally had a well-appointed

interior, and was the joy of the third
lord of Halifax who lived at Stansted
House. Later it gained a reputation as
a resort for ladies and gentlemen of
ill-fame and as a signalling tower for
illegal shipping in Chichester harbour; Lord Halifax then ordered its
destruction. **Views** over Chichester
Harbour and to the Isle of Wight.
(d) **The Avenue** 1½-mile-long
beech avenue, which Pevsner held to
be one of the best in England. Daniel
Defoe visited it in 1724 and wrote
that Portsmouth harbour and
Spithead were visible.
(e) **Stansted House** (open to public;
fee) For the quickest way to the
entrance, turn right immediately
before woods restart, along woodland
fence at edge of field; turn right on to
track at end, then immediately left.
The house was rebuilt by Sir Reginald
Blomfield in the neo-Wren style in
the early 1900s, after the 17th- and
18th-century house was destroyed by
fire. Adjoining is the Gothick-style
chapel, built out of remains of the
original (late 15th-century) house,
consecrated at a service attended by
Keats. The grounds also include a
Dutch rose garden and an arboretum.

Clayton windmills and Wolstonbury Hills

Contributed by Brian Edwards
Recommended by Pat and Roy
Galbraith, Andrew Bailey,
W E Gilbert, D J Unwin

Enclosed pasture and rough grassland slopes on the northern escarpment of the South Downs, with views over the Weald. A short stiff climb to Wolstonbury Hill. Route-finding quite easy; most paths and tracks well defined.

Length 5 miles (8km), 2½ hours
Difficulty 2–3
Start Pyecombe church, 300 yards N of junction of A23 and A273, 5 miles N of Brighton. Roadside parking. Grid reference TQ 292126
By train Hassocks (1 mile off route). Take footpath to Clayton immediately E of railway line
OS maps 1:50,000 198; 1:25,000 TQ 21/31
Refreshments Jack and Jill Inn, Clayton

WALK DIRECTIONS

1 (a) At crossroads, with church on right, proceed into School Lane. Follow until main road (A273) and turn left on footpath alongside road to signpost opposite entrance to Pyecombe Golf Club **2**. Cross A273 on to bridleway with South Downs Way signpost, and go across Pyecombe golf course.

3 At end of golf course go through

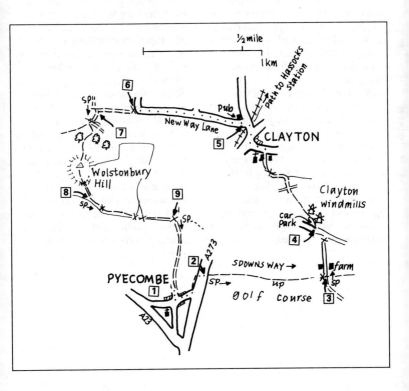

gate, then immediately turn left at South Downs Way signpost. This track leads through farm, then soon through metal gate; continue straight on towards windmills (**b**); ignore track which joins from right. Go down track past mills and turn right into car park **4**.

Take gate at corner of car park, by concrete bridleway signpost. Go downhill to Clayton village, aiming slightly to right of Clayton church at farm buildings. Halfway down hill continue on depressed grassy track veering slightly right, ignoring cross-track near fence corner. After 130 yards track becomes more defined and curves to the left down-hill. Go through iron gate marked 'Private land keep to bridleway'. Follow track to tarmac lane passing house on your right and farmyard on left. Turn left along lane, past church (**c**), to reach main road (A273), which cross carefully. Turn right, then immediately left over the railway bridge (**d**).

5 Immediately after railway bridge turn left along New Way Lane and follow for ½ mile. **6** Where road turns sharply to the right, continue ahead through gates (signposted as bridleway). **7** After ¼ mile track turns left (signposted). Pass further signpost and over stile. Take narrow path going half left up steep bank (ignore wide track going sharp left). Follow path through woods, where it becomes more defined, and then on

to open downland. Follow path steeply to the trig. point summit (**e**), the continue down on other side over stile and follow track to reach signpost **8**. Turn left, shortly passing through metal gate, and continue with fence on right. Pass through another metal gate ¼ mile later, and continue to further metal gate **9**. Turn right (signposted bridleway) and follow track to Pyecombe.

WHAT TO LOOK OUT FOR
(**a**) **Pyecombe** The tapsel gate into the churchyard has a shepherd's crook handle; the old building opposite used to be a forge famed for its crook-making (the post of the forge sign is still there).
(**b**) **Clayton windmills** 'Jill' is the white post mill, moved in the 1820s from Patcham by a team of oxen; 'Jack' is the black tower mill.
(**c**) **Clayton church** Contains some fine 12th-century wall-paintings. Its plan and chancel arch are Saxon (probably 11th-century).
(**d**) **Clayton tunnel** 1¼ miles long, with a castellated portal, and a cottage built directly over it.
(**e**) **Wolstonbury Hill** On top is an Iron Age hillfort, unusual in the respect that the ditch is inside the rampart. Its builders used the 'downward build' method of construction, throwing earth from the excavated ditch downhill. The enclosure within it may be connected with the working of Wealden iron ore.

Friston and the Seven Sisters

Contributed by Andrew Bailey
Recommended by Ian Wilson,
D Marsh

One of the most attractive stretches of coastal scenery in the South-east of England, with a section of mixed woodland in Friston Forest and two smart, pretty villages. Some of the up and down along the cliffs omitted by taking the shorter route. Good for wild flowers in spring. Route-finding moderately easy, mostly on defined paths and tracks; keep well clear of the cliff edge.

Length *Full walk* 7½ miles (12km), 4 hours
Difficulty 3–4
Shorter walk 6½ miles (10.5km), 3 hours
Difficulty 3
Start Seven Sisters Country Park (car park; free) at Exceat on A259, 6 miles W of Eastbourne and 2 miles E of Seaford. Grid reference TV 518995
OS maps 1:50,000 199; 1:25,000 TV 49/59/69
Refreshments Tiger Inn, East Dean

WALK DIRECTIONS

1 Leave car park and turn right along A259 for 60 yards (**a**). At bus stop, cross road on to track between buildings, cross stile and ascend steep grassy field straight ahead to flint wall. Cross wall and proceed into Friston Forest along path signposted West Dean. Descend long flight of steps to village (**b**) **2**.

At corner of tarmac lane turn right and follow lane round past houses and then into Friston Forest. (Just before Friston Forest sign, lane on left leads 100 yards to church and rectory.) Keep forward to follow signs to Friston. **3** Bear right at fork just after second white house. Continue straight along broad grassy track, ignoring side turnings. **4** After 1½ miles, track meets tarmac lane at

T-junction with private drive opposite. Turn left and follow lane which bends round to right. 40 yards before second vehicle passing-point, leave lane and take gate in wall on right to enter field. Bear half left across field (no path) and pass through small gate in wall on far side **5**. Cross lane and go over stile into next field, which cross half left, making for top far left corner. Cross stile and enter wood. Emerge on to A259 at Friston **6**. Cross A259, go down lane opposite, signposted Crowlink.

For shorter walk follow lane through NT car park then to cluster of houses at Crowlink. Carry straight on, ignoring turning on right signed Crowlink House. Lane becomes track and then, just beyond last house, grassy footpath which leads on to path along the Seven Sisters (**d**). Turn right here and continue directions from **10**.

For full walk follow lane for 40 yards, then enter churchyard on left through tapsel gate. Proceed through churchyard and leave by far right corner. Walk downhill to East Dean through grassy combe. Go through gate on to surfaced lane. At T-junction turn right and in a few yards reach the village green (**c**). **7** Leave village green at south corner near shop and post office. (To visit church, fork left into Lower Street.)

Fork right into Went Way. At end of lane proceed straight on through gate on to path signposted Birling Gap. At corner of garden go straight on, ignoring cross-track. Ascend through wood and emerge on to open downland (Went Hill) **8**. Make for prominent small barn. At barn, turn right for 25 yards then left on to slightly sunken track which descends gradually towards sea. **9** When track bends sharply to left after ⅓ mile, leave it and proceed straight on through gate and down grassy field to gate/stile. Cross stile and bear half right to another gate. Go through this gate and turn right; you are now back on the path along the Seven Sisters (**d**). Follow coast for 2 miles.

10 When descending from last 'Sister', first make for shingle beach at Cuckmere Haven, then, just before ground steepens markedly, bear half right downhill and make for prominent wide grassy track on flat ground between lagoon on left and

steep bank on right (**e**). Follow grassy track until it joins concrete track. Follow concrete track back to Exceat and car park.

WHAT TO LOOK OUT FOR
(**a**) **Exceat** Formerly a sizeable village, hit hard by the Black Death.
(**b**) **West Dean** By the fine Norman church is the 13th-century rectory, one of the oldest continually inhabited houses in Britain. King

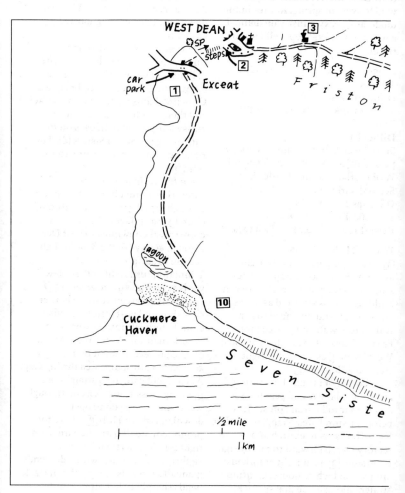

Alfred is thought to have had a manor-house here, quite possibly at the ruined house by the dovecote in the village centre.

(c) **East Dean** Attractive flint-walled cottages surround the village green; nearby is the simple Norman church with its Saxon tower.

(d) **Seven Sisters** A series of seven chalk spurs with dry valleys between, abruptly cut off to form sheer cliffs, just W of the culmination of the South Downs at Beachy Head. From here to Cuckmere Haven is good for bird-watching. **Flora** Small hare's ear, moon carrot, least lettuce, orchids, rampion, gentians, thistles, and others.

(e) **Cuckmere Haven** Near the river mouth a Roman burial ground and mammoth's tusk have been found. The lagoon marshland, alluvial grassland and shingle bank are a rich habitat for wildlife and flora.

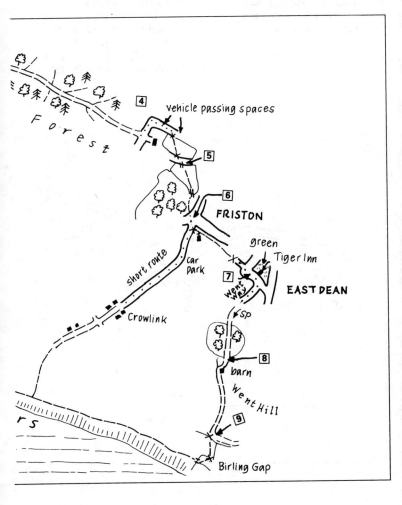

Glynde, Mount Caburn and Lewes

Contributed by J A Walton
Recommended by Andrew Bailey,
Pat and Roy Galbraith

Over open downland with extensive views over the Weald, descending to take in Glynde, then going up past fine vantage (and picnic) point above the Ouse Valley. Paths across downland sometimes ploughed out; route-finding moderately easy. Railway stations at either end of walk enable it to be split in two.

Length *Full walk* 7 miles (11km), 3½ hours

Short walk omitting Glynde
5½ miles (9km), 2½ hours
Difficulty 2
Start *Both walks* Lewes station. Car parking at station or in town
By train Lewes or Glynde
OS maps 1:50,000 198;
1:25,000 TQ 40/50 and TQ 41/51
Refreshments Trevor Arms, Glynde (just beyond railway bridge); numerous pubs and cafés in Lewes

WALK DIRECTIONS

1 (a) Emerge from Lewes station and turn right over railway bridge then right into Lansdowne Place, which leads into Friars Walk. Continue down to first set of traffic lights and

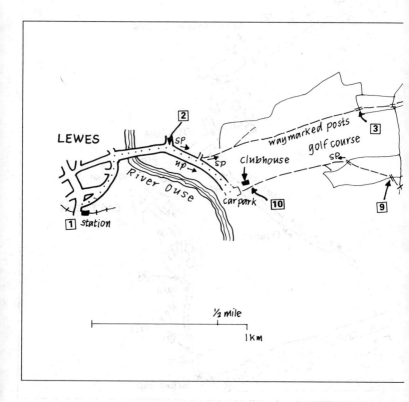

turn right into main street to cross over River Ouse and reach junction **2**. Go straight across and up steep tarmac lane signposted to golf course. About half-way up, take track on left waymarked to Ringmer and Glyndebourne; follow Glyndebourne arrow to turn immediately right and emerge on to golf course. Follow series of waymarks (posts) across golf course.

3 On leaving course via stile, keep straight on across two fields with steep-sided valley on your right (**b**). Keep straight on, past copse on your left, until dew pond **4**. Turn sharp right and follow track (**c**) towards and past small chalkpit, after which take left fork of tracks so that copse is to left. Ignore next left turn which follows perimeter of copse, but continue forwards across stile and proceed straight ahead, with fence on right.

5 *For short walk omitting Glynde* keep straight on.

For full walk turn left at first grass strip separating arable fields, opposite gate in fence. This leads on to cart-track, which leads through Glynde Estates farm buildings to emerge on to road opposite Glynde Place (**d**) **6**. Turn right on road and follow through Glynde village (**e**); then right into Ramscombe Lane. A few yards after village shop, cross stile on right marked 'Lewes

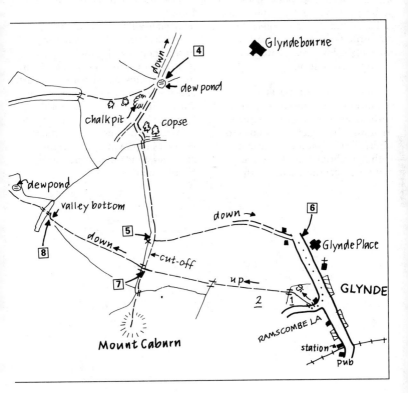

2½ miles' and follow path half left across field to next stile, then continue in same direction across second field. Slope gets progressively steeper and after the next stile it is quite steep on grass strip between two arable fields.

[7] At top, just before next stile, detour left to Mount Caburn (f). Return to main path, turn left over stile, then steeply downhill to valley bottom [8]. Left over stile and across to another in 100 yards, passing dew pond on right 350 yards later, then through gate and across stile shortly beyond [9].

Walk diagonally across and up slope of next field, to stile, beyond which turn left and follow signs until path comes in from left; ignore this and keep straight on to golf club-house [10]. Go through car park to road. Walk down road, enter Lewes and return to station.

WHAT TO LOOK OUT FOR

(a) **Lewes** Handsome country town with Georgian (and earlier) streets. An unusually high proportion of its timber-framed buildings are faced with sham brick faces known as mathematical tiles, added to the exteriors in the 18th century, when brickwork was a status symbol. The tell-tale thinness of the bricks is occasionally apparent at the corners of the buildings.

(b) **View** on left (N) over the Weald towards the Ashdown Forest.

(c) **View** of Glyndebourne Festival Theatre. John Christie established the annual opera festival in 1934 in his Tudor manor-house; the opera-house was built later. After suspension during the Second World war, performances started up again in 1950.

(d) **Glynde Place** (open to public; fee) Stately Elizabethan mansion, now the home of Viscount Hampden. In its panelled long gallery are portraits by Lely and Zoffany, and a cartoon by Rubens.

(e) **Glynde village** Its unusual classical church was designed in 1765 by Sir Thomas Robinson.

(f) **Mount Caburn**, on which a 3.5 acre hillfort, enclosed by a visible rampart and ditch, commands a view of the Ouse Valley. The fort was probably occupied between 500BC and AD50; a model can be seen in the Barbican House Museum in Lewes. Coins, brooches, beads and Celtic pottery have been found.

Hartfield and Pooh country

Contributed by Paul Bilson
Recommended by Simon Watts,
D Marsh, J Wells, W E Gilbert, Roy
and Pat Galbraith, K J Wright, B H
Marcusson, B Edwards,
J Empson-Ridler and M Vingoe,
Andrew Bailey, R Pullinger,
M G Bruce

**Through unspoilt countryside
associated with Winnie the Pooh,
using woodland tracks, field paths, an
old railway line and quiet lanes. Field
paths not all defined, and directions
are quite involved but route-finding
moderately easy.**

Length 7 miles (11km), 3½ hours
Difficulty 2–3
Start Hartfield, 2 miles S of A264
(East Grinstead to Tunbridge Wells).
Limited roadside parking. Grid
reference TQ 478357
OS maps 1:50,000 188;
1:25,000 TQ 43/53
Refreshments Anchor and Hay
Waggon, both in Hartfield; Dorset
Arms, Withyham; Gallipot Inn at 10

WALK DIRECTIONS

1 Take lane between Anchor and
Hay Waggon inns, turn left after 100
yards through archway and pass along
left side of churchyard. After 50 yards
continue on tarmac path past school
on your right, and go through
kissing-gate after another 50 yards.
Bear half left towards far corner of
field (avoiding tarmac path) heading
for kissing-gate to emerge by road
junction. Take B2026 ahead, signposted Edenbridge. After 200 yards
(just before bridge) turn right on path
through gate, leading past house on
your right (**a**). **2** 50 yards later turn
right, signposted Forest Way. This
leads to old railway line. Follow for ¾
mile, ignoring first path crossing over
old railway after ½ mile.

3 Where second path crosses over
old railway, turn right over stile

marked with Wealdway sign (yellow
'WW'). Proceed towards gate 50 yards
to left of two barns and then forward
to tarmac lane. Turn left over bridge,
then immediately right up lane
which continues to follow Wealdway, signposted Withyham church
(**b**). Follow lane 1¼ miles, ignoring all
turns to right. **4** Cross over
cattle-grids and 50 yards later, just
after estate cottages (Fisher's Gate),
turn left by gate (clearly signposted)
and follow path between fences
which turns right into woods after 50
yards. At junction of lanes, take lane
straight ahead. Ignore left turn after
30 yards and, 75 yards later, fork right
by cottage. After 120 yards fork right
again, still on lane, where forestry
track continues ahead.

5 At junction of tracks, with
entrance to Kovacs Lodge on right,
keep straight on (waymarked
Wealdway), following track inside
northern edge of Five Hundred Acre
Wood (**c**). Ignore turnings to left
which lead further into woods, and 30
yards after crossing small footbridge
turn right uphill 30 yards to edge of
wood. Then turn right and follow
path to road opposite Tile Barn
Cottage **6**. Turn right for 80 yards
along road then turn sharp left on
track into Tile Barn Farm. Turn
immediately left after first barn and
keep straight on for 150 yards. Go
through furthest left of three gates.
Proceed alongside hedge on right and
after 100 yards enter next field.

Cross field and continue in same
direction (no path) to pick up the
well-defined path in woodland
opposite (starting 200 yards from top
of left-hand corner of field). After 50
yards take middle of three paths, soon
leading over hurdle and into paddock.
Continue to gate 50 yards away, in far
corner of field. Turn left along edge of
field and cross hurdle 50 yards ahead.
Turn right on track leading to corner
of tarmac lane **7**.

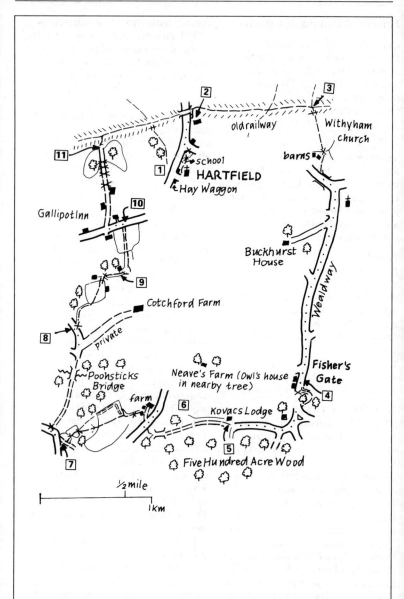

Carry straight on along lane for 50 yards and turn right through gate. This track leads down ¼ mile to Poohsticks Bridge (**d**). Cross bridge and 300 yards later keep straight on at staggered junction formed by track on left and (30 yards later) lane on right (**e**). **8** 100 yards further on turn right through gate into field. Follow left edge of field, turn right at the end (still at edge of field) and cross stile at corner of woods. Cross field diagonally, aiming for stile to left of prominent brick house. Cross tarmac path and turn right through gate, taking path along edge of woodland.

9 After 130 yards turn right at fence in front of house; then cross stile and turn immediately left alongside fence which swings round left after 150 yards. Cross stile and continue to gate at far end of field then follow track down to road **10**. Turn left along road for 140 yards, ignoring turn on right to Culvers after 40 yards. Opposite Landhurst House turn right and follow track to Culvers Farm. Keep straight on through farm, through four gates and enter wood.

11 Emerge from other side of wood, bear half right to gate leading to old railway embankment, along which turn right. After 300 yards leave old railway for stile on right, and take path straight on following line of posts on your left and then line of trees on your right. Cross stile and follow path to Hartfield.

WHAT TO LOOK OUT FOR
(**a**) The house was once **Hartfield station**. The route soon leads along the former branch line from East Three Bridges to Tunbridge Wells.
(**b**) **Withyham church** Mainly 14th-century with 17th-century rebuilding, it has monuments to members of the Sackville family.
(**c**) Pooh buffs will guess that **Five Hundred Acre Wood** is the 'Hundred Acre Wood' of A.A. Milne's stories.
(**d**) The bridge where Pooh and the others played at dropping sticks into the water in *The House at Pooh Corner*.
(**e**) The Milne family lived at **Cotchford Farm**, away to the right (not open to public).

Fairlight Glen and Hastings Old Town

Recommended by Pat and Roy Galbraith, Andrew Bailey

Outstanding stretch of coast, well frequented but wild, with a mixture of bracken, heather and grassland on sloping cliffs above the sea, screened from development inland by woodland. Good waymarks make route-finding through a dense network of paths moderately easy.

Length 4½ miles (7km), 2 hours
Difficulty 2
Start Large car park in Hastings Old Town, at E end of Hastings seafront near net houses and cliff railway
OS maps 1:50,000 199;
1:25,000 TQ 81/91
Refreshments Dolphin Inn at start and many others further into Hastings

WALK DIRECTIONS
1 From seafront in Old Town by net houses (**a**), climb Tamarisk Steps (immediately by Dolphin Inn). First section of steps leads to lane at Lindsell Cottages. Walk along lane for 25 yards, then go up second section of steps on right, leading past top station of cliff railway. Follow sign to Cliff Walks and Glens (bollard 1; of many bollards here, those along coast are marked 'For help, note bollard number and ring 999 . . .') along coastal path with sports fields on left. Follow coastal path for 1¾ miles to bollard 11 near Lover's Seat. (Steep final approach to the Lover's Seat area can be avoided by turning inland earlier at bollard 8, signposted Fairlight Glen (Upper). This leads to top of glen (bollard 9), at **3**.)

2 After visiting Lover's Seat return to bollard 11 and follow signs to Fairlight Glen (Upper) and Barley Lane. This leads to top of glen (bollard 9) **3**.

Continue 600 yards along track

between fences to emerge on to tarmac lane (Barley Lane) **4**. Left on lane for 400 yards, then opposite footpath signposted to Ore, turn left along track (unsignposted). After 40 yards keep straight on over stile where track veers left into private garden. **5** Path soon enters woodland; after 200 yards fork right downhill. After 80 yards continue right downhill at fork. After another 150 yards path passes close by reservoir on your right.

6 200 yards beyond reservoir, reach bollard 5 and turn right to take path signposted Barley Lane. This path crosses over stream, then goes steeply uphill near caravan park. At stile 50 yards before reaching Barley Lane, take path to left across open ground overlooking Ecclesbourne

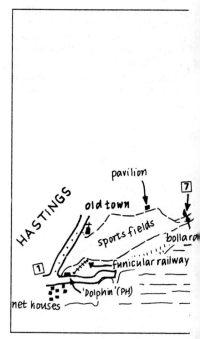

Glen on your left. Path is rather faint at first but later becomes much more defined. Keep straight on, ignoring any paths to left and right. Finally rejoin coastal path walked earlier, at bollard 2.

7 As alternative to retracing steps, turn right uphill along right-hand edge of sports field. At top right-hand corner turn left, passing in front of pavilion. Descend on track to lower section of playing field. At far right-hand corner turn left, and after 50 yards turn right downhill to Hastings Old Town (**b**). From here there are a number of interesting alleys leading back to seafront.

WHAT TO LOOK OUT FOR

(**a**) **Net houses** Tall wooden sheds, a storage place for nets and tackle, built high to save land. Suffered a serious fire in 1961 but were partially reconstructed later. Fish market on Sunday mornings.

(**b**) **Hastings Old Town** The old, fishing part of Hastings, consisting of Main Street, All Saints Street and a warren of alleys on the hillside. The town was one of the original five Cinque Ports that supplied ships for the King's navy in return for privileges in medieval times; the others were Romney, Hythe, Dover and Sandwich (Winchelsea and Rye were added later). In 1854, painter Dante Gabriel Rossetti stayed in what is now the bar of the Cutter Hotel, while his future wife (whom he married in Hastings six years later) lodged in town.

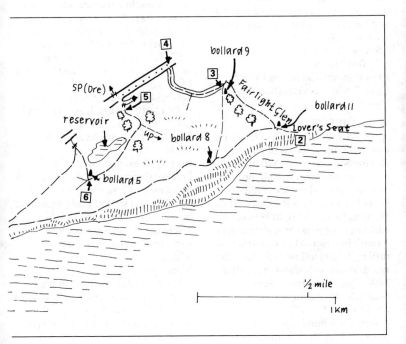

West Hoathly and Selsfield Common

Contributed by Herbert Tout
Recommended by Andrew Bailey,
B Marcusson, Pat and Roy Galbraith,
Deidre Fraser, D Marsh

Pasture with patches of deciduous woodland, just elevated enough to get good views over the Weald and the South Downs. Not all field paths defined, and directions should be followed with care.

Length 6 miles (9.5km), 3 hours. *With extension round lake at end 6½ miles (10.5km), 3 hours*
Difficulty 2
Start West Hoathly, 1 mile off B2028, 7 miles ESE of Crawley. Car parking either in village (not always easy at weekends, especially in summer) or in picnic site car park between village and Vinols Cross Inn (see map; grid reference TQ 367326)
OS maps 1:50,000 187; 1:25,000 TQ 23/33
Refreshments Cat Inn and Vinols Cross Inn at West Hoathly; White Hart Inn at **4**

WALK DIRECTIONS

1 (a) With West Hoathly church on your left, take road out of village, passing bowling green. Where road veers left, continue straight on ¾ mile on lane and track to Philpots School and Farm (well signed). **2** At Philpots Farm turn right between buildings and pass through iron gate. At path junction 30 yards further on turn right, and follow path through woods over footbridge and into field. Follow public footpath signs across fields, aiming just right of Chiddinglye Farm **3** .

With farm buildings on left, proceed along track to major junction of several tracks beside farm. Take track on left downhill, leaving farm buildings on left. Ignore path on right through iron gate after 25 yards,

opposite private drive. After further 100 yards go through iron gate on right (red paint marks). Follow footpath signs to T-junction with track, turn left to emerge on to B2028, with White Hart Inn on left **4** .

Turn right on road for 30 yards, then left on track to Old House Farm. After ¼ mile, just before reaching farm, turn left on path between hedges (FP sign). Follow path over stream, through some trees and across large field to stile close to Great Strudgate Farm. Path across field is not defined but the finger-post on footpath sign gives direction. **5** Do not cross stile on far side of field but turn very sharp right and, taking direction from finger-post, recross field aiming for right-hand side of small wood (obvious cut-off is not a right of way). Follow footpath signs across fields and emerge on to B2028. Turn right along road for 300 yards.

6 Take second turn left, signed Selsfield Common (NT) and Selsfield Place (ignore private road to Old Selsfield). After 170 yards, at entrance to Old Mill Cottage, leave track and take path half left through wood. **7** At path T-junction after 230 yards, turn right through woods to farm. Proceed through farm and along track for ¼ mile to T-junction with road **8** . Turn left for 250 yards, then right into drive of Moatlands and then immediately left (signposted) along path through woods to T-junction with track near Gravetye Manor **9** (b).

For direct route back turn right. Follow track to its end near The Moat. Cross stile and take path straight ahead across fields (finger-posts give direction). Enter wood, cross foot-bridge and at T-junction turn right uphill. Then follow path out of wood and across fields to West Hoathly.

For Gravetye Lower Lake turn left.

Follow track past Stable House. At T-junction of lanes (with entrance to Gravetye Manor on right) cross straight over on to path and follow field edge downhill to gate on left and public footpath on right. Leave public footpath here, make ½ mile circuit of Gravetye Lower Lake and rejoin public footpath at same point. Then continue along field edge, through wood (ignore path joining from right) and across further fields to West Hoathly.

WHAT TO LOOK OUT FOR
(a) **West Hoathly** The half-timbered 15th-century Priest's House is a domestic museum, including furniture and needlework (fee). Elsewhere, some pleasant tile-hung cottages, and a fine manor-house opposite the church.
(b) **Gravetye Manor** Late-Elizabethan manor-house, now a hotel. Horticulturalist William Robinson, author of *The English Flower Garden*, lived here and lavished his skill on the garden (open Tue and Fri).

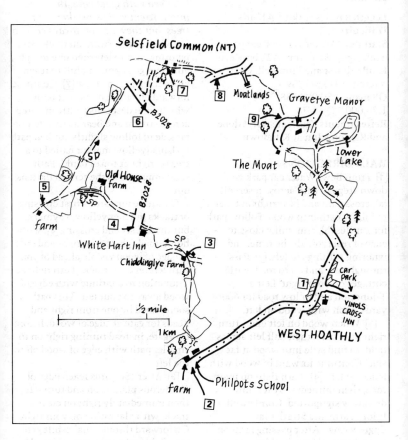

183

Bewl Water and Scotney Castle

Opens with two miles of waterside walking (very unusual for southern England), followed by field and woodland paths to the village of Kilndown. Skirts Scotney Castle, mostly through open parkland, before following a minor road and crossing fields to return. Route-finding tricky between 5 and 10, especially in woodland; follow directions carefully.

Length 8 miles (13km), 4 hours
Difficulty 2–3
Start Bewl Water visitors' car park (fee). Signposted from A21 between Lamberhurst and Flimwell. Grid reference TQ 677339
OS maps 1:50,000 188; 1:25,000 TQ 63/73
Refreshments Kiosk at start; Globe and Rainbow Inn at Kilndown

WALK DIRECTIONS

1 From Bewl Water car park go down steps to dam across reservoir (a); cross dam and bear right at far end to follow path into wood. Follow path for 2 miles (b), remaining close to edge of reservoir all the time, and ignoring turnings to left. 2 Pass through gate and on to road, with cottages on your right. Left at T-junction and follow road for 600 yards, soon with wood on left.

3 When wood on left ends, turn right over stile, then half left across field, to find stile into wood at far side. Continue forward in wood with fence on left. 4 Turn right on main road, then immediately left into driveway signposted 'Combewell Priory Farm and Strathallan Engineering'. After passing farm on your right and farm buildings on left, reach T-junction of tracks 5.

Turn left on sunken grassy track, which soon swings left then right into field. 50 yards beyond right-hand

bend bear quarter right (path indistinct at first) to find clear path into woods. Follow this to junction of tracks with pond on left and earth bank stretching ahead of you. Turn right at this junction and pass through gate into field 6. Go forward over earth-bridge and turn right, to follow with fence on right. Where fence bends away to right, continue and make for gate in corner of field, leading into wood.

NB The route should now be followed with great care; there are intermittent yellow markers on the trees, but they are not always easy to see. Continue forward on track, first ignoring turn to left then one to right; you soon go slightly uphill to reach cross-track at top of rise 7. Continue forward on rather indistinct path which soon descends to stream. Step across stream and bear quarter left on far side to follow slightly sunken path up bank (yellow marker nailed to a tree on right at top of bank). Path soon improves as the terrain flattens out.

Continue forward at first crossing of tracks (further yellow waymark), but then at second crossing 8, with home-made shelter on right and stile at edge of wood visible ahead of you, turn left on clear track. Turn right at T-junction to continue with edge of wood away to your left. This path is soon joined by one from right and heads for gate at edge of wood. Ignore this gate, instead turning right on to smaller path with edge of wood off to the left.

9 After 150 yards reach edge of coniferous plantation and turn left then immediately right on clear track, with plantation on your right. Go forward through makeshift gate into field and head for stile straight ahead 10. Turn left on unsurfaced lane; continue forward on reaching road, on to footpath between gardens. Turn right on road, soon passing

Kilndown church (**c**) and Globe and Rainbow Inn on your right **11**.

Opposite pub turn left on to signposted public footpath. Forward over stile, ignoring cross-track. After 100 yards bear half right into wood, following yellow arrow on to clear track that twists and turns. Cross stile at edge of wood and bear quarter right to footbridge on far side of first field. Head quarter left across second field (**d**), to stile, then forward in third field (**e**) to follow line of trees. **12** Over stile at top of field, and turn left on to road.

After 75 yards turn right over stile (signposted Lamberhurst), and bear half left across field, heading for stile in far corner of field (ignore gate on nearby skyline). Forward over stile into next field (**f**) and head for right-hand end of evenly spaced avenue of trees. Turn left on reaching this, soon dropping downhill with fence and wood on your right. **13** Continue forward when fence bends away to the right, making for stile in far right-hand corner of field. Over stile and into wood, soon emerging on to road (**g**). Cross road and pass

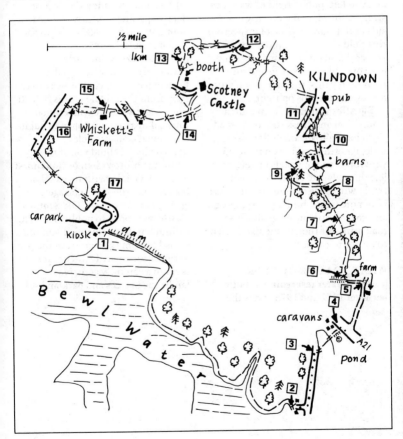

through metal gate into field; bear quarter left following direction of marker arrow (path indistinct) and head for stone bridge at bottom. **14** Turn right on grassy crossing track just before bridge. Pass through 2 gates and farmyard to reach road.

Cross road to take path opposite, first following right-hand edge of field. After 75 yards turn right through gap in hedge, then turn immediately left to proceed with hedge on left. **15** Forward over unmetalled drive, continuing with hedge on left. Where hedge swings away to left, public right of way goes straight ahead; make for stile at far side of field (at the time of inspection this field was heavily ploughed, and it was easier to divert round left-hand edge of field). Cross stile and turn right for 5 yards, then left, soon with fences and gardens on right.

16 After 200 yards, turn right at T-junction and cross stile on to road. Turn left on road, and follow for ¼ mile, ignoring turning on right. 75 yards after end of woods on left, turn left through gate on to clear field track, with edge of field on left. Cross two more fields (bridleway signposts), and go over stile into wood. **17** At road, turn left then immediately right to return to car park.

WHAT TO LOOK OUT FOR
(a) **Bewl Water reservoir** was built between 1972 and 1975 and is the largest in the southern Water Authority's regon. There is a path most of the way round its 15-mile perimeter.

(b) **Chingley Furnace** A collection of ancient buildings on the far side of the reservoir is a fine relic of the ancient Wealden iron industry. Built in 1558, it used water power to drive the bellows and hammers.

(c) **Kilndown church** Early Victorian, but notable for its sumptuous array of fittings and decorations, all aiming to reproduce (if not surpass) their medieval counterparts.

(d) The **'new' Scotney Castle** (not open to public) is clearly visible to your left. Built in 1837–1844 in the Tudor style, by Salvin.

(e) **Finchcocks** A fine early 18th-century three-storeyed house built of red brick, visible away to the right from the middle of this field. It houses an extensive collection of musical instruments (open to public; occasional concerts held).

(f) If you look behind you at this point, the hilltop town of **Goudhurst** is clearly visible, with its weather-boarded and tile-hung cottages.

(g) The entrance to the **Old Scotney Castle** (NT; open to public; fee) is just to your left down this road; not much is visible from the route, but the part 14th-century, part 17th-century ruin is set in a carefully contrived landscape of trees and parkland.

Fairwarp and theAshdown Forest

Heathland, some mixed woodland and a small village, then a short ascent to the summit of Camp Hill before a long, gentle descent, part over heath and farmland, part through woodland. Finishes with a short stretch of heathland on way back into Nutley and the main road. Going is mostly easy, but route-finding quite complicated on intricate network of heath and forest tracks (follow directions carefully). Central section follows Wealdway.

Length 9 miles (14.5km) 4½ hours
Difficulty 3
Start Nutley church, in centre of village, on A22 between East Grinstead and Uckfield
OS maps 1:50,000 187 and 188, or 198 and 188; 1:25,000 TQ 42/52 and TQ 43/53

WALK DIRECTIONS

1 With Nutley church behind you, turn right through centre of village. Take first turning on left (Clockhouse Lane) and, when tarmac road turns left into housing estate, continue forward on unmetalled track, keeping left after 50 yards to pass between scattered houses. Where tarmac starts again, just after house called Forest Edge, fork left on clear paths with marker post on left. Keep left where major track joins from right, and fork left 50 yards further on. Path then continues downhill to cross stream **2**.

Continue forward up rise beyond. Later passing under hurdles and continuing to farm driveway (to Upper Misbourne Farm) **3**. Cross driveway and follow fence on right. Where fence ends, pick up major track which merges from left. 120 yards beyond, where main track swings half right, turn half left on to heath track (indistinct at first, but soon become clear), crossing stream and rising up hill beyond.

Continue forward over second stream (**a**) and on to broad track straight ahead. Pass over a cross-track to reach gravel drive leading to house (Spring Garden) **4**.

Do not follow drive by fork left on unmade track, and turn right on broad cross-track after ¼ mile, soon crossing gravel drive. (Tower of Fairwarp church is soon visible on left). After about ⅓ mile turn left at obvious fork to reach road **5**. Turn left on road and turn left again on major road. Then turn immediately right after bus shelter, into lane signposted 'Fairwarp: narrow road'. Follow road through village (Foresters Arms is on left). ½ mile beyond end of village where road swings right (and by entrance to Oldlands Hall), turn left on minor road.

(For next 2½ miles this route follows Wealdway long-distance path, marked by short wooden posts with notches cut in the top to show the direction of the path.) **6** 50 yards beyond road junction, turn half left between hedges, keeping close to hedge on right where they diverge. Beyond end of hedge, continue half left on well-defined path that winds over heathland. Continue forward over cross-track, with footbridge on left. **7** 300 yards further on, turn right on narrow path uphill (marker post 5 yards to right of main track). Turn left on broad track for 150 yards, then fork right (marker post) crossing metalled track after a further 200 yards. Turn left on second metalled track at the bottom **8**.

When metalled track swings right into cottage grounds, continue forward on grassy path with hedge on right, soon crossing footbridge into wood. At end of wood, where maintrack swings half left, turn half right on clear narrow path heading up hill through bracken. Cross broad

187

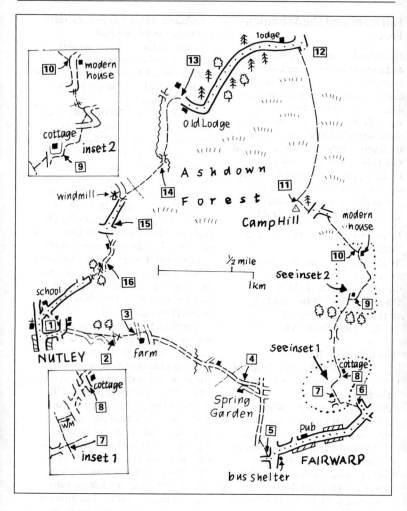

gravel track and continue forward with hedge and cottage garden on left.
9 Keep left at corner of hedge and turn right opposite cottage. keep forward over cross-track, and turn left on to gravel track 50 yards further on. This very soon bears right: turn sharp left here, then turn right after 10 yards to cross stile (yellow marker). Proceed alongside hedge on left, then left over further stile after 20 yards. Turn right on to tarmac track.

10 Where this swings right, just beyond modern house, continue half left across grassy heath to reach road. Turn left on road, to reach junction after 20 yards. Continue straight ahead on path to right of signpost. This soon brings you to isolated clump of trees (Camp Hill) **11**. Turn right just beyond bench to follow broad track which heads straight across heath, keeping roughly parallel to main road 300–400 yard away on right. Continue on this for 1 mile avoiding side tracks to reach road just by driveway to Old Lodge **12**. Turn sharp left onto Old Lodge driveway. and follow tarmac drive for ¾ mile. **13** After passing large gabled stone house (Old Lodge) continue on track between hedges. Just before track crosses stone footbridge, turn left on signposted footpath, passing between hedge and stream. At end of hedge, turn half left on clear path through wood. Turn left after crossing footbridge and continue forward through gate, ignoring paths to left. **14** At fork 35 yards from gate bear right. Path soon rises out of wood and onto heath. Continue forward uphill, ignoring all cross-tracks, then enter a narrow path in trees. Turn left over stile at end of track, by restored windmill (**b**). Follow track to road **15**.

Cross road and take path on edge of heath straight ahead; at track after 150 yards turn right, and proceed with heath on your left and houses on right. Continue on track downhill, passing a small isolated house (Brackendale). **16** Just beyond house, where track swings left, turn right following hedge on right to pass round wooden hurdle and into wood. Pass through gate at end of wood and continue forward on unmade road, which soon brings you back to the centre of Nutley.

WHAT TO LOOK OUT FOR
(**a**) A small stone walled enclosure known as **the Airmen's Grave**, containing a memorial to six airmen whose plane crashed at the spot in 1941, is reached by taking a left-hand path at the second stream and walking uphill for about 200 yards.
(**b**) **Nutley windmill** (open to public; fee). The oldest working windmill in Sussex, restored by local enthusiasts after 65 years of disuse.

189

Mad Jack Fuller's monument and Bateman's

Leads from Burwash to a grassy hillside looking over a Wealden landscape of gentle pasture, small ponds and woods, including some coniferous plantations; one fine view near Brightling. One section of road-walking (the forest path which could have avoided some of this was closed at time of writing because of felling operations). Route-finding quite involved, with undefined routes across fields and networks of forest tracks.

Length 9 miles (14.5km), 4½ hours
Difficulty 3
Start Burwash, on A265 between Heathfield and Hawkhurst, and 15 miles S of Tunbridge Wells. Free car park in village centre.
OS maps 1:50,000 199; 1:25,000 TQ 62/72
Refreshments Pubs and tea-rooms in Burwash; Fuller's Arms (shortly before Brightling); tea-room at Bateman's, when house is open

WALK DIRECTIONS

1 (**a**) From car park return to village street, turn right and follow to church, where pass through gate into churchyard. Keep right of church porch then fork left 30 yards later to reach small gate at end of churchyard. Follow left edge of first field to gate ahead, beyond which bear quarter right in second field, slightly downhill; stile soon becomes visible. Beyond stile proceed downhill for 25 yards, then left over stile to enter third field **2** .

Follow left edge to gate 30 yards to right of left-hand corner (just to right of pond which is beyond hedge). Turn right beyond gate, and bear diagonally down fourth field for gate in bottom (left) corner, then half left in fifth field to (waymarked) stile in hedgerow on left. In sixth field head

up half right to corner of woodland fence on skyline, then continue direction to stile **3** . Bear diagonally across seventh field to stile in bottom left corner, then proceed along left edge of eighth field to stile/footbridge at end. Beyond footbridge bear half left across ninth field making for gate at highest point of field. Continue same direction (half left) across tenth field to gate/stile (house visible ahead), beyond which turn right in eleventh field, along right edge.

4 At the top of field join tarmac farm road, turn right along it, follow ½ mile. Turn right at road, then after 150 yards left on to farm road signed Socknersh Manor. **5** 600 yards later reach manor buildings (signs indicate area private except for bridleway) and keep forward until level with manor itself (**b**), then follow road as it bends right. This leads into woods, past lake, then later past another house and finally reaches B-road **6** .

Turn right along road (**c**). Pass pub at next crossroads, then 600 yards later, where road bends markedly left, and just before metal posts in verge, pass through kissing-gate on your right, then turn left uphill, with hedge on left. **7** Where hedge veers left bear half right, towards nearest electricity pole, to reach fence, along which turn left, uphill. At end of field, cross stile on right (**d**), and cross the paddock diagonally to reach gate in front of house. Turn right on track, to reach road at Brightling (**e**) **8** . Turn right on road (**f**).

After ½ miles, and 100 yards before house ahead, take the signposted bridleway on the right (undefined), heading across field at 90 degrees to road, roughly bisecting the distance between two electricity poles. **9** Pass into woodland at corner of field, to find clear path. **10** After ½ mile pass under aerial ropeway and continue direction, soon with fence on left, then 200 yards later, at bottom of slope, cross stile on left. Path (indistinct) descends, bending slightly right after 100 yards, to stile and stream at bottom of valley. Beyond stream follow left edge of field uphill, until taking stile on left at end of field and at top of slope. Path beyond it leads to road **11**.

Turn right on road, then after 100 yards take gate on left into forest. Immediately fork left, continue over cross-track after 130 yards and 130 yards later turn right at T-junction, then sharp left 30 yards later. Follow to next T-junction at which **12** turn left. Track bends right; 50 yards after it bends left, turn right. Track bends left after 150 yards, soon dips to cross stream and leads up to junction of tracks **13**.

Keep forward on wide track leading slightly uphill. After 400 yards reach

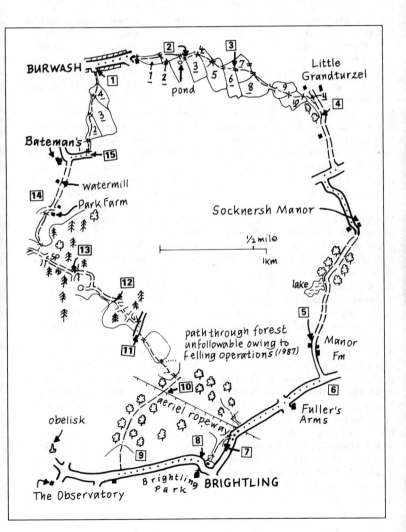

complex of tracks by signpost; turn 90 degrees right on to narrow track leading down to gate at end of forest. Beyond it descend by left edge of field and **14**, just before three-gabled farm at bottom, take gate on left, then turn right on farm road. Ignore right by farm, and continue, soon past oast-house (**g**) and then to reach corner of road by Bateman's (**h**).

Turn right, opposite front of Bateman's, on road. **15** After 300 yards take signposted gate/stile on left; follow right edge of first field to stile, then bear quarter right in the second field, aiming for right-hand corner of woodland, then proceed forward to stile in right-hand corner.

Keep forward along left edge of third field and maintain the same direction across fourth field, heading for nearest (lone) tree, in hedgerow ahead. Do not cross hedgerow but turn left (still in fourth field), with hedge on right, to stile at top, then proceed to car park.

WHAT TO LOOK OUT FOR

(**a**) **Burwash** Handsome village with smart and well-preserved cottages, including Rampyndene House (1699). At its eastern end the Norman church of St Bartholomew.

(**b**) **Socknersh Manor** (not open to public) Brick and timber-frame, early 17th-century; described by Pevsner as 'the perfect Christmas card subject'.

(**c**) The road crosses over an **aerial ropeway**, still in use serving the British Gypsum Mines, ¾ mile to the right. The ropeway leads to the main Hastings railway line.

(**d**) At the top of the rise, turn round for a **view** of the Weald.

(**e**) **Brightling** Opposite the church is the former Fuller's Arms. The owner, 'Mad Jack' Fuller of Brightling Park (the manor just behind the church)

agreed to move the pub to its present position out of sight of the church, on condition that the rector allow him to build his own mausoleum in the churchyard. This he built in 1810 in the form of a colossal pyramid, and allegedly he is seated inside, wearing a top-hat and holding a bottle of claret. Fuller was an MP as well as a landowner, and saved Bodiam Castle from possible demolition by purchasing it.

(**f**) From the road is a view of Mad Jack Fuller's **obelisk**, one of his many follies, possibly built in imitation of Cleopatra's Needle which had been presented to Britain to mark the coronation of George IV. If, instead of turning off into the field, you continue along the road for 150 yards, Fuller's 'Observatory' comes into view; this rotunda was built by Robert Smirke for the observing not of stars but of Fuller himself – his servants were to watch from here for his carriage from Westminster, so that food, drink, slippers and so on would be ready on his arrival at the house.

(**g**) Behind the old oast-house on the left is a restored **water mill**, part of Bateman's (see below); flour is still ground in it and is on sale. Close to it is one of the oldest working water-driven turbines, installed by Rudyard Kipling to provide Bateman's with electricity.

(**h**) **Bateman's** (NT; open to public; fee) Home of Rudyard Kipling between 1902 and 1936, with the writer's rooms, including his study, left as they were then, and his 1928 Rolls-Royce still in the garage. Among the works he wrote here were *Puck of Pook's Hill* and *Rewards and Fairies*, both set in the area around Burwash. The house itself was built in 1634.

CENTRAL ENGLAND

Berkshire, Buckinghamshire, Cheshire, Derbyshire,
Gloucestershire, Hereford & Worcester, Oxfordshire,
Shropshire, Staffordshire, Warwickshire

This large region stretches from the western fringes of London to the
Welsh border, and, very roughly, from the M4 to the fringes of the
Peak District and the River Mersey. Cheshire (excluding those parts of
the county in the Peak District) and North Shropshire are of
predominantly lowland scenery, but enhanced by some very pretty
black and white villages, and by the small, abrupt Peckforton Hills,
Grinshill and Kerridge Hill, which give outstanding views. South
Shropshire is more obviously a walker's landscape, giving well-varied
hill walks. The two main ranges are the Long Mynd/Stiperstones ridge
and the rather mellower hills further east, including Caer Caradoc and
Wenlock Edge. The county of Hereford and Worcester harbours some
first-rate scenery, especially round the edges of the old county of
Herefordshire. To the east is the moorland ridge of the Malverns
which looks enormous until you are close up to it; to the south the
spectacular wooded Wye Valley Gorge; to the west the imposing
semi-uplands of the Welsh border; and to the north some unspoilt and
attractive small hills between Leominster and Ludlow. The Hereford
plain (which lies in between all these) has some charming black and
white villages. What was Worcestershire has rather less material for
good walks; the Abberley Hills and the small hills (Lickey and Clent)
near Birmingham are exceptions.

The Cotswolds is the name given to the area roughly bounded by
Stratford-on-Avon, Cheltenham, Bath, Witney and Banbury, though
precise definitions of its extent differ. Most of the best walks are on
the Cotswold escarpment, the steep western edge of the area,
rewarding not just for the views westwards towards Wales but for its
varied scenery, characterised by bold grassy slopes and steep, narrow
valleys. The scarp is followed for most of its length by a long-distance
path, the Cotswold Way. The Stroud Valley is one of the deepest
valleys in the Cotswolds and provides some pleasant walking on its
wooded and grassy hillsides. But elsewhere the Cotswolds are not well
endowed with good walks: much of the area is now dominated by
featureless expanses of farmland (including a lot of improved arable),

although there are occasional pockets of lusher scenery, such as near Chedworth.

The south-eastern corner of the region is taken up by the Chilterns and the Thames Valley. The chalk downlands of the Chilterns are at their most dramatic in the steep rough grazing slopes of the escarpments (for instance Coombe Hill), from which there are views across the vast plains of the South Midlands. Deeper in are secretive valleys, large beech woods, fine country houses and many well-groomed old world villages with pleasant pubs. Public rights of way seem to be in good shape, though bridleways inevitably get churned up by horses and are very sticky after rain. The Thames Valley has almost classical river scenery, and where its hinterland has escaped development there is lush lowland scenery at the west ends of the Chilterns, making for excellent round walks.

To the north and west of the region is the region's one National Park, the Peak District, an area of varied and unspoilt scenery virtually encircled by large industrial towns. It has two distinct landscapes, the White Peak and the Dark Peak. The first, which fills most of the southern half of the Park, gets its name from grey limestone; it consists of a high and empty tableland of dry-stone walled pasture fields, interrupted by deep, narrow valleys. Of the latter, Dove Dale is the most spectacular and though normally very crowded, deserves to be seen. The Dark Peak takes up most of the northern part of the Park. This is the landscape of millstone grit, a dark rock which has resulted in grim and rather austere rounded hills (many of them tough to walk over, requiring a compass and an appetite for bog-leaping). The highest point of the Park is Kinder Scout (2,038ft), a large area of blanket bog; it can be a nasty surprise for anyone walking the Pennine Way, which begins at nearby Edale. Many of the Dark Peak's valleys have been flooded by reservoirs, some quite attractive, such as Ladybower. Overall the Peak District has something to offer most walkers, though it doesn't have any really dramatic mountain scenery. It has three stately homes – the parklands of two of which have provided good round walks featured in this book. There are pleasant stone villages, a few show-caves (near Castleton), wild flowers in the White Peak, and excellently maintained footpaths.

BERKSHIRE

Culham Court and Henley Regatta course

Contributed by Peter Nevell
Recommended by Ian Wilson,
B A White

Follows the world-famous regatta course along the banks of a very beautiful stretch of the Thames, which though seen from the bridge at the start is reserved for the second half of the walk. Woodland and unspoilt farmland in the first half. Most paths well defined; route-finding quite easy.

Length 7 miles (11km), 3½ hours
Difficulty 2
Start Bridge at Henley-on-Thames
OS maps 1:50,000 175;
1:25,000 SU 68/78
Refreshments Full range in Henley;
Five Horseshoes (after point [2]);
Flower Pot Hotel, Aston

WALK DIRECTIONS

[1] (a) From Henley Bridge walk along left-hand footway of A423 over bridge (away from Henley), passing the Little Angel Inn and then allotments below on left, to end of footway; here turn left up flight of steps into the woodland. Shortly cross over track and continue climbing path between iron railings. [2] At wire-fenced plantation ahead bear right, cross over track and follow well-defined woodland path (b), shortly bearing left to reach house on left with long wooden fence. Turn left along road for about 20 yards, then [3] turn right through small wooden gate across field to stile, and across second field to further stile. Follow enclosed path into well-defined winding woodland path.

[4] On reaching white gate turn left to follow track and then grass path with fence on left and hedge on right, to arrive at road (take care). Turn right

along Aston Lane to junction with main road (A423); here turn immediately left over stile into field and follow edge of field with conifers and houses on right. [5] At end of houses, turn left into track along edge of field with large trees and then a hedge on right. Just before copse ahead, turn right through gap in hedge and continue along edge of next field with hedge on left, and then fence on left after right turn, to reach stile at tarmac farm road [6].

Turn left along road and shortly after fork left at small clump of fenced trees; at bottom of dip in drive up to Culham Court (c) turn sharp right along gravel track. [7] Just before overhead wires converge, turn sharp left into field at stile adjacent to metal gate and continue along edge of field with fence on right. At end of fence, go through middle of field to stile just to right of railings around Culham Court (d), then, keeping iron railings on left, pass through two iron gates and over another stile.

Bear immediately right through middle of long narrow field to iron gate just to left of distant farm building, then follow tarmac track ahead down to road [8]. Turn right at T-junction. At centre of Aston village, where road bends left, take minor cul-de-sac down to river [9]. Turn left along towpath, passing Hambleden Lock (e); the Greenlands estate, seen on opposite bank (f); Temple Island (g); and Fawley Court, also opposite, to return, along regatta course (h), to Henley.

WHAT TO LOOK OUT FOR

(a) **Henley** has a strong flavour of Edwardian elegance and comfort, and repays exploration. The first Oxford and Cambridge Boat Race was rowed here in 1829 (Oxford won). (b) This is a particularly rewarding

195

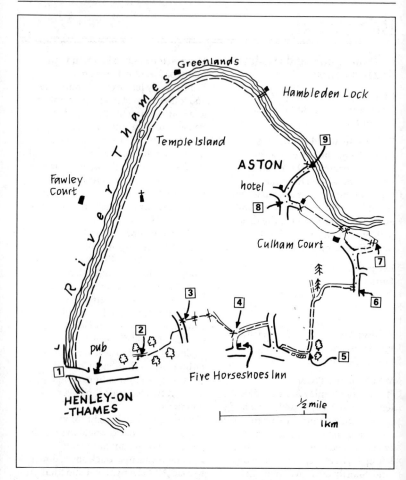

walk in **spring**, in bluebell time: they are here in great numbers.

(**c**) **Culham Court** (1770-1) Pleasing example of neo-classical style.

(**d**) The grass to either side of this stretch of path is full of daffodils in season.

(**e**) A short detour across the river at Hambleden Lock is recommended; attractive weather-boarded watermill and mill house on opposite bank.

(**f**) **Greenlands** Victorian mansion in the Italian style, formerly the home of

Viscount Hambleden.

(**g**) **The Temple** was designed by James Wyatt to improve the view from Fawley Court, which he classicised in 1771. The Court has gardens by Capability Brown.

(**h**) **Henley Royal Regatta** was established in 1839 as 'a source of amusement and gratification to the neighbourhood and the public in general'. It acquired the 'Royal' from the Prince Consort's patronage in 1851.

Combe Wood and Inkpen Hill

*Contributed by Chris John
Recommended by R K Barnett,
Mr and Mrs D W Power, Barry
Hendricksen, J F M Kaye*

**Through the game reserve of Combe
Wood (keep dogs on a lead) then, after
a short stretch on tarmac lanes and
farm tracks, reaches the edge of the
chalk escarpment with views over
the South Midlands. Finishes off with
a descent over rolling downland to
Combe. A short section of road-
walking. All tracks well defined;
route-finding easy.**

Length *Full walk* 7½ miles (12km),
3 hours
Shorter walk omitting Buttermere
5½ miles (9km), 2 hours
Difficulty 2
Start Church at Combe village,
between Inkpen and Netherton. Park
by church. Grid reference SU 368607
OS maps 1:50,000 174; 1:25,000
SU 25/35 and SU 26/36

WALK DIRECTIONS

1 Take track up past church (**a**). At
top (½ mile) continue forward as
signposted at crossing of tracks, then
drop down into Combe Wood. Avoid
side turns (mostly marked private) and
follow for another mile to reach
junction of tracks at bottom, with
signposts pointing left and right 2.
Turn right, following track along
bottom of valley. After 500 yards this
leaves woods 3.

For shorter walk turn right uphill,
with woodland fence on right. 3/1
After ¾ mile cross stile. Continue
forward, on track bending round left
to reach a prominent corner of
woodland where footpath sign points
the way you have come. Keep right,
at corner, following right edge of
field. 3/2 At break in hedge on
right, and as indicated by marker
arrow, change to other side of hedge.
Follow until reaching junction of

tracks with bridleway signpost pointing the way you have come. This is
point 8. Turn right to continue.

For full walk fork quarter right,
following track along valley, soon
joined by woods on left. 4 After ½
mile, where woods end on left, reach
junction of tracks and turn left on
track between fences. Follow into
hamlet of Buttermere to reach
T-junction with phone box on right
in hamlet 5. Turn right on road,
avoid immediate left turn, but follow
road 500 yards to cottages 6.

Turn right here, down 'no through
road' (road sign). At end, 30 yards
beyond last house, take left fork,
following track on to escarpment. 7
At cross-track after 200 yards turn
right. After 1½ miles reach crossing
of tracks 8. With track marked
bridleway on your right, continue
forward (both tracks ahead come
round to same point a little further
on). Follow track (**b**), past Combe
Gibbet (**c**) and down to road 9. Cross
road, continue through car park and
pick up track at far side signposted
'Wayfarers Walk, Emsworth 70'. This
leads over Walbury Hill (**d**); after ¾
mile reaches corner of road 10.

Turn sharp right to take track
between gateposts (just opposite left
bend in road), across middle of field
and descending (village of Combe
visible below). Where hawthorn
bushes appear on left, drop down into
well defined track between them and
descend to Combe, avoiding left turn
after 150 yards 11. Track becomes
tarmac lane; continue forward past
cottages, avoiding left turn by
thatched cottage to reach Y-junction
of lanes 12. Turn left along road
(signposted Linkenholt and Netherton) and follow as far as hairpin bend
just below church.

WHAT TO LOOK OUT FOR

(**a**) Behind the 13th-century church is
Manor Farm, an 18th-century

rebuilding of an older house in which Charles II stayed, en route to Marlborough. A pretty gazebo in the garden is dated 1667 and is visible from the walk.

(b) **View** Over the Kennet Valley. N to Lambourn Downs; NE to hills of the Thames Valley, E of Newbury and Greenham Common airfield.

(c) **Combe Gibbet** Replica of earlier gibbets that have been chopped down by anti-capital punishment demonstrators and blown over by the wind. Probably sited deliberately within view of the travellers along this track, for whom the bodies which hanged from it acted as a warning. It stands on a 200ft-long prehistoric burial mound.

(d) **Walbury Hill** At 974ft the highest point in Berkshire, encircled by the just-discernible ramparts of Walbury Camp, which covers an 82-acre site, the largest hillfort in Berkshire.

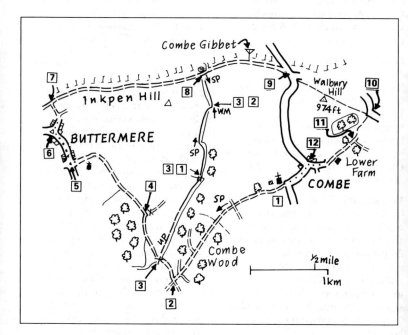

BUCKINGHAMSHIRE

Bradenham and West Wycombe

Recommended by A Callender

Tracks through Chiltern beech woods lead from a secluded village to an exceptionally fine (albeit more discovered) one. Care needed with busy main roads. Waymarks make route-finding quite easy.

Length 3½ miles (5.5km), 1½ hours
Difficulty 1–2
Start Bradenham, just off A4010, 1½ miles N of roundabout with A40 and 3½ miles NW of High Wycombe. Park by village green at end nearest church. Grid reference SU 827971
OS maps 1:50,000 165 and 175; 1:25,000 SU 89/99
Refreshments Pub at Bradenham; three pubs at West Wycombe

WALK DIRECTIONS

1 (**a**) Standing with church behind you and road on right, turn left across green to pavilion, at which turn left on gravel track which runs alongside boundary wall of Bradenham Manor. After 200 yards, at corner of wall on left and immediately before footpath/bridleway sign, turn right uphill on narrow woodland path initially just inside edge of woods (avoid wider track half right actually next to signpost). This path is waymarked throughout – look for white painted arrows on trees ahead. After 200 yards it forks left further into woods, and 200 yards later continues forward at crossing of tracks in hollow.

2 200 yards after this, avoid waymarked stile up on left and follow path ahead for another ½ mile as it eventually descends, to leave woods by stile **3**. Bear straight down/half left, cross railway with care, then continue same direction to cross road and

proceed (still half left) across large field. In far left-hand corner emerge by gate on to tarmac lane and turn left into West Wycombe village (**b**). Turn right at main road through village.

4 Turn sharp right on tarmac lane just after last house on right in village, opposite entrance to West Wycombe Park (avoid road signed to Bledlow Ridge) and follow up as far as school, where lane bends right. Here continue straight uphill on grassland (no path), to turn right on meeting chalky cross-track by trees. After climbing on this a little further, West Wycombe church (**c**) and mausoleum (**d**) are visible on left. Turn left uphill to pass around left side of them and leave by gate at other side of churchyard **5**.

Continue forward on wide track which soon becomes surfaced; just after it bends right take signposted footpath on left. This too is way-marked with white arrows: avoid any paths on left and continue forward at cross-track by 'Keep your dog on a lead' sign, after ¾ mile. **6** ½ mile beyond this pass cottage. Immediately after, turn right on footpath leading steeply downhill, initially with fence on right, soon leaving woods by stile. Descend close to right edge of field, to reach gate in corner. Cross railway, proceed across next field to main road and back to Bradenham.

WHAT TO LOOK OUT FOR

(**a**) **Bradenham** At the top of the sloping NT-owned village green stands an imposing brick-fronted manor house, *c.*1670, with the Victorianised church of St Botolph beside.
(**b**) **West Wycombe** Attractive village with a main street of predominantly 17th- and 18th-century cottages, among them Church Loft (with clock),

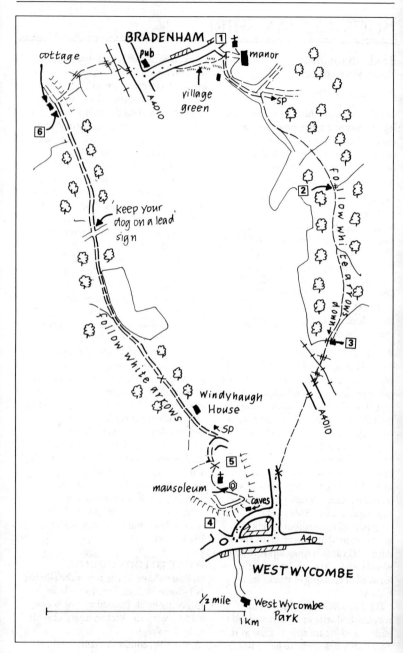

thought to have been built by monks of Bisham Priory in 1417 for use as a guest-house. The village was bought by the Royal Society of Arts, in order to save the place from road-widening, and was handed over to the NT in 1934. S of the road is the Palladian mansion of West Wycombe Park (NT; open to public; fee), built for Sir John Dashwood in 1765 in the style of Robert Adam, and containing fine painted ceilings; is its superb park, landscaped by Repton (1803), has a number of classical temples. On the hillside immediately behind the main street is the grand 18th-century entrance to the man-made West Wycombe caves (open to public; fee), created in 1750–2 by Sir Francis Dashwood and probably used by him for his Hell Fire Club, a brother-hood set up for whoring, drinking and black magic rituals for one or two weeks of the year.

(c) **Mausoleum** Gigantic, hexagonal, roofless structure (which you can't enter, only peer into), built 1763–4 to a design by John Bastard (architect of most of Blandford Forum, Dorset, which was rebuilt in the 18th century). Contains memorials to the Dashwood, Despencer and other families.

(d) **Church of St Lawrence** Originally medieval, but re-modelled in the 18th century. Situated well above West Wycombe, as it used to be the parish church of Haveringdon (which has since disappeared). It is capped by a hollow ball covered with gold leaf, another meeting-place for Sir Francis Dashwood's club.

Hampden House and Coombe Hill

Contributed by Alastair Macgeorge
Recommended by Ian Wilson,
F C Mattinson

Rural countryside within easy access of West London, through varied farmland and mixed woods and past three remote country pubs. A good climax to the walk at Coombe Hill. Take care with directions from ⑥ to ⑦ and from ⑩ to ⑪.

Length 10 miles (16km), 5 hours
Difficulty 3
Start Ellesborough, on B4010, 2 miles W of Wendover. Roadside parking. Grid reference SP 836067
By train Wendover. Turn right out of station and follow road 200 yards to T-junction. Turn right and follow road over railway. After 400 yards, where road bends right, take footpath ahead leading up to Coombe Hill. After ¾ mile reach monument on Coombe Hill and start walk at ⑮
OS maps 1:50,000 165; 1:25,000 SP 80/90
Refreshments Plough Inn, Lower Cadsden; Rising Sun at Little Hampden (no walking boots allowed inside); The Fox, Dunsmere

WALK DIRECTIONS

① With Ellesborough church behind you, turn right on B4010 for 30 yards, passing bus-stop, then turn left over stile on footpath running across field. Pass into next field by stile and bear quarter right uphill, skirting hill which is on left and picking up well-defined path after 200 yards leading into woods by stile, then soon out of woods. ② After 200 yards, path enters second woodland, and 200 yards into wood reaches gravel track. Cross gravel track and pass over stile/gate opposite leading into field. Turn half right across field (no path) to reach stile (not the one already in view) on far side with

acorn marker (denoting Ridgeway Path). Cross stile and continue on well-defined Ridgeway Path, forking left after 250 yards.

③ After ¼ mile cross stile to reach sunken trackway. Turn right downhill for 20 yards, then left on narrow path which leads down to Lower Cadsden. Turn left along road and follow to Plough Inn, just after which ④ leave road (which bends left) for track straight ahead; ignore Ridgeway, which is sharper right. After 300 yards take middle of three paths (waymarked with arrow), to cross hurdle and immediately ascend slope. After 400 yards cross stile and continue straight on, now having entered Hampden estate. Follow marker arrows.

⑤ ½ mile later, path veers left to leave woods by gate, emerging on tarmac drive opposite wooden cottages by Solinger Farm. Turn right on drive and after 200 yards, where drive veers left, turn right through gate. Turn left immediately after gate, on path, following marker arrows. ⑥ After 400 yards turn half right where track comes in obliquely from left, and 150 yards later avoid dropping down to well-marked track on right but maintain same direction, still following marker arrows. After 150 yards cross cart-track and 30 yards later cross stile ⑦.

Turn left after stile on straight path alongside line of ancient woodland on left (Grim's Ditch (**a**)), soon emerging from wood to follow left edge of field. After ½ mile turn left through gate heading towards Hampden House (**b**), and pass through second gate, leading on to tarmac lane. Follow lane, passing church and leaving estate 300 yards later by gatehouse ⑧. Immediately after gatehouse, by road junction, turn left over stile to cross field (path undefined) to stile. In second field continue same direction heading for gate at bottom left-hand

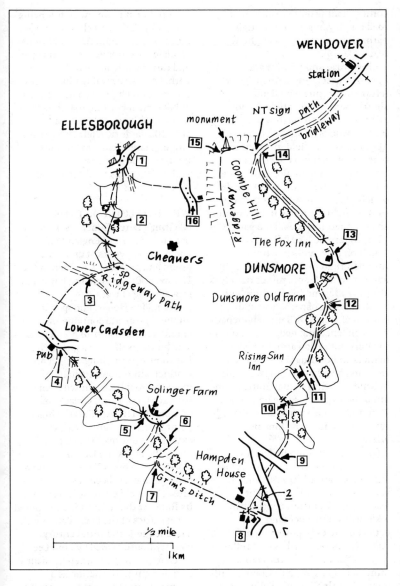

If you have a walk to suggest for any subsequent edition of the Holiday
Which? Good Walks Guide, *please send it to us. We need a rough sketch map
and a brief description of the walk's attractions. Directions are not necessary.
All walks must be in Great Britain, Northern Ireland, the Isle of Man or the
Channel Islands and should fit the criteria given in the Introduction
(see page 7). Please write to:* Holiday Which? Good Walks Guide, Consumers'
Association, 14 Buckingham Street, London WC2N 6DS.

corner, leading on to road. Left on road for 20 yards, then turn right on path, alongside hedge on right, to reach road 9.

Cross road and follow path opposite, ascending with hedge on left then entering woodland on left shortly before end of field. Follow arrow markers through woods, leaving woods by stile on other side 10. Emerge into field, turn left to bottom (near) left-hand corner of field, and turn right alongside hedge for 80 yards. Reaching stile in hedge on left, do not cross it, but turn right to cross field. At top of field continue ahead and follow woodland path 200 yards to tarmac lane 11.

Left on lane, and after 100 yards turn half right on bridleway (roughly opposite pub). Ignore minor right fork after ¼ mile, and ½ mile from pub reach crossing of paths/tracks at bottom of slope 12. Turn left on path between fence and hedge, and follow to Dunsmore Old Farm. Just before main farm buildings cross stile on right and bear half left to two fields by stiles. In third field maintain same direction to gate leading on to road. Turn right on road, and after 50 yards turn left, signposted Dunsmore village.

13 After passing The Fox Inn continue ahead on bridleway. Avoid stile on left after 100 yards and, 50 yards later, avoid gate on right leading into field, but continue over wide stile on to woodland path between fences 14. After ¾ mile reach T-junction with wide bridle-way at edge of woods, turn left and immediately right on to Coombe Hill (marked with NT sign). Follow path to Coombe Hill monument (c) 15.

Turn left at monument, following Ridgeway Path with slope immed-iately on your right. After 400 yards reach fence crossing direction of path, and turn right to leave Ridgeway Path. Drop sharply downhill, follow-ing fence on left, and continue ahead at NT sign at bottom, to follow track to road 16. Turn right on road, and after 100 yards turn left on footpath, crossing large field. On far side of field, cross stile and turn right. Follow 200 yards to Ellesborough village.

WHAT TO LOOK OUT FOR

(a) **Grim's Ditch** Generic Saxon term used in this part of England for ancient earthworks of unknown origin and purpose. The ditch in the Hampden Estate is marked by a long straight line of trees.

(b) **Hampden House** (not open to public) The estate contains an extensive and beautiful beech forest. The house itself, now a girls' school, has some eye-catching 18th-century Gothick alterations. Its hall has a medieval roof transplanted from a barn at Manor Farm, Great Kimble.

(c) **Coombe Hill** At 852ft the highest point in the Chilterns, with an extensive view over the Oxfordshire plain, the Berkshire Downs and the Cotswolds. This NT-owned stretch of downland has been designated a Site of Special Scientific Interest for its **flora**. At the summit is a memorial to casualties of the Boer War. ¾ mile S is Chequers, the 16th-century country house owned by Lord Lee of Fareham until 1921, when he made it over as a gift to the nation as a country house for prime ministers.

CHESHIRE

Beeston Castle and the Peckforton Hills

Contributed by Brian Marsden
Recommended by Dr J Morley

The isolated Peckforton Hills rise out of the Cheshire plain to culminate in high crags topped by ruined Beeston Castle. Outward route crosses pastureland with distant views of castle; return is through parkland and coniferous and deciduous woodland, with one modest ascent. Easy going underfoot, but outward route is over a complicated series of field paths (some undefined) – follow directions carefully; return route easy to find, the last part on well-marked tracks

Length 6 miles (9.5km), 3 hours
Difficulty 2
Start Pheasant Inn, Higher Burwardsley, 10 miles SE of Chester. From centre of Burwardsley village, signposted Higher Burwardsley. This leads to crossroads and phone box; Pheasant Inn is on left. Grid reference SJ 523565
OS maps 1:50,000 117; 1:25,000 SJ 45/55
Refreshments Pheasant Inn (bar and bistro; children allowed in part of pub) and Cheshire Candle Factory (restaurant), both in Higher Burwardsley; occasionally, refreshment caravan in Beeston Castle car park

WALK DIRECTIONS

1 With Pheasant Inn behind you, turn left to reach crossroads and turn right on road downhill. After 250 yards turn right on metalled farm track signposted Outlanes Farm. Just before farm turn right over stile in hedge (yellow waymark) and follow left edge of first field. Left over stile just beyond large metal barn, and forward into second field with wood on right.

Over bridge with two stiles, then half right uphill to corner of third field **2**. Half left in fourth field, following sign to Tattenhall Lanes (path undefined, but heads towards farm, aiming for stile to left of metal gate). Over stile, then half right to stile on right side of fifth field. Turn right again in sixth field, proceeding alongside hedge on right to reach two stiles and bridge in corner. Half right after second stile, to cross further stile into wood **3**.

Turn left over stile, proceeding along side of seventh field, with edge of wood on your right. Half right over next stile to find stile on right-hand side of eighth field. Over this stile into copse, then forward following yellow way-markings to emerge at edge of large (ninth) field. Half left in this field heading for post bearing yellow waymarking; pass this and continue to far corner of field, at which **4** tracks converge from sharp left and sharp right; continue half left on well-marked track with edge of wood on right, signposted Beeston. Track later becomes tarmac road between houses.

5 150 yards after last house (large, half-timbered, called Moat House) turn left on path signposted Beeston Castle, over ladder-stile, then over two more stiles to reach tarmac lane **6**. Turn left on lane, then immediately right over stile and into wood. Path soon crosses further stile; beyond this turn right with high stone wall on left, to reach road soon after, with car park on right **7**.

(*For Beeston Castle* continue forward on road for 100 yards – main entrance is on left. After visiting castle, turn right out of entrance to return to this point.)

Turn right on road and, after ¼ mile, left at T-junction and left again at second T-junction. After 100 yards

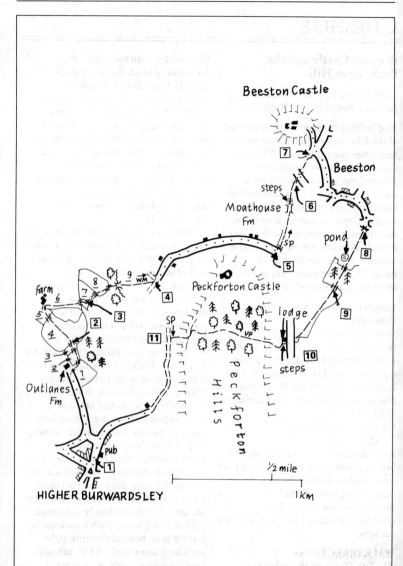

turn right on road signposted Bunbury, then after 150 yards, where road bends left, turn right on unmetalled track. Cross stile to left of gate, and forward over cross-track through gate into field **8**. Half left in field, heading for middle of small coniferous wood on far side. Path skirts to left of pond to reach gate and stile on edge of wood.

9 On reaching far end of wood emerge into field by stile and head just to left of distinctive gatehouse building with tower. In far corner of field turn right, so that fence is on left, then continue half left to find stile in corner of field, which brings you out to road just to left of gatehouse **10**. Cross road and continue up stone steps to find signposted path into wood. Continue on waymarked path through wooded grounds of Peckforton Castle, avoiding all paths marked 'private'.

After about ½ mile path drops steeply downhill; ¼ mile further on reach junction of tracks at edge of wood **11**. Turn left on broad track signposted Bulkeley Hill. After ¼ mile, fork right on track signposted Burwardsley, which later becomes tarmacked and brings you out in front of Pheasant Inn.

WHAT TO LOOK OUT FOR
(a) **Beeston Castle** (English Heritage; open to public; fee) Ruin of a 13th-century castle built by the Earl of Chester, with much of its curtain wall and gatehouse surviving. Impregnably sited 740ft up an isolated, steep-sided conical hill. **View** W to Clwydian Range (1,818ft); N to Merseyside (including Liverpool Cathedral); ENE to the Peak District beyond Macclesfield; S to the Wrekin (1,334ft); SW to the Berwyn (2,712ft).
(b) **Peckforton Castle** (not open to public; only visible from a distance) Massive and medieval in appearance, complete with turrets, moat and gatehouse, sited high up on the Peckforton Hills, and designed 1844-50 by Salvin for the first Lord Tollemache at a cost of £60,000. Tollemache built a large number of farmhouses and estate cottages in the area.

Ingersley Vale and Kerridge Hill

Based on contributions from Jenny Pharo and J B Roe
Recommended by Brian Marsden, Andrew Ward, Mr and Mrs R F Maddock, W P Quayle, Richard Banks, Dr John Morley

A brief exploration of the western edge of the Peak District with views from pasture fields on the outward leg and vast panoramas for one mile along the moorland ridge of Kerridge Hill. Route-finding tricky from 4 to 5, otherwise easy.

Length 3½ miles (5.5km), 1½ hours
Difficulty 2–3
Start Crown Inn, Church Lane, Bollington, off B5090. From A523 (Stockport to Macclesfield) take turning for Bollington. Carry on through this long village passing under railway bridge and the canal aqueduct (by sign to Pott Shrigley); ¼ mile later turn right at Turners Arms down Church Lane. Crown Inn is on left at end. Roadside parking. Grid reference SJ 939777
OS maps 1:50,000 118;
1:25,000 Outdoor Leisure 24
Refreshments Pubs and cafés in Bollington

WALK DIRECTIONS

1 (a) From Church Lane with Crown Inn on left, turn left on lane, soon past mill pond on your right. At fork just before old mill ahead (now used by Rainow Textiles) fork right slightly uphill on track. Avoid any further right forks uphill but carry on to group of cottages at end of track 2. Continue forward through gate to find path leading half left up to small gate, then bear quarter left across first field to stone stile. Continue on paved path to far left-hand corner of second field and next stile, beyond which turn right, with wall on right, on clear path which changes to other

side of wall by next stone stile; this leads down between fences to reach road at edge of Rainow village 3.

Turn right on road and after 100 yards (just before road bends left downhill) cross stile on left. Follow right edge of two fields (Kerridge Hill is in front of you) and cross footbridge beyond 4. (In this section, your objective is to pick up well-defined grassy track 130 yards away, not yet visible, which contours hillside). Bear half right uphill beyond footbridge for 30 yards then, just before nearest electicity pole, bear left steeply uphill (no path). 5 After 100 yards reach grassy track and turn left on it to pass through gate. Immediately beyond gate do not continue ahead on track but bear quarter right uphill on narrow path which passes through narrow gate in wall ahead (b).

6 At end of next field, path enters scrubby woodland. 300 yards later, and 20 yards before disused kissing-gate by wall ahead, turn sharp right uphill on wide path. Enter area of gorse then continue on to ridge of Kerridge Hill (c). 7 At far end of ridge is White Nancy (d); here bear quarter left steeply downhill to Bollington past small fenced area, then cross track to follow path on edge of fields on to residential road. Continue straight on down road to reach Crown Inn.

WHAT TO LOOK OUT FOR

(a) **Bollington** Former mill town with terraced stone cottages; a mill passed near the start, dated 1809, is still used for making textiles. The path through fields S of the town is paved with flagstones, dating from the time when mill-workers used it as a route to and from Bollington.
(b) Chimney of the ruined **Cow Mill** is visible down to left.
(c) **View** W across the Cheshire plain to the Clwydian Range (about 50 miles away); NW to Manchester, just

S of which the aeroplanes of Manchester airport can often be seen. **(d) White Nancy** Bell-shaped white obelisk at northern end of Kerridge Hill, immediately above Bollington.

Thought to have been built to commemorate the Battle of Waterloo, 'Nancy' being the horse that pulled the stones to the top of the hill when the monument was built.

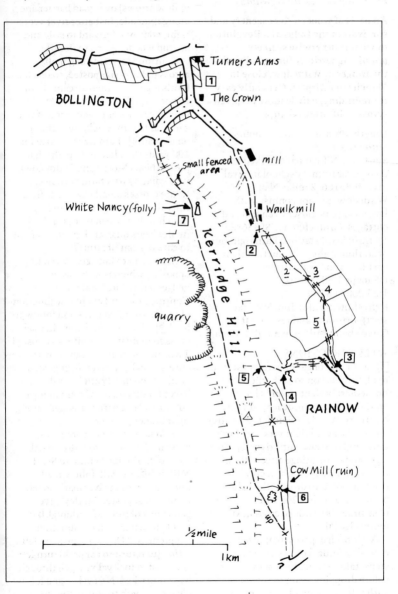

The River Bollin and Quarry Bank Mill

Contributed by Andrew Ward
Recommended by Dr John Morley,
Brian Marsden, Paul Newman

An oasis of wooded river scenery and survivals of the Industrial Revolution in what is otherwise scarcely promising territory for a good walk – the fringes of Wilmslow, close to Manchester Airport. Generally easy route-finding; a little more involved across fields from ④ to ⑧.

Length 5½ miles (9km), 2 hours
Difficulty 1
Start Free NT car park (locked at dusk) near primary school in Styal, just off B5166, 2 miles N of Wilmslow. Do not confuse with larger car park closer to chapel and cottages. Grid reference SJ 836835.
By train Styal station. Turn right out of station, right at T-junction then first left into Styal village
OS maps 1:50,000 109; 1:25,000 SJ 88/98
Refreshments Ship Inn, Styal (at start); tea-room and restaurant at Quarrybank Mill (when mill is open)

WALK DIRECTIONS

1 (**a**) At end of car park furthest from road, turn left on to path, then immediately right. Avoid chapel gate on right, but continue forward into Northern Woods. Avoid left fork after 150 yards, avoid right fork 150 yards later, and descend until river **2**. Turn right and cross bridge after 300 yards, then turn left to climb steeply through wood to drop to the valley bottom again after 200 yards. Continue 300 yards to cross next footbridge **3**.

After bridge, path (signposted Oversley Bridge) rises steeply up steps, taking route high above river before dropping again to riverside. Path follows riverside for 1 mile to road at Oversley Bridge **4**. Turn left

to cross bridge and take path to right at end of far bridge parapet. After 50 yards cross busy A538 road, and take path opposite (signposted Castle Hill, Morley Green; soon marked by yellow arrows) over road barrier and along riverside. Just after river veers right, continue forward to stile and ascend wooded slope to field **5**.

Continue forward (diagonally across field) as signposted, to reach footbridge over small stream. Turn left on to path signposted to Morley Green, pass through left-hand of two gates on to farm track, then emerge on to road **6**. Turn right on road for 100 yards then left on to path (signposted Nans Moss Lane/Wilmslow), immediately past farm entrance. Route crosses small triangular field, runs along left edge of two fields, then briefly beween fences and finally bears quarter right across field to gate in front of farm **7**.

Cross road to take grassy track opposite, which runs between hedges, signposted Wilmslow. Continue forward at oblique junction of tracks after 200 yards and follow to road **8**. Turn left, and at main road cross to footpath opposite (signposted Twinnies Bridge). As soon as path enters woods, turn left (signposted again). Woodland path leads down to River Bollin and turns right along it. 500 yards later path turns right along right branch of river.

9 Where river next branches, cross bridge on left to follow north bank of Bollin for ¾ mile to Styal Mill (**b**) **10**. At mill, follow road uphill away from river (path on left by mill, signposted Morley, gives good view of front of building). **11** Just before road reaches junction (Apprentices' House is ahead on left), *either* (to return to car park) turn left (signposted to Styal village), through barrier marked 'No cycles' and follow clear field path to starting-point *or* (to return to station) continue forward

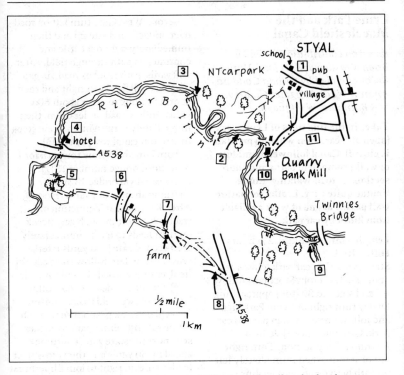

past Apprentices' House on surfaced path between wooden railings
and straight on at junction of tarmac
lanes. At road junction turn left;
Station Road is first on right.

WHAT TO LOOK OUT FOR
(a) **Styal village** Model dwellings built
to house Samuel Grey's workforce
who were employed at Quarry Bank

Mill; shop, chapel and school were
built at the same time.
(b) **Quarrybank Mill** (NT, open to
public; fee) Handsome building in a
pretty woodland and river setting.
Built by Samuel Grey of Belfast in
1784, for cotton spinning. Inside is a
display about the Greys and the
cotton industry. Nearby are the
manager's and apprentices' houses.

Lyme Park and the Macclesfield Canal

Based on contributions from Dr Brian Marsden and Dr John Morley Recommended by Gillian Goddard, Andrew Ward, Margaret Godfrey, D R Burnham, W P Quayle

Takes in the fine trees of Lyme Park (open all year, even when Lyme Hall is closed). Canal followed in middle of walk; some field paths and short sections of road-walking. Route-finding quite easy. Leaflet for nature trail passed at end of walk available from kiosk by car park.

Length 6 miles (9.5km), 2½ hours
Difficulty 1
Start Lyme Hall car park (closes at 7pm), Disley. From Stockport follow A6 and signs to Buxton; approaching Disley turn right at Lyme Park sign and follow drive through park to car park. Grid reference SJ 963824.
By train Disley station. Turn right out of station, then immediately left up path between fences leading through woods to road. Turn right on this quiet residential road and follow to gate-house at Lyme Park, then continue forward, crossing main park drive, following signs to Elmerhurst Trail until crossing ladder-stile on left
OS maps 1:50,000 109; 1:25,000 SJ 88/98
Refreshments Café by lake near car park in Lyme Park; tea-room in Lyme Hall

WALK DIRECTIONS

1 Leave car park with Lyme Hall behind you and lake in front, and follow road to left, which then bears half right uphill. **2** At top of rise take right fork, then after 30 yards fork left to viewpoint (a). At 'Cars prohibited beyond this point' sign, turn left on grassy track leading into woods via Knott Gate **3**. Follow track through woods for about ¾ mile and arrive at West Gate **4**.

Beyond West Gate turn left on road over bridge, cross stream and then immediately right over stile and continue on path through field. After 100 yards, path reaches road via gap in stone wall **5**. Turn right and then continue along road for about 600 yards. Follow road under canal, then immediately turn right up stone steps to arrive at canal towpath (b) **6**.

Turn left, and follow towpath for 1 mile, until bridge number 13 **7**. Cross canal via bridge 13 and continue ahead along farm track. **8** After 300 yards, at T-junction of tracks, turn left through gate (track on right leads to farm). Immediately after second gate (100 yards later), cross stile on left, follow right edge of field, entering woods by stile at end.

9 On other side of woods follow left edge of two fields, then continue forward on track past house to reach estate gate **10**. Enter park by ladder-stile next to estate gate, continue ahead for 50 yards and then cross next ladder-stile on right to join Elmerhurst Trail (signposted from opposite direction). Follow the trail through woodland (c) (clear signposts all the way) to arrive back in Lyme Park car park from the lake side. In the final few hundred yards, this trail meets a nature trail (d).

WHAT TO LOOK OUT FOR

(a) **View** NW over Stockport and central Manchester; W across Cheshire.
(b) **Macclesfield Canal** 26½ miles long, designed by Thomas Telford. Connects the Peak Forest and Trent and Mersey Canals.
(c) **Lyme Park** (NT open to public all year; no fee) Deer Park with celebrated collection of trees and shrubs, some very rare. In the park stands the Cage, an Elizabethan construction with 18th-century alterations, used probably both as a vantage watchtower for the hunt and

as a place where anyone caught poaching could be detained.

(**d**) **Lyme Hall** (NT; house open to public; fee; garden open to public all year; fee) Elizabethan house partly remodelled in 1725 by Italian architect Giacomo Leoni, whose design for the S front (overlooking the lake) is one of the finest examples of the English Palladian style. The hall was the home of the Leigh family for 600 years until given to the NT in 1947. Adjacent are the rose garden and orangery, the latter containing fig trees, camellias and palms.

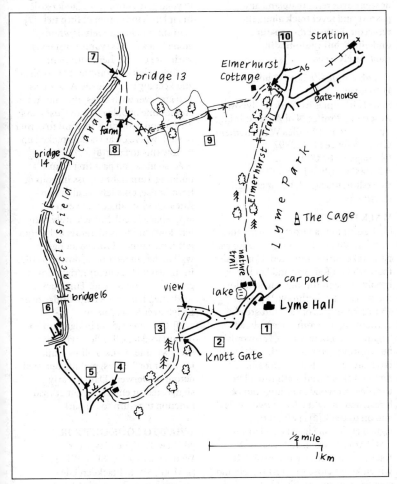

DERBYSHIRE

Ladybower Reservoir

Recommended by Michael Elstob

A good varied walk with a 600ft ascent through coniferous forest, a gradual descent over remote upland and pasture and level track along the reservoir. Paths across pasture undefined, but route-finding moderately easy.

Length 6 miles (9.5km), 3 hours
Difficulty 2
Start Fairholmes car park, Ladybower Reservoir, 2 miles N of A6 road-bridge over reservoir, 12 miles W of Sheffield. Grid reference SK 172897
OS maps 1:50,000 110;
1:25,000 Outdoor Leisure 1
Refreshments Snack bar at car park by starting-point

WALK DIRECTIONS

1 Return to road from car park and turn left. Opposite left entrance to car park, take path signposted 'Concession footpath Old Railway and Locker-brook'. Ascend through forest following signs to Lockerbrook. **2** After 15 to 20 minutes of easy but steady climbing ignore minor path ahead (signposted 'Lockerbrook Farm only') but continue on main path. 100 yards later, and 20 yards after crossing remains of old wall, path turns left to stile over wooden railings out of forest, across right edge of two fields and on to track **3** . Left on track signed Hope via Hagg Farm Hostel.

4 After ½ mile, at crossing of tracks, take narrow path up on left which keeps close to forest on left and soon merges into track. **5** At end of first (large) field continue forward, signposted Ladybower, avoiding path over ladder-stile on left leading into forest. Continue along edge of forest in second field, but in middle of third field, track leaves forest

edge to head for gate on skyline **6** (**a**). Continue forward over skyline on snaking grassy path across fourth field – not very well defined, but once over brow of hill, gate is visible ahead. Beyond gate continue to ladder-stile in far left-hand corner of fifth field **7** .

In sixth field turn left downhill along fence for 100 yards until level with gate on left; here turn right, aiming to left of prominent crags ahead and keeping on the level. As soon as you are level with crags, the faint track crosses line of old wall (now just grassy hump) and continues forward to corner of wall, where clear track is picked up. Follow this to farm **8** .

As soon as you pass first farm building, turn right to pass in front of farm-house, take left-hand of two gates, cross small pen and enter strip-shaped field. Immediately turn left down hill to ladder-stile in bottom left-hand corner. Proceed alongside wall on left in next field, down to stile. In third field bear quarter right down to gate leading on to road. Turn right on road, then left across road–bridge over Ladybower Reservoir (**b**).

9 On other side of bridge turn left on surfaced lane (bridleway) which soon becomes track. Follow bank of reservoir for 2 miles, making optional detour to Derwent Dam (clearly signposted) at end. Turn left at road junction to return to car park.

WHAT TO LOOK OUT FOR

(**a**) **View** To right, NW, over Woodlands Valley; SE to Win Hill (1,516ft); SW to Blackden Edge.
(**b**) **Ladybower Reservoir** 13 miles round its perimeter. When built in 1943-5 it swallowed two villages, thirteen farms and five miles of road. The spire of Derwent church stood above the water level until demolition in 1959.

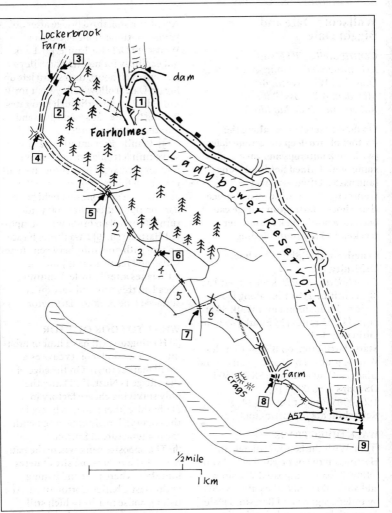

Lockerbrook
Farm
3
dam
2
1
Fairholmes
4
Ladybower Reservoir
1
5
2
3 6
4
5
6
7
crags
farm
8
A57
9

½ mile
1 Km

Wolfscote Dale and Biggin Dale

Contributed by P J Mead
Recommended by Margaret Godfrey,
Dorothea Whitworth, Brian
Marsden, A E Moss, Paul Bilson,
Robert and Linda Maddock

On mainly level paths along the bottom of two deep limestone dales (with rock outcrops and caves), plus some well-defined field and woodland paths. Often very wet: wellington boots are a better choice than shoes. Hartington village can become a bottleneck at summer weekends. Easy route-finding.

Length 5 miles (8km), 2½ hours
Difficulty 1–2
For a full day's walk keep forward at
3 , continue 1½ miles along Dove Dale to Milldale and join Walk 84 at point 3 ; 15 miles (25.5km), 7½ hours
Difficulty 3–4
Start Hartington, on B5054 15 miles W of Matlock. Free parking on central triangle. Grid reference SK 128604
OS maps 1:50,000 119;
1:25,000 Outdoor Leisure 24
Refreshments In Hartington

WALK DIRECTIONS

1 (a) With the central triangle in Hartington to your right, behind you, follow B5054, signposted Warslow, and after 100 yards take path on left by toilets, signposted Beresford Dale. The path bears right behind toilets, and after running along right edge of two fields crosses path running between walls and continues opposite through squeeze-stile. Clearly marked path leads round hill, through three fields and is waymarked by posts. Follow this into woods and over footbridge, at river (b). 2 300 yards later recross river by second footbridge, and turn right to follow riverside path which now runs along the bottom of Wolfscote Dale (c).

Avoid crossing third bridge after 300 yards; continue along bottom of Wolfscote Dale for 1 mile. 3 Look out carefully for meeting of valleys (easy to overshoot), turn sharp left up Biggin Dale. Follow valley floor for ¾ mile (d). Path goes through two gates, leaving NT area at second gate and entering nature reserve.

4 ¼ mile after entering nature reserve turn left (signposted Hartington). Immediately pass through small gate; path follows bottom of valley ahead. Proceed alongside field boundary on right, then after 200 yards turn left uphill on bridleway, signposted Hartington. 5 Pass through gate on top; path now runs between stone walls, and reaches cross junction with lanes after ½ mile. Continue ahead on this tiny and very quiet surfaced lane back to Hartington.

WHAT TO LOOK OUT FOR

(a) **Hartington** Still has a hint of urbanity, as a reminder of its days as a small market town. On the edge of the village is Nuttall's Dairy, the only surviving cheese factory in Derbyshire (there used to be six in the county), largely concerned with the manufacture of Stilton.
(b) The opposite bank where the path reaches the river is the site of **Beresford Hall**, where poet and fishing enthusiast Charles Cotton lived. At a fishing house nearby (which still stands) he and his friend and collaborator Izaak Walton fished, inspiring Cotton to add to Walton's *The Compleat Angler.*
(c) **Wolfscote Dale** Gets its name from the obvious, as a haunt of wolves. Striking exposed limestone formations. **Flora** Meadow-sweet, meadow cranesbill and celandine grow on the turfy meadows.
(d) **Biggin Dale** Dry valley, containing a nature reserve. **Flora** Characteristic limestone-loving plants.

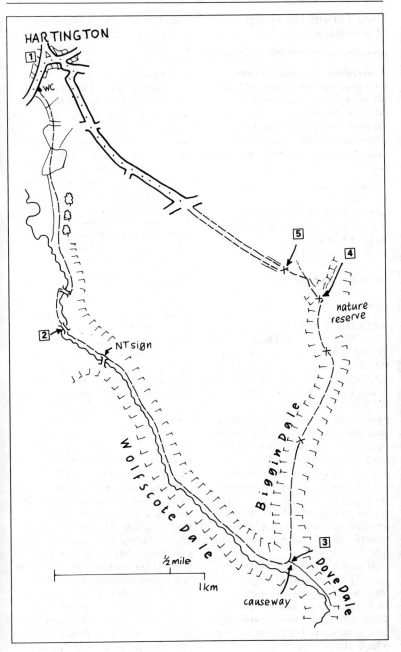

High Tor and the Heights of Abraham

Contributed by Dorothea Whitworth

A precipitous, wooded river gorge with good viewpoints and old lead mines. Ascent can be avoided by taking cable-car across valley. Paths via High Tor and the Heights of Abraham are subject to opening hours (see page 540). Some residential roads. Route-finding easy.

Length 4½ miles (7km), 2 hours
Difficulty 2
Start Matlock Park near Matlock station; walk down A6 (Dale Road) to Ye Olde English Hotel
OS maps 1:50,000 119; 1:25,000 Outdoor Leisure 24
Refreshments Plenty in Matlock; cafés at High Tor and Heights of Abraham

WALK DIRECTIONS
1 (a) Take Old English Road beside Ye Olde English Hotel, and leave it for tarmac footpath leading past small car park. Cross footbridge over River Derwent (b) and turn right. Walk through Matlock recreation park past children's boating-lake (on your left) and minature train (on your right). Continue out of park and for a few yards on narrow road, then almost immediately take gate on right. Cross narrow footbridge and turn right again to follow path which rejoins main river. On reaching junction with large footbridge over river on right, do not cross it but turn left.

2 Pass under railway bridge, ascend path ahead until it reaches road, at which point turn sharply back right through gateway into High Tor grounds (pay fee either at kiosk or at Summit Café). Follow grassy path which climbs steadily.

3 From café at summit, before continuing walk, detour to actual summit (right side of café). Walk

continues on path below and to left of café, and becomes narrow tarmac driveway. It descends past old Roman lead workings on your right, then into woods. Just before driveway exits from grounds at kiosk and gate, turn sharp right on to woodland path and wind down until you reach cable-car base station **4**. (To avoid a second and much steeper climb, you can use cable-car to point **6**.) Continue down past cable-car station (c), under railway bridge and across river by footbridge, to enter outskirts of Matlock Bath. Cross main road and turn left along it, and after a few minutes take first turning right (Holme Road). Climb steeply, ignoring right fork, and continue climbing parallel with cable-car lines.

5 As road starts to level out, turn right into Masson Road, take first (small) turning left and you will see an entrance lodge and gate into the Heights of Abraham (d) (if closed, retrace steps to **5**, continue uphill on Upperwood Road until **7**). Tarmac path zigzags steeply uphill and under wooden footbridge which you will later cross. Keep climbing until you reach the Great Rutland Cavern Nestus Mine (e), Hillside Tavern and viewpoint. Proceed, ascending steeply by path or steps, to Tree Tops Visitor Centre **6**.

At this point you are close to the cable-car summit station. (Climb to top of nearby Prospect Tower for a bird's eye view of the surroundings. Entrance to the Masson mine (f) is just behind and right of Tree Tops Centre.) Retrace steps downhill as far as junction immediately below the Hillside Tavern. Here turn right and descend by another path down to gatehouse and on to road. Turn left and descend a few yards, then **7** turn left on fenced footpath leading up through woods and crossing above-mentioned footbridge. Path soon levels out, passes under the

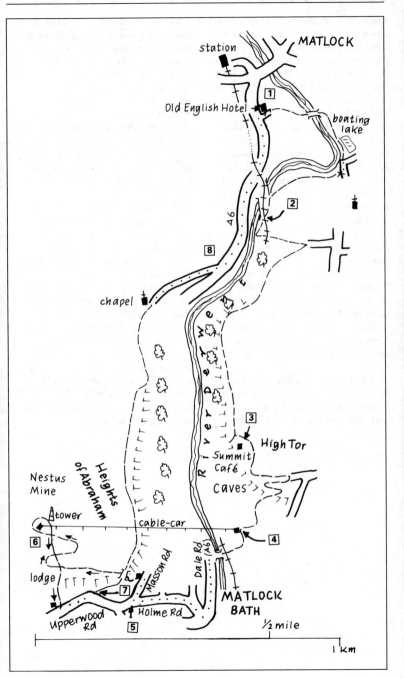

cable-car lines and continues up and down on side of hill. Emerge on to farm track and continue downhill, passing St Johns Chapel (**g**). **8** Rejoin A6 on outskirts of Matlock and turn left along it, and follow back to start.

WHAT TO LOOK OUT FOR

(**a**) **Matlock** The warm springs that make Matlock a spa were discovered in 1698. Daniel Defoe paid a visit in 1724 and said 'This bath would be much more frequented than it is, if a bad stony road which leads to it and no good accommodation when you are there, did not hinder.' However, he much approved of High Tor, 'the prodigious height of this tor . . . was to me more a wonder than any of the rest in the Peak.' Byron was a frequent visitor in the following century and said 'I can assure you there are things in Derbyshire as noble as Greece or Switzerland'.
View Over Derwent Valley with ruins of Riber Castle on hillside away to left.

(**b**) **River Derwent**'s initial course ran south-east from Matlock Bridge, but after the surface of grit and shale had been eroded it cut a course directly south through the underlying limestone. This created the dramatic gorge, which is rich in ferns, including moonwort, brittle bladder, maidenhair and green spleenwort.

(**c**) **Cable-car** See page 540 for operation times.

(**d**) The **Heights of Abraham** are named after the heights scaled by Wolfe's army at the Battle of Quebec in 1759, and are said to have been named by one of Wolfe's surviving officers.

(**e**) **Rutland Cavern** (open to public; fee) Consists largely of lead-mine workings, some of which date from the 15th century, but it contains some natural features, including the 80ft high Nestus Grotto.

(**f**) **Masson Cavern** (open to public; fee) Formerly mined, now open as a show-cave. It includes the Great Cavern, 130ft long and 30ft high and wide, whose roof holds a mass of large calcite crystals, some nearly a foot long. Some Roman excavations.

(**g**) **St John's chapel** (usually locked) Built into the side of the cliff in 1897, by Guy Dawker; has Arts and Crafts style furnishings inside.

Edensor and the Chatsworth Estate

Recommended by Michael Elstob, J S Freem

Leads through pasture and over a gentle wooded hillside before emerging into the landscaped parklands of the Chatsworth Estate, reaching first the estate village and then the bridge by the house itself. Concludes along the grassy banks of the Derwent. Field paths undefined; directions should be followed with care.

Length 7 miles (11km), 3 hours
Difficulty 2
Start Calton Lees car park (free), between Rowsley and Baslow on B6012. Well signposted. Grid reference SK 259686
OS maps 1:50,000 119; 1:25,000 Outdoor leisure 24
Refreshments Cafés in Edensor and Chatsworth House; Peacock Inn and shop in Rowsley

WALK DIRECTIONS

[1] Take minor road at bottom of car park leading away from B6012, soon passing between gate-posts marked 'no through road'. At T-junction turn left and pass group of cottages (Calton Lees). Just after last cottage cross steps over wall on left, follow left edge of first field leaving it by ladder-stile on left just before end [2]. Turn right to continue same direction across second field to gate, and in third (large) field continue forward on narrow path to gate in wall ahead [3].

Fourth field is inverted 'L' shape; continue ahead, round corner, and just before end cross stile on right into woods. Path into Rowsley village is now easy to follow as it runs along bank of river. Just before reaching road it goes under old railway bridge (**a**). [4] At road, turn right. Follow

road uphill; at top of village, it becomes bridleway, and continues to ascend.

[5] After ½ mile keep left through woods by metal barrier. [6] ½ mile later, at next junction of tracks turn right uphill through woods (avoiding main track half right, which descends gently, between walls). Ascend for 300 yards to oblique T-junction of forest tracks, turn left and after 80 yards take next track on right. [7] After joining wall follow footpath sign across enclosed grassy area, through woods, to emerge by ladder-stile into field [8].

Turn left on path, initially with forest fence on left, and continue to signpost. At signpost turn right downhill on path (heading for fold with water troughs) which soon follows posts with yellow marker arrows. [9] At bottom of field pass through gate between belts of woodland, and turn right, proceeding with woods on right. At bottom right-hand corner of field (just after woods end), do not pass through gate but turn left, alongside wall on right, then enter woods ahead by gate.

[10] At other side of woods you are in Chatsworth Park, with house visible half right. There is free access for walkers in this part of the park, so descend half right by any way you like towards spire of Edensor church (slightly hidden by trees, but very soon becomes visible).

[11] Find small gate 50 yards to left of churchyard, leading between fences to village. Turn right through village (**b**), past gatehouse, cross main road and take path opposite/half right by prominent tree. This leads to bridge in front of Chatsworth House (**c**) [12]. Stay on near side of bridge and turn right along right side of river. [13] After 1 mile, by ruined stone estate building, bear half right up to gate leading to Calton Lees car park.

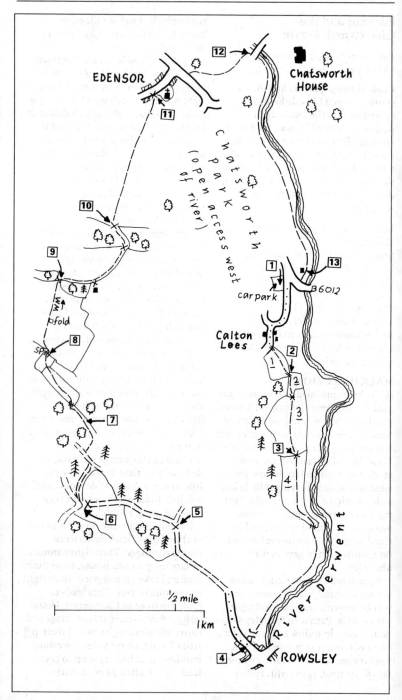

WHAT TO LOOK OUT FOR

(a) **Bridge** of the scenic Peak District line (Matlock to Buxton via Miller's Dale) which closed in the 1960s. Crystal Palace designer Sir Joseph Paxton built Rowsley station and the four adjacent Midland Cottages for the railway, and it was probably his influence that finally persuaded the Duke of Devonshire to allow the line to be extended to cross his estate.

(b) **Edensor** Estate village for Chatsworth, transplanted from its former site closer to the house, made up of ornate 19th-century cottages enclosed by an ornamental gateway at the bottom end. The village was probably the work of Paxton. Gilbert Scott built the impressive (if sombre) Early English-style church in 1867;

Paxton's tomb is in the churchyard.

(c) **Chatsworth House** (open to public; fee) Majestic country seat of the Dukes of Devonshire. Originally Elizabethan, the house was extensively remodelled in classical style in 1687–9 by William Talman, a contemporary of Christopher Wren; with later work by Thomas Archer (1705) and Jeffry Wyatville (1820s). The estate was landscaped in the 1760s by Capability Brown, who altered the course of the river. The Great Conservatory, Lily Houses and greenhouses are by Paxton. Hedge maze, fountains and cascades in the grounds. **Birds** Common sandpipers, grey wagtails, yellow wagtails, siskins, nuthatch, tufted ducks, kingfishers, dippers, herons.

The River Derwent and Padley Chapel

Contributed by J H Bradley
Recommended by B H and
M J James, Archibald McGlen,
P R Gurnell

An easy riverside path through meadows (with wild flowers in spring and early summer) and woods; abundant birdlife, including herons, dippers and mallard. Route ascends slightly for views down the valley. A little road-walking. Easy route-finding.

Length 5½ miles (9km), 2½ hours
Difficulty 1
Start Hathersage station, just S of A625 (Chapel-en-le-Frith to Sheffield); take Bakewell road from centre of Hathersage. Grid reference SK 233811
OS maps 1:50,000 110 and 119; 1:25,000 SK 28/38 and Outdoor Leisure 24
Refreshments Pubs and tea-rooms in Hathersage

WALK DIRECTIONS

1 (**a**) From Hathersage station follow station approach down to B6001. Cross half right to go down Dore Lane, under railway bridge, until lodge of Nether Hall **2**. Turn left over stone stile beside farm gate and proceed along farm track. After 100 yards where track turns right, continue forward, crossing stile in hedgerow ahead. Continue along this path with fence on right which is followed until road **3**. Cross road and take signposted lane opposite, through double gates which lead to farm **4**.

Pass immediately to right of farmhouse and enter field by gate; continue forward, joining river-bank after 300 yards then continuing along it and soon into woodland. **5** On emerging from woods, continue beside river across two fields and, at

tree-lined boundary of second field, cross stile but do not cross bridge over stream **6**. Instead, turn left uphill, proceeding with wall on left, up past double telegraph pole (can be marshy for a few yards) then continue beside wall along left edge of two fields as far as ruined stone hut **7**.

Turn right on to well-defined track leading towards railway line. Cross bridge near railway to junction with another track **8**. Turn right, and follow track 100 yards to Padley Chapel (**b**). Retrace steps to junction of tracks and continue straight ahead, taking track which soon becomes path and passes through mixture of fields and woods, rising gently up hillside for 1 mile. Crags of Millstone Edge are away to right.

9 At main road turn right and take first turning left 50 yards later. Follow road, with wood on right. After 300 yards, where wood ends, take track on left by sign to Scraperlow Hall Farm. **10** Where track emerges from between stone walls turn left on to path, proceeding with wall on left to corner of field then over wooden stile and into wood. Follow path downhill through wood with stone wall down on left.

11 At bottom (far) left-hand corner of wood, descend steeply to pass through wicket gate in fence and follow track down to main road **12**. Cross over to pavement and turn left. Go uphill along road for 80 yards and pass through a narrow gap in wall on right just beyond bus-stop, then through gate and on to path leading downhill through field along remains of stone wall. **13** At bottom turn right along back fences of row of houses emerging on to small road. Turn left to reach B6001 at station approach.

WHAT TO LOOK OUT FOR

(**a**) **Hathersage** The area used to be famous for producing millstones. In

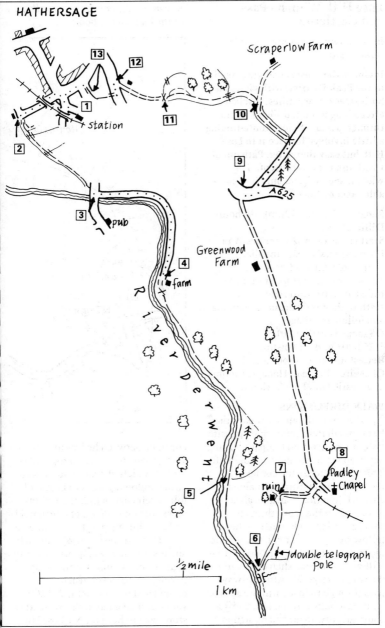

HATHERSAGE

the churchyard is a 19th-century tombstone to Little John (of Robin Hood's gang). Hathersage was the village of Morton in *Jane Eyre*.

(**b**) **Padley chapel** Just about all that remains of a manor-house owned in the 16th century by the Fitzherbert family.

225

Lose Hill, Winnats Pass and Castleton

Based on an idea contributed by Mike Braid

Includes the most scenic ridge walk in the Peak District, with views on both sides for two miles; reached after a long but not difficult climb through pasture fields. Route-finding a little involved for ascent to Lose Hill, but easy thereafter. Path out of Castleton very wet just after 9 **when inspected, and only just passable. Ascent 1,000ft.**

Length 7½ miles (12km), 3½ hours
Difficulty 3
Start Hope, on A625, 4 miles W of Hathersage. Car park in village, well signposted. Grid reference SK 171835. *By train* Hope station, ¾ mile E of start (turn right out of station, then right again at main road, and follow to village).
OS maps 1:50,000 110;
1:25,000 Outdoor Leisure 1
Refreshments Tea-rooms and Cheshire Cheese in Hope; tea-rooms and Castle Hotel in Castleton

WALK DIRECTIONS

1 (**a**) Turn right out of car park then left immediately before and opposite Woodroofe Arms on footpath leading between walls, signposted Lose Hill. This soon reaches the corner of a residential road; turn right along it and at T-junction continue ahead (school is on the right) through squeeze-stile beside gate into field; follow right edge of field. Cross series of small fields by squeeze-stiles (Lose Hill visible ahead), then cross railway (**b**) by footbridge 2 . After railway pass through field, continue ahead on lane, past bungalow on left, and 13 continue forward at end by signpost (Castleton Road right, Edale Road left) to enter field by stile.

Follow right edge of field for 150 yards, then turn right by signpost to

Key maps, pinpointing the walks, are at the back of the book.

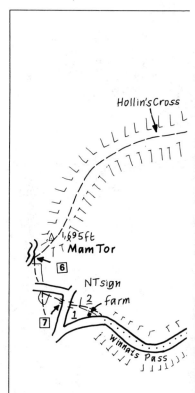

continue between hedges for 50 yards, then cross stile on right. Make for stile to left of nearest stone barn ahead, following signs to Lose Hill: follow left edge of first three fields, cross stile on left edge of fourth field and continue up past barn to emerge by ladder-stile on track 4 . Turn left, and just by farm bear quarter right to signpost on skyline. Continue up beyond it – soon you reach dilapidated wall on right, and 200 yards later bear half right by isolated stone post to head for NT Lose Hill Pike sign 5 .

Continue up to ridge to summit of Lose Hill (**c**), then left along ridge for 2½ miles to trig. point on Mam Tor,

Special interest lists at the back of the book give opening times for castles, houses, museums and gardens passed on the walks.

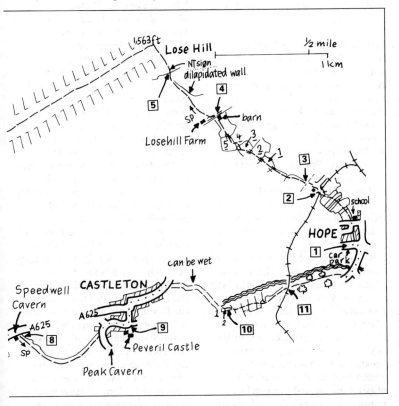

at end of ridge, beyond which path descends steeply down to road **6**. Immediately before reaching road turn left down steps to stile and descend to stile ahead. Cross road and cross stile slightly to left by NT Windy Knoll sign (**d**). After 20 yards fork left on grassy path aiming for distant farm. **7** Cross stile and road beyond, and continue forward across stile by Winnats Head Farm NT sign, aiming for gate just to left of farm ahead. In second field follow right edge, signposted Winnats Pass, and turn left on reaching the Pass to follow verge alongside road at bottom of gorge (**e**).

8 30 yards after Speedwell Cavern

(**f**) turn right through gate, on path signposted to Castleton. Proceed, with wall on left, to village (**g**). **9** Turn left at grass triangle in centre of Castleton and turn right at main road. At end of village, just before road bends left, turn right on track signposted Hope. This soon becomes field path.

10 In second field, path leaves river and leads to stile. Cross three small fields in quick succession (making for squeeze-tiles ahead) then, by signpost to Hope in next field, continue forward, to be joined by fence on left after 30 yards; follow left edge of field round to stile leading over railway. **11** After crossing railway, route is easy to find and path is well defined, and leads along edge of trees above river to road. Turn left into Hope village.

WHAT TO LOOK OUT FOR

(a) **Hope** Recently expanded village with 15th-century church containing two tombstones in the aisle floor marked by huntsman's horn and arrow motifs, probably in memory of wood-reeves who managed the Royal Forest of the Peak.

(b) **Private line**, connecting main railway with Bradwell cement works, 1½ miles away.

(c) **Lose Hill/Mam Tor Ridge** Impressive ridge with views on the right (N) of the Vale of Edale and the upland plateau of Kinder Scout, and on the left (S) over the Hope Valley. Lose Hill was probably named after a battle in AD626 where the Kings of Wessex, who camped on nearby Win Hill, were victorious over the King of Northumbria, who camped here. Mam Tor, capped by the ramparts of Derbyshire's largest Iron Age hillfort, is known as 'shivering mountain' because of its frequent landslips, which happen when the solid bands of gritstone are undermined by the removal of softer shales underneath. As a result, part of the A625 has been closed for some years. **View** Right, of the Vale of Edale with the upland plateau of Kinder Scout beyond; on left over the Hope Valley.

(d) **Windy Knoll** In a cave near Winnats Pass, woolly rhinoceros, bear and wolf bones have been found.

(e) **Winnats Pass** Deep limestone gorge with a former turnpike road running along its bottom, reputedly haunted by the ghosts of two runaway lovers who were robbed and murdered by Castleton miners, and whose bodies were thrown down a mine near Speedwell Cavern.

(f) **Speedwell Cavern** (open to public; fee), mined for lead in the 18th century, now a show-cave reached by boat along an underground river.

(g) **Castleton** Predominantly of ancient grey stone cottages, looked over by the ruins of Peveril Castle (open to public, fee). The castle keep, of which the walls are at their original height, was built by Henry II in 1176. It controlled the village and the Royal Forest, and was used as a hunting-lodge until the 15th century. In the SW corner of Castleton is the entrance to what was called the Devil's Arse, euphemistically re-named Peak Cavern by the Victorians. At 60ft high and 100ft wide, it is the largest cave entrance in the country, and well worth walking up to even if you don't want to go in.

Monsal Dale and Miller's Dale

Contributed by Dorothea Whitworth
Recommended by Michael Elstob,
Brian and Mary James

Along a river gorge that competes with Dove Dale as the favourite in the Peak District, but which is large enough to absorb its visitors, many of whom visit the famous viewpoint at Monsal Head. Especially interesting for its limestone flora and relics of the cotton industry. Rises out of the valley to follow green tracks between dry-stone walled pasture. Mostly on defined tracks and paths; easy route-finding. Final descent can be slippery after rain.

Length *Full walk* 8 miles (13km), 4 hours
Difficulty 3
Short walk omitting Miller's Dale
3½ miles (5.5km), 1¾ hours
Difficulty 2
Start White Lodge car park and picnic site on A6, 4 mies NW of Bakewell (fee; honesty box). Grid reference SK 171702. If car park is full, park at pay-and-display car park at Monsal Head and start at **3**
OS maps 1:50,000 119; 1:25,000 Outdoor Leisure 24
Refreshments Monsal Head Hotel and café, both at Monsal Head; Angler's Rest in Miller's Dale (detour as described)

WALK DIRECTIONS

1 From car park take narrow path by honesty box down to main A6 road. Cross and go through break in wall opposite and down stone steps. Cross field to stream, go over stepping-stones and stile. Turn right and follow path straight ahead, parallel to river, which is down on your right. This is Monsal Dale (**a**). **2** After ¾ mile bear right off path and cross over the footbridge and continue with river on left past weir/waterfall.

Path climbs steeply through woodlands and continues high above river to Monsal Head **3**. From Monsal Head return to path and continue steeply downhill, signposted to viaduct. Take first path to left and cross the river by high viaduct. You are now on old railway line and Monsal Trail.

For short walk immediately after viaduct turn left uphill through gate (signposted Brushfield). After 200 yards walled path turns right and then continues to ascend on clearly defined track (mainly walled on both sides). After ¾ mile reach signpost to Monsal Dale via Brushfield Hough (on left). This is point **12**.

For full walk continue along Monsal Trail for ¾ mile until blocked-off tunnel. Cross stile on right and continue downhill on well-trodden narrow path. Follow down to Cressbrook Mill and footbridge over river by weir/waterfall (**b**) **4**. Turn left, cross second footbridge and take river-side path along under cliffs with the river on left. Continue along this concessionary footpath through gorge of Miller's Dale (**c**). **5** After 1 mile reach Litton Mill, where track leads to right over bridge and then immediately left into factory road. Continue through stone gateway into hamlet of Litton Mill. Continue straight ahead for 50 yards. **6** Turn left into alleyway beside house (signposted 'Trail 200 yards, public footpath to Taddington 1½ miles'). Cross river by footbridge, climb steps and path to rejoin old railway line. Turn right and follow under railway bridge. (Note old grey stone cottage on skyline, a landmark you will shortly climb up to). **7** After ½ mile, path reaches waymark pointing down right to Miller's Dale.

For optional detour to Angler's Rest, Miller's Dale (adds 1½ miles total) follow path down steeply, cross river by footbridge, turn left on lane

229

to reach hamlet of Miller's Dale, then retrace steps.

To continue main walk go up steps opposite waymark on left (leaving Monsal Trail) and over stile through wall. Path then climbs steeply uphill for 100 yards (with dilapidated wall on left) before bending right and continuing diagonally uphill through trees and bushes, and over a low wall into Derbyshire Naturalists' Trust land (**d**), and again steeply uphill to tumbledown old stone cottage (previously mentioned) 8 . Cross over wall, past cottage on your right and proceed through gate ahead. Follow track beside wall across two fields and exit on to wide farm track. Continue on down to barn, then turn immediately sharp left on track. 9 After ½ mile track turns right. Follow this farm track which runs down mostly between walls.

10 After ⅔ mile, pass Top Farm on your right. 200 yards later at next group of farms, where track ahead bends right and becomes tarmacked, turn left through gate to pass in front of farm. After ascending gently for 200 yards, path levels out and follows along top of tree line with wall up left. 11 200 yards later, at end of trees, path goes through gate into steep-sided field and makes straight across to lone tree on skyline opposite, by signpost for Monsal Dale via Brushfield Hough 12 .

By signpost (on right), bear half right (or sharp left if you have taken the short walk) into field between tree (left) and wall (right). Cross field diagonally, go through gap in wall. Continue with wall on left down to tree line. Continue straight on through gate, then forward with wall on right to another large gap, and past farm buildings on left 13 . Left through farm gate and immediately right through farmyard and out through another gate.

Cross small walled field, through

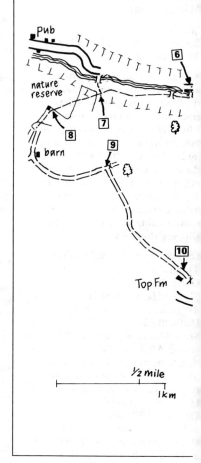

gate into larger walled field. Path joins farm track. Continue along track for 150 yards then, just before track turns right, look for steps over wall in corner on your left. Cross wall, bear right and follow narrow but well-defined path. Very soon you can see starting-place, down below on your right. Path descends steeply, mostly through woodland. At bottom turn right, cross stream and return to start.

WHAT TO LOOK OUT FOR
(**a**) **Monsal Dale** Rich **flora**, typical of

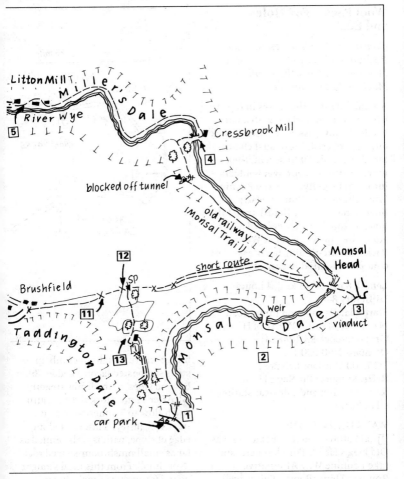

limestone country: orchids, meadow saxifrage, red campion, violets, wood anemone, lily of the valley, forget-me-not, marsh marigold. **Birds** Coots, moorhens, dippers, spotted flycatchers, willow warblers. The Monsal Trail follows the course of the former St Pancras to Manchester railway (Buxton to Matlock section closed in 1968) over the five-arched viaduct which dominates the valley. (b) **Cressbrook Mill** Cotton mill established by Robert Arkwright, rebuilt by William Newton (1815), a benevolent man who treated his 200 orphan employees with a kindness unusual in his time. Litton Mill, the next mill in the valley, had by contrast a notorious reputation for its treatment of apprentices; the death rate among them was very high. (c) **Miller's Dale** The Wye is a famous trout river; numerous waterfowl, and water-voles are common. (d) **Nature reserve** Access to paths only; permit required otherwise. **Flora** Characteristic limestone plants, including thyme, marjoram and rock rose. Some butterflies, notably common blue.

231

Wool Packs, Fox Holes and Edale

Contributed by Brian Hathaway
Recommended by Michael Elstob,
Dorothea Whitworth, Archibald
McGlen, Judith Samson

An upland route that takes in the
fringes of the moorland plateau of
Kinder Scout, passing a series of rock
outcrops of great individual character. One steady 700ft ascent, then a
more testing descent over boulders
into a rocky gully. Uses the Pennine
Way Alternative Route (clearly defined across pasture fields), then follows reasonably well-defined paths
along the top (less clear at Wool
Packs). Route-finding fairly easy, but
compass essential in case of mist.

Length 8 miles (13 km), 4 hours
Difficulty 3–4
Start Edale station, on minor road
N of A625, 4 miles WNW of Hope.
Grid reference SK 124853
OS maps 1:50,000 110;
1:25,000 Outdoor Leisure 1
Refreshments Old Nag's Head,
Ramblers' Inn and café near station,
all at Edale

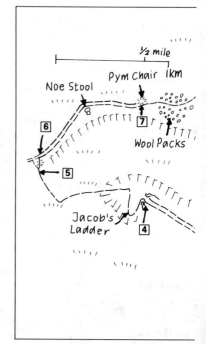

WALK DIRECTIONS
1 (**a**) Follow road into Edale as far as
Old Nag's Head. Turn left here, and
take Pennine Way Alternative
Route to Upper Booth. This is well
waymarked, and the route across
fields is easy to find. **2** In sixth field
ignore path on right, but continue
forward, soon descending half left
towards farmhouses (Upper Booth);
make down for bottom right-hand
corner of field to reach track leading
to them. After 20 yards, turn left at
T-junction of tracks, and follow
through farmyard to tarmac lane by
telephone box **3** .

Turn right on lane, signposted
Pennine Way, and follow past Lee
Farm, where lane becomes track. **4**
¾ mile after farm cross stream by

bridge and turn right to climb up
steps signposted Jacob's Ladder (**b**).
Beyond steps, path climbs steadily.
5 After ½ mile fork right at cairn
and follow to T-junction of peat
tracks (**c**), (**d**) **6** . Turn right along
edge of slope; path is well defined as
far as small mushroom-shaped rock
(Noe Stool). From this head straight
on to large group of rocks (Pym
Chair), still keeping close to edge of
slope **7** . Beyond Pym Chair, bear
quarter left towards highest of large
number of weathered rocks known as
Wool Packs; although this is a
complicated area, there is a path
leading between the rocks, or you can
make your way round them.

Beyond Wool Packs soon pick up
edge of slope on your right, and 300
yards later descend gully to cross
stream **8**. After stream immediately
turn right on path which follows
stream down on your right for a few
yards before climbing over brow of

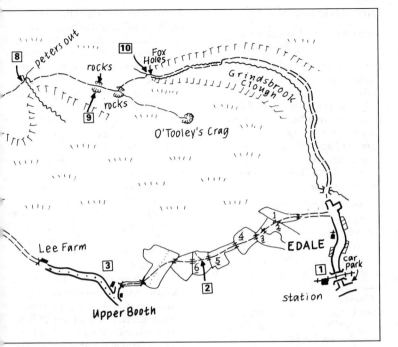

hill. 9 After ½ mile reach another rocky outcrop, and at next (smaller) outcrop 200 yards later bear half left on well trodden path leading gently downhill to deep rocky gully known as Fox Holes. Scramble down it 10.

Turn right alongside stream at bottom of Fox Holes (this is the Pennine Way, but no path is visible for the first few hundred yards). Soon pick up path on left side which follows gully back to Edale.

WHAT TO LOOK OUT FOR

(a) **Pennine Way** Starts here and runs 270 miles up the Pennine Chain to Kirk Yetholm in the Scottish borders. The longest long-distance path after the South-West Peninsula Coast Path. Created 1951-65.

(b) **Jacob's Ladder** Recently built steps beyond the packhorse bridge follow the route hacked out by Jacob Marshall, an 18th-century trades-man who used this short cut while his pony zigzagged up the hillside.

(c) **Kinder Scout** The 20-square mile expanse of peat lags before you is one of the best and largest examples of a blanket bog in the country (though it is being denuded as the peat erodes). The Pennine Way crosses this featureless table, but it is a long and extremely challenging slog, needing very careful compass-reading to cross it. In the 1930s this was the scene of a mass trespass, when ramblers protested about the denial of public access to the countryside, before access areas, long-distance paths, National Parks and registered rights of way came into existence. **Birds** Curlew, dunlin, golden plover, ring ouzel, merlin, red grouse.

(d) For a good **view** W towards Hayfield and Kinder Reservoir, detour forward for five minutes to top of slope.

233

Dove Dale and Milldale

Contributed by Dorothea Whitworth
Recommended by Brian Marsden

Incorporates one of the most dramatic gorges in the Peak District and some quiet wooded and dry-stone walled slopes. Ends with a descent from the side of Bunster Hill. Very easy route-finding as far as the hamlet of Milldale, then less frequented paths (but mostly well defined). Dove Dale is best avoided on busy summer Sundays.

Length *Full walk* 7 miles (11km), 3½ hours.
Difficulty 2–3
Shorter walk omitting Milldale
5 miles (8km), 2½ hours. (For 15-mile walk in Dove Dale incorporating this walk, see special note on Walk 77).
Difficulty 2–3
Start Large car park in Dove Dale, 5 miles NW of Ashbourne. Grid reference SK 146509
OS Maps 1:50,000 119;
1:25,000 Outdoor Leisure 24
Refreshments Izaak Walton Hotel near start; caravan in car park selling snacks and drinks; shop at Milldale with tables inside and out, serves hot and cold drinks and snacks; Air Cottage on hilltop serves tea in garden on warm summer days.

WALK DIRECTIONS

1 Leave car park on path passing to left of toilets. In one minute cross over wooden footbridge on right. Turn left, follow rough path beside river entering gorge, and follow clear path along Dove Dale (**a**) for 2 miles.

2 *For shorter walk* cross over bridge, turn right, follow path 200 yards. Look for waymarker with arrow to Ilam and take narrow path uphill in woodland; this is point **6**.

For full walk do not cross bridge but continue along riverside path. Scenery gradually becomes less dramatic and gorge less high. Cross

stone bridge into small hamlet of Milldale (**b**) **3**. Walk continues on narrow path which leaves hamlet on left just past toilets. Zigzag up small, grassy hill. Turn left and follow path alongside wall. Keep following this narrow path across a steeply sloping field, through gap in wall and steeply uphill through small wood. Cross open field, making for steps over wall to left of stone hut **4**.

Maintain direction across three fields, descending to reach river's edge, then continue for ½ mile close to river. **5** Go through gap in wall into Hurts Wood, then after 200 yards take narrow path on right signposted Ilam **6** (if you reach the footbridge over River Dove you have overshot by 200 yards).

Follow path up through woods. At top, path bears left and runs along inside top of woods with wire fence (farm boundary) above right. Follow path for ½ mile along top of hill, keeping farm boundary close to your right. **7** At end of woodland cross ladder-stile on right, then turn left and cross another ladder-stile over wall into field. Follow farm track towards house (Air Cottage) ahead. **8** At Air Cottage keep on main track which bears right, over cattle-grid, aiming across field towards gate. Immediately before gate turn left uphill between walls.

9 At top of rise pass through gate and continue forward with wall on right to reach NT sign by stile. Cross stile, turn right downhill, with wall on right. **10** 50 yards before bottom reach stile in wall on right; do not cross it but turn left on path which crosses side of Bunster Hill to reach saddle of hillside ahead (track well defined here) **11**. Cross saddle and descend steeply. At bottom proceed a few yards to left and then cross next stile on right into field. Cross fields diagonally to stiles going toward Izaak Walton Hotel. When in field

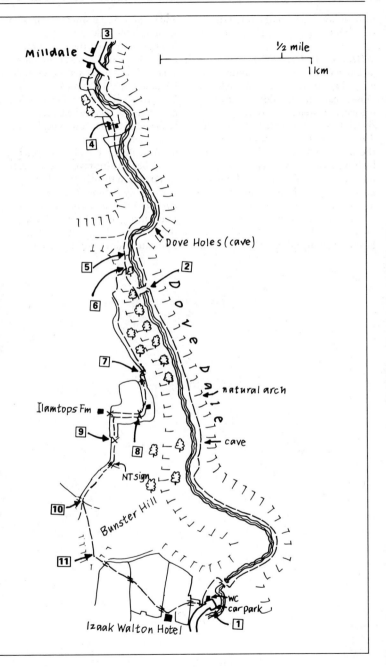

Milldale

3

½ mile

1 km

4

Dove Holes (cave)

5

2

6

D o v e   D a l e

7

natural arch

Ilamtops Fm

9

cave

8

NT sign

10

Bunster Hill

11

WC
car park

1

Izaak Walton Hotel

235

nearest hotel, bear half left to stile
which returns to Dove Dale car park.

WHAT TO LOOK OUT FOR

(a) **Dove Dale** Limestone ravine
gouged out by the action of the River
Dove. Features, in order they are
passed, are: stepping-stones over
river; Dove Dale Castle (crag) on left;
Twelve Apostles (remnants of spurs,
the sides of which have been cut off
by frost action leaving isolated
pinnacles) on right and on left Lover's
Leap (a 130ft high spur from which a
jilted girl in the 18th century
attempted suicide by jumping off,
only to have her fall broken by
bushes, leaving her a little scratched

and surprised). Tissington Spires on
right, Jacob's Ladder on left;
Reynard's Cave on right (natural
arch, 40ft high); Lion's Head Rock
(shaped like a lion – path goes under
it); Ilam Rock (120ft rock) on left;
Pickering Tor on right; Dove Holes
(two shallow caves, the larger 30ft
high and 55ft wide) on right; Raven's
Tor on left.

(b) **Milldale** Izaak Walton stayed here,
and it became his favourite place. It
inspired him to write the classic
work on fly-fishing, *The Compleat
Angler or the Contemplative Man's
Recreation* (1653). Viator's Bridge –
the packhorse bridge at Milldale –
also dates from about this time.

Calke Abbey Park and Staunton Harold

Contributed by Dorothea and Tiny Whitworth
Recommended by Pauline and Barry Haynes

Takes in two country mansions, their parkland and a succession of ponds and small lakes, with woodland, farmland and a short stretch of road providing the link. Not all field paths defined, but route-finding reasonably easy.

Length *Full walk* 6 miles (9.5km), 2¾ hours
Difficulty 2
Short walk omitting Staunton Harold 4 miles (6.5km), 2 hours
Difficulty 1
Start Middle Lodge in Calke Abbey Park. 9 miles S of Derby. Entrance to park from A514 in village of Ticknall (one way traffic); car park is ¼ mile into park. Grid reference SK 362229
OS maps 1:50,000 128; 1:25,000 SK 22/23
Refreshments Saracen's Head coffee-shop in Staunton Harold Hall; Staunton Stables Tea-room in craft centre

WALK DIRECTIONS

[1] From car park return to Middle Lodge, pass beneath archway and turn left. Proceed alongside fence for 60 yards and then cross stile on left. Proceed ahead down left side of first field, then cross stile into wood Follow woodland path 80 yards to next stile, then forward along left edge of second and third fields. [2] Leave third field by far left-hand corner. In fourth field, standing with farmhouse away quarter left, continue ahead, aiming for middle of far hedge/fence and leave field by gate on to road. Left on road, and follow for 500 yards.

[3] Immediately after road bends sharp right, cross stile on left by footpath sign. By keeping alongside fence on your left, proceed across four fields. [4] Emerge by gates on to road and turn left along road for 100 yards. *For short walk* proceed along road for another 100 yards to point [9]. *For full walk* turn right up lane, past Saracen's Head, to farm at top of rise. Look for metal field-gate on left, opposite side of farmhouse (if padlocked, climb sturdy wooden fence). Cross small area beside old brick barn and climb fence into field ahead (easiest access is to right of barn, by climbing wooden fence) (a). Proceed across first field, beside left-hand hedge, at end of which leave via fence into second field [5].

Continue in same direction across second and third fields with woodland fence on right. At far side of third field pass through gate, step over low fence just beyond into fourth field and continue alongside hedge on right. [6] When level with houses turn left on track, then after 40 yards turn right on wide farm track. Proceed past back of nurseries, and then with woods on your left for ⅓ mile, until reaching strip of woodland which comes across from right [7].

Proceed a few more yards, then just before stream take narrow woodland path on left. Proceed with stream on right at first; path then bends left, and winds round to beside small lake on right. Cross shallow stream by wooden plank. [8] Emerge from wood on to lawns. Continue beside lake past Staunton Harold church (b). Turn up left and pass Staunton Harold Hall on your left. Cross car-parking area and turn left on tarmac drive, past craft centre and nurseries, and follow ⅔ mile (c) to road junction [9].

Turn right and follow road, ignoring right turn after ⅔ mile. [10] Turn left back into Calke Abbey Park (through exit gate for cars). Proceed up tarmac drive, passing church, then down past abbey (d) to stable block behind. Where drive hairpins left, proceed ahead into abbey car park. Leave car park by gate on left. Turn right and continue with fence on right. Proceed steeply downhill to Thatch House Pond, joining path and steps coming from left.

Cross over fence to right, past weir, and follow path alongside and above narrow lake. Path bends left around end of water. Proceed uphill on grassy path turning left half way up hill and 35 yards past second electricity post [11]. Path winds through bracken to reach gate. Pass through gate into field/parkland and continue on path which bears slightly left and crosses to top edge of tree line. Continue ahead to cross stile. Turn right for a few yards to top of track, then follow track downhill to car park.

WHAT TO LOOK OUT FOR

(a) The right of way passes to the left of the barn, but there were two broken (and not really usable) gates to contend with at inspection. The ensuing section across fields lacks gates or stiles, at time of writing, but the fences are quite low and reasonably manageable.

(b) **Staunton Harold** Formerly a village; only the hall (now with craft centre) and church remain, in a beautiful lake and parkland setting. The hall was originally Jacobean, but was altered in 1700, then largely rebuilt in the Palladian style by the fifth Earl of Ferrers, from 1763 onwards. The Ferrers sold up and left in 1954, and the hall would have faced demolition had it not been taken over by Group-Captain Leonard Cheshire as a Cheshire Home. The church (NT) was rebuilt by Sir Robert Shirley between 1653 and 1665, as a gesture of defiance against Cromwell. An inscription

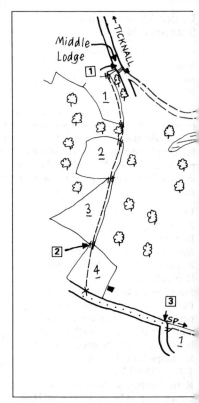

above the entrance reads, 'When all things sacred were throughout the nation Either demollisht or profaned'. Its ceiling paintings, woodwork and fittings are all from the mid 17th century; the organ and fine iron chancel screen were added in the early 18th century.

(c) A public right of way shown on OS maps going N of here through Dimminsdale has, unfortunately, been extinguished.

(d) **Calke Abbey** (recently taken over by the NT; due to open to public 1989) Classical mansion built in 1703 on the site of priory founded soon after the Norman Conquest. Stands in a 500-acre deer park. St Giles church, in the grounds, has a fine monument to Sir John Harpour and his wife.

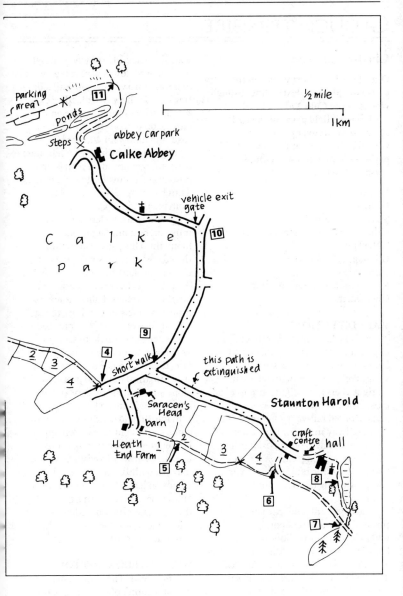

GLOUCESTERSHIRE

Chedworth Villa

One of the best short walks on the Cotswold plateau, descending through woods to the Coln Valley. Road-walking and field paths in the early stages; descent over pasture to Chedworth village at end. Most field paths undefined but route-finding reasonably easy.

Length 4 miles (6.5km), 1½ hours
Difficulty 1–2
Start Seven Tuns Inn at N end of village, close to church. Grid reference SP 052120
OS maps 1:50,000 163; 1:25,000 SP 01/11
Refreshments Seven Tuns Inn, Chedworth

WALK DIRECTIONS

1 (a) Take lane immediately to right of pub, and after only 5 yards turn half left on footpath to cross stile after 20 yards. Follow top of field: where fence on right veers away right, turn left and cross stile to enter strip of woodland (course of old railway). On other side of old railway make for left end of terrace of cottages on opposite hillside, by proceeding wall on left to bottom, crossing bridge over stream and continuing up to road by cottages **2**.

Cross road, and take path opposite through gate (to left of cottages), which leads uphill following right-hand side of field to stile at far end, and then is sunken and leads to road. Turn right on road. Pass large barns on your left after 500 yards, then count two fields on your left after these barns. Second field has small covered water-tank close to road: take second gate on left (into third field) (b **3**).

Cross field, and edge of woodland soon appears on right. Follow stone

wall alongside edge of wood on right to bottom of hollow where gateway leads half right into wood. Ignore all side tracks and follow woodland track for ½ mile to pass through gate and emerge on to road **4**. Turn left on road, and follow for 200 yards to 90-degree bend by house on left; here carry straight ahead on path (signposted) and follow for ½ mile to road. Turn left on road, signposted to Roman villa only (c).

5 Take path on left of modern museum building (signposted public footpath). This path leads uphill through woods, passing under old railway by short tunnel after 100 yards. **6** 150 yards later turn sharp left at junction of tracks. Follow track for ½ mile, ignoring side turnings, to reach stile at edge of wood **7**. Continue ahead across first field to stile on skyline. In second field maintain direction with fence on right; cross stile into third field and proceed alongside wall on left to next gate ahead (avoid gate on left).

In fourth field continue ahead to stone stile (avoid stile on left) **8**. Follow steps down through copse. Emerge by stile into pasture, and make downhill, keeping parallel to woods on left. Where you see house on right at bottom, turn right through gate/stile immediately before it and follow lane to pass church and return to start.

WHAT TO LOOK OUT FOR

(a) **Chedworth** The church, in a pleasant corner of this large, scattered village, has a Norman font and a wine-glass-shaped 15th-century pulpit. The turret at the SE corner of the nave bears the date 1485 in Arabic numerals, a very early use of these, and a reminder that the Cotswold wool trade brought in traders and

ideas from distant parts.
(**b**) This right of way was not
signposted from the road and was
ploughed out when we checked it.
(**c**) **Chedworth Roman villa** (NT; open
to public; fee) Romano-British villa
excavated 1864–66 with bath-house
and pavements, plus a museum. David
Verey describes it as 'one of the few
villa sites in Britain to retain an
atmosphere of rural peace – Virgil
would have approved of it'.

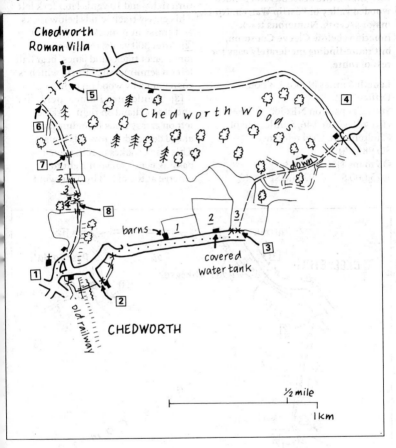

Cleeve Common and Postlip Warren

Takes in the highest point in the Cotswolds. Easy walking on the plateau top, on tracks across springy turf, then route descends steep-sided wooded valley of Postlip Warren. No major ascents. Numerous track junctions below Cleeve Common, but route-finding moderately easy for rest of route.

Length 6 miles (9.5km), 3 hours
Difficulty 2
Start Car park on NE side of Cleeve Hill village on A46, 5 miles NE of Cheltenham. Grid reference SO 985270
OS maps 1;50,000 163; 1:25,000 SO 82/92 and SP 02/12

WALK DIRECTIONS

1 From car park follow road downhill for 30 yards, then turn left opposite bus shelter and phone box, over gate/stile (signposted public path) to follow track. After 10 yards turn right, and 10 yards later fork left. This grassy track winds below rocks and grassy hummocks on your left.

2 After 300 yards, reach 5-way junction of tracks and lanes; bear half left on semi-metalled track, which is soon joined by wood on right.

3 ½ mile later, immediately after end of woodland on right, fork half left on grassy track (avoiding lane ahead descending towards houses). This track snakes uphill, soon passing bench on your right to emerge at top of hill by 'Cotswold

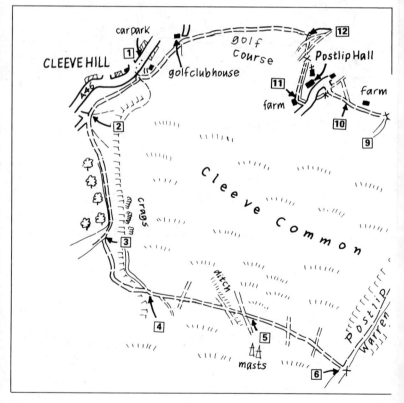

242

Way new route' marker post (**a**) 4.
Continue direction (avoiding oblique
cross-track which heads towards
masts away to right). Track is well
defined, and follow it across open
grassland, ignoring all cross-tracks.

5 After ¾ mile track reaches edge
of gorse area on left (joining track
from left: keep forward along it).
Continue same direction (edge of
gorse immediately veers away half
left) to reach gate in stone wall after
¾ mile 6. Do not pass through gate,
but turn left, descending with wall on
right. After ½ mile, cross stile
(waymarked) into wood, and 7 200
yards later turn right (marker post)
and 50 yards later turn sharp left on
woodland track. This descends gently
to pass house (Woodpeckers).

8 100 yards beyond Woodpeckers,
where wooden railing on left ceases,
turn sharp left through gate (blue
arrow marker) and follow path down
to stream (**b**). After crossing stream,
ascend alongside fence on left,
towards brow of hill. 9 Near top,
pass through gate on left (blue
marker) and maintain direction on
farm track which shortly passes farm.
10 200 yards after farm, avoid right
fork and 100 yards later (50 yards
before cottages ahead) turn left (**c**)
through gate (yellow marker). Keep
alongside wall on right, cross track
200 yards later and pass through gates
opposite.

11 Where wall on right veers right,
continue to follow it on track which
leads through gate, to emerge on open
land. Continue straight on and avoid
all side-tracks. Pass through gate at
top 12. This track leads to starting-
point – avoid right turn after 200
yards and ¼ mile later pass golf club-
house on your right to take track by
'Tewkesbury Council – no golfing'
sign; avoid tarmac track on r.ght soon
after, but take rough track on right
immediately beyond which leads
down to gate and starting-point.

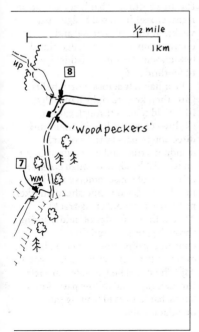

WHAT TO LOOK OUT FOR
(**a**) Water permeating through the
oolitic Cotswold limestone has
lubricated the impermeable clay
foundations, resulting in an unstable
slope and large-scale landslips. The
scarp slope caused by this has been
eroded back and troughs have been
created – including the embayments
in which Cheltenham and
Winchcombe stand, and the valley of
Postlip Warren. **View** W across the
Severn to the Forest of Dean, with the
Sugar Loaf and Black Mountains
beyond. Further to the right is the
jagged outline of the Malverns and
further right still, Birmingham.
(**b**) **View** of Winchcombe, with
Sudeley Castle further right.
(**c**) **Postlip Hall** (not open to public), a
16th- to early 17th-century
manor-house with a restored Norman
chapel in its grounds.

Shenberrow Hill and Stanton

**Climbs quickly to follow farm tracks
along the Cotswold ridge, with views
of the Vale of Evesham, Bredon Hill
and the Malverns. Drops down
through partly wooded pasture into
Stanton, to return over pasture, with
views of the escarpment from below.
Directions for this last stage should
be followed carefully; route not
always visible on the ground.**

Length 5 miles (8km), 2½ hours
Difficulty 2
Start Buckland, 12 miles NE of
Cheltenham and 1 mile E of A46.
Grid reference SP 084360
OS maps 1:50,000 150;
1:25,000 SP 03/13
Refreshments Mount Inn, Stanton
(with garden)

WALK DIRECTIONS

1 Take road to left of Buckland
church (**a**), and follow it out of village
centre, soon ascending and passing
ponds; eventually road becomes unmetalled and near top of rise curves
right (avoid left turn). **2** ½ mile after
top of rise, pass through gate, and
immediately beyond it turn right on
track signposted Shenberrow Hill and
Stanton. Follow track through fields
for ¾ mile, to T-junction of tracks **3**.
Turn left on track for 10 yards, then
turn sharp right over cattle-grid (blue
arrow marker). Follow this (over
Shenberrow Hill with its hillfort) for
½ mile.

4 Where main track veers left to
house, continue straight ahead
through gate (yellow marker). Ignore
cross-track after 20 yards but make
for marker post ahead; path then
swings right to follow bottom of dry
valley. **5** After 300 yards fork left
(marker post), soon passing fenced
drain, and cross stile in corner of
field. Keep to right side of field,
passing stone outhouse after 100
yards, and cross stile (yellow marker)

on your right soon after. Beyond
stile, bear immediately half left on
faint path, aiming to right of lake in
distance, to reach stile which leads
between fences to second stile **6**.

After second stile ascend ahead for
20 yards to reach track. Turn left and
follow into and through Stanton
village (Mount Inn is on first turning
right) (**b**). **7** Turn right by stone
cross in centre of village, follow lane
50 yards, then turn left into churchyard. Follow path to left of church
and take path between stone walls
on other side of churchyard. Cross
stile into first field and maintain
direction (no path) aiming for stile
in far corner ahead. Follow path
along left edge of second field,
still maintaining direction, to
stile/stones over stream **8**.

In third field bear half right to
corner of hedge immediately ahead,
then continue half right (ignoring
track quarter right which runs ap-
proximately parallel to hedge)
towards bottom of bank of trees up on
right; cross line of old hedge (still
visible at time of writing) and
continue up to stile in hedge ahead
(which soon becomes visible) leading
to footbridge **9**.

Bear half left across fourth field to
gate, then keep to right-hand edge of
fifth field to pass through gate on
skyline; cross sixth field, maintain
direction to pass to right of large
deciduous tree, and continue straight
on to stile, heading through copse. At
other side of copse, emerge by ditch
into field **10**. Continue ahead (marker
post) to gate (avoid cross-track).
Then follow left edge of field, passing
through gate/stile and then
continuing direction. Fence on left
eventually meets with hedge beyond.
11 Where this hedge ends, turn left
through gate, and follow path down
(along bank) to road leading into
Buckland village.

WHAT TO LOOK OUT FOR
(a) Buckland church Has 13th-century arcades and 16th-century panelling; happily, the 'restorers' passed it by. The rectory nearby is largely medieval.
(b) Stanton Pretty example of a North Cotswold village, which owes much to the care of Sir Philip Stott, a land-owner and architect. In the centre is the village cross, which has a 17th-century sundial on its medieval base. The church is Norman and Perpendicular, and has 20th-century furnishings by Sir Ninian Comper, whose strawberry symbol can be seen in the stained glass.

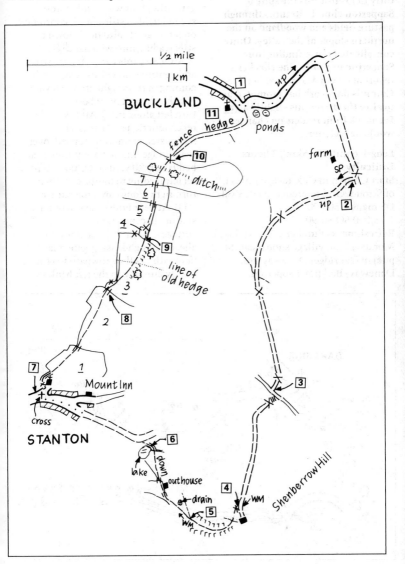

The Thames and Severn Canal and Sapperton

Recommended by D J Sutton

An exploration of the narrow and secluded Stroud Valley, along the towpath of the derelict canal on the valley floor, then heading up over turfy fields towards the spire of Sapperton church. Returns through pasture fields and woodland on the northern slopes of the valley. Quite complicated route-finding from Sapperton onwards; one checker's report of recent Manpower Services Commission work has prompted us to alter the directions slightly at [11]. Feedback from readers on changes would be welcome.

Length 6 miles (9.5km), 3 hours
Difficulty 2
Start Church in Oakridge, 6 miles E of Stroud. Grid reference SO 913033
OS maps 1:50,000 163;
1:25,000 SO 80/90
Refreshments Butcher's Arms (closed Mondays) and village shop (near the pub) in Oakridge; Daneway Inn, Daneway; Bell Inn, Sapperton.

WALK DIRECTIONS

[1] Start on small green by entrance to church, with church immediately down to left and school on right, and bear half right to find path at end of green, leading between cottages, and between walls, to stile (with yellow waymark). Turn half left following left edge of first field to reach gate/stile; follow 10 yards across second field to stile ahead; continue on left edge of third field, down to stile leading into woodland [2] .

After 30 yards turn left over stile, and continue downhill (avoid path coming in from right after 150 yards). Reach tarmac lane at bottom and turn left along it. [3] After ¼ mile reach junction and turn right, signposted Frampton Mansell, over road-bridge. Immediately after, road bends left; 20 yards later take steps on left leading to footbridge; then turn right along canal towpath (**a**).

[4] At next bridge pass to other side of old canal, taking track past cottages; 30 yards later continue ahead through kissing-gate, marked 'footpath'. Follow towpath for 1 mile, finally crossing to the left bank by

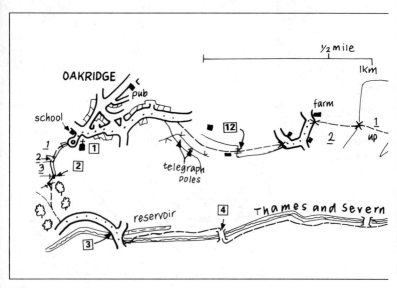

wooden bridge, then emerging on road by Daneway Inn **5**. Cross to other side of bridge and continue along other side of the towpath, signposted Sapperton; course of canal is now through pub car park.

6 After ½ mile, path crosses over mouth of canal tunnel (**b**) and leads up to stile. Bear quarter right uphill across field, heading for spire of Sapperton church and soon passing to right of stone shelter. At stile at top, path continues on left to churchyard **7**. Continue through churchyard to reach road (**c**).

Turn left on road and follow it downhill, turning left at junction after 100 yards. Continue, avoiding right turns; where road leads to house on left, keep right (signposted public footpath), cross stream and then cross traces of old canal (with remains of lock just visible), to enter woodland. 50 yards after bridge, avoid sharp left turn, and 50 yards later, take fork left uphill.

8 After 200 yards turn left at crossing of tracks. Follow tracks along level, avoiding any right turns (avoid sharp right after 200 yards and

2 tracks on right at junction 300 yards later) and continue until road **9** (**d**). Turn left on road, but immediately cross gate/stile on right, then follow track winding half left round side of hill. After 50 yards, cross stile on left (avoid stile on right) and follow path across grassland, at far end of which gate/stile leads on to road **10**.

Turn right on road, passing driveway on right after 250 yards. 100 yards later, fork half left on stony driveway. 50 yards on, find gap in hedge on left of drive opposite garden of house. Go through gap and follow path between hedges, soon to follow left edge of field. On reaching wooden fence at foot of hill, cross stile on left. Cross field for 20 yards, to gate and over footbridge **11**. After footbridge bear straight on up to stile leading into woodland. Pass through woodland to take gate into field: bear half right across first field (no path), aiming towards buildings and heading through gate in hedge ahead on skyline. In second field head for gate immediately to left of metal barn.

Emerge on to lane and turn left along it. Avoid left turning marked

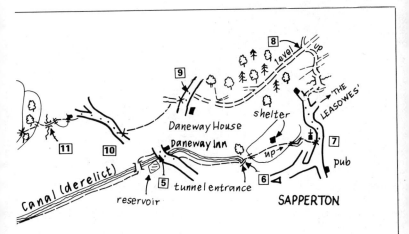

'Unsuitable for motors' after 200 yards, but 100 yards later, where road bends right, keep ahead through gate (yellow waymark). Path follows left edge of field and is well defined.
12 On far side of field, cross stile and bear quarter right (path undefined) uphill, following telegraph poles. At junction at top (with farmhouse away to right), continue forward along left edge of field to find gate leading on to road. Turn left on road and follow road through Oakridge and to Oakridge church (turnings up on right take you through middle of village).

WHAT TO LOOK OUT FOR
(a) The derelict **Thames and Severn Canal** functioned from 1789 until 1911. Further on is one of its feeder reservoirs, followed by the Daneway Inn, a canalside pub by the site of a former flight of locks.
(b) **Canal tunnel** with grand embattled parapet. The tunnel leads SW for two miles, to emerge at a pub near Coates.
(c) **Sapperton** Ernest Gimson and the brothers Barnsley, followers of the Arts and Crafts movement, settled here at the beginning of this century and built a number of cottages in the village in traditional style, including Upper Dorvel House, Leasowes, Beechanger, number 40a on the Green, and the village hall. The church was largely remodelled in the early 18th century and contains bench-ends with Jacobean caryatids, transplanted from Sapperton House after it was demolished in the 1730s. Poet John Masefield lived at Pinbury House during the Second World War.
(d) A few yards left is **Daneway House**, a medieval manor that Lord Bathurst allowed the Barnsley brothers and Ernest Gimson to use as a workshop for producing and exhibiting Arts and Crafts style furniture.

HEREFORD & WORCESTER

Symonds Yat and the Chickenwire Bridge

Contributed by Mrs I Southall

A good walk for children, providing they don't mind the 400ft climb uphill to the Symonds Yat Rock viewpoint at the end. Involves two crossings of river – by a ferry pulled across by a wire, and later over a wire suspension bridge (quite safe, despite creakiness). Between these, follows level tracks along the wooded Wye Gorge (where there are often abseilers and canoeists). Good waymarking throughout; route-finding easy. Ferry operates daily, all year. Can be joined to Walk 129 from the suspension bridge, for a full day's walk.

Length 3½ miles (5.5km), 1½ hours
Difficulty 2
Start The Symonds Yat Forestry Commission car park, on B4432 3 miles NNW of Coleford; on right side of road as approached from Coleford (no parking in village or at Symonds Yat West). Grid reference SO 564158
OS maps 1:50,000 162; 1:25,000 Outdoor Leisure 14
Refreshments Various in Symonds Yat East

WALK DIRECTIONS

1 From car park turn right on road (away from Coleford), then after 50 yards left on to track with 'no entry' road signs. Follow this, pass to right of toilets and continue forward past refreshment cabin (Wye Valley Walk sign). Continue 50 yards beyond cabin to pick up waymarked path (following yellow arrows). Descend steeply to cross-track, turn left and immediately right to continue down.

2 At T-junction of paths (with chalet-style house visible ahead), turn left, descending to road by river. Turn right to Saracen's Head Inn.

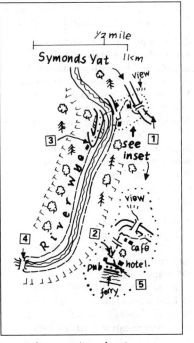

Locate ferryman (in pub or just outside), cross river by ferry, walk up to lane. Left on to lane and follow for 200 yards, soon ascending slightly. **3** Where lane bends sharp right, continue forward past Woodlea (guest-house). Follow track along river gorge to suspension bridge.

4 Cross bridge, turn left on other side and follow back to Symonds Yat East. **5** Retrace steps to car park by taking path just to right of entrance to Forest View Hotel and turn right up steps (waymarked) opposite chalet-style house behind trees. ¼ mile later turn right up steps (waymarked) and ascend to grassy track, turn left and immediately right up to refreshment kiosk. From here it is two minutes' walk to viewpoint. Keeping to left of kiosk, cross wooden bridge over road, turn left on other side, to reach Symonds Yat Rock.

249

The Malvern Hills and Eastnor Castle

Contributed by Humphrey Southall
Recommended by Ronald Locke

Takes in perhaps the most interesting part of the main Malvern ridge (a bold moorland ridge with vast views), but also includes the lower and wooded Ledbury Hills. Passes a number of sites of literary or historical importance, including the Iron Age hillfort at the British Camp, the highest point on the walk, and the mock-medieval Eastnor Castle. Route-finding quite involved; directions should be followed carefully.

Length 13 miles (21km), 6½ hours
Difficulty 3–4
Start Ledbury town centre, by the half-timbered Market House
OS maps 1:50,000 149 and 150; 1:25,000 SO 63/73 and SO 64/74
Refreshments Full range in Ledbury; Horse and Jockey, Colwall; refreshment hut at British Camp car park

WALK DIRECTIONS

1 From Market House (**a**) walk up Church Lane (not Church *Street*). At top, turn half left on path through small park (**b**); at exit turn slightly left, then turn right on road for 50 yards, past entrance to John Masefield High School, ignoring left turn (Homend Crescent) and continue up steps into wood **2**.

Ascend path as it bends left, avoiding two minor paths, but when path begins to level out take major path to right, leading to edge of wood. After ⅓ mile reach road at junction (**c**). Cross road and follow minor road opposite for 200 yards; bear left at footpath sign into small farmyard, then immediately right into field **3**. Ascend field to wood, between hedges at first, then through right-hand gate with hedge on left

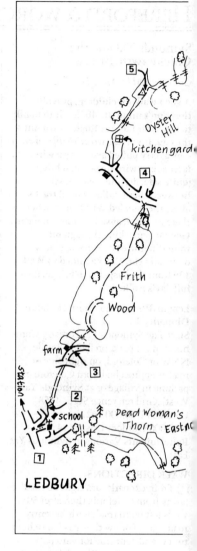

For an account of rights of access in the countryside – and how to complain if a public right of way is unusable – see the 'law and practice' section on page 17.

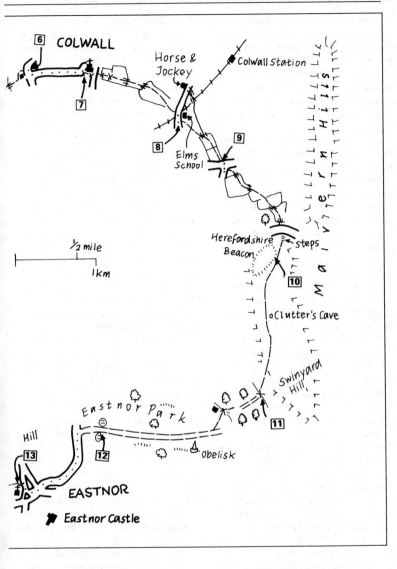

If you have a walk to suggest for any subsequent edition of the Holiday Which? Good Walks Guide, *please send it to us. We need a rough sketch map and a brief summary of the walk's attractions. Directions are not necessary. The address to write to is on page 10.*

and enter woods by stile. Path goes over minor shoulder then turns left at T-junction with wider path. Follow path above field, but when field ends and major path turns right, take minor path steeply left up on to ridge and then continue forward along ridge; at end, path descends through field to gate and road **4**.

Left along road and proceed for ¼ mile until entrance to Hope End on right. Go over stile to left of drive and follow footpath across field (**d**) to cross stile by edge of wood into second field, then continue to trig. point at summit of Oyster Hill **5**. From summit, continue forward along, and drop down, steep bank, to turn right along cross-track on near side of iron railing fence. When track veers right, continue forward along fence over grass to first of series of stiles. Maintain same direction to emerge by house on to road **6**.

Turn right on road then left after 25 yards into road signposted Colwall Church. Follow for ½ mile. **7** When road bends left, enter churchyard by gate (**e**). Cross churchyard and leave by opposite gate, maintaining direction, then take path opposite, between two houses. Follow path through succession of fields. In fourth field bend slightly to right and exit on to drive of Brockbury Hall. Follow drive to road by railway bridge **8**.

For Horse and Jockey turn left on to road for ¼ mile. Turn right on leaving pub then, shortly left on footpath signposted British Camp, cross railway line, continue over field beyond, to playing field. Skirt to stile in far right-hand corner, continue straight ahead over series of stiles to reach road opposite Oldcastle Farm at **9**. *Otherwise* ascend steps from drive to road over bridge, take path on left after Elms school, then cross playing field and two fields to road opposite entrance Oldcastle Farm **9**.

Cross road and enter Oldcastle

Farm drive, but turn off left immediately and follow hedge. Continue into second field, then over stile in left-hand hedgerow, just beyond crest of rise, into third field. Continuing uphill in roughly same direction, cross large field, aiming to right of prominent new house, and ascend past toilets at British Camp car park to road. Turn right and cross A449 to steps at right-hand end of large car park. Follow steps and tarmac path to summit of British Camp/Herefordshire Beacon (**f**) **10**.

From summit descend slightly and follow ridge; at end of ridge, make steep descent bearing left to Cutter's Cave (**g**) and continue forward on path. Descend slightly to saddle, ignoring track which crosses ridgeway. Follow ridge to Swinyard Hill for ⅓ mile, then beyond crest of hill descend to right, following path to gate into wood **11**.

Ignoring first gate on right, take track through wood, turn right over stile by second gate, in clearing, and bear left on track to gate, with keeper's cottage on right. Go through gate and continue on track to obelisk (**h**). **12** Cross bottom of valley between two lakes, then bend left and rise to join tarmac drive; follow to main road opposite gates to Eastnor Castle. Unless visiting castle (**i**), cross main road and bear right into Eastnor village; keep to right of village green and follow road past church, turning left on to footpath beside entrance to Eastnor Court **13**.

Follow path along left-hand edge of field, rising to obtain view of Eastnor village; at crest, path turns right and down, with Eastnor Hill on right. Cross field on track, then enter wood for short distance. At end of wood cross stile then ascend field, passing ruins at Dead Woman's Thorn to right; go through belt of trees and cross further field, then enter wood by gate on right. Follow path down through wood, ignoring forestry tracks that cut across path, which becomes increasingly cut into the hillside.

At bottom, gate and short lane leads to main road. Cross to footway and turn left, following road until past police staton and Magistrates Court, then right on path leading to Ledbury churchyard; turn left, and back to starting-point.

WHAT TO LOOK OUT FOR

(**a**) The half-timbered, 16th-century **Market House** is attributed to John Abel, King's carpenter by appointment to Charles I. More half-timbering in **Church Lane**, one of the most perfect medieval streets in England.

(**b**) **Ledbury church** Largely early 14th-century with a detached tower bearing a Georgian spire. Masefield wrote of its 'golden vane surveying half the shire'.

(**c**) **Knapp Lane**, away to the left, descends to Ledbury station. At its foot is Knapp House, Masefield's birthplace (1878). His narrative poem *The Everlasting Mercy* is set in the area covered by this walk.

(**d**) To the right is the site of **Hope End**, the family home of Elizabeth Barrett Browning between 1810 and 1825. The house has gone but the

curiously oriental stables and kitchen garden remain.

(**e**) **Colwall church** Has a Norman doorway and some Early English work. W H Auden was a schoolmaster at Colwall in the 1930s.

(**f**) This is one of the most spectacular hillforts in Britain. The original **Iron Age fort** consisted of an 8-acre enclosure on the highest part of the hill, ringed by a bank and ditch. Later it was enlarged, and in the 11th or 12th century a Norman castle motte was raised on the summit. Among the many who have treasured this marvellous place was the composer Edward Elgar, who walked here often. **View** SW to the Sugar Loaf (1,955ft); W to the Black Mountains (2,338ft) and the Brecon Beacons (2,906ft); WNW to Radnor Forest (216ft); NW to Titterston Clee Hill (1,750ft); E to Bredon Hill (961ft); SE to the Cotswolds (979ft); SSW to the Forest of Dean.

(**g**) This is a medieval **shepherd's shelter**, cut into the rock.

(**h**) The **obelisk** is a memorial to the Seymour-Cocks family of Eastnor castle.

(**i**) **Eastnor Castle** Not medieval (despite its appearance), but early 19th-century: the work of Smirke and Pugin between 1812 and 1851. For opening times, phone Ledbury 2304.

Witley Court and Abberley Hill

Contributed by Humphrey Southall
Recommended by Ronald Locke

Wooded hills and quiet farmland, later descends into Abberley Park. Follow directions carefully, especially in woodland sections.

Length 6 miles (9.5km), 3 hours
Difficulty 3
Start Hundred House, Great Witley, on A451 and A443, 11 miles NW of Worcester. Grid reference SO 752662
OS maps 1:50,000 150; 1:25,000 SO 66/76
Refreshments Hundred House and post office shop, Great Witley

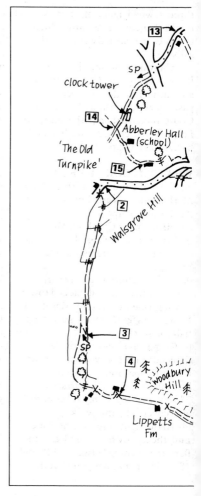

WALK DIRECTIONS

1 From Hundred House (**a**) cross road to gate by phone box with public footpath signpost. Go through gate then bear right across field, heading for stile that can be seen on skyline. Go through gate on to sunken road and over stile on opposite bank. Maintain direction across field to another pair of stiles. Bear left on road beyond for 400 yards, until reaching minor road on left at house called The Old Turnpike **2**. Turn up minor road for 50 yards, then left through gate into field. Cross field to well-defined path up shoulder of Walsgrove Hill, starting at corner of wood. Ascend hill by path, then turn right along summit path, through succession of small fields with wide views to right (**b**).

3 At signpost, follow direction right, then left into wood till stile is reached. Cross and continue up field, ignoring gate on right, and bear slightly left, to gate leading uphill to farm **4**. Pass in front of farm (**c**), then enter wood by gate. Continue forward on path running just inside wood, leading to Lippetts Farm. Pass to left of farm, then re-enter wood by gate. Continue around side of Woodbury

Hill (**d**), on overgrown track, and descend with path to stile and into field next to house. Continue down field to second stile and road **5**.

Turn right along road for 300 yards, then left down tree-lined track and descend to derelict farm buildings. Continue on track as it bends right then curves round edge of large field, then past a second building and up minor ridge, where it meets another track coming up from right **6**. Turn left on this and follow for ½ mile to junction with main drive of Witley

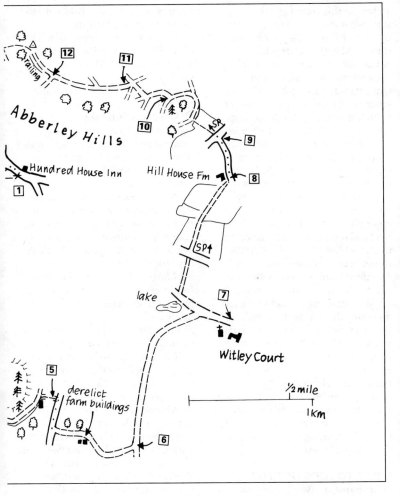

Court. Detour right to visit house and church (e) **7**.

Return along drive past point where it was joined earlier and descend into minor valley with pool on left, turning right on to another track as soon as drive starts to ascend again. Follow track across field to road and cross to footpath signposted Redmarley. Follow track over rise to Hillhouse Farm, then **8** swing around to right of farm buildings and descend steeply on tarmac road to another small valley, passing

between pools. Continue on road as it ascends to another main road, and cross to footpath signposted Abberley Hill **9**.

Cross field and when track divides at edge of wood take right-hand fork. Follow this, keeping edge of wood on left, and take next left fork which runs up on to a shoulder, where another path joins from left, and then ascends shoulder steeply (f). **10** At top of rise, turn left on track which after 200 yards descends slightly, then turns to left while in minor valley. At this corner (**g**) take somewhat overgrown path steeply uphill following valley, to summit ridge of Abberley. Here join path which follows ridge and turn left [**11**].

Continue along ridge for ½ mile, ignoring side paths. [**12**] At obvious junction of paths keep right, and at further junction just beyond, keep left. When path picks up line of iron fence continue to follow this, keeping it on left-hand side, to reach trig. point on summit. Beyond summit, bear down slope to left to reach well-defined path below, leading down end of hill to join minor road just right of house [**13**]. Turn left on road and follow downhill. At bottom, cross A443 and follow bridlewalk immediately opposite, signposted Stamford Road. This runs directly below Abberley Hall clock tower (**h**).

[**14**] At crossing of tracks turn left and immediately right on track, passing under footbridge and skirting school buildings. Beyond buildings continue along sunken trackway. At junction turn left to pass behind range of farm buildings. [**15**] At clearing with pond on left, turn right round back of house and over stile on to track leading shortly down to road. Cross and turn right on footway back to Hundred House.

WHAT TO LOOK OUT FOR

(**a**) **Hundred House** This very substantial Georgian inn has a photograph on the wall inside showing a visiting party of cyclists at the end of the last century. Among them is young Stanley Baldwin, later to become Prime Minister.

(**b**) **View** Over the Teme valley. The Clee hills are beyond, and in clear weather the Black Mountains can be seen.

(**c**) There may be peacocks on the roof here.

(**d**) **Woodbury Hill** Large figure-of-eight-shaped Iron Age fort, surrounded by rampart, ditch and bank. Reached by footpath from Lippetts Farm; return to the farm to continue the walk.

(**e**) **Witley Court** Spectacular ruined Victorian mansion, once one of the richest houses in England, with two enormous fountains in the gardens. The attached Church of St Michael is described by Pevsner in *The Buildings of England* as 'the most Italian and the most baroque church interior in England'. Not to be missed.

(**f**) **View** Back over the Severn Valley to Bredon Hill and the Cotswolds.

(**g**) This point has to be identified carefully; perhaps the feet of those who follow the walk will make the path uphill more distinct.

(**h**) **Abberley Hall** Home of William Walsh, an 18th-century poet remembered chiefly for his friendship with Dryden, Addison and Pope. One of the paths is named Addison's Walk, and Pope is known to have been invited to the Hall in 1707. The house was re-built in the 19th century and the clock tower added in 1883. The hall is now a private school.

Old Radnor and Hergest Ridge

Recommended by Brian Hathaway, Andrew Lowe, Kenneth McQueen, Peter Sidaway

Contrasting views east into pastoral England and west into the hill-country of Wales. Mainly through pasture and woodland early on, then later ascends an old drovers' track which winds up behind Hanter Hill. For the climax, an exhilarating but easy walk along Hergest Ridge, with views on three sides. Route-finding rather involved in the early stages (though Offa's Dyke Path waymarks help) as field paths are undefined, but becomes easier.

Length 10 miles (16km), 5 hours
Difficulty 4
Start Kington just off the A44, 18m W of Leominster
OS maps 1:50,000 148;
1:25,000 SO 25/35
Refreshments Harp Inn, Old Radnor (behind church) – an ancient inn, rescued from dereliction by the Landmark Trust in 1972. Pubs and cafés in Kington

WALK DIRECTIONS

1 From the Swan Hotel in Kington enter the square containing war memorial, leave it at far left-hand corner, enter second square and turn right at T-junction at far end. Follow road ignoring side turns: it soon merges into Crooked Well (road). At end, cross footbridge, then cross A44. Take signposted Offa's Dyke Path (ODP) opposite; track leads uphill.
2 After 200 yards take ODP-signposted gate on right, leading up to track between hedges, which in turn leads up to gate into field. Continue forward, up rise to wooden gate leading to fenced path, into hamlet of Bradnor Green (**a**).

Continue forward 50 yards to ODP signpost, then bear half left for 80 yards to next ODP signpost. Continue on path leading immediately to left of houses, soon to reach golf course **3**. Continue forward across golf course aiming for left end of line of trees, where gate/stile on other side of road leads to walled track.

Fork left after 50 yards, enter first field and make for stile (stiles are waymarked by acorns in this section) in top right-hand corner, just to left of small wood. Bear half left in second field to next stile. Continue forward in third field to stile. In fourth field, stile is in bottom far right corner, just above trees. Forward in fifth field, over rise to next stile and signpost **4**. Bear quarter right across sixth field as signposted, soon with fence/hedge on right, looking out for prominent ODP signpost on skyline (half left).

Enter seventh field and bear half left to signpost (which soon comes into view ahead). Signpost and stile are on grassy bank which is Offa's Dyke (**b**); turn left along top of dyke. **5** By next belt of trees follow dyke as it bends left at sheepfold. At end of next field, just before woodland ahead, fork left on wide track which cuts through line of dyke and descends.

6 After 200 yards track passes through gate; 30 yards later fork left (signposted ODP). 100 yards later reach ODP signpost at base of hill, turn left to leave ODP. Descend to fence, turn right along it. **7** After 600 yards take gate on left and bear down to gate beyond and immediately to left of ruined building **8**. Follow right edge of two fields to road. Cross road, take gate opposite and make for gate in top right-hand corner of field (**c**) by turning right along hedge.

9 Beyond gate turn right; proceed with hedge on right for 500 yards to wooden barrier; do not cross barrier but turn left with trees on right, to forestry gate with 'Fire' notice. Continue 300 yards to reach forestry track **10**. Right on forestry track, and follow to A44. Cross road, take road opposite/slightly to left. Turn right at junction after 80 yards, to enter quarry (**d**). **11** After 70 yards reach junction of roads at top of quarry.

If quarry is not operating turn right and keep right, passing 'helmets must be worn beyond this point' sign, and then under double overhead conveyor belt; keep right beyond conveyor, initially alongside fence and, where trees begin, fork right on narrow path leading to kissing-gate into field. Follow field path towards house; 25 yards before house, bear half left, keeping close to fence on right and ignoring track on other side of fence. At the end of field, pass through gate on to road, turn left up to Old Radnor.

If quarry is operating (dangerous to pass under moving conveyors), take 'public road' signed straight ahead. Right at first junction (you will return to this point) and right again at next junction to ascend to Old Radnor.

12 With Old Radnor church porch (**e**) on your right, take road ahead out of Old Radnor. Take first left, after ¼ mile, then right at next junction to descend to hamlet of Burlingjobb **13**. Cross main road (**f**) by phone box and take cul-de-sac opposite, to farm **14**. Do not enter farm (on left) but turn right through gate, then left under power lines to join track which ascends round shoulder of Hanter Hill (on your right).

15 After 600 yards fork right to leave hedge on left. Track ascends towards Hergest Ridge (prominent long hill ahead). **16** Reach complex of tracks by corner of fence and turn left on wide grassy track to ascend to Hergest Ridge (**g**). Towards top fork left, and at top turn right at T-junction with wide track (race-course). **17** 50 yards later, turn sharp left; track descends gently along ridge for 1½ miles to gate, then

along lane (**h**), down to road **18**. Turn right on road, back into Kington.

WHAT TO LOOK OUT FOR
(**a**) **Bradnor Hill** (1,284ft) Site of England's highest golf course. Bradnor Green is a scattered hamlet on the NT-owned common. **Views** into England: ENE to Titterstone Clee Hill (1,750ft) (near Ludlow); E to the jagged Malvern ridge (1,114ft); S to the Black Mountains (2,338ft); SW to the Brecon Beacons (2,906ft).
(**b**) **Offa's Dyke** Well-preserved section of the boundary, built *c.* AD840 by Offa, King of Mercia.
(**c**) Right of way is actually half right to kink in hedgerow, but stile is missing at that point.
(**d**) **Old Radnor limestone quarries** Worked since the late 18th century; limestone formerly quarried for

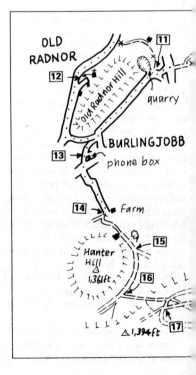

agriculture, now for road works.
(e) Old Radnor church One of Wales's finest churches. Contains a magnificent medieval screen, a monolithic font (carved from one of five stones from a nearby pre-Christian stone circle) and Britain's oldest surviving organ case. The church and a few houses are the remains of what was the capital of Radnorshire, before New Radnor, built as a planned town a few miles away in the 11th century, took over.
(f) New Radnor branch line Opened 1875, closed in the 1950s, it ran from Titley Junction (beyond Kington) to New Radnor (or rather ½ mile short of the latter, as the railway company ran out of money). A former crossing-keeper's cottage stands by the B-road, which here uses the route of the railway.

(g) Hergest Ridge ½ mile wide near Kington, but narrow enough to straddle at its westernmost end a tear-drop shaped grassy ridge capped by a racecourse, used since 1824 for annual trotting races. **Views** S to the Black Mountains; N to Radnor Forest (2,166ft); NE to scarp of Clee Hill in Shropshire; E to the Malverns and, in clear weather, to the Cotswolds beyond. Elgar is believed to have been inspired to write his Introduction and Allegro for Strings while walking here.
(h) Hergest Croft gardens (open to public; fee) Passed after ¼ mile. Created by local banker William Hartland Banks between 1896 and his death in 1930. Included a collection of exotic temperate shrubs and trees, a rockery and bog garden, an azalea garden and greenhouses.

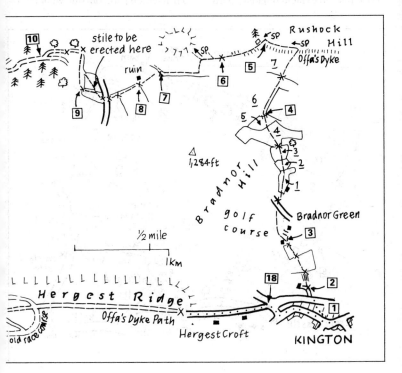

Bircher Common, Croft Ambrey and Croft Castle

Contributed by Ronald Locke

Takes in an outstanding viewpoint, some ancient trees and a medieval-cum-Gothick country house. All paths well defined; route-finding moderately easy.

Length 5 miles (8km), 2½ hours
Difficulty 2
Start Free NT car park on Bircher Common, just N of B4362 and 5 miles NNW of Leominster; 1 mile W of B4361 (Ludlow to Leominster). Grid reference SO 466661
OS maps 1:50,000 137, 148 or 149; 1:25,000 SO 46/56

WALK DIRECTIONS

1 From parking place take metalled track on right, after a few yards forking left on to stony track. After 100 yards leave track for grassy path

on left over common, aiming for buildings ahead, where it rejoins tarmac track by chapel **2**. Turn left along it, and at first junction of paths go straight ahead, keeping pond immediately on right, following path which leads uphill towards right-hand edge of wood on skyline.

3 On reaching wood, path joins broad grassy track. Turn right along it, skirting edge of wood. Follow for 500 yards. **4** Where track turns sharp left, continue forward on grassy path with beeches and wire fence on right. Path soon veers left into grassy field. Follow length of field (path indistinct) aiming for point ahead where two belts of woodland meet one another. **5** At junction of ways at end of field, do not enter wood, but take path on right (past notice relating to use of horses on common), and through gate on to path beyond. Turn left on path, outside woodland

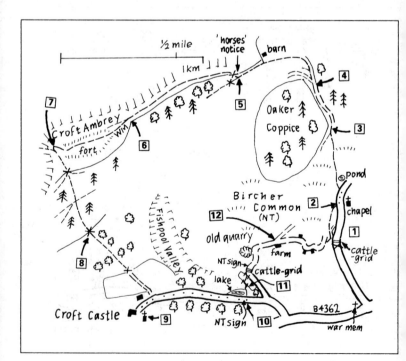

fence and follow along crest of
Leinthall Common, for ½ mile 6.

Just beyond two large ancient
beeches take well-trodden path on
left, steeply uphill with blue
waymarkings, to Croft Ambrey (**a**).
Continue along of hillfort 7. At far
end, path leads down again. Follow
this, ignoring sharp right turn
downhill, to junction by gate bearing
blue waymark, and go through gate
into wood. Follow path ahead. 8
Where path emerges by gate/stile into
field with ancient chestnut trees (**b**)
on left, continue across field in same
direction (path indistinct) to another
line of chestnuts (path becomes
clearer), and then across field. Passing
through gate, path becomes track
crossing parkland of Croft Castle.

At T-junction, with farm buildings
on right, turn left, and soon go over
cattle-grid to entrance gate of Croft
Castle (**c**) (**d**) 9. From castle gateway
follow avenue directly ahead for ½
mile (beech avenue at first then,
beyond cattle-grid, oak avenue) 10.
Leave avenue at NT sign on left,
labelled Fishpool Valley. Take grassy
path half left between two oaks
(avoid track sharp left). Path descends
gently to pass right end of lake. At far
side leave lake: do not follow long
side of lake but continue forward
(faint path) through strip of woodland
up to cross stile into field 11.

Cross stile and continue across
field to next stile, and on to metalled
lane. Turn left over cattle-grid, then
right on broad stony track past NT
sign, keeping sign to left. Track
swings left near farm buildings, then
right at abandoned quarry. 12 At

Highwood Farm take right fork of
tracks, continuing previous direction
to pass two houses and deviate left
round garden of third house; track
then bears left uphill back to parking
place.

WHAT TO LOOK OUT FOR
(**a**) **Croft Ambrey** An Iron Age hillfort
with a total area of about 40 acres,
which was occupied from about 450
BC to its destruction, probably in
AD 48. The inner part of the fort was
surrounded by a rampart and ditch
and contained rows of rectangular
wooden huts, serving as houses,
granaries and other stores. While it
was inhabited it underwent many
changes (excavation has revealed 15
successive sets of gate-posts at one
entrance) and was eventually used as
a Romano-British sanctuary, after it
ceased to be a fort. Fine **view** W to
Radnor Forest, N to Shropshire hills.
(**b**) These **Spanish chestnuts** are about
350 years old.
(**c**) The **Church of St Michael and All
Angels** is close to the Great Door of
the castle. It contains the exceptionally fine early 16th-century tomb
of Sir Richard Croft. The model for
the church was at nearby Shobdon, an
18th-century church with a wedding-
cake Gothick interior.
(**d**) Originally a Norman border castle,
Croft Castle (NT; open to public; fee)
is like a fortified manor-house and is
mainly 14th- and 15th-century, with
substantial 18th-century Gothick
alterations. It has been occupied by
the Croft family continually since
the Norman Conquest, except for the
period 1750-1923.

Lickey Hills and Bittell Reservoirs

Based on contributions from Janice Mason and T E Pennall Recommended by D J Sutton, Dorothea Whitworth, A Duxbury, G H Carpenter

Over farmland and wooded hills, with opportunities for bird-watching by the reservoirs, and only the view from the Lickey Hills to remind of the proximity to Birmingham. Most field paths are signposted and defined, but some care needed with the numerous woodland path junctions.

Length 5 miles (8km), 2½ hours
Difficulty 2
Start Barnt Green station, 5 miles NW of Redditch (platform 4 exit). From Birmingham direction take B4120 to Barnt Green, turn right immediately after railway bridge, into main village street. Park at station. Grid reference SP 006737
OS maps 1:50,000 139; 1:25,000 SO 87/97 and SP 07/17
Refreshments Victoria Inn and shops in Barnt Green

WALK DIRECTIONS

1 From station car park proceed down to road, turn left, then right along B4120. Take first left (Margesson Drive). Where road bends left after 50 yards, keep straight on/slightly to left through entrance in fence (signposted Bittell Farm Road). Keep to right of sports club buildings, behind which path follows hedge into field **2**. Follow left edge of first and second fields. Bear half right in third field, passing immediately to right of copse in centre of field, to gate and on to road **3**.

Continue forward along road (ignoring road on right and private road on left), past reservoirs (**a**) and uphill past farm on right, immediately after which **4** take gate/stile on the left, just before house (signposted Upper Bittell Reservoir), leading to track between fence (left) and hedge (right). Where fence on left swings away, keep alongside fence on right through group of trees to stile. Beyond stile continue forward along reservoir until just before boat club, where path turns left away from reservoir to reach pond 50 yards later **5**. Turn right on bridleway in front of pond and follow ½ mile to T-junction with farm road, at which turn left. Road passes under railway, then past church on left.

6 Just before first house on left take gate/stile on right (signposted Barnt Green Road). Follow trees on right side of field, at end of which turn left on grassy path leading to stile. Cross tarmac path beyond, take

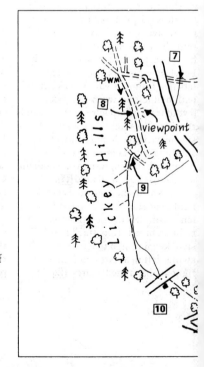

stile opposite and continue forward, along fence on right edge of field. **7** At end of field cross stile, follow path between fences to road. Cross road, take ascending woodland path opposite. After 100 yards turn right on to cross-track and ascend for 250 yards; track then levels – ignore two right turns then turn sharp left on to wide waymarked track. Ascend gently to viewpoint (**b**) (huge pole on left), after which **8** continue on same track, soon descending.

After 350 yards, and just before track is about to bend left, take waymarked path on right, descending to steps. At bottom of steps turn right. **9** 30 yards later turn left by post number 6, down steps. Path crosses bridge after 100 yards. From here ignore all right turns and follow path which runs roughly parallel to edge of woodland, occasionally reaching it. **10** Left on road, then immediately right up wooden steps. Follow woodland path back to station (station footbridge is always open).

WHAT TO LOOK OUT FOR
(**a**) The **reservoirs** are the habitat for wildfowl: tufted duck, waders, great crested grebe, pochard; in winter, wigeon, teal, snipe and golden-eye.
(**b**) **Lickey Hills** Hillside of mixed woodland, some of which is a fragment of the primeval forest that once covered this area. One side of the hill was used centuries ago as a shooting range, and ancient cannonballs have since been found. **View** E and NE over Birmingham and the farmland immediately S of it.

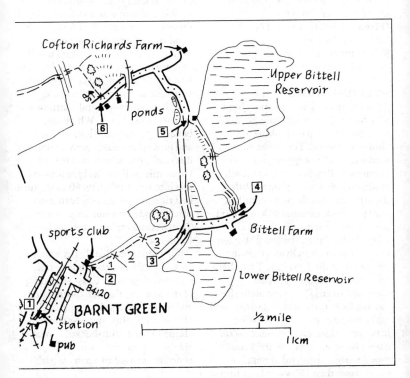

OXFORDSHIRE

The Sinodun Hills and Dorchester-on-Thames

Varied figure-of-eight walk on steep grassy hills, Thames footbridges, riverside towpath, field paths and forest tracks. Route-finding and going underfoot easy throughout; two short ascents.

Length 5 miles (8km), 2½ hours
Difficulty 2–3
Start Sinodun Hills car park, near Brightwell-cum-Sotwell. From Wallingford take A4130 Didcot road for 3 miles, and turn right on minor road signposted Wittenhams, Appleford and Abingdon. After ½ mile turn right again, signposted Wittenham Clumps. Car park is ½ mile further on, on right
OS maps 1:50,000 164 or 174; 1:25,000 SU 49/59
Refreshments Tea-room and several pubs in Dorchester

WALK DIRECTIONS

[1] With gateway to car park behind you, turn right through gate, then half left along grassy path making for clump of trees (a). Turn right on reaching fence at edge of trees, and continue with fence on left to reach bench and viewpoint plinth. With these behind you, head downhill on grassy path for gate and stile. Forward, with hedge on left.

[2] Turn right on road, and bear left beyond end of churchyard. Continue forward over three bridges. Turn sharp left after last bridge on to path alongside river. [3] Immediately after passing lock, turn right across field and make for gate on far side. Forward between hedges, on path which soon passes between dykes (b) and bends round to right. Forward at next cross-track, then 150 yards later turn left on field path heading for houses.

[4] Left on lane and continue for 300 yards. Just beyond end of thatched cottage on left (Port House), and just before number 19 on right, turn right on path between walls to reach Dorchester High Street (c) by garage [5]. Turn right along High Street for 200 yards (d) and fork right in front of Fleur de Lys public house. Left at end of road, on narrow path between fence and wall, then right on road, passing Roman Catholic chapel on your left.

[6] Fork right at village green and continue to thatched cottage at end of road. Turn right on path, then left on unmade road. Continue forward over cross-track, and on to field path with hedge on left. [7] Cross stile in corner of field and continue forward with Dyke Hills on right. Pick up left-hand edge of next field just beyond pillbox, and continue forward to stile in fence opposite when hedge bends to left. Head for right end of bridge and turn right along towpath to lock.

[8] Recross bridges and continue up lane towards church. Where road bends right, turn half-left, over stile and forward on grassy path, making for diagonally opposite corner of field. Cross stile (yellow and blue arrows) and into wood. [9] After 80 yards, turn half right round wooden barrier, to reach broad forest ride after ¼ mile. Turn left and make for gate and stile at top of rise.

[10] Turn immediately right after crossing stile, and continue uphill with wood on right. Cross stile at top of rise and pass through fortifications and over grass to stile at edge of clump of trees. Over this, and pass through clump to reach a further stile on far side. Cross one more stile and continue forward to reach car park.

WHAT TO LOOK OUT FOR

(a) **Wittenham Clumps** Extensive views over the Thames, the Chilterns and the Berkshire Downs.

(b) **Dyke Hills** Remains of the ramparts of an Iron Age town, situated on a bend in the river.

(c) **Dorchester** Once a staging-post on the road from London to Oxford (two imposing coaching-inns – the White Hart and the George – survive). Now a backwater, bypassed by traffic, with fine ancient buildings, some timber-framed, some gabled, some tiled, some thatched, many of them occupied by antique shops.

(d) **Dorchester Abbey** (beyond lych-gate) An Augustinian foundation, dating from the 12th century but greatly extended in the 13th and 14th centuries. Imposing interior has fine stained glass with unusual tracery and some magnificent arcades.

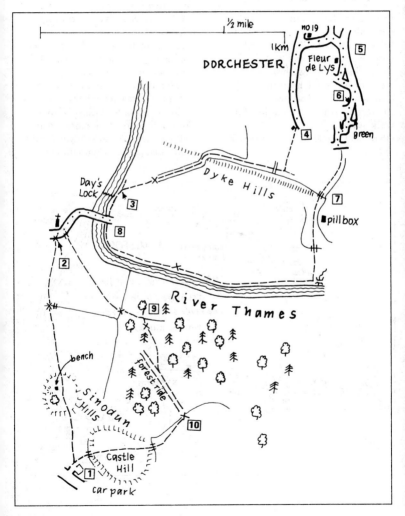

Streatley, the Ridgway and Unhill Wood

In three distinct sections: on a grassy Thames-side path to Streatley; then over field paths, farm tracks and minor roads on to the Berkshire Downs, mostly following the Ridgway long-distance path; finally, a gentle descent over remote woodland paths, farm tracks and field paths. Mostly easy route-finding, though care needed in the last stretch; easy underfoot, with one brisk ascent.

Length 8 miles (13km), 4 hours
Difficulty 2–3
Start Moulsford village, on A329 between Streatley and Wallingford. Car parking by phone box next to recreation ground in centre of village. Grid reference SU 591838
By train Goring and Streatley. Join walk at point **2**
OS maps 1:50,000 174; 1:25,000 SU 48/58

Refreshments Beetle and Wedge Hotel, Moulsford (serves afternoon teas); Bull Inn, Streatley; Miller of Mansfield and John Barleycorn in Goring, just off route

WALK DIRECTIONS

1 With recreation ground behind you, turn right along main road. Left after 200 yards on lane signposted to Beetle and Wedge Hotel, which soon brings you to hotel (**a**) and river. Turn right along river, and follow towpath for 2 miles.

Where river-path ends, turn right inland on path between fences, soon emerging on to lane with path emerging from right. Continue forward, keeping churchyard on right, then bear left in front of main entrance to church to reach High Street in middle of Streatley village **2** (**b**). Turn right on road, and forward at traffic lights. 100 yards beyond traffic lights, just past Old Schoolhouse,

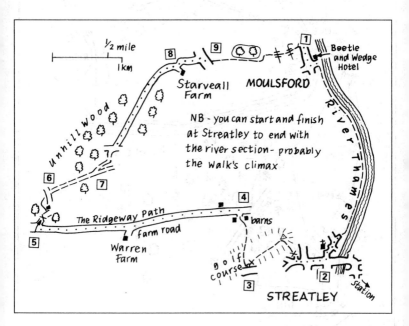

turn right on gravel drive uphill. Where drive divides, forward through gate by NT sign, and continue uphill on grassy path to reach trig. point (**c**). Left at trig. point, walking alongside fence on right, to pass through gate into small car park. Follow right-hand grassy bank of car park, and where bank ends turn sharp right on sunken path (by footpath sign) **3**.

Continue downhill across fairway of golf course (watching for flying golf balls!), following line of old sunken path. Cross a second fairway and, immediately beyond this, bear half left and head for signpost by gap in hedge with barns beyond. Pass to right of barns to reach road **4**. Left on road (part of the Ridgway long-distance route). After 1 mile, by entrance to Warren Farm, fork right on unsurfaced track. After further mile, just after field track merges from left, turn sharp right on track, which soon reaches gate at edge of wood **5**.

Continue into wood, ignoring 'No thoroughfare' sign (this is a public right of way). Immediately after isolated cottage, turn left (path undefined) and, after 50 yards, turn right through gap in fence, on to clear woodland path. After ¼ mile emerge at clearing with a number of paths branching off **6**. Continue forward on gravel drive, with woods on left and with mostly grassland on right. After ½ mile grass area starts to open up on left too. 20 yards beyond this point, **7** fork left on grassy track, which soon swings left into wood, first uphill then downhill.

Soon after emerging from wood reach T-junction of tracks and turn right; 50 yards further on join gravel track and fork left. Continue along clear track, first uphill, then downhill, for 1¼ miles, avoiding side turnings, to reach farm buildings **8**. Turn left in front of pair of semi-detached cottages in farmyard, and continue along lane to reach main road (A417) **9**.

Turn right on road and immediately left by public footpath sign. Path first follows the old field boundary, heading for corner of wood. Continue with edge of wood on left, turning left when wood ends, and right 50 yards later. Cross 2 stiles; after second turn right on path. After 30 yards turn sharp left to cross recreation ground and return to starting-point.

WHAT TO LOOK OUT FOR
(**a**) **Beetle and Wedge Hotel** Named after the tools used for splitting trees into planks before they were floated down the Thames to London – the 'beetle' was a mallet used to hit the wedge. H G Wells stayed here while writing *The History of Mr Polly*; it appears in the book as the Potwell Inn.
(**b**) **Streatley** Handsome, mostly 18th-century, village with a main street at right-angles to the river. The three-storeyed Streatley House, on the left, is a particularly fine Georgian house with an imposing doorway.
(**c**) **Lough Down** Views of the Thames and the Goring Gap.

Goring Heath and Mapledurham

A quiet and completely rural route, first over farm tracks and through beechwoods, then along track above the Thames to Mapledurham; returns over field paths (including one modest ascent) and through more woods. Route-finding generally easy, though care needed in woodland sections; some waymarking.

Length 6½ miles (10.5km), 3 hours
Difficulty 2
Start Goring Heath post office, 5½ miles NW of Reading. From Reading take A4074 signposted Wallingford. After 5 miles turn left on B4526 signposted 'Goring 5' and take first turning on left, signposted Goring Heath. Post office is ½ mile further on at cross-roads. Roadside parking. Grid reference SU 657792
OS maps 1:50,000 175; 1:25,000 SU 67/77
Refreshments General store at Goring Heath; King Charles's Head, ½ mile off route, on road between **1** and **6**

WALK DIRECTIONS

1 Take track to right of post office, through gate, soon passing houses on your right. Where houses end, bear half-right on tarmac lane which soon crosses common land. Forward over cross-track, but 200 yards after this – just before long, low flint building with two gables – turn right through gate, and left in field, following left edge, to find stile into wood **2**.

Forward into wood, alongside fence on left for 30 yards, then half right downhill. After 200 yards turn left on clear cross-track which soon swings round to right to bottom of valley and edge of wood. **3** Left on major track, which soon climbs uphill. Left on cross-track at top of hill, and continue steeply downhill between banks, avoiding side turnings.

4 At bottom of hill take left-hand of 3 parallel tracks divided by yew hedges, and continue for ½ mile (**a**) to wrought-iron gate. Through gate and continue on path for further ½ mile to road. Turn right on road, and pass through village (**b**) to water's edge, church (**c**) and watermill **5**.

From watermill retrace steps through village, and continue on road for ¼ mile beyond village. Where road bends right, keep forward on farm track (signposted Goring Heath 1½). 50 yards beyond cottages on right, turn right uphill on farm track with hedge on right. 50 yards before end of field, cross stile on right then turn left on farm track. Pass to right of farm buildings to reach road **6**.

Turn right on road, and then immediately left over stile. Follow fence on left of field, and cross over stile into wood. Path later passes between gardens to reach gravel drive **7**. Left on gravel drive and forward over cross-track. Where drive swings right to thatched cottage, keep forward on path between hedges. Keep to right of pond just inside wood, and turn left just before fence on far side of wood. Continue with fence on right for ¼ mile (path waymarked by white arrows).

8 Just before end of wood on right, find stile in fence. Do not cross this, but instead turn half left (again following white arrows), and 100 yards further on fork right (more white arrows). Continue forward, ignoring cross-tracks, to reach road **9**. Cross road and take path opposite between fences (yellow arrow). Cross stile at end and follow left edge of field. Where first field on left ends, turn half right, making for gate at right end of hedge. Turn left to proceed alongside hedge on left, over stile, and continue on path between hedges to emerge on to open land with almshouses on left **10** (**d**).

Left in front of almshouses, and at

end of them turn half right on grassy ride to right of driveway signed to 'The Chantry', and follow back to starting-point.

WHAT TO LOOK OUT FOR

(a) **Hardwick House** Just off path to right; restored, part early 16th-, part 17th-century house, irregularly shaped and gabled, built of brick. (Not open to public.)

(b) **Mapledurham** Small village with attractive 17th-and 19th-century buildings, including early 17th-century almshouses and a fine early Georgian mill house (not open to public). The working watermill (open to public) is one of the oldest corn and grist mills on the Thames.

(c) **Mapledurham House** (open to public; fee). Large Elizabethan house dating from end of 16th century; visited by Alexander Pope, who was a friend and correspondent of Mary and Martha Blount, (who lived here). The house was used by the BBC in the serialisation of *The Forsyte Saga*.

(d) **Alnutt's Hospital** Eight single-storey almshouses, founded by Henry Alnutt, Lord Mayor of London, in 1724; grouped round a courtyard, with a chapel in the middle.

Shropshire

Grinshill

*Recommended by Mrs J Wilbraham,
Mr and Mrs R F Maddock*

**A real surprise in the pastoral farmland
of north Shropshire. Heads along edges
of fields towards Clive church, over
and around Grinshill, along a quiet
country road, followed by a track
through parkland, then between two
lakes in woods. Field paths not
defined, but route-finding is
reasonably easy.**

Length *Full walk* 4 miles (6.5km),
2 hours
Difficulty 1–2
Short walk from church in Clive (point
4) 1½ miles (3km), 1 hour
Difficulty 1
Start Yorton railway station, off B5476
3 miles S of Wem; free car park

WALK DIRECTIONS

1 Leave car park and turn right along
road, passing farm on your left after
100 yards. 100 yards after farm turn
left through gate into first field. Head
for makeshift stile opposite,
immediately to left and behind
telegraph pole; reach it by walking
alongside hedge on left. Beyond stile,
continue 20 yards through small
fenced enclosure, taking right-hand of
two gates **2**. Enter second field,
proceed alongside hedge on left,
heading towards church spire. Pass
through left-hand of two gates at top of
field. Follow track between hedges (if
overgrown, turn into field on left
immediately after passing through
gate, keeping alongside hedge on right
until meeting fence, then turn right
through gate). After 300 yards path
becomes tarmacked and reaches
T-junction with tarmac lane at edge of
Clive village **3**.

Turn left on lane, and after 40 yards
turn right past metal barrier on to
path. After 50 yards, at corner of road,
follow road ahead 30 yards to
T-junction. Turn right on road and
immediately left before church **4**,
following stone track up on to
Grinshill Hill (**a**). After 300 yards pass
school on left, and 100 yards later fork
right by 'Motor cycling prohibited'
sign. Follow path to trig. point,
view-indicator and radio beacon.
Retrace steps for 100 yards then fork
right, following path for 100 yards to
turn right at T-junction of paths.

5 After 30 yards turn right at
T-junction with track running along
edge of wood. Follow for ½ mile to
T-junction with tarmac lane **6**. Turn
right, and after 50 yards turn left
(immediately after derelict cottage),
keeping car park on right. After 30
yards path becomes sunken track (if
muddy, use path immediately above it
veering round to right downhill. After
200 yards, after steepest part of slope,
turn sharp left to double back. **7** After
300 yards turn right on main
(descending) path; avoid fainter path
that continues same direction ahead.
Path now runs along bottom of woods
(avoid turnings on right).

8 After 600 yards, and just after
Crofters Hill (bungalow) on left, turn
right at junction of tracks (or left for
Grinshill village (**b**) and Elephant and
Castle Inn). At T-junction with track
40 yards later, turn right. **9** After ½
mile reach road, with Clive church on
right. Turn left, and follow road for ½
mile. **10** At T-junction turn left for 10
yards, then turn right through double
gates. After 20 yards take left of two
gates and take track that runs alongside fence on right through parkland.

11 After 300 yards cross tarmac
track and pass through gate opposite.
Bear quarter right, aiming for gate just
beyond far end of wall. Enter next field
and maintain direction alongside

For a key to the symbols used on the maps, and for an explanation of the difficulty grading, see the inside front cover.

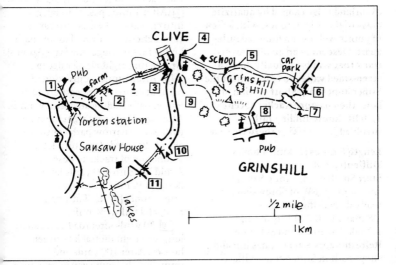

grounds of Sansaw House, to reach stile leading between lakes in wood. 30 yards after lakes, reach railway embankment, turn right through gate, then immediately left up steps to cross railway. Descend steps opposite to enter field. Maintain direction across field, heading for gate in far right-hand corner. Emerge on to tarmac lane, turn right and follow lane (c) ½ mile to T-junction. Turn right, passing under railway, and Yorton station is immediately on right.

WHAT TO LOOK OUT FOR

(a) **Grinshill** Small hill of birch and scrub, with views from its trig. point over the S Shropshire hills (see view-indicator). Quarrying for Grinshill sandstone – used by the Romans in building Wroxeter (Uriconium) – and for copper has

created 200ft drops in places.

(b) **Grinshill village** Has some handsome houses, including the 17th-century manor-house (near the church); half-timbered Step House; and Stone Grange (by the cricket pitch), a house built in 1617 as a retreat for masters and pupils of Shrewsbury school for whenever plague hit the town.

(c) A field path avoids some lane walking, but was overgrown when checked. Turn right along lane as described in text, passing church on your left after 400 yards; road then bends left; 50 yards later turn right through gate. Proceed alongside hedge on right to skirt field, and cross opposite fence (by stile and railway line) by steps. Cross field to gate, emerge on to lane and turn left to reach Yorton station.

Snailbeach and the Stiperstones

Recommended by J F Harrold, M D Bishop, Stephen Banfield

Moorland ridge capped by quartzite crags of the Stiperstones, with a view of points well over a hundred miles apart. Descent is on an old drovers' track that winds gradually down a steep-sided valley to emerge near the Stiperstones Inn. Short section of lane, then pasture tracks. Ascent 1,300ft. Route-finding rather involved ③ and ④ ; otherwise easy.

Length 8 miles (13km), 4 hours
Difficulty 3–4
Start Snailbeach, 1 mile S of A488 and 10 miles SW of Shrewsbury; roadside parking
OS maps 1:50,000 126 and 137; 1:25,000 SJ 20/30 and SO 29/39
Refreshments Stiperstones Inn and shop, both in Stiperstones village

WALK DIRECTIONS

① (**a**) From Snailbeach village ascend lane by spoil heaps, signposted Lords Hill. Ignore side tracks. **②** After ½ mile reach T-junction and turn right. 50 yards later turn left on track through gate and pass chapel on your right. 70 yards after chapel avoid left fork. Track passes under power lines, proceeds alongside fence on your right and ½ mile later passes through narrow strip of woodland.

③ On other side of woodland, track crosses field to gate in far corner (to right of derelict cottage). Pass through gate and pick up grassy track that leads, with fence on your left, to next gate. 30 yards after gate keep half right, avoiding gate on left. **④** After 200 yards reach protruding corner of wall: avoid right fork that follows wall but fork half left up to skyline.

⑤ After ¾ mile turn left at crossing of paths at cairn, then fork right 50 yards later. **⑥** After 200

yards, continue ahead through gate, descending to track. Turn right on track and after 50 yards avoid turning left to house. Continue on grassy track across field and through woods. **⑦** After 1 mile, pass through gate into car park. 50 yards into car park turn right over stile and follow path up to crags on ridge (the Stiperstones). At top, turn right along ridge (**b**).

⑧ After 1 mile, at junction of paths at cairn (passed earlier), turn left on path leading steeply downhill. After 350 yards veer right, on main path where narrow path continues ahead. 200 yards later turn left at T-junction of tracks to descend. Avoid left turn 400 yards later and descend ½ mile to village of Stiperstones **⑨** (**c**). Turn right on road, and follow ¾ mile.

⑩ 20 yards after road veers sharp left, turn right on track between houses. After 100 yards and immediately before cattle-grid, turn left over stile, ascend with fence on right into woods for 50 yards, then turn left on well-defined path. After 500 yards, by house, fork right at major staggered junction of tracks, passing old mine workings and chimneys. Follow until meeting lane and then turn left downhill to starting-place.

WHAT TO LOOK OUT FOR

(**a**) **Snailbeach** The dazzling white spoil heaps, which look like snowy mountains from a distance, are the remains of a once-thriving lead-mining industry centred on Snailbeach, The Bog in the Stiperstones and Shelve Hill. Evidence of Roman lead-mining has been found in the area, and by the 12th century lead was being transported from Shelve as far as Wiltshire. The activity peaked in the 18th and 19th centuries, when landlords enticed squatters on to their common land by charging them

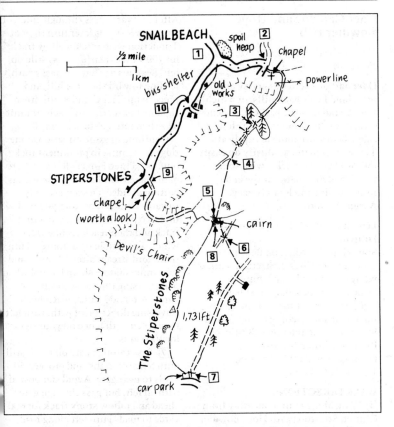

SNAILBEACH
spoil heap
chapel
½ mile
1km
bus shelter
old works
power line
1
2
10
3
4
STIPERSTONES
9
5
chapel
(worth a look)
cairn
6
Devil's Chair
8
The Stiperstones
1,731ft
car park
7

a 6d or 1s annual rent so that the demand for mining and quarry labour could be met. Remnants of these communities can still be seen on and around the hill; rails from the long-since closed mineral railway to Pontesbury are still in place, and on re-entering the village at the end of the walk, the route passes a number of shafts, derelict chimneys and an engine-house.

(b) **The Stiperstones** Series of quartzite outcrops. The first reached is known as the Devil's Chair, surrounded by boulders which are said to have fallen from the Devil's leather apron when its strings broke; he now sits there hoping his weight will sink the Chair into the ground, which event is supposed to bring about the immediate ruination of England. The story also says that an instant thunderstorm takes place whenever anyone sits on the Chair, and that on a hot day the wind carries a whiff of the Devil's brimstone.

View NW the Berwyn (2712ft); NNW the Clwydian Range (1,818ft); NE the W edge of the Peak District, NNE The Wrekin (1,334ft), SE The Long Mynd (1,694ft); S Hay Bluff in the Black Mountains (2,220ft); SSW Radnor Forest (2,166ft); SW the Brecon Beacons (2,906ft); WSW nearby Corndon Hill (1,683ft).

(c) The OS map shows a Road Used as a Public Path from here to Crowsnest, which would avoid some road-walking, but seems to have disappeared (if it was ever visible).

273

Caer Caradoc and Hope Bowdler Hill

Contributed by A F Harrold
Recommended by D J Sutton

Over part of a series of grassy and moorland hog's back hills, of which Caer Caradoc is the highest. Ascends steeply to the summit, then along a ridge, before dropping abruptly at Three Fingers Rock. Mostly on easily followed grassy tracks, with some undefined field paths at the end; route-finding moderately easy. Ascent 1,000ft.

Length 7 miles (11km), 3 hours
Difficulty 3–4
Start Hope Bowdler, on B4371, 1½ miles ESE of Church Stretton. Park in village or in lay-by on Church Stretton side of village (just before signpost on right to Chelmick and Ragdon if approaching from Church Stretton). Grid reference SO 475925
By train Church Stretton
OS maps 1:50,000 137 or 138; 1:25,000 SO 49/59

WALK DIRECTIONS

1 Walk along main road away from Church Stretton (with Hope Bowdler church away to your right). Avoid some road-walking by turning up drive on left running in front of houses, and rejoining road by path. 20 yards after rejoining road (after end of houses), turn left through gate leading uphill **2**. After 600 yards track passes through gate; keep straight ahead, soon crossing small stream. Track eventually veers to left around base of hill on your left, then **3** descends and is joined by fence on right; ignore path on right through gate, but follow path steeply downhill, with hawthorn hedge on right. After 200 yards, path veers away from hawthorn hedge and then descends down towards gate **4**.

Pass through gate and after 50 yards turn right at T-junction of paths.

After 250 yards pass through group of trees and 50 yards later turn right at T-junction with track. Follow track for 400 yards, then **5** cross stile on left. Bear quarter left on grassy path, leading towards brow of hill, and proceed up Caer Caradoc Hill (turn right just past crags to reach summit (a) – then retrace steps to crags).

Continue in same direction along ridge for ½ mile to prominent rock outcrop (Three Fingers Rock), where path makes half left turn along final portion of ridge. Descend steeply towards track. At bottom you will find two parallel tracks; cross first track and then reach second track, which was visible from top **6**. Turn right, ford stream after 30 yards, and turn immediately sharp left uphill on path, passing through gate after 50 yards. After 500 yards, reach fence traversing direction of path: turn left, to proceed with fence on your right for 100 yards.

7 Pass through gate on right, still with fence on right, and proceed 50 yards to next gate. Avoid signposted path on left, but pass through gate ahead and follow stony track for 600 yards to road. Turn left along road and after 30 yards **8** cross narrow stile on left marked with yellow arrow. Turn half right, heading for stile in far left-hand corner. In second field head across field to stile, walking parallel to road. In third field, track soon becomes well defined and follows bottom right-hand side of field. Pass through gate and follow track to Hope Bowdler village.

WHAT TO LOOK OUT FOR

(a) Caer Caradoc (1,506ft) Capped by the grassy ramparts of a hillfort. Caradoc is the Welsh form of Caractacus, who, according to legend made his last stand here against the Romans in AD50 (though the account given by Tacitus, the Roman historian, doesn't tally with this). **View** N to the Cheshire Plain; NE to the Wrekin (1,334ft) and the Peak District a long way beyond; SE to Wenlock Edge and Brown Clee Hill (1,772ft) with Titterstone Clee (1,750ft) beyond; W to the Long Mynd which blocks out anything more distant; NNW to Ruabon Mountain (1,677ft) near Wrexham.

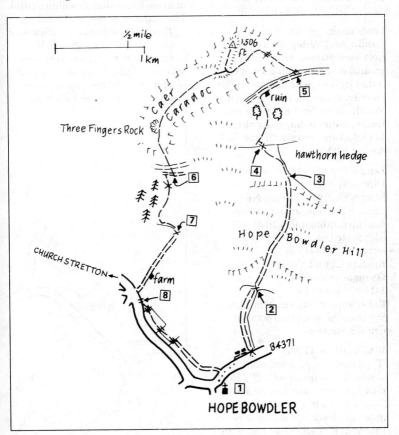

Cardingmill Valley and Ashes Hollow

Contributed by J F Harrold
Recommended by M D Bishop,
Brian Hathaway, Dorothea and
Tiny Whitworth, G J Fox

Leads up the bottom of the Cardingmill Valley, then one mile over open plateau, followed by a gradual descent looking down into Ashes Hollow, with Callow Hollow (another deep valley) on the right. Mostly on well-defined paths and tracks; route-finding fairly obvious, but take care between 3 and 8. Ascent 1,000ft.

Length 10 miles (16km), 4 hours
Difficulty 3–4
Start NT car park ½ mile NE of Church Stretton, at end of tarmac road up Cardingmill Valley (signposted from B4370). Grid reference SO 441948
By train Church Stretton
OS maps 1:50,000 137; 1:25,000 SO 49/59
Refreshments Ragleth Arms, Little Stretton; pubs and tea-rooms in Church Stretton

WALK DIRECTIONS
1 (**a**) From car park follow path alongside stream, uphill. **2** After ½ mile ignore tributary steam and footpath on left. After another ½ mile path levels out on top of moorland and **3** reaches junction with broader track (marker post) (**b**). Turn left on broad track. **4** After 400 yards (just beyond area of rushes on left marking source of stream), take broad earth track bearing left. (Avoid grassy track turning more sharply left just before area of rushes.) Follow for 300 yards to T-junction with road **5**.

Left on road, then almost immediately take the narrow path on the right. This is the Port Way (**c**), an ancient track overgrown with heather, rather like a ditch, 2 to 3ft

below level of surrounding ground. Initially path runs to left of old track; soon you can walk on line of track itself. **6** After ½ mile turn left on broad stony track which crosses at right angles, leading downhill to road. Turn right on or alongside road.

7 After ⅔ mile reach small area of grass, with trees, known as Pole Cottage (no cottage there anymore, only a corrugated-iron barn) on your right. 100 yards later turn left on to broad earth track, then turn left at

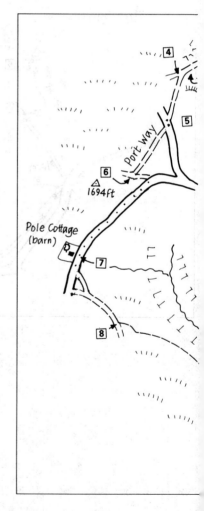

T-junction of tracks. **8** After ¼ mile fork left on to narrower track. Follow it downhill around shoulders of hills for 2 miles to reach stream beyond gate **9**. Step over stream; proceed on tarmac lane which soon bends right. At junction (**d**), turn left to reach B4370 **10**.

Turn left on road in direction of Church Stretton. After ¾ mile a row of houses begins on left, screened by high hedge. **11** 300 yards later, where hedge ends, turn left into small gap before next row of houses begins. Enter woods, and follow path to right, rising behind next houses, running roughly parallel to B4370.

12 After ½ mile emerge on and continue forward along road, with houses on left, following it round sharp right-hand bend. Immediately enter small car park on left and go through wicket-gate behind it into field signed 'Rectory Field & Wood, property of CC, public access and nature trail'.

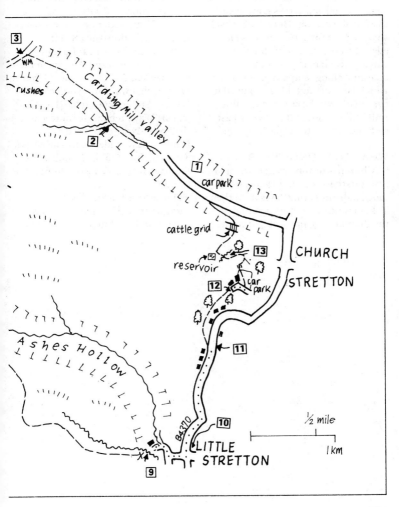

277

Follow path straight ahead uphill to far left-hand corner of field, and cross stile into wood. Continue forward for short distance between birches to join path at right angles, where turn right. In a few yards this is joined by path from right; keep left on main path, and left again at the next junction, shortly after. Path now descends through beeches, and down flight of rough steps to stream **13**.

Cross stream by clapper-bridge (which is actually an old gravestone) then proceed uphill on path to stile at edge of wood and across grass ahead, to edge of reservoir. Here double back sharply right on path that runs along edge of woods. Continue for 300 yards to reach road; cross this and continue along footpath opposite, which bends to left downhill until it eventually reaches road in Cardingmill Valley. Turn left and walk past café and houses to car park.

WHAT TO LOOK OUT FOR

(a) **Church Stretton** Small town; a hill resort in the 1880s and 1890s; its mock half-timbering dates from then. Takes its name from its position on the Roman road, or 'street', running between the Roman settlements of Wroxeter and Leintwardine. The church is a mixture of 12th-century Norman and 17th-century, with a 14th-century roof. The walled-up N door has a Saxon fertility symbol above it.

(b) **View** (from various points at the top) NE, the Wrekin (1,334ft); E, on the other side of Church Stretton, are The Lawley (1,236ft) and Caer Caradoc (1,506ft); SE the long ridge of Wenlock Edge, with Brown Clee Hill (1,772ft; the highest point in Shropshire) beyond; and Titterstone Clee Hill (1,750ft; with mushroom-shaped radar installations) just S of it; S Bringewood Chase near Ludlow; SW Black Mountains and W of them the twin-peaked Brecon Beacons (2,906ft); W into what was Montgomeryshire; NW the Stiperstones ridge (1,731ft).

(c) **Port Way** Prehistoric route across the Long Mynd, once used by Neolithic axe traders, recognised as a King's highway in the Middle Ages. Periodically marked with Bronze Age tumuli.

(d) **Little Stretton** Small village with some pretty half-timbered cottages, and a thatched church built in 1903.

STAFFORDSHIRE

Lud's Church and the Dane Valley

Contributed by Kevin Hall
Recommended by Dorothea and Tiny
Whitworth, Dr J Morley,
K E Pimperton, G A Johnson,
T C Freedman, B F Calladine

**Fairly short, but covers open farm-
land, mixed forests and upland moors
on the outward leg, with a more
enclosed rocky river valley return.
Some surprises, including a tiny chasm
hidden just inside the forest. Mostly
signposted and route is quite easy to
follow.**

Length 6 miles (9.5km), 3 hours
Difficulty 2
Start Wincle, Cheshire, on minor road
2 miles S of A54 (Buxton to
Congleton), 7 miles SE of Macclesfield.
Roadside parking near Ship Inn or near
river-bridge. Grid reference SJ 963652
OS maps 1:50,000 118;
1:25,000 Outdoor Leisure 24
Refreshments Two pubs in Wincle

WALK DIRECTIONS

1 From Wincle village follow road
downhill for ¼ mile. **2** Cross bridge
over River Dane and, after 100 yards,
turn left up path signposted Gradbach.
After 50 yards cross tarmac drive, then
turn left and immediately right up
path leading through field and over
stile into woods. **3** After 300 yards
emerge from woods by stile and turn
half left to cross field and head for
Hangingstone Farm **4**.

Turn left uphill on track between
barn on left and farmhouse on right.
After 100 yards reach gate and turn
right on track skirting bottom of
moorland. Pass through gate 200 yards
later (ignoring right turn). Pass cottage,
and 100 yards later keep straight on
through gate/stile with wall on right
(ignoring right fork).

5 After 100 yards enter Roaches
Estate at sign (**a**) and keep right,
proceeding with wall on right for 1¼
miles. **6** Just before path reaches road
turn left downhill, initially with

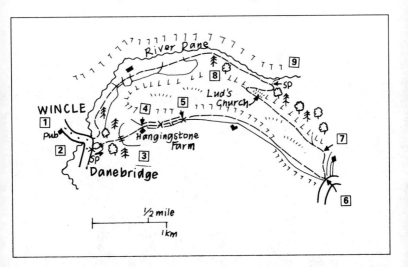

wall on right. **7** After ¼ mile turn left on well-defined path running just inside edge of woods; do not take path leading into heart of woods. **8** After ¾ mile path passes rocky gorge known as Lud's Church (**b**), and descends steeply to right.

9 After ¼ mile and 50 yards before river, turn left, signposted Danebridge. From here route is well signposted and easy to follow, as path runs parallel to river. On emerging from woods after ½ mile path bears half left away from river to stile past cottage on your right. (There has been some footpath erosion here; keep to alternative route if signs direct you to do so.) After ½ mile path re-enters woods; ½ mile later it reaches road at Danebridge. Turn right to return to starting-point.

WHAT TO LOOK OUT FOR
(**a**) **Roaches Estate** Wallabies escaped from a private house nearby in the 1940s. Some of them survived and bred, and a few pairs still exist (we didn't spot any on inspection, but have been assured that they frequent the thickets above the River Dane). Feral wallabies also breed in the Ashdown Forest in Sussex.
(**b**) **Lud's Church** A landslip created this small rocky cleft. In Richard II's time, persecuted religious dissenters known as the Lollards used it as a secret meeting place, and services were conducted by a Walter Ludank, who may have given it its name.

Dimmings Dale and the Ranger

Contributed by Barry Calladine
Recommended by J S Freem,
Dorothea Whitworth, R F Casterton

A wooded valley with rock outcrops, explored by an easy riverside path passing ponds and a former smelting mill soon after the start. Ascends gently along a farm track to the Ranger, with views of Alton Towers and over the other side of the Churnet Valley. All tracks well defined; easy route-finding. Good for families with small children.

Length 3½ miles (5.5km), 1¾ hours
Difficulty 1–2
Start Free parking space by the Ramblers' Retreat coffee-house, near River Churnet, 1 mile NW of Alton. Follow Alton Towers signs through Alton, and turn left off main road just before River Churnet; parking is on left, after 1 mile
OS maps 1:50,000 119 or 128; 1:25,000 SK 04/14
Refreshments Ramblers' Retreat coffee-house

WALK DIRECTIONS

[1] Pass to right of Ramblers' Retreat and immediately fork left to follow wide track, keeping left of the old smelting mill and small lake. Proceed on track alongside stream on your right for 1 mile, along steep-sided valley of Dimmings Dale. [2] Leave track and cross to right side of water on wide path between two narrow lakes. Path proceeds up valley, later recrossing stream by narrow concrete footbridges. [3] Emerge on to tarmac lane, turn right on it and proceed up-hill (passing Old Furnace Farm). [4] After 500 yards turn right on to the track signposted to the Ranger and Alton. Follow track uphill.

[5] After ½ mile, where main track bends off right to farm, continue forward, descending towards trees. 200 yards later pass through gateway to youth hostel, but beyond it immediately keep forward (ignoring right turn leading to youth hostel). Proceed downhill on rough (sometimes wet) path signposted Staffordshire Way. Almost immediately, path divides again at cross-tracks. Continue ahead down through Ousal Dale and back to start.

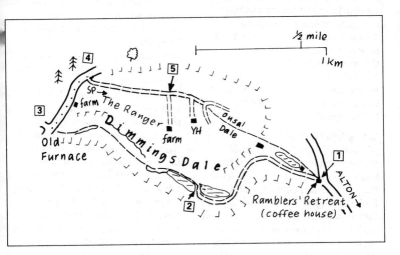

WARWICKSHIRE

The Grand Union Canal and Packwood House

Contributed by I M Firth
Recommended by R R Taylor

Canals and the splendid avenue approaching Packwood House supply just enough ingredients for a good round walk. Roads and pasture fields for the link sections. Not all field paths are defined, but route-finding quite easy.

Length *Full walk* 7 miles (11km), 3½ hours
Short walk 4 miles (6.5km), 2 hours
Difficulty 1
Start Brome Hall car park (grid reference SP 186710) by canal at Lapworth. From Hockley Heath take B4439 SE, pass Boot Inn on left after 2 miles; car park/picnic area is ½ mile further on, on right of road down Brome Hall Lane, just before canal and railway bridge. Leave car park on canal and reservoir side, turn right on towpath.
By train Lapworth station. Emerge from station, turn right on road in front of station, right at T-junction, then pass over canal and reservoir, then left on towpath.
OS maps 1:50,000 139; 1:25,000 SP 07/17
Refreshments Punch Bowl Inn, Boot Inn, Black Boy Inn and shop (see map for locations)

WALK DIRECTIONS

1 Follow towpath along canal/reservoir to cross first bridge at the junction of the Stratford-upon-Avon Canal (right) and Grand Union Canal Link (left). Take left-hand canal, past lock number 20. **2** Reach T-junction with Grand Union Canal proper; cross bridge to turn left, with canal on right. **3** Reach next bridge (number 66).
For short walk turn left on to road,

follow ½ mile to pass over railway. This is point **7**.
For full walk continue along towpath. **4** At next bridge (number 67; Chessetts Wood) towpath continues on other side. Pass under next bridge; Black Boy Inn is at following bridge. Retrace steps to Chessetts Wood bridge, turn right on to road, then left at T-junction. **5** 50 yards later take Valley Lane on left, follow to Valley Farm, ignoring right turns. Continue forward at farm, where road ends, following track for 30 yards. **6** Continue forward where track bends right into farm buildings, crossing waymarked stile. Follow right edge of first field to stile 20 yards to left of far right-hand corner. Continue forward along left edge of next four fields, then follow path to road. Turn right on road, soon over railway **7**. Immediately after, turn right on private road (The Grove). After 100 yards reach house and take waymarked gate/stile on right. Bear half left to corner of hedge 30 yards away then proceed with hedge on right to skirt garden and pass to far end of house, where stile leads on to drive. Cross drive, take waymarked kissing-gate opposite/slightly to right and follow left edge of field until road **8**. Turn right on road and, after 200 yards, left over gate/stile (NT sign Packwood Avenue). Follow path along the avenue to Packwood House (a) **9**.

With avenue on left and house on right, follow road, taking signs for Lapworth; ignore first left after 500 yards, but fork left 400 yards later and left again at B4439, to cross canal **10**. Immediately turn left down to towpath (either by stile on left or, rather easier, by path on other side of road, leading to towpath, then right, under bridge).

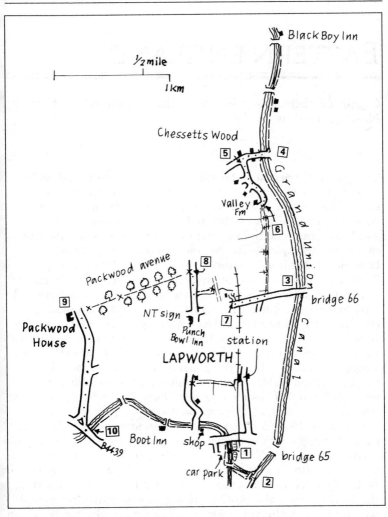

To return to car park follow towpath back to start.

To return to Lapworth station follow towpath to next road-bridge, then turn left on road. Road bends left, then right, past half-timbered house on right. 150 yards later, just before next house on right, take kissing-gate on right. Follow left edge of two fields to stile in left-hand corner at end, where path leads into station by footbridge.

WHAT TO LOOK OUT FOR
(a) **Packwood House** (NT; open to public; fee) Timber-framed house built *c.* 1560, with a fine yew garden representing the Sermon on the Mount – its avenue is called Multitude Walk, there are twelve 'apostles' and four 'evangelists', and the gigantic yew symbolises Christ. The Carolean garden contains four gazebos, the oldest *c.* 1680.

EASTERN ENGLAND

Cambridgeshire, Essex, Hertfordshire, Leicestershire, Norfolk, Nottinghamshire, Suffolk

Though not the richest part of the country for good walks, there are some highly rewarding pockets of countryside in this region. The coast of East Anglia, with its vast skyscapes and profuse birdlife, harbours some excellent walks, and there are unspoilt areas of parkland in the eastern shires that make for easy walking. Much of the region is completely flat, but there are a few areas of hilly farmland. Agricultural improvement has changed the landscape drastically in places, with enormous, hedgeless fields becoming a frequent sight. Hertfordshire has a few good pockets, notably around Ayot St Lawrence – an area of parkland and traditional-looking farmland with some pretty villages; not surprisingly, a lot of people walk here. Ivinghoe Beacon is the tip of the Chilterns and well worth walking to; from its summit you get an enormous view. In Essex, we struggled to find a walk meriting inclusion, but found one, albeit short, at Saffron Walden. Cambridgeshire is also something of a walker's desert, but has a fine oasis at Wicken Fen, where you can see what the fens were like before reclamation.

Suffolk and Norfolk have a handful of glorious coastal walks, particularly appealing to the naturalist and anyone with a love of wide open expanses, though it's hard to find interesting inland sections coinciding with the best of the coast. We tried hard to find a good walk in the Norfolk Broads, but there simply aren't enough paths skirting the Broads to make this possible (all suggestions gratefully received; see page 10). Lincolnshire is dominated by the Lincolnshire Wolds, an area of gentle chalk hills with a character of its own. It's much quieter and more remote than the chalk country of southern England, with enough trees and pasture fields to give variety. Waymarking on the walks we tried was good. Leicestershire and Nottinghamshire have some attractive estates, for instance Calke Abbey Park and Clumber Park (in the Dukeries), and elsewhere are a handful of unspoilt hilly landscapes, such as Burrough Hill, and some interesting roughish land in Bradgate Park, in the hunting country of Charnwood Forest.

CAMBRIDGESHIRE

Wicken Fen

Contributed by Ted Capell
Recommended by Vanessa Kelley,
Sheila and John Benfield

Of special interest for bird-life and botany; gives an idea of the Fens as they were before drainage and reclamation. Goes round Wicken Fen on tracks and a quiet tarmac lane. Easy route-finding.

Length 5 miles (8km), 2 hours
Difficulty 1
Start Wicken Fen nature reserve, just S of A1123; turn off at W end of village of Wicken, 8 miles S of Ely. Grid reference TL 565706
OS maps 1:50,000 154; 1:25,000 TL 46/56 and TL 47/57
Refreshments Maid's Head at Wicken

WALK DIRECTIONS

1 (a) Turn left out of car park, then immediately right, before first cottage, along clearly defined track. Follow track for ½ mile. *N.B. Avoid*
well defined track veering off to left after ¼ mile, but keep straight on. **2** As track veers off to right, turn left over stile, and so along wide green track, skirting nature reserve on left. After 1¼ miles pass through gate and emerge on to road **3** . (b) Turn left down road for ¾ mile into Upware. **4** At Upware, do not cross bridge but turn left along tow-path on left bank of Burwell Lode.

5 After 500 yards, cross bridge over Wicken Lode, immediately turn left into NT property. Continue along bank of Wicken Lode for 1½ miles, where New River enters Wicken Lode. **6** Ignore bridge, left, crossing New River (this leads straight back to car park) but continue along river bank. After ½ mile, cross stile and continue along metalled path below river bank, for another ¼ mile.

7 Cross bridge by wind-pump, follow path to right, away from river and into Wicken. Turn left on to main road, and return to car-park via Lode Lane and village.

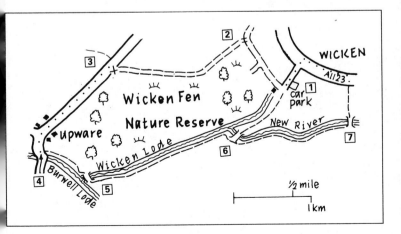

WHAT TO LOOK OUT FOR

(a) **Wicken Fen** (NT; open to public; fee) The oldest nature reserve in Britain, whose 700 acres of near-natural fenland are home to a great variety of **birds,** from warblers nesting in the scrub to waterfowl on the meres and waterways. A range of fenland plants can be seen too. A walk inside the reserve is strongly recommended either before or after the main walk.

(b) The OS map shows a right of way crossing the field ahead and then bearing left to Upware. When we checked the walk the path had disappeared under plough. If it has been reinstated it offers an alternative to the following stretch of road.

ESSEX

Saffron Walden and Audley End

Contributed by Don Unwin

A short walk with much to see, through the medieval streets of Saffron Walden and on grassy tracks through the parkland of Audley End House. Partly along country roads, with a pavement or wide grassy verge. Easy route-finding.

Length 3 miles (5km), 1½ hours

Difficulty 1

Start Market Place, Saffron Walden. Pay-and-display car park on common; alleyway opposite is signposted to tourist information (in market place)

OS maps 1:50,000 154; 1:25,000 TL 43/53

Refreshments Various in Saffron Walden; tea-room in Audley End House (when house is open)

WALK DIRECTIONS

1 (a) From Market Place, with tourist information/town hall on your left, take Market Hill (street ahead) leading to crossroads; turn left (Church Street) b), then first right, a cul-de-sac leading into churchyard (c). Take tarmac path past left end of church, then continue right on main path (still beside church) to leave at opposite side of churchyard, opposite museum entrance (d). Turn left into street (Castle Street).

2 Take path on right, signposted Bridge End Gardens (e); this leads down between walls. Fork left, after 50 yards passing through gateway (to which you will return). Explore garden, return towards gateway, turning right just before it on to path leading to Bridge Street **3**. Left into Bridge Street (f). **4** Turn right into Abbey Lane (opposite George Street), and where road turns right continue forward through estate gates; fork right,

then 10 yards later take the centre of three paths, leading across first field to gate, then between fences, past sewage works and to kissing-gate **5**.

Enter next field and follow right-hand edge to next kissing-gate. Path then leads through trees, along stream, to estate road **6**. Left on road, follow to main road **7**. Left on main road (g), past front of Audley End House (h). **8** Take first road on left (signposted Audley End). This passes miniature railway (i) and Audley End village (j) (both on right).

9 ½ mile after Audley End village turn left at gate-house. After 20 yards keep forward at crossing of tracks, and ignore faint left fork 50 yards later. Follow back to Abbey Lane gate-house, then proceed to town centre.

WHAT TO LOOK OUT FOR

(a) **Saffron Walden** Originally Cheyping Walden, the town prospered and grew in the Middle Ages as a centre of the saffron industry, the yellow pigment from the saffron crocus being used in cloth-making, food-colouring and medicine. The industry survived here until the 18th century. It has also been a wool- and cotton-weaving town. Many of its medieval streets are virtually intact, particularly in the NW part of town, where there is barely a window out of place. Much notable pargeting – the craft of decorating external plaster walls. Just S of market place is a small complex of lanes known as the Rows, whose names – Butcher, Market, Mercer – betray their origins as medieval market areas. On the far side of the common is an ancient, cobweb-like turf maze, of unknown date and purpose (possibly ornamental, or for monks or pilgrims to do penance, by crawling round); the common was used for a Royal Tournament in 1252.

(**b**) **Sun Inn** (on left; no longer an inn) Boasts the best example of pargeting in the town, representing a fight between Tom Hickathrift, a carter of quite tremendous strength who could raise a haystack on his pitch-fork, and the Wisbech Giant, who is shielding himself with a wheel and axle. Cromwell may have stayed here while holding meetings in the church during the Civil War.

(**c**) **St Mary the Virgin** largest parish church in Essex, 200ft long, with a spacious nave; mainly Perpendicular (15th to early 16th century), partly restored later; its soaring tower was added in 1832.

(**d**) **Museum** Mainly of local and natural history.

(**e**) **Bridge End Gardens** Elegant example of late-18th to early-19th-century gardening, started in 1790 by Atkinson Francis Gibson. Its hedge maze, added in 1838–9, is now being replanted.

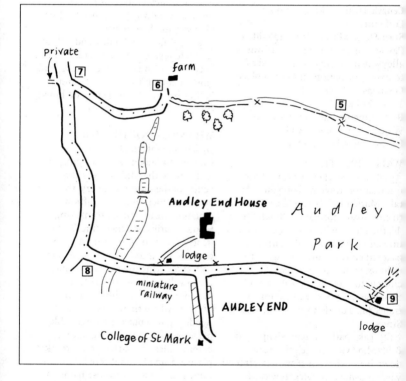

(**f**) **Youth Hostel** (on right) Early 16th-century half-timbered town-house, with a carved dragon-post and two oriel windows. Formerly used as a malting; its oak-wheel sack-hoist is still in position.

(**g**) Up on the right, just visible, is a **circular temple**, designed by Robert Adam to commemorate the British successes in the Seven Years War (1756-63).

(**h**) On the left, stable block, and **Audley End House** (English Heritage;

open to public; fee). Vast Jacobean mansion altered by Vanbrugh in the early 18th-century. Built on the site of Benedictine Monastery of Walden, which was given by Henry VIII to Lord Audley after the Dissolution.

(**i**) **Miniature railway** (runs Sun and bank hols) 1½-mile ride through woods.

(**j**) **Audley End** Georgian estate village to Audley End House. Fine Elizabethan almshouses (College of St Mark) just visible at far end of street.

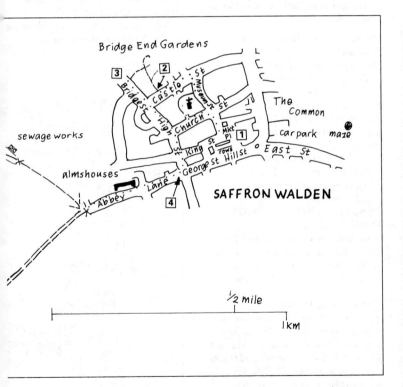

HERTFORDSHIRE

Brocket Park and Ayot St Lawrence

Starts on a path into the woods of the Brocket Estate, leading on to landscaped parkland and the miniature valley of the River Lea (here not much more than a brook), which winds its way between marshes to Waterend. A fine parkland avenue leads from Lamer House towards Ayot St Lawrence, then route finishes along farmland tracks.

Length 8 miles (13km), 4 hours
Difficulty 2
Start Ayot Green, immediately W of A1(M), 3½ miles N of Hatfield. Take B197 (which runs closely parallel to A1(M) from Welwyn southwards), and turn off at signpost to Ayot St Lawrence and Ayot St Peter. After crossing bridge over motorway, immediately turn left (into Brickwall Close) and park on roadside by Waggoners' Inn. Grid reference TL 221140
OS maps 1:50,000 166; 1:25,000 TL 01/11 and TL 21/31
Refreshments Waggoners Inn, Ayot Green; Brocket Arms (also serves teas on Sun afternoons 3.30pm to 5.30pm, Easter to Sept), Ayot St Lawrence

WALK DIRECTIONS

1 (**a**) From Waggoners' Inn take stile opposite and slightly to left; follow path, soon into woods of Brocket Park.
2 After ¼ mile, at junction of tracks near edge of woods fork right as waymarked, and proceed to stile, to emerge into field. Keep forward, alongside fence on right. At end of field cross stile and turn sharp right (or continue along edge of next field for view of lake from bridge – then retrace steps) over estate road for path signposted to Waterend. Proceed between fences.

3 On reaching estate road again, cross it and turn left through small waymarked gate into field. Proceed initially alongside fence on left, then maintain same direction over rise where fence bears left (path is barely visible) (**b**). Pass close to estate buildings and head across to gate/stile just visible on edge of woodland. Enter wood, follow yellow marker arrows, ignoring any left turns, soon descending to junction of tracks **4**.

Continue forward on track following edge of the woods, then soon into

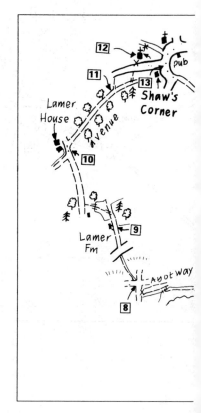

fields. **5** After ⅓ mile, reach road at Waterend (**c**); turn right on road, then left after 50 yards on signposted bridleway. **6** After ¼ mile, where main track bends right, cross way-marked stile to continue ahead parallel with brook. Track soon enters field, following left edge.

7 Beyond stile, continue forward following power lines, and leave field by stile in far right-hand corner, just to right of last power post. Beyond it, turn left on track, follow to gate at end of field, beyond which turn right at T-junction of tracks. **8** After 130 yards turn left at track junction, then 75 yards later turn right by yellow arrow marker post. Ascend bank to

stile and follow path beyond. At road, cross to track opposite.

9 Shortly after trees begin on right, ignore left turn to farm but keep ahead on grassy track for 100 yards, then cross stile on left. Keep along left side of line of trees, then leave field by stile in far left-hand corner, into woods. Turn right, following woodland path until reaching hard track, along which turn right.

10 After ⅓ mile track merges into tarmac estate road: proceed along it for 100 yards, then fork right (left is 'Private', into Lamer House (**d**)). Track runs along avenue of trees. **11** Where avenue ends, keep right on main track, ignoring gate/stile ahead, which is

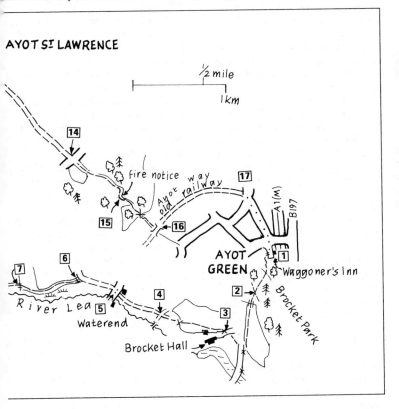

AYOT S⁺ LAWRENCE

½ mile

1 km

signposted Ayot St Lawrence. Proceed just inside edge of woods, ignoring turnings to right, then at end of second field on left, and 50 yards before track emerges into field, take stile on left, and follow right edge of field to road. Turn right on road, then take next track on left, signposted St Lawrence's Church (**e**).

12 With façade of church behind you, turn left through ornate iron gates, then turn right on grassy track and follow to road. Turn left for Ayot St Lawrence village, but to continue turn right on road. **13** At Shaw's Corner ignore right turn but keep forward, signposted Wheathamp-stead. Road soon bends left, then, where it bends right 20 yards later, keep forward on the signposted bridleway.

14 ¾ mile later cross road and take bridleway opposite alongside woods. Soon, fence on right ends. **15** At end of (large) field, track bends right (still alongside woods, past fire notice on your left), then 100 yards later bears left to leave field and enter woods: keep forward, soon emerging into field by gate. Track follows left edge of field for 50 yards, then bears left into next field, following right edge in same direction.

16 Where old railway bridge crosses track, take path on right up to it and turn left on to old railway track (**f**) (this is a permissive path only; in the unlikely event of it being closed, proceed under railway bridge, and follow track to road. Left on road, then take first right to Ayot Green). **17** Reach road-junction, take signposted road ahead for Ayot Green and follow to start.

WHAT TO LOOK OUT FOR
(**a**) **Ayot Green** Consists of about a dozen cottages flanking a tree-fringed triangular common.
(**b**) **View** of Brocket Hall, an 18th-

century red-brick mansion designed by George Paine; stands above the Broadwater, an ornamental lake crossed by stone bridge.
(**c**) **Waterend** A ford and a couple of houses. One is the Water End House, a fine brick manor-house (1610); the other (across the brook) is the medieval White Cottage.
(**d**) **Lamer House** Only a pretty stable-block is visible from the route. Apsley Cherry Garrard, co-traveller with Scott on the doomed Antarctic journey and author of *The Worst Journey in the World* (a title reputedly inspired by Shaw) lived here. Lamer Park has now lost some of its parkland feel, but retains a good avenue along its NE approach.
(**e**) **Ayot St Lawrence** George Bernard Shaw lived at the new rectory, which he renamed Shaw's Corner (NT; open to public; fee), from 1906 until his death in 1950. Personal items inside include his walking-sticks and notebooks. Shaw allegedly settled here because of an epitaph in the churchyard to a woman who died at 70, which said simply, 'Her life was short'; he thought that a village considering 70 a short life must be a good one to live in. There are two churches: the first encountered is the new one, designed by Revett in 1778–9, its giant portico modelled on the Temple of Apollo at Delos; its position completes a vista from Lamer House. The second church is a Gothick, ivy-clad ruin. Other note-worthy buildings in the village are Ayot House (three-storey, early 18th-century) and the half-timbered cottages adjoining the pub.
(**f**) **Old railway** Opened in 1860, linking Hatfield and Dunstable via Welwyn and Wheathampstead; closed to passenger traffic in 1965. When the gravel workings nearby were shut in 1971, it ceased operation completely.

Ivinghoe Beacon and the Ashridge Estate

Contributed by Alastair Macgeorge Recommended by F C Mattinson, J Moore, D Fraser, Ian, Sandra and Gordon Wilson

Largely over chalk downland (in parts with enough scrub and rough grassland to make it feel like true upland) in the first half of the route, then through the fine woodlands of the NT-owned Ashridge Estate; arable farmland near start and end of walk. Very muddy after wet weather. Route-finding moderately easy, on defined path and tracks.

Length 8½ miles (13.5km), 4 hours
Difficulty 3
Start Tring station, 2 miles E of Tring, 5 miles NW of Berkhamsted. Grid reference SP 951122
OS maps 1:50,000 165; 1:25,000 SP 81/91
Refreshments Greyhound Inn and (opposite) Town Farm tea-room in Aldbury; teas at Bridgewater Monument at summer weekends; cream teas at hotel by Tring station

WALK DIRECTIONS

1 Turn right out of station, crossing railway. Avoid road-turning on left after 300 yards, but 100 yards later turn left on tarmac track (signposted Ridgeway Path). Where track bends left, after 50 yards, keep straight on, following grassy path to reach junction of paths after a few yards **2**. Turn left through gate, signposted Ridgeway Path and follow Ridgeway Path signs where given. Path runs first between hedges, then **3** turns half right at junction as signposted, and then ascends to turn left up wooden steps at next signpost, and continues through woods (waymarks on trees – avoid side-turnings).

4 After ½ mile, path emerges on to downland by stile. Follow well-marked grassy bank (**a**), which leads uphill. **5** Just where bank is about to descend, keep to the top of slope to follow faint grassy path alongside fence on right down to road **6**. Turn left on road, then right after 50 yards, on track signposted Ridgeway. After crossing field, track passes over gate/stile and ascends steeply to the second gate/stile. **7** 300 yards beyond gate, where main track turns right, keep straight on, initially with fence on left. Reach road and cross to take left-hand of two tracks opposite, a broad grassy track which leads to summit of Ivinghoe Beacon (**b**). Turn right at trig. point and follow to stile. Do not cross stile, but turn right, initially along fence on left and retrace steps to road **8**.

Just before road take path on left, which runs parallel to road as far as NT car park at top of hill (if path is too muddy, alternative route can be found closer to road). Turn left on road and after 250 yards turn right at second NT sign, signposted to Clipper Down Cottage, with waymark on post. Follow this broad track for ½ mile until it forks just short of cottage. **9** Take left fork immediately in front of cottage and continue along track for further mile, avoiding all side-turnings.

10 Pass log cabin and NT sign 50 yards down to your right. 200 yards after log cabin, at post marked with yellow horseshoe, turn half right towards clearing, soon crossing wooden footbridge over gully. Continue forward on this track: Bridgewater Monument soon comes into view (**c**) **11**. Take track between cottage (on your left) and Bridgewater Monument (right). Follow track downhill through woods, ignoring forks on left, to Aldbury village centre (**d**) **12**.

From Aldbury village centre take lane just to left of Greyhound Inn. Cross stile on right at end of lane, cross small playing-field to stile in

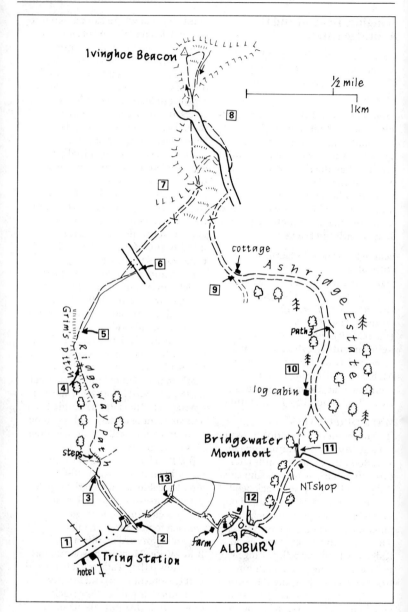

Ivinghoe Beacon

½ mile

1km

8

7

6

cottage

Ashridge Estate

9

Grims Ditch

Ridgeway Path

5

path 3

4

10

log cabin

steps

Bridgewater Monument

11

3

13

NT shop

12

1

2

farm

ALDBURY

Tring Station

hotel

left-hand corner, and emerge into large field. Turn left along bottom of field and turn right on meeting fence. Circuit field, passing gate into farmyard (do not enter). At top of field turn left through gate, then turn immediately right, with fence now on right as far as stile, beyond which **13** left on path between fences. After ¼ mile pass through gate and maintain same direction across field to gate in hedge. Turn left and retrace steps to Tring station.

WHAT TO LOOK OUT FOR

(a) The **bank** is called 'Grim's Ditch'. A long earthwork that runs for 25 miles through the Chilterns, it probably dates from the Iron Age, and was apparently a boundary mark.
(b) **Ivinghoe Beacon** Starting-point for the long-distance Ridgeway Path that runs 85 miles to Overton Hill near Avebury in Wiltshire. **View** Over a large slice of the Midlands; eight counties are visible on a clear day.
(c) **The Bridgewater Monument** (NT; open to public) Tall column (which you can climb when it is open) to the third Duke of Bridgewater, the canal builder. Ashridge Nature Walks are nearby (leaflet from NT information centre). There is a sanctuary of fallow and muntjac deer.
(d) **Aldbury** 16th- and 17th-century cottages (including an old bakehouse) grouped around a triangular green with duckpond, stocks and early 19th-century whipping-post. Stocks House nearby was the home of the suffragette and writer Mrs Humphrey Ward, aunt of author Aldous Huxley and scientist Julian Huxley.

Wilstone and Marsworth Reservoirs and the Grand Union Canal

Contributed by Alastair Macgeorge
Recommended by Keith
Chamberlain, A Callender, Mr and
Mrs S F Parker, Donald Kenrick

An unusual circuit, almost entirely on towpaths of the Grand Union Canal and its branches (including a derelict one), plus the banks of its feeder reservoirs (good for bird-watching). Short link sections across farmland and along roads. Easy route-finding, though field path just after the start is undefined. Walk starting from Tring station follows canal all the way to reach main walk.

Length 5 miles (8km), 2 hours;
8 miles (13 km), 3 hours if starting
from Tring station

Difficulty 1
Start Village centre, Wilstone
(¼ mile off B489 and 8 miles E of
Aylesbury). Grid reference
SP 905140
By train Tring station. Turn left out
of station and follow road past hotel,
and after 200 yards turn right on
towpath along right side of canal. At
first bridge (¾ mile) cross to other
side of canal. Continue under second
bridge ½ mile later. After 400 yards
cross footbridge to take right branch
of canals. Start at ⑦
OS maps 1:50,000 165;
1:25,000 SP 81/91
Refreshments Half Moon, Wilstone;
Grand Junction Inn, near ⑦ (see
map); White Lion Inn at ⑧

WALK DIRECTIONS
① With the Half Moon pub on your
left follow street out of village. 100

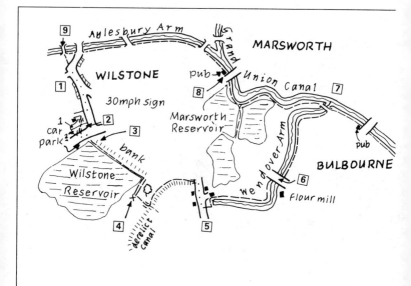

yards after end of speed derestriction signs at edge of village, take track on right through gate. After 30 yards, immediately after track crosses low bridge, turn sharp left over stile and cross field (no path), making for gate. **2** In second field continue same direction to stile in far left-hand corner. This emerges on B489; cross with great care, turn left to point 50 yards along road where break in fence on right allows access to top of embankment of Wilstone Reservoir **3**. Turn left along embankment for ½ mile. After left-hand corner of reservoir track passes belt of trees and reaches T-junction of tracks; turn right.

4 After 300 yards, at gate signed 'no footpath', turn left on path between hedges, leading up to stile. Cross stile, then left along derelict (drained) canal. After 500 yards turn right on road, follow for 200 yards

past houses (Little Tring), then **5** turn left, signposted 'footpath', to pick up drained canal. Just where canal proper starts, cross to left-hand tow-path (**a**). **6** After ½ mile cross to right-hand towpath by bridge. Follow for ½ mile to junction with main portion of Grand Union Canal.

7 *For Tring station*, turn right. *To continue to Wilstone*, cross bridge to left-hand towpath (**b**). Follow the towpath for ¾ mile, passing reservoir on your left (**c**), to bridge number 132 (number is on plaque above arch of bridge). **8** Cross road and continue on towpath opposite, passing White Lion Inn. Take left fork of canals after 300 yards. Follow left-hand towpath for 1 mile (**d**).

9 200 yards after passing under bridge 3, and just by footbridge turn left to leave canal for footpath leading to houses at edge of Wilstone village. Turn right on reaching road; this leads to village centre.

WHAT TO LOOK OUT FOR
(**a**) **Tringford pumping station** Marks the navigable extent of the Wendover Arm. Built by the Grand Junction Canal company to pump water from the Marsworth, Wilstone and Tringford reservoirs.
(**b**) On opposite bank, the **Bulbourne workshops**, where craftsmen make traditional wooden lock-gates.
(**c**) **Marsworth Reservoirs** Divided by a dyke which you can walk along. **Birds** Wild fowl and waterside population, principally black tern and great crested grebe.
(**d**) **Birds** by and near canal: reed and sedge warblers, little grebe, yellow wagtail, flycatchers , moorhen, coot, tufted duck, water rail, mistle thrush, kingfisher, tawny and barn owl, reed bunting, heron.

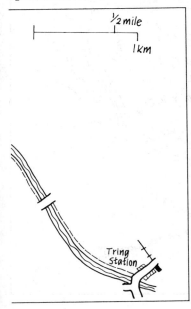

½ mile

1 km

Tring station

LEICESTERSHIRE

Bradgate Park

Contributed by Diane Crawley
Recommended by Dorothea
Whitworth

One of a number of medieval hunting parks in Charnwood Forest. Route covers roughish heathland with rock outcrops, then follows estate road (free from traffic) for return. Many path junctions, but some waymarking and plenty of landmarks; route-finding quite easy.

Length 4 miles (6.5km), 2 hours
Difficulty 1–2
Start Car park (fee) just inside

Bradgate Park, 5 miles NW of Leicester; turn off B5327 at Newton Linford church. Grid reference SK 523098
OS maps 1:50,000 129 and 140; 1:25,000 SK 40/50 and SK 41/51

WALK DIRECTIONS

1 (a) Go through gate into park and immediately leave road for path on left beside wall. Path passes through gap in wall, after which four paths branch off: take second from left and follow uphill through bracken until reaching war memorial at top of hill **2**. Proceed ahead to enclosure of trees (ignore descending paths), to enter it by

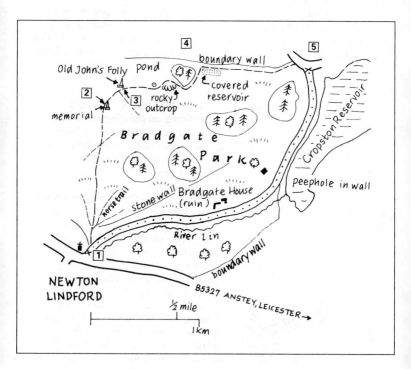

gap in wall, then follow path to gateway in wall visible at other end. Proceed to Old John's Folly (**b**) and view-indicator ③.

Turn right (eastwards; view-indicator gives compass direction) downhill to nearer small round pond. Pass to right of pond and continue ahead to rocky outcrop, just beyond which turn right alongside woodland wall to follow path, first uphill, then bending left and downhill.

Where wall bends left again, fork right to leave wall, making for left end of large oblong gravel area (covering underground reservoir) ④. Turn right, and follow path alongside boundary wall. ⑤ Just beyond house, pass through gap in wall on your right and follow horse trail to reach car park. Turn right on to tarmac park road, follow (**c**) back to start.

WHAT TO LOOK OUT FOR

(**a**) **Bradgate Park** Never formally landscaped as parkland, but retained as a hunting reserve; it was presented to the city and county of Leicester by a private benefactor, Charles

Bennion, in 1928. In addition to the folly and the ruins of the house it contains fallow and red deer and some fine oak trees. Information centre at car park.

(**b**) **Old John's Folly** Commemorates a retainer who died in a bonfire accident at the 21st birthday party of the Earl of Stanford in 1786. From this 700ft vantage-point a panoramic **view** over Charnwood Forest.

(**c**) On the left, after ½ mile, a peep-hole in the wall gives a view over **Cropston Reservoir**. About ½ mile on are the ruins of **Bradgate House** (open to public; fee), birthplace of Lady Jane Grey (1537–54), the nine-day Queen of England. The house was built by her grandfather. Captured for the Royalists by Prince Rupert during the Civil War, it was visited by William III in 1696. Early in the following century it was destroyed by fire and abandoned. Originally a moated house, built of brick with stone quoins, only the chapel and two towers survive. Peacocks and fantail pigeons can be seen on the walls.

Burrough Hill

Contributed by Mrs S Wilson
Recommended by D Crawley, Deirdre
Fraser, I D W MacSporran, Dorothea
Whitworth

Escarpment (capped by a hillfort)
of pasture and woodlands, with
quiet tarmac lanes around its
base. Permissive path from 1 to
6 may very occasionally be closed.
Route-finding quite easy, with
waymarking for most of ridge
section.

Length 5 miles (8km), 2 hours
Difficulty 1–2

Start Burrough Hill car park, 6 miles S
of Melton Mowbray on minor road
between Burrough on the Hill and
Somerby (car park signed, though not
very clearly if approached from W).
Grid reference SK 767115
OS maps 1:50,000 129;
1:25,000 SK 61/71

WALK DIRECTIONS

1 From car park take gate beside
toilets and follow farm track past farm
buildings on your left, then past
information board with map. Detour
to top of fort and view-indicator (**a**) (or
save this for end of walk) and return to
information board. Proceed along

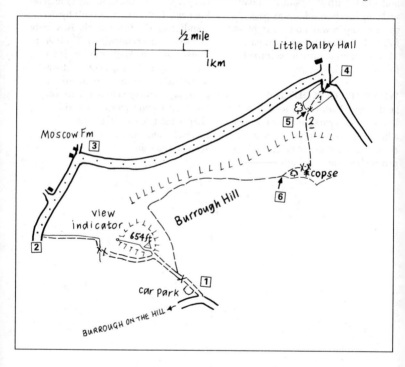

path, which soon descends with fence on left, passing through two sets of gates, then proceed along right edge of field alongside hedge. **2** Turn right along road and fork right 350 yards later (signposted Little Dalby).

3 After another 350 yards, turn right, signposted Little Dalby and Pickwell. Follow this tarmac lane for 1½ miles (**b**). **4** 100 yards after lane bends sharply right, pass through gate on right (signposted Somerby). Cross first field diagonally left to gate in far corner; cross bridge beyond, and ascend bank into second field **5**.

Bear right and proceed uphill on grassy path between fields aiming for copse 350 yards ahead. At top of field, pass through gate, turn right and proceed through second gate, then bear left uphill keeping copse on left.

Make for prominent signboard on skyline **6**. Turn right on to path by board (marked Dalby Hills Path), and follow back to starting-place; path is clearly waymarked all the way.

WHAT TO LOOK OUT FOR

(**a**) **Burrough Hill** Nearly 600ft above sea-level, capped by the largest Iron Age hillfort in Leicestershire. In early Roman times this may have been the local capital, before Leicester. View-indicator on top.

(**b**) **Little Dalby Hall** (away to the left) Built by William Hartopp c.1580, with wings added later, and much remodelled in 1838, then partially rebuilt in recent times. In the early 1700s the Hartopps' housekeeper, a Mrs Orton, perfected the recipe for Stilton cheese here.

Foxton Locks and Saddington Reservoir

Contributed by P M Roberts
Recommended by Diane Crawley,
Dorothea Whitworth, Dianne Clarke

**Canalside walk with views of
undulating farmland, passing
Saddington Reservoir. Route-finding
reasonably easy through fields. Area
atrracts a fair number of visitors at
summer weekends.**

Length 7½ miles (12km), 3½ hours
Difficulty 1–2
Start Foxton Locks car park, Foxton,
3½ miles NW of Market Harborough.
From Market Harborough take A6 N
for 2 miles, turn left at crossroads,
continue past Gartree Prison and
Foxton primary school, take second
left (signposted Gumley). Car park is
after ½ mile, on left. Grid reference
SP 692892
OS maps 1:50,000 141;
1:25,000 SP 68/78 and SP 69/79
Refreshments Pub, cafe and shop at
Foxton Locks (bridge 61); Bell Inn,
Gumley

WALK DIRECTIONS

1 Take path beside car park
entrance and follow footpath to
Grand Union canal, at which turn
right on towpath, under road-bridge,
then cross to other side of canal by
adjacent footbridge. Proceed along
towpath on left side of canal (**a**),
under bridge number 61, then over
bridge number 62, beyond which
towpath follows right-hand side of
canal.

2 At next footbridge cross canal
(Gumley village, which you will
shortly reach, is visible on hillside
ahead). Proceed forward on right edge
of first field, alongside hedge, and
cross fence in far right-hand corner
(obstructed by single strand of barbed
wire at time of checking: if it is still
there, you are entitled to take gate
further to left to enter second field;

see map). In second field head for gate
to left of sewage works **3**. Aim for
left end of line of trees on far side of
third field, where signpost for
Gumley points direction over fence
(**b**); then turn sharp left in fourth field
to proceed alongside trees, bending
left 20 yards later at corner, then
continuing alongside them.

Cross single strand fence into fifth
field, still alongside trees, until
kissing-gate, beyond which proceed
to road in Gumley (**c**). Turn right on
road and, where it bends left,
continue forward through gate on
track (**d**) which leads to left of church,
through trees and to kissing-gate **4**.
Emerge into field, make for gate in far
right-hand corner, then left on road
for 200 yards. **5** Take next turn on
right, then turn right again at
crossroads 100 yards later through
gate (signposted 'Gated road to
Saddington'). After 1 mile road passes
alongside Saddington reservoir and
yacht club.

6 Where road dips into hollow,
turn right at bottom and cross
footbridge over dyke (signposted).
Continue to next signpost, visible
further up field on your right (and to
right of footbridge 150 yards ahead),
proceeding in long and narrow first
field parallel to stream on your left
and raised dyke on your right. Beyond
this signpost, the path continues
alongside dyke on right. At end of
field cross stile beside stream into
second field. Continue forward, with
trees on left to reach gate into third
field.

7 Soon cross stream by plank
bridge, and bear slightly left on path,
keeping fence on your left. Pass under
the canal aqueduct (which leaks),
then over stile beside gate, then
immediately cross stile on left to
follow right edge of field. After 50
yards path bends left between two
ash trees and crosses stile to emerge
on canal towpath. Turn left and

follow towpath 3½ miles back to start (**e**).

WHAT TO LOOK OUT FOR

(**a**) **Foxton Locks** Two staircases of five locks each, over which the canal drops 75 feet in ¼ mile; fed by small reservoirs adjacent. The locks were opened in 1814 and provide the link between the East Midlands coalfields and London.

(**b**) Another single-strand barbed wire fence here at time of checking.

(**c**) **Gumley** Originally a Saxon settlement; King Aethelbald of Mercia held a council here in AD749. Near the Bell Inn is a preserved Victorian butchery, with original equipment.

(**d**) The track was once the **main road** through Gumley; the road was diverted to its present course when Gumley Hall was built in 1764. The hall, which was on the right of the track between the church and stable block, was demolished in 1964, though its Italianate clock tower survives.

(**e**) As you return uphill by locks, look out for the remains of the **Foxton inclined plane** on your left. It was a late-19th-century attempt at by-passing the locks and saving water, but only operated for 10 years. The locks had in the meantime fallen into disrepair and were renovated in 1908; the inclined plane closed in 1910 and was dismantled in 1928. The remains of it are being restored by the Foxton Inclined Plane Trust; further information available at the shop at the bottom lock. Models of the two features are on show at the museum in Market Harborough.

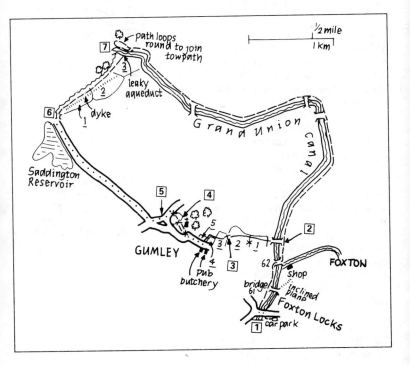

LINCOLNSHIRE

Tennyson's birthplace and the Central Wolds

Contributed by Martyn Bishop
Recommended by Eleanor Nannestad,
Janice Josiffe, B H and M J James

Some of the quietest parts of the Wolds. Six villages on the way, with the remotest of the scenery coming after Tetford. Route-finding moderate.

Length 11 miles (17.5km), 5 hours
Difficulty 3
Start Fulletby, 4 miles NE of Horncastle, by petrol station. Roadside parking. Grid reference TF 296733
OS maps 1:50,000 122;
1:25,000 TF 27/37
Refreshments Cross Keys Inn, White Hart Inn and shop, Tetford; Blue Bell, Belchford

WALK DIRECTIONS

[1] With petrol station on left, follow road to T-junction. Turn right, then after 300 yards take track on left, signposted bridleway. Track descends; 150 yards before bottom of slope, where track bends to the left, and immediately before copse begins on right, cross ditch on right and bear half left on other side, keeping close to copse on your left. [2] After 30 yards emerge into field: ahead is prominent triangular top of Hoe Hill. Do not make for it, but bear half right aiming just to right of nearest bushes. On reaching them (by waymarker post) turn left, with bushes and ditch on right, and at corner after 30 yards, turn right (still with ditch on right).

[3] 200 yards later, just before the end of the field, cross ditch on right by waymarker post and continue up slope ahead to reach edge of field 20 yards later. Bear half left, aiming 100 yards to the right of group of trees, to find gate at right extremity of hedgerow. In

next field keep well to left of trees ahead by bearing quarter left (soon fence away to right comes into view). Leave field by gate in far right-hand corner [4]. Turn left on road then immediately right, signposted Ashby Puerorum (**a**). After ½ mile turn right, for Ashby Puerorum (**b**). Keep left just before church, then turn right at T-junction. Take next right turn, signposted Stainsby only.

[5] After 600 yards fork left just after large barn (signposted public footpath)

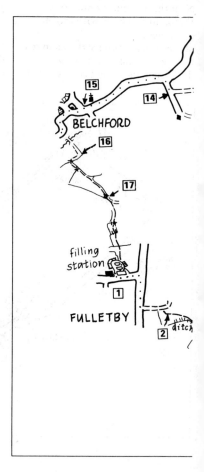

and 50 yards later keep left, passing between old brick barn (on your right) and modern barn (left), beyond which enter field, to follow farm track downhill. **6** After 200 yards, and immediately after track bends right through break in hedge turn left (waymarked) proceeding alongside hedge on left. On reaching corner of hedge, right of way proceeds quarter left, aiming for left-hand side of small conifer plantation (it may be easier in practice to follow edge of field to this point), just in front of which **7** cross footbridge and proceed to left of plantation to pick up track leading

uphill to village of Bag Enderby (**c**). Turn left when level with thatched cottage (turn right to see village) on track.

On entering first field keep forward along right edge. After 300 yards, by electricity post, cross neck of field to stile ahead. Proceed down slope in second field to stile by electricity post, then ascend third field to gate in front of farm. Enter farmyard, turn right and keep right, to pass through gate and on to road. Left on road into Somersby (**d**) **8**. Ignore right turn just before church and ignore left turn ½ mile later. Road bends right (soon past quarry on right) then left, then

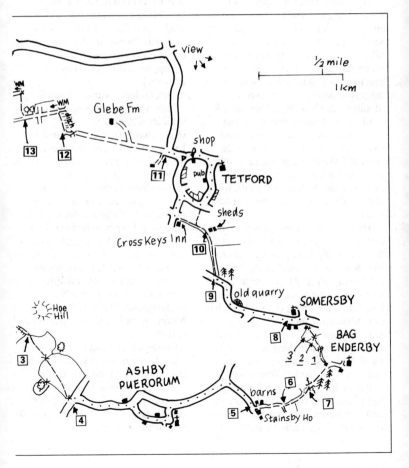

passes small pine wood on your right.

9 At end of pine wood, turn right on track (signposted) into right-hand of two fields. Where track ends, continue forward with hedge on left. **10** Keep to left of sheds, follow left edge of two fields and proceed to road (*NB In second field after sheds, grassy track on right by electricity pole leads directly into Tetford, though this is not a right of way*). Turn right on road and turn right at next junction then left, signposted Louth. Proceed through Tetford village (**e**), keeping left by church, and right at next fork, then turn right by grassy triangle.

11 After 100 yards, where road bends right, forward (**f**) on track (ignore immediate left fork to farm). After 600 yards keep left at fork (signposted) and, where track ends, maintain direction alongside hedge on left to reach gate and footbridge **12**, beyond which turn right (waymarked); very soon alongside ditch on right, then after 300 yards turn left on signposted grassy track. After 300 yards keep forward over cross-track, now with trees on right. **13** Where trees end, turn right (waymarked), ascending on track alongside ditch. After 300 yards, when level with gate on right, turn left on track.

14 Reach farm road, turn right along it then left at T-junction. Follow into Belchford. **15** After passing church turn left (Dams Lane; Viking Way ('VW') waymark). After ¼ mile, 20 yards after road swings right (and just before metal barrier), cross stile on left (VW waymark), for path between fences. Cross footbridge, take stile on right and turn left alongside fence, on clear track. **16** At top of field turn right on cross-track (VW waymark), and after 100 yards turn left through right-hand of two gates (VW signpost and waymark). Continue forward over two fields alongside fence (soon becomes a hedge) on left.

17 At far corner of second field cross stile and turn left on track. Fork right by signpost and electricity pole after 80 yards, continuing alongside hedge on right (VW waymark). Cross stile just before bottom of rise, and immediately turn left to cross second stile. Bear quarter right to stile at bottom of field (VW waymark). Forward in next field, making for lower of two radio masts. Cross stile, to find stile in top corner. Left on road, then take third turning right and first left by post-box to return to start.

WHAT TO LOOK OUT FOR

(**a**) A bungalow on the left has a **gate** made out of farming implements.
(**b**) **Ashby Puerorum** 'Ashby of the boys'; previously its revenues went to support choirboys at Lincoln cathedral.
(**c**) **Bag Enderby** Attractive small village, where Tennyson's father was vicar (as well as at Somersby). The church has been much restored, but has an interesting medieval font adorned with quaint carvings. The old rectory and hall are nearby.
(**d**) **Somersby** Tennyson was born in the Georgian rectory (not open to the public) in 1809; he was baptised in the church and as a boy used to toll the bell. Inside the church are his clay pipes and quill pen. Next to the rectory is Manor Farm (1722; attributed to Vanbrugh) built in an embattled style, with four towers. Its plan bears a striking resemblance to Vanbrugh's Nunnery, built at Greenwich a year earlier.
(**e**) **Tetford** Dr Johnson is said to have played skittles at the White Hart Inn.
(**f**) For a **view** of Lincoln cathedral, Boston Stump and the sea, continue on the road for ¾ mile to the top of the hill (from where you can follow roads to Belchford; see map).

Louth, Raithby and Hubbard's Hill

Unspoilt hilly farmland and woodland, with some parkland and a lake at South Elkington Hall. Then follows an almost traffic-free road with wide grass verges. Follows stream for final section, ending in the deep wooded valley of Hubbard's Hill. Waymarked most of the way, making route-finding quite easy.

Length 10 miles (16km), 4½ hours
Difficulty 2–3
Start Louth town centre, in Westgate, by church spire
OS maps 1:50,000 122; 1:25,000 TF 28/38
Refreshments Full range in Louth

WALK DIRECTIONS

1 (a) With spire of Louth church immediately behind you, continue forward along Westgate, soon passing the Wheatsheaf Inn. Bear right at junction, and keep right on main road when it curves round to right. After it crosses stream take second right turn, by sign for Deighton Close school. Continue up drive, ignoring all side turns.

2 Where drive bends right by farm buildings, go forward on grassy track, soon with hedge on right. Continue with hedge (later fence) on right. Cross over farm road, then proceed along right edge of field, past a second farm, to reach woods at end. Pass through gate into wood, in which keep forward, ignoring side turnings. After emerging from wood continue on grassy field track down to road **3**.

Cross the road and go over the stile opposite. Turn quarter right and head for gate at bottom of valley. Forward through gate and make for further gate on skyline **4**. Forward into large open field at top, on track, then soon maintain same direction on reaching corner of tarmac farm track. This track later bends round to right and passes barns on your right. 300 yards beyond barns, and at corner of fence on your right, turn right through gate into field **5**.

Bear half left across field, down to woodland fence which runs along bottom edge, and proceed alongside fence to wide gate at far end, ignoring right turn but following track which bends left around end of lake across parkland. **6** (b) Just before it reaches main road, turn left on unsurfaced road, then turn right in front of estate buildings. Turn right at T-junction, and immediately left to reach tarmac road by church institute. Left on road which bends left immediately after church. Left over stile just after church (signposted public footpath). Forward with fence on left, and on reaching trees turn right down to stile into wood **7**.

Keep right following waymarks, then 30 yards later take leftmost path at three-way fork. 100 yards later path bends left over footbridge and turns right immediately afterwards. Go forward after 200 yards over cross-track (signposted bridleway). **8** ¼ mile later, where main track bears left, go forward over footbridge and through waymarked gate beyond to leave woods, and turn quarter right to follow grassy field-track alongside trees on right. Just before sewage treatment works, cross gate/stile on right, turn right on track and 30 yards later turn left on tarmac lane.

9 300 yards later take next left turn and follow to main road. Cross road to track opposite. Where main track bends right into copse, keep forward on grassy track down to bottom of the slope, where it crosses bridge and turns right, proceeding alongside ditch. **10** 80 yards after fence begins on right, turn half left on grassy track, heading for barns, where turn left, passing immediately to left of barn. 50 yards later, turn left on farm road.

307

11 After 500 yards turn left at T-junction with road. Follow road for 1 mile, then turn right to descend to hamlet of Hallington; immediately ignore left turn uphill but take next left, then just after post-box in hamlet turn left again. **12** Fork right after 30 yards to follow driveway into Home Farm. Pass between farmhouse (right) and stables (left); exit by gate. Cross first field to gate ahead, then forward along left edge of second field to cross stile in far left corner **13**.

Cross track (c) and keep forward (signposted) to end of field, where turn left along hedge, then after 100 yards cross stile on right. Make across field aiming to left of leftmost house ahead. Find gate and emerge opposite Raithby church (d) **14**. From church re-enter field through which you came, retrace steps alongside fence on left for 50 yards, and at its corner bear half right, aiming for leftmost of nearby houses, reaching it via the footbridge.

Keep just to left of this house, cross stile and cross track beyond it, then immediately turn left along edge of field (which immediately rises above level of track). Keep alongside the hedgerow and **15** 300 yards into

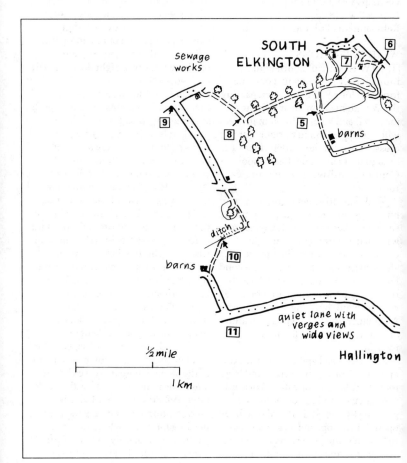

second field cross waymarked stile on left into wood. Cross old railway track to take waymarked path opposite/slightly to right. After 100 yards, turn left at path junction. Path leads to stile, beyond which follow stream on your left to road **16**.

Cross road to gate opposite and follow path alongside stream (or up steps for high-level route if preferred). **17** When path joins road turn right on it, then immediately left on path which soon crosses bridge to rejoin road. 80 yards later take gate on left (marked 'no cycling'), cross park and return to Louth church.

WHAT TO LOOK OUT FOR

(**a**) **Louth** Red-brick market town with some good Georgian streets, including some particularly well-preserved houses in Westgate. The soaring spire of its large church can be seen for miles around.

(**b**) **South Elkington** Approached through the landscaped parkland of its 19th-century hall.

(**c**) The building on the right is the former **Hallington railway station**, on a line which ran Louth to Bardney.

(**d**) **Raithby church** Gothick, built 1839. Has grotesque corbels inside and out; contains a barrel organ.

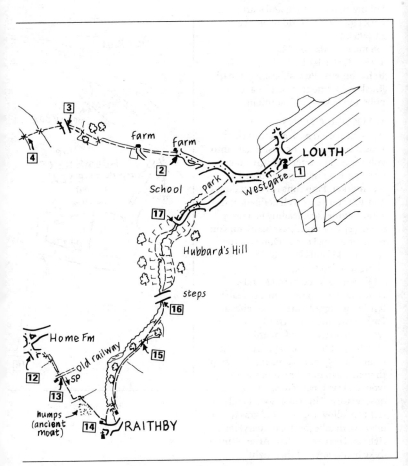

NORFOLK

Gore Point and Thornham

Contributed by Dorothea Whitworth

A mostly level walk on quiet sand dunes and along raised dykes, skirting a bird sanctuary and river estuary; good sandy beach near the start. Pleasant sea views on inland section, too. Some road-walking, all on minor lanes.

Length 7 miles (11km), 2½ hours
Difficulty 1
Start Holme-next-the-sea, just N of A149, 3 miles NE of Hunstanton. Follow signs to beach and start at car park close to sea. Grid reference SF 698439
OS maps 1:50,000 132;
1:25,000 SF 64/74
Refreshments Pub, shop and car park kiosk in Holme-next-the-Sea; two pubs and baker's in Thornham

WALK DIRECTIONS

1 (**a**) Leave car park and turn right. Pass through opening beside gate into golf course and after 100 yards take coast path on right beside board and waymarker. Path runs between dunes and golf course, is well defined, and soon waymarked, leading up grassy slope. **2** Continue past house on your right, entering Holme Dunes nature reserve 200 yards later (**b**). Proceed along wooden track.

3 Where wooden track ends, continue across grassy area to reach left-hand edge of pine woods ahead. Path continues through edge of pine woods. Shortly, wooden bird-watching observatory appears up on right, then **4** path turns right up steps then immediately left along another wooden track, past entrance to observatory. This track soon bends right to follow top of raised grassy dyke, with lake (bird sanctuary) on right and estuary on left. After ½ mile dyke bends left and then right.

5 When bridge appears on left, cross it; on other side keep right, following track which passes between two inlets.Track becomes tarmac road. Proceed along it, take next turning on left; Lifeboat Inn is immediately on right **6**. Continue through Thornham village, keeping right at next junction, to reach main road (A149). Turn right along it, then **7** take second turning on left, a minor road signposted 'Ringstead 3 miles'. Take next right, signposted

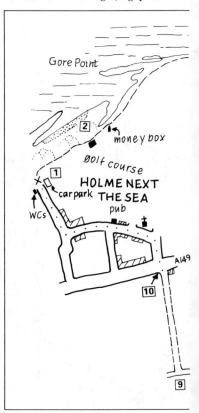

'Ringstead 2½ miles'. **8** After ½ mile, ignore minor right turn, and 175 yards later continue forward on track, where road bears left (**c**). **9** After ½ mile turn right and follow farm track downhill. **10** Reach A149, cross it and take road opposite. Follow lane which soon bends left, then passes church and pub. At T-junction, turn right and proceed back to start.

WHAT TO LOOK OUT FOR

(**a**) **Holme-next-the-Sea**. Terminus of the ancient Peddar's Way, which heads almost dead straight NNW from near Ixworth in Suffolk. Why it ended here is uncertain; perhaps a ferry crossed the Wash to Lincolnshire. It now forms part of an official long-distance path.

(**b**) Coast is of great interest for its wide variety of **birds**, including hoopoes, wrynecks and ospreys, as well as some rarities – among them collared flycatcher, red-rumped swallow and nutcracker. Permit required for visiting the adjacent reserves; on sale at Holme Bird Observatory.

(**c**) **View** of the sail-less tower windmill at Ringstead, straight ahead (W).

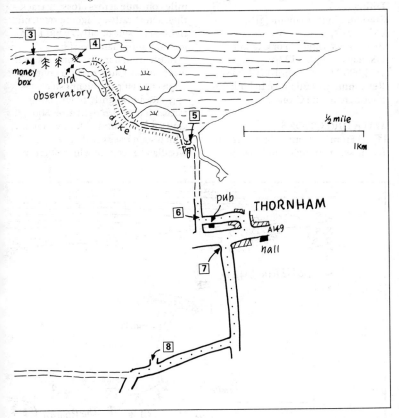

Sheringham and Cromer

Over small hills (though at just over 300ft, the highest in the county) with bracken heathland and pine woods, returning from Cromer along wide sand and pebble beach at foot of crumbling sandy cliffs. Can be treated as two linear walks by using trains or buses between Cromer and Sheringham. Inland sections all waymarked (North Norfolk Coast Path) apart from initial stages out of Sheringham; easy route-finding.

Length 9 miles (14.5km), 4½ hours
Difficulty 3
Start Sheringham (point **1**) or Cromer (**9**)
By train Sheringham or Cromer
OS maps 1:50,000 133;
1:25,000 TG 04/14 and TG 23/33
Refreshments Full range in both Sheringham and Cromer

WALK DIRECTIONS

1 (**a**) From seafront in Sheringham, facing sea, turn right, picking up concrete esplanade, which soon passes shelter on your left. 150 yards later, by last building (toilet block), and just before grassy cliffs begin, turn right up steps. Continue to corner of residential road, at which turn left on to path between fences.

2 Where path emerges from fences, keep forward close to cliff-top, on path leading to trig. point visible ahead, beyond which descend steps. At bottom of slope, pass field on your right, and at end of field (300 yards after trig. point) turn right along grassy path between fields. After ¼ mile continue across crossing track then across railway; ignore track on right on far side of railway but keep forward until main road **3**.

Route from here to Cromer is well waymarked. Cross road for continuation of coast path, signposted opposite and slightly to left, along tarmac lane. Turn right after 300 yards at junction, and follow track, which soon rises gently towards woodland at edge of which **4** turn

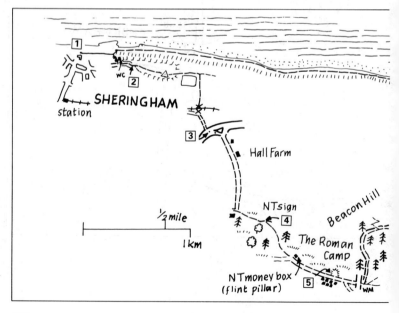

left by NT sign. Fork right 100 yards later by next NT sign, and follow clear track up through woods. Keep forward at junction 500 yards later (NT flint pillar on left). **5** Track passes NT car park, flagpole and viewpoint at Roman Camp (**b**) on your left (opposite entrance to caravan site); 50 yards later fork left, follow to and across road, and take first left turn (waymarked), after 30 yards. Track descends steadily, leaving forest after ½ mile, then runs between hedges.

6 Just after track emerges from hedges, ignore left fork, but keep forward, soon continuing between hedges, through gate and along right edge of field. At end of field, take gate ahead, continue across grassy area to farm track, along which turn left and immediately sharp right. Continue between hedges. **7** Keep left after 300 yards between hedges, ignoring breaks on either side. 150 yards later keep forward on joining corner of track and follow to road. Cross to track between hedges opposite, under

railway arch: follow up rise, ignoring track between hedges opposite, under railway arch: follow up rise, ignoring turns; Cromer (**c**) comes into view.

8 Keep forward on joining tarmac lane, follow to main road, along which turn left into Cromer. **9** From seafront in Cromer, facing sea, turn left and follow esplanade. Where esplanade ends, continue on beach to Sheringham.

WHAT TO LOOK OUT FOR
(**a**) **Sheringham** Sedate seaside resort at the top of miniature sandy cliffs.
(**b**) **Roman Camp** Probably not Roman at all; the grassy humps may be connected with Saxon or medieval iron-smelting. **View** Over the coast and of the way you have come.
(**c**) **Cromer** Small resort with a pier; near the seafront are a couple of winding lanes that hark back to its days as a fishing village before it expanded in the railway age. Still famous for its crabs. In the centre, the massive flint church, 15th-century but rather over-restored inside.

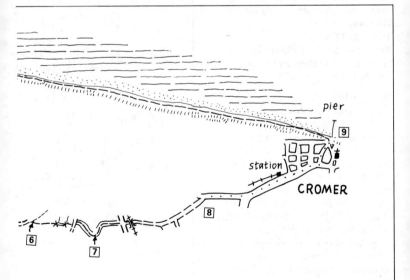

Holkham Hall and Burnham Overy Staithe

*Based on a contribution from
J W Taylor*
*Recommended by Ronald Locke,
F C Smale, F Schumann*

Starts off through parkland before following country roads and farm tracks past a watermill and windmill to reach small natural harbour of Overy Staithe; return route follows top of a dyke overlooking the largest salt-marsh in Europe, and then takes you out on a huge sandy beach fringed with dunes and pine trees. Roads across Holkham Park closed to pedestrians for about two hours a week in shooting season (notices displayed). Easy route-finding.

Length 10 miles (16km), 5 hours
Difficulty 2–3
Start Holkham, on A165 1½ miles W of Wells-next-the-Sea. Car park on N side of road, opposite signed entrance for Bygones museum/Holkham Hall (fee in summer); if full, second car park in Holkham village by estate gate. Grid reference TF 891446
OS maps 1:50,000 132;
1:25,000 TF 84/94
Refreshments Victoria Hotel, Holkham; The Hero and shop at Burnham Overy Staithe

WALK DIRECTIONS

1 From car park (**a**) go back to main road, cross it and continue along minor road opposite, through Holkham estate village and enter Holkham Hall estate via gates, beyond which keep forward. **2** ¼ mile later keep right at T-junction (left is private) and follow estate road past Holkham Hall (**b**), immediately after which road bends left by lake.

3 At end of lake, fork right (**c**) (signposted to garden centre). Road soon leads over cattle-grid, shortly beyond which keep forward at junction, ignoring right turn signposted to

garden centre but continuing forward to leave estate by lodge at West Gate. Beyond, proceed to B-road **4**. Turn left on road and follow for 1 mile.

5 At village of Burnham Overy Town, immediately before houses begin on right side of road, turn right on to signposted farm track. At end of field turn left, picking up track between hedges. **6** On joining corner of road, turn immediately left, on enclosed path leading to church (**d**), then through churchyard to road; turn right on road, then after 75 yards turn right at junction, signposted Burnham Overy Staithe.

7 100 yards later, where road bends right, turn left into track

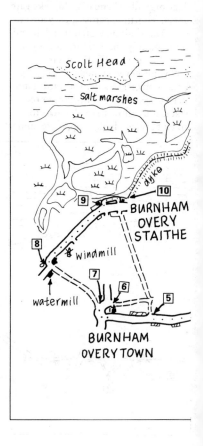

314

between hedges. On emerging into field, keep forward alongside hedge on your right, until reaching road by water mill (**e**) 8 . Turn right on road (**f**), and follow to Burnham Overy Staithe. 9 Take first turn on left in village to quayside (**g**) and where road bends right inland, keep forward on gravel path leading to raised dyke beyond nature reserve sign (**h**). 10 Left on dyke, follow 1½ miles to sand dunes, where duckboards lead through dunes to beach 11 .

Turn right along beach (**i**). 12 Pine woods soon begin on your right; keep parallel to them and walk along beach for 2½ miles in all until reaching Holkham Gap 13 , a prominent V-shaped break in corner of woods (which now extend some way out to left). At Gap, head inland on wide path, soon on duckboards, back to car park.

WHAT TO LOOK OUT FOR
(**a**) Just before the main road is reached, the site of little **Holkham station** is passed on the left. This used to be on the branch line from Heacham to Wells, washed out in the disastrous flood of 1953 and never reinstated.
(**b**) **Holkham Hall** In the Palladian style, with gardens landscaped by Capability Brown. It was the home of Thomas Coke, the great 'improving

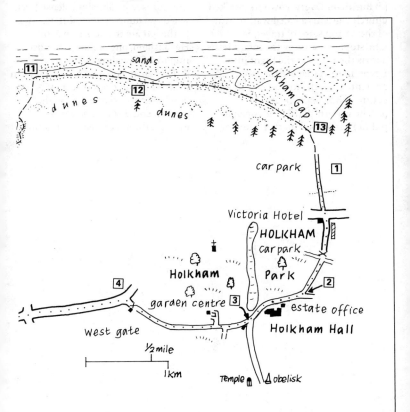

landlord' who inspired agricultural progress in the 18th and early 19th centuries. By his experiments in breeding, by manuring and by adopting rotation farming he improved the value of his land ten-fold. His annual 'sheep-shearings' attracted agriculturists from all over Britain and became an important means of spreading knowledge of new methods. The tall column in the park was raised as a memorial to him by his neighbours.

(**c**) Just after the lake, straight ahead, is a thatched 17th-century **ice house** with Dutch gables. Ice would be cut from the lake in winter and stored in it for use in the summer.

(**d**) **Burnham Overy Town** Its crooked church contains a faded wall-painting of the patron saint of travel, St Christopher, carrying the infant Jesus across the water in the flight into Egypt. In the village is the foot of an ancient cross, the former commercial centre of Burnham Overy.

(**e**) The **watermill** (NT; not open to public) has a flood marker showing the depth of water in the 1953 floods.

(**f**) On the right is a fine six-storey **tower mill** (NT; not open to public), built in 1816 and rescued in the 1920s after it had been tail-winded in a storm and had its machinery wrecked.

(**g**) **Burnham Overy Staithe** Once a flourishing little harbour with a regular packet-boat from London; traces of berths and warehouses can still be seen. Nelson, born at Burnham Thorpe, sailed here as a boy. It was also the home of Captain Woodget of the *Cutty Sark*.

(**h**) These **marshes** are of international importance ecologically. Apart from the prolific **birds**, the area shows all the stages in establishing dense larch woods on dunes and mud-flats. Away to the left are the dunes on Scolt Head Island, one of Europe's most important breeding places for terns.

(**i**) This great expanse of sand has been used for filming desert scenes. A beachcomber's paradise: the shells, starfish and assorted objects washed up from the sea can be a distraction.

NOTTINGHAMSHIRE

Clumber Park

Contributed by Dorothea Whitworth
Recommended by B H and M J James

Gentle walk in landscaped parkland with fine trees (predominantly oak, beech, Spanish chestnut and lime), and some newer coniferous plantations. Tracks mostly well defined; easy route-finding.

Length 4 ½ miles (7km), 2 hours
Difficulty 1
Start Car park (fee; free for NT members) close to Hardwick village, inside Clumber Park, 5 miles SE of Worksop. Turn off A614 4 miles N of Ollerton, opposite Normanton Inn to enter Clumber Park by Normanton Gate; follow park road which turns right and descends to cross ford, then passes Hardwick village. Take first left after houses and go downhill to car park on left before lake. Grid reference SK 636755
OS maps 1:50,000 120;
1:25,000 SK 67/77
Refreshments NT café in park, after point **7**.

WALK DIRECTIONS

1 (A) From car park, walk along wide lakeside path in clockwise direction, with lake on right (**b**). **2** Cross over footbridge above weir. Continue on well-defined path bearing left and slightly uphill, away from lake. Path soon reaches fence at edge of forest, then runs alongside fence on right, just inside forest. **3** After ¼ mile, where fence ends, path divides into three (saw-mill just visible on left, set back in trees). Take centre one, which bears half right, and follow across open parkland until it meets tarmac estate road **4**.

Turn right on road. After 200 yards, take gate on left into pine woods (occasionally, woodland is closed for felling; if so, proceed along road to bridge over lake at **7**. Immediately fork right and follow track for 500 yards. **5** At T-junction, turn right, now with thick pine woods on right and mixed woodland on left. **6** After 600 yards reach next junction, at edge of pine woods. Turn right, keeping edge of pines still on your right and follow this path for ½ mile until rejoining estate road at Clumber Bridge **7**.

Cross over bridge and turn immediately right on to path near lake. Follow until level with cafe, church and site of house (**c**). After visiting them, rejoin lakeside path and follow through church grounds and terrace garden path. At end of lakeside path and just before small wooden bridge, turn left and go up through trees to gate out of church grounds.

Cross field, go through another gate into woodland. Turn right and follow woodland path, then immediately right again and follow path back to lake. Continue around lake, passing through grove of rhododendrons, to reach start.

WHAT TO LOOK OUT FOR

(**a**) **Clumber Park** Former seat of the Dukes of Newcastle and one of the four estates that constitute the Dukeries, the others being Worksop, Thoresby and Welbeck. Between the two World Wars the public was denied access to the park, and in the Second World War it was used as an ammunition dump. Happily, the NT has taken it over and opened it up. Large areas are managed forestry, and are occasionally closed during felling operations.
(**b**) **Birds** on the lake include Canadian geese, mallards, tufted ducks, coots, moorhens, swans and pochards.

(c) **Clumber House** Built in 1770 and demolished in 1937. John Murray, in his *Handbook for Travellers* (1892), wrote: 'The park was laid out, planted, and in fact created, by the great-great-grandfather of the present Duke. The house, though of stone, is not imposing externally, from want of height; but it has comfort and splendour within. In 1879 nearly all the rooms were consumed by fire. It has been replaced by a fine Central Hall in classic style by Charles Barry. The State Dining-room will accommodate 150 guests.' Its near-priceless collection of pictures, which includes works by Rembrandt, Rubens, Raphael, Vandyck, Holbein, Dürer and Gainsborough, is on exhibition at the Nottingham Castle Museum. Its Victorian church of St Mary stands intact.

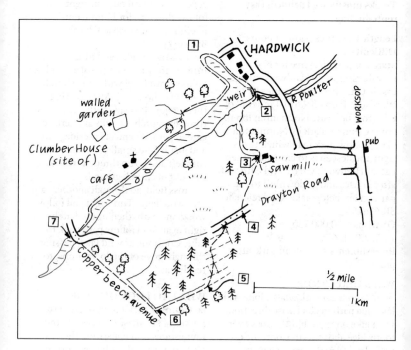

SUFFOLK

Aldeburgh and Thorpeness

Contributed by Keith Chamberlain

Of special interest for bird- and plant-life. All on the level, yet quite varied, leading along an old railway track, through heathland, past a lake near Thorpeness and along a shingle beach. One section on road. Easy route-finding.

Length 5½ miles (9km), 2 hours
Difficulty 1–2
Start Moot Hall at N edge of Aldeburgh
OS maps 1:50,000 156; 1:25,000 TM 44/45
Refreshments Various pubs and the celebrated Fish and Chip Shop at Aldeburgh. The Dolphin and a café (opposite the Meare, an artificial lake) at Thorpeness

WALK DIRECTIONS

1 (**a**) From Moot Hall cross to Mill Inn opposite, and take road to left of it, signposted A12. Just before church take gate into churchyard and follow path to wooden kissing-gate on far side. Continue along enclosed path beyond, ignoring a right turn after 200 yards, to take wooden kissing-gate leading to caravan site **2** . Cross to tarmac track on the far side of toilet block ahead, ignoring track on near side. Turn left through the caravan site to stile leading to abandoned railway track, on which turn right. Follow for ½ mile.

3 Where railway track is barred by metal gate take signposted track on left over stile, past houses to main road. Turn right along road for 500 yards. **4** At dip in road, turn right alongside brick wall signposted public footpath to Thorpeness. Wall is succeeded by garden hedge. Where it ends, do not continue on track past nature reserve notices, but

look for narrow path bearing left and passing through small copse on to area of gorsy heathland (**b**). Continue along this path to edge of reedbeds.

5 Turn right at junction of paths, with reedbeds now on left. Path winds through banks of gorse and broom. **6** After ½ mile turn left on path at T-junction through wood to rejoin old railway, on which turn left and follow for short distance, crossing small river by low walled bridge. **7** On leaving wood turn right on footpath across garden of ex-railway cottage and follow along edge of golf course and by left side of Meare. Path passes to left of clubhouse and on to track. Follow track between House in the Clouds and windmill (**c**) into Thorpeness itself (**d**).

8 Turn right on reaching tarmac road and walk round edge of Meare; cross road by café and go down to beach (**e**). Turn right and walk either along beach proper or path at back. Latter is best for flowers, insects and birds.

WHAT TO LOOK OUT FOR

(**a**) **Aldeburgh** Birthplace of the 18th-century poet George Crabbe, and the home of Benjamin Britten, whose opera *Peter Grimes*, set on this coast, was based on a character in Crabbe's poem *The Borough*. The walk passes two buildings of particular interest, the 16th-century timber-framed Moot Hall and the church of St Peter and St Paul (largely 16th-century interior; ship auctions used to be held inside at that period), but the rest of the town also deserves exploration.

(**b**) **North Warren** RSPB nature reserve of 250 acres (leaflet from Minsmere, further up the coast towards Dunwich). It provides a varied habitat of heath, woodland and wetland, attracting a range of **birds** including

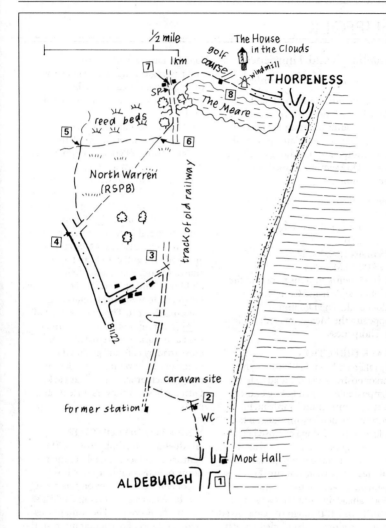

willow, reed and sedge warblers, redpolls, bitterns, linnets and stonechats, with occasional marsh harriers and bearded tits. The wetter areas have marsh marigolds, meadowsweet and yellow iris; just south of Sluice Cottage a small patch of marsh orchids can be seen in season (late spring to early summer).

(c) The **windmill** (open to public) dates from 1803. Originally a corn mill, it was moved to its present site to pump water to the House in the Clouds, the curious disguised water tower opposite.

(d) **Thorpeness** Built between 1910 and 1930s as a planned seaside resort adjoining the Meare, an artifical lake of 65 acres. Weather-boarding and timber-framing give the village an individual character.

(e) **Birds** Terns and ringed plovers. **Flora** Yellow horned poppies, sea holly and rare sea-pea.

The Gipping Valley, Badley Church and Needham Market Church

Contributed by D A Allen
Recommended by P J Keeble, T W Hoskins, D Dastur

River scenery and old water mills, with a landscaped parkland track leading to the site of Badley Hall. Brief optional extension takes in the river and lake south of the town. Some road-walking. Quite easy route-finding.

Length 6 miles (9.5km), 3 hours; 7 miles (11 km), 3½ hours with extension S of Needham Market
Difficulty 1
Start Needham Market, on B1113 8 miles NW of Ipswich. Free car parking in station yard, or (Sundays only) in High Street.
OS maps 1:50,000 155; 1:25,000 TM 05/15
Refreshments Needham Market

WALK DIRECTIONS

1 From station yard cross railway by tunnel to left of station building. Emerging into sports ground, half left to wooden hut. Just beyond hut find beginning of narrow road which goes alongside railway. Follow past old maltings to reach River Gipping (**a**) on right. Cross river by footbridge, turn left, follow tarmac path on right-hand side of river for 200 yards, then fork left on to grassy path leading to road-bridge. Go under bridge and follow river bank, passing Ravens Farm on opposite bank after ½ mile (ignore footbridge here).

2 1 mile later, cross river at bridge by derelict lock and turn right along track leading towards buildings of Badley Mill. After 200 yards turn left along faint path leading to footbridge visible from track. Cross bridge and turn right for a few yards over grassy area to reach unmetalled track, on

which turn left. Pass under railway and emerge on to B1113 **3**. Turn left along road (heading back towards Needham) for 300 yards, then right on road (Badley Walk) by bungalows. At last bungalow on right continue along footpath to right of it. Follow for ¾ mile through thicket, along former main approach to Badley Hall.

4 Emerge into field at end of thicket and continue in same direction. After 100 yards you see Badley Hall in front of you (**b**). **5** At Hall and church turn sharp left to farm road (**c**). Follow this 1 mile to reach B1113 **6**. Turn right on road and follow for ½ mile to outskirts of town, then *either* continue along road back to start *or* take route via footpaths to get better view of Hawks Mill, a fine water-mill. **7** For this route turn left off road at Gypsy Lane. Go over level crossing and continue on farm track towards Ravens Farm. **8** Turn right 100 yards beyond railway on to footpath across middle of field, parallel to railway. At end of field continue along track in same direction, past stables on left and Valley House on right. Emerge on to one of mill by-pass channels of Gipping before seeing Hawks Mill through willows on left. At road turn right, under railway bridge and uphill to High Street (whichever route, do not miss Needham Market church (**d**)).

9 *For extension by River Gipping and lake S of Needham Market* go from station yard under railway and turn right along the lake shore. Turn left at road, passing tall, weather-boarded Bosmere Mill. Just beyond mill cross road and go through wide iron gate on right, leading to path along Gipping Alderson Lake on right. Follow riverside for as long as you fancy, then retrace steps.

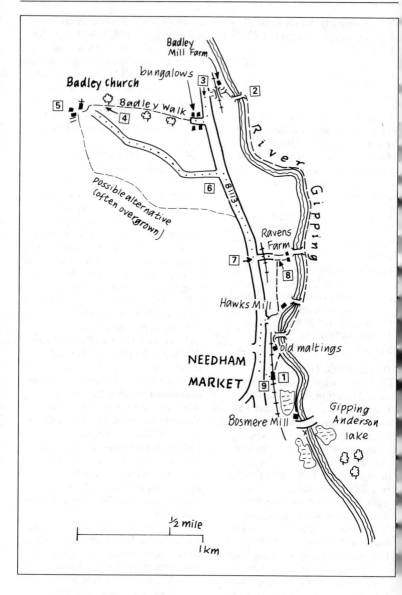

Badley
Mill Farm

bungalows

Badley church

Badley Walk

River Gipping

possible alternative
(often overgrown)

Ravens
Farm

Hawks Mill

old maltings

NEEDHAM
MARKET

Bosmere Mill

Gipping
Anderson
lake

½ mile

1 km

WHAT TO LOOK OUT FOR

(a) The **River Gipping**, which later becomes the Orwell, was canalised in 1793 to connect Stowmarket with Ipswich Docks. With the coming of the railway in 1847, navigation declined rapidly, but the walk offers evidence of the river's former importance. Ravens Farm was used by bargees as an inn.

(b) **Badley Hall and church** Elizabeth I is reputed to have ridden along Badley Walk, the approach to Badley Hall, a house now in a state of decay and only a fraction of its former size. In front of the Hall stands Badley church, an unspoilt medieval church which escaped Victorian restoration and retains its 17th-century latched box pews. No church in the county is more remote. It is often locked, but fortunately the clear glass of the windows makes it possible to enjoy the interior from outside.

(c) At Badley the OS map suggests a footpath route back to Needham, and the waymarkings near the church add encouragement. When our checker tried this, however, he found himself engulfed by shoulder-high nettles and had to retire defeated to follow the more sober route described in the text. Valiant spirits might yet succeed where he failed, though, especially in the spring.

(d) **Needham Market High Street** Many of the houses are Tudor, in most cases hiding behind Georgian façades. The parish church has a nondescript and unviting exterior, but inside is a hammer-beam roof described as 'the culminating achievement of the English carpenter'. As Pevsner's *Buildings of England: Suffolk* says, 'The eye scarcely believes what it sees, and has a hard if worthwhile job in working out how this unique effect could be attained'.

Dunwich and Minsmere

Contributed by Stephen Brough
Recommended by Sheila and John
Benfield, Keith Chamberlain,
P J Keeble

Through low-level heathland and marsh scenery, outstanding for its natural history; a glimpse of the sea at Dunwich. Route-finding generally easy, but care needed on Dunwich Heath.

Length 8 miles (13km), 4 hours
Difficulty 2–3
Start Eel's Foot Inn, Eastbridge,
2 miles N of Leiston. Grid reference
TM 453662
OS maps 1:50,000 156;
1:25,000 TM 46 and TM 47/57
Refreshments Eel's Foot Inn, at Eastbridge; Ship Inn and Flora's Café, at Dunwich (the latter is a Suffolk institution; the fish is freshly caught and you can wait on the beach for it to be cooked)

WALK DIRECTIONS

1 Standing with Eel's Foot Inn behind you, turn left along metalled lane and after 100 yards take track on left signposted 'Minsmere Sluice 1½ miles'. Follow for a few yards to green footpath sign indicating narrow grassy footpath to right. **2** At fork after 500 yards, avoid path on left leading to bridge over dyke, and continue straight ahead. Where path is blocked by gates, take second gate on left with stile beside. On far side bear right, up grassy rise heading for sea wall.

3 At sluice-gate by sea wall turn left and walk for 1 mile with sea on right and Minsmere reserve on left (**a**). **4** Just before car park on the hill-top to the right of coastguard cottages, turn left inland following waterway.

5 After ½ mile, path makes right turn (**b**). 100 yards later turn left, and after further 200 yards turn right and

follow waymarked path for Dunwich. **6** ½ mile later turn right at oblique T-junction with path. **7** Cross road ½ mile later and follow path to the outskirts of Dunwich, at which turn right towards sea on road; where road bends left, keep forward on sandy track leading into Dunwich (**c**) **8**.

From Flora's Café (on beach), take road inland for short distance and bear right along road in front of inn for 300 yards, to church. At junction take farm track signposted Walnut Tree and Apple Tree. Follow track, which becomes path and then forest ride. Ignore all cross-paths. **9** Keep right at junction with another ride on left. When ride bears away right at edge of wood, take track straight ahead on to Westleton Heath (**d**). Stony track leads on for ½ mile.

10 On meeting road, continue forward, and follow road for ¼ mile. **11** Take first turn left by RSPB sign, and then second right, signposted bridleway. When path meets tarmac lane, cross to far side and take grassy track left, signposted public footpath (ignore path straight ahead). **12** After ½ mile, track enters wood and passes straight through it, bearing right on far side and becoming tarmacked. At Dam Bridge, just before East Bridge, the Minsmere New Cut is crossed, a place of great interest for its bird- and plant-life (**e**). Eastbridge village is shortly beyond.

WHAT TO LOOK OUT FOR

(**a**) **Minsmere** RSPB reserve of 1,500 acres. Its freshwater marsh attracts an exceptional number of **birds**, including bitterns and bearded tits, and provides a habitat for the rare marsh sow thistle, hemp agrimony, marsh mallows and orchids. It also has heathland (a stronghold for the nightjar) and woodland, supporting nightingales, owls and all three varieties of British woodpecker. Over 280 species of birds have been

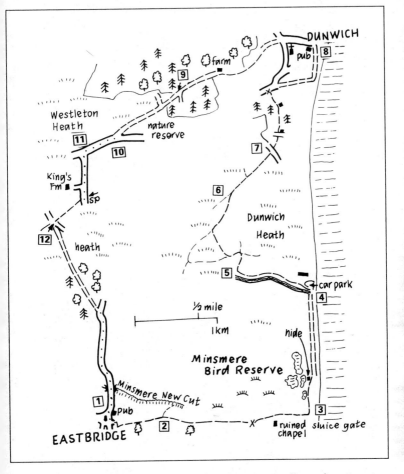

recorded here, some 200 of which are seen annually. There is a hide for public use; entry to the rest of the reserve is by permit only.

(**b**) **Dunwich Heath** (NT) Fine example of the Sandlings, great coastal heathlands that were once the grazing grounds for the sheep that provided the wool on which Suffolk's prosperity was built. The sheep have gone, but the heath is still a fine sight when the gorse and heather are in bloom, and there are many small mammals and insects.

(**c**) **Dunwich** Once an important town with a flourishing port and nine churches, now a village where imagination must supply a vision of what has been swallowed up by the sea. A visit to the small museum helps.

(**d**) **Westleton Heath nature reserve** Another vestige of the East Suffolk heathlands. Its **birds** include stone curlews, nightjars, red-backed shrike and woodlarks, while the **flora** includes a number of heathland rarities. The stony track followed is a surviving Roman carriage-way.

(**e**) A detour to the right, along the waterway, is recommended for bird-watchers and botanists who want to see yet more.

NORTH-WEST ENGLAND

Cumbria, Greater Manchester, Isle of Man

All but four of the featured walks for this region are in the Lake District, which inevitably dominates the north-west for the walker. However, the rest of the region is by no means all industrial, and we suspect the *Guide*'s dearth of walks, especially in Lancashire, is unjustified. We did have suggestions for routes in the Forest of Bowland and on the moors just north of Manchester, but these were given the thumbs down by *Holiday Which?* readers who tried them out. Recommendations for good walks in Lancashire would be particularly welcome (see page 10).

The Lake District is the most visited of the National Parks. Though not the most dramatic area in Britain – both Snowdonia and the Scottish Highlands have grander and more desolate mountain scenery – it has an unequalled sense of proportion, and the best range of walking anywhere. It is only about thirty miles across, but packs in enormous variety, and feels much larger. Though the tourist centres are inundated with visitors and some paths are well walked, it is possible to escape from the crowds completely once you're on foot. The topography of the area lends itself admirably to round walks, so much so that it can be hard to decide where to begin. There are plenty of easy walks around and near the lakes, particularly in the south, where there is a delightfully varied but gentle patch of countryside to the west of Lake Windermere. There are also some rewarding, though fairly easy, fell walks in Borrowdale and around Grasmere and Ambleside, and around Derwent Water.

The biggest attraction for more ambitious walkers is the mountainous area bounded by Eskdale to the south, Wasdale to the west, Borrowdale to the north and Great Langdale to the east: this is the main mountain group (including the highest mountains in England, Scafell Pike and Scafell), which gives some outstanding walking, much of it on high ridges. Most of these involve quite sharp hauls, and should be taken quite slowly; in all but the worst weather (for which, regrettably, the Lake District is renowned) the rewards are magnificent. Paths are often well defined (less so on mountain tops), and sometimes eroded. Sometimes the public right of way shown on OS maps doesn't match properly the well-trodden path on the ground – you may have to follow what you see on the ground rather than what's on the map. Generally, access to the main mountain areas of the

Lakes is less of a problem than in other parts of the country, as very large tracts of land belong to the National Trust or to public bodies who allow open access.

On the fringes of the Lakes are some worthwhile excursions, for example to Morecambe Bay, a vast area of mudflats with small hills surrounding it, and Arnside Knott, from which there is a good view of the Lakeland fells. The north-west coast is followed closely by the railway for much of the way, and there isn't much for the walker along it, though the section between Whithaven and St Bees is interesting, particularly for bird-watching. The finest coastal scenery in the north-west is without doubt on the Isle of Man (which we have included in this English section even though the island is autonomous); it can rival the best of the Cornish and Pembrokeshire coasts. Inland can be rewarding too, with hills having something of the character of the Pennines. A network of public footpaths exists, and some areas are completely open to walkers.

CUMBRIA

Morecambe Bay and Arnside Knott

Recommended by Mr and Mrs W A Comstive

Follows the sandy and rocky shores edging the huge mud-flats of Morecambe Bay (rich in birdlife) and ascends Arnside Knott, a wooded hill with fine views over the bay and into the Lake District. Route cleverly avoids caravan sites. Paths and tracks mostly well defined; route-finding quite easy. Rocks on shore can be slippery.

Length 6½ miles (10km), 3 hours
Difficulty 2–3
Start Arnside, Morecambe Bay. Car park (grid reference SD 454786) at end of B5282. Follow B-road through Arnside, keeping right at end at 'no through road' sign by Albion Hotel. *By train* Arnside station, on the Lancaster to Barrow line. Turn right out of station, and after 50 yards turn left on path signposted to church. Keep forward at church, on path signposted Silverdale Road. 300 yards later, cross road and take path opposite to emerge at T-junction opposite police station. Turn right to esplanade road and turn left along it
OS maps 1:50,000 97; 1:25,000 SD 37/47
Refreshments Pubs and cafés in Arnside

WALK DIRECTIONS

1 Follow esplanade road to end, then forward on path signposted New Barns Bay, alongside beach (**a**). **2** After ½ mile path reaches bay with house on other side. Cross to far side, pass to right of house, then either follow beach or pick up path just inside woods above beach, 150 yards after house. **3** At next bay, pick up path running at top of low cliffs on

other side of bay. Just before cliffs, narrow path leads on to it; follow signs to Far Arnside.

4 ¾ mile later fork left through gate (right fork leads to beach). Track soon leads into caravan site; avoid side turns, track soon becomes lane and turns left through hamlet of Far Arnside. **5** At T-junction with road take path opposite, signposted Silverdale, proceeding with wall on right across first field then forward and up to pass through small gate at far side of second field. Bear half left, making your own way to service road in caravan site. Turn left along it.
6 Opposite sharp right turn with another service road (with 'no entry' road-sign), take grassy track half left by wooden electricity pole. Follow ¼ mile to ruined tower (**b**) **7**.

Turn left in front of tower on track down to farm. Pass through gate by farm, signposted Arnside, taking farm road to reach road **8**. Cross road and pass through gate opposite, with NT sign for Arnside Knott (**c**). Follow woodland path uphill for ½ mile, then turn right on path marked 'This is a footpath, not a bridleway; walkers only please'. Ascend to T-junction of paths by bench, then right to viewpoint (**d**).

9 300 yards after viewpoint take stile on left on to grassy hillside. Turn half right to wall on your right, then follow it down to ladder-stile. Cross into woods then emerge on to road. **10** Turn left on road, which soon bends sharp right. Turn right at next junction and follow to Silverdale Road (signposted).

For car park turn left and follow back to waterfront.

For railway station turn right and after ¼ mile take path on left by Our Lady of Lourdes Chapel and descend to road. Turn left to reach station.

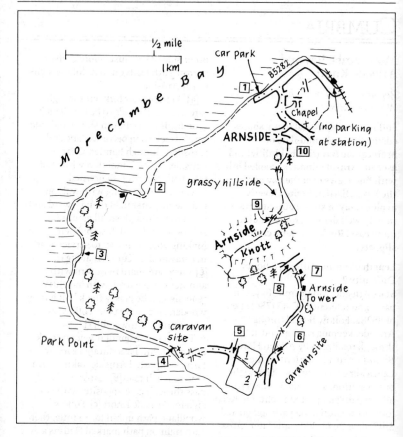

WHAT TO LOOK OUT FOR

(a) **Morecambe Bay** One of the fastest incoming tides in Britain crosses this vast expanse of sand and mud-flats. Though extremely dangerous to walk across without a detailed knowledge of the tides, it can be safely crossed, with a guide, from Kents Bank near Grange-over-Sands to Hest Bank, between Carnforth and Morecambe (about 8 miles in all). Ask at local tourist offices if you are interested in trying it. **Birds** Over 200,000 waders (the largest estuary population in Britain): mallard, curlew, shoveller, redshank, shelduck, oystercatcher, ringed plover, dunlin, diver, pink-footed goose, merlin, knot, godwit, eider, wigeon.

(b) **Arnside Tower** Ruined pele tower – a four-storey building with what was a five-storey tower. Remains of the parapet are visible, but the internal floors have collapsed. Probably 15th-century; built as a defence.

(c) **Arnside Knott** Has a yew grove and some uncommon grasses and ferns, among then adder's tongue. **Birds** Redwing, woodcock, greenfinch, hawkfinch, fieldfare.

(d) **View** Over Morecambe Bay, with Grange-over-Sands to the W; NW to the southern fells of the Lake District, including the Old Man of Coniston; E to Shap Fell, the Howgills and the Forest of Bowland.

The Cumbrian Coast Path, Whitehaven to St Bees

Contributed by Mr and Mrs P R Gurnell

Along the sheer sandstone cliffs of a little-known part of the Cumbrian coast, especially good for bird-watching (best in the breeding season – spring and early summer). From Whitehaven the route becomes increasingly countrified and remote, with views of the Scottish coast and the Isle of Man. Waymarking rather scant in initial stages when walk was inspected; care needed with directions. Take care with children, as there are sheer unfenced drops from the cliffs. Check bus or train times for return, before travelling.

Length 8 miles (13km), 4 hours
Difficulty 3
Start By harbour, Whitehaven. Return by bus or train from St Bees to Whitehaven
OS maps 1:50,000 89; 1:25,000 NX 90/91
Refreshments Various in Whitehaven and St Bees

WALK DIRECTIONS

1 (**a**) From left (S) side of harbour take road around it, soon leading round to old cannon (**b**), (**c**), then continue on tarmac path which doubles back above harbour and leads up to castellated look-out. **2** By ruined Fan House (information board), turn sharp right up residential road, then keep forward on, 'no through road' after 100 yards where principal road bends left. This leads under railway arch to emerge by derelict cottage (**d**). Turn left 10 yards before cottage, on path which runs with fence on right (path not very clear but route is obvious).

3 After ½ mile fork left on cinder track (right fork is coloured red by sandstone, and leads to old mine), rising to perimeter fence of colliery.

Follow this to join concrete road, then 30 yards later branch right over area of coal spoil, proceeding with fence on left. Path soon becomes clearer, crossing and recrossing fence on left by stiles.

4 ½ mile later reach small perimeter fence (ahead); avoid stile (sharp left) and proceed forwards to cross conveyor belt by footbridge. Path continues ahead, and soon winds uphill through bracken (**e**). **5** Turn right at T-junction of paths by Cumbria Way memorial stone. **6** Take small gate to right of bungalow, passing above quarry then along cliffs.

7 Keep to right of lighthouse, taking stile beside fog-warning station. Several viewpoints for bird-watching are passed on right, by stiles (**f**). **8** Where path dips down to cove (**g**), take low stile/steps 50 yards inland, and follow obvious path uphill, then along to St Bees (**h**). Turn left on road by hotel, and follow to St Bees station.

WHAT TO LOOK OUT FOR

(**a**) **Whitehaven** Former coal port, the earliest post-medieval planned town in Britain. It retains the original grid street layout, 17th-century, and there are some distinctive terraces (being preserved). The harbour, from where coal used to be shipped to Ireland, has some gruff character in its piers and bonded warehouses.
(**b**) The **cannon** may have come from a ship sunk by an 18th-century Scottish anarchist, Paul Jones, who fought for the colonists in the American War of Independence and launched an attack on Whitehaven harbour in 1778 – the first invasion of the British mainland since 1066.
(**c**) The **candlestick chimney** of the Wellington Pit is nearby, the first of seven former coal mines passed. It operated between 1840 and 1932 and suffered a notorious accident in 1910

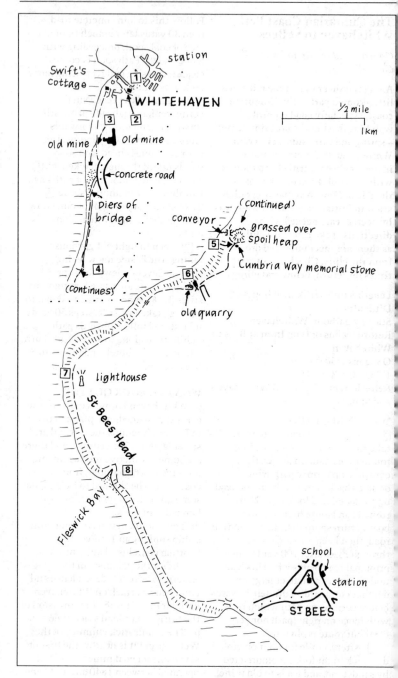

when 136 miners were killed. Next is Haig Colliery, the last to close in Cumbria, in 1984. Then Saltom, which went one mile out to sea (opened 1729, the first undersea pit in England; remains of buildings on beach); Ravenhill (1737); Kells; Ladysmith; and Croft (opened 1774).

(**d**) This 17th-century house was the childhood home of Jonathan Swift, author of *Gulliver's Travels*.

(**e**) **Flora** Various cliff plants on the walk, attributable to differences in aspect and geology; they include rock sea-lavender, thrift, bloody cranes-bill, golden saxifrage.

(**f**) **St Bees Head nature reserve** Birds: 5,000 breed here, including a few pairs of black guillemots – the only colony in England. More abundant seabirds are auks, guillemots, razorbills, puffins, shags, herring gulls, fulmars, kittiwakes.

(**g**) The cove is **Fleswick Bay**, which contains semi-precious stones. Not surprisingly – considering its isolation – it has been a smugglers' beach.

(**h**) **St Bees** Here a legendary 7th-century Irish princess – to whom 'as much land as was covered by snow on Midsummer Day' was granted – founded a priory. After Dissolution in 1536, the church became the parish church; fine Norman doorway. On the S side, enveloped in a lead-lined tomb, was found in 1981 the perfectly preserved body of a 14th-century lord, since dubbed St Bees Man. Opposite the church is St Bees school (founded 1583), with some of the original buildings surviving in its quadrangle.

Eskdale and Stanley Ghyll Waterfall

On the level through woods and pasture, with occasional glimpses up Eskdale, passing a romantic waterfall near the end. Completes the circuit by a trip on the narrow-gauge railway from Boot to The Green (see Special interest lists at back for when it runs). A section of quiet road at the start. Route-finding quite easy. Sturdy and easily managed stepping-stones crossed at the end; suitable footwear advisable (alternative route given in case stones are submerged).

Length 3 miles (5km), 1½ hours
Difficulty 1
Start The Green railway station, Eskdale Green (Ravenglass and Eskdale Railway), 3 miles W of Boot and 7 miles W of Hardknott Pass. Grid reference SD 146998. Small car park at station for rail patrons (free). Large car park at Boot (fee), by station. If using latter, take train before walk. Grid reference NY 173003
OS maps 1:50,000 89 and 96 or 90 and 96; 1:25,000 Outdoor Leisure 6
Refreshments Brook café, pub and railway café at Boot; King George IV Inn near Eskdale Green; Bower House, Eskdale Green (not on route)

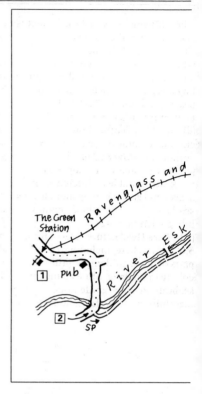

WALK DIRECTIONS

1 Turn right out of The Green station, ignore first left turn, then **2** left on to track (signposted Boot), immediately after road crosses river. Follow obvious track close to river. **3** After ¾ mile track bears half right to gate into woodland. Proceed, avoiding side turns: after ½ mile avoid left fork. **4** Leave woods by gate. **5** Just before entering next woodland (signposted to Boot) turn right (between walls) then immediately left through gate with sign for Stanley Ghyll Force beyond (**a**). At stream, make a mental note of this point as you will return to it, and turn

right up stream to reach Stanley Ghyll Force (falls) by succession of footbridges.

6 Retrace steps to Boot signpost and take this path through woods, over footbridge and across field to reach corner of stone wall (signpost). Turn left, proceeding with wall on right, to reach small gate by stream. **7** Cross stream by stepping-stones (if you don't fancy this there is a stone footbridge ¾ mile further along stream, to right, and path on both banks (**b**)). On far bank, follow track past church. 100 yards later, avoid left fork and follow to road. Boot village (and mill) is ahead; station is to left (**c**).

WHAT TO LOOK OUT FOR

(**a**) **Stanley Ghyll** Perhaps the finest setting for a waterfall in the Lake

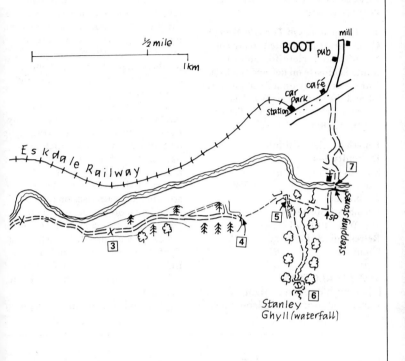

District – a precipitous wooded
chasm with luxuriant ferns, crossed
by a series of footbridges. Total fall
is 60ft.
(**b**) If avoiding the stepping-stones,
the route is obvious for ¾ mile as far
as the footbridge (do not try to cross
dangerous skeleton of old railway
bridge passed after only ¼ mile); on
other bank route continues close to
river for a short distance, but
continues one field away from the
river before rejoining it.
(**c**) **Ravenglass and Eskdale Railway**
(small museum at Ravenglass, by
station) Operated from 1875 to 1913
to take iron ore from the mines near
Boot (on N side of valley) to the
Furness railway at Ravenglass; excur-
sion trains were put on at weekends
and Bank Holidays. Following floo-
ding in 1912 the railway was relaid
as 15-inch gauge in 1915. In
September 1960 local enthusiasts
outbid scrap merchants for it in an
auction and a new railway company
was formed to run the line as a tourist
attraction. One of the original
carriages survives as a garden shed in
Ravenglass.

Levers Water and Coniston copper mines

The lower slopes of The Old Man of Coniston are designated an area of historical and scientific interest. Route is mostly on defined tracks and paths, but briefly undefined just after ③ and the turn-off at ⑥ needs care. Keep well clear of any mine shafts. Ascent 1,100ft.

Length 4 miles (6.5km), 2½ hours
Difficulty 3–4
Start By road-bridge in centre of Coniston, on A593 8 miles SW of Ambleside
OS maps 1:50,000 96 or 97; 1:25,000 Outdoor Leisure 6
Refreshments Pubs and cafés in Coniston

WALK DIRECTIONS

① (**a**) With Bull Inn on right, cross bridge, and turn right up lane signed to Sun Inn. At Sun Inn, turn right on farm track and beyond farm take gate into field ②. Track ascends gently (**b**). Ignore bridge over stream on right after ½ mile. Path becomes rougher (**c**), then passes through gate and ascends more steeply to reach stile ¼ mile later.

③ 300 yards after stile, look out for (but do not take) prominent stony track on left. 40 yards later, turn right on another stony track which soon narrows to path as it ascends. At top of slope (with waterfall before you) bear right, down to footbridge over stream; clear path rises on to low shoulder on other side. Ascend to point where reservoir is seen below you (**d**) ④. Continue forward (pass to right of small fenced area) then turn right along reservoir path. A spectacularly deep shaft is immediately on the right.

⑤ At end of reservoir turn right on

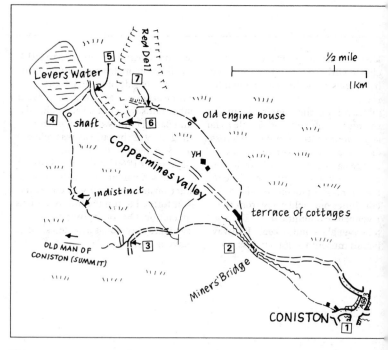

clear path that descends towards Coniston; view opens up, suddenly (e). **6** After 300 yards look out for level grassy/stony path on left, immediately after end of hillside on left: it contours around hillside to lead into next valley, Red Dell. Follow to valley floor (f) **7**.

Turn right on path at bottom of valley. Path crosses stream and passes more ruined copper-mine works (g) before descending to track by incongruous-looking terrace of houses. Follow track down to Coniston, walking on other side of stream from which you ascended.

WHAT TO LOOK OUT FOR

(a) **Coniston** Writer and social reformer John Ruskin, who lived at Brantwood on the other side of the lake from 1871 to his death in 1900, preferred burial in the Coniston churchyard to Westminster Abbey. The Ruskin Museum in the village contains some mementoes.

(b) **Coppermines Valley** Scene of intense mining activity from about 1599 to 1942, with a renewed attempt at opening up the mines in 1954. Various companies have operated here, including the Company of Mines Royal in early times, then later the Macclesfield Copper Company and Barratt's, a Cornish mining company. The surface deposits were removed early on, and tunnelling for deeper deposits took place in the 17th century, when skilled Austrian and German miners were employed. By the end of the 19th century tunnelling reached 1,230ft and several hundred miners were employed.

(c) The Youth Hostel which soon comes into view ahead was once the **mine office** and manager's house; just above it are the Bonsor Mine dressing floors.

(d) The two richest veins of copper were at **Paddy's End**, here at Levers Water, and **Bonsor** (which you soon pass). The shafts here are deep and extremely dangerous, and the ground unstable. Do not stray from the route.

(e) **View** Over Coniston Water, with Grizedale Forest as the backdrop. The lake was where Donald Campbell was killed in 1967 trying to break the world water-speed record in *Bluebird*.

(f) **Bonsor mine** (Red Dell) Behind you, to the right (on the slope from which you have just descended) is the former Thriddle Incline. The path then immediately passes the remains of an old wheel shaft on your right.

(g) **Bonsor East mine** (18th-century) Remains of shaft (on left) and wheel shaft (right).

Around Windermere

Through unspoilt woods by England's longest lake; returns along level track close to lakeside. Thorough sign-posting, but care needed with route-finding just after 4. Ascent 700ft, all at beginning.

Length 5 miles (8km), 2½ hours
Difficulty 2–3
Start Ferry terminal (Ferry House) on W bank of Windermere, by Far Sawrey.
From Windermere take A592 S through Bowness, and turn off on to B5285 (signposted to Coniston and Hawkshead via Ferry). Park here and take ferry (operates daily, usually every 15 minutes until late evening; small fee for foot passengers)
From Coniston direction use NT car park marked on map. Grid reference SD 387953
OS maps 1:50,000 97;
1:25,000 Outdoor Leisure 7
Refreshments At both ferry terminals

WALK DIRECTIONS

1 *From ferry terminal on W bank of Windermere* follow road 300 yards to T-junction, turn left then 20 yards later turn right (steps in wall) on path signposted Claife Heights.

From NT car park, with the lake behind you, take the path in the far right-hand corner of the car park, signposted Claife Heights.

Both paths ascend to ruined house (The Station). Path narrows, but is very clear and well waymarked as it rises through mixed woodland (**a**). 2 After ½ mile, at top of slope, turn right at T-junction of paths, sign-

posted Hawkshead. 3 ¾ mile later pass through gate and turn left on track, signposted Hawkshead and Sawrey. Track (walled) passes through gate after 200 yards: immediately before next gate turn right on track between walls, signposted to Hawkshead. Follow obvious path, avoiding side turns.

4 After ¾ mile path rises to the highest point of walk, and dilapidated stone wall becomes visible close to right of path. At the top, turn right, signposted Bell Grange; view over Windermere opens out (**b**). 5 After ½ mile reach T-junction with semi-cobbled path, and turn right downhill, signposted Bell Grange. 6 At bottom (house on left), turn right on track and follow close to shore of lake back to start.

WHAT TO LOOK OUT FOR

(**a**) Legend has it that the woods here are haunted by a Lakeland goblin known as the Crier of Claife.
(**b**) **View** Over Windermere, with Wansfell Pike at its N end. The longest lake in England, 10½ miles. Prominent among its islands is Belle Isle, named after Isabella Curwen who bought the house on it for a knock-down price in 1776 – the builder was ridiculed by his friends for its circular design (the first house of this shape to be built in England). In an earlier house on the island lived Robert Phillipson, a Cavalier, also known as Robert the Devil, whose hilted sword still hangs in Kendal church; he left it there after he stormed a church service in pursuit of Roundheads in the Civil War.

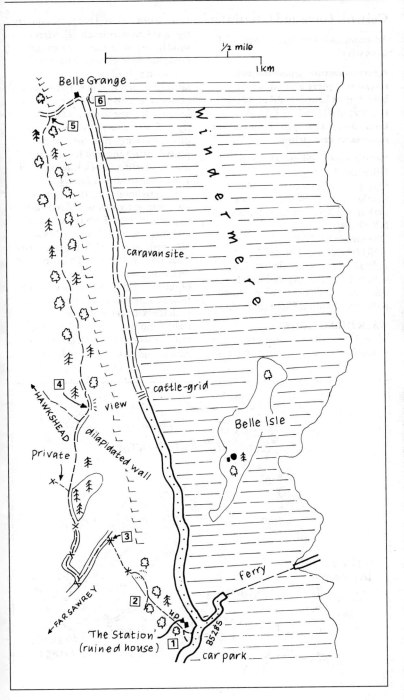

½ mile

1 km

Belle Grange

6

5

Windermere

caravan site

4

HAWKSHEAD

view

cattle-grid

dilapidated wall

Belle Isle

Private

X

3

X

FAR SAWREY

ferry

2

up

The Station
(ruined house)

1

B5285

car park

Colwith Force and Elterwater

Recommended by Mr and Mrs W A Comstive

A mix of pasture, woodland and riverside scenery against the backdrop of Langdale Pikes, passing two waterfalls and the lake of Elterwater. Route quite involved but reasonably easy to find.

Length 5 miles (8km), 2½ hours
Difficulty 2
Start Elterwater, just off B5343, 5 miles W of Ambleside. Free car park in village centre. Grid reference NY 328048
OS maps 1:50,000 90; 1:25,000 Outdoor Leisure 7
Refreshments Britannia Inn, Elterwater; Three Shires Inn, Little Langdale; Rosewood Tea Gardens and Skelwith Bridge Hotel, Skelwith Bridge

WALK DIRECTIONS

1 (a) From village centre, cross road bridge over river, turn right on tarmac lane on other side. This passes quarry tips and becomes track. 2 After ½ mile ignore footbridge over river, but continue on track which now swings left (soon uphill), shortly reaching farm on your left, where track swings abruptly left. 50 yards later, turn right on track leading to quarry buildings. 3 At T-junction in front of main quarry building, turn right (signposted 'path') and fork left at last quarry building. Track leads through woods and to tarmac lane 4.

Turn right on lane, then immediately left on narrow woodland path opposite cottage. Path then ascends, crossing wider track after 100 yards. 600 yards later reach T-junction with track on edge of forest 5. Turn right on track, through gate. At beginning of second field on left leave track to take kissing-gate/gate on left. Clear path leads diagonally to far right-hand corner (stile). 50 yards later, cross steps in wall and follow path alongside fence on right to pass

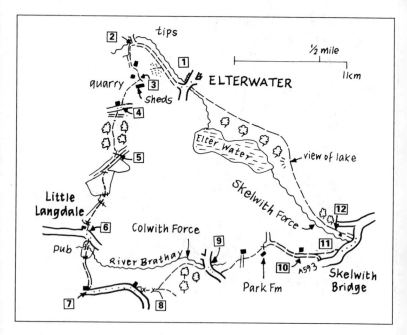

through farm via double gates, then bear left down to road at edge of Little Langdale **6**.

Turn left on road and after 80 yards turn right over stile. Path leads down to footbridge then up to stile in the right-hand corner of wall ahead, then ascends to farm. **7** Turn left on lane just behind farm and follow to next farm, at which pass through the farmyard, turn right at end then left through gate (just before cattle-grid). Path leads half right to next gate, then follows left edge of field to gate into wood **8**. Immediately fork left down to waterfall (Colwith Force) (**b**). Then follow stream to reach road **9**.

Turn right on road, then after 50 yards left over stile, signposted Skelwith Bridge. Path leads across field, up through woods and then across fields to farm. Cross driveway and continue over stile opposite, taking clear paths across fields to next farm, at which continue forward past farmhouse to gate, then follow track downhill (fork right after 50 yards, signposted Skelwith Bridge). **10** After ¼ mile, pass house on your left, and 100 yards later ignore

track which veers right to gate, but continue ahead on path leading through woods and emerging on road at hamlet of Skelwith Bridge **11**. Left on road then left immediately after road-bridge. Fork right after 50 yards by entrance to Kirkstone Galleries, soon picking up path into woods **12**. Path is now unmistakable – it passes Skelwith Force (waterfall), emerges into pasture and reaches end of (lake) Elterwater (enjoy the view when you can; the path doesn't come close to lake again (**c**)). Follow back to start.

WHAT TO LOOK OUT FOR

(**a**) **Elterwater** Pleasant village of bluish-grey stone cottages by an attractive green. Juniper wood used to be burned here to make charcoal for the local gunpowder industry. Slate quarrying still takes place nearby, and there are slateworks at Skelwith Bridge.

(**b**) **Colwith Force** A series of small waterfalls in a wooded glen, dropping 90ft in all.

(**c**) **View** Over Elterwater to Lingmoor Fell (1,530ft), with Langdale Pikes 2,403ft beyond.

Rydal and Grasmere

Recommended by W A Comstive

A literary pilgrimage, taking in two of Wordsworth's homes and his burial place, plus two lakes joined by the River Rothay. Very popular with visitors, but the setting remains practically unchanged since Wordsworth's time. All tracks and paths well defined and signposted; easy route-finding.

Length 5 miles (8km), 2 hours
Difficulty 1
Start Grasmere, just off A591, 4 miles NW of Ambleside (three car parks in village; fee)
OS maps 1:50,000 90;
1:25,000 Outdoor Leisure 7
Refreshments Pubs and tea-rooms in Grasmere

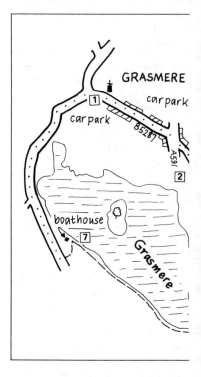

WALK DIRECTIONS

1 (a) With church on left follow road over bridge through Grasmere. **2** Cross main road to the lane opposite, signposted Dove Cottage (b). Follow lane, avoiding side turns. **3** After 600 yards continue forward ('no through road to motors'). ¼ mile later, lane becomes track. Follow this through pasture and woodland (track forks after ½ mile, with left fork ascending along high stone wall: forks rejoin) to village of Rydal **4**.

Turn right on tarmac lane (Rydal Mount (c) is soon on right and follow to main road. Turn right along it, then 300 yards later turn left on to footbridge. Path immediately swings right **5**. Path follows river, then side of lake (d).

6 After path ascends away from Rydal Water, look out for and take path entering woods on your right, ignoring sign to Grasmere (straight on). Descend to footbridge; do not cross, but turn left along river, then follow shore of Grasmere (lake) (e). **7** Path turns away from lake by stone boathouse. Emerge on to tarmac lane and turn right into Grasmere.

WHAT TO LOOK OUT FOR

(a) **Grasmere** (village) Wordsworth described it as 'the loveliest spot that man hath ever found'. He lived in the village for 14 years, first at Dove Cottage (1799-1808), then at Allan Bank, later at the Rectory and finally at Rydal Mount, until his death in 1850. He, his wife, Mary and sister, Dorothy, are all buried in Grasmere churchyard.

Grasmere is also famous for its annual sports (which include Cumberland wrestling and races up Butter Crag), its gingerbread and its St Oswald Day rush-bearing procession on August 5 – a north country

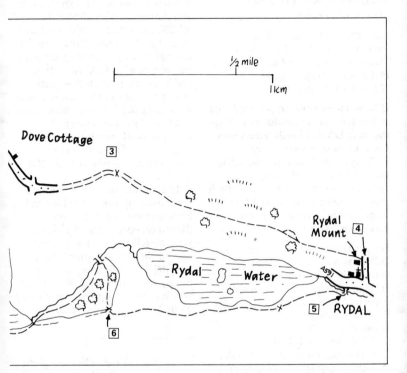

tradition of bringing rushes into the church for strewing on the floor.

(**b**) **Dove Cottage** (open to public; fee) Home of the Wordsworths until 1808, then of their friend De Quincey, author of *Confessions of an English Opium Eater*. The museum next door contains several of Wordsworth's possessions.

(**c**) **Rydal Mount** Wordsworth's home for the last 37 years of his life (open to public; fee).

(**d**) **Rydal Water** Good for watching wildfowl. **Flora** Along the banks of the River Rothay, which connects the two lakes, is alder buckthorn, a species local to the Lakes. **View** Over the water to Nab Farm, where De Quincey used to visit Margaret Simpson, to the strong disapproval of the Wordsworths, who thought her too low-born. Beyond is Heron Pike (2,003ft).

(**e**) **Grasmere** (lake) The island in the middle is a drumlin, a hillock of boulder debris left behind by glaciation. **Flora** Butterwort (insect-eating), enchanter's nightshade. **Birds** Dippers, grey and pied wagtails, sandpipers.

343

Wansfell Pike, Troutbeck and Ambleside

Contributed by C Laughton
Recommended by C J Morris, Peter
Danks, Jan and John Ansell,
D A Allen, Charles Crane,
G H Brown, Mr and Mrs C Stamp

Climbs a minor peak at the north end of Windermere, somewhat apart from the main Lakeland Fells. Fine views. Pasture tracks and some road-walking for the link sections. All on defined paths, mostly signposted; route-finding quite easy. Ascent 400ft through Skelghyll Wood and 1,000ft from Troutbeck to summit; then a very steep descent.

Length 6 miles (9½km), 3½ hours
Difficulty 3–4
Start Ambleside, either town centre, at **1**, or car park at S end of town, opposite Hayes Garden Centre, at **2**. Parking at both points (fee).
OS maps 1:50,000 90;
1:25,000 Outdoor Leisure 7
Refreshments Plenty at Ambleside; Post Office and Stores, Troutbeck (drinks can be enjoyed on a bench outside); the Mortal Man, Troutbeck; Queens Head (¼ mile off route) at Town Head, NE of Troutbeck

WALK DIRECTIONS

1 From town centre, with bus station on right, follow Lake Road (high street), then fork left into Old Lake Road. **2** Proceed past car park on right after ¼ mile, and 100 yards before main road turn left up steep narrow lane signposted Jenkyn Crag. **3** After ½ mile lane bends left into private house: keep forward on hard track. This follows contour of hill. **4** Track enters woodlands (**a**) (NT sign) and 150 yards later branches left uphill over bridge; avoid left turn 30 yards later and follow to Jenkyn Crag, (signposted right from path; 2 minute detour) **5**.

Return to woodland path and fol-

low it out of wood, through farmland and through farm (High Skelghyll). **6** 200 yards after farm, cross stream by bridge, then immediately turn left through gate signposted Troutbeck. Ignore minor left fork after 30 yards and by keeping right follow path which rises to join walled track: turn right along it. **7** After ¼ mile ignore right fork by wooden seat and continue until reaching road at Troutbeck (**b**) **8**. For detour to Townend house, turn right for 200 yards (**c**).

To continue, turn left along road for ½ mile. **9** Take gated lane on left between farm buildings on left (fingerpost opposite for Ambleside via Wansfell). Follow track uphill, passing through gate after ½ mile, then **10** 220 yards later, turn left through gate signposted Wansfell, which gives access to path over peaty ground (very clearly marked with

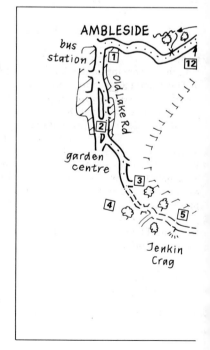

cairns, and soon well defined) leading to summit of Wansfell Pike (**d**) [11]. From trig. point continue ahead to cross wall by stile, and descend carefully on steep, well-defined path leading towards Ambleside. At bottom cross two stiles within 200 yards to emerge on to tarmac lane [12].

Turn left, towards Ambleside: shortly after lane passes through gate, look out for metal turnstile on right, entrance to Stock Ghyll Waterfall (**e**). After viewing falls, continue on lane back to start.

WHAT TO LOOK OUT FOR
(**a**) **Skelghyll Wood** Mixed woodland of oak and exotic firs (including Sequoia and Hondo Spruce). **View** From Jenkyn Crag over Windermere.
(**b**) **Troutbeck** Scattered village with a number of roadside wells, each given a saint's name and a Victorian stone surround. The inn sign of Mortal Man, with its jingle, was painted by Julius Caesar Ibbetson, who lived in the village 1801–05.
(**c**) **Townend** (NT; open to public; fee) Marvellously unspoilt yeoman's house (c. 1626), the home of the Browne family for over 300 years until it was handed over to the Trust in 1944.
(**d**) **View** Down Windermere, with Grizedale Forest on the W side and, SW, standing on its own, the small conical hill of Latterbarrow (803ft); beyond it, Hawkshead village – further right is the Old Man of Coniston (2,631ft), W Scafell Pike (3,206ft), Rydal Water and Grasmere; NW Fairfield (2,863ft); N the Kirkstone Pass with Place Fell (2,154ft) at its far end; NE, across the Troutbeck valley, High Street (2,663ft).
(**e**) **Stock Ghyll waterfall** Popular beauty spot, with pretty falls in a fine woodland setting.

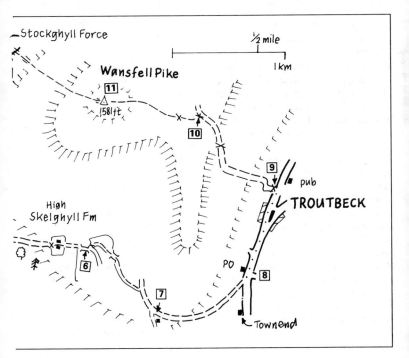

345

Haweswater and High Street

Recommended by J G Rawlinson

**Takes in an outstanding viewpoint;
best on a very clear day. Ascent to
High Street is past a tarn set beneath
crags; descent is down a grassland
ridge to Haweswater. Path rather
faint shortly after 3, otherwise route
is quite easy to find in clear weather;
compass essential in case of mist.
Ascent 1,700ft.**

Length 8 miles (13km), 4 hours
Difficulty 4
Start Car park at S end of Haweswater
(end of road). Grid reference
NY 469107
OS maps 1:50,000 90;
1:25,000 Outdoor Leisure 5

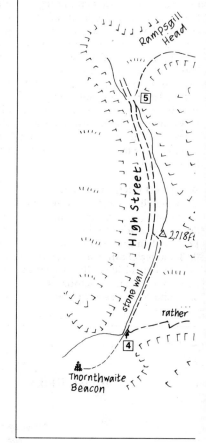

WALK DIRECTIONS

1 (**a**) With reservoir on right proceed
to gate at end of road/car park. After
50 yards continue forward,
signposted Kentmere. Path soon
rises, along stream on right. 2 At
small lake (Small Water), take
well-marked path around right side of
lake. Path ascends to shoulder 3.
Turn right at crossing of paths, along
shoulder, on fairly clear path marked
by cairns. After ½ mile it passes over
crag with large cairn and becomes
less distinct, but from here path to
top of grassy ridge can be seen ahead
(*NB prominent cairn half left,
Thornthwaite Beacon, is not
trig.point but makes a worthwhile
detour*).

Ascend to wall (**b**) 4. Turn right
along wall to trig.point, at which turn
left (downhill, path undefined),
reaching track after 150 yards. This is
High Street (Roman road): turn right
along it (**c**). 5 After ½ mile, and 100
yards after track crosses stone wall,
turn right by cairn. This track
ascends a little, but soon descends (**d**).
After ¼ mile path is undefined for
200 yards (route obvious in clear
weather): if misty, take care to bear

half left where path gives out (ahead
is a sheer drop), joining clear path
after 200 yards.

6 At bottom, by reservoir, turn
right just before fence (boggy area;
path unclear) to cross bridge. Route
back from here is easy to find: clear
path across pasture with ruined stone
walls, then through trees where it
turns right, and finally runs parallel
to banks of Haweswater, to return to
start.

WHAT TO LOOK OUT FOR

(**a**) Before the valley was flooded by
the reservoir, this area, Mardale, was

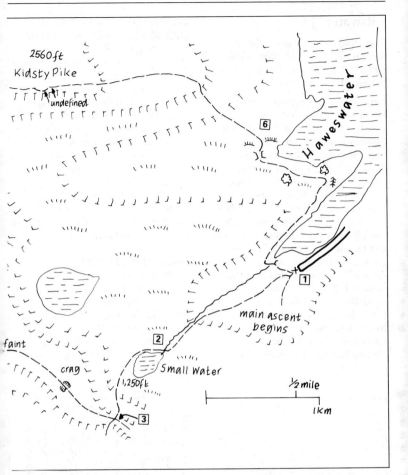

so remote that it harboured outlaws who had their own dynasty of 'kings' from 1209 until 1885. The first King of Mardale was Hugh Holme, who reputedly fled to a cave in Rigindale after conspiring against King John.

(**b**) **View** Very extensive, into Lancashire, with Blackpool Tower and Heysham nuclear power station to S. SSW over much of Windermere, with its N end blotted out by Wans-fell Pike (1,581ft). SW is the Old Man of Coniston (2,631ft) then, left to right, Crinkle Crags (2,816ft), Bowfell (2,960ft), Scafell Pike (3,206ft), Langdale Pikes (2,403ft), Great Gable (2,949ft), Fairfield (2,863ft), Helvellyn (3,116ft), Skiddaw (3,054ft) and Blencathra (2,847ft).

(**c**) **High Street** High-level Roman road that connected the fort at Brocavum near Penrith with the one at Galava near Ambleside, on Windermere. The track is in fact pre-Roman, possibly a neolithic route for the stone-axe 'factory' on Langdale Pikes.

(**d**) For a **view** over Ullswater and Martindale Common, turn left where track is about to descend over the grassland (no path) for a few yards, to Rampsgill Head.

347

Ullswater

*Contributed by Brian Rochester
Recommended by Dominic Farley,
E J Dixon, C J Morris, Jan and John
Ansell, J G Rawlinson*

Rates among the region's finest
lake-shore walks, and there are
usually plenty of ramblers along it.
Returns either via steamer or by path
over the saddle of Place Fell, to
descend through Boredale – less
distinguished scenically, but adds
some valley landscape to the walk.
One optional ascent, up Hallin Fell, is
worth postponing to the end of the
walk if you plan to park at Howtown
and return to it. Some quiet road-
walking in Boredale. Route-finding
easy; a little care needed over the
saddle of Place Fell. Ascents: 750ft
up Hallin Fell, 600ft up towards Place
Fell. Check ferry times before travelling: telephone Ullswater Navigation on Kendal 21626 or Glenridding 229. Services are occasionally
cancelled.

Length 8 miles (13km), 4 hours
Difficulty 2 (3 if including ½ hour
detour to Hallin Fell).
With extension via Boredale 15 miles
(24km), 7½ hours
Difficulty 3-4
Start Howtown Pier, Ullswater, 8
miles SW of Penrith (small car park).
Take minor road along E side of lake
from Pooley Bridge or take steamer
from Pooley Bridge or Glenridding.
Grid reference NY 443198
OS maps 1:50,000 90;
1:25,000 Outdoor Leisure 5
Refreshments Howtown Hotel at
Howtown; various pubs and hotels in
Patterdale and Glenridding

WALK DIRECTIONS
[1] With lake on right follow lakeside
path. After 200 yards ignore left turn
beyond second kissing-gate and turn
left 50 yards later, signposted Patterdale. Follow path 100 yards up steps
to emerge at base of Hallin Fell [2] .

To ascend Hallin Fell turn left for
¼ mile and fork right uphill after

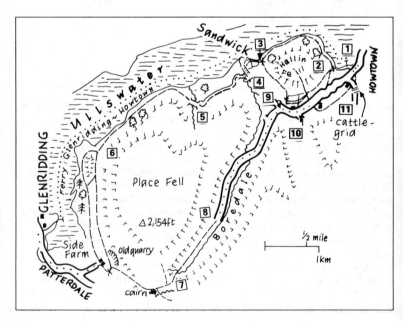

30 yards. Just before reaching road turn right uphill for 200 yards and right again before gate to ascend with wall on left, then proceed to summit (**a**). Take same route to descend, but keep by wall all the way, crossing it 30 yards before lane by stile signposted Patterdale. Enter field and turn half right to cross waymarked stile. Continue in same direction across next field; pass through kissing-gate and turn right up hill on path, soon with wall on left. After ½ mile enter woods and continue (with wall on left) to lakeside. Turn left through kissing-gate at ③.

To avoid Hallin Fell turn right along lakeside path to kissing-gate after 1 mile ③ (**b**). Cross three fields making for gates; go over bridge, and carry on to road at Sandwick ④. Turn left on road, then right after 30 yards on to path signposted Patterdale, proceeding with wall on your right.

⑤ After ¾ mile cross footbridge and bear uphill, keeping wall on right. ½ mile later enter woodland. ⑥ After ½ mile, emerge from woods in front of Silver Crags.

To finish at Glenridding continue forward on main path. 1 mile later turn right at Side Farm and follow prominent farm track. At main road turn right and follow ½ mile to Glenridding (**c**).

To continue via Boredale turn left sharply uphill by cairn on left, follow rise up and then descend; keep left at next fork. Pass cavern and waterfall on your left and 100 yards later pass through old quarry, then proceed uphill on track, ignoring left fork after 300 yards at bench. ⑦ After ½ mile proceed on path (sometimes indistinct) over saddle of hill. At saddle keep left, skirting hill which is on left; avoid path crossing stream

and, 100 yards later, ignore path on left leading up hillside (Place Fell). After ¼ mile path becomes defined track and drops down into Boredale.

⑧ ½ mile later continue past farm, on tarmac track. ⑨ After 1 mile fork right, signposted Howtown. ½ mile later cross bridge and take tarmac lane uphill directly ahead. Fork left after 200 yards, just past Hawes Farm on left. ⑩ After 175 yards turn right by church, proceeding with churchyard wall on left for 50 yards and then continuing same direction straight up hillock (no path).

After 100 yards turn left along prominent track on right of valley floor. ⑪ After ½ mile track is joined by wall on left and drops to surfaced track. Turn left over cattle-grid. Follow for 200 yards then fork right in front of house, taking the path alongside steam. At road turn right to starting-point.

WHAT TO LOOK OUT FOR

(**a**) **Hallin Fell** View over most of Ullswater, the Lake District's second longest lake. NW across the lake, the nearest peak is Gowbarrow (1434ft); the waterfall, Aira Force, is hidden just to the left of it. SW away from the lake, but running roughly parallel to the shore is the valley of Boredale; S are the low hills of Martindale Common.

(**b**) **Birds** Dipper, ring ouzel, meadow pipit, whinchat, wheatear, wagtail, redpoll, sandpiper, kestrel, buzzard, peregrine, raven, spotted flycatcher, woodpecker, goldcrest, jackdaw.

(**c**) Both the lake steamers are Victorian: *Lady of the Lake* was launched in 1877, and *Raven* in 1880. They were converted from steam to oil in the 1930s.

Watendlath Beck and Lodore Falls

Based on a contribution from Geoff Peacock

After an ascent to Watendlath Tarn, follows a stream through semi-wooded landscape, then into deeper woods where the stream tumbles over a precipice. Final section crosses duckboards over low-lying ground (can get flooded) near the southern end of Derwent Water, with the Eel Crags/Cat Bells ridge directly ahead. Two stretches along road (main road has a pavement). All paths well defined, partially signposted; route-finding quite easy. Ascent 850ft.

Length 6 miles (9.5km), 3 hours
Difficulty 3
Start Car park (free) on B5289 5 miles S of Keswick, on left, shortly after passing bridge on your right to village of Grange. Grid reference NY 253168
OS maps 1:50,000 89 or 90; 1:25,000 Outdoor Leisure 4
Refreshments Café at Watendlath; tea-room and Borrowdale Hotel at Lodore; Grange Café, Borrowdale; Gates Hotel and restaurant at Grange.

WALK DIRECTIONS

1 From car park entrance take signposted footpath to Bowder Stone (a). On exit from Bowder Stone, continue on road for ¼ mile then

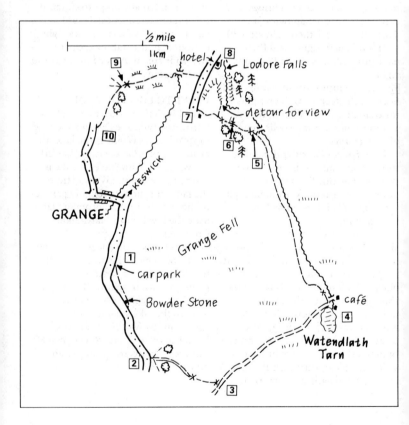

round corner take footpath on left, through gate with NT sign for Grange Fell. **2** After 20 yards continue forward at junction of paths, taking path uphill with stone wall on right. Path bends right, out of trees and through gate.

3 After ¼ mile, after second gate, turn left on track uphill leading to Watendlath Tarn (**b**) **4**. From tarn, retrace steps to bridge, beyond which immediately turn right and follow path signposted Lodore. Path runs close to stream. **5** After 1 mile avoid crossing bridge but fork left, shortly into woods by gate. **6** At stile ¼ mile later, immediately turn left on path, shortly leading to gate. 200 yards after gate, minor fork on right leads to crag (view of gorge of Watendlath Beck), from which retrace steps. Main path descends into Borrowdale, reaching gate to right of hotel **7**.

Turn right on road. After ¼ mile look for (but do not take, for the moment) track on left signposted Manesty. Continue on road for another 100 yards, then turn right, round back of Lodore Swiss Hotel to see Lodore Falls (**c**) **8**. Retrace steps to track signposted Manesty: this leads across fields to bridge, then across marshy area by duckboards (*NB if in flood, use B-road to Grange instead*). **9** 50 yards after small gate, take leftmost of three tracks, and 20 yards later keep left again on track along avenue of oaks. **10** At road turn left into Grange, then right on main road to starting-point.

WHAT TO LOOK OUT FOR
(**a**) **Bowder Stone** Vast boulder, 30ft by 60ft, with steps built up it.
(**b**) **Watendlath Tarn** Small lake with packhorse bridge nearby. Greenhow Farm here was the birthplace of Judith Paris, heroine of Hugh Walpole's *Rogue Herries*.
(**c**) **Lodore Falls** (always open, small fee, honesty box). Precipitous site, but little water except after heavy storms.

Eel Crags and Borrowdale

It may be best to let the weather forecast influence where to start, so that the ridge portion of the walk coincides with clear weather. A steep slog up Tongue Gill Valley (with loose quarry spoil for the final portion), then views from the grassy ridge. Wooded riverside walking along Borrowdale, linking Grange to Seatoller. Path briefly ill defined just after ④, but otherwise route is quite clear on the ground; route-finding quite easy in clear weather, though compass essential, in case of mist. Ascent 1,800ft.

Length 9 miles (14.5km), 5 hours
Difficulty 4–5
Start *From Seatoller* (if you want the ascent first) on B5289 1 mile W of Borrowdale and 1 mile E of beginning of Honister Pass; grid reference NY 246137. Free car park
From Grange (if you want the river path first) just off B5289 1 mile S of Derwent Water. Grid reference NY 254175. Limited roadside parking. From river-bridge enter village, take left turn in village centre, signposted Seatoller. Follow walk directions from ⑧/①
OS maps 1:50,000 89 or 90; 1:25,000 Outdoor Leisure 4
Refreshments Yew Tree Inn and Café, Seatoller; Grange café and Gates Hotel (with restaurant) in Grange

WALK DIRECTIONS

① *From Seatoller* turn right out of car park and follow road uphill for 200 yards. At left bend in road, climb up to kissing-gate on right. Do not proceed to next gate (30 yards away) but turn left before it, uphill with wall on right, on clear path. ② Cross track after 300 yards and continue up half left on wide grassy path (cairned) leading to gate. Beyond it turn right on level path with wall on right and follow for ¾ mile, crossing two bridges.

③ 30 yards before third bridge, turn left on clear path ascending left side of Tongue Gill Valley (obvious). After passing two makeshift bridges on right in first ½ mile, path leaves stream to aim for old quarry workings up quarter left and towards head of valley. Continue beyond old quarry to reach fence at top ④. Cross fence by leftmost of three stiles and bear quarter left, descending slightly (path just visible but not very good) for ¼ mile. Just before edge of ridge and before stream, pick up well-defined track and turn right on it up to large cairn at summit of High Spy (**a**) ⑤.

Beyond summit, continue along left edge of mountain ridge for 2 miles, avoiding bearing right. Path is easy to find and descends slightly. ⑥ Bear down towards next portion of ridge with two big humps ahead (Catbells). Immediately before path ascends on to them, turn right on another path, descending steeply with wooden railing on right. Avoid two sharp left turns and descend to gate/stile ⑦. Immediately before gate/stile, turn right on narrow path signposted Seatoller (permissive path). This soon runs alongside small conifer plantation, then ½ mile later follows left edge of deciduous wood. ⑧ At end of wood, turn left over stile and proceed with woodland wall on left down to track.

For Grange village (refreshments; alternative starting point) ignore this track and continue straight on through gate into semi-wooded pasture. Bear quarter left around hillock to gate at bottom (path barely defined), and turn right into village. ⑧/① Turn right just after church, on lane signposted Seatoller. After ¼ mile, at next junction, turn left on to track.

For direct route, avoiding Grange keep right, to follow track downhill, which soon leads through farm and becomes lane. 400 yards later, turn

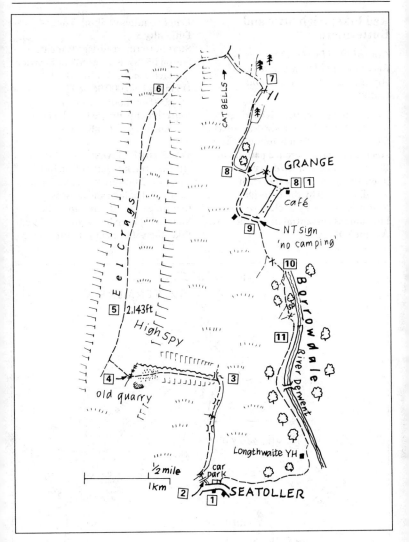

right on track.

9 Track soon passes NT sign 'no camping'. Just after it joins river, fork left (signposted Rosthwaite; right is to Seatoller, up through gates). 200 yards after gate, track bends right, away from river and soon joins old stone wall on left, crossing it 30 yards later. After ¼ mile, fork left (signposted) on narrow path. Path leaves wood by gate and soon rejoins river. Follow past cottage, then avoid bridge on left and continue past Longthwaite Youth Hostel. Path is easy to follow to Seatoller car park.

WHAT TO LOOK OUT FOR
(**a**) **View** E over Derwent Water to High Seat (1,996ft) and Helvellyn (3,116ft); N to Skiddaw (3,054ft), W to Hindscarth (2,385ft), SW to nearby Dale Head (2,473ft).

Red Pike, High Stile and Buttermere

*Contributed by Mrs D I Johnson
Recommended by Jan and John
Ansell, Geoff Peacock, Diana
Crawley*

**Rugged and dramatic, with a ridge
path for 1½ miles. Steady descent as
far as Bleaberry Tarn is followed by a
steeper and rather eroded path up to
Red Pike. A very steep descent
(requiring particular care), then
woodland path by the lakeside.
Route-finding easy in clear weather
but compass essential in case of mist.
Ascent 2,400ft.**

Length 6 miles (9.5km), 5 hours
Difficulty 5
Start Buttermere village (car park;
fee) on B5289, 8 miles SW of Keswick.
Grid reference NY 176170
OS maps 1:50,000 96 or 97;
1:25,000 Outdoor Leisure 4
Refreshments Bridge Hotel, Fish Inn
and snack bar, all in Buttermere

WALK DIRECTIONS
1 Take track to left of Fish Inn,
signposted Buttermere Lake. Track
passes end of lake and crosses
footbridge. 2 20 yards after the
footbridge, keep left, signposted Red
Pike, then after next gate turn sharp

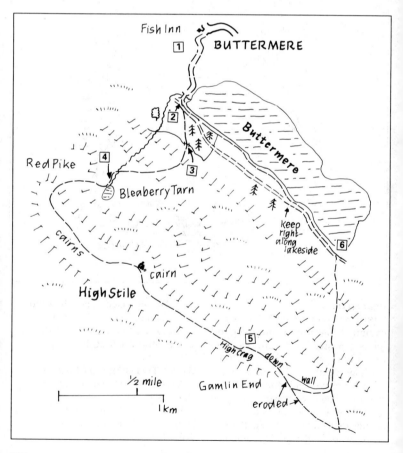

right, also signposted Red Pike. Ascend through woods. [3] Path leaves forest by stile, and is clearly marked and cairned as it soon swings right over stream then up to lake [4] Take obvious path to right of lake, ascending to ridge up on right then continuing up to first summit, Red Pike (**a**). Follow ridge around to left towards next summit (High Stile). Path is well marked with cairns but rougher: keep close to left edge with tarn down on left. High Stile and next summit, High Crag, are minor ascents. [5] After High Crag, path (very eroded) descends steeply for ¼ mile.

Then *either* (immediate descent) 200 yards before tarn, fork left on to narrow path for the descent. Path soon joins wall. On reaching corner of wall turn left to reach clear track (200 yards). *Or*, if you prefer, con-tinue up to next summit, descend beyond it to crossing of paths and turn left; the two routes meet.

[6] At bottom turn left along lakeside path and follow to end of lake, then retrace steps by turning right to starting-point.

WHAT TO LOOK OUT FOR
(**a**) **View** Several lakes are visible: Buttermere below, Crummockwater to left of it and Loweswater further left still; Derwent Water and Ennerdale also in view. Of the peaks, N is Grasmoor (2,791ft) and Skiddaw (3,054ft); NE, on other side of Buttermere, is Robinson (2,417ft); E is Helvellyn (3,116ft); SE Great Gable (2,949ft); SSE Scafell Pike (3,206ft), S to Pillar (2,927ft) and Steeple (2,760ft); WSW up the valley to Ennerdale.

Cat Bells and Derwent Water

Along a moorland ridge of three humps, with views over Derwent Water; the lake's partly wooded south-western shore provides the return route. A modest climb, but a route that every walker visiting the Lake District should try. All on well-defined and signposted paths (though ridge rather eroded) – keep to path; easy route-finding. Ascent 1,050ft.

Length 4 miles (6.5km), 2 hours
Difficulty 3
Start Small car park by Cat Bells (free). From Keswick take B5289/A66 W, turn off through Portinscale and follow signs to Grange. Look out for sign for 'Grange 2¾': ½ mile later, road crosses cattle-grid; fork right just beyond (signposted car park and Skelgill). Car park is 150 yards further on left. Grid reference NY 246212
OS maps 1:50,000 89 or 90; 1:25,000 Outdoor Leisure 4

WALK DIRECTIONS

1 Take path from car park sign-posted Cat Bells. This zigzags up ridge and passes two hillocks 2 . Third hillock is bigger and the highest point of walk (**a**). Path then descends, and 3 ¼ mile later, turn left just before path ahead ascends. Follow to bottom ignoring two sharp left turns. 4 Turn left on road, then after 200 yards take gate on right by NT sign and pillar-box. Track leads through woods to emerge by cottage 5 .

Continue forward (signposted Brandelhow). After second cottage, path leads up to enter woods by gate. Soon reach shore and follow it (**b**). 6 After ½ mile path enters field by gate; follow shore round. At next bay, path swings inland (signposted) and bends right, through neck of woodland. Follow up across field to tarmac lane 7 . Turn right on lane. 100 yards after passing Hawes End House (up on left), taking kissing-gate on left to lead up to cattle-grid. Turn left to car park.

WHAT TO LOOK OUT FOR

(**a**) **View** E over Derwent Water to Helvellyn (3,116ft); S along the continuation of the ridge to Eel Crags and High Spy (2,143 ft) and to Pike O'Stickle (2,323 ft); W over the Newlands Valley with the Crag Hill/Causey Pike ridge ending abruptly in a prominent pyramidal triangle; N to Skiddaw (3,054 ft).
(**b**) **Derwent Water** 3½ miles long from N to S, with Keswick close to its N end and Borrowdale at the other. Of its three largest islands, St Herbert's Island is the southernmost; remains of the cell inhabited in the 7th century by St Herbert are still extant. Further N are Lord's Island and Rampsholme, both of which were once inhabited. In the Beatrix Potter stories, Squirrel Nutkin crossed Derwent Water on a raft.

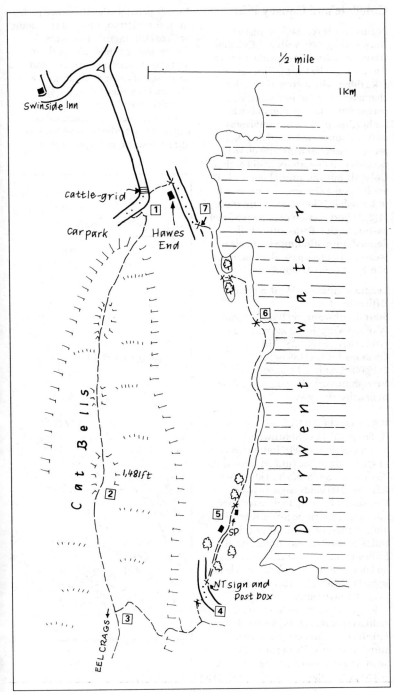

Swinside Inn

cattle-grid

Car park

1

Hawes
End

7

½ mile

1 km

D e r w e n t W a t e r

Cat Bells

1,481ft

2

6

5

SP

NT sign and
Dost box

4

3

EEL CRAGS

Coledale and Causey Pike

Begins on a level track along the steep-sided grassy valley of Coledale; starts ascending close to old mines at Force Crag. The Crag Hill/Causey Pike ridge, which gives the walk the character of real mountaineering, is reasonably safe, but demands a head for heights. (For a more ambitious outward route via Grisedale Pike, proceed out of Braithwaite on road described in directions, avoid path to Coledale but continue along road 200 yards to take signposted path on left to Grisedale Pike; rejoin main route at ②.) Short section of quiet road and pasture at end. Paths quite well defined; route-finding easy in clear weather, but compass esential in case of mist. Ascent 2,500ft.

Length 9 miles (14.5km), 5 hours
Difficulty 4–5
Start Braithwaite, on B5292, 3 miles W of Keswick. Roadside parking. Grid reference NY 232236
OS maps 1:50,000 89 or 90; 1:25,000 Outdoor Leisure 4
Refreshments Pubs, tea-room, shop in Braithwaite only.

WALK DIRECTIONS

① From B5292 in Braithwaite with Royal Oak Inn on left, follow road out of village (ignoring turn on left signed 'Coledale – no through road'). Turn left after 200 yards, signposted to Coledale (NT sign). Path leads up to join track; continue forward on this, along valley, on level. After 1½ miles, just before old mines ahead, follow main track which bends left and descends to cross ford, then leads uphill to reach shoulder of hill. Path (well defined) turns left (**a**) ②.

Ridge path soon follows stream on right as it enters grassy valley. Follow ½ mile to its highest point, then ③ turn left at crossing of paths. Path soon leads out to reach edge of slope, with spectacular views below. ④ After

½ mile path joins well-defined path (turn sharp left to detour to trig. point of Crag Hill; then retrace steps). Follow well-defined ridge path: it descends (ignore cross-tracks) and then ascends, reaching summit of Causey Pike after 1 mile (**b**) ⑤.

Path descends steeply towards final portion of ridge; here (at cairn) you can decide whether to take left fork (direct descent, not too steep) or con-

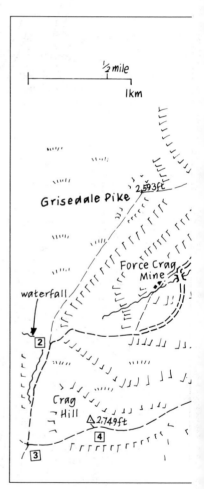

tinue along ridge (steep descent at end, and a little longer). Both lead down to emerge on road by stone bridge 6. Turn left on road. After ½ mile take path on left signposted Braithwaite, which leads slightly uphill; finally pass through farm buildings to take farm track back to Braithwaite.

WHAT TO LOOK OUT FOR

(**a**) **View** Briefly opens out W down Gasgale Valley, bounded to N by Hopegill Head (2,525ft) and S by Grasmoor (2,791ft).

(**b**) **View** N to Hopegill Head and Grisedale Pike (2,593 ft); SW to Grasmoor, S to Robinson (2,417ft): SE to Eel Crags (2,143ft): Rigg Beck immediately below to S; E over Derwent Water to Helvellyn (3,116ft).

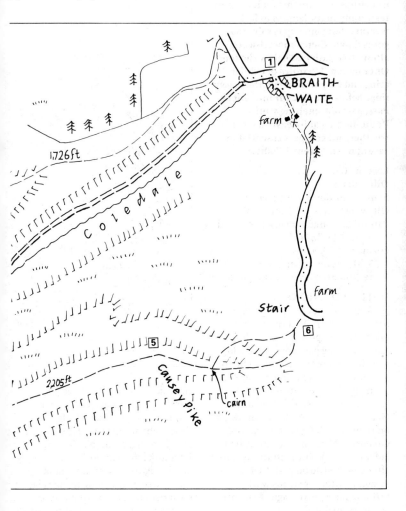

Helvellyn via Striding Edge and Sticks Pass

Recommended by J G Rawlinson, W A Comstive

Route makes the most of the spectacular scenery around Red Tarn and follows Striding Edge, a rocky and exposed knife-edge ridge that demands a light scramble up to the summit. Care needed up the Edge: numerous monuments on it are grim testimony to its dangers in bad weather, but going up is safer than going down; there is a well-worn alternative path just below the top. Once on top, 1½ miles of exhilarating and easy walking on the grassy ridge before the descent into Sticks Pass, past old smelting works. Route-finding quite easy in clear weather, but compass essential in case of mist. Ascent 2,750ft.

Length 10 miles (16km), 6 hours
Difficulty 5
Start Glenridding, near S end of Ullswater, on A592 1 mile NW of Patterdale. Large car park (fee). Grid reference NY 387169
OS maps 1:50,000 90;
1:25,000 Outdoor Leisure 5
Refreshments Various in Glenridding

WALK DIRECTIONS

1 Return from car park to main road. Turn right then right again, taking road opposite Glenridding Hotel, leading past post office and soon becoming track. Fork right after ¼ mile, signposted Greenside, Red Tarn. 2 Turn left at T-junction (¼ mile), signposted Greenside, Helvellyn via Mires Beck. Ignore gate on right after 200 yards, signposted Greenside Mine, but continue up to ladder-stile 3. Turn left immediately after ladder-stile on path that ascends steadily. After it reaches wall, Striding Edge (next stage of ascent) becomes visible ahead.

Ascend to top; take great care on

For an account of rights of access in the countryside – and how to complain if a public right of way is unusable – see the 'law and practice' section on page 17.

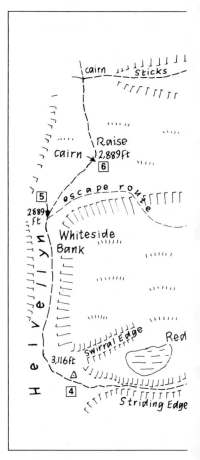

final stages of Striding Edge (**a**) (if windy, take obvious parallel path a few feet to right of top of edge). 4 Turn right at top, past stone shelter and then trig. point (**b**). 200 yards later fork left (right fork leads steeply down ridge of Swirral Edge) and follow easy track along top of ridge: it soon rises to cairn on first minor summit (Lower Man), then turns half right, descending then ascending to

For a key to the symbols used on the maps, and for an explanation of the difficulty grading, see the inside front cover.

Special interest lists at the back of the book give opening times for castles, houses, museums and gardens passed on the walks.

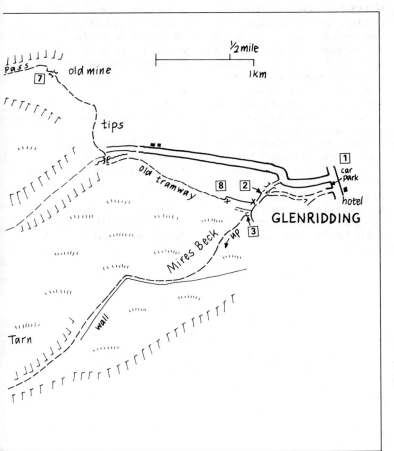

cairn on next minor summit (Whiteside Bank) [5]. Fork left (or right for escape route in bad weather – path soon descends and rejoins route at point [7]).

[6] Third summit (Raise) is capped by rocks, and route is less visible, though obvious in clear weather. Gently descending path is faint but well marked with cairns. After ½ mile, just before path rises, turn

right at small rough cairn on clear path leading down off ridge. This is Sticks Pass, which descends to reach old mine workings after 1 mile [7].

Path bends right at mines, then left: follow cairned path out of mines, across footbridge on right and downhill. Just after it crosses old channel (former leat), track is undefined, but continue down to footbridge over stream. Turn left.

8 ½ mile later turn left where way ahead is barred. Follow track down valley to ladder-stile crossed at start of walk and retrace steps to start.

WHAT TO LOOK OUT FOR
(a) Striding and Swirral Edges
Together form a giant corrie, gouged out by glaciers during the Ice Age. As on many other Lake District peaks, this hollow is on the E side of the mountain, relatively hidden from the sun, and sheltered from snow-laden winds coming in from the W. The gouging action of ice in this hollow, together with further hollows N and S, created the knife-edge ridges. Immediately below is **Red Tarn**, an 80ft-deep lake, raised by a low dam of boulders in 1860 to supply water to the lead mines of Glenridding.
(b) View E to the Eden Valley, Cross Fell (2,930ft) and much of the Pennine chain, from the Scottish Borders to Ingleborough. S to Morecambe Bay and the Lancashire coast; SSW the Old Man of Coniston (2,631ft); SW Scafell Pike (3,206ft); WNW Grisedale Pike (2,593ft); NW, Solway Firth and the Dumfries Hills; NNW Skiddaw (3,054ft). Among the monuments on top of Helvellyn is one to commemorate the landing of an aeroplane on the summit in 1926.
(c) Helvellyn
> It was a cove, a huge recess
> That keeps, till June, December's
>   snow;
> A lofty precipice in front,
> A silent tarn below!
> Far in the bosom of Helvellyn,
> Remote from public road or
>   dwelling,
> Pathway, or cultivated land;
> From trace of human foot or hand.

Fidelity, William Wordsworth

GREATER MANCHESTER

Marple Locks, the Peak Forest Canal and Cobden Edge

Contributed by Richard Watts
Recommended by Gillian Goddard,
David and Margaret Burnham,
Andrew Ward, Margaret Godfrey,
Dr John Morley, D Rock, Mr and
Mrs R F Maddock

Canal towpath leading out of suburban Marple, with green hillsides soon appearing ahead, then pasture hillside, moorland and golf course, with short sections of quiet road-walking. Route-finding quite easy, but take care with directions from 7 to 9.

Length 7 miles (11km), 3 hours
Difficulty 2–3
Start Marple station, on A626 (on left if you are coming from Stockport); car park. Grid reference SJ 963893
OS maps 1:50,000 109; 1:25,000 SJ 88/98
Refreshments Plenty in Marple; post office at Strines (on Sundays); Fox Inn at Brook Bottom

WALK DIRECTIONS

1 Turn right out of station and at canal turn left on to towpath along right-hand side of canal and walk past locks (**a**). **2** At junction of canals (**b**), cross bridge and turn left along towpath to take left-hand branch. **3** After 300 yards cross to other side of canal by bridge. Follow towpath for another 1½ miles. **4** Turn left 150 yards after passing swing bridge (and 50 yards after passing through metal barriers on towpath), down into the cutting along track.

5 Cross main road near Strines post office and take road opposite (Station Road) towards Strines station (**c**).
6 After passing under railway by bridge, immediately continue forward (avoiding left fork) on track,

which rises to village of Brook Bottom. Follow road to left through village, and left again opposite post-box on lane signposted bridleway, up past Methodist chapel. **7** At highest point of road, turn right over wooden stile, ascend with wall on left and in 50 yards pass through squeeze-stile on left. After 20 yards, by near end of long shed, bear half right on narrow rising path.

8 At top of first rise, path climbs past footpath signpost pointing way you have come, and rises steadily alongside dry-stone wall on right. Follow this wall past Higher Capstone Farm, climbing steeply behind farm to gate **9**. Turn left along track. **10** Detour to cross (immediately up on right) for view (**d**). Return to and continue along track and immediately turn left at lane junction, descend until you reach golf course on right: enter it between wooden posts **11**.

Follow right (top) edge of golf course, soon along grassy track. After 300 yards keep on main track which bends left (avoiding the narrow path ahead, leading to a wide stile). On reaching stony track turn right along it past car park and then sharp left (signposted to scout camp at Linnet Clough). **12** Go straight on at end of surfaced road along track (signposted Marple), which descends gently (**e**).

13 At bottom, fork left at the road junction ('Roman Lakes Bird Sanctuary' sign on tree ahead), over river, and ascending to cross railway just as it enters tunnel (**f**). **14** At residential road turn right to return to starting-place (signposted Marple station).

WHAT TO LOOK OUT FOR

(**a**) Top part of 16-lock flight known as **Marple Locks**, which was not completed until 1804, four years after the canal began to operate. In the

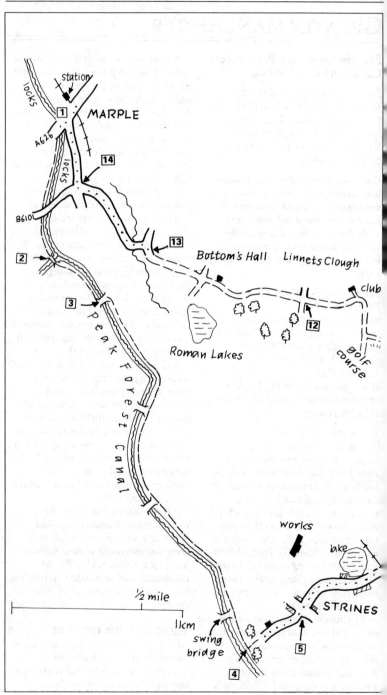

meantime, a tramway operated between Marple Junction and Buxworth Basin, and limestone from Doveholes had to be unloaded and reloaded. A recommended diversion at the end of the walk is to walk down the lower part of the flight and follow the canal to the triple-arched/100ft high Marple aqueduct.
(**b**) Junction of **Peak Forest Canal** (left, which turns to beyond Whaley Bridge) and the **Macclesfield Canal** (designed by Telford), opened 1831.
(**c**) **Mill pond** on left (with dovecote), formerly supplied works nearby.
(**d**) **View** Peak District to E and SE, including Kinder Scout (E, 2,088ft) and Chinley Churn (SE, 1,483ft); S to the moors beyond Lyme Park; SW the Cheshire Plains; W and NW across Stockport and Manchester.
(**e**) Towards bottom of slope, on left, is **Bottom's Hall**, which once housed the apprentices for Samuel Oldknow's Mellor Mill (built 1790) nearby. The lake beyond (next left turn, for detour), known as Roman Lakes, was the mill pond.
(**f**) **Beechwood** Derelict house on the right was built by the Manchester, Sheffield and Lincolnshire Railway in 1850, right over the tunnel.

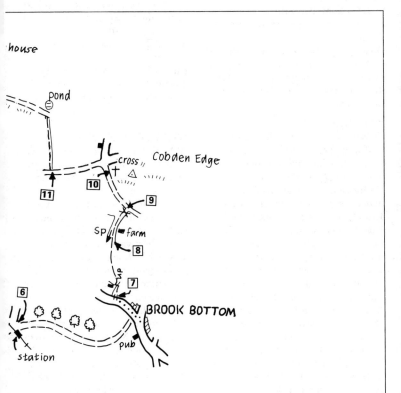

ISLE OF MAN

Spanish Head and Cregneish

*Based on a contribution from
D H T Wood
Recommended by C Oldham*

**Along cliff-tops of exceptional beauty,
with the added interest of the Calf
of Man. Good views inland, too,
notably from the quiet road beyond
Cregneish. Field path at end is briefly
undefined, but route-finding
throughout easy.**

Length 6½ miles (10.5km), 3 hours
Difficulty 3
Start Seafront, Port Erin
By train Port Erin (Isle of Man Steam
Railway)
OS maps 1:50,000 95; 1:25,000 Rights
of Way map for Isle of Man (published
by Isle of Man Highways Authority)
Refreshments Full range in Port Erin;
café at point ③

WALK DIRECTIONS
① With sea on right, follow seafront
road around bay. Beyond pier, road
divides; fork left following one-way
traffic sign. ② Just before red-brick
Marine Biological Station (**a**), take
signposted path on left which leads
behind generator and up steps. Path
soon leads between fences, then turns
left at sea, alongside fence. On
emerging into open, keep left alongside
fence then wall. Proceed along cliff
path for 2 miles (**b**).

③ Beyond café, path proceeds by
flagpole. Follow cliff-top, around first
headland, then steeply up on to
Spanish Head (**c**); continue along
cliff-top. ④ On reaching NT sign for
Spanish Head (facing other way), cross
ladder-stile. Left, alongside wall, to
huts, is continuation of route, but first
detour ahead a few yards to turn right
through gate opposite derelict building
to see the Chasms (**d**).

Return, and follow the above-
mentioned path to huts; continue on
tarmac lane towards Cregneish. ⑤
Fork left in village (**e**), proceed to main
road and turn left then immediately
right (**f**) (signposted Port Erin). After
250 yards, road passes pond on your
left; 150 yards later make up to fence
up on right which encloses stone circle
(**g**). Return to road, proceed down it,
then ⑥ , 150 yards later, fork right on
to moorland track (parallel to road).
Ignore side turns and follow track
down, soon between walls, then
reaching stile.

Carry on across field towards Port
Erin seafront, leaving this large field
by signposted stile in bottom left
corner. ⑦ Half-way down next field
cross stile on left and proceed on
path to driveway, where turn right
downhill. At end, turn left on road
then right at T-junction and proceed
to start.

WHAT TO LOOK OUT FOR
(**a**) **Marine Biological Station** Attached
to Liverpool University, researching
into fish breeding to keep up stock of
fish in the sea.
(**b**) Soon the view ahead opens up
over the **Calf of Man**. The island is
an NT bird sanctuary; **birds** include
Manx shearwaters and puffins.
(**c**) **Spanish Head** Large headland which
gets its name from a false story that
ships from the Spanish Armada were
wrecked on it.
(**d**) **The Chasms** Remarkable series of
rifts, probably caused by earth
movements. Most are no more than a
few feet wide but plummet the full
depth of the 200ft cliffs and further;
cliff-top **view** of the cliff and rocks
from E side. Take great care here,
particularly with children.
(**e**) **Cregneish** The single-storey
thatched dwellings are historical
monuments and form the Manx

If you have a walk to suggest for any subsequent edition of the Holiday Which? Good Walks Guide, *please send it to us. We need a rough sketch map and a brief description of the walk's attractions. Directions are not necessary. All walks must be in Great Britain, Northern Ireland, the Isle of Man or the Channel Islands and should fit the criteria given in the Introduction (see page 7). Please write to:* Holiday Which? Good Walks Guide, *Consumers' Association, 14 Buckingham Street, London WC2N 6DS.*

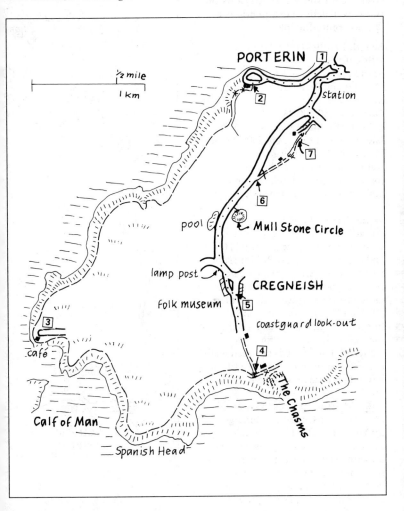

open-air museum.

(f) **View** of the southern hills, including NE to South Barrule, the highest of them at 1586ft.

(g) **Mull Circle** Stone circle, late neolithic or early Bronze Age, consisting of twelve cists, grouped in pairs. **View** over Calf of Man, Port Erin.

Glen Maye, Corrin's Folly and Peel Castle

More than just a good cliff walk, with plenty to see. Can shorten route by taking bus back from Peel (a regular service at time of writing), but the old railway track is easy to walk and has river and hillside views. All paths and tracks well defined except briefly at 3 ; easy route-finding.

Length 10 miles (16km), 5 hours
Difficulty 3–4
Start St John's, on A1 between Douglas and Peel. Grid reference SC 277818
OS maps 1:50,000 95;
1:25,000 Rights of Way map for the Isle of Man (published by Isle of Man Highways Authority)
Refreshments Pubs and shop in St John's; Waterfall Hotel, café and shop at Glenmaye; full range in Peel

WALK DIRECTIONS

1 (**a**) Take the road signposted Castletown, opposite Tynwald Hill and to left of Tynwald Hill Inn, soon past Farmers' Arms, then take next right, signposted Patrick. 50 yards later, just after bridge, take next left.
2 After ½ mile, just after end of forest on right, take track on right, marked as 'Unsuitable for motor vehicles'. This ascends between walls (**b**); after 1 mile ignore ladder-stile on left but proceed now alongside fence on left.

3 Where fence ends by gate and sea view opens out ahead, emerge into open grassland. Continue in same direction across grass. Path is undefined but on reaching corner of remains of stone wall it becomes better defined, heading to right of ruined building and soon between walls. 4 Emerge on to tarmac lane. Turn right on lane, which bends left after 20 yards (ignore track ahead). Descend 1 mile to Glenmaye.

5 At village turn left on road, then

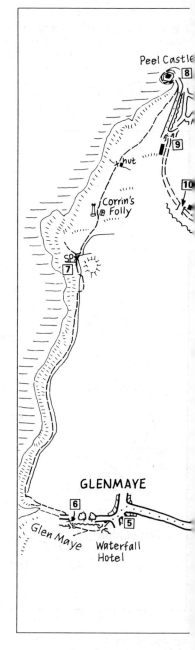

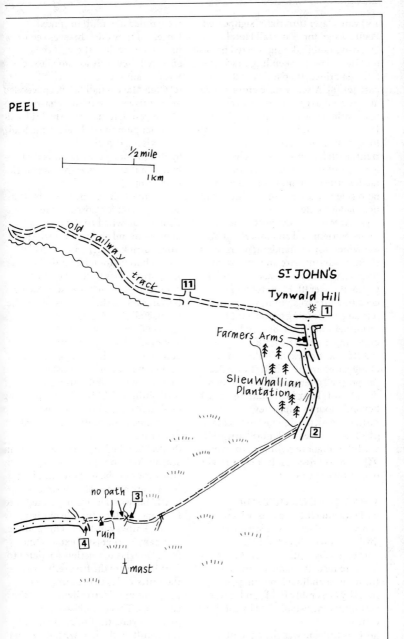

PEEL

½ mile

1 km

old railway track

11

St JOHN'S

Tynwald Hill

☼ 1

Farmers Arms

SlieuWhallian Plantation

2

no path

3

ruin

4

△ mast

150 yards later turn right (signposted Peel) by sign for Waterfall Hotel. Opposite hotel take signposted path for Glen Maye, descending to waterfalls via bridge, then follow riverside path (**c**). **6** After ¼ mile cross bridge (**d**), proceed to gate, cross road and take path opposite (signposted Peel). Path ascends and soon leads to sea; at fork, bear right, close to fence on right. Path follows close to cliff edge for 1½ miles (**e**), then takes iron ladder-stile on right, to proceed on land side of wall, rejoining cliff-top by next ladder-stile.

7 At footpath signpost, where fields on right end and moorland hill (on which tower stands) appears, pass through kissing-gate and turn right on grassy path, which soon bears left to reach tower (**f**). From tower proceed to white trig. point, where turn left on path leading to the left of prominent hut, then descend to Peel, emerging near castle (**g**) **8**.

After visiting castle follow road along harbour, cross bridge into Peel (**h**), proceed over quayside road then **9** 30 yards later turn sharp right just beyond Moore's Kipperies, on old railway track (**i**), signposted Glenfaba. **10** Track passes under bridge (**j**); 300 yards later ignore right fork to river. **11** At next cross-track, keep straight over, proceed to start.

WHAT TO LOOK OUT FOR

(**a**) **Tynwald Hill** The grassy steps capped by a flagpole constitute the 'hill' from which, on Old Midsummer's Day (July 5), new Manx laws are read. Its name is derived from the Scandinavian 'thing-vollr', literally 'assembly field', and it was certainly long established by the 11th century.

(**b**) This **hillside** was the ancient scene of witch persecution. Suspects were rolled downhill in spiked barrels; if they died this was seen as a judgement against them; if they survived they were assumed to be witches anyway.

(**c**) **Glen Maye** Small but deep wooded glen with a waterfall in a chasm.

(**d**) On your left just after the bridge is a former **pumping-wheel** for the lead mines (see plaque).

(**e**) **Birds** Among the sea-birds that breed on these cliffs is the rare black guillemot.

(**f**) **Corrin's Folly** Stone tower built as a mausoleum for Corrin, a Freechurchman who had the remains of his wife and children transferred from Patrick churchyard to the enclosed burial ground next to the tower; the purpose was to show that non-consecrated ground was suitable for burial. Among the hills visible to the E, Snaefell (2,036ft) can just be seen.

(**g**) **Peel Castle** (open to public; fee) Approached by a causeway. If you don't have the chance to go inside, best seen from the signposted footpath which skirts its curtain wall. Built by William le Scrope, King of Man from 1392 to 1399. Inside is the ruined 13th-century cathedral of St German.

(**h**) **Peel** Smoked kippers are on sale in season (May to Sept) from the smokeries by the harbour. Leading from it are a maze of tiny streets.

(**i**) **Old railway** The former Douglas to Peel line, built by the Isle of Man Steam Railway in 1873. This and the company's other (still extant) line from Douglas to Castletown (later to Port Erin) were the first railways in the British Isles to use automatic coupling and electric lighting in the carriages. This line closed in 1965.

(**j**) Just beyond the bridge, a former **watermill** on the left, with its wheel still in place.

NORTH-EAST ENGLAND

Northumberland, Yorkshire

This region includes some of England's finest upland scenery,
especially in its three National Parks. Two of these – the Yorkshire
Dales and Northumberland – form part of the Pennine chain. There is
some fine mountain country outside the National Parks, too, in the
wild and remote Northern Pennines. Away from the main mountain
areas, the region has less obvious appeal for the walker, though there
are lower ranges of hills, such as the Howardian Hills in Yorkshire,
while Northumberland has a majestically empty and unspoilt
coastline.

The Yorkshire Dales are known for their distinctive limestone
landscape, which includes man-made constructions – dry-stone walls
and stone barns – as well as many natural features: jagged white scars,
rocky limestone pavements, crag-lined gorges, caves and potholes.
Particularly fine is the area round Malham, where it is possible to take
in, as part of a single short walk, Malham Cove, a limestone pavement
and Goredale Scar. Further west, the scenery becomes wilder and
more desolate, and the second highest mountain in this section of the
Pennines, Ingleborough, is a major attraction for walkers, sometimes
climbed with its two neighbours, Pen-y-Ghent and Whernside (the
highest of the three) as part of the tough Three Peaks Walk. There is
more fine scenery further north, in grand, pastoral Wensleydale, with
its pretty waterfalls, and in narrow, austere Swaledale, with its stone
barns and tiny, remote villages.

Some fifty miles of the Pennine Way crosses the Dales. North of the
Dales, the Way passes through increasingly empty and desolate
mountain scenery – much of it offering walks too tough for this book
– before reaching Hadrian's Wall and the Northumberland National
Park, through which it also passes for fifty miles. Much of this
National Park will appeal only to the keen fell-walker, and has few
easy or clear paths, but the bold grassy ridges of the Cheviot Hills offer
plenty of rewarding routes which aren't too difficult in dry conditions.
For easier walking, there is a superb, twenty-mile stretch of Hadrian's
Wall, most of it snaking along the great crags of the Whin Sill. We
haven't succeeded in identifying a really good round walk that takes
in the Wall, but in summer, at least, there is a bus you can use to
return to your starting point. Outside the Park, there is easy walking

along Northumberland's low-lying but distinctive coast, which has some dramatic castles and vast sandy beaches.

The region's third National Park, the North York Moors, includes the largest expanse of heather moorland in England: it is plateau-like rather than mountainous, and there is no point within its boundaries over 1,500ft. The main massif is crossed by numerous ancient trackways that provide easy walking and some views of broad and lonely horizons. The plateau is cut into by a series of lush green dales dotted with neat red-roofed villages and isolated farmsteads built in local yellow stone. But more dramatic scenery lies round the edges of the Park, three sides of which are followed by the area's main long-distance path, the Cleveland Way. On the western and northern sides, the land drops away precipitously, to give spectacular views; on the eastern side, the moorland rarely extends as far as the coast, but there are fine cliffs, including the highest on the east coast, at 660ft, and some intriguing and chaotic landslips, as at Ravenscar. Regrettably, some parts of the Park, notably in the south-east, have been covered with dull coniferous forests.

We conclude with an apology to County Durham, for which we haven't included any walks. Even though there is dramatic moorland in the west of the county and some impressive river scenery around Durham city, we haven't so far found any round walks worth recommending. We would be especially pleased to have suggestions – see page 10.

NORTHUMBERLAND

Hulne Park, Alnwick

Easily managed tour of parkland owned by Alnwick Castle. All on tracks; easy route-finding. No public rights of way in the park, but public access is allowed on its drives and tracks on Saturdays and Sundays, 11am until dusk; at other times, ask at the estate office, Alnwick Castle (open in normal office hours, even when castle is closed to visitors) for a free permit. No dogs.

Length 8 miles (13km), 3½ hours
Difficulty 1–2
Start Entrance, Alnwick Castle
OS maps 1:50,000 81;
1:25,000 NU 01/11
Refreshments Plenty in Alnwick

WALK DIRECTIONS

1 (**a**) With castle entrance behind you, follow street ahead (Bailiffgate). 30 yards after passing Northumberland Street on your left, keep left into no-through road, soon to reach gatehouse, then follow estate drive ½ mile. **2** 50 yards after lodge on left, turn half right on track downhill (not sharp right, signed 'Park Cottage').

3 Left at T-junction. To view abbey gateway (**b**) look out for bridge on right after ¼ mile, approached by narrow path. Cross bridge, right on track on other side through parkland with river on right. Retrace steps from gateway.

4 ½ mile later (¼ mile after diversion to abbey gateway) turn half right at oblique T-junction, into parkland by gate after 100 yards. Track leads past bridge: do not cross, but follow ¼ mile to next bridge **5**. Cross bridge, fork left. Track follows close to river for 1½ miles. **6** Hulne Priory (**c**) comes into view up on right, but no track leads to it from river (not

open to public, though you are welcome to walk outside the walls at weekends).

7 Take next bridge on left after passing priory. Track ascends gently. **8** Reach tarmac estate drive (farm visible away to left) and turn right. After 50 yards turn right at triangular T-junction. **9** Take next left turn (opposite sentry hut). Ignore next left turn and ascend gently to Brizlee Tower (just to right of track). (**d**)

10 Continue forward on track, soon passing viewpoint with stone bench/ standing stone (**e**). **11** 150 yards after viewpoint turn left at crossing of tracks, in woods: follow round past cave (**f**) to rejoin point reached earlier **12**. Turn right on track, downhill. **13** Turn right on tarmac estate drive, and follow back to start (**g**).

WHAT TO LOOK OUT FOR

(**a**) **Alnwick** By the river is the huge castle (open to public; fee), Norman with 18th- and 19th-century restoration. There are two town gates (the one with the Percy Lion is 15th-century), an 18th-century market hall and bridge of the same period.
(**b**) **Abbey gatehouse** The only visible remnant of the abbey, a 14th-century archway under four projecting towers, highly ornamented on its side. Heraldic shields just below the castellations.
(**c**) **Priory** A Carmelite foundation of *c.* 1240, with a 15th-century tower and a handsome 18th-century farmhouse inside its curtain wall. The Carmelite monks eked out a stark existence: their own coffins furnished their cells and they were required to dig daily a shovelful of earth for their graves. The principal church in the priory has a rare pre-Christian Tau cross.
(**d**) **Brizlee Tower** Gothick folly erected in 1781 by the first Duke of

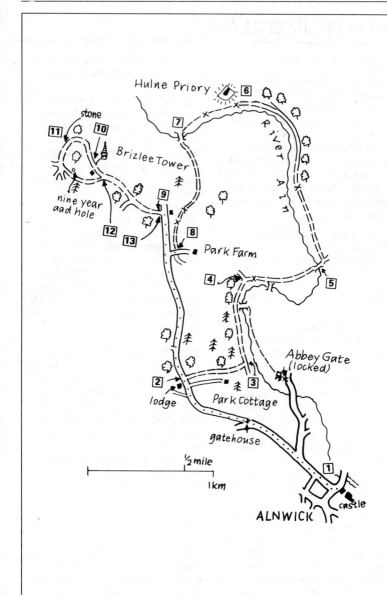

Hulne Priory 6

7

stone

11 10

Brizlee Tower

nine year
aad hole

9

12 13

8

Park Farm

River Aln

4 ✕ 5

Abbey Gate
(locked)

2

lodge

3

Park Cottage

gatehouse

½ mile

1 km

1

castle

ALNWICK

Northumberland. On it is inscribed in Latin, 'Look around yourself; I have measured out everything here: my commands and my planting; I have even planted many of the trees with my own hands'.

(e) **View** Over the Cheviots, with the coast beyond Alnwick to the right.

(f) **Cave** Known as the 'nine year aad hole', a natural cave with the stone figure of a hermit placed by its entrance. Three robbers allegedly once hid here with their booty; two killed each other off, then the third died, leaving the whereabouts of the treasure (and the provenance of the story) uncertain.

(g) If you have time, turn left at the end of the walk, down to the river bridge; a path on the right on the far side of the river gives a good view of the **castle**.

The Central Cheviots: The Street and Windy Gyle

Contributed by Dr and Mrs A P J Lake
Recommended by Rosemary Royle

Genuinely remote, over grassy hills and a ridge along the national boundary, looking far into Scotland. About a mile of peaty land on top, sometimes boggy. Patches of forestry on the return, otherwise grassy hillsides and a very quiet tarmac lane along the River Coquet at end. All on defined tracks; route-finding quite easy in clear weather but compass essential in case of mist. Ascent 1,000ft.

Length 12 miles (19km), 5 hours
Difficulty 3–4 (4 in boggy conditions)
Start Coquet Valley, 13 miles NW of Rothbury. Follow lane NW from Alwinton for 6 miles (signposted Windyhaugh), pass through tiny hamlet of Lounges Knowle (look out for school and phone box) and park just before next bridge over tributary stream ½ mile further on, at junction of lane with track off to the right. Grid reference NT 860115
OS maps 1:50,000 80;
1:25,000 NT 81/91

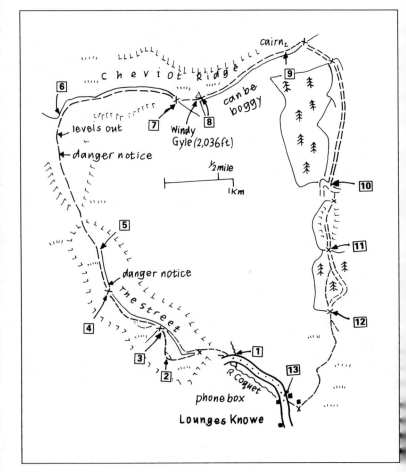

WALK DIRECTIONS

1 From parking area, cross bridge then turn right through gate (signposted the Street) (**a**). Track ascends steadily, bends left through gate/stile after 600 yards, beyond which it keeps right, roughly parallel to fence away to right. **2** ¼ mile after passing corner of fence away to right, follow track as it bends right, along ridge. **3** Track regains fence, passes through gate; 75 yards after gate, take either fork (they rejoin). Track is sometimes indistinct, but route along ridge is obvious in clear weather.

4 After ½ mile track reaches corner of fence on your right. Keep forward alongside fence. **5** Where fence ends, track bends quarter left uphill, soon descends to bottom of dip, then track is very clear as it ascends. **6** ¼ mile after track levels, it reaches corner of fence; track continues quarter right (Windy Gyle, your objective, is the right-hand of two summits half right). Path is soon joined by fence on left; follow for ¾ mile.

7 Pass through gate: track leads ahead up to Windy Gyle (**b**) **8**. Continue forward from summit, walking alongside fence on right (boggy after rain, but manageable). **9** Pass large cairn after 600 yards and, 300 yards later, turn right through gate, following track leading away from fence, downhill, for 1½ miles.
10 At T-junction turn left on hard track then right after 50 yards, on to track leading to gate after 200 yards. Ascend middle of ridge ahead (track indistinct until ridge descends), track soon descends into plantation **11**.

Ascend forestry track for 250 yards, then fork right where main track levels out. **12** Leave plantation by gate at far end, then forward on track. Track soon descends into valley on right, then ascends a little before reaching hut. Then descend to road **13**. Turn right on road, back to start.

WHAT TO LOOK OUT FOR

(**a**) **The Street** An ancient drovers' track, rising from the Coquet Valley over to Hownam, on the Scottish side. Leads you up on to a delightful ridge almost immediately.

(**b**) **Windy Gyle** Can usually be counted on living up to its name; offers one of the best views on the border (the fence is the national boundary; the summit is just in Scotland). N, towards the Lammermuir Hills (1,755ft); NW to the Moorfoot Hills (2,137ft); immediately E to the Cheviot itself (2,674ft); SW to the Pennines, including Cross Fell (2,930ft). At the trig.point is Russell's Cairn, named after an English knight who was murdered here by the Scots in 1585 on a day of truce. The cairn itself is much older.

Ross Back Sands

Contributed by J Hawgood
Recommended by Mr and Mrs V R
Beasley, J Philpots

Beyond the sand dunes, a vast
beach of golden sand with Bamburgh
and Holy Island castles visible
across the water at either end and the
Cheviots in view inland; excellent
bird-watching towards the Lindis-
farne nature reserve (particularly
at low tide when birds are feeding).
At 'springtide at high' (every two
weeks), sea covers sand south of
marker obelisks to form an island
for about 1½ hours; times of spring
tides can be checked by telephon-
ing coastguard (091-257 2691; 24-
hour service). Farm tracks and a
quiet road for the link section.
Easy route-finding.

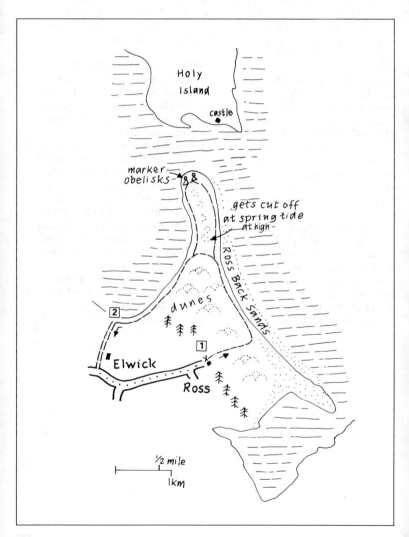

Length 5 or 6½ miles (8 or 10.5km),
2½ or 3½ hours
Difficulty 2
Start Ross, 3 miles E of A1, 14 miles N
of Alnwick and 18 miles S of
Berwick-on-Tweed. Park at end of
road. Grid reference NU 135373
OS maps 1:50,000 75; 1:25,000 NU
04/14 and NU 13/23

WALK DIRECTIONS

1 From Ross, walk to end of lane
and continue direction on path
through dunes to beach. Turn left to
follow coast round, skirting sand
dunes; if desired continue up to
northern most tip by marker
obelisks. Follow coast for about 4
miles (a).

2 Turn inland to left along
cart-track to Elwick. Turn left on
tarmac lane; keep left after 300 yards
at junction and follow lane 1 mile to
starting-place.

WHAT TO LOOK OUT FOR
(a) **Ross Back Sands** One of the
loneliest beaches on the English east
coast. **Birds** include fulmar, petrel,
black-headed gull, wader, godwit,
curlew, oystercatcher, turnstone,
dunlin, knot and eider duck.
Views N to Holy Island, the cradle
of Christianity in England, where
Aidan, a missionary from Iona,
arrived in AD635 at the invitation of
Oswald, King of Northumbria. The
island is three miles long and a mile
wide, with the castle and priory at its
S end. The castle was restored by Sir
Edwin Lutyens.

Dunstanburgh Castle and Craster

*Contributed by Rosemary Royle
Recommended by J G Pells*

Keeps for the second half of the walk the coast path, past the ruin of Dunstanburgh Castle (melodramatic when we were there in thick mist; if closed, it is still rewarding to walk round its curtain wall) and ending at a large sandy beach. Uses level farmland tracks and field paths for the first half. Easy route-finding.

Length 4½ miles (7km), 2 hours
Difficulty 1
Start Dunstansteads (small car park by gate at end of road); grid reference NU 245225. From S end of Embleton, on B1399 9 miles S of Bamburgh, take road E, signposted Dunstansteads and Dunstanburgh Castle.
Or Craster (car park, fee), at point ⑤
OS maps 1:50,000 75 and 81; 1:25,000 NU 21/22
Refreshments Jolly Fisherman, Craster, by harbour

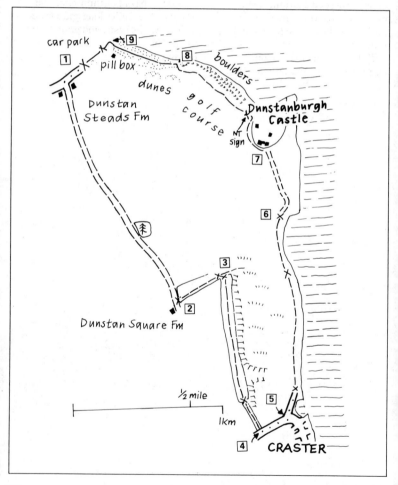

WALK DIRECTIONS

1 Follow road inland, then turn left in front of farm (signposted Dunstan Square) through farmyard and on to concrete farm road for 1 mile. **2** Left at next farm, through gate opposite first barn on right, (signposted Craster); track follows right edge of field. **3** Through gate at end of field, forward for 30 yards, then right through gate. Keep on left side of long field, with gorse-clad crags on left. Pass into second field by gate and follow path to road **4**.

Left on road, to quayside in Craster (**a**) **5**. With quay on right, follow road along seafront. Where road ends, keep forward through gate (signposted coastal path/Dunstanburgh Castle). Follow shore (no path, but easy walking across turf). **6** After two more gates, track begins, bends inland, and heads for gate of castle keep. **7** Left at keep, to skirt inland around castle (**b**). Beyond castle, rejoin coast and enter golf course by gate (NT sign).

8 Where boulders on beach below end, descend to beach. **9** 400 yards later, just after a point level with concrete pillbox (just visible in dunes), left through gap to take track to gate at starting-point.

WHAT TO LOOK OUT FOR

(**a**) **Craster** Still very much a fishing village; you can buy Craster kippers here in season (May to Sept). The harbour, atmospheric rather than picturesque, was built in 1906 as a memorial to Captain Craster (killed in India, 1904), who lived locally. The concrete hopper here is a reminder of the whinstone quarrying that took place in the village until the 1930s.

(**b**) **Dunstanburgh Castle** (English Heritage, open to public; fee) Largest of the Northumbrian castles, situated right by the coast on a slight rise. A long and virtually intact curtain wall encompasses the ruined keep and Lilburn Tower. An important stronghold during the Wars of the Roses. Started by Earl Thomas in 1313, and later fortified against the incursion of Scots who had a try at storming it (unsuccessfully) in 1834. It fell into decline in the late 15th century.

YORKSHIRE

Castle Howard Estate

Based on a contribution from Geoffrey White

Through the woods and landscaped parklands of one of England's great country houses, rising to the ridge of the Howardian Hills – a gentle escarpment overlooking the Vale of Pickering and the North York Moors. Takes a quiet road at the start. Paths mostly well defined; route-finding moderately easy.

Length 6½ miles (10.5km), 3 hours
Difficulty 2
Start Large lay-by 1 mile N of Castle Howard by gatehouse on main estate avenue (100 yards S of crossroads where E turning is signposted Coneysthorpe), 5 miles W of Malton. Free parking. Grid reference SE 707712
OS maps 1:50,000 100; 1:25,000 SE 67/77
Refreshments Shop at Coneysthorpe; café at Castle Howard, 1 mile off route

WALK DIRECTIONS

1 Turn left out of lay-by, then left at crossroads (signposted Terrington). Follow road (very quiet) for ¾ mile. 2 Where road bends left, keep straight on, on track signposted bridleway. 3 After 300 yards, turn right on track waymarked by arrows. Keep left at junction 150 yards later. Left again at next junction 150 yards after this (waymarked) and keep right 20 yards later (waymarked). Follow to gate 4.

Beyond gate, follow track across parkland to gate ahead, then uphill through woods (ignore cross-track after 100 yards). 5 Turn right at top of ridge by waymarkers. 6 Cross road to track opposite (a) (b). 7 After 1½ miles path leads through small

gate and follows right edge of field, leaving it by waymarked stile in right-hand corner. Head half right (farmhouse ahead) to corner of fence, then proceed alongside fence on left to stile 8.

Turn right on farm track. At end cross road, take signposted bridleway via gate opposite, and turn left in field; faint grassy path gradually diverges from hedge on left, and where bank of trees immediately on right ends, track becomes very clear and zigzags downhill. Castle Howard Mausoleum (prominent round classical building) is visible on skyline, with (smaller) temple to right of it (c).

9 After ½ mile, keep right (left leads to farm). 10 ½ mile later, and ¼ mile after woodland begins on left, turn right at junction of tracks as waymarked (ahead leads to gate marked private). 11 At gate at top (turn round for view of Castle Howard) turn left on road past Coneysthorpe hamlet (d) and back to start.

WHAT TO LOOK OUT FOR

(a) An arresting view of **Castle Howard**. The palatial house is of strikingly original design for the early 17th century. No one really knows who designed it: Vanbrugh was appointed as designer, but at that time he is not known to have had any architectural experience; his career had until then been a military one. Hawksmoor, who had already had a great deal of experience as an architect, was brought in as clerk of works, and it is quite likely that the design was by both men. Hawksmoor had been working for Wren since he was 18, and Castle Howard was very probably modelled on Wren's proposed plan for Hampton Court (which never got beyond the drawing board). The

building is familiar to many as the house used in the television adaptation of *Brideshead Revisited*.
(**b**) Shortly after, view on left opens out across the **Vale of Pickering** (much of which is also owned by the Castle Howard Estate) to the N York Moors.
(**c**) **Mausoleum and temple** The mausoleum is huge and majestic, with 20 columns encircling a rotunda.

Designed by Hawksmoor in 1731, it was not completed until after his death. The Temple of the Four Winds was built 1724–6 in the Pailadian style from a design by Vanbrugh.
(**d**) **Coneysthorpe** Built for the estate around an oblong green, at the top of which is a handsome classical chapel (1835).

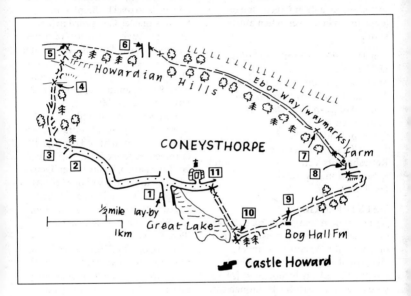

Hardraw Force

Recommended by Michael Elstob

The most impressive waterfall in the Dales (reached through back door of a pub). Negligible ascent, yet fine views down Wensleydale. Includes short sections along road. Route-finding a little tricky just after ⁴; elsewhere field paths are well defined or route is obvious. Small fee for visiting waterfall, payable at Green Dragon Inn (open in daylight even when pub is shut).

Length 4 miles (6.5km), 1½ hours
Difficulty 1–2
Start Hawes town centre, on A684 34 miles W of Northallerton. Car park at E end of town, near Dales information centre (fee)
OS maps 1:50,000 98; 1:25,000 Outdoor Leisure 30
Refreshments Various in Hawes; hotel in Simonstone; pub and café at Hardraw

WALK DIRECTIONS

1 From town centre take road to right of Midland Bank, soon passing church on your right. At bottom turn left, signposted Hardraw, on road which crosses old railway by bridge (**a**). **2** 80 yards after bridge turn left through gate signposted Pennine Way. On rejoining road turn left along road and cross bridge. **3** 150 yards after bridge, turn right through gate, signposted Sedbusk. Follow path to cross footbridge, ascend up to gap-stile, then continue up to top right-hand corner of field to emerge by stile on to road **4**.

Turn right on road, then immediately left over stile. Take care to find route in this field (the only difficult route-finding in the walk): turn right along bottom of field for 20 yards, then bear half left, skirting base of grassy hillock, ascending gently to find stile in stone wall ahead. Continue forward quarter left across

second field to ladder-stile, then forward to stile beyond stone barn **5**. Turn right on lane into Sedbusk, then 100 yards later turn left at lane junction into centre of hamlet **6**.

Turn left opposite phone box on path signposted Simonstone. Path leads across series of small fields; aim for stiles ahead (easy to find) (**b**). **7** After ¾ mile path becomes farm track and leads to road by hamlet of Simonstone (**c**). Cross road to lane opposite. After passing row of cottages continue forward to stile, cross hotel driveway beyond and cross next stile. Head down on path following right edge of field, aiming just right of farmhouse ahead **8**.

Turn left by house and follow clear footpath, signposted Hardraw, Green Dragon Inn on right and pay (small) entrance fee to see Hardraw Force (**d**). **9** Take path opposite Green Dragon (slightly to right), by phone box. After 20 yards leave track ahead for path paved with flagstones leading along left edge of field. This clear path (Pennine Way) leads ½ mile across fields to road **10**. Turn right on road, retracing steps over bridge crossed at start of walk, and remember to take field path on right 150 yards after bridge.

WHAT TO LOOK OUT FOR

(**a**) Site of **Hawes station**, which was originally owned jointly by the North East and Midland Railways. The line, built in 1877, connected Leyburn to the Carlisle/Settle line at Garsdale until closure in 1964.
(**b**) **View** Down Wensleydale, with Wether Fell (2,015ft) beyond Hawes, and Addleborough (1,564ft) behind you, sharply to the left.
(**c**) You can see the **Upper Hardraw Falls** (pleasantly set in woodland, but modest compared to Hardraw Force) by turning right on road at Simonstone; where road bends right, take

track on left into woods and around the falls.

(**d**) **Hardraw Force** At 96ft high, the highest waterfall above ground in England, caused by the erosion of soft shales adjacent to the harder limestone. The Victorian tightrope walker Blondin crossed the falls; a brass band competition was held here in 1885, and periodically ever since (the original terraces for the audience are still visible); and the falls have twice been recorded as freezing completely, in 1739 and 1880.

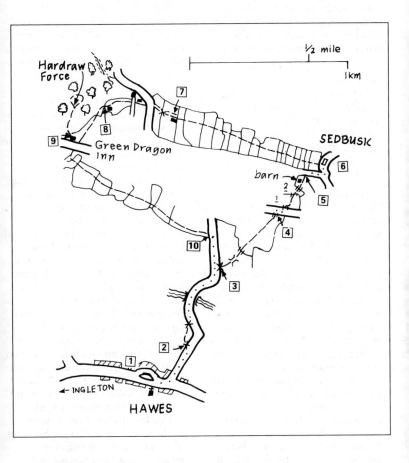

Upper Swaledale and Kisdon Hill

Contributed by Geoffrey White

Fine river scenery and waterfalls; mellow rather than rugged, in spite of the steepness of the Swaledale slopes. After a modest ascent from Keld, return is on grassy tracks over Kisdon Hill. Paths and tracks generally well defined; route-finding quite easy.

Length 5½ miles (9km), 3 hours
Difficulty 2
Start Muker, 20 miles W of Richmond on B6270; roadside parking. Grid reference SD 909978
OS maps 1:50,000 98 and 91, or 98 and 92; 1:25,000 Outdoor Leisure 30
Refreshments Shop and pub in Muker; water tap in square at Keld

WALK DIRECTIONS

1 From B6270 take minor road uphill into village centre and keep to right of post office (**a**). 30 yards later turn right, signposted Gunnerside. This leads into field where clear path leads through five fields, then cross bridge over Swale and turn left **2**. Walk along turf or track to follow river upstream. **3** After 1 mile, reach Swinner Gill with its deep gorge, waterfalls and footbridge (**b**). Cross bridge, immediately forking right on upper track on rising out of Swinner Gill (**c**).

4 After ¾ mile pass through gate, and 100 yards later fork left downhill to cross two bridges, the second crossing the Swale itself. **5** 200 yards later, reach Pennine Way sign at T-junction of paths. Turn right to continue (or detour left for views of Kisdon Force (**d**), forking left again as signposted after ¼ mile, then retrace steps). Path soon enters square at Keld **6** (**e**). Turn left through village, take first left fork and turn left again at T-junction by phone box.

7 After 300 yards fork left on to track (signposted Muker) by side of barn. Follow this walled track which very soon turns uphill and becomes more gradual after passing farmhouse up on your left (**f**). **8** At end of second (long) field after passing that farm, continue half left (signposted Muker) to pick up track between walls on other side of pasture. **9** Where walled section ends, continue forward on grassy track and on reaching corner of wall proceed with wall on left down towards Muker (**g**). Join surfaced lane further down, and continue down to start.

WHAT TO LOOK OUT FOR

(**a**) **Muker** Tightly clustered around its Elizabethan church. Pioneer botanists Cherry and Richard Kearton, who were born nearby at Thwaite, went to school here (commemorative tablets on either side of the school door). They were the first to use photographs for illustrating botanical books.
(**b**) The hillside on the right is dotted with relics – shafts, workings and spoil heaps – of the Swaledale **lead-mining industry**; it once accounted for most of Yorkshire's lead output. When the industry (which dated from medieval times) declined at the end of the last century, huge depopulation followed. Just after crossing Swinner Gill you will pass a ruined smelt mill, part of the Beldi Hill mines; a little further on a leat (channel) runs close to the path: this comes down the hill from the old workings, and used to operate a water wheel in the mine dressing works.
(**c**) **Crackpot Hall** Ruin up on the hill on the right, named after the Norse for 'hole of the crows', though the meaning of its name was not fully appreciated until the 1950s, when a cave entrance to Fairy Hole (Crackpot Cave) was discovered.
(**d**) **Kisdon Force** Well worth the short detour from the route, not so much for the waterfall itself as for its situation, deep in a rocky gorge.
(**e**) **Keld** On the other side of the square an entrance leads into a farm-

yard, at the far end of which is a good view down into another waterfall, Catrake Force.

(f) Kisdon Hill Name means 'little detached (hill)'. It was cut off from the main upland mass to the E when glacial ice blocked the Swale and diverted it to cut its present course around the E side of the hill. **View** ahead (S) is towards Lovely Seat

(2,213ft) and, away to the right (SW), Great Shunner Fell (2,349ft).

(g) The Pennine Way coming in from the left and the final part of the walk into Muker follow the old **corpse way**. This was the route coffin-bearers used from Muker to the church at Grinton, before the church at Muker was built in 1580. Stone slabs were placed at intervals.

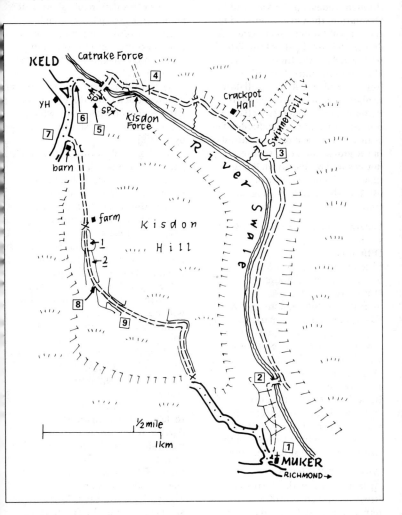

Simon's Seat

Based on a contribution from
Mark Denham
Recommended by Dr T S Worthy,
Michael Elstob, R C S Wilson,
Martyn Bishop, S R Pearce, Gary
Smerdon-White, John Hone

**One of the most varied walks in
Yorkshire. Ascends gradually
through woods, up the Valley of
Desolation, then over moorland to
the crags of Simon's Seat. After the
descent follows banks of the Wharfe,
with woods in the final sections.
Shorter route omits Simon's Seat,
following edge of Barden Fell down to
road, then continues down to river.
Paths and tracks mostly well defined;
route-finding quite easy. Barden Fell
is an access area, closed on Saturdays
in the grouse-shooting season;
notices will be displayed. For information telephone estate office
(Bolton Abbey 227). No dogs at any
time.**

Length *Full walk* 8½ miles (13.5 km),
4½ hours
Difficulty 3
Shorter walk omitting Simon's Seat
5½ miles (9km), 3 hours
Difficulty 2
Start Bolton Abbey, 6 miles NW of
Ilkley, in riverside car park (fee) at N
end of village. Turn off B6160 by
ornamental fountain. Notices tell
you if Barden Fell is closed to public
OS maps 1:50,000 104;
1:25,000 SE 05/15
Refreshments Pavilion at start and
end of walk (Cavendish Tower);
tea-room by post office, Bolton
Abbey; tea-room at Howgill; pub
(with restaurant) at Barden Tower

WALK DIRECTIONS

1 (**a**) From car park on banks of
River Wharfe cross bridge at
refreshment pavilion and continue
straight ahead for 70 yards on other
side, avoiding riverside footpath.

Turn left at crossroads then, after 300
yards, turn right on narrow path
opposite five rough stone bollards
on verge.

2 Where path rejoins road, turn
right on path, immediately leaving
road and passing through gate on
right side of cottage. Head across field
to gate in wall ahead. Track is now
well defined and descends, entering
Valley of Desolation (**b**). **3** At waterfall it climbs steep bank on right and
descends to cross footbridge. Ignore
right forks but continue on main
track which ascends to ladder-stile to
enter forest.

4 10 yards beyond stile turn right
on forest track immediately forking
left, keeping on main track which
ascends to leave forest after ½ mile
by stile **5**.

For shorter walk turn left on track
(later becomes path), walking
alongside wall on your left at edge of
moorland. ¾ mile later cross
ladder-stile on left, follow stony track
down to road and then turn right
along it. At road junction ½ mile
later turn left and 200 yards later fork
right on path following river, soon
reaching Barden Bridge at **10**.

For full walk continue forward
across moorland on prominent track
which ascends gently and passes
stone table after ½ mile. Shortly
after, turn right at T-junction of
tracks and follow cairn-marked track
to Simon's Seat (**c**) **6**. Turn left
on rough track signposted Howgill
and Barden.

7 ¾ mile later, track bends right
to descend between forest walls.
After ½ mile turn right by barn on
right, signposted Barden. Descend to
tarmac lane (café is 200 yards on
right). **8** Cross lane and descend on
track opposite until road. Cross road,
take path opposite and slightly to left,
signposted Barden Bridge. Keep left
on path along wall on reaching River
Wharfe. **9** Follow riverside path.

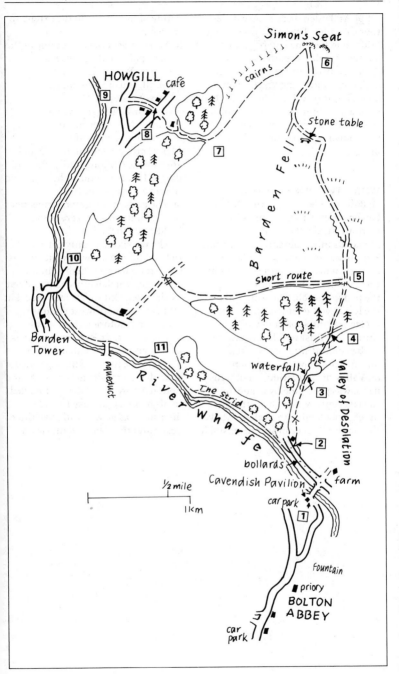

Simon's Seat

cairns

6

HOWGILL   café

9

8

7

Stone table

Barden Fell

Short route

5

10

Barden Tower

11

aqueduct

River Wharfe

The strid

waterfall

Valley of Desolation

4

3

2

bollards

Cavendish Pavilion

farm

car park

1

½ mile

1 km

fountain

priory

BOLTON ABBEY

car park

10 At Barden Bridge you can de-tour to Barden Tower (**d**) by crossing bridge and keeping left. **11** After another 2 miles (**e**) path enters woods (**f**): take any of a number of criss-cross paths, still following line of river, emerging at road 1 mile later. Turn right across bridge and take path on right signposted Bolton Abbey/Cavendish, which leads back to bridge.

WHAT TO LOOK OUT FOR

(**a**) **Bolton Abbey** Part of the Duke of Devonshire's Chatsworth Estates; glorious parkland and among England's most romantic abbey ruins. The abbey, which was founded by Augustinian canons in 1151, retains the nave of its church, now used as the parish church. The waterfall on the left as you re-emerge on to the bridge was the subject of works by Turner and Ruskin. The area teems with people at summer weekends, but the landscape absorbs them.

(**b**) **Valley of Desolation** Lugubrious name was prompted by a landslip in the last century, which destroyed much woodland in the valley. Above the waterfall you can see the unstable nature of the slope and the extent of the slippage.

(**c**) **Simon's Seat** Rocky outcrop at the highest point of the grouse moors; view over Wharfedale towards Burnsall, and of Skyreholme, a tributary valley.

(**d**) **Barden Tower** (always open; free) Ruined three-storey hunting-lodge overlooking the Wharfe. 11th-century, restored in 1485 and 1685 by the Clifford family. **Barden Bridge** Three graceful arches span the river; constructed in 1659.

(**e**) The path passes a stone **aqueduct** bearing water from reservoirs in Nidderdale to Bradford.

(**f**) The **woods** are mainly oak woods, rich in bird-life. Down by the river is the Strid, a narrow channel in the gritstone, which has been gouged out by the river. Only a few feet wide, but 30ft deep; its narrowest point is the Strid Jump, notorious for looking much easier to cross than it really is; a lot of people have fallen down it. The Boy of Egremond managed to do so with fatal results in the 1100s, and Bolton Abbey was allegedly founded in his memory (an easy legend to dismantle, as he was still alive three years after the abbey's foundation).

Mastiles Lane and Kilnsey Moor

Contributed by Ed Hopkins
Recommended by R C Hibbert

Limestone scenery with many of its distinctive features: dry-stone walls, springy turf, subterranean streams, stone pavements, rock outcrops and dew ponds. Not a particularly demanding walk, though most paths across pasture are undefined and route-finding is quite tricky, particularly in the early stages.

Length 12 miles (19km), 6 hours
Difficulty 3
Start Grassington, 8 miles N of Skipton on B6265
OS maps 1:50,000 98; 1:25,000 Outdoor Leisure 10
Refreshments Pubs and cafés at Grassington; pubs at Kilnsey and Threshfield

WALK DIRECTIONS

1 (a) Walk up Main Street and, 100 yards after post office, turn left down Chapel Street. After 300 yards, where road veers left, continue ahead on path through farmyard, signposted Conistone. Turn left immediately behind farm, as signposted. Arriving in field, turn right on track, again signposted Conistone, with stone wall on right. Clear track leads to gate and into second field, towards end of which track becomes indistinct; maintain direction to stone stile **2**.

In third field, locate slight outward protrusion in corner of wall opposite and somewhat to left: head for it by walking alongside wall on your right, to find stone stile just to left of protrusion. Proceed across fourth field, with wall on right, to next stile to enter open pasture **3**. Your objective is to pick up line of long stone wall not yet visible, up on right: continue ahead for 50 yards,

then turn left on more prominent track for 20 yards and turn right up path at point where main track veers sharp left, soon walking parallel to stone wall on right. **4** After ½ mile pass pond; 100 yards later cross wall on right by steps. Bear half left across field, through gate after 250 yards. Continue half left and 200 yards later cross ladder-stile **5**. Carry straight on for 300 yards to stile ahead. At end of next field, keep straight on as indicated by fingerpost, until path veers round to right, past head of rocky gorge on your left. Immediately after gorge cross ladder-stile sharp left, and another after 200 yards. Follow path to, and then along bottom of, gorge (b). After 200 yards pass through gate and into Conistone village **6**.

Turn right on road, signposted Kilnsey, to cross River Wharfe by road-bridge. After 600 yards turn left at T-junction (c), for 50 yards. **7** Turn right by bungalow. Follow track past farm on your right. After 100 yards fork left over stream; 30 yards later pass through gate (stream still on right). At barn, 400 yards on, fork right on path which veers round to left. At far top corner of field, cross wall on right by step **8**. Turn left on track (Mastiles Lane) (d) and fork left after 200 yards.

After ¼ mile fork right through gate. **9** After ½ mile turn left at gate signposted Bordley, walking with wall on left. After 300 yards continue forward at junction of tracks **10** After ½ mile (just where track ahead dips down through gate to Bordley) turn left, signposted Threshfield. Proceed with wall on right for 300 yards to bottom of valley. Turn left, keeping wall on right for 50 yards, and cross wall by steps **11**. Head uphill alongside wall on your right. After 350 yards continue forward where wall on right veers away half right. Cross remains of stone wall

391

after 150 yards and keep parallel to wall 100 yards to your right.

12 After 400 yards cross three small fields by stiles to reach large field. Continue in same direction and on far side of field cross stile 30 yards to right of stone barn **13**. Cross bridleway and follow signposted footpath, immediately crossing fence to proceed with wall on right. After 100 yards, just before farm, cross wall by steps on right. Continue 30 yards up to gate, past farm on your left, then uphill between walls as signposted. After 100 yards turn left (signposted) into field, with wall on left. After 200 yards pass to left of ruined farmhouse and make for bottom right-hand corner of field. Cross steps and follow well-defined path which runs parallel to stream for ½ mile and then crosses it **14**. Go

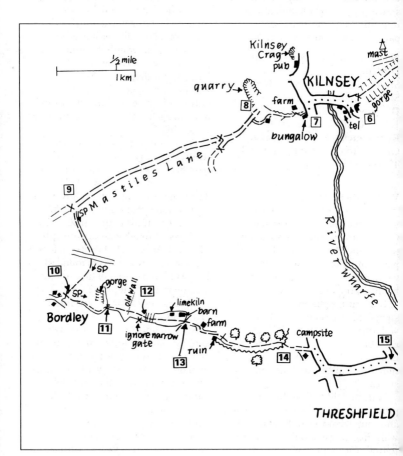

over stile into camp-site. Fork left after 100 yards into caravan area and take stony track just to left of house. After ¼ mile turn right along road and left at crossroads, signposted Grassington. **15** After ¾ mile turn right on road for 150 yards into Threshfield village (**e**). Turn left opposite Old Hall Inn up road to T-junction 150 yards on **16**. Turn right along B6160. After 100 yards turn left on to bridleway, signposted Threshfield School. Cross railway bridge (**f**) and continue in same direction.

17 After 300 yards (at school) turn left along road for 175 yards, then sharp right through narrow gate, to follow path along bank of River Wharfe. After ¼ mile cross river by footbridge and continue on path ½ mile to Grassington, turning left at road at top to return to starting-point.

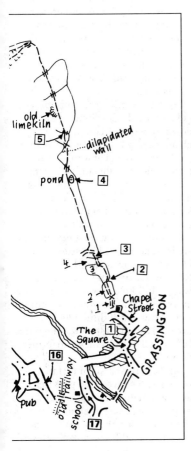

WHAT TO LOOK OUT FOR

(**a**) **Grassington** Bustling stone village with a market square and a medieval bridge. In the 18th and early 19th centuries it was a prosperous lead-mining centre; traces of mining survive on the moors to the N.
(**b**) This gorge, **Conistone Dib**, is a good example of a limestone dry valley, formed by glacial melt-water.
(**c**) **Kilnsey** Centre of the great Pennine estate of Fountains Abbey; sheep were brought here along Mastiles Lane for shearing. Behind the Tennant Arms is the former Kilnsey Hall, built 1648 (now a barn). The highlight of the annual village show is a race up Kilnsey Crag, the imposing limestone mass, a truncated spur shaped by glaciation, and the largest overhang in Britain.
(**d**) **Mastiles Lane** Formerly Strete Gate, an ancient way, probably pre-Roman. In the Middle Ages it was used by monks of Fountains Abbey to reach the abbey's lands in Malham and the Lake District. Controversy raged in the 1960s when it was proposed that it should be tarmacked for motor traffic; happily it remains a green lane.
(**e**) **Threshfield** Former centre of the Wharfedale besom (broom) industry; a small village with stocks on green.
(**f**) **Old railway line** Former branch line from Grassington to Skipton, a section of which has recently re-opened as a private steam railway.

Arncliffe and Moor End Fell

Recommended by Michael Elstob

Leads from one dale to another via grassy upland, with some fine stone villages at the bottom and a riverside path. Could vary the route after 8 by descending to Starbotton and following path by Wharfe back to start. Not all paths defined; follow directions carefully.

Length 8½ miles (13.5km), 4 hours
Difficulty 3–4
Start Kettlewell, on B6160 14 miles N of Skipton. Car park by River Wharfe, at W end of village (fee). Grid reference SD 967723
OS maps 1:50,000 98; 1:25,000 Outdoor Leisure 10
Refreshments Three pubs at Kettlewell. Hotel and café at Arncliffe.

WALK DIRECTIONS

1 (**a**) Turn right out of car park and cross River Wharfe by road-bridge, follow road uphill for 300 yards then, just before Kettlewell village sign (facing other way), fork right through gate on track signposted Hawkswick. This ascends steadily, following yellow marker dots, soon through woodland. At end of woodland continue to follow markers (half right uphill through old enclosures) to reach ladder-stile. Path continues across first large field to next stile **2**.

Continue forward in second field (path eventually becomes indistinct) and, after ½ mile, look out for and cross ladder-stile over wall away to right **3**. Continue forward downhill, on path which bends right 150 yards later (signposted). Descend into hamlet of Hawkswick **4**. Turn right on road through Hawkswick, and shortly after last house cross foot-bridge on left, then immediately turn right (signposted Arncliffe). Path

alongside river is waymarked (**b**). It crosses two footbridges over tributaries in first ½ mile; after second footbridge turn right on edge of field to rejoin river bank.

5 30 yards after leaving bank turn right through gate and immediately left to head for distant stile. Thereafter continue forward until entering village of Arncliffe via waymarked gate on left (church tower is visible just beyond) **6**. To continue walk, turn right on road across bridge (turn left to see village (**c**)). At T-junction turn left, then 300 yards later turn right past farm, signposted to Starbotton. Track is waymarked and ascends steadily.

7 After 1 mile, reach summit at ladder-stile (**d**). Continue forward, downhill with wall on right, changing to other side of wall 300 yards later. At end of wall, continue forward down to distant wall: gateway is 50 yards to left of projecting corner of wall **8**. Head on down, keeping just to left of prominent ruined semi-circular walled enclosure, and turn right beyond it; signpost beyond ladder-stile ahead (do not cross) identifies direction for Kettlewell. After 100 yards, cross wall by low hole in wall (old dog-gate) and continue across fields heading for farm. Near end of third field path is diverted through gap in wall on right; follow yellow markings into former farmyard.

9 Turn right at (former) farm, taking path between old pens (left) and barn (right). Proceed on path alongside wall on left along bottom of field; path soon becomes track and descends steadily towards Kettlewell. At bottom of steepest part of descent, and once level with crags up on right, track reaches gate; continue forward, with wall on left, to reach wood just outside Kettlewell.

WHAT TO LOOK OUT FOR

(**a**) **Kettlewell** Close-knit and compact stone village, formerly very prosperous when three abbeys – Fountains, Bolton and Coverham – all had property here; it was also a lead-mining centre.

(**b**) **River Skirfare** Birds include herons, kingfishers, mallard, oystercatchers, wagtails, sandpipers and dippers.

(**c**) **Arncliffe** Its name means 'eagle's cliff'. Sleepy stone village (familiar to viewers of the television series *Emmerdale Farm*) grouped around a long green with entrances into it from all points of the compass so that villagers could bring in their live-stock from the surrounding pastures in time of attack. S of the village is a well-preserved Celtic field system, with traces of rectangular and circular enclosures.

(**d**) **View** Down Wharfedale, with Great Whernside (2,308ft) straight ahead; village of Starbotton down to left.

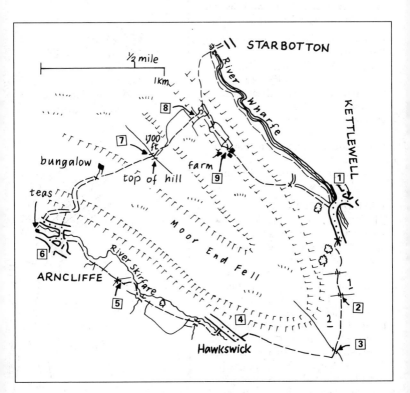

Gordale Scar and Malham Cove

Based on a contribution from Jack Crewe
Recommended by Michael Elstob

A much-visited area (best avoided at summer weekends if you want it to yourself). Three remarkable natural features: Gordale Scar, the limestone pavement and Malham Cove; also takes in some wooded river scenery at Janet's Foss. Short sections of field paths undefined, but route-finding quite easy. Watch your footing as you cross the limestone pavement.

Length 4 miles (6.5km), 2 hours
Difficulty 1–2
Start Malham, 11 miles NW of Skipton. Large car park (fee) at information centre in village. Grid reference SD 900626
OS maps 1:50,000 98; 1:25,000 Outdoor Leisure 2
Refreshments Pub, café and hotel at Malham. Occasionally, refreshment van at entrance to Gordale Scar (high season)

WALK DIRECTIONS

1 Turn left out of car park and into village, turning right over bridge opposite Buck's Inn. After bridge immediately turn right again, doubling back on track, alongside river, leading to stile. Follow this well-trodden path across two fields, then turn left on path signposted Janet's Foss (ignoring path signposted Pennine Way, half right). Path is well signposted and after two fields proceeds alongside river on right. **2** After ½ mile path enters Janet's Foss (wooded gorge) by kissing-gate and NT sign (a). After passing waterfall it continues up to road **3**.

Turn right along road and 150 yards later turn left through gate, signposted Gordale Scar (avoiding, for the moment, first path on left, signposted Malham Cove). Follow up to water-

falls (b) **4**. After viewing Gordale Scar retrace steps to road, turn right, then after 50 yards cross bridge on right and stile beyond it, signposted Malham Cove. Bear immediately half left across first field to corner of wall (yellow marker posts) then continue forward with wall on right to ladder-stile **5**. In second field, continue forward to cross ladder-stile in top right-hand corner and

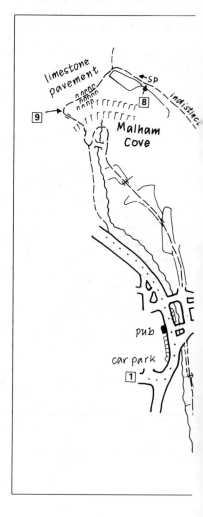

turn left to proceed on clear path with wall on left.

6 ¼ mile later, at corner of wall on left, path continues forward to wall ahead, turns right, then crosses ladder-stile on left 50 yards later, to emerge on road **7**. Turn right on road, then immediately left over stile signposted Malham Cove. Path ascends quarter right over a small rise, from where you can see signpost at top of next rise ¼ mile away; head towards it on grassy path. **8** At signpost to Malham Cove turn left, soon reaching stile and continuing forward (signposted footpath), ignoring path on right, signposted to Malham Tarn. Cross limestone pavement (path undefined), taking care not to stray too far from edge (**c**).

9 At information sign about pavement, head down left to double

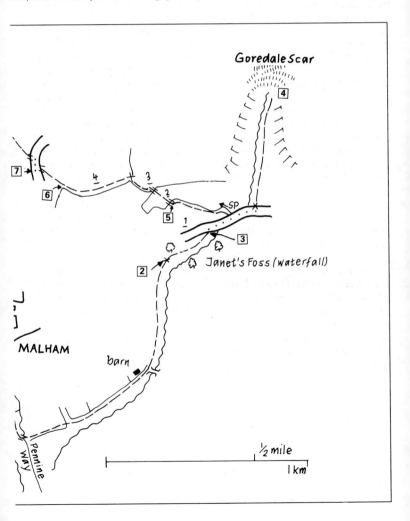

Goredale Scar

Janet's Foss (waterfall)

MALHAM

barn

Pennine way

½ mile
1 km

ladder-stiles. Path then descends steeply to foot of Malham Cove (**d**). At bottom turn left to view cove, then retrace steps and *either* follow well-marked track across fields to lane at edge of Malham (this track teems with visitors at peak times) *or* (if you want more seclusion) 30 yards before Cove, cross stream by stones and follow the left bank. At stile continue forward uphill, cross two fields in direction of signposts heading for ladder-stiles, and in third field continue forward to wall at top (left side) of field and follow easy path back to Malham.

WHAT TO LOOK OUT FOR

(**a**) **Janet's Foss** Wooded gorge, rich in insect, bird and plant life, leading to the Foss (or force) itself, a modest waterfall flowing over a very fine cone of tufa (a limestone incrustation). The cave just behind is the home of Janet, queen of the fairies.

(**b**) **Gordale Scar** Remains hidden until the last moment. Gordale Beck performs a double jump from a stone 'window'. The limestone cliff, standing on the Mid-Craven Fault, was eroded by the stream, which then disappeared underground. The roof of the cavern, which was gouged out, has now collapsed, exposing the stream once more. The scene made a strong impression on early Romantic English landscape artists, including James Ward, whose painting of the Scar (1815) is now in the Tate Gallery. A public footpath leads right up the Scar, but it looks like a good way of damaging yourself.

(**c**) **Limestone pavement** Caused by the dissolving effect of rainwater; often likened to an outsized bar of white chocolate. The fissures are 'grykes' and the blocks are 'clints'. The grykes harbour a number of plants (some rare), including hart's tongue, geranium, wood sorrel, rue, asplenium, enchanter's nightshade and wood garlic.

(**d**) **Malham Cove** 250ft high at its highest point, an inland cliff of limestone, representing one stage before what has happened at Gordale Scar: the cliff has been eroded by the stream, which has now vanished underground, but its cavern has not collapsed yet. The stream re-emerges at the foot of the cove. Probably most of the rock at the bottom was scoured away by glacial action. One of the cove's most significant visits was by Charles Kingsley, who joked that the black lichen marks on the rock could have been caused by a chimney sweep falling over the edge. He later enlarged this idea into the plot of *The Water Babies*, in which Tom, the sweep, meets the water babies in the River Aire. Ruskin and Wordsworth wrote about Malham Cove and in 1786 John Hurtley recorded the excellence of its five-fold echo: 'a most pleasing effect in a calm and clear evening from a French horn or any other instrument'.

Ingleborough and Gaping Gill

Contributed by Graham Fullarton
Recommended by R C Hibbert,
B H and M J James

Takes in one of England's grandest views, from the flat top of Ingleborough summit, followed by a descent studded with potholes and other limestone features, including Gaping Gill, a rocky gorge, and Ingleborough Cave. A leisurely ascent at the start, apart from the short slog to the summit. Mostly on well-defined paths, but in mist finding the way off the summit is difficult; compass essential. Check bus times before travelling, for trip back.

Length 8 miles (13km), 5 hours
Difficulty 3–4
Start Ingleton, at car park by information centre on A65. Finish at Clapham; return by bus (frequent service)
OS maps 1:50,000 98; 1:25,000 Outdoor Leisure 2
Refreshments Pubs and cafés in Ingleton; New Inn, Clapham

WALK DIRECTIONS

1 From car park by information centre in Ingleton turn right on road through village and up to T-junction, then left along road signposted Hawes. Just beyond last house on right, turn right, signposted Ingleborough. Track ascends alongside wall on right for 50 yards, but then be sure to bear half left up to gateway in left-hand corner of pasture 2. Track runs between walls, then ½ mile later continues gently uphill to Ingleborough (a). Last portion of ascent is much steeper, track is rougher and marked by cairns.

3 At top (b), continue forward between trig. point (right) and stone shelter (left) to reach small cairn on edge. Turn right along edge, passing large cairn after 200 yards; turn left at next cairn to find track leading down to prominent ridge and then (less well-defined) up to Little Ingleborough, the minor peak. At top of rise, look down for track descending quarter left, and identify fenced hollow ¼ mile distant (not very prominent but identifiable further down), just to left of main track. This is Gaping Gill; minor path leads straight to it (c) 4.

With Ingleborough behind you and Gaping Gill on left, turn right on path, and then left 100 yards later, rejoining main track to continue descent. No difficulty finding route from here: ¼ mile later it crosses ladder-stile and path turns on right beyond. It is very clear as it descends through rocky gorge and soon passes entrance to Ingleborough Cave (d). At woods, ½ mile later, route enters nature reserve (e). 5 At road turn left and follow through Clapham to T-junction at end. Bus-stop is on right, by post office.

WHAT TO LOOK OUT FOR

(a) As Ingleborough comes into view the layering of **millstone grit** and **limestone** is apparent. The rocks change rapidly as you ascend: Silurian slates, Great Scar limestone, shales, sandstones and finally limestone on the flat summit, all bedded horizontally.

(b) **Summit** See view-indicator by stone shelter: E to Ribblehead railway viaduct, on the Carlisle line, and the flat-topped Pen y Ghent (2,278ft); NW to Whernside (2,416ft); S to Forest of Bowland (1,839ft). On a clear day, over Morecambe Bay and into the Lake District. The summit is the site of an Iron Age hill village; you can still just make out the hut circles. Quite a lot of it survived well into the 19th century, when someone had the idea of demolishing it and using the stones to build a tower, which then promptly fell to pieces.

Ingleborough, Whernside and Pen y Ghent together constitute the Three Peaks, the mountain group famous as a challenge route: two schoolmasters were the first to walk the 27-mile circuit in a day in 1887. It has since been the target for thousands of walkers and athletes; the record time is just under 2½ hours.

(c) **Gaping Gill** Above ground, a sink 20ft by 8ft. The stream plunges out of sight into a 340ft underground waterfall, the highest in Britain. St Paul's Cathedral could fit easily into the huge chamber at the bottom. Occasionally (in the 10 days before the spring and summer bank

holidays), you can be lowered by winching-chair into the chamber. The organisers drily point out that the descent is free; you only pay to come up again.

(d) **Ingleborough Cave** (open to public; fee) A show-cave ever since J W Farrer opened it in 1837. Has a great sculptured canyon known as the Long Gallery, very fine concretions, underground pools and 15 miles of connecting tunnels and chambers leading to Gaping Gill.

(e) **Reginald Farrer trail** Landscaped trees, at their best in spring and autumn; pay fee at cottage at far end.

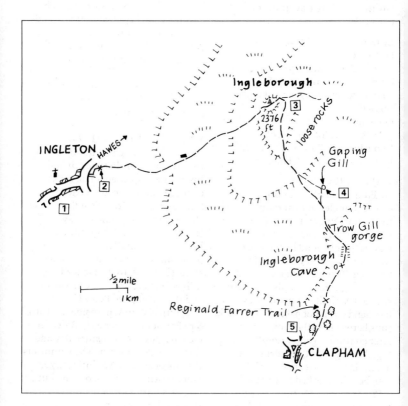

Upper Nidderdale

Contributed by John Hone
Recommended by Dr and Mrs T S
Worthy

**A high-level moorland track follows
east side of dale, coming down to
cross end of Scar House Reservoir.
Track then runs mostly between
dry-stone walls to Middlesmoor;
return to Lofthouse across pasture
fields. Care needed with directions
just after 2 and 4; otherwise
route-finding easy. Ascent 1,200ft.**

Length 11 miles (17.5km), 5 hours
Difficulty 4
Start Lofthouse, on minor road

6 miles NW of Pateley Bridge,
19 miles NW of Harrogate. Car park in
front of village hall, near post office.
Grid reference SE 102735
OS maps 1:50,000 99;
1:25,000 Outdoor Leisure 30
Refreshments Pub and shops in
Middlesmoor

WALK DIRECTIONS
1 With car park behind you, turn
right up village street, past war
memorial. 150 yards beyond end of
village fork left on to track, signposted Nidderdale. After first gate
avoid right fork up through gate, and
do the same at second gate. ½ mile
later, track reaches Thrope Farm 2.

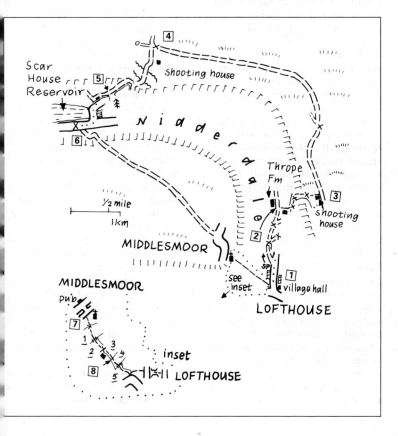

Turn right immediately before farm, keeping pens on your right, through gate and then alongside stone barn on right. From barn bear uphill (path undefined) to gate in fence ahead. Beyond gate turn left along fence to pass through second gate after 50 yards, then immediately turn right on path to ascend hill steeply, with fence on right. 50 yards later forest appears on right of path, and path bends left and ascends to gate. Continue up (no path) to shooting-house on skyline ③.

Just behind shooting-house, find clear track and turn left along it. After 1 mile this passes through gate. Continue forward beyond it, avoiding descending left fork. Track is quite straightforward to follow. ④ After another 2 miles reach gate with 'bridlepath only, no motorcycles' sign. Turn left immediately beyond, on to cross-track (a). This turns right after 200 yards (shooting-house on left beyond wall).

In next ½ mile track dips down twice to cross streams in small ravines: 100 yards after second stream, reach wall and turn sharp right uphill away from wall. Track rises to reach gate then continues across moor to reach corner of wall 300 yards later ⑤. Continue forward, alongside wall on left. Track soon descends, and after ¼ mile turn sharp left by 'private road' sign to descend to road at Scar House reservoir (b). Turn right to cross reservoir dam, and on other side turn right.

⑥ Turn sharp left just before gate, signposted Nidderdale Way. Route for next 2 miles to Middlesmoor is obvious. ⑦ At Middlesmoor (c), pass through village, forking left on cobbled lane just after passing pub on your right. At end of lane, turn right to find path to right of churchyard,

signposted Lofthouse. Steps lead across first field aiming for squeeze-stile. Clear path follows left edge of second field, then continues forward past farm to enter third field, following right edge to next squeeze-stile ⑧.

In fourth field, continue forward along right edge to cross stile 30 yards to left of far right-hand corner, then bear quarter left across fifth field to stile leading on to corner of road. Turn immediately left through kissing-gate signposted Nidd Head, and cross next road for signposted footpath that crosses footbridge (d) and leads up into Lofthouse.

WHAT TO LOOK OUT FOR

(a) 150 yards straight on is a fenced **mine shaft** of immense depth (try dropping a stone down it).

(b) **Scar House and Angram Reservoirs** Developed to provide water for Bradford; 30 million gallons are piped daily, via the River Wharfe aqueduct near Bolton Abbey. The road crossed on the far side of the dam is the line of the former Nidderdale light railway. Built in 1907 for transporting materials for the construction of the dams, it carried passengers for a brief period, and closed on completion of the Scar House Reservoir in 1936.

(c) **Middlesmoor** Perched on a hilltop overlooking the confluence of the Nidder and How Stean valleys, a collection of cottages huddled round a few cobbled streets. Church of St Chad dominates the view for miles around, though close up it is something of a disappointment; entirely 19th-century, though it contains an 11th-century Saxon cross-head.

(d) Just before the river bridge, recross the light railway and pass close to the former **Lofthouse station**.

Sutton Bank and Gormire Lake

Recommended by Alan Williams

The inland cliff of Sutton Bank is seen first from its wooded base, then after a steepish 500ft ascent, from its level top. Takes in part of Gormire Lake, a rich habitat for plant- and bird-life. Mostly on well-defined paths and tracks, though less clear just after 8 ; route-finding moderately easy.

Length 7½ miles (12km), 3½ hours
Difficulty 3
Start Small car park (free) ½ mile N of Kilburn and 7 miles E of Thirsk. Take road leading N out of Kilburn, signposted White Horse Bank/Old Stead, turn left after ½ mile, signposted White Horse Bank. Car park is 150 yards on left, by 'parking ½ mile' sign (referring to next car park). Grid reference SE 515806
OS maps 1:50,000 100; 1:25,000 Outdoor Leisure 26
Refreshments Café/kiosk at Sutton Bank car park

WALK DIRECTIONS

1 Turn right out of the car park (towards Kilburn) then, after 30 yards, right on to track. 2 Keep forward after 200 yards where main track turns left to farm. Track narrows to path, enters woods, then widens. 3 Continue forward on joining stony forest track. Ignore grassy right fork at top of rise. 4 After ¼ mile, fork left (at fork of stony forest tracks).

5 After ½ mile, farmland appears briefly on right of track. 50 yards later, where track bends left, turn right on narrow path signposted 'bridleway' (signpost was rickety at inspection), soon emerging into field (a). Continue forward towards farm. 6 Left along fence in front of farm, then right after 100 yards, over waymarked stile. Left on farm road. 7 Turn right on main road, then left

on farm road after 100 yards. Keep forward at farm, soon on rutted grassy track across field to gate 8 .

Turn right beyond gate, descending alongside fence on right (no path) into woods; here, pick up clear path, crossing stile on right after 50 yards. Beyond stile, path leads to left, then bends right, then bends left again (at rough T-junction of paths) to ascend steadily. 9 After 250 yards lake comes into view; descend to lakeside path, turn right along it (b). After end of lake, and 50 yards before the gate ahead, turn left to pick up path following other side of lake.

10 Beyond end of lake path crosses wooden duckboards; ignore the signposted turn to Garbutt Wood on right (c), but 20 yards later turn right, signposted Thirlby Bank. Path winds uphill for ¾ mile – the hardest part of the walk. 11 Turn sharp right at top of ridge (d), and follow to road 12 . Turn left on main road (information centre/refreshments to left) then right 30 yards later, signposted White Horse Walk.

13 After 1 mile, pass hill-carving of the White Horse (e), then immediately descend by steps on right, to main car park. Continue out of car park and on to road. 14 Turn right on road, follow to car park.

WHAT TO LOOK OUT FOR

(a) **View** The Jurassic sandstone cliffs on your right were undercut by glacial melt-water running between the ice mass on the plain (where you are now) and the escarpment.
(b) **Lake Gormire** One of only three natural lakes in Yorkshire (the others are Semerwater and Malham Tarn); alleged to be bottomless. Glacial landslips dammed the flow of glacial melt-water (see (a)) to create the lake. **Birds** Important breeding-place for wildfowl, including wild ducks, coots and great-crested grebes. Some rare **flora**, including tufted loosestrife. On

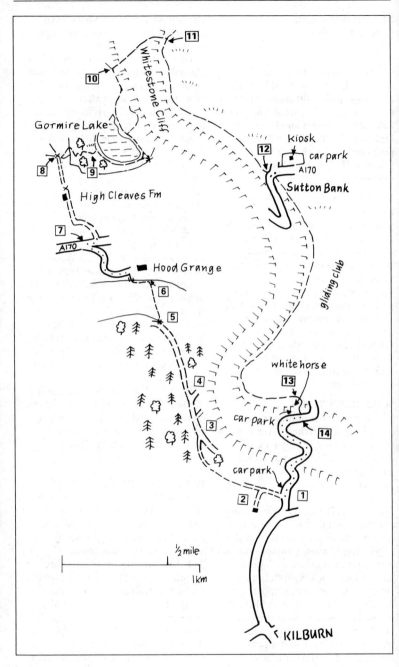

the far side you pass the edge of Garbutts Wood, a nature reserve of mixed woodland which supports various wildlife, in particular, badgers, deer and foxes.

(**c**) Alan Williams recommends taking the Garbutt Wood path here and following the nature trail below the escarpment and then up the sloping path to the ridge. This has the advantage of breaking up the climb and giving a view of the cliff itself. The disadvantage is that you miss the views from Whitestone Cliff, 'though there are plenty of views from the rest of the ridge path'.

(**d**) **Whitestone Cliff** and **Sutton Bank** View over Plain of York and Vale of Mowbray to the Pennines, including Great Whernside (2,308ft) in the Yorkshire Dales, and Penhill (1,792ft) just N of it; S to York Minster and the cooling towers of Ferrybridge power station 35 miles away. **Birds** include merlins, harriers and, occasionally, peregrine falcons. At Sutton Bank there may be gliders from the adjacent airfield; you are told to 'beware of hanging towlines'.

(**e**) **The White Horse** Carved into the hill, measuring 314ft by 228ft. It was marked out by the schoolmaster and pupils of Kilburn school in 1857.

Ryedale and Rievaulx Abbey

Recommended by T S and H J Worthy

Begins through flat farmland on a plateau, but suddenly reaches the partly wooded valley of Ryedale, with the slopes framing a view of the ruins of Rievaulx Abbey. Returns along a quiet road, then past fish ponds and through woods and fields. Not all field paths well defined, but route-finding moderately easy.

Length 6 miles (9.5km), 2½ hours
Difficulty 2
Start Village green, Old Byland, 8 miles ENE of Thirsk. From top of Sutton Bank on A170 (Helmsley to Thirsk), take minor road leading NE and follow signposts to Cold Kirby, immediately before which turn left on narrow road to Old Byland. Grid reference SE 550858
OS maps 1:50,000 100; 1:25,000 Outdoor Leisure 26
Refreshments Ice-cream and teas at cottage 150 yards from Rievaulx Abbey

WALK DIRECTIONS

1 (a) From village green, with phone box on left, follow road up to T-junction, at which turn right. 200 yards later, opposite last house, turn left over ladder-stile (by footpath signpost). Follow left edge of two fields **2**. At end of second field turn right (signposted) and proceed with fence on left through four more fields. **3** Emerge on to track (ignore gate away to right). Keep forward, heading towards barn ¼ mile away (b). At barn continue forward (track undefined for short distance), and head down towards farm (c).

4 Just before farm turn right along farm approach road and proceed above River Rye with views towards Rievaulx Abbey (d). **5** After ¾ mile take next turn left down track leading to bridge over River Rye. **6** 150

yards past bridge take stile signposted Rievaulx into field on right. Keep close by river and follow yellow markers, over two stiles in close succession (e), then along left edge of fields. Track then leads towards Abbey.

7 *To detour* to Rievaulx Terraces (f) turn left up to B-road for ½ mile to terraces entrance. *To continue* turn right on road through Rievaulx village, past Abbey entrance on left (g) to reach T-junction at Rievaulx

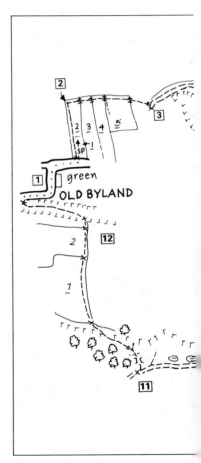

Bridge ½ mile later **8**. Turn right over bridge, still following road. You are now on the Cleveland Way. **9** After 500 yards ignore turning on right to Old Byland but continue straight ahead. **10** ½ mile later take track on right leading to gate (acorn sign). This leads through woodland and past fish-breeding ponds on right.

11 After ½ mile, just before gate ahead, turn right (acorn sign) over footbridge, and into woods by kissing-gate. 10 yards beyond kissing-gate take right-hand path at fork, then immediately ignore another right fork but continue to stile and across another stile/bridge. Follow the path uphill to left through woods and ¼ mile ahead follow Old Byland signpost through gate at top of rise, to walk alongside hedge on right edge of two fields. Old Byland shortly comes into view.

12 Cross farm approach road and go through another gate ahead. Path then turns to left down gradual slope

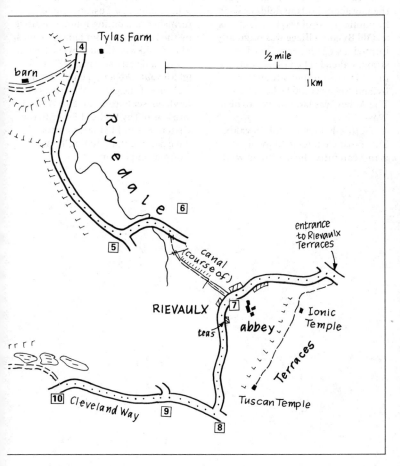

to valley bottom and then up other side to gate in fence bordering road (or cut off small corner by turning right up to electricity pole). Turn right and return to village green at Old Byland.

WHAT TO LOOK OUT FOR
(**a**) **Old Byland church** has well-preserved Norman work. Saxon sundial outside is inscribed 'Huscarl made me for Sumerlethi'.
(**b**) Checkers on two occasions have reported a **'bull in field' sign** here, but it appears to a bluff (see page 19 for the law about bulls in fields crossed by public rights of way).
(**c**) **Old Byland village** was originally located near Tylas Farm, the farm straight ahead. The village was moved to its present site so that Byland Abbey could be built here. The Abbey was later moved to near Wass.
(**d**) Picture-book views of **Rievaulx.** Like most Cistercian foundations, it is in a carefully chosen site in wild country with a water supply. In the Abbey's heyday the valley would have been richly wooded.
(**e**) Between these stiles you cross the line of an old **canal**, built as an additional water supply to Rievaulx Abbey.
(**f**) **Rievaulx Terraces** (NT; open to public; fee) Fine example of 18th-century landscaping; created as a pleasure garden by Thomas Duncombe in 1758. A grassy terrace with trees, ½ mile long, it has a mock temple at either end, one Tuscan, the other Ionic. The Tuscan temple, furnished as a dining-room, was used by the Duncombes for family picnics. Many wild woodland flowers, best in spring and early summer (NT; fee).
(**g**) **Rievaulx Abbey** (open to public; fee) One of the great abbey ruins of England, set N to S (not E to W) on a site granted by Walter l'Espec to the Cistercians in 1131. Many artists have painted it, including Turner, Cotman and Girtin.

Crosscliff and the Bridestones

Contributed by S G McCluskey
Recommended by John Hone,
Brian Marsden, Geoffrey White,
Mr and Mrs B H James, M Futers

**Lonely moors punctuated by some
striking features, including the
conical hill Whinny Nab, the
Bridestones and a number of ancient
cairns. One section through planted
forestry is quickly passed thanks to
good waymarking. All tracks and
paths well defined, except briefly,
just before** 12.

Length 9 miles (14.5km), 4½ hours
Difficulty 2–3
Start Car park 8 miles NNE of
Pickering on A169, ¼ mile S of the
Saltergate Inn. Car park on right of
road as you come from Pickering, just
before road hairpins steeply downhill.
Grid reference SE 853937
OS maps 1:50,000 94;
1:25,000 Outdoor Leisure 27
Refreshments Saltergate Inn, just N
of start

WALK DIRECTIONS

1 From car park turn right on to
main road for 100 yards (in Whitby
direction), then turn right on
signposted public footpath. 2 150
yards later go through gate then
immediately left on track following
edge of plantation on your left. 50
yards after next gate track bends
right, away from plantation. 3
¼ mile after next gate avoid left fork,
downhill. Track soon descends to
reach Malo Cross (**a**) 4. Turn right,
in front of cross, on clear moorland
track which leads along valley, with
forest away to left. At gate, track
narrows to path, and reaches second
gate ½ mile after cross. Continue up
towards farm, crossing stile to
emerge on farm track 5.

Turn left on track downhill (away

from farm), heading towards the
prominent hillock, Blakey Topping
(which you can climb), in front of
which track bends right. 6 300 yards
later, by standing stones, track bends
left through gate (**b**). Track bends
right 200 yards later, then crosses
moorland (**c**). 7 Pass farm and cross
stream by bridge (just to left of track);
follow track for another ½ mile to
T-junction. Turn right and follow the
track which ascends through trees to
the junction of five tracks at top of
ridge 8.

Turn sharp right (path is narrow at
first) and immediately reach the
Crosscliff viewpoint and blue marker
post (**d**). From the view-indicator
continue on same path for 600 yards.
Look for further blue marker posts.
9 After less than 10 minutes' walking, turn left as directed by marker
and follow the posts 1 mile through
forest to road 10. Turn left, then right
through car park and along right side
of Staindale Water, soon emerging on
road. Turn left along it, and 300 yards
later turn right by sign with map of
Staindale, into another car park. Head
across picnic area towards NT sign,
then towards second sign, for
Bridestones (**e**) 11.

Immediately fork left up slope,
through trees to Low Bridestones.
Follow path down across small ravine
and up to High Bridestones. Turn
right at T-junction by these. At final
Bridestone path narrows and follows
moorland hillside, with valley of
Dovedale down on left. ½ mile later
path turns right, and where it peters
out make your own way across the
heather, heading towards left corner
of forest 300 yards ahead. Turn left on
track just before forest. 12 Keep
straight on where track comes in
sharply from right (**f**). 13 10 minutes'
walking brings you to the end of the
moorland at edge of escarpment.
Keep forward on farm road, back to
car park.

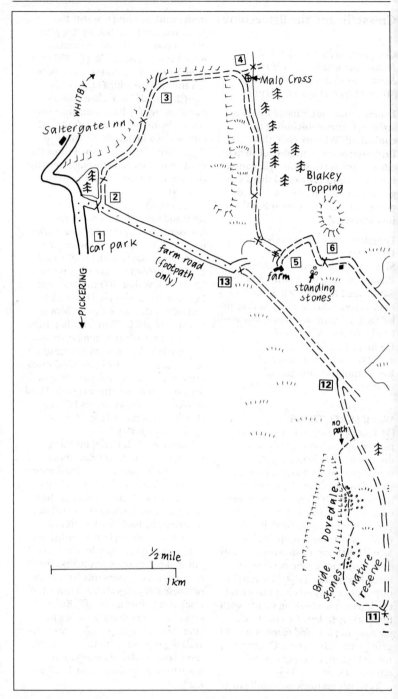

WHAT TO LOOK OUT FOR

(**a**) One of several ancient crosses on the North York Moors, and almost intact, **Malo Cross** is an ancient waymark on the old salt route, along which salt for preserving fish was carried to Whitby.

(**b**) **Standing stones** Three still upright stones, formerly part of a stone circle; other stones visible nearby. They were probably erected between 1600 and 1000BC.

(**c**) The moorland here has been deliberately conserved to retain landscape variety. Away to the left, on a spur above the stream, are nearly a hundred ancient **cairns**.

(**d**) The view is described on the indicator; most of it by now familiar. Away to right, the ballistic missile early warning system radomes, three giant golfball-like structures, each of a diameter of 140ft; erected 1961–2.

(**e**) **Bridestones nature reserve** Entered through an oak wood, a surviving fragment of the great forest that covered the area before early settlers burned it down. On the moorland beyond, the Bridestones, two groups of weathered Jurassic sandstone rocks, whose mushroom shape is due to alternating bands of hard siliceous and weak calcareous rock. Formed about 60,000 years ago, they will eventually weather away completely.

(**f**) Final stretch is along an ancient packhorse track called **the Old Wife's Way**. At the car park at the end, cross over to get a view into the Hole of Horcum, the deep valley of Levisham Beck.

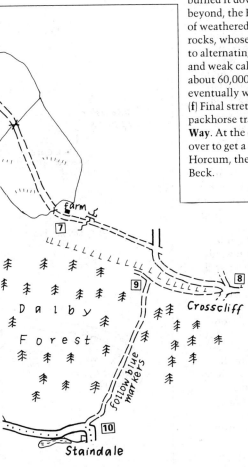

Roseberry Topping

*Based on contributions from
Geoffrey White, R C S Wilson*

**A small hill that looks like a pudding
basin, with a 360-degree view from
the top. Approached by moorland
tracks, with a short section at the
edge of planted forest. Easy
route-finding.**

Length 4 miles (6.5km), 2 hours
Difficulty 1–2
Start Free car parks at Gribdale Gate,
2 miles E of Great Ayton or 1 mile E
of railway station
By train Great Ayton (Whitby to
Darlington line). Turn right out of
station, on road. ¾ mile later, at
hamlet of Gribdale Terrace, keep
straight on where road bends left, to
enter field by stile, then follow left
edge of fields up to car parks. Grid
reference NZ 592110
OS maps 1:50,000 93 and 94;
1:25,000 Outdoor Leisure 26

WALK DIRECTIONS

1 From car park nearer to Great
Ayton, cross cattle-grid and turn half
left on to track signposted bridleway
(not sharper left, up steps, signposted
Cleveland Way). Track rises
on to moorland. **2** After ¼ mile,
avoid left fork which leads towards
forest. 120 yards later keep forward
at junction of tracks. Track curves
round (a) to reach corner of forest
(¾ mile) **3**.

   Turn left at corner of forest, on
wide track (which is continuation of
road). **4** After 1 mile, reach forest.
Pass through gate, then immediately left on track (this is the Cleveland Way) which follows (inside)
edge of forest. **5** Pass through
gate in wall on left ½ mile later
to follow track gently uphill over
moorland.

   6 After ½ mile, reach gate at
corner of forest; sharp left is return
route. Pass through gate and ascend

to Roseberry Topping, the prominent
hill ¼ mile away (b) **7**. Retrace steps
from Roseberry Topping to gate at
corner of woodland, then turn right
and follow track alongside wall back
to car park.

WHAT TO LOOK OUT FOR

(a) **View** Right (SE) down over
Lonsdale, towards the North York
Moors railway near Kildale.
(b) **Roseberry Topping** Once thought
to be Yorkshire's highest mountain

1½ miles high, according to an 18th-century play). It is in fact only 1,057ft, but the panorama extends right round: N and NE to Teesside (Tees transporter bridge, Redcar steelworks and Hartlepool over the estuary); W over the Vale of York and towards the Pennines; S along the scarp edge of the North York Moors. The nearest hill S is topped by huge (60ft) stone monument (its size is its main distinction) to Captain Cook, put up by Robert Campion, a Whitby banker, in 1827. Cook went to school in Great Ayton (the schoolhouse is now a Cook museum) and had his first job at Airey Holme farm, the right-hand of the two nearest farms to the S. The quarries on Roseberry were for ironstone and whinstone extraction; this was one of the most intensively worked areas in N England. The terrace of cottages passed between Great Ayton station and the car park were built for quarrymen.

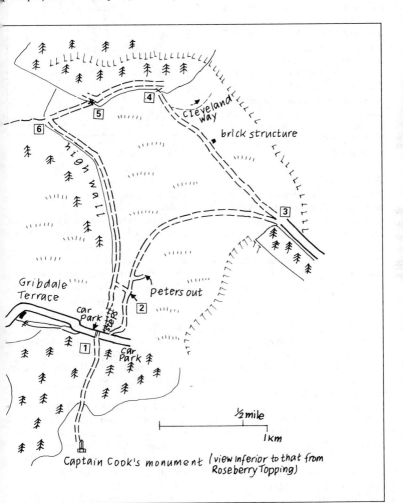

Captain Cook's monument (view inferior to that from Roseberry Topping)

North York Moors Railway and Mallyan Spout

A short exploration of the original route of this railway as far as Beck Hole; return by steam or diesel train (check times before starting). Pasture and woodland, with a fine waterfall near the end. All on defined paths and tracks; route-finding quite easy.

Length 4½ miles (7km), 2 hours
Difficulty 1
Start Grosmont station (North Yorks Moors Railway and BR), 7 miles SW of Whitby. Large car park (fee). Return by North York Moors Railway from Goathland. Grid reference NZ 828052
OS maps 1:50,000 94; 1:25,000 Outdoor Leisure 27
Refreshments Station Tavern and café at station, Grosmont; Beech Hall Inn (bar food, teas), Beck Hole; Mallyan and Goathland Hotels, Goathland

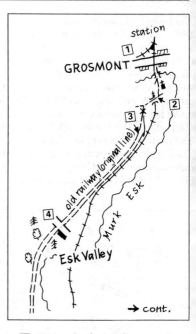

WALK DIRECTIONS

1 Left out of station car park on to road, then right just after level crossing, signposted Goathland/Loco Shed. Path crosses small suspension bridge, then immediately forks: fork left (signposted Goathland) up past church (**a**). **2** When level with end of churchyard, reach T-junction of paths and turn right (soon past viewpoint for watching trains) 100 yards later, left through gate (signposted public footpath). Path soon descends alongside fence to railway (**b**) **3**.

At railway (and loco yard) you are now following old railway track (soon leaving working railway). ½ mile later reach road at hamlet of Esk Valley (**c**) **4**. Cross road, continue on old railway line opposite. Follow for 1½ miles. **5** Turn right just after gate/stile (signposted Egton Bridge). Do not cross railway bridge 30 yards later, but turn left, signposted Goathland (**d**).

6 100 yards after path crosses artificial stepping stones, keep straight on, signposted Goathland; left turn to Beck Hole is optional for pub/teas. 80 yards later, opposite Incline Cottage (**e**), turn right through gate marked 'To the Mallyan'. Clear path proceeds alongside fence on right, uphill then later downhill. **7** After ½ mile reach signpost for Mallyan Spout ahead, Goathland left. Follow river 200 yards to Mallyan Spout (**f**). Retrace steps to signpost and take path uphill to Goathland. **8** Left on road (**g**), then fork right ½ mile later in centre of village. Railway station is 600 yards along, on left of road.

WHAT TO LOOK OUT FOR

(**a**) **Grosmont church** Its original building was funded by the railway company, which sold cheap day tickets to a fête in the village in 1839. Building started the next year; it was rebuilt 1879–80.
(**b**) On descending to the level of the

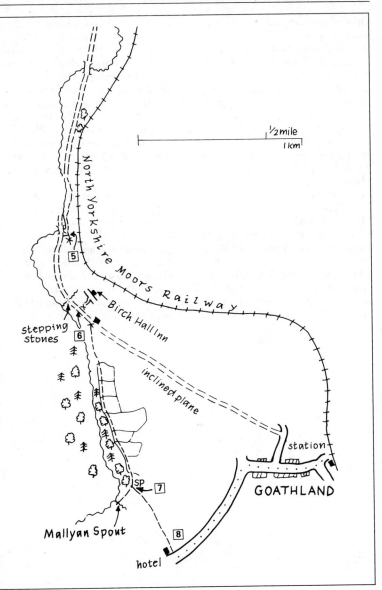

1/2 mile
1 km

North Yorkshire Moors Railway

5

Birch Hall Inn

stepping
stones

6

inclined plane

station

7 SP

GOATHLAND

Mallyan Spout

8

hotel

railway, you join the course of the original railway, opened in 1836 as the **Whitby and Pickering Railway**, running for its first 11 years as a horse-drawn tramway. The working ('deviation') line on the left has a siding with a sizeable collection of old carriages and locomotives.

(**c**) **Esk Valley** An incongruous terrace of cottages, built for workers at the local ironstone and whinstone mines. 1 mile later, in the wood, the path climbs steps; piers of the old railway bridge are visible on the opposite bank of the river.

(**d**) Soon pass **Beck Hole station** (signboard). Closed in 1865, it had a brief renaissance between 1908 and 1914.

(**e**) **Incline Cottage** Originally a railway cottage (remains of an original sleeper is below one of its windows), getting its name from the inclined portion of the original line which rises beyond it. The incline (which you can follow to Goathland if you prefer to omit Mallyan Spout) runs from here up a 1 in 15 slope to Goathland; it was fraught with problems, being too steep for horses or steam traction, and in 1865 the deviation line was built by blasting away large sections of bedrock. The line closed in 1965, but was reopened by a private company of enthusiasts in 1973.

(**f**) **Mallyan Spout** (take care on slippery rocks) A 70ft cascade of a tributary stream into the wooded Eller Beck.

(**g**) **Goathland** A long village street with wide grassy verges, grazed by sheep. Occasionally a venue for traditional sword-dancing. At summer weekends the parked cars outnumber even the sheep.

Robin Hood's Bay

Contributed by Alan Williams

First along the old railway line to Robin Hood's Bay – which ranks among England's prettiest seaside villages – then back along the beach and sandstone cliffs. The Whitby–Robin Hood's Bay–Ravenscar–Scarborough bus service can be used to split walk in two. All paths well defined and signposted or waymarked; easy route-finding.

Length 7½ miles (12km), 3½ hours
Difficulty 2
Start Car park (free) at Ravenscar (large demarcated verge by road, by entrance drive to Raven Hall Hotel), midway between Scarborough and Whitby. Grid reference NZ 980016
OS maps 1:50,000 94;
1:25,000 Outdoor Leisure 27
Refreshments Hotel and café at Ravenscar; plenty of pubs and tea-rooms in Robin Hood's Bay; house on old railway track (1 mile from start) occasionally serves tea – look out for noticeboards

WALK DIRECTIONS

1 (**a**) From road/car parking area, with entrance to Raven Hall Hotel behind you, take second path on right, signposted Cleveland Way and leading past NT shop/information centre. Ignore right turn after 100 yards by NT sign. **2** 100 yards later turn left by geological trail post, to lead on to old railway track (**b**). Follow for 3 (easy) miles (**c**).

3 Descend to road by steps and take steps opposite to regain old railway (avoid immediate path fork on left). **4** After 1 mile cross road and continue on old railway opposite. **5** 500 yards later take ladder-stile on right, signposted public footpath. Bear half left across field to gate in left-hand corner. Proceed alongside fence on left through two fields; path becomes clearly trodden and leads

¼ mile into Robin Hood's Bay (**d**) (**e**).

6 *If high tide* take right turn immediately before road ends at rocky foreshore in village, leading up stone steps, then 50 yards later keep right (signposted 'cliff path'). In first mile, path descends to two inlets, crossing footbridge each time.

If low tide descend to foreshore/beach and turn right along it. After ½ mile pass Boggle Hole Youth Hostel and footbridge at inlet on right, then 500 yards later leave beach for next footbridge in next inlet, to maintain direction up path with handrail.

7 Path ascends to road. Continue forward along it for 300 yards then left over stile (Cleveland Way signpost) on to cliff-top. **8** After ½ mile, turn right as signposted, to leave cliff-top, walking alongside fence on left. 50 yards before end of field, left over stile. Clear path follows right edge of field to reach gate, then forward on track, keeping left 50 yards later (signposted Cleveland Way). **9** ½ mile later, fork right as waymarked and follow back to start.

WHAT TO LOOK OUT FOR

(**a**) **Ravenscar** Planned as an Edwardian seaside resort. Pavements, roads and drains were laid out, but the distance to the beach and the unstable ground deterred developers from building villas. If you find the place intriguing, go and look at the failed parade of shops in Station Road. The Raven Hall Hotel is much older, dating from the 18th century; built on the site of a Roman signal station.

(**b**) Old **alum quarries** and overgrown **spoil heaps** are visible on the left, and it is possible to make out lines of shale, sandstone and ironstone. The alum, processed with human urine shipped in from London beer-houses, was used as a fixer for dyes. A good

417

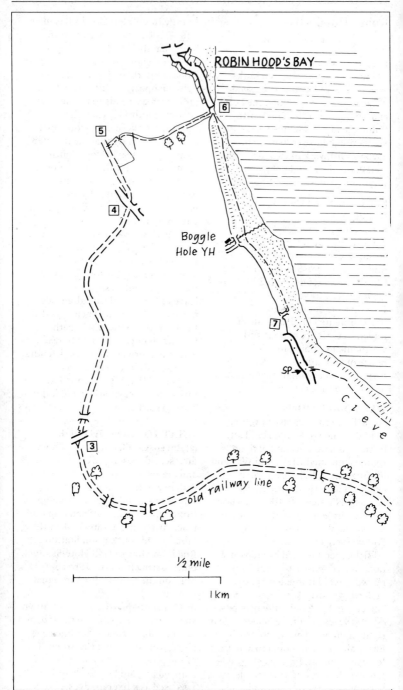

ROBIN HOOD'S BAY

6

5

4

Boggle
Hole YH

7

SP

Cleve

3

old railway line

½ mile

1 km

place for fossil-collecting.

(c) **Old railway line** Used to run along the Yorkshire coast, from Seamer Junction, near Scarborough, to Whitby and beyond, to Saltburn. Opened in 1885, closed 1965.

(d) **Robin Hood's Bay** So steep that the window of one house looks on to the roof of its neighbour. It was one of the most notorious spots for smuggling on the E coast, and many of the houses have smugglers' cupboards – recesses between the party walls for hiding in when the excise men were at large. Robin Hood is said to have kept his boats here for use as getaways, and he is also supposed to have seen off some marauding Danish pirates at the request of Abbot Richard of Whitby, in the mid 12th century. Some houses in the village have curious bow windows, called coffin windows, built so that passers-by could pay their last respects.

(e) **Beach** Expanse of sand and rock pools, another excellent place for fossils.

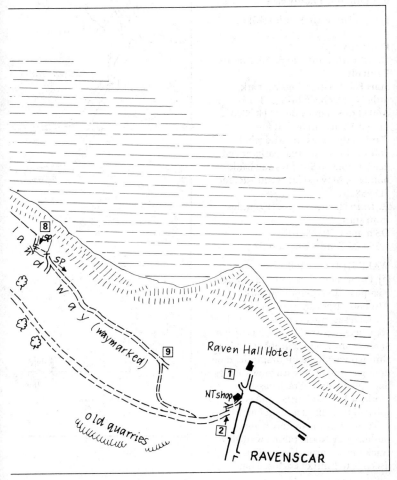

Hebden Dale and Hardcastle Crags

Contributed by Mark Denham
Recommended by Michael Elstob

A figure-of-eight route based on two dales and the moorland lying in between, following a level riverside path along wooded Hebden Dale past the outcrops of Hardcastle Crags and a ruined mill at the end. A permissive moorland path is followed in the second loop (closed off some days in shooting season; notices displayed), past reservoirs. Paths well defined; route-finding mainly easy.

Length *Full walk* 8 miles (13km), 4½ hours
Difficulty 2–3
Short walk 4 miles (6.5km), 2 hours
Difficulty 2
Start Hardcastle Crags car park, 1 mile N of Hebden Bridge. Take A6033 to Keighley out of Hebden Bridge, then turn off left for Hardcastle Crags and Midgehole. Follow this road to car parks at end (fee payable on Sundays and bank holidays, May to Oct). Grid reference SD 988291
By train Hebden Bridge (1¼ miles from start)
OS maps 1:50,000 103; 1:25,000 Outdoor Leisure 21

WALK DIRECTIONS

1 From car park follow road to right (signposted 'Overspill car park'). After 80 yards turn right on road through secondary car park, which soon becomes track and leads up left side of valley. This climbs steadily up through woodland for first mile, then emerges into open with views across and down valley. Track passes working farm at Laithe, and is follwed to disused farm at Nook **2**.

Turn left immediately before buildings at Nook, taking walled track uphill through gate. This ascends to limit of enclosed land,

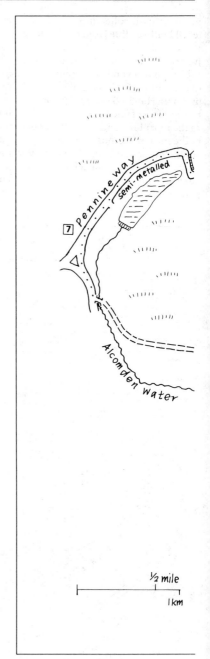

½ mile

1 km

420

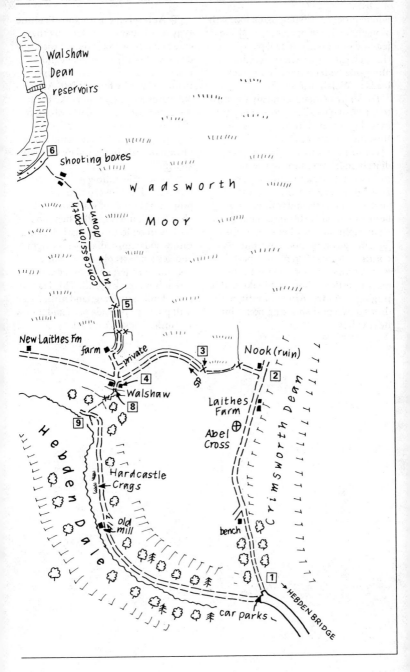

Walshaw Dean reservoirs

6 shooting boxes

W a d s w o r t h

M o o r

concession path down up

5

New Laithes Fm

farm

private

3

Nook (ruin)

2

4

Walshaw

8

9

Laithes Farm

Abel Cross ⊕

H e b d e n   D a l e

Hardcastle Crags

old mill

C r i m s w o r t h   D e a n

bench

1

car parks

HEBDEN BRIDGE

where proceed on signposted footpath along left edge of open moor. ③ On leaving moor (signposted) pass through gate and then turn right, alongside wall on right. This track leads to Walshaw farm ④.

For short walk enter farmyard, turn left, to leave left-hand corner of yard by stile indicated by footpath sign. Resume directions at ⑧.

For full walk turn right immediately in front of farmhouse and follow track back towards moor. Fork left after 200 yards (right is signed as private) and immediately before next farm 100 yards later, turn sharp right on track between walls. ⑤ Emerge on to moorland and continue forward on narrow path, which crosses moorland for 1 mile (easy to follow, though it looks as if it might peter out). After summit, path drops down past shooting-boxes into next valley.

⑥ At reservoir, path joins Pennine Way. Cross dam, keep left on other side and follow Water Board road down valley. ⑦ ¼ mile beyond reservoirs, at first junction, leave Pennine Way by forking left. After 400 yards leave road and take track on left across bridge. Follow back to Walshaw. In farmyard at Walshaw turn right, to leave right-hand corner of yard by stile indicated by footpath sign ⑧.

Beyond stile, follow path directly downhill. Keep just to right of projecting corner of wall 100 yards ahead (path undefined). Then proceed with wall on left to find gate leading into woods. Immediately fork right and descend steeply. ⑨ At valley bottom, turn left and immediately fork left on track uphill. This leads past Hardcastle Crags and mill. After mill pick up riverside path and follow 1¼ miles back to car park.

SCOTLAND

The hardened hill-walker will need little introduction to Scotland's dramatic lakes, mountains and islands. But to those less passionate about scree-running and wading through knee-deep bogs, the vast stretches of open hillside and pathless moorland can seem rather daunting. Don't let this put you off: tucked away in all the scenic splendour are some excellent round walks with the added bonuses of comparatively unrestricted access (see page 20), limited agricultural 'improvement', pubs open all day, and some very quiet roads (even on some A-roads, you'll be unlucky to see more than a couple of cars an hour). On the other hand, the Scottish path network is quite sparse (though perhaps not as sparse as OS maps show it to be) and there are only two official long-distance paths, the West Highland Way and the Southern Upland Way. This, coupled with the fact that a lot of the mountain scenery is on a huge scale and is difficult terrain (which often makes it hard to get much variety in a day or half a day) means good round walks in Scotland take some finding.

In the north, the Highlands and Islands region includes much of Scotland's most famous dramatic scenery. Much of the walking in this area is well beyond the scope of this book and we have to confess that there isn't a single walk in the Scottish section that takes you up a 'munro' (a mountain over 3,000ft). But there are some excellent walks over quite manageable terrain that give you a real flavour of the Highlands, and it isn't necessary to stick to the many forestry tracks in the area, which are easy enough to walk on but can get monotonous. The Central Lowlands are mostly anything but low, and there are some justifiably popular walking areas near the large urban centres, with good paths. Further south are the Southern Uplands – an area of medium-sized green hills which merge into Northumberland. There are however, still some gaps on our Scottish walks map – notably in Dumfries and Galloway, and the islands of Mull and Arran. Suggestions are particularly welcome for these areas; see page 10.

BORDERS

Scott's View, the Wallace statue and Dryburgh Abbey

Recommended by Tim Kirby

Characteristic Border landscape of unspoilt river valley and green hills, with fine views over southern Scotland and into Northumberland. Can be nettly in high summer soon after 6; avoid by using road. Paths mainly well defined and route-finding easy, but involved from 9 to 12; can also be avoided by using road.

Length 7 miles (11km), 3½ hours
Difficulty 2
Start St Boswells, 4 miles E of Melrose. Park by village hall and phone box
OS maps 1:50,000 74;
1:25,000 NT 43/53 and NT 63/73
Refreshments Tea-room on route close to Dryburgh Abbey near end of walk; various in St Boswells

WALK DIRECTIONS

1 With village hall on right, follow main street for 30 yards and take first right (waymark). Track narrows to path; at T-junction of paths after 100 yards turn right. (a) 2 100 yards later, fork left by second bench; and 100 yards later ignore left fork, but follow to edge of golf course then continue along river bank (no path visible). 3 30 yards before far side of golf course, turn right over strip of course, picking up plank bridge and clear path, 50 yards later. Follow path for 1 mile.

4 Path ascends to bridge. Turn left on it to cross river, and follow road for ¼ mile. 5 Take first left, signposted Dryburgh Abbey. At hamlet of Clintmains keep straight on (signposted Brotherstone) where principal road bends left. 6 Follow road 250 yards, then keep forward on track where road bends right. *NB after ¾ mile, for a short stretch, track can*

get overgrown in high summer, though it is usually quite penetrable; if you prefer, continue on road – see map. 7 Shortly after track bends right, reach gate, turn left on track to continue to road. Left on road and right at next road junction to lay-by and viewpoint (b). The best view is had by continuing on road 50 yards beyond lay-by, then turning sharp right through gate; take first track on right (150 yards) and make your way to prominent pointed stone on summit. 8 Retrace steps to the lay-by and back along the road for ¼ mile.

9 Just after road bends left and right, and opposite rocky outcrop, take gate on right leading on to track (this more complicated section through fields can be omitted by continuing on road for 1 mile, then turning right between stone gate-posts on woodland track to reach Wallace statue, which is point 12).

In second field, keep close to left edge (grassy track) to reach gate into woodlands. 10 30 yards later keep forward at junction of tracks, follow to corner of forest fence on left (100 yards) then turn left up along fence to pass through small gate ahead. Continue forward through field to gate at far end and then across second field (gap) and third field, keeping close to wall on the left.

11 Where wall on left is replaced by fence, take small gate on left, and continue direction with fence on right. 50 yards after woods begin on right, take gate on right; path leads to Wallace statue (c) 12.

Just before statue, take path downhill. Right on road at bottom. 13 Detour ahead down Dryburgh Abbey Hotel drive to see abbey (d). *To continue*, with hotel drive ahead, turn right down road (no-through road), leading down to footbridge; just

If you find that a walk's directions are no longer accurate, please let us know; in particular, signposts, stiles, field boundaries and buildings can change. If a path is impenetrable or has been ploughed out, it is well worth complaining to the rights of way section of the District Council. For details of the council's duties in footpath upkeep, and for an account of the law and practice concerning walking in the countryside, see the special section on page 17.

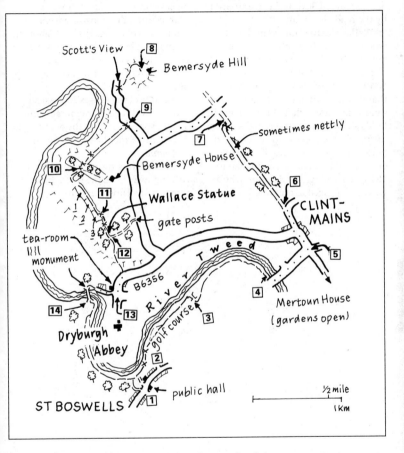

before crossing footbridge, detour up bank on right to see Temple of the Muses (**e**). **14** Turn left on far river bank, on track. 150 yards later take narrow path on right (ahead leads to river), and follow for ¾ mile.
Path crosses bridge (**f**), and leads away from river to enter St Boswells. Take

first road on left to return to start.

WHAT TO LOOK OUT FOR
(**a**) As soon as you reach the Tweed, a view of **Dryburgh Abbey** on the opposite bank of the river.
(**b**) **Scott's View** In particular, of the Eildon Hills, the triple-peaked mass on

the far side of Tweedsdale. Under the central one, King Arthur's knights are supposed to be lying asleep 'awaiting Scotland's time of need'. From the summit of the hill by the viewpoint, good views across the Borders into Northumberland; S to Rubers Law; SW to Ettrick Forest; W to the Upper Tweedsdale Hills. On Sir Walter Scott's funeral day, the hearse stopped by the road viewpoint.

(c) **Wallace statue** Hidden in the woods, 20ft high, its plinth raising it to almost 40ft. The 'great patriot hero, ill-requited chief' is William Wallace, a Scottish patriot commemorated in many forms, but none as bizarre as this sandstone monolith. In his left hand he holds an enormous stone shield, and in his right what appears to be a similarly outsized ice-cream cone. The statue, erected by the 11th Earl of Buchan in 1814, and sculpted by a mason who was also engaged in building Scott's house at Abbotsford, has been described as 'an atrocious effigy to the hero who suffers much from the clumsy worship of his Scottish admirers.'

(d) **Dryburgh Abbey** (open to public; fee) Go into the grounds if you want to see it, as it is not visible again on this walk. Best known as the final resting place of Sir Walter Scott, it was a 12th-century Premonstratensian foundation of the Augustian Canon of Alnwick. It burned down four times in two centuries and was besieged in 1540, but remains a ruin of exceptional beauty.

(e) **Temple of the Muses** A classical rotunda built to commemorate James Thompson, who wrote the poetic cycle *The Seasons* and the words of *Rule Britannia*.

(f) On the left of the path, just before turning away from the river, the remains of a **Howitzer** gun.

CENTRAL

Achray Forest and Loch Drunkie

In the heart of the Trossachs, nearly all on sheltered forestry tracks. Some attractive picnic sites, especially at Larch Point (signposted). Partly waymarked; easy route-finding.

Length 6 miles (9.5km), 2½ hours
Difficulty 1–2
Start Car park at start of Achray Forest Drive, 3 miles N of Aberfoyle on A821. Grid reference NN 523043
OS maps 1:50,000 57; 1:25,000 NN 40/50

WALK DIRECTIONS

1 Walk past cabin at entrance to forest drive (**a**) and continue along drive for ¾ mile. **2** After passing small cutting on right reach post marked 'The Quarry' and turn right on side track, passing wooden barrier. **3** Turn right on main forest drive and follow with the shore of loch on right.

4 Just after children's playground turn right past wooden toilet hut and keep right to follow waymarked path along loch shore. **5** Turn right at T-junction, following sign for Spruce Glen, then keep right when this joins forest drive. **6** After ¼ mile fork left just after the car park on left, past wooden barrier and on to minor track. **7** Turn right at T-junction (downhill) and straight on at next junction, heading uphill.

8 After ¾ mile reach cross-track and continue forward on narrow path marked with wooden post and green and yellow waymarking. **9** Straight over at road, through barrier and up to viewpoint **10** (**b**). Retrace steps to road, and turn right to start.

WHAT TO LOOK OUT FOR

(**a**) **Achray Forest Drive** Costs £1 for vehicles; no charge for pedestrians.
(**b**) **View** Over the Trossachs: W to E Lochs Katrine, Achray and Venachar; WNW Ben Venue (2,386ft), NE Ben Ledi (2,882ft).

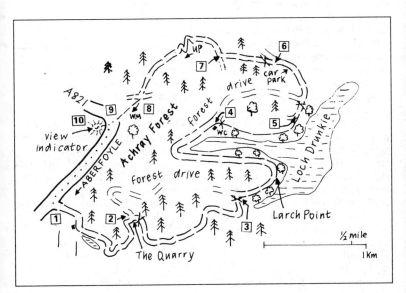

Bracklinn Falls and Callander Crags

Callander Crags is a gently rising, knife-edge-shaped hill; a rocky path leads to the summit and viewpoint, then drops abruptly through forest back to the start. Residential roads to begin with, then quiet farm road and pasture. Briefly undefined just after **8**; otherwise route-finding is quite easy.

Length 7 miles (11km), 3 hours
Difficulty 3
Start Callander town centre, by church (by square at centre of town)
OS maps 1:50,000 57;
1:25,000 NN 60/70
Refreshments Pubs and cafés in Callander

Key maps, pinpointing the walks, are at the back of the book.

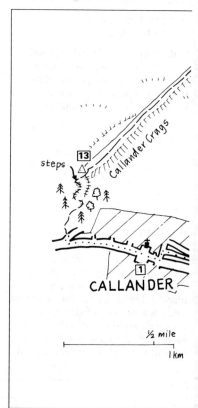

WALK DIRECTIONS

1 With parish church on left, follow main street, take first left (North Church Street) then first right (Craigard Road). **2** At end of road, left over bridge (old railway), then first right (Aveland Road). Before you turn, look out for Arden House (**a**) (furthest house uphill on left). **3** Where road bends right, continue forward on track. 75 yards later, turn left (opposite end of residential road on right) to enter golf course, then right after 30 yards along bottom edge of course (no path).

4 After ¼ mile cross stream by small bridge (just before hut on left). 40 yards later, turn right through gate, forward towards house to next gate, then left on path (old railway track) (**b**). **5** Emerge on road, turn right. Keep right at next T-junction and 50 yards later turn left on path rejoining old railway track. Ignore side-turns and follow to reach road **6**. Left on road, and immediately left again at fork of farm roads. Follow for ¾ mile.

7 Fork left on track, signposted West Bracklinn. **8** Left through gate

opposite bungalow, then bear half right (no path) up to left corner of wall in front of farm. Turn right along wall, keeping farm on right, and follow past farm to gate **9**. Half left beyond gate (no path) aiming for right corner of woodland, at which pass through gate then, 10 yards later, take metal gate on left. Follow narrow path leading along top edge of woodland and soon ascending gently to reach bridge over Bracklinn Falls (**c**) **10**.

Cross bridge, continue up clear path avoiding side turns, through double kissing-gates and later alongside woods. **11** Reach road,

Special interest lists at the back of the book give opening times for castles, houses, museums and gardens passed on the walks.

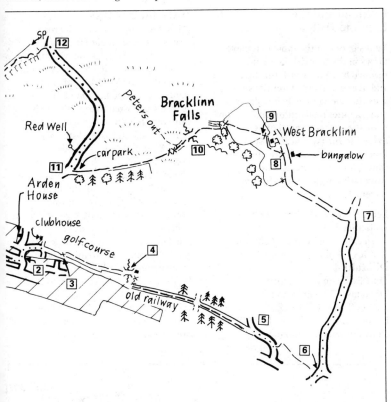

turn right uphill (**d**). **12** After ¾ mile turn left in front of small hill, on path signposted Callander Crags. Path ascents to ridge, then along ridge following fence on right. **13** Path continues from crag (viewpoint) (**e**). Ignore first flight of steps on left, but take second flight 50 yards later and descend to Callander.

WHAT TO LOOK OUT FOR

(**a**) **Arden House** Used in the TV series *Doctor Finlay's Casebook* as the home of Doctors Cameron and Finlay.

(**b**) **Old railway line** Former Caledonian Railway, a link between Dunblane and Balquhidder Junction.

(**c**) **Bracklinn Falls** In Scots dialect, the 'speckled' pool, mentioned in Scott's *The Lady of the Lake*. Best after a prolonged period of rain.

(**d**) On the left, a signposted path to the **red well**, a chalybeate spring (presumed to be health-giving). Here you can sample some rusty-tasting water from a ladle that looks as if it has been there since the well was restored in 1924.

(**e**) **View** N to Ben Vorlich (3,231ft); E to the Ochils (2,364ft) and the Forth Plain; S to the Campsie Fells (1,897ft); SW to Loch Venachar; W to Ben Ledi (2,882ft; nearest peak).

FIFE

Falkland and the Lomond Hills

Takes in one of the most extensive
views in the Scottish Lowlands,
reached by a steep path through woods
and over grassland. After the summit,
a section along ridge before descent
along a quiet road (unfortunately, no
path alternative at present). Can
extend to the twin peak of West
Lomond via an easy there-and-back
route along ridge track. Thorough
waymarking; easy route-finding.
Ascent 1,200ft.

Length 4 miles (6.5km), 2½ hours
Difficulty 3–4
With extension to West Lomond
9 miles (14.5km), 4½ hours
Difficulty 4
Start Falkland town centre
OS maps 1:50,000 58 and 59;
1:25,000 NO 20/30 and,
for W Lomond Hill only, NO 00/10
Refreshments In Falkland only

WALK DIRECTIONS

1 (**a**) From main street take road
opposite church and to right of
Covenanters' Hotel, soon past factory
on left. **2** Where road ends, continue
forward on track. Fork right after 50
yards, signposted Lomond Hills. Path
is well signposted to top. 100 yards
later turn left up steps (signposted) to
enter woods, and ascend steadily.

   3 After path leaves woods it
continues uphill with forest on right,
then when grassy hill (summit of East
Lomond) is visible, half right path
leads to it (**b**). **4** From summit
continue on prominent grassy track on
other side, leading towards next
summit, West Lomond. Track soon
passes through gate to merge with
track between walls. Keep forward.
5 Reach road. *For extension to West
Lomond*, turn right on road, then left
on track after 100 yards and follow 2½
miles to West Lomond, then retrace
steps to road, turn left down it

and follow to Falkland. *For walk returning directly to Falkland*, turn right on road, descend to start.

WHAT TO LOOK OUT FOR

(a) **Falkland** Ancient royal burgh, a fetching town of cobbled streets and old houses dominated by the Renaissance palace (NTS; open to public; fee), with its gardens, chapel and 16th-century tennis court. It was a hunting palace of the Stuart kings, in particular a favourite residence of James V and his daughter, Mary Queen of Scots.

(b) **View** On a clear day, most of southern Scotland, notably W to Ben Lomond (3,194ft), Ben More (3,852ft) and the Trossachs; NW to Ben Lawers (beyond Loch Tay; 3,984ft); E over the Fife coast; S to the Pentlands (beyond Edinburgh; 1,898ft). View-indicator at the summit.

GRAMPIAN

Morrone from Braemar

A short mountain ascent to a view of most of the main range of the Cairngorms. Takes a steepish path up, then a short section of track before dropping to a quiet road for the return to Braemar. All paths and tracks well defined; easy route-finding. Ascent 1,650ft.

Length 6½ miles (10.5km), 3½ hours
Difficulty 4
Start Braemar, on A93 17 miles W of Ballater
OS maps 1:50,000 43;
1:25,000 NO 08/18 and NO 09/19
Refreshments Tea-shops and hotels in Braemar

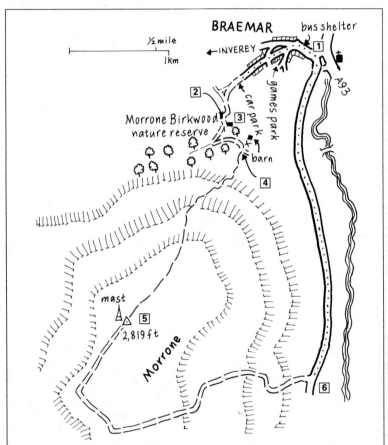

WALK DIRECTIONS

1 (**a**) Follow village street through Braemar (signposted Inverey from A93) until road forks in front of Haggart's shop (bus shelter on right). Fork left, immediately ignoring further turning on left, and follow road out of village.

2 Road becomes track just past car park. Fork left 100 yards later, then take the next left (around left side of triangle of tracks).

3 150 yards after passing house, fork right by nature reserve post (**b**). 200 yards later keep left (on level) along main track, where another track comes in from right. **4** After 200 yards turn uphill opposite gate/barns on left of track. Clear path leads to summit; where path divides as you climb, keep to most trodden path.

5 At top (**c**), keep forward. Track leads along ridge for a while before dropping down to left. **6** Left along road at bottom, and follow into Braemar.

WHAT TO LOOK OUT FOR

(**a**) **Braemar** A large village, which became a fashionable place to stay when Queen Victoria had Balmoral Castle built, six miles away. Every September the Highland Gathering takes place in Princess Royal Park; the famous event includes caber tossing, piping and athletics. Robert Louis Stevenson stayed here in 1881 and wrote *Treasure Island*.

(**b**) **Morrone Birkwood nature reserve** The finest subalpine birch wood in Britain, sharing several characteristics with woodlands in Norway. **Flora** Lime-rich soils, the protection from grazing provided by juniper bushes and many damp hollows encourage the growth of over 280 species of plants, some rarely found in such conditions, including alpine cinquefoil, alpine rush, three-flowered rush, small white orchid and numerous lichens.

(**c**) **Morrone summit** 2,819ft, though its name is a corruption of 'munro', which denotes a mountain over 3,000ft. The path is well stamped down by Highland Games competitors in the race from Braemar to the top; the record time stands at 24 minutes 58 seconds. **View** NW to the main Cairngorm mass; N to Beinn a'Bhuird (3,924ft) and Ben Avon (3,843ft); W to Dee Valley; SE to Lochnagar Hills; E to Glen Callater.

The Southern Cairngorms: Glen Dee and Glen Lui

Leads along level valley floors into the wilds of the Cairngorms to reach the southern end of the Lairig Ghru pass. Scenery on huge scale (but still changing slowly as you proceed), with a backdrop of mountains beyond the immediate moorland valleys. Worthwhile at end to scramble down the wooded bank to the Linn of Dee, a small chasm with rock pools. It is possible to hire bicycles from the garage at Braemar, from where the start is an easy 40-minute ride. All paths quite well defined, but can be boggy after rain from ② to ③; easy route-finding.

Length 14 miles (22.5km), 7 hours
Difficulty 3–4
Start Linn of Dee, 6 miles W of Braemar. Take road signposted Inverey from Braemar; Linn of Dee is the signed bridge 1½ miles beyond Inverey. Continue across bridge; car park is on left after 200 yards. Grid reference NO 061897
OS maps 1:50,000 43; 1:25,000 NO 09/19 and Outdoor Leisure 3

WALK DIRECTIONS

① From car park retrace steps towards bridge. Where road bends left to cross river, continue forward on track signposted Glen Geldie and Glen Tilt; level track leads to bridge

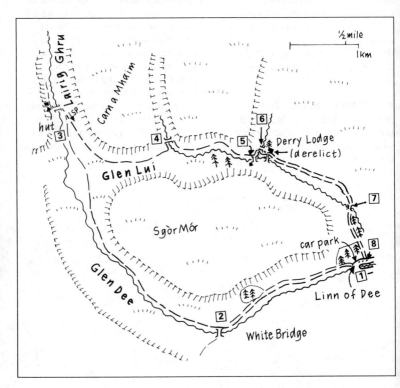

after 1½ miles (**a**) ☐2. Do not cross
bridge, but keep forward (signposted
Aviemore by Lairig Ghru). Path leads
up Glen Dee, with river on left; keep
forward, stepping across streams
where necessary. Path is distinct, but
can be boggy after wet weather.

☐3 After two hours' walking,
mountain-rescue hut is visible ahead
(**b**). 300 yards before bridge leading to
hut, turn right, up to signpost,
following path for Braemar via Derry
Lodge; path contours hill and is easy
to follow (**c**). ☐4 On reaching river,
turn left on path above river, to
footbridge, then follow path downstream on far bank (*or* cross by
stones, with care, to avoid detour).
Path follows river down towards
trees.

☐5 Pass house on opposite bank of
river, then follow river round; soon
footbridge is visible away to left by
two huts ☐6. Cross footbridge
(signposted Braemar) and turn right
on far bank to pick up track just
behind nearer (larger) hut. Track
passes old hunting-lodge; ignore right
turn down to bridge 200 yards later.

☐7 After 1½ miles, cross bridge
over river. ☐8 Right on road, back to
start; *or* scramble down to the river

for a riverside path back to the Linn
of Dee.

WHAT TO LOOK OUT FOR
(**a**) Left over bridge leads down **Glen
Tilt**, a long lonely route which
reaches civilisation at Blair Atholl,
20 miles away.
(**b**) **View** Ahead into the Lairig Ghru
and the heart of the Cairngorms – the
towering peak immediately W is the
Devil's Point (3,303ft); Lairig Ghru
passes up between Braeriach (left,
4,248ft) and Ben Macdui (4,296ft)
before descending to Aviemore. The
Cairngorm range is Britain's largest
nature reserve, containing several
wildlife rarities, including golden
eagles, peregrine falcons and reindeer
(reintroduced). **Flora** includes arctic
and starwort mouse-ear, alpine
hair-grass, hare's foot sedge and
mountain hawkweed, plus some
rather more montane species,
including alpine saw-wort, purple
saxifrage and roseroot.
(**c**) In this valley are some fine **Scots
pines** by the river, a surviving
fragment of the great Caledonian
Forest that once covered Scotland,
and which almost disappeared after
the Highland Clearances.

Mither Tap, Bennachie

A 1,698ft summit on a heathery plateau, towering above an enormous lowland area, reached by an undemanding ascent through planted forestry. All tracks well defined; plenty of coloured marker posts. Easy route-finding.

Length 6½ miles (10.5km), 3 hours

Difficulty 3
Start Rowantree car park, 7 miles W of Inverurie. From Inverurie take A 96 NW 2½ miles, then turn left, signposted Chapel of Garioch, after which continue ahead until signpost on left to Rowantree car park. Grid reference NJ 693245
OS maps 1:50,000 38; 1:25,000 NJ 62/72

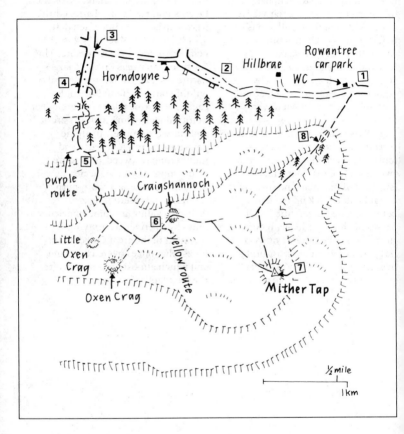

WALK DIRECTIONS

1 From car park follow track which is continuation of road, passing to left of toilets. Ignore side turns and follow track (**a**), with woods on left. After ½ mile fork left (still with woods on left), where right fork leads to house. **2** Where track becomes road (house on left), proceed along it for 80 yards then keep forward on track, as road bends right. **3** Left at T-junction with road.

4 Just beyond the Forestry Commission sign turn left on track signposted 'bus park', which then bends right and leads to information board with map. Follow yellow trail (shown by yellow markers on posts) from here, ascending 200 yards to track, then turn right and immediately left. Yellow posts are well placed. **5** Emerge on to moorland; follow yellow posts towards nearest peak on left (Craigshannoch). **6**

Leave yellow trail and climb over Craigshannoch, then continue on obvious path along edge of ridge to major summit, Mither Tap. Notice track descending to left of your path from summit; this is return route.

7 Descend from summit (**b**) (if you have lost your bearings, it's the path heading N – see view-indicator on summit for compass direction) along side of main ridge before turning right on to path along wooded spur. **8** Just as woods start, path divides into three, but paths soon merge again. Descend to the car park.

WHAT TO LOOK OUT FOR

(**a**) Now a green lane, this track was once the **Aberdeen turnpike** road.
(**b**) **View** Described on view-indicator at summit. Includes Aberdeen, the Watch Tower, the sea, Binnack Moor and the outlying peaks of the Cairngorms.

HIGHLAND

Loch na Creitheach and the Eastern Cuillins

A there-and-back route along the coast path, leading straight to one of Britain's most challenging mountain ranges. Reaches a climax at Loch na Creitheach, where you will see why we are not recommending an expedition further into the Cuillins. A good walk for one of Skye's many inclement days, as the coast is often sheltered and quite low, and the going underfoot is easy. Easy route-finding.

Length 8 miles (13km), 4 hours;
4 miles (6.5km) each way
Difficulty 3
Start Elgol, at the end of the A881,
14 miles SW of Broadford. Small car park opposite signposted turning to Glasnakillie. Grid reference
NG 518136
OS maps 1:50,000 32;
1:25,000 Outdoor Leisure 8
Refreshments Shop at Elgol

WALK DIRECTIONS

1 From car park follow road uphill 300 yards to cluster of cottages, near top of steep portion of road, then turn left on stony track which passes two-storey house after 100 yards. Do not keep on the track to the second house, but change to the far side of fence on your right, where path leads along bottom (left) edge of two fields to gate **2**. Path ahead is easy to find as it contours above coast (**a**).

3 After descending into first large bay, path continues up on far side, along edge of low cliffs. (**b**) **4** At next bay, follow to prominently placed Camasunary farmhouse (**c**) (noting the way you have come, as you will come back the same route). Cross stream by bridge below waterfall.

5 Turn right just before reaching

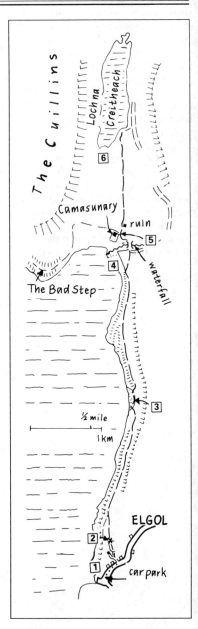

438

Camasunary (a working farm, partly surrounded by a ruined one), to pick up stony path leading past second ruin. Proceed to Loch na Creitheach (**d**) [6]. Retrace steps from loch.

WHAT TO LOOK OUT FOR

(**a**) ½ mile out of Elgol, on a promontory, is a small **cave** where Bonnie Prince Charlie hid before leaving Skye for ever. The promontory, known as Sharp Seat, used to be a haunt of childless women who came here in the hope that they would become fertile.
(**b**) **View** W to the nearby island of Soay (4 miles), and N of it, the Cuillins, including Gars Bheinn

(2,934ft) and Sgurr Alasdair (3,257ft); 12 miles SW, the island of Rhum.
(**c**) **View** The continuation of the coast path beyond Camasunary follows the aptly named Bad Step (more of a climbing route than a path) to the entrance of Loch Coruisk. It requires walking on a high ledge, with a sheer drop on the seaward side and little more than a narrow cleft to hang on to; a slip on the wet rocks is usually fatal.
(**d**) **View** Reveals some of the brutal beauty of the Cuillins. Left to right: Trodhu (1,623ft); Marsco (at the far end of the loch, 2,414ft); Bla Bheinn (3,044ft).

Southern Skye shores and Loch Slapin

Low coastline and some slightly boggy moorland. Easily managed in comparison to most circular walks on the island; the 40 minutes' walk along the A881 (very quiet unfenced road) can be avoided by catching the daily post-bus – check times at Broadford tourist office. Some care needed with path junctions through quarry at start. An intermittent moorland path to the coast, with a hard track for the last two miles before joining road; route-finding moderately easy.

Length 9 miles (14.5km), 4½ hours
Difficulty 3–4
Start Ruined chapel at Suardal, 2 miles SW of Broadford, Skye. Take A881 out of Broadford. After 2 miles road passes three houses; cemetery is ¼ mile further on right. Roadside parking. Grid reference NG 617207
OS maps 1:50,000 32; 1:25,000 Outdoor Leisure 8

WALK DIRECTIONS

1 Follow road towards Broadford.
2 Pass first house (bungalow), then after 50 yards turn right through gate on to track. 3 Where track reaches old crofter's cottage bear half left (no path) across stream, up bank, to reach grassy former railway track after 30 yards. Turn right along this. 4 Keep to left fork after ¼ mile. Track passes through old marble quarry and rises for ¼ mile (a).

5 Near end of quarry ignore wide grassy track on right (incline of old railway) leading gently downhill, but bear half left on path passing large spoil heap after 50 yards. 6 30 yards after spoil heap ignore minor left fork. Keep left on main path 100 yards later. Path through moorland is boggy but passable and maintains same direction, soon crossing fence and continuing along bottom of

small valley, then on right side of valley.

7 Reach shore, turn right along it (b). First stream is crossed by stone bridge within walls of old croft (ruined) (c); subsequent streams can be stepped across and require no jumping. Avoid walking on rocky foreshore; clear path runs just inland from it. 8 Metal (covered) sheep-pen comes into view; your objective is the stony track leading from far side of it. Reach fence above the pen, turn right and follow fence. 9 Once level with deserted stone croft down on left, take small gate on left (the second passed) down to croft (d), by which turn right on track, and follow for 2 miles (e).

10 Ignore driveways on right and 30 yards later, left. 11 Turn right on A-road; follow back to start.

WHAT TO LOOK OUT FOR

(a) A working marble quarry is passed at the end of the walk. **Flora** Two types of Alpine flower – white-petalled mountain avens (May) and yellow mountain saxifrage (August).
(b) **View** Across Loch Eishort (a sea-loch) to the southernmost part of Skye. 17m SW, out to sea, the island of Rhum.
(c) The **ruined huts** are all that remain of the old crofting settlement of Borreraig, an extreme example of the eviction of crofting communities in the 19th century. On Skye nearly 7,000 families were made homeless between 1840 and 1883.
(d) The croft, now empty, is the last remnant of the settlement of Suishnish. Writing in 1904, a university professor recalled the scene in 1852:

'On gaining the top of one of the hills on the south side of the valley, I could see a long and motley procession winding along the road that leads north from Suishnish . . .

it was a miscellaneous gathering of at least three generations of crofters. There were old men and women, too feeble to walk, who were placed in carts; the younger members of the community on foot were carrying their bundles of clothes and household effects, while the children, with looks of alarm, walked alongside . . . Everyone was in tears.'

(e) **View** Across Loch Slapin towards Bla Bheinn (3,046ft).

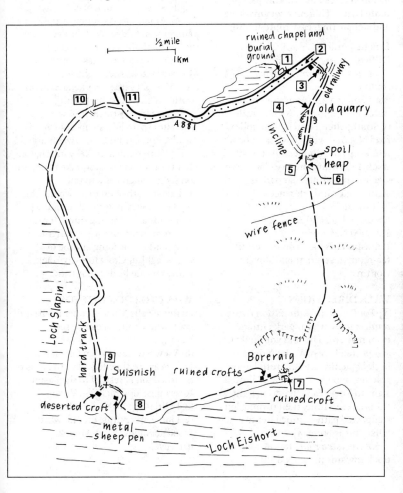

Rogie Falls

Takes in a fine waterfall and an excellent viewpoint, via generally easy paths and tracks in coniferous Torrachilty Forest. Rough riverside path (crosses rock at ③; easy if wearing suitable footwear), avoidable by forest track and walking part of route twice. Thorough waymarking and signposting; easy route-finding.

Length 4 miles (6.5km), 2 hours
Difficulty *On riverside path* 3
On Forestry Commission (easy) route 1–2
Start Forestry Commission car park ¼ mile N of Contin on A832, 2 miles SW of Strathpeffer. From Contin follow road N; out of village where it bends left, keep straight on along forestry track, following Forestry Commission sign to Torrachilty; car park is signposted. Grid reference NH 454567
OS maps 1:50,000 26; 1:25,000 NH 45/55
Refreshments None on route, but tea-room, restaurant and shop in Contin

WALK DIRECTIONS

1 *For Forestry Commission (easy) route* stand with car park entrance from main road behind you, and take signposted Forest Walk on right at back of picnic area, and turn left on reaching next forest track. Follow signs to Rogie Falls; ignoring right turns after ¼ mile, then turning left on signposted path ¾ mile later to reach falls. This is point **4**.

For riverside route follow forestry track towards main road. **2**

Opposite first forestry hut on left, turn right down steps. Keep right at bottom on path that is soon joined by forest fence on right. Path is slightly overgrown by gorse, but is easy to follow. **3** Where path emerges by rocks, cross rocks with care, aiming for continuation of path slightly up to right, soon to rejoin fence.

4 At falls (**a**), do not cross the suspension bridge. With bridge on left follow path for 50 yards (retracing steps if you came on easy route via forestry track), then right at path junction. 50 yards later keep to main path which bends sharp left. **5** Turn right on forestry track, follow ¾ mile. **6** Turn sharp left, signposted 'forest walk'. Route from here is waymarked.

7 Turn right after 300 yards. Ignore left turn 200 yards later; take next path on right, which leads to tall ladder-stile, then on to viewpoint (**b**) **8**. Left at viewpoint to descend. **9** 150 yards after passing through gate into semi-open area (**c**), fork right (waymark misleading at time of checking). **10** Cross forestry track; path opposite leads to car park.

WHAT TO LOOK OUT FOR

(**a**) **Rogie Falls** Much-frequented beauty spot, where salmon can be seen leaping in July.
(**b**) **View** S towards Glen Orrin; E to hills near Strathpeffer; W to the hills of Strathconon Forest; N to the Easter Ross range, of which Ben Wyvis (3,433ft) is the highest in view.
(**c**) **Flora** Early purple orchid, white wood anemone, lady's smock, cat's eye.

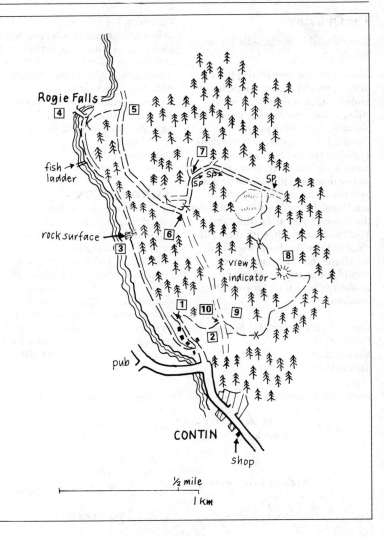

Rogie Falls

4

5

fish ladder

7

SP

SP

SP

rock surface

3

6

8

view indicator

1

10

9

2

pub

CONTIN

shop

½ mile

1 km

The Quiraing

Contributed by Andrew Leslie and Nils Blythe

One of the more unearthly places in Britain, a rocky chasm caused by geological faulting between rocky cliffs, and a series of stone towers and pinnacles (including the 120ft 'Needle'). Return over outward route, as path peters out after a mile; can make walk into a circuit by climbing on to a moorland hillside for a view over the Quiraing and towards the sea. Rough but reasonably level along the chasm; boggy and pathless over Meall na Suiramach, with sheer cliffs off to the left. Route obvious along the chasm, but moorland return should not be attempted in poor visibility. Not a walk for young children.

Length 2 miles (3km), 1½ hours
Difficulty 3
Via alternative return route
3 miles (5km), 2½ hours

Difficulty 3–4
Start Car park (not signed as such) by Quiraing, on minor road between Uig and Brogaig. From Uig, take A855 N, which bends right at end of village; ¼ mile later turn right on minor road which hairpins steeply down after 3½ miles into gorge; car park is on right shortly after. Grid reference NG 443682
OS maps 1:50,000 23; 1:25,000 NG 46/56

WALK DIRECTIONS

1 Cross road, take well-trodden path through picnic area, leading below cliffs and past complex of stone towers and pinnacles.

2 Where path peters out, *either* retrace steps *or* ascend cliff on left (which has now become an easily climbed grassy slope) and double back to ascend to trig. point on Meall na Suiramach (no path). At trig. point bear SW along contour to reach road, then left on road to reach car park.

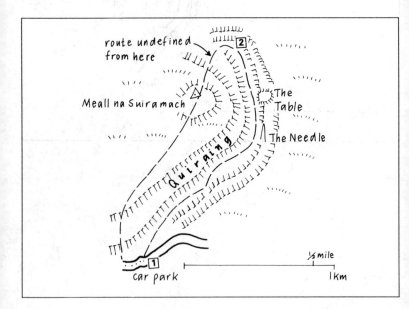

444

Glen Coe and Glen Etive

A good non-mountaineering round walk in an otherwise demanding upland area, leading through or past seven glens. Follows valley floors all the way, with close-up views of some daunting-looking peaks. Boggy (but passable) from ⁊7⁊ to ⁊8⁊; don't expect to return with dry feet. Not all paths defined, but valley floors are obvious; easy route-finding. Ascent 2,100ft: 800ft gently up Lairig Eilde, then 1,300ft more steeply from Dalness up Lairig Gartain.

Length 11 miles (17.5km), 7 hours
Difficulty 4
Start Lay-by on A82, 3¾ miles E of Glen Coe NT visitor centre and just where road enters small rocky gorge (¼ mile after first house on left). On left side of road as you come from NT visitor centre. Grid reference NN 181565
OS maps 1:50,000 41; 1:25,000 NN 05/15

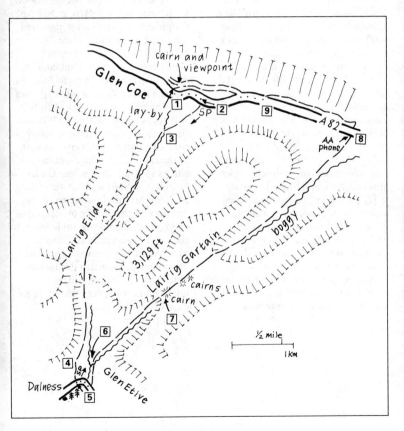

445

WALK DIRECTIONS

1 Left on main road for 600 yards.

2 Turn right on stony path signposted to Loch Etive head. Path rises for ¼ mile then descends into valley.

3 Cross stream by easy natural stepping-stones as soon as it is reached. Clear path continues on right side of stream and later recrosses it. Path leads to the top of the valley and descends into valley ahead.

4 Towards bottom of descent make down to road, reaching it near driveway with cattle-grid at small larch wood **5**. Left along road (ignore signpost after 200 yards for footpath to Glen Coe (**a**)) for 300 yards, across road-bridge, then turn left (no path) and follow contour of hill round, with stream down on left. **6** About 100 yards after passing confluence of streams cross right-hand river where safe, and ascend a few yards to reach well-defined path which leads parallel to right-hand stream, following it up to its source. Keep to left side of stream; path becomes intermittent, and route steepens.

7 At top by large cairn proceed down valley past further cairns. Shortly after river begins (away to right), pick up path (boggy) and follow down glen to reach main road by car park and AA box **8**. Cross road, continue on other side (no path for 30 yards) to reach remains of old road (track covered with prominent strip of heather); turn left on it. **9** On rejoining main road proceed along it for 250 yards before picking up track on right. Follow for ¾ mile to cairn and viewpoint (**b**), at which take narrow path on left down to car park.

WHAT TO LOOK OUT FOR

(**a**) The signposted route crosses the stream at a potentially ankle-twisting point, so we suggest this easier alternative.

(**b**) **Glen Coe** A vast glacial trough whose steep sides rise to over 3,000ft from near sea-level. Here in 1692 the Campbells of Glenlyon slaughtered the Macdonalds of Glencoe, ostensibly under the orders of William III. When the Highlanders failed to accept William and Mary in place of James VII of Scotland (James II of England), the last day of 1691 was set as an ultimatum by William III. Macdonald tried unsuccessfully to find a magistrate to receive his oath at the last minute, then sent his papers to Edinburgh, where Under Secretary of State and Master of Stair Sir John Dalrymple suppressed them. Jumping on the chance of making an example of them, Dalrymple issued the order to slaughter the clan Macdonald. Forty perished and three years later the Scottish Parliament voted that the killing had been unlawful murder, yet Dalrymple got off with dismissal.

LOTHIAN

The Pentland Hills

Recommended by Tim Kirby, Geoff Peacock

Remote-feeling moorland hills just outside Edinburgh. Take either the low-level walk past reservoirs and a waterfall, or the high-level ridge walk with excellent views in all directions. A familiar area to Robert Louis Stevenson, whose childhood home was at Swanston at the north-east end of the range. Most paths well defined. Ascent (high-level walk) 1,500ft (2,000ft if entire ridge is walked).

Length *Low-level walk* 7½ miles (12km), 3 hours
Difficulty 3
High-level ridge walk 12½ miles (20km), 7 hours
Difficulty 4–5
Start Balerno, just S of A70, 8 miles WSW of Edinburgh. Turn left off A70 into Balerno along Bridge Road. Just after High School turn left (signed Malleny House) along Main Street, which soon becomes Bavelaw Road. Follow road uphill, then turn left immediately after copy-paper factory, into Harlaw Road. Follow road ¾ mile and, 300 yards after it bends left, turn right up track opposite Harlaw Farm. Park at end of track by footpath signpost to Glencorse reservoir. Grid reference NT 182655.

(Frequent bus services to Balerno from Edinburgh. Alight at stop after High School. Follow road up to copy-paper factory, then turn left along Harlaw Road. After ¾ mile, just where lane veers left, turn half right to pass through gap-stile, following narrow path between fields on left and woods on right. After 400 yards pass through gap-stile and emerge on to tarmac lane.

Turn left on track for 300 yards until reaching T-junction with track, signposted Glencorse. This is point **1**. Turn right to start route.)
OS maps 1:50,000 66;
1:25,000 NT 06/16 and NT 26/36
Refreshments Flotterstone Inn (½ mile off high-level route; 1¼ miles off low-level route)

WALK DIRECTIONS

1 Follow track ahead, signposted to Glencorse reservoir. After 300 yards fork left across field (as indicated by white arrow on post) to meet wall on other side, at which point path turns right, following wall **2**. Proceed gently uphill, passing through gate after ¼ mile, and then continuing direction to and through second gate at right-hand corner of another wall. Continue in same direction over saddle of hill. Descend ¾ mile to reservoir **3**.

For low-level route via Logan reservoir turn right and follow road **3** /**1** beside reservoir (**a**). **3** /**2** Just after cottage beyond end of second reservoir cross small bridge (on left) but then maintain same direction with stream now immediately on right. Valley narrows; after ½ mile, waterfall comes into view on left. **3** /**3** Reach head of valley and make for right-hand corner of wall crossing it. Path beyond is fairly clear and runs six feet above boggy area which is down on left. At ladder-stile, path becomes clearer and snakes towards trees, just before which reach meadows. Continue forward to cross ladder-stile over wall, picking up clear track beyond. Track bends left and then right. Emerge on to road leading through avenue of trees. Continue directions from **10**.

For high-level walk turn left on road skirting reservoir. **4** 300 yards after reservoir ends and after houses,

turn right through kissing-gate (just
before large gate) and follow
well-marked stony track which
descends to stream and then turns
left.

5 After 400 yards and two gates,
wall appears on right (**b**). Turn right
immediately before wall begins. Cross
small footbridge, and immediately
turn right, keeping by stream, crossing tributary after 50 yards and
ascending hillock between the two
streams which marks beginning of
highest Pentland ridge. Follow path,
ascending ridge steeply, and crossing
fence on right by stile after 500 yards
6. Ridge path ascends two peaks (**c**),
Turnhouse Hill (topped by small cairn)
and Carnethy Hill (larger cairn), before
dropping 400ft to reach well-defined
cross-path by gate **7**.

To descend via Logan Burn (escape
route if bad weather; also pleasant
valley path along Logan Burn) turn
right and follow path to stream near
cottage to bottom of valley, at which
turn left, picking up directions at
3/**2**.

To continue high-level walk
continue ahead to ascend to trig. point.
After trig. point path bears quarter
right and to lesser peaks of East Kip
and West Kip, and then descends
steeply to junction of tracks marked by
signpost **8**. Turn right on wide track,
which bends right after ½ mile and
climbs low ridge. **9** After 1½ miles
enter woods by gate. 30 yards later,
turn right on track, and 50 yards
later turn left on road along avenue of
trees.

10 At end of avenue (**d**); road crosses
reservoir. 200 yards after which, turn
right opposite lay-by, on wide track.
After 250 yards this is joined by
semi-tarmacked track coming in from
left; keep straight on, following edge of
reservoir. **11** At end of reservoir, turn
right for 50 yards towards weir,
then left around left edge of
second reservoir. At far end, path

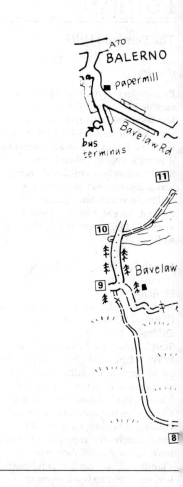

continues over long narrow bridge
and round right-hand side of house,
passing between wooden hurdles.
Emerge on to tarmac lane; turn
right (or turn left, then, at corner
of lane, pass through gap-stile if you
want to get the bus back to Edinburgh
from Balerno) and follow lane 300
yards to reach T-junction with track by
car park.

WHAT TO LOOK OUT FOR
(**a**) Half way along Logan Lee
Reservoir, up on the right, are the

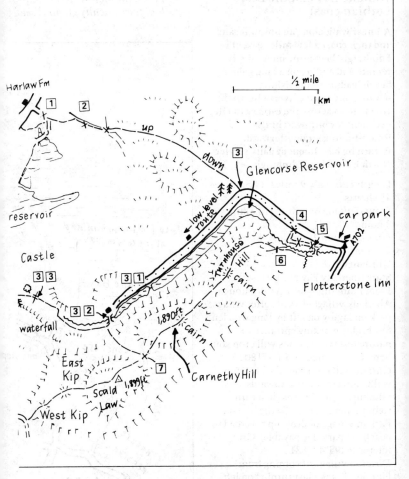

remains of **Howlet's House**, a medieval priest's house with its own chapel; some of the vaulted roof remains. Belonged to St Catherine's chapel, a 13th-century chapel that has now been submerged by the reservoir.
(**b**) To detour via Flotterstone Inn continue along track, passing through gate after 200 yards. Turn right along road to reach Flotterstone Inn. Then retrace as required (back to reservoir for low-level walk; or turn left after 200 yards where wall on left ends, for

high-level ridge walk).
(**c**) View S across the Borders to the Cheviot range (2,674ft); SE to the Moorfoot Hills (2,137ft); E to the Lammermuir Hills (1,755ft); N across the Firth of Forth to the conical Lomond Hills (1,713ft) in Fife; and NNW to the abrupt ridge of the Ochil Hills (2,364ft).
(**d**) The avenue is the entrance for **Bavelaw Castle** (hidden in the trees; not open to public). Most of the present building is 17th-century.

449

Gullane Bay and the East Lothian coast

A linear walk along an unspoilt sand and rock coast a few miles east of Edinburgh, becoming increasingly remote and ending on a long golden beach leading to the fishing -cum-resort town of North Berwick. Good views across the estuary to Fife; excellent for bird-watching. Route-finding straightforward. Return by bus; frequent daily service North Berwick to Edinburgh.

Length *Full walk* 9 miles (14.5km), 4½ hours
From Gullane 6½ miles (10.5km), 3 hours
From Dirleton 2½ miles (4km), 2 hours
Difficulty 1–2
Start Aberlady Bay nature reserve. From Edinburgh, take A198 through Aberlady village; ¼ mile after village, park on lay-by on left by long wooden footbridge marking entrance to nature reserve. The bus will drop you here. Grid reference NT 471805
Gullane village. From the bus-stop walk along main road towards Edinburgh for 50 yards then turn right up road signed 'To the beach'. Park in village or drive up this road to beach car park (fee payable). Grid reference NT 477831
Dirleton village. If coming from Edinburgh, take last turning on left, signposted Yellow Craig. Car park just before beach. Grid reference NT 515855
OS maps 1:50,000 66; 1:25,000 NT 48/58/68
Refreshments Tea-shops and pubs in Gullane, North Berwick and Dirleton; Waggon Inn, Aberlady

WALK DIRECTIONS
None needed, once you have found the coast. Keep to path as signposted from Aberlady Bay; avoid turning inland on to the golf course. If

For a key to the map symbols, and details of the difficulty grading, see inside front cover.

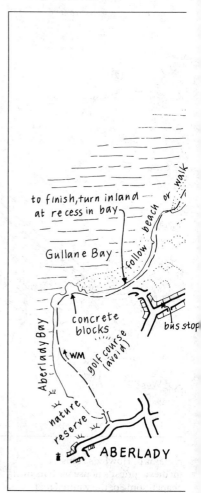

you want to finish at Gullane or Dirleton, see map for where to turn inland; if finishing at North Berwick, keep on beach, and strike inland when level with church tower.

WHAT TO LOOK OUT FOR
(a) **Aberlady Bay nature reserve**. Notable for its **birds**; 55 species are recorded as breeding here. In winter,

Though we have tried to find walks all round the country, some areas are not represented and suggestions for walks in these areas would be welcome. The address to write to is on page 10.

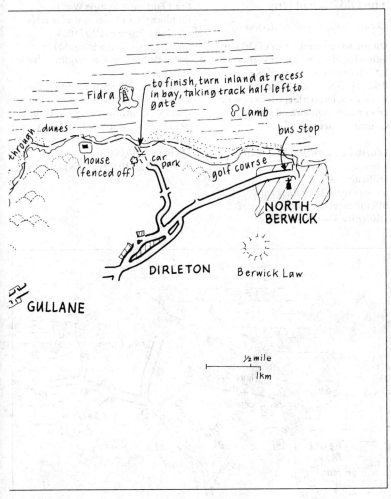

thousands of scoter can be seen just out of the bay. Other species include eider, shelduck, ringed plover, grebes, divers, wigeon, mallard, dunlin and godwit. **Flora** Lichen, grasses, saltmarsh mosses, marsh orchids, bog pimpernel and moonwort.
(**b**) **Gullane Bay** Also notable for **birds**, including large flocks of sea-duck and scoter. **Views** across to

Fife. The nearest island is Fidra, which supports a colony of terns. The towering island further east is Bass Rock, a famous place for gannets; puffins live here, too. Daily boat trips in summer to Bass Rock from North Berwick.
(**c**) Inland, the abrupt and distinctive hill is **Berwick Law** which, like Bass Rock, is a volcanic plug.

ORKNEY

The Old Man of Hoy

Contributed by Bob Anderson

On the westernmost part of Orkney, following cliffs from near sea-level to 1,150ft (the highest sea cliffs in Britain). Track well defined to Rackwick, but both versions of walk cross pathless moorland after $\boxed{4}$**. Compass essential.**

Length *Full walk* 9 miles (14.5km), 5 hours
Difficulty 4–5
Shorter walk from Rackwick
5½ miles (9km), 3 hours
Difficulty 3–4

Start *Full walk* ¼ mile W of Hoy Outdoor Centre, where road bends to N. Grid reference HY 223034
Shorter walk Rackwick (grid reference HY 202985). Car parking at both start points
(Ferry from Orkney mainland, either from Stromness to Honess near the Outdoor Centre (passenger ferry only), or from Honton (near Ophir) to Lyness (vehicles).)
OS maps 1:50,000 7;
1:25,000 HY 10/20 (covers part only)

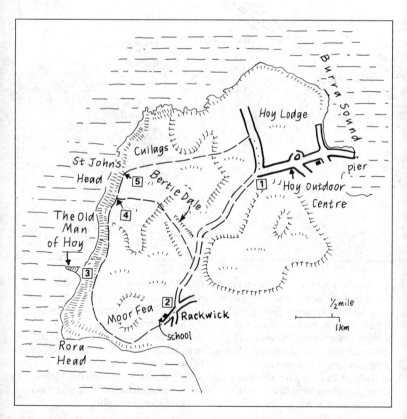

WALK DIRECTIONS

1 From corner of lane follow path along valley to continue direction of lane from Hoy Outdoor centre, arriving at hamlet of Rackwick after 3 miles. Turn right on lane and **2** fork right, past Rackwick school, heading towards sea. Turn right along coast. **3** After 1 mile reach The Old Man of Hoy (**a**).

For shorter walk continue up coast for 1 mile after The Old Man of Hoy, then **4** turn right over moors down Bertie Dale. At stream at bottom turn right into Rackwick, on well-defined track.

For full walk follow coast for 2 miles after The Old Man of Hoy then **5** turn right, just after path ceases to climb (this is St John's Head). Keeping ridge on your right traverse moor (no path), then descend steeply downhill to lane. Turn right to starting-point.

WHAT TO LOOK OUT FOR

(**a**) **The Old Man of Hoy** A 450ft pillar or stack, detached from the mainland by coastal erosion. First climbed in 1966, and in 1967 the BBC made a film of six climbers tackling it by three different routes.

STRATHCLYDE

Falls of Clyde and New Lanark

Follows woodland paths immediately above a series of waterfalls and takes in the pioneer Industrial Revolution settlement of New Lanark. Best done as a there-and-back walk starting from Corehouse nature reserve car park; if you prefer a circular walk start at Lanark (adds some road-walking and a section along wood-land tracks). Paths and tracks clearly defined; easy route-finding.

Length *Linear walk* (there and back; highly recommended) 6 miles (9.5km), 3½ hours
Difficulty 2–3
Circular walk 8 miles (13km), 4 hours
Difficulty 2–3
Start *Linear walk* Corehouse nature reserve car parks; grid reference NS 878414. Take A72 W out of Lanark and turn left through Kirkfieldbank after river bridge. ¼ mile later, at end of village, fork left. Where road swings right after 1 mile, continue ahead on track to car park at end. To join walk take left-hand track leading into nature reserve, by signs. After 200 yards turn right, signposted to the falls. This is point 6.
Circular walk Lanark town centre
OS maps 1:50,000 71 or 72; 1:25,000 NS 84/94
Refreshments Plenty in Lanark; teas at village shop, New Lanark; shop at Kirkfieldbank

WALK DIRECTIONS
1 From main street in Lanark make your way down to parish church. Turn half left in front of it into Castlegate, follow 300 yards down to entrance gates of Castlebank Park on left 2. Make your way through the park: turn right opposite gatehouse, then right by Castlebank House to rejoin road. Road becomes path, descending to reach road by bridge 3. Turn left, across bridge, then left again on other side, on residential road in Kirkfieldbank.

4 After ¼ mile, and 80 yards before speed derestriction signs, turn left through estate gates by gatehouse. Follow forestry track for 1½ miles, ignoring side turns. 5 At crossing of tracks (left is private, leading to house) turn right. 200 yards later, and 30 yards after gate on left, turn left (sign-posted to the falls; sign facing other way) 6.

Path crosses field, enters woods. Turn left on path signposted Corra Linn, and just before next gate turn right on to path. Immediately right is the continuation, but first turn left for a dramatic first view of falls (**a**), just beyond ruins of Corra Castle (**b**). Retrace steps and follow path along top of gorge. 7 Left over sluice-bridge, then immediately left on other side, on woodland path above gorge. 8 After 1 mile fork left, at end of section of concrete/metal railing, down steps to electricity station. Continue forward on track and follow to New Lanark (**c**).

9 *For linear walk* retrace steps.
For circular walk continue on road through end of village; avoid side turns and proceed for 1 mile back to start.

WHAT TO LOOK OUT FOR
(**a**) **Falls of Clyde** A wild and romantic wooded gorge with huge cliffs; when the sluice-gates from the hydro-electric station are opened, the torrent is extremely fierce. **Flora** Purple and meadow saxifrage, butterwort, lesser celandine, dog's mercury, campion, marsh marigold, marsh orchid, wood vetch, grass wood millet, woundwort. **Birds** Woodpeckers, tits, warblers and chiff-chaffs.

Advice on how to complain if a stile is broken or missing, or if a public right of way is unusable, is given in the section on page 17 – 'Walking in the countryside, law and practice'.

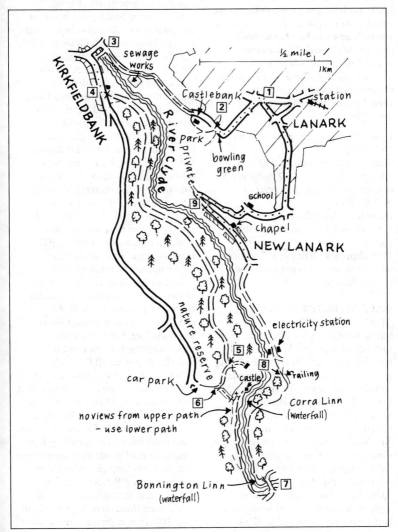

(b) Corra Castle Perched high above the gorge, the former stronghold of the Bannatyre family.

(c) New Lanark Early industrial settlement, pioneered in 1784 by Arkwright and Dale to accommodate Arkwright's enormous cotton-spinning mill, which was worked until 1968. Industrialist Robert Owen managed New Lanark from 1800 and built the school, institute, counting house, store and nursery buildings. Trail leaflet available at visitor centre.

A tour of the Craignish Peninsula

Starts off along easy farm tracks, but later involves some scrambling along a rocky shore (you may have to heave yourself up on to low bank above shore at high tide). Then a steep grassy hill (300ft), with a view of nearly all the islands in the Sound of Jura. Finishes along a quiet road. Path undefined from 5 until 12.

Length 8 miles (13km), 4½ hours
Difficulty 4
Start Ardfern village on B8002 on Craignish Peninsula, 12 miles NNW of Lochgilphead. Grid reference NM 805044
OS maps 1:50,000 55;
1:25,000 NR 60/70 (not available at time of writing)
Refreshments Galley of Lorne (hotel with bar also serves teas) and shop, both at Ardfern

WALK DIRECTIONS

1 With Galley of Lorne on right follow loch shore for 100 yards, then first left, signposted Ardlarach. 2 Fork left on track after ½ mile where road ends. 600 yards later ignore left fork. 3 Continue forward past Lunga House on your left (large castle-style house). 150 yards later turn left past Ardfern riding centre. 4 150 yards later, where track bends right, turn left through gate. Track follows right edge of first field, left edge of second, then crosses stream by bridge, soon to cross open land.

5 At farmstead (track ends), bear half right from corner of wall (no path) aiming between two hillocks 100 yards away. Keep forward, aiming for prominent rocky inlet 400 yards below. Best route is to keep left of rock 50 yards away; intermittent path leads down towards stream, then follows stream down to sea 6.

Follow rocky shore with great care

(difficult for about ¼ mile; slightly better on grassy bank just above shore). Route then gets easier. 7 Cross to far side of next bay (a), walking along beach (which avoids crossing fence). At end of beach make for gate leading into field away to left (just below and to left of grassy hummock) 8. Half left across field, aiming for gate in far left-hand corner. Keep forward up along fence on left in second field (b), at end of which gate leads to house 9.

Follow track round right side of house; just before far end of house turn right through gate into field, follow right edge of field 50 yards, to pass through gap on right, then half left up to shoulder of hill, crossing tumbledown wall. From here make your own way to summit of hill (about ten minutes' walk) (c). 10 From summit, with sea before you, locate nearest farmhouse on left (which you will reach). Now, with farmhouse before you, bear quarter right downhill to join wall. At right-hand end of wall (just above steep slope on right), wall can be crossed easily; take care not to dislodge any stones 11.

Beyond wall, walk close to steep slope on right; soon gap in wall ahead comes into view. Pass through it and bear towards gate in far left corner of field, by farmhouse 12. Turn right on farm road; follow for ¾ mile. 13 At next farm road bends left; ignore right turn 30 yards later (d), follow ¼ mile to next house 14. Keep ahead on grassy track, through gate after 30 yards, then through field on track, to road. 15 Turn right on road for 250 yards, then left to view chapel (e). 16 Turn right out of chapel entrance (retracing steps) and follow (quiet) lochside road (f) for 2 miles back to start.

WHAT TO LOOK OUT FOR

(a) The bay, called **Bay of the Field of**

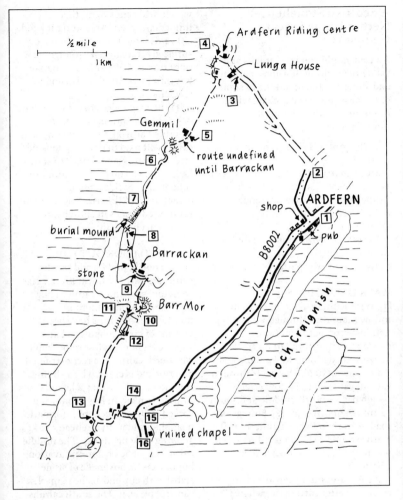

Heads, is where the Celts once fought a fierce battle with Viking invaders. The hummocks you are walking towards are the mounds where the dead were buried.

(**b**) Just opposite a sheep-pen (which is on your left) in the second field is a small fallen **slab**, on a barely noticeable grassy mound. Called Leac an Duine Choir (Stone of the Just Man), rough carvings are visible on it; legend has it the stone can speak.

(**c**) **View** The islands, left to right (S to N), are Jura (its N end), Scarba (crescent-shaped; the highest in view), Luing (in foreground), Lunga (almost joined on to Scarba) and Shuna (with a prominent house on it).

(**d**) Just to the right is **Craignish Castle** (private, built in the 19th century), detour not worthwhile.

(**e**) Ruined 12th-century chapel on lochside, with good examples of **sculptured stones** (medieval tombstones).

(**f**) **View** Across Loch Craignish, with its numerous islands (none of which are inhabited).

457

A Scottish Stonehenge: Nether Largie Linear Cemetery

An easy ramble on level tracks and estate roads through woods, parkland and along a sea-loch, taking in some of the best-preserved archaelogical monuments in Scotland. Easy route-finding.

Length 7 miles (11km), 3 hours
Difficulty 1
Start Kilmartin, on A816 6 miles N of Lochgilphead. Car park opposite Kilmartin Hotel. Grid reference NR 835988
OS maps 1:50,000 55; 1:25,000 NR 79/89 (not available at time of writing)
Refreshments Kilmartin Hotel

WALK DIRECTIONS

1 With Kilmartin Hotel on right, follow main road through village. **2** Left just after petrol station, over cattle-grid, then fork left on track across left edge of field. Pass through gate at end of field. Sharp left through gate 40 yards later. Follow track which passes north, middle and south cairns (signposted) (**a**). **3** Emerge on road, turn right (**b**), to T-junction **4**. Turn right on road, then left on track where road bends to the right after 150 yards.

5 After ½ mile keep ahead on track just after cattle-grid, where main track bends right to house. **6** Turn right opposite lodge. Track crosses left edge of field (**c**). Track soon leads into woods, across bridge and into fields, at first following electricity poles then bearing left to emerge by gate and lodge on to surfaced driveway **7**. Turn right on driveway, follow to Duntrune Castle (**d**).

8 Retrace steps from castle, pass lodge (point **7**) and continue on driveway. **9** Left at T-junction to follow estate road to farmhouses, at which road bends right, then immediately left. At next right bend (50 yards later) keep straight on, on surfaced estate road (**e**). **10** Ignore right turn and 50 yards later ignore left turn by estate church, soon to reach lodge (**f**).

11 Beyond lodge cross road to lane opposite (for optional detour to Ri-cruin cairn (**g**), turn right on road; cairn is off road to right, signposted after 300 yards) and retrace to start, keeping ahead on track by primary school to go back past linear cemetery. At Kilmartin church visit sculptured stones in churchyard and crosses in church (**h**),(**i**).

WHAT TO LOOK OUT FOR

(**a**) The **north, middle and south cairns** are part of a linear Bronze Age cemetery stretching 1 mile. The purpose of the alignment is unknown. The cairns have been victims of grave robbing; what survives is nonetheless rem .kable. The **north cairn** has a reconstructed exterior and is entered by a sliding trap-door, under which a ladder leads into a chamber. In it is a tomb and carved slab; an excellent information board helps identify axehead marks and ring and cup motifs. The **middle cairn** was robbed before excavation, but one cist (a box made of stone slabs) with cup and axehead marks can still be seen. The **south cairn** is the most striking of all and, at 134ft long, one of the largest in Britain. The chamber itself is 19ft long, and entered by an opening between stone slabs. Urns and coffins would have been placed here; graves of the Beaker Folk were excavated here in the 19th century.

(**b**) **Templewood Circles** (On the right of road). The incomplete circle was never finished, and replaced a wood circle. The main circle consists of 17 uprights, with one orange-coloured stone with a carved spiral

motif; this seems likely to have been to do with sun worship.
(**c**) On the right in this field is **Kilchoan**, a burial-chamber with a Bronze Age cist.
(**d**) **Duntrune Castle** (not open to public) 13th-century, originally the residence of the Campbells, taken over by the Malcolms of Poltalloch, who still live here. A dismal tale concerns a piper who, in 1644, was sent out by the MacDonalds to spy on the castle; he was caught, had his hands cut off and was immured alive. The legend was confirmed when, in the course of building work in the 19th century, workmen found a handless skeleton of a young man between the walls. **View** SW to Isle of Jura, S to Knapdale Forest on the mainland.
(**e**) The sinister ruin of **New Poltalloch House** becomes visible on left. Built for Neil Malcolm in 1849 at

a cost of £100,000, it fell into ruin in the 1950s.
(**f**) Just before the lodge, a **Bronze Age cist** is visible up on bank on left.
(**g**) **Ri-cruin cairn** Stands in trees. Thoroughly plundered, but two cists remain among the stones.
(**h**) **Kilmartin church** Building itself is of little consequence but inside is Kilmartin Cross, an early Celtic cross that is one of the oldest images of Christ to be found in Britain. The beardless face, short hair and right angles of the arms indicate it is from the 10th century. A medieval cross stands alongside. Under a cover in the churchyard are sculptured stones – locally carved medieval tombstones.
(**i**) If you haven't reached saturation point, there is one more cairn to see. Return to petrol station where walk started and turn left just before it by the signpost to **Glebe cairn**, which soon comes into view.

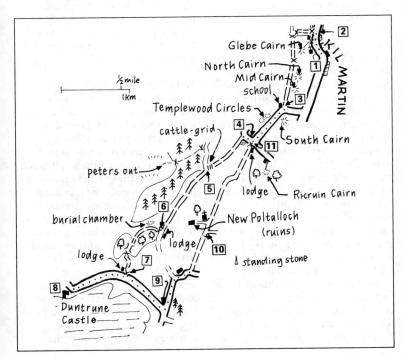

Inveraray and Dunchuach Tower

Incorporates stretches of pasture and planted forestry (some semi-open). Steady ascent to tower on the wooded hill just above Inveraray Castle, then level estate tracks past the castle itself. Mostly on well-defined paths and tracks; route-finding moderately easy.

Length 6 miles (9.5km), 3 hours
Difficulty 2–3
Start Inverary town centre, on A83 24 miles NE of Lochgilphead
OS maps 1:50,000 56; 1:25,000 NN 00/10 and NN 01/11
Refreshments Argyll Arms (Johnson and Boswell came here on their Highland tour in 1773) and George Inn, both in Inveraray; tea-room in Inveraray Castle

WALK DIRECTIONS

1 (a) From quay in front of Inveraray tourist information office follow up Main Street, pass round left of church and continue along loch shore (b). Right immediately past petrol station, then fork right after 40 yards and turn right again at T-junction (Sinclair Avenue). Follow this round as it bends left through housing estate called Barn Park.

2 Where metalled road ends, turn right on stony track, then turn immediately left through gate to follow left edge of field. Through iron kissing-gate, then left on track inside wood. Continue for ½ mile, ignoring turnings to left. **3** Immediately before water-treatment station, fork right on track into woods. Continue through woods for ⅓ mile. **4** Turn right on wide forestry track. Follow for 1 mile, ignoring all side tracks.

5 Cross road and continue forward on track, soon passing through complex of workshops and cottages (c). Where track bends right, just beyond end of complex, turn left on road over bridge. Keep right on other side, and 100 yards later fork left on track. **6** After further 150 yards reach gate and, 150 yards later, coloured waymarking arrows at edge of wood on right; turn left here on grassy field track, and soon turn left on major track, through gate into wood (d). 80 yards into wood, fork right, and continue on stony track which winds uphill to reach tower at top of Dunchuach (e) **7**.

From tower, retrace steps for 100 yards back to waymarker post just below woods. 20 yards further on, turn right on narrow path, first through grass, then descending steeply into wood. After ¼ mile, left at junction of paths, continuing steeply downhill. Just after short flight of steps, reach forestry track, turn right on it then sharp left after 100 yards on narrow waymarked path.

8 Right on track at edge of woods.
9 Left at T-junction, to pass over bridge. Continue along tarmac driveway, past Inveraray Castle on left (f) to return to starting-point, ignoring right turns.

WHAT TO LOOK OUT FOR

(a) **Inveraray** Transplanted from its old location near the castle when the Duke of Argyll decided he didn't want the town on his doorstep. Though it has lost its role as an important centre for the woollen and fishing industries, and as a centre of judiciary, it remains an intact and handsomely conserved example of 18th-century town planning. Several reminders of former land use in its street names, such as Factory Land (site of old woollen factory), Ferry Land (where there was some accommodation for the ferryman) and Relief Land (the tenements for the poor). A survival of the Old Town is the medieval Mercat's Cross, removed from its old site to the

quayside end of the Main Street in the 1830s. At the other end of the Main Street is the imposing classical church (built 1794–1804), originally divided into two so that services could be held in Gaelic and English.
(b) **Raised beach** As you leave the town, the flat, low land to the right shows the original level of the beach.
(c) **Malt Land** Partly abandoned group of workshops and farm buildings.
(d) **Arboretum** A varied tree collection, partly exotic; fully described in a nature trail leaflet available at the castle. Just after entering woods you pass on the left the remains of a lime kiln, which until 1912 produced agricultural lime for use on the estate. At point 6, on the left of the path, is an enormous

Western red cedar, with the largest girth of any red cedar in Scotland.
Flowers Orchids, speedwell, greater stitchwort, pimpernel. **Birds** Jackdaws, buzzards, woodwarblers, spotted flycatchers, skylarks, meadow pipits. **Mammals** Wild cats, badgers, red squirrels, deer.
(e) **View**, principally over Loch Fyne. In the distance, Ben Vorlich (to the E, 3,093ft), Ben Bhuide (NE, 3,112ft) and others. The tower on top was built as a picturesque imitation ruin in 1748, to add to the vista from the castle, from which it appears in silhouette.
(f) **Inveraray Castle** (open to public; fee) Built in 1743 for the third Duke of Argyll to a design by William Adam, to replace the old castle which had by then become a ruin.

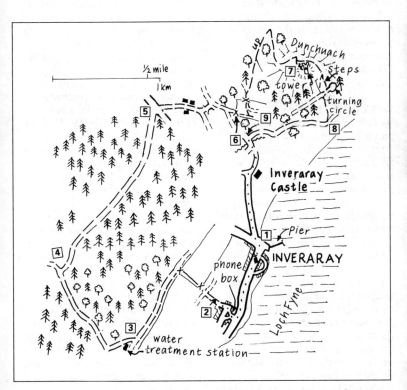

Isle of Kerrera

Takes in the entire southern half of
an island of small green hills. Careful
timing needed in order to get ferry
back to mainland; check times before
departure. Exceptional views in final
section from Gylen Castle. Mostly on
tracks, with a short undefined section
after 6, then along the coast path;
route-finding quite easy.

Length 8 miles (13km), 4½ hours
Difficulty 2–3
Start Isle of Kerrera, reached by ferry
from 2 miles SW of Oban. Follow
road along coast, past Kilbowie
Hostel; terminal is just after next
group of two houses and marked by
'telegraph cable' indicator-post. Ferry
times on small notice board;
alternatively, check with Oban
Information Centre (telephone Oban
63122). No service after 5pm, or on
Sundays (at time of writing). Grid
reference NM 835283
OS maps 1:50,000 49;
1:25,000 NM 62/72 and NM 82/92

WALK DIRECTIONS

1 From ferry, follow road up past
phone box, and fork right 100 yards
later on to track. Ignore left turn to
farm after ¼ mile. 2 After ½ mile
from start, keep forward through
gate, ignoring track on right. 3
¾ mile later, track reaches cottage.
(a) Keep just to right of cottage, then
forward immediately past ruined
barns on left, picking up grassy track
which contours hillside then follows
bottom of small valley.

4 Emerge at next cottage (away to
your left); continue forward to gate
then along track. 5 After ¾ mile,
pass next cottage. *NB If you're in a
hurry to catch the ferry back, follow
track back to start, though in doing
this you'll miss the castle, followed
by the finest part of the walk.*

50 yards later, just as track is about
to ascend, turn right through gate

into field (no path) and head towards
sea. Soon castle comes into view:
make for it. (b) 6 At castle, locate
cave above shore away to left (200
yards to left of prominent pinnacle).
Head for grassy valley beyond,
keeping to left of cave (no path, but
going is easy). Follow valley to cross
right-hand end of tumbledown wall
ahead, then rejoin shore. View opens
out dramatically (c).

7 Follow clear path which runs
close to shore (below cliffs) for 1 mile
(passing lighthouse out on right,
¾ mile). 8 Reach large bay (with
cottages) and rejoin track; turn right
along it (d), to starting-place.

WHAT TO LOOK OUT FOR

(**a**) **View** W across to the Isle of Mull,
including Dùn da Ghaoithe (2,512ft);
N to the low-lying isle of Lismore;
beyond it, several peaks on Morven,
one of the remotest parts of the
mainland; Glencoe allegedly visible
to the NE.
(**b**) **Gylen Castle** (or Castle of the
Springs) Spectacularly perched on
pillar of rock overlooking a bay of low
cliffs, built 1587 by the MacDougalls
of Dunollie and destroyed by the
covenanting troops of General Leslie
in 1647. A tower and internal
staircase remain; its only visitors
now are sheep and the occasional
walker.
(**c**) **View** SW to the Isle of Seil and the
Garvellachs; S to the mainland to
which Seil is almost joined; and, once
you have rounded the corner, E across
the Sound of Kerrera; NE to Oban.
(**d**) The **farmhouse** soon passed up on
the left, close to the field, is where
Alexander II of Scotland died during a
visit to Dunollie. At Horseshoe Bay,
where you pick up the ferry, King
Haakon of Norway gathered his fleet
in 1263 before the battle of Largs in
the Clyde, in which the Scots were
victorious.

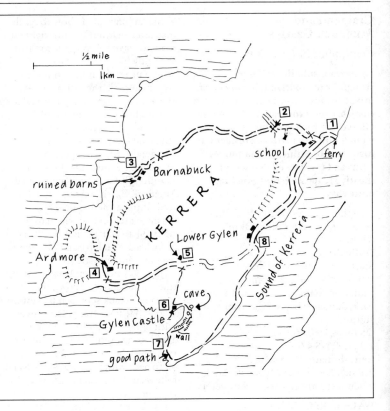

Craigend and Mugdock Castles

Contributed by John White

Leads from suburban Glasgow straight into moorland; further on are mixed woods, three lochs, two ruined castles, a reservoir path and a view of Glasgow, which feels miles away. Comes down to earth at a residential road close to Milngavie station. All paths and tracks well defined and mostly signposted; route-finding quite easy.

Length 5½ miles (9km), 2½ hours
With extension 8 miles (13km), 4 hours
Difficulty 1
Start Milngavie (pronounced 'Mulguy') station, 23 minutes by train from Glasgow Central. Large car park. Sundays: bus services only (to station)
OS maps 1:50,000 64; 1:25,000 NS 47/57
Refreshments Milngavie only (though possibly at Mugdock Castle when restoration work is complete)

WALK DIRECTIONS

1 With station entrance behind you, turn left, under pedestrian tunnel. West Highland Way (WHW) begins here (map displayed), and is clearly signposted or waymarked with thistle motifs; Allander Way signposts are also followed. Follow Station Road beyond tunnel, down main pedestrian street in Milngavie, turning right just after crossing river (signpost), down ramp, right on road then immediately left on signposted tarmac path.

2 After 300 yards turn left as signed (yellow arrow), then after 50 yards turn right, along riverside (waymarked). **3** WHW turns right to leave river after 500 yards (waymark), turning left 300 yards later at T-junction (waymarked). **4** Straight on after ¼ mile (signposted Mugdock Wood) at junction. Follow to reach road after ¾ mile **5**. Turn right on road, to leave WHW. (*For extension see below*)

6 Turn right after ½ mile, into Kyber car park, then turn left after 30 yards through gate (but first detour ahead a few yards for view of Glasgow) on track signposted Craigend Castle (**b**). **7** Turn right at Craigend Castle (signposted Mugdock Castle) and follow track for ½ mile. **8** Turn right (signposted Mugdock Castle) on to path, which leads into and across field to kissing-gate, beyond which fork right. **9** Reach T-junction with track (castle on left), and turn left to pass in front of castle (**c**).

10 200 yards later, keep on main track as it bends left down to lochside. Track soon bends right into woods. **11** Just after passing level with house (visible away to left), avoid stone bridge on left leading to iron gates, but fork left 20 yards later on to path which crosses stream and follows it, then reaches road **12**. Turn right on road.

13 At bottom of hill pass through gateway in reservoir wall on left, then right along reservoir path (**d**); follow to buildings. **14** Turn left on road at far end, past waterworks building on left (**e**), then turn right at ornamental garden into driveway. **15** 200 yards before (locked) gates ahead, take parallel residential road on right to keep in same direction. **16** Right at road junction at bottom, into Moor Road. **17** Left at T-junction (Buchanan Street); follow back to start.

For extension, from **5** , turn left on road, then right after 30 yards through kissing-gate, continuing on WHW; track passes lake after ½ mile. On reaching small lake on left, keep forward on track (waymark misleading at time of writing), reaching turning-circle after 100

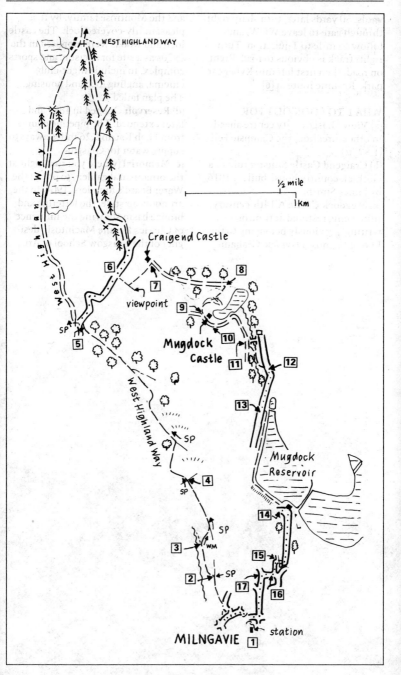

yards. 50 yards later, turn sharp right through gate to leave WHW, and follow ½ mile to T-junction. Turn right; track is obvious to road. Right on road, then first left into Kyber car park. Resume route at **6**.

WHAT TO LOOK OUT FOR
(a) **View** Glasgow city centre ahead; in other direction, the Campsie Fells (1,897ft).
(b) **Craigend Castle** Sinister ruin of a Gothick country house built *c.* 1816 by James Smith.
(c) **Mugdock Castle** A 14th-century ruin (being restored at time of writing) previously belonging to the Earl of Lennox, David de Grahame and the Montrose family. By it, a pleasant lily-covered loch. The castle, loch and woods were proposed in the 1970s as a site for a leisure and sports complex, to include night-club, cinema, angling loch and housing. The plan failed.
(d) **Reservoir** Opened in 1859 and later extended. The pipeline comes from Loch Katrine, 26 miles away, to supply water for Glasgow.
(e) **Memorial** (where you turn right at the ornamental garden) to one of the Water Board's founders, 1904. In the art nouveau style, the lettering and bronze basin showing the influence of Charles Rennie Macintosh, designer of the Glasgow School of Art.

TAYSIDE

Knock of Crieff and the Shaggie Burn

Easy woodland paths, farm tracks and estate roads, with distant views of wilder terrain. Route undefined between 6 and 8, and directions are a little involved; follow with care. Nature trail leaflet (covering part of walk) available from Crieff Tourist Office.

Length 6 miles (9.5km), 3 hours
Difficulty 3
Start James Square, Crieff
OS maps 1:50,000 52 or 58;
1:25,000 NN 82/92
Refreshments Full range in Crieff

WALK DIRECTIONS

1 (a) From centre of Crieff take Hill Street, diagonally across James Square from Tourist Information Office, and just to the right of the Drummond Arms Hotel. Left and immediately right at first crossroads, along Knock Road. Continue same direction, ignoring turns to left; road soon becomes unmetalled track. **2** Left on narrow path 20 yards before kissing-gate, to proceed with fence on left. Path merges with track near house after 50 yards: turn left along it, then 40 yards later, pick up narrow path running along fence on left.

Immediately after field on left ends, fork right into wood, and fork right again after 40 yards. Path soon joins fence on left to follow edge of wood. After ¼ mile track enters second wood. **3** 150 yards later, fork right at first junction of tracks in this wood. (You are now on the Culcrieff Nature Trail, marked with numbered posts.) Left at next junction of tracks, then straight on by post number 4 (left leads to farm). Follow main track as it winds gradually downhill between fields.

4 Keep sharp right on main track

by point 8 on nature trail (leaving trail which continues ahead on narrow path). 100 yards later turn right through metal gate, to follow stream and edge of field on left. Through further gate, then follow path, first through woodland, then along bottom of quarry. Keep left in centre of quarry to follow wide track across wooden bridge to road **5**.

Turn right on road for 150 yards, then fork right on to estate track, with lodge on left ('private road – no entry' sign on this track refers to vehicles and walkers are welcome). Follow estate track for 1 mile, and turn right on to main drive in front of Monzie Castle (b). **6** Take first gate on right after small bridge adorned with four pointed stone towers, and turn immediately right with fence on right. Follow edge of field round to find partially collapsed (but very robust) wooden bridge across ditch on far side (it is 80 yards to left of far right-hand corner; there is prominent heap of boulders on far side of bridge). Cross this carefully and follow left side of next field. Turn right at top of field, proceeding with fence on left.

7 In far right corner of field (as viewed from bridge), turn left through gate/stile, and bear half right to cross open moorland. There is no defined path over this, but it helps to keep Monzie Castle and last gate you have turned through in a straight line behind you. This brings you to wooden kissing-gate at edge of wood ahead (if you have passed through bracken to reach edge of wood, you have gone too far to the left; if you've had to lose height, you're too far right) **8**. Into wood, then proceed alongside fence on left. Path is indistinct at first, but soon improves after path merges from right.

After 250 yards forward over cross-track on to clear path, and right

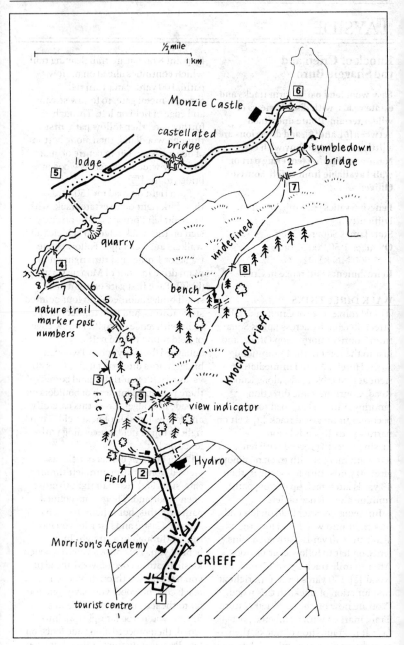

at first fork to reach viewpoint and view-indicator table (**c**) **9**. Continue direction on leaving viewpoint on broad path downhill between two benches to left and one to right. Turn right at first fork (after 200 yards, on entering woods), left at second one, just after passing two benches. Forward over wide track at edge of wood, through gate to follow left-hand edge of field. Cross driveway to Hydro Hotel (**d**), and continue direction, later on road, to return to centre of Crieff.

WHAT TO LOOK OUT FOR
(**a**) **Crieff** Formerly one of the two great 'trysts' or cattle-markets of Scotland (the other was at Stenhousemuir), where Highland drovers brought their cattle and buyers travelled in from the S. After the town was burnt down by the Highlanders in the Jacobite Rebellion of 1716, James Drummond laid out James Square. In 1746, during his retreat to Culloden, Bonnie Prince Charlie held a council of war in the

Drummond Arms (which has since been rebuilt).
(**b**) **Monzie Castle** (not open to public) Georgian in character, but largely rebuilt at the turn of the century. Approached by a rather theatrical castellated bridge.
(**c**) **Knock of Crieff** A wooded sandstone hill with a view-indicator pointing out some of the SE Highland peaks, including Ben Vorlich (3,231ft) and Ben Chonzie (3,048ft). To its S is a hill where the 'kind gallows' once stood, on which Highland cattle thieves were hung by the Stewarts of Strathearn.
(**d**) **Strathearn Hydro** Established in 1868 for people who wanted to take its health-giving waters, it is a large establishment with much character, including a vast lounge and a wrought-iron balcony somewhat reminiscent of the 'cure' resorts of Vichy and Baden-Baden. Serves tea and coffee.

Kinnoull Hill and the Tay Valley

A wooded hill on the edge of Perth, flat on top but precipitous on one side, capped by two stone follies. One stretch of road-walking, though road is quiet and there are good views beyond Kinfauns Castle to the Tay. Full walk is a figure of eight route; short one takes the southern loop via Kinnoull Tower. Trail leaflets available from Perth Tourist Office. Thoroughly waymarked; easy route-finding.

Length *Full walk* 6 miles (9.5km), 3 hours
Short walk 3½ miles (5.5km), 1½ hours
Difficulty 1
Start Quarry car park, Kinnoull Hill, 1 mile E of Perth. From tourist information centre in Perth follow main road with river on your right, then cross next road-bridge. Turn right on other side, then first left, just after Isle of Skye Hotel, into Manse Road. At end of road turn right at crossroads into Hatton Road. Car park is 150 yards after end of built-up area, signposted on right of road. Grid reference NO 134235
OS maps 1:50,000 53 or 58: 1:25,000 NO 02/12

WALK DIRECTIONS

1 Return to entrance of car park, turn right on path signposted 'children's walk'. Follow yellow marker posts, past viewpoint and forking right by house, then turning left 100 yards later into woods. Many paths exist in woods: look out for further yellow marker posts. Just before reaching wider track, path passes brown marker post (for 'nature walk', which here duplicates 'children's walk') **2** . Turn left on this track and follow to gate leading on to road **3** .

For short walk turn sharp right immediately before reaching road, signposted 'tower walk'; this is **8** .

For full walk turn right on road, and look out soon for Binnhill Tower in woods ahead, just to right of road. **4** Turn right on track leading into woods for detour to Binnhill Tower (**a**). Track passes through barrier: fork left beyond, follow to tower. Retrace steps to road. Turn right to continue along road for 250 yards. **5** Left on track, signposted Coronation Road (**b**). Track leads to deserted cottages, bends left through gate between them. Follow left edge of field ahead, to gate in far left-hand corner.

6 Keep forward beyond gate, at first with fence on left, and then forward on path marked with yellow marker posts (horseshoe motifs). At end of forest, path turns right (waymarked), then 50 yards later turn left through gate, signposted Coronation Road, to enter forest.
7 After ¼ mile turn left, following

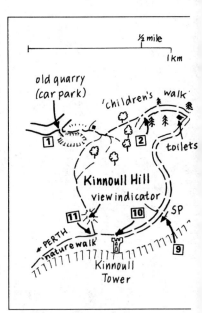

470

sign to Jubilee car park and Corsie Hill. Keep forward after 250 yards, ignoring track sharp left. Keep forward again after a further 200 yards, ignoring track sharp right, then fork right 50 yards later (yellow marker post). Continue to barrier then follow track along edge of woods gently downhill to road. Left on road then 100 yards later right through gate **8**.

Fork left beyond gate (signposted for 'tower walk'). **9** After ¾ mile turn left, signposted Kinnoull Tower (**c**). **10** Forward at tower along cliff-top. **11** At cliff viewpoint turn right towards view-indicator. (If you started on foot from Perth, you can follow cliff-path all the way back; keep left at **11**, ignore all subsequent right turns.) Just to right of indicator pick up yellow waymarks ('children's walk'). Path forks right, then leads through woods. ½ mile later turn right (waymarked) at junction. Follow path ahead back to car park (ignoring next waymarked turn on right, of course).

WHAT TO LOOK OUT FOR

(**a**) **Binnhill Tower** Stone tower built in the 18th century as a picturesque imitation ruin. Lord Gray and the ninth Earl of Kinnoull decided after a trip up the Rhine that the Tay could do with its own romantic castles, and built Binnhill and Kinnoull Towers at the top of the cliffs above the river.
(**b**) **Coronation Road** Also known as the King's Highway. Connected the former royal city of Scone and Abernethy, another Pictish capital, from AD 700 to 1050 (though the road is possibly older than this).
(**c**) **Kinnoull Tower** and **Hill** The tower, like Binnhill, is a folly. Near it is a stone table where the ninth Earl of Kinnoull used to picnic and enjoy the view over the Tay and to the Ochils. Excellent panorama in all directions from summit of hill.

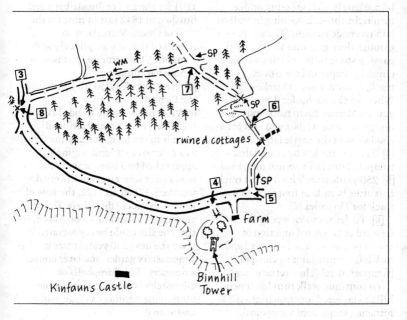

Kenmore and the banks of the Tay

Along an avenue of chestnut trees by the banks of the Tay and on a higher-level forestry track giving fine views of Taymouth Castle and Loch Tay. One very leisurely 300ft climb, otherwise all on the level. Easy route-finding.

Length 4½ miles (7km), 2 hours
With detour to viewpoint at end
5½ miles (9km), 2½ hours
Difficulty 1
Start Kenmore village square, at E end of Loch Tay. Park here; larger car park at lakeside near S end of village (both car parks free). Grid reference NN 773455
OS maps 1:50,000 51 or 52;
1:25,000 NN 64/74
Refreshments Kenmore Hotel, Kenmore

WALK DIRECTIONS

[1] (a) With church away to the left, follow main road out of village. Immediately after crossing bridge turn right through opening in wall to join riverside path (b). [2] Path passes through deer-gate into woods, soon passing stone folly (which you can climb by steps) and continues, as track, along avenue of birches. [3] When level with bridge down on right you can detour down bank and across bridge to castle (c) (but you will get a good view of the castle later).
[4] Track turns left by castellated parapet. Turn right on reaching road. [5] 250 yards later left on forest track. Left after ¼ mile at first fork, follow track for 1½ miles (d).

[6] To detour to viewpoint keep forward at staggered junction of tracks (signposted 'Viewpoint') and fork left ½ mile later to viewpoint (signposted) (e). Then retrace steps.

To continue walk turn left downhill at staggered junction (right if retracing steps from viewpoint),

and turn sharp left at next junction. [7] Just after barrier/forestry map turn right on path. [8] Turn right on reaching road and follow back into Kenmore, avoiding right turns.

WHAT TO LOOK OUT FOR

(a) **Kenmore** Its present location is due to landowner Colin Campbell of Glenorchy who, in the 16th century, decided that the village, its church and inhabitants should be moved from a few miles further up the Tay. His plan was not realised fully, however, until 1760, when the present estate village of model dwellings was built. Tenants lived here rent-free on condition that they carried on a trade and kept their houses clean.
(b) **River Tay** A ceremony every January marks the start of the salmon season, and an annual raft race from Kenmore is held in June.
(c) **Taymouth Castle** Gothick steel-blue extravaganza, begun in 1801 for the Earl of Breadalbane and finished in 1842 just in time for the visit of Queen Victoria, who remarked that it was 'princely and romantic'. Unfortunately, it is now somewhat run-down.
(d) **View** Over Taymouth Castle and the E end of Loch Tay.
(e) **View** Below is the wooded Isle of Loch Tay, one of many artificial islands in the loch, built by the Celts as a defensive site and originally approached by a causeway that is now under water (except in very dry weather). When, in 1122, the wife of King Alexander I died there, the King granted the island to Scone Abbey, so that the site could be consecrated. Over the next 200 years it was used as a monastery garden and later housed a nunnery. The Campbells of Glenorchy (who were responsible for moving Kenmore village) had a castle on it.

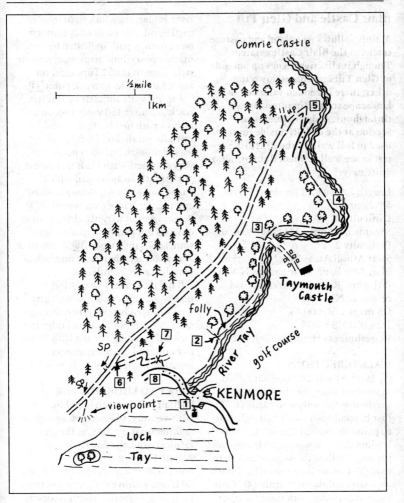

Blair Castle and Glen Tilt

Mainly follows woodland and pasture tracks of the Blair Castle estate. Though it effectively goes up one side of Glen Tilt and comes down the other, there is enough variation in landscape to sustain interest throughout. A short, quiet road section at the end. Riverside route used in full walk is undefined; other tracks are well defined. Route-finding quite easy.

Length *Full walk* 11 miles (17.5km), 5½ hours
Difficulty 3
Short walk 7 miles (11km), 3½ hours
Difficulty 2
Start Atholl Arms Hotel (by station), Blair Atholl, off A9 6½ miles NW of Pitlochry. Roadside parking. Grid reference NN 870654
OS maps 1:50,000 43;
1:25,000 NS 86/96
Refreshments Hotels in Blair Atholl

WALK DIRECTIONS

1 With Atholl Arms on left follow main road, then take first right by gatehouse and follow to castle (**a**). **2** Just beyond castle turn half right on to path (signposted Diana's Grove) leading through woods (**b**). Ignore side turnings, follow to gateway and on to road **3**. Cross road to woodland track opposite, follow for ¾ mile. **4** Turn right over bridge, fork right on other side, soon to reach deer-gate. **5** Fork left 50 yards after deer-gate; track ascends gently. Keep left at next fork, 100 yards later.

6 Leave woods by gate (**c**), and continue on grassy track along top of hill. Re-enter woods by gate and descend gently past large pond on right. Ignore sharp right turn over bridge soon after pond. **7** Take next fork right and descend to cross small stream by bridge. **8** Just after bridge pass through gate.

For short walk fork right, cross river-bridge, then fork right over cattle-grid. 200 yards later turn left on to narrow path indicated by marker posts (blue arrows), ascend to stile, then to track. Turn right on track for ¾ mile, to reach point **11**.

For full walk fork left up forestry track and after 150 yards fork on to narrow path just to right of, and initially parallel to, forest track (easily missed, but soon becomes very distinct). Path leads into forest (fork right as waymarked after 100 yards), out of forest, through fields and then to bridge over waterfall **9**. Beyond waterfall route along river is obvious but path is a little rougher, sometimes indistinct. **10** Cross river at next bridge, then right on track (**d**). Fork left after ¾ mile.

11 Track enters woods. **12** ¼ mile into woods fork right through gate. Track descends gently, bending right after ¾ mile. Follow over bridge then forward to emerge on road **13**. Turn right on road, then left at next junction, signposted 'Blair Atholl ½'.

WHAT TO LOOK OUT FOR

(**a**) **Blair Castle** (open to public; fee) 13th-century, of historical as well as architectural interest, as the chief residence of Earls and Dukes of Atholl. House guests have included Edward III and Mary Queen of Scots.
(**b**) **Diana's Grove** Collection of trees, including some fine conifers (described by notice on gate) planted in 1737. Has a statue of Diana (1861).
(**c**) **View** Over the sizeable Blair estate, an area of forest plantation and moorland used for grouse-shooting and deer-stalking. The valley was farmed, in narrow strips, until the last century by tenant farmers, remains of whose crofts can be seen in places. (**d**) By the bridge is **Marble Lodge**, called after a nearby outcrop of green marble that also went to make the fireplace in the castle's great hall.

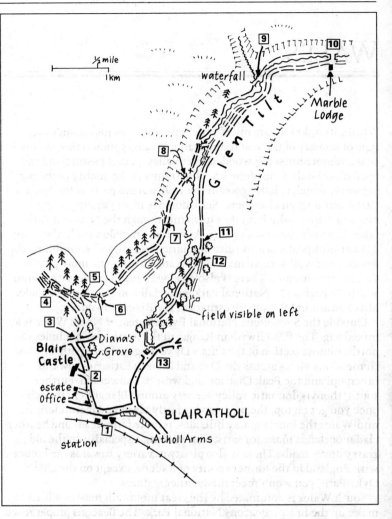

WALES

Within its 8,000 square miles Wales encompasses just about every type of scenery of interest to the walker – craggy mountains, dramatic coast, remote hillsides, wooded river valleys, quiet pastureland and open moorlands. One of the few constraints is the quality of the path network, which is fairly good in the well-walked parts of the National Parks, but uneven elsewhere. Snowdonia is most famous for the mountain from which it takes its name, though the National Park takes in a very much wider area. As well as Snowdon itself, the many 3,000ft-plus peaks nearby offer dramatic walking and scrambling: the selection of walks we've made deliberately avoids the more popular ascents and circuits. There is also good walking in the less frequented southern part of the National Park, especially on the slopes of Cader Idris and around the superb estuary of the River Mawddach.

Outside the Snowdonia National Park the rest of North Wales is a mixed bag. The fine Clwydian Range, in the north-east, includes the northernmost section of the Offa's Dyke long-distance path, and has tremendous views across the Dee and Mersey Estuaries towards Liverpool and the Peak District, and west to Snowdonia. Further south, there is dramatic valley scenery around Llangollen, though once you get on top, the moorland is fairly bleak and featureless. In mid-Wales the lonely grassy hillsides, remote farmsteads and heather-clad moorlands make for satisfying walking, especially on the old grassy drove roads. There is also plenty of variety towards the border with England in the former county of Radnor; except on the Offa's Dyke Path, you won't meet many other walkers.

South Wales is dominated by the great mountain masses which make up the Brecon Beacons National Park. The Beacons proper reach nearly 3,000ft; their grassy, horseshoe-shaped ridges offer exception-ally fine walks. Between the Beacons and the English border, the National Park takes in the high sandstone plateau of the Black Moun-tains, cut into by a series of narrow valleys to leave a series of ridges in between. West of the Beacons, but still within the National Park, the rolling grassy (and strikingly unforested) hills of the Fforest Fawr have on their fringes a series of impressive waterfalls in the valleys of the Hepste, Mellte and the Neath. Generally, we were disappointed by the quality of footpaths in the Brecon Beacons National Park – we didn't find them as well signposted or maintained as in most other National Parks, and we found a surprising number blocked or hard to follow.

Elsewhere in South Wales, there is fine coast walking in Glamorgan, particularly on the cliff-tops of the Gower Peninsula, though you have to pick your routes carefully. The mining valleys may not appeal to everyone but, with their abrupt hillsides, secluded forests and remote moorlands, they provide some pleasant walking; one of the most scenic parts is around Afan Argoed. Then, on the eastern edge of Wales there's the dramatic lower Wye Valley, where the river has carved a sinuous course between steeply wooded slopes.

Wales's third National Park, the Pembrokeshire Coast, embraces almost two hundred miles of consistently beautiful coast, with barely a break in the long-distance coastal path. The path network inland is a bit sparse, but there are still plenty of opportunities for good round walks. In the south, the cliffs are lower and flatter, there are impressive river estuaries, and the farmland inland is lush and green. Best of all, though, are the round walks on the peninsulas, such as Strumble Head and Marloes, from where the sea, dotted with rocks and tiny islands, stretches away in all directions.

CLWYD

Vale of Llangollen and Castell Dinas Bran

On two levels along a steep-sided valley – by a canal, then up on the Panorama Walk (though the walk's best view is from the scant ruin on Castell Dinas Bran). Directions should be followed with care from **3** until Offa's Dyke Path is picked up; otherwise easy route-finding.

Length 5½ miles (9km), 2½ hours
Difficulty 2
Start Llangollen, by river-bridge (next to steam railway station)
OS maps 1:50,000 117;
1:25,000 SJ 24/34
Refreshments Full range in Llangollen; Sun Inn, Trevor

WALK DIRECTIONS

1 (**a**) Cross bridge over River Dee, turn right on A539 then immediately left up lane. Follow until canal bridge, turning on to towpath just before bridge. Turn right on towpath (**b**), which after 1½ miles bends right under main road: leave canal by crossing next bridge **2**. Cross main road, taking lane slightly to right by pub. Follow uphill for ¼ mile then, where lane bends sharp left, continue forward on left-hand of two tracks.

After ¼ mile, and 50 yards after passing through second gate, reach hairpin corner of track at edge of trees; turn left and **3** 50 yards later turn right over stile. Then continue forward, alongside fence on right. At corner of fence, continue forward another 30 yards into trees, then pick up path leading half right alongside old stone wall, to cross stile into denser forest. Ascend path: after 130 yards ignore first sharp left turn but take second sharp left 150 yards later, by acorn waymarker on tree (indicating Offa's Dyke Path). Follow up to

reach stile on to tarmac lane (the Panorama Walk) **4**.

Turn left on lane for 1½ miles. Ignore sharp left turn after 1 mile (**c**). **5** When level with Castell Dinas (ruined castle on isolated hill on your left), turn left over cattle-grid and 50 yards later cross stile on right to ascend to top of hill (**d**). Keep to right side of castle ruins at top, descend on to prominent stony track leading down on to grassy ridge (Llangollen is away to left).

6 At end of ridge, once level with house on left, join stony track and pass through gate. Continue forward at junction of tracks 100 yards later

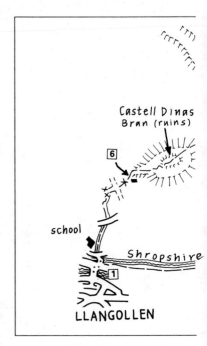

Castell Dinas Bran (ruins)

school

Shropshire

LLANGOLLEN

and at end, pass through left-hand of two gates. Clear path then leads along left edge of field, across lane and through gate opposite, finally emerging above canal bridge where towpath was first picked up. Turn left back into Llangollen.

WHAT TO LOOK OUT FOR

(a) **Llangollen** Its international fame as the headquarters of the Eisteddfod has made it a busy tourist centre. Two features of note: the carved oak ceiling in the 13th-century church and the four-arched stone bridge (built 1345-46 by John Trevor), one of the 'seven wonders of Wales'.

(b) **Llangollen Canal** Runs 46 miles from the Shropshire Union Canal at Hurleston to Llantisilio just N of Llangollen, where it is fed by the Dee via Telford's engineered 'Horseshoe Falls'. A few miles E is Telford's Pontcysyllte Aqueduct, 120ft high and 100ft long.

(c) **View** Right, of the limestone terraces of the Eglwyseg escarpment, which culminates at World's End to the N.

(d) **Castell Dinas Bran** ('Crow Castle') An 8th-century ruin crowning a steep-sided hillock above the Vale of Llangollen. Originally built for Eliseg Prince of Powys, it was occupied in the 13th century by Griffith, son of Madoc, who sided with Henry III and thus betrayed his country. **View** E down the Dee Valley towards the Pontcysyllte Aqueduct.

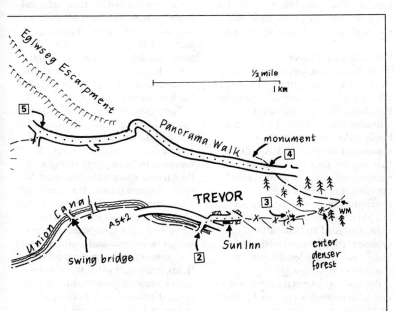

Gop Hill, Graig Fawr and Dyserth Falls

A tour of the northernmost end of the Clwydian Range, and just about the northernmost part of the Offa's Dyke Path. Only rises to 820ft but there are nonetheless extensive views. Pasture fields and moorland edge, with an old railway track in the final stages. Route-finding intricate (field paths sometimes undefined) but not difficult.

Length 10 miles (16km), 5 hours
Difficulty 3
Start Dyserth, on A5151, 3 miles S of Prestatyn. Car park in village
OS maps 1:50,000 116;
1:25,000 SJ 07/17 and SJ 08/18
Refreshments Pubs and cafés at Dyserth; Blue Lion Inn at Cwm; shop and Crown Inn at Trelawnyd; shop and Eagle and Child at Gwaenysgor

WALK DIRECTIONS

[1] (a) Make your way up main street (A5151) and turn right into Foel Road. Where road forks, keep left in Upper Foel Road. [2] 200 yards after rejoining lower road and where road bends right, keep forward on signposted footpath, at first a drive, then beyond stile continues as narrow path along bottom of woods. On emerging from woods via stile continue direction along contour of hill (do not ascend) to stile. Beyond stile cross road and take stile opposite, then proceed with hedgerow on your left (no path) to reach gate on skyline [3].

Beyond gate maintain direction, in line with prominent isolated house on hillside ahead, and soon descending. 50 yards before road and houses turn left to find well-defined path leading just below woods to stile, beyond which turn right along hedgerow to stile. Emerge on road by Blue Lion Inn at Cwm [4]. Turn left on road, then left immediately before church, over signposted stile. Keep alongside churchyard wall, but where it bends half right, bear half left to stile into woods. Proceed on woodland path to stile at top, then keep forward alongside hedge on left until stile on to tarmac lane. Cross lane to stile opposite (immediately to left of electricity post). Proceed along right edge of field to makeshift stile at end [5].

Continue forward across second field to gate ahead and bear half right across third field to makeshift stile in break in hedge ahead. Cross track and take Offa's Dyke Path, over stile opposite. Continue forward, along slight valley in first field, to stile, then follow left edge of second field to cross stile at end [6]. Emerge on to track between hedges, turn right and follow to road. Left on road, then take waymarked stile after 20 yards, bearing half left across field towards trees, just before which keep to left side of hedgerow and proceed to stile, then continue on path, soon reaching track between hedges [7].

Turn right on track. After 400 yards ignore sharp right turn, continue past waterworks then take next right. [8] 400 yards later, where main track veers left to house, keep straight on, then ignore sharp right turn after 200 yards. Proceed for another ½ mile. [9] Turn left at T-junction of tracks, then 50 yards later cross stile on right. Cross first field, alongside remains of hedgerow on right and maintain same direction across second and third fields, aiming for gates ahead in line with bottom of churchyard. Turn left on road, proceed up to main road in village of Trelawynyd. [10] Turn right on road, then left on road signposted Llanasa, by clock tower. Just before road bends right at top of village take driveway on left (signposted public footpath), soon keeping just to right of garage ahead, then cross stile into scrubby land. Bear half right, uphill

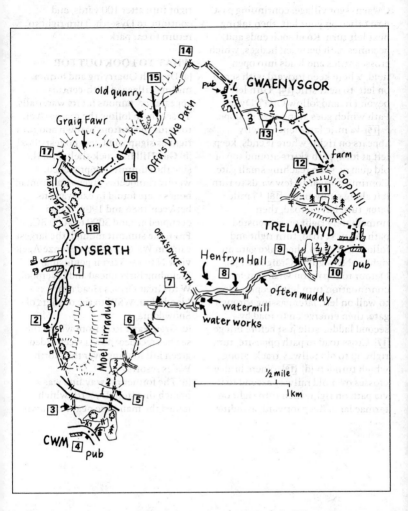

(path soon gives out) aiming for summit, a grassy tump between two bands of woodland, and approached via stile.

11 From summit (**b**), retrace steps to stile, then turn right keeping close to woodland wall, and soon descending. At bottom cross stile, turn right on to farm track, then immediately fork left on to track skirting base of hill. **12** When level with farm on left, fork left into farmyard, in centre of which turn left

on to farm road. At T-junction turn left, then cross stile on right after 30 yards. Bear half left (no path) across first field, up to corner of hedgerow opposite and proceed along it with hedge on right to leave field by stile in top corner **13**.

Maintain same direction in second field, crossing stile 50 yards left of right end of stone wall. Proceed across third field to leave by gate in far right-hand corner. Beyond, turn right on road, follow through

Gwaenysgor village, continuing past post office on your left, then taking next left turn. Road soon ends and becomes path between hedges, which crosses stiles and leads into open field, where keep forward with scrub on left, to next stile **14**. Turn left beyond it, and follow Offa's Dyke Path which goes along edge of slope.

15 ¼ mile later fence briefly appears on right; where it ends, keep left at fork; path skirts around top of old quarry, soon reaching small gate. Continue forward a few yards to turn left along stony track. **16** ¼ mile later, turn left on road, then immediately right on signposted path. At next road, turn right and follow 150 yards, then take gate on right at NT sign for Graig Fawr (**c**). Detour to top if you wish, but for continuation turn left, keeping close to wall on left, later passing through gate, then emerge on to road by second ladder-stile just before bridge **17**. Cross road to path opposite, turn right up to old railway track, along which turn left (**d**). **18** Where bridge crosses over old railway ascend to it via path on right, then turn right on tarmac lane. Keep forward, avoiding

right turn after 100 yards, and continue to Dyserth. Turn right to return to car park.

WHAT TO LOOK OUT FOR
(**a**) **Dyserth** Quarrying and former milling village of 19th-century appearance, famous for its waterfalls. To see them follow the main street towards the bottom of town and turn right as signposted (fee; honesty box).
(**b**) **Gop Hill** In a rock shelter on the side the summit is approached, woolly rhinoceros, hyena and human bones were found in excavations between 1886 and 1908; it was occupied around 3000 to 4000 BC. From the summit mound (the largest cairn in Wales; possibly Bronze Age) **view** N to the Wirral peninsula, including Birkenhead and Liverpool; W to Great Ormes Head near Llandudno; WSW to the outliers of Snowdonia.
(**c**) **Graig Fawr** Reef from which the sea has receded, now a steep-sided green hill looking over the North Wales resorts.
(**d**) The former **railway line** was a branch line from Dyserth which joined the main line near Prestatyn.

DYFED

Devil's Bridge, the Rheidol Valley and Parson's Bridge

Contributed by D E Hoare

Through a wooded valley, with distant views of the gorge. Starts from terminus station of British Rail's quaintest line, along which route soon passes for a few yards; periodically emerges on to pasture. Full walk uses easy farm and forestry tracks from Parson's Bridge into next valley; shorter walk follows quiet A-road for three miles back to start. Route from 6 to 9 sporadically waymarked when inspected, but care required from 7 until 9.

Length *Full walk* 9 miles (14.5km), 4½ hours.
Shorter walk 7½ miles (12km), 4 hours
Difficulty 3
Start Devil's Bridge station (narrow-gauge; summer only) on A4120 12 miles E of Aberystwyth. Parking at station, on roadside or near Devil's Bridge Hotel. Grid reference SN 738769
OS maps 1:50,000 135; 1:25,000 SN 67/77
Refreshments Café at post office, Hafod Arms Hotel and tea-room, station kiosk, all in Devil's Bridge; Old Rectory, Ysbyty Cynfyn, sometimes serves teas.

WALK DIRECTIONS

1 Turn right out of Devil's Bridge station. Follow road towards Aberystwyth for 400 yards. At end of village, immediately past second of two bungalows, turn right through gate into field. Proceed alongside fence on right, then at corner of fence continue forward on narrow path (soon becomes wider). 80 yards after path bends left into trees, avoid right fork (which leads to gate on to railway line). Shortly, path drops down to stile, beyond which continue 50 yards alongside railway to gate on to railway (**a**), which cross for gate opposite leading into nature reserve.

2 After 100 yards fork left to take stile back on to railway and follow railway for 120 yards, then pass under wire fence on right (no stile at time of writing, but fence deliberately tied up for easy access) on to path descending through wood to stile into rough pasture. Follow clear path through next gate, then **3** turn right downhill alongside woods on right to gate over footbridge over River Rheidol. On far side of bridge, turn right along road past old mine (**b**).

4 After ¼ mile, after climbing slope, where road turns left, keep forward on stony track past two cottages on left and go through gate into forest. Shortly, area of open pasture appears on right. Pass alongside this and 200 yards before end of clearing take left fork into trees and ascend slowly through wood. **5** Cross stile (**c**) and turn left steeply up path alongside fence. Path soon veers right, reaching gate/stile after ¼ mile. Continue forward on track for ¾ mile.

6 At farm (on your left), turn right through gate into field and head down field (keeping 50 yards from fence on left) to footbridge at bottom; cross it and ascend path to stile to emerge on to tarmac lane **7**. Turn left along lane. After ¼ mile turn right at junction (**d**) then after 50 yards, at Ystumtuen village sign, turn right over stile. Follow grassy path on right side of small valley (path barely defined but keep forward) and at brow of hill, lake on left comes into view. After lake, cross stile ahead and follow path to join fence coming in from left. Continue alongside fence and watch for stile over it (broken at time of checking). Cross stile and continue with fence now on right.

8 After 200 yards take second gate on right. Route is difficult to find here. 200 yards half left is small stone circle (ancient cairn): make for it and at cairn, by bearing quarter right, proceed downhill (keeping distant wooded gorge initially half left). Once you have descended steepest part of slope, you will see stile signed 'path'. Beyond it, descend alongside fence on right past ruined barn and proceed to stile into coniferous wood. Just inside wood, pick up clear path down to stile 300 yards on. Shortly after stile, reach stony path and turn left (still down-

hill) to Parson's Bridge (**e**) **9**.

Cross bridge and on other side immediately bear left through gate and up path, zigzagging steeply up through forest. At second zigzag (sharp left), ignore faint path ahead and keep to main path up to left. Emerge from wood through gate and follow path between walls and fences to church at Ysbyty Cynfyn (**f**) **10**.

For shorter walk turn right on road, and follow back to start.

For full walk turn left on road for 300 yards, then right on farm track just before 'road narrows' sign. This ascends gently for 1 mile, turning right

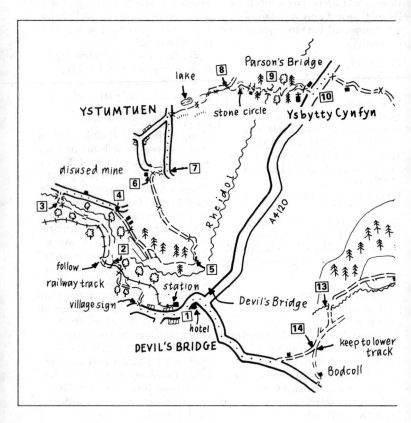

just after farm and finally enters forest by gate. **11** 20 yards later fork right on to path which descends steeply through forest. Cross forest track after ¼ mile, taking path opposite, 20 yards to right.

12 After ¼ mile, at next forestry track, turn left, and 200 yards later turn sharp right at junction of tracks. Follow this level track along bottom of forest. **13** After 1½ miles track bends left to cross bridge and through gate immediately after. **14** ¼ mile later fork right on to lower of two tracks leading past cottage and up to road. Turn right to Devil's Bridge (**g**).

½ mile

1 km

WHAT TO LOOK OUT FOR
(**a**) **Vale of Rheidol railway**
Narrow-gauge steam railway, opened in 1902 to serve Rheidol Valley zinc mines, and since being threatened with closure in 1954 has become a major tourist attraction run by BR.
(**b**) Remains of Rheidol United **iron oxide and lead mines**.
(**c**) Continue ahead for a few paces for a good view of the **Mynach Falls**.
(**d**) Straight ahead are the ruins of the barracks for **Ystumtuen** lead mines, which were worked from the 16th century until the early 20th century.
(**e**) **Parson's Bridge** Modern bridge across a rocky chasm gouged out by the River Rheidol (one of Britain's swiftest rivers, it falls 1,750ft in 28 miles from its source at Plynlimon to the sea at Aberystwyth). The original bridge was named because it was used by clergymen on their way to conduct services at Ysbyty Cynfyn, and was just a precarious plank hung by chains.
(**f**) **Ysbyty Cynfyn** In the churchyard and wall are five standing stones, part of a pre-Christian stone circle. Many Welsh churchyards are roughly circular and this may indicate that the sites have been of special religious significance for thousands of years. A tombstone here marks the grave of the first recorded quadruplets in Wales.
(**g**) **Devil's Bridge** (fee; obtain disc from nearby kiosk to get through turnstile) Three bridges, one on top of the other, span the gorge created by the Mynach Falls. Each bridge represents a different level of the road: below the present one is an 18th-century stone structure, and below that a 12th-century one, probably built by monks from Strata Florida Abbey.

Bosherston lily ponds and St Govan's Chapel

An easy walk for everyone, with the lily ponds, a sandy beach, then a level section along the coast to the improbably placed chapel of St Govan's. Takes a quiet road back to the start. Easy route-finding. Coast path is occasionally closed for army firing practice: if so, red flags will be flying and you can make obvious circuit of the lily ponds and omit the chapel. For details of firing times, see notice board by pub in Bosherston, or telephone Castlemartin (064 65) 321.

Length 4 miles (6.5km), 1½ hours
Difficulty 1
Start Bosherston village car park, by church (free). From Pembroke take B4319 S, then after 4 miles turn left on to minor road signposted Bosherston and St Govan's (signpost not very clear at time of inspection – watch for previous turning, which is signposted Broad Haven and Freshwater East. Bosherston turning is ½ mile further on). Grid reference SR 967948
OS maps 1:50,000 158; 1:25,000 SR 89/99
Refreshments St Govan's Inn, Bosherston

WALK DIRECTIONS

[1] From car park take the footpath signposted to lily ponds. At bottom of slope avoid steps on right, continuing forward to cross bridge over pond (**a**). Path first follows edge of pond, then rises over small hill to pass over second bridge. [2] Turn right over third, wide bridge, and follow path to reach top of beach [3].

Head out across sand, beyond line of dunes, turn right, then take steps on right at end of dunes. These bring you to wooden gate (with toilets, NT information booth and car park just beyond). Turn sharp left before this gate, on surfaced track, continuing

direction to stile after it ceases to be surfaced. [4] Coast path brings you to second stile at edge of MoD land. If red flag is flying here, retrace steps to Bosherston; if red flag isn't flying, continue along coast path to wooden stile at corner of car park. Cross stile and over to surfaced track beyond.

[5] Tarmac path to left of this point leads out to St Govan's Head: unless you want to detour to it, keep right here, heading for post with star on top. Go down steps to right of star to reach St Govan's Chapel, St Govan's Well and rocky cove beyond (**b**). Climb up steps and continue forward on to road inland. Follow for 1 mile back to Bosherston.

WHAT TO LOOK OUT FOR

(**a**) **Lily ponds** 80 acres of artificially created ponds, of great beauty at any time of year but particularly when the lilies are in bloom (June and July). Formerly part of the vast Stackpole Estate, the house of which was demolished in 1967. Besides lilies, **flora** includes stonewort, ploughman's spikenard, black bryony, wild thyme, cowslips. **Birds** Coots, woodpeckers, kingfishers, moorhens, teals, and several species of duck. Also: roach, pike; emperor dragonflies and blue damsel flies.
(**b**) **St Govan's Chapel** Primitive and amazingly situated at the foot of cliffs – from the top it is totally hidden from view. In the 5th century it was a hermit's cell; the occupier might have been St Gobhen or Cofen, wife of the King of Glamorgan, or (later) Sir Gawain, one of the Knights of the Round Table, who became a hermit after King Arthur's death. The stone bench and altar are the only surviving parts of the cell, now incorporated in the minuscule 13th-century chapel. A pilgrimage place in medieval times, because of the alleged curative powers for eye trouble of the red mud in a holy well nearby (now dry).

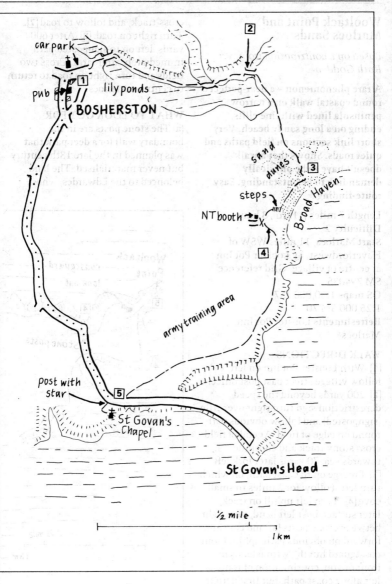

car park

pub

BOSHERSTON

lily ponds

1

2

sand dunes

3

Broad Haven

steps

NT booth

4

army training area

Woodback Point

Stone posts

post with star

5

St Govan's Chapel

St Govan's Head

½ mile

1 km

487

Wooltack Point and Marloes Sands

Based on a contribution from Ruth Godden

A rare phenomenon – a near-perfect round coastal walk on a narrow peninsula lined with fine cliffs, ending on a long sandy beach. Very short link sections on field paths and quiet roads. Shows that a walk doesn't have to be physically demanding to be outstanding. Easy route-finding.

Length 7 miles (11km), 3 hours
Difficulty 2
Start Marloes, 11 miles WSW of Haverfordwest, by Lobster Pot Inn at centre of village. Grid reference SM 794085
OS maps 1:50,000 157; 1:25,000 SM 70
Refreshments Lobster Pot Inn, Marloes

WALK DIRECTIONS

1 With Lobster Pot Inn on left, follow village street past post office.
2 200 yards beyond the speed derestriction sign turn right over stile (signposted) and follow obvious path round on edge of field. At end of field cross stony track and continue towards sea. 70 yards later fork left.
3 Emerge on to coast path, on which turn left. Follow for 2 miles to small cove **4**. Turn left uphill on track, later surfaced. At left bend, turn right between stone posts (**a**), and continue forward on obvious path uphill. From coastguard hut (**b**), with islands in front of you, continuation of route is left along coast path, but first detour down on to rocky headland (this is Wooltack Point) **5**.

Retrace steps downhill and fork right on to coast path. After 1 mile along cliff-top you get close-up views of big rocky island (Gateholm Island) (**c**). ½ mile beyond this, the path descends to gully **6**. Turn left on to

cross-track, and follow to road **7**. Turn right on road. **8** After 600 yards, left on to signposted path immediately after farm. Cross two fields and turn right on road to return to centre of Marloes.

WHAT TO LOOK OUT FOR

(**a**) The **stone posts** are in the boundary wall for a deer park that was planned in the late 18th century but never materialised. The land belonged to the Edwardes, whose

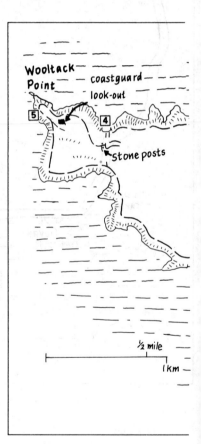

488

family seat was at Wolf's Castle; the estate was broken up in the 1920s.
(**b**) **View** To the right (N), St David's Head; straight ahead Skomer Island, with The Neck (just joined on to it) in front (W), and Midland Isle foremost. Further away, and to the left (SW), Skokholm Island. The islands are important bird habitats, supporting the largest concentration of Manx shearwaters in Britain (135,000 pairs). Skomer is also famous for puffins and Skokholm for storm petrels. Grey Atlantic seals can sometimes be seen on the rocks (breeding time is autumn). The islands and the 'deer park' are all flat-topped – the result of wave erosion when sea-level was 200ft higher than it is today.
(**c**) **Gateholm Island** At low tide remains are visible of the paddle-steamer *Albion* (the first to be bought by a Bristol Channel port), wrecked on its voyage of delivery in 1840. In the 7th century, the island was in-habited, probably by monks.

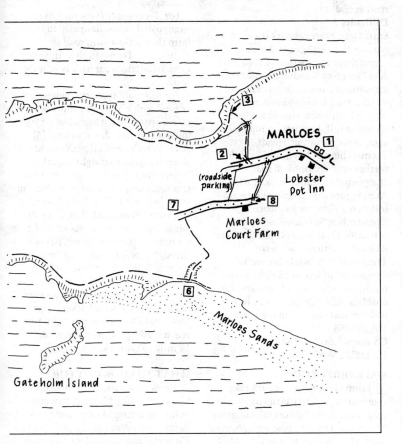

Garn Fawr and Strumble Head

Contributed by Ruth Godden

Cliff path along a deeply indented coastline, then moorland. Starts off spectacularly with a very short ascent to the Iron Age hillfort on Garn Fawr, looking down over Pwll Deri Bay. Tracks across pasture and moorland well defined; easy route-finding.

Length 6½ miles (10km), 3 hours (can be shortened to 5½ miles by using road at end)
Difficulty 3
Start Garn Fawr car park (free), 5 miles W of Fishguard. From roundabout at junction of A40 and A487 just S of Goodwick, take exit signposted Goodwick. In centre of village, take left-hand turn signposted Llanwnda/Strumble Head. At top of hill, bear left on road signposted Strumble Head/ Tremarchog/ St Nicholas. ½ mile further on keep right on road signposted Strumble Head/Pwllderi. At next junction continue forward following signs for Pwllderi/ Tremarchog/St Nicholas (road to Strumble Head goes off to right here). At next junction, Pwllderi/ Tremarchog/St Nicholas are all signposted to left: turn right at this point, soon passing 'Unsuitable for coaches' sign. Car park is on left ½ mile up this road. Grid reference SM 899388
OS maps 1:50,000 157; 1:25,000 SM 83/93

WALK DIRECTIONS

1 From Garn Fawr car park take signposted path to top of large rocky crag, Garn Fawr hillfort (heading due W towards the sea), past trig. point on right, then descending other side. **2** Reach tarmac lane, turn right. 100 yards later cross next lane to take driveway with YHA sign. **3** After 20 yards turn right and follow coast path for 2¼ miles (**a**), finally passing Strumble Head lighthouse, some way below. Path eventually disgorges on to tarmac lane by Strumble Head car park **4**. Turn right along lane and follow for 200 yards. Where lane swings round to right, continue forward on coast path. **5** After ¾ mile, reach T-junction at Porthsychan Bay, the second large bay reached.

For direct route back turn right (signposted public footpath) to reach farm then follow farm road to T-junction. Turn left, then right at next T-junction; car park is ¾ mile further on.

For full walk turn left (signposted coastal path). After 50 yards keep on coastal path which branches off right (do not continue down to bay). **6** After ½ mile, coastal path reaches stone bungalow on right of path. Turn right through small gate, to go through bungalow garden, picking up track beyond. Follow ¾ mile to road **7**. Turn left on road, then after 50 yards, right into farm (via second gate on right). After farmhouse, pass up through gate, pick up track between hedges. Follow ¼ mile up to foot of moorland. **8** Turn right to follow close to fence at bottom of moorland, on grassy path, which soon crosses fence and swings left and right, to reach road **9**. Turn left on road, ¼ mile to car park.

WHAT TO LOOK OUT FOR

(**a**) **Birds** Along the coast, numerous birds, including Manx shearwaters (which breed on Skomer and Skokholm islands), sea-ducks and divers. Choughs, fulmars and herring-gulls breed here.

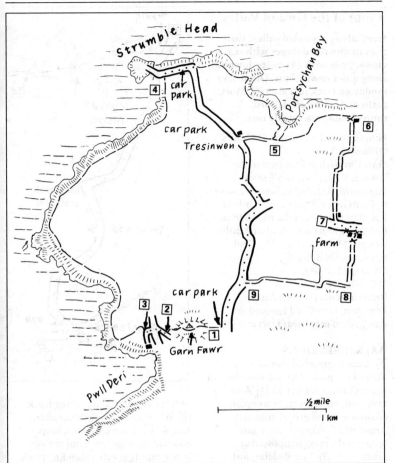

A tour of the Gwaun Valley

Starts along a wooded valley, then rises to moorland slopes with sea views. Ends with 1¾ miles downhill, along quiet tarmac lane. Often very muddy on track just after 8. Most paths and tracks are defined: route-finding reasonably easy.

Length 10 miles (16km), 4½ hours
Difficulty 3
Start Car park at Pontfaen in the Gwaun Valley, 5 miles ESE of Fishguard. Turn off valley road at sign to Pontfaen; car park is 50 yards on left. Alternatively take B4313 from Fishguard and turn left after 3 miles by sign 'Maenclochog 7½'. Grid reference SN 025340
OS maps 1:50,000 145; 1:25,000 SN 03/13
Refreshments Dyffryn Arms, Pontfaen; Dan Coed tea-garden (marked on map) near start of walk

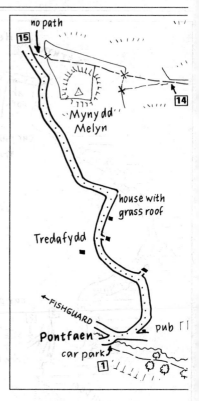

WALK DIRECTIONS

1 Take signposted footpath out of back of car park. Path follows close to River Gwaun, on left (**a**). 2 After 1 mile path emerges from woodland, crosses footbridge over tributary (signposted). 50 yards after gate, ignore right fork (signposted as bridleway). 3 ½ mile later, fork right. Path immediately passes ruined cottage down on your left and rises to stile, then leads up to ponds by farm (**b**) 4. Keep to right side of ponds, cross stile and turn right on track. 5 Left on road, then left 50 yards later at T-junction.

6 After ¾ mile cross stile on left (signposted), opposite Gellifawr Country House Hotel. Follow right edge of field, to cross stile at far right-hand corner, then immediately left along it, through gate. Follow clear path through woods. 7 At road turn left, follow 100 yards, then keep straight on where road bends left, on track to Llanerch Farm. Keep to left

of farm, through gate, taking track. 8 Where main track bends sharp left, 40 yards beyond farm, keep forward through left-hand of two gates, taking gently ascending track just inside woods.

9 After ½ mile, on leaving woods (houses visible ahead), turn left at junction of tracks. Follow uphill, soon between fences. 10 At open moorland (**c**) keep forward past right-hand of two prominent rocky outcrops, crossing stile on skyline. Pass through gate on right just beyond 11. Turn left, proceeding with fence on left.

12 After ¼ mile, on reaching corner of fence, turn left, still following fence, and avoid crossing stile at next corner, but turn right, still alongside fence. 13 At road cross to gate opposite (signposted public

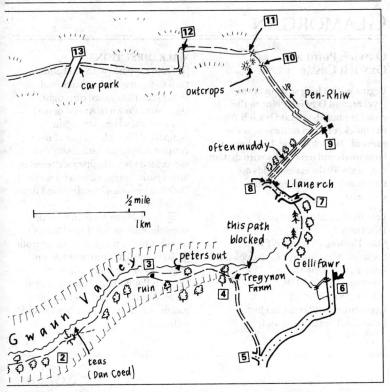

footpath). Path runs alongside wall on right. **14** After ½ mile, where wall ends, fork right, heading to the right-hand of two gates in fence ahead (**d**). At gate, path becomes track, and at second gate bear quarter right (no path) to next gate **15**. Turn left on road, follow 1¾ miles (**e**) down to the starting-point.

WHAT TO LOOK OUT FOR

(**a**) **Gwaun Valley** Deep, wooded 8½-mile-long valley, cut out by the action of glacial melt-water now the course of the modest River Gwaun, which starts in the nearby Preseli range and reaches the sea at Fishguard. Otters can be found in part of the valley. **Birds** include willow and wood warblers, chiff-chaffs, ravens and buzzards. In the 1850s the legendary Black Dog of Baal, a ferocious jet-black dog-cum-monster terrorised the valley.

(**b**) The path shown on OS maps from Tregynon (053345) to Coed Gelli-fawr (057347) is currently overgrown and unusable; it would cut out about a mile.

(**c**) Away to the right on this hillside is **Carningli**, a fine prehistoric hillfort, surrounded by traces of ancient enclosures and hut-circles. The rock here, bluestone, is the type used for the building of Stonehenge; the stone was probably transported naturally by glacier and deposited near the Mendips, from where men moved it to the site in Wiltshire.

(**d**) **Views** N towards St David's and Dinas Heads; S to Preseli.

(**e**) Road-walking necessary all the way back; the path from Tredafydd to Ponfaen post office is obstructed.

GLAMORGAN

Oxwich Point and Oxwich Castle

Begins with a long section at sea-level around Oxwich Point to the popular sandy beach at Oxwich Bay; the quicker return route is past the ruins of Oxwich Castle. Finishes on farm roads and field paths with distant sea views. Paths across fields are undefined; route-finding other-wise easy.

Length 5½ miles (9km), 2½ hours
Difficulty 1
Start Horton, 15 miles WSW of Swansea. Car park by beach (fee). Grid reference SS 475856.
OS maps 1:50,000 159; 1:25,000 SS 48/58/68
Refreshments Various in Horton; kiosks and hotel in Oxwich

WALK DIRECTIONS

1 From car park, with sea behind you, turn right on road. Just after road swings left (100 yards) turn right, signposted Oxwich. At end of road continue ahead on path, again signposted Oxwich. At end of road continue ahead on path (again signposted Oxwich; distance refers to a direct path cutting off coastal section). Path follows coast closely (avoid turns inland) (**a**).

2 After 2½ miles path rises up steps through woods (**b**) and bends round at top of rise, following contour.
3 300 yards later turn right down steps at post number 5, signposted Oxwich Point in direction you have come. At bottom path swings left, passes church (**c**) and reaches Oxwich village (**d**) **4**.

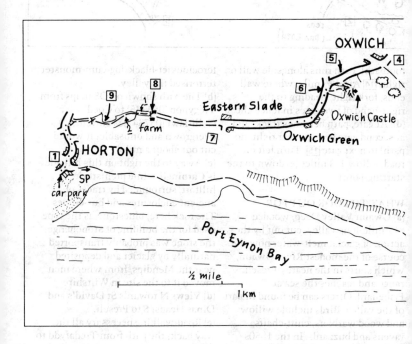

494

Turn left at crossroads in Oxwich (signposted to camp-site). **5** Take third signposted footpath on left (all are signposted to Oxwich Point), indicating 'Oxwich Point 2.1km'. 30 yards later fork right, and 50 yards later turn right through gate (for close-up view of castle (**e**) take next left through farmyard), and half right to stile in far right-hand corner of field **6**. Left on road.

7 ¾ mile later, after second hamlet, road becomes unsurfaced track, signposted 'Western Slade Farm, footpath only'. **8** Continue through farm, take gate/stile, marked Horton, into field. Forward, with fence on left to right-hand of two stiles. In second field, pick up path running close to hedge on right.

9 At end of hedge bear quarter right, keeping to right of house with two chimneys in distance, to find gate. Forward on track and, 150 yards later,

left at T-junction (road visible on right) then immediately turn right to reach road. Left on road, into centre of Horton.

WHAT TO LOOK OUT FOR

(**a**) The coast displays a **degraded cliff line** – the slopes to the left of the path are eroded cliffs – and a **wave-cut platform**, where the drop in sea-level has left a noticeable shelf. **View** Lundy Island, and across the Channel to Exmoor and Morte Point.

(**b**) **Oxwich Bay nature reserve** Splendid sweep of golden sands in the bay itself, plus rocks and dunes flanked by woodlands and saltmarsh. Woods are predominantly oak, ash and beech, with an understorey of hazel and holly; in spring, bluebells, ramsons, wood anemones, dog-violets and lesser celandines.

(**c**) **St Illtyd's church** (often closed) By itself in the woods, just above the beach. Tiny, mostly Norman, and possibly the site of a 9th-century hermit cell occupied by St Illtyd. Contains 14th-century effigies of a knight and lady, thought to be from the de la Mere family.

(**d**) **Oxwich** In the village centre is The Nook, where the preacher John Wesley stayed between 1664 and 1671.

(**e**) **Oxwich Castle** Fortified manor-house, built 1541. May soon be open to public.

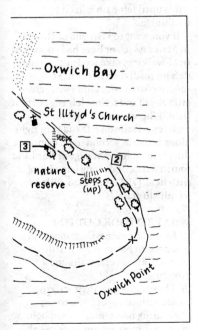

Nash Point and
St Donat's Castle

**Offers some striking cliff scenery and
views across the Bristol Channel,
with two wooded combes inland and
an optional there-and-back extension
along the coast as far as St Donat's
Castle. Quite safe for children along
the cliff path, which is fenced on its
seaward side; route reaches sea-level
at a small cove at Nash Point. Paths
across fields undefined, but route-
finding made easy by exemplary
waymarking (even telling you
which side of the field to follow).**

Length 4½ miles (7km), 2½ hours
With extension to St Donat's
7 miles (13km), 3½ hours
Difficulty 2
Start Grass triangle in Monknash,
¾ mile N of Marcross and 4 miles
WNW of Llantwit Major. Grid
reference SS 921706
OS maps 1:50,000 170;
1:25,000 SS 87/96/97
Refreshments Plough and Harrow,
Monknash; kiosk sometimes in
summer at Nash Point; Horseshoe
Inn, Marcross

WALK DIRECTIONS

1 From T-junction, with minor road
behind you, turn left along road
towards Bridgend. After 300 yards
cross stile on left, signposted
Blaen-y-cwm, opposite first right
turn. Turn left beyond stile, along
wall of building (forge) then continue
direction across field to waymarked
stile. In second field continue forward
keeping immediately to right of
prominent ruins of monastic grange
(**a**), to find stile. Continue and cross
third field to point where hedge
meets stone wall: cross stile, and
emerge on track.

2 Turn right on track, ford stream
then immediately turn left on path
running just above stream (or follow
left edge of field – routes merge). At

end of field cross stile and follow left
edge of second and third fields. Avoid
footbridge on left in third field but
continue to stile, through paddock
and on to tarmac lane **3**.

Left on lane, through gate/stile,
then after 50 yards turn right on track
into Blaen-y-cwm nature reserve.
Follow track through woods and then
along valley towards sea. **4** 50 yards
before gate leading to beach, turn left
up narrow path to reach cliff-top.
Follow cliff-top alongside fence on
right, crossing stiles as necessary (**b**).

5 Just before Nash Point
lighthouses ahead (**c**), path descends
into valley. Turn left along valley to
continue (or detour to lighthouses,
and to St Donat's Castle (**d**) 1½ miles
beyond, via coast path). After 150
yards reach woods and fork right (left
is nature trail; both paths lead to
same place, but left fork unusable
owing to impassable stepping-stones
at time of checking). Follow path 600
yards until left path joins it by
footbridge.

If you want to visit pub or church
in Marcross (**e**), or have had enough of
field-walking, take road at this point
(left on road, then left at next
junction to finish). Otherwise, cross
stile ahead and follow left edge of first
field. Where wooded bank on left
ends, cross stile on left and turn right
along hedge in second field. Continue
direction along right edge of third and
fourth fields, and along left edge of
fifth field. **7** Left on road, follow
¾ mile to start.

WHAT TO LOOK OUT FOR

(**a**) Ruins of a **monastic grange** that
belonged to Neath Abbey. Still
standing are several walls and a
dovecote.
(**b**) These cliffs owe their striking
candy-striped appearance to
alternating horizontal beds of light
grey lias limestone and dark, weaker
shale. Vertical joints in the limestone

have created fissures and blow-holes, some of which have enough wind being forced up them to blow away a hat placed over the top.

(c) **Nash Point** The two lighthouses were built in 1836 in line with the sandbank just SW of Nash Point as a navigational aid (buoys had yet to be invented), following the wreck of the *Frolic*, in which 60 lives were lost. They still contain the original lenses for magnifying the beam. Sadly the taller lighthouse will have been automated by the time this book is published, and will no longer be open to the public.

(d) **St Donat's Castle** (occasionally open to public) Built *c.* 1300 by the Stradling family and restored in the early 20th century; within the medieval castle is a 15th/17th-century country house. In the grounds are cavalry barracks and, near the cliffs, a look-out tower used as a shipwrecker's tower by a lord of Dunraven who, in the 15th century, unwittingly lured his own two sons to be wrecked on the rocks below. From 1925 the castle was owned by American newspaper millionaire William Randolph Hearst; since 1962 it has been the headquarters of Atlantic College.

(e) **Marcross church** Norman, restored. To the right of the porch is a leper's window, through which those suffering from infectious diseases could follow the service. A pillar in the churchyard is the surviving stump of an ancient sundial.

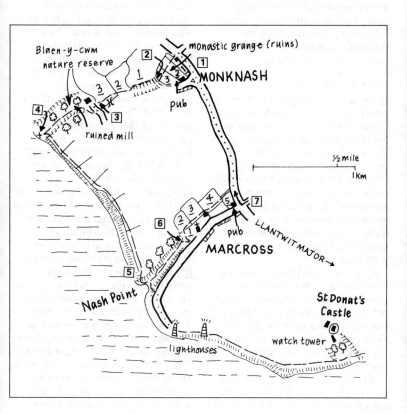

The Afan Valley and Cymmer

Gives a good impression of South Wales's industrial past. Begins over grassy upland, then descends through forest plantations to Cymmer for the easy return route along an old railway track close to the river banks. One complicated section through forestry, between 6 and 9, otherwise route-finding easy. Ascent 700ft.

Length 7½ miles (12km), 3½ hours
Difficulty 3
Start Afan Argoed County Park and Welsh Miners' Museum car park, on A4107, 5 miles NE of Port Talbot. Well signposted from road.
Grid reference SS 821951
OS maps 1:50,000 170;
1:25,000 SS 89/99
Refreshments Café at museum at start; 'Refreshment Rooms' (pub) at old station, Cymmer (converted single-storey station in village centre); shops in Cymmer

WALK DIRECTIONS

1 (a) Turn left out of car park, taking tarmac lane leading uphill to farmhouse. Tarmac ceases here; continue uphill on grassy track between banks. 2 After 600 yards track bends left after passing through gates in wall. 100 yards later, wall on left ends; 30 yards later fork right on grassy track leading uphill. 3 Reach edge of wood, keep forward, with wood on right. ¼ mile after end of wood, track runs alongside second tongue of woodland.

4 Where track reaches gate into forest ahead, do not enter forest, but turn left with forest on right. At end of forest cross stile into grassland: proceed on track keeping close to fence on left. View opens out on right over Maesteg. 5 After next stile, track is indistinct: continue alongside fence on left, gently uphill. At top of rise, track becomes clear, and drops to crossing of tracks (ignore

gate on left) then rises up toward forest ahead.

6 100 yards before forest, take right fork (left fork passes through gate) to continue along fence to gate on skyline. Through gate, enter forest: ignore cross-tracks (i) immediately, (ii) after 50 yards, (iii) after another 140 yards, keeping forward each time on track or narrow path. 7 100 yards later, path merges into stony track. Follow it downhill, keeping right as main track bends right after 150 yards, and 150 yards later turn left down open strip (firebreak), heading towards bridge.

8 Turn right on track halfway down slope, by second set of power lines (where modern building in front of bridge comes into view). After 220 yards, and 30 yards before third electricity pole, fork left on to path, which leads to top of bank. Turn left along it to descend to left end of Cymmer village 9. Turn right on main road, into village (b). Take first left then turn right on long residential street to walk parallel to main road. Turn left on rejoining main road, then immediately left again (no through road) on road leading down to concrete bridge 10.

Turn left after bridge. When level with old railway bridge 300 yards later, drop down to level grassy track just below road on left. This is the old railway (c). Keeping on level follow this for 2 miles. Pass villages of Abercregan (up on right) and then Dyffryn (left, on other side of river). 11 Next village on other bank of river, Cynonville, comes into view as you pass between two stone pillars (remains of bridge). 30 yards later, look out for orange marker post on left, and find path by it leading down to riverside track. Turn right along it.

12 Where woods ahead open out to grassy area, fork left over grass and cross bridge, then up steps, to turn left at top of steps and left at next

cross-junction in front of iron bridge. Use stone bridge ahead to reach road up on right and emerge by entrance to car park.

WHAT TO LOOK OUT FOR

(a) **Afan Argoed Welsh Miners' Museum** (fee) Simulated coal faces plus pit gear, old photographs and miners' equipment and personal belongings.

(b) **Cymmer** Mining village of sombre stone-built terraces, dominated by its 107ft-high viaduct (opened in 1878), one of the last surviving metal viaducts in Wales. It connected the mineral line on the N bank of the river with the Great Western Railway.

(c) **Old railway line** The South Wales Mineral Railway, planned in 1861 by Brunel in broad gauge, and converted to standard gauge 11 years later. Its final section closed in 1970.

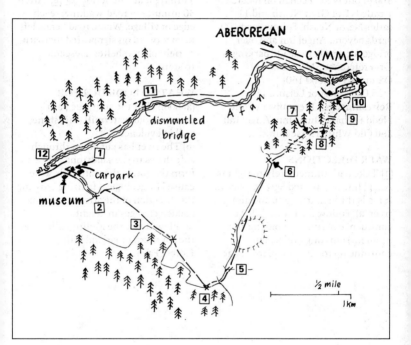

Neath Vale: the Brecon Beacons waterfall country

Takes in a tremendous series of waterfalls, whose torrents get more violent as you proceed along the wooded Neath Gorge. Returns along a quiet open road. Can be slippery in places; suitable footwear essential. Easy route-finding.

Length 5½ miles (9km), 3 hours
Difficulty 2–3
Start Pont Nedd Fechan on B4242 1 mile NE of Glyn Neath and 11 miles NE of Neath. Follow road 100 yards beyond Angel Inn and over bridge for ample roadside parking. Grid reference SN 901077
OS maps 1:50,000 160; 1:25,000 Outdoor Leisure 11
Refreshments Three pubs in Pont Nedd Fechan: Dinas Inn, Angel Inn and Old White Horse Inn

WALK DIRECTIONS

1 Take path immediately to right of Angel Inn, signposted Sgwd Gwladys: it leads through iron gate and along river (**a**). Follow for 1 mile. **2** At confluence of rivers, avoid (for the moment) crossing bridge, but continue up to viewing-platform at Sgwd Gwladys, a fine waterfall. Return to cross bridge, then turn right on other side, to follow river upstream. Path ascends a little and river becomes more dramatic (**b**). **3** After ½ mile take care in fording small stream by waterfall on left (retrace steps to start if you don't feel confident).

4 ¾ mile later emerge from wood and make for road beyond car park. Turn right on road over bridge. **5** Turn right at T-junction (**c**). **6** After 30 minutes of road-walking, reach edge of village. Where road bends left, keep forward on signposted footpath to right of bus shelter. Descend to start.

WHAT TO LOOK OUT FOR

(**a**) Soon after the start, the path passes an old **watermill** (millstones still in evidence).
(**b**) The river has cut down through soft shales to the sandstone below to form the **gorge**; the waterfalls were caused by geological faulting crossing the direction of the stream, causing sudden changes in height.
(**c**) **Views** Over the Mellte Valley and the southern moorland hills of Fforest Fawr.

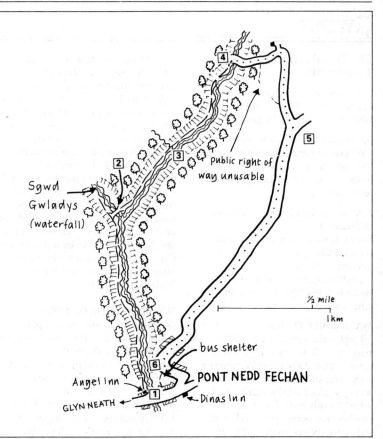

Sgwd Gwladys (waterfall)

public right of way unusable

½ mile
1 km

bus shelter

PONT NEDD FECHAN

Angel Inn

GLYN NEATH ←

Dinas Inn

GWENT

The Wyndcliff and Tintern Abbey

Contributed by George Phipson
Recommended by W R Roberts, Ian
Wilson and family, Richard Cassling

In the heavily wooded Wye Gorge, with classic views where it opens out. Ends on Chepstow's Regency iron bridge. All on waymarked paths; easy route-finding.

Length 13 miles (21km), 6½ hours
Difficulty 3–4
Start Car park at Chepstow Castle
By train Chepstow
OS maps 1:50,000 162;
1:25,000 Outdoor Leisure 14
Refreshments Wide selection in
Chepstow and Tintern

WALK DIRECTIONS

1 (**a**) Go through castle grounds, passing castle on your right, and turn right at road. Take second turning on right after 400 yards (signposted Wye Valley walk). Pass through car park after 50 yards and follow yellow marker arrows through woods with River Wye below on right. **2** After 2 miles cross road and continue opposite up 365 steps to Eagle's Nest viewpoint on The Wyndcliff (signposted) (**b**); yellow arrows here mark a less steep ascent round to the left.

3 1 mile later, path makes steep descent and turns right, on track, soon emerging into field. Turn left as indicated. After 50 yards, turn right across field (waymarked), then into and through woods. **4** At Tintern, take lane between Anchor Hotel and abbey (**c**), and turn left along river path which soon leads back to main road. Turn right on road, then after 100 yards turn right over footbridge. Follow yellow arrow markings, ¾ mile

up to Devil's Pulpit (**d**). From here carefully follow the Offa's Dyke markings for most of the way back.

5 After 2 miles, turn right on road as signposted, then, after 600 yards and opposite entrance to Bough Cliff House, turn left on path as signposted. ½ mile later turn left on road. **6** After ¼ mile, by number 2 Broadrock Cottage, take Offa's Dyke Path on right (**e**). ½ mile later rejoin main road, turn right along it for 50 yards then take gate on right to resume on path. After ¾ mile, cross main road and follow path between walls. Ignore Offa's Dyke Path signposting to left after 100 yards, and continue to cross bridge and return to start.

WHAT TO LOOK OUT FOR

(**a**) **Chepstow Castle** (open to public; fee) Substantial and imposing ruin of a stronghold founded by William Fitz-Osborn and enlarged in the 13th century. It contains four courts, a gatehouse and three towers.

(**b**) **The Wyndcliff** View of the Severn Estuary and Forest of Dean, and over nine former counties (rather fewer since counties were amalgamated). A rich and varied **flora** of limestone-loving plants under a cover of beech, ash, lime, yew and oak trees. **Birds** Woodpecker, pied flycatcher, nightingale, redstart, buzzard.

(**c**) **Tintern Abbey** (open to public; fee) Ruined Cistercian foundation whose beauty and setting captivated Wordsworth. The abbey was founded in 1131 and its church was built in the 13th century.

(**d**) **Devil's Pulpit** View of the abbey ruins far below.

(**e**) **Wintour's Leap** 300ft sheer drop into the Wye, one of the dizziest views in the gorge.

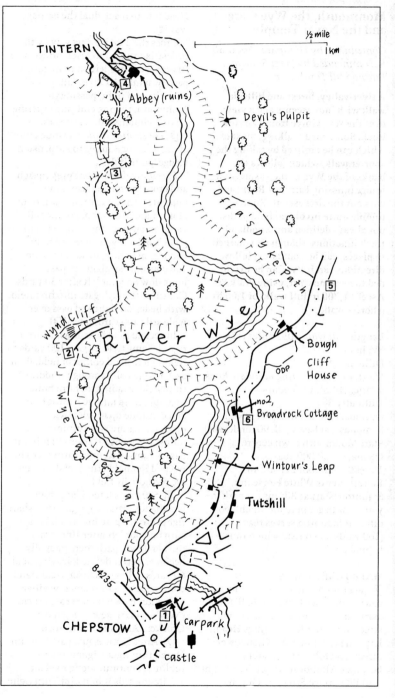

TINTERN

½ mile

1 km

4

Abbey (ruins)

Devil's Pulpit

Offa's Dyke Path

Wynd Cliff

3

River Wye

2

5

Bough Cliff House

ODP

Wye Walk

6 no 2, Broadrock Cottage

Wintour's Leap

Tutshill

B4235

CHEPSTOW

1

car park

castle

503

Monmouth, the Wye Gorge and the Naval Temple

Contributed by Humphrey Southall
Recommended by Peter Sidaway,
Eric and Jill Tomlinson

A river-valley, forest and hillside walk with four ascents and a view over the Wye Gorge from Fairview Rock. Some road-walking, most of which can be omitted by taking the shorter walk, which follows the banks of the Wye to the suspension bridge (missing Fairview Rock) and cuts out the first ascent. Route-finding quite involved: field paths not always defined and woodland track junctions, though waymarked in places, can be confusing; follow directions carefully. Can be extended to Symonds Yat, using Walk 90. Ascent 1,700 ft (full walk) or 1,000ft (shorter walk).

Length *Full walk* 10½ miles (17km), 5½ hours
Difficulty 4
Shorter walk omitting Fairview Rock 9 miles (14.5km), 5 hours
Difficulty 3–4
Optional extension of either walk to Symonds Yat (see Walk 90 for details)
Start Monmouth town centre
OS maps 1:50,000 162;
1:25,000 Outdoor Leisure 14
Refreshments White Horse Inn, Staunton (start at Biblins car park if you want to get here for lunch); post office at Staunton serves teas (100 yards down road which runs behind pub)

WALK DIRECTIONS

1 (a) From Agincourt Square in town centre, with market hall/Rolls statue on left, proceed down main street, take first left by Kings Head; left at next T-junction (Glendower Street) and follow this; later it becomes Almhouse Street. Turn right into Wyebridge Street by Queens Head Inn, to reach dual the carriage-way **2**.

Cross the dual carriageway by the pedestrian tunnel to reach bridge over River Wye. Turn left on to metalled path (waymarked Wye Valley Walk) with river on right, passing the Monmouth rowing club and entering Dixton churchyard ¾ mile later.

3 *For shorter walk* continue close along river for 3 miles to suspension bridge (point **10**).

For full walk turn left past church and cross main road, using gap opposite entry to church. Turn right along main road, then left after 60 yards on tarmac lane signposted to golf club. Follow lane round right bend; at next (left) bend leave lane and continue straight on, past bungalow on your left after 50 yards. Continue through gate into first field, with hedge on right and pass over wide stile 100 yards ahead **4**.

In second field bear down quarter right leaving field by gate 100 yards to right of left-hand corner of field. Path ascends opposite through middle of third field, heading for farm buildings. **5** Cross tarmac road at farm and continue up rough track opposite. Ignore side turnings and follow track ahead; after 1¼ miles it passes ruins of Kennel Farm on right. Beyond Kennel Farm, woods on right are replaced by fields.

6 600 yards later, just before woodlands restart on right, turn sharp right through gate into field. Pass barn on your left after 100 yards; further down, path then gradually becomes better defined, leaving field 60 yards to left of bottom right-hand corner. Descend to Ganarew village, past church on left and cross bridge over dual carriageway, signposted Crockers Ash; and follow road.

7 After ½ mile, just past Doward Hotel, turn right (signposted to Biblins). Continue along road for 1 mile towards Biblins. **8** Turn right down track just after sign on tree on right marked 'Private lane – no parking'. After 200 yards avoid the turning left into quarry, and 200 yards later ignore turning on right which runs along edge of forest. Path leads on to gradually descending waymarked walk (**b**). Follow yellow arrows up on to viewpoint (Fairview Rock) and down to Seven Sisters crags. **9** At bottom, turn left along river for ½ mile.

10 Cross river by wire suspension bridge. *For extension to Symonds Yat* cross bridge and follow river to Symonds Yat East (village), where you can detour to Symonds Yat rock: see Walk 90 for details.

To continue walk turn left on other side of river, for 30 yards, then turn right steeply uphill. After 200 yards turn right at T-junction with path (route is waymarked with yellow arrows as far as Staunton, but waymarks are not all readily seen). After ¼ mile path ceases ascending

on passing (second) wooden barrier on right; 100 yards later, turn right (uphill) at junction. **11** 200 yards later turn right on forestry track, then immediately left on to another track. Follow for 150 yards, and where track bends left, turn right on to grassy track. Track bends left after 100 yards, and reaches forestry track 130 yards later **12**. Turn left on to this, then immediately right, on path leading to view over forest. Just before view, fork right; path descends and skirts huge crag (**c**), turns right down through deep woods, then passes another large crag (**d**) and descends to track **13**.

Turn left on track, and ½ mile later look out for waymarked path on left. Ascend for ¼ mile, then fork right. Follow to Staunton village **14**. From Staunton, with White Horse Inn on your left, follow main road to end of village, then turn left, opposite last house on right, up tarmac lane. After 75 yards, immediately after gate, turn

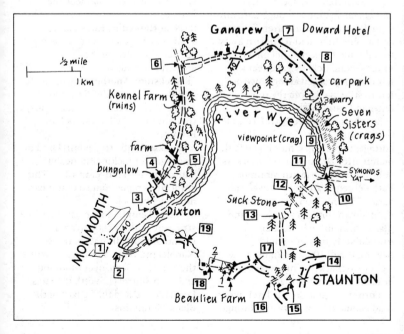

right on path indicated by yellow arrow to ascend.

15 Pass trig. point on your right (**e**) and proceed alongside wall on right, on path signposted to Redbrook. After 150 yards turn right on surfaced track, which immediately bends left in front of house; after 30 yards turn right on another surfaced track; follow for 50 yards, then fork left to gate. Do not pass through gate but turn right on track between cottage (left) and outhouse (right). After 100 yards, by wooden electricity post, turn right on path, and follow 100 yards to T-junction with track **16**.

Turn right on track for 40 yards and turn left on partially concealed path (50 yards before conifers begin ahead on left side of track), and descend to road. Turn left on main road, for 250 yards, crossing county boundary into Gwent, then turn left up lane signposted Monmouth. **17** After 350 yards, just after Graygill House on right, turn right (signposted Kymin and Naval Temple) through gate into field. Ignore right fork after 75 yards and ascend first field with barn away to right and fence parallel on left. Enter second field by gate near top left corner, proceed along fence on left to stile just before the top left-hand corner **18**.

Bear half left to see Naval Temple (**f**), then turn right, past castellated cottage, to pick up Offa's Dyke Path on left after 70 yards (acorn markers/ yellow arrows), back to Monmouth. Path descends, to cross stile after 50 yards. 75 yards later cross stile on right, down through woods to lane **19**. Turn right on lane, then immediately right into field (waymarked); 100 yards later, fork right (waymarked), into woods, then descend to corner of road.

Turn right, and ¼ mile later, where road bends right, go forward through gate (signposted) on track, to leave field by waymarked kissing-gate at far end (ignore gate in far left corner). Descend to road and continue down to Wye bridge in Monmouth.

WHAT TO LOOK OUT FOR

(**a**) **Monmouth** Strategically sited at the confluence of the Wye and Monnow, with a much-photographed medieval bridge over the latter (looking more like something out of provincial France than the Welsh Marches). Henry V was born here, hence the name Agincourt Square for the town centre. In the square is a statue of Charles Rolls of Rolls-Royce (inventor of the internal combustion engine), holding a model aeroplane.

(**b**) A cave passed on the left is called **King Arthur's cave**, though it has nothing to do with him. In 1870, excavations uncovered skeletons and Roman pottery; under the floor were bear and beaver bones and below them were bones of mammoth, woolly rhinoceros, reindeer and hyena.

(**c**) **Near Harkening Rock** Large sandstone boulder, whose concave surface allegedly catches and amplifies sounds.

(**d**) **Suckstone** Another very large boulder, measuring 60ft by 40ft by 26ft, estimated to weigh 4,000 tons; thought to be the largest rock in Britain.

(**e**) **Buckstone** (by trig. point) Used to be a logan (or rocking) stone, but vandals pushed it over in 1885. The authorities replaced it so that it can no longer be rocked.

(**f**) **Naval Temple** Rustic pavilion-like structure built in 1800 to commemorate the admirals of the Napoleonic Wars. **View** of much of the Forest of Dean, over Monmouth, and W to Skirrid (1,596ft), the Sugar Loaf (1,955ft) and the SE part of the Black Mountains.

Clytha Castle and the River Usk

Based on a contribution from Peter Sidaway
Recommended by Andrew Lowe, Alan Williams, P M Hopper

Leads out over a quiet hillside, to return along the River Usk. One section along a small tarmac lane, with views of Skirrid and the Sugar Loaf. Field paths not defined, but waymarking very thorough; route-finding quite easy.

Length 7 miles (11km), 3½ hours
Difficulty 2–3.
Start NT car park ¼ mile S of old A40, 5 miles SE of Abergavenny. Turn off S on road signposted to Bettws Newydd; car park is ¼ mile on right. Grid reference SO 362086
OS maps 1:50,000 161; 1:25,000 SO 20/30
Refreshments Black Bear Inn, Bettws Newydd (in village centre, 600 yards off route); Chain Bridge Inn (300 yards off route)

WALK DIRECTIONS

1 From car park turn left on to road. After 50 yards turn right through gate into field, signposted Camp Coed y Bwnyd. Ascend alongside fence on right (no path) to reach woodland fence, at which turn left to skirt wood (waymarked), on path which then climbs bank (waymarked) to emerge with Clytha Castle (**a**) visible ahead. Head for stile 100 yards to left of castle and cross stile into woods. Cross track after 20 yards and continue through woods to stile into field **2**.

Path leads ahead to prominent white waymark post on opposite side of first field, at which turn left, with fence on right. Leave field by corner, cross to the other side of fence and continue forward through the waymarked gate into second field. Turn right with hedge on right to

skirt field; at right-hand corner turn left uphill, still skirting field with trees on right. Enter third field by waymarked stile and continue forward along right edge to next stile, beyond which path leads 40 yards to tarmac lane **3**.

Turn right on lane. Ignore left turn after 500 yards (**b**). Follow road to next T-junction **4**. Left on road for 20 yards, then cross stile on right (signposted Bettws church). Bear half right (no path) towards further of two electricity poles, reaching waymarked stile in top corner. Forward in second field, alongside hedge on left. Turn left in third field, proceeding alongside hedge on left to end of field, then turn right along fence to enter churchyard by waymarked stile (**c**) **5**.

For Black Bear Inn take main gate out of churchyard; left on lane, then right at T-junction. Inn is ¼ mile on, on left of road. Turn left at crossroads beyond inn, follow for ½ mile to reach point **7**.

To continue turn left on reaching church porch, to cross waymarked stile into field. Bear half left (no path) to gate in bottom left-hand corner, at far end of small conifer plantation. Emerge on road, turn left, and after 100 yards take next track on right, opposite house.

6 After 100 yards, just beyond house, turn left through waymarked gate and proceed alongside fence on left to skirt first field for ¼ mile, to cross waymarked stile on left. In second field turn right (waymark confusing at inspection) and follow, with hedge on right, to gate into wood, beyond which clear track leads down to road (wood is Priory Woods nature reserve). Left on road, follow for ¼ mile (*for Chain Bridge Inn* continue down lane another ¼ mile).

7 Cross stile on right (signposted Clytha Park 4km/Usk Valley Walk), just where woods begin on right. Path

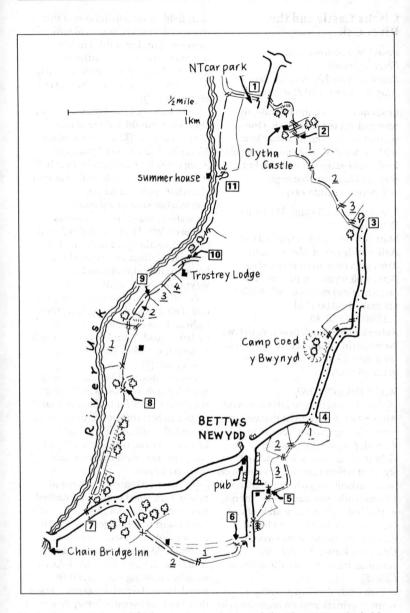

leads along top of woods before descending to gate into field. (There are waymarks for the Usk Valley Walk, and most of route back to start is easy to find.) Continue forward, along foot of wooded slope, with field down on left. After 500 yards, field appears on right, then woods reappear on right.

⑧ Enter woods by gate and after 50 yards turn left through waymarked gate, as main track veers right, to enter field. Follow right edge of first field, leave by left (waymarked) of two gates/stiles at far end. Path soon leads into second field; keep forward along left edge, leaving it by waymarked stile in far right-hand corner 9.

Turn left into third field, along fence towards farm, and continue across left edge of (small) fourth field to pass farm. Track leads ahead through woods; after 80 yards keep forward on joining stony track, and where track bends right (after 50 yards) keep forward over waymarked stile 10. Path leads high above river, then enters field: keep forward, along left edge, crossing waymarked stile, on left just before far end of field: this descends to river level.

Follow river to electricity lines level with summerhouse on opposite bank 11. Turn right, away from river, to cross tributary stream by waymarked gate/bridge, then rejoin riverside; follow river bank through

this long field, and at end cross stile, turn right on track between hedges and follow back to car park.

WHAT TO LOOK OUT FOR
(**a**) **Clytha Castle** (not open to public) Small, Gothick-castle-style country house built by William Jones in 1790 to take his mind off the death of his wife three years earlier.
(**b**) After 130 yards, a stile on your right is signposted to **Camp Coed y Bwynyd**, an Iron Age hillfort of which the ramparts are visible; it is now under a dense cover of trees and there are no views from it. To reach it, proceed beyond barn to ladder-stile into woods.
(**c**) **Bettws Newydd church** 15th-century, virtually untouched, containing a Welsh-style rood screen and a musicians' gallery of the same period. In the churchyard (which is circular, so that the Devil could find no corners by which to enter) is a 30ft wide, 1,000-year-old yew.

Vale of Ewyas and Llanthony Abbey

Approaches abbey ruins via grassy fields in the curving Vale of Ewyas. After the ascent (fairly steep at first but then steady), on the eastern ridge of the Black Mountains, with views extending into England. Paths undefined across fields and directions should be followed carefully; route along ridge is obvious. Ascent 1,000ft.

Length 11 miles (17.5km), 4½ hours
Difficulty 3–4
Start *Either* Cwmyoy (very limited roadside parking) on minor road 8 miles N of Abergavenny. Grid reference SO 299233 *Or* free car park at Llanthony Abbey, on B4423 10 miles N of Abergavenny. Grid reference SO 289278; start walk at 9
OS maps 1:50,000 161; 1:25,000 Outdoor Leisure 13
Refreshments Abbey Hotel, Llanthony; Queen's Head, Cwmyoy (just off route; outside village)

WALK DIRECTIONS

1 From Cwmyoy phone box, with phone box on right, take next left, follow 'no through road' uphill, past entrance to Cwmyoy church (**a**), to T-junction. Turn left, passing church down on left. When level with end of churchyard turn right on sunken path (signposted Graig) that ascends 150 yards to junction of paths. Turn left and continue in this direction, initially between fences, then, after gate, with fence on left only.

2 Just after fording small stream (can be dry in summer) path passes through gate and into open field. Continue forward for 130 yards on clear path; cottage comes into view ahead. Turn left on path beween line of trees (left) and grassy bank (right). This is joined by fence on left after 80 yards; follow past the first stone farmhouse on left.

3 At second farmhouse (100 yards later), pass through farmyard in front of farmhouse to gate ahead (avoid left turn in farmyard). Cross first (small) field to gate ahead. In second field bear half left (no path) to find stile 50 yards above bottom left-hand corner. Immediately turn left in third field (waymarked), alongside fence on left to skirt field; this soon leads into trees, where clear path leads to gate/stile (ignore footbridge away to left) 4.

Bear quarter right across fourth field, along foot of rough grassy slope, to stile. Proceed across fifth field to next stile. Follow left edge of sixth field, to leave by waymarked stile 80 yards to right of far left-hand corner, at which make towards ruined farmstead, ¼ mile ahead 5. Pass through yard of ruined farmstead to gate on far side. Proceed forward on the level across first field through line of trees, and forward to gate. Continue across second field to next gate then forward along right edge of third and fourth fields. Two gates lead on to track: follow into next farm 6.

Keep forward through gate beyond farm; track follows left of two fields. Bear quarter right (no path) across third field to enter left-hand of two fields by gate/stile. Proceed alongside hedge on right into fourth field, then forward to stile 50 yards to left of right-hand corner 7. Follow right edge of fifth field and maintain direction across centre of sixth field to gate/stile. Emerge on road 8.

Turn right on road, and take next right (signposted Llanthony Abbey). 9 (**b**) With church on left and abbey and Court Farm on right follow road: where it bends left back down to B-road, keep forward through gate/stile and turn right on track. In second field, turn right (signposted Longtown), with abbey wall on right. In third field bear half left uphill (signposted Longtown) aiming for waymarked gate/stile at top of field, into woods **10**.

Clear path leads up through woods, at other end of which take stile on left (immediately before path reaches gate) out of woods. Ascend alongside fence on right to gate ahead. Turn right on path, with wall on right. **11** After 600 yards path leaves wall, ascending steadily towards ridge.

12 At top of ridge turn right on

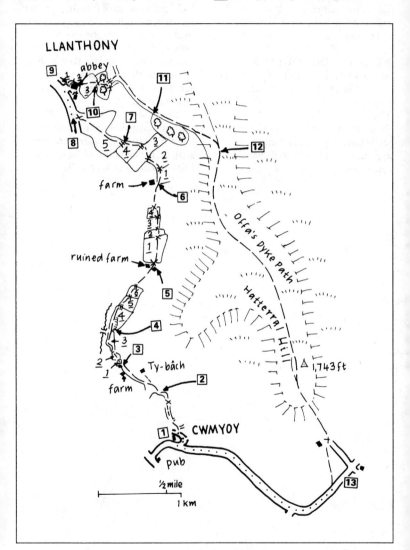

track (Offa's Dyke Path, no waymarks), and follow for 2½ miles with views on both sides (**c**), eventually past trig. point and then descending. Later track becomes surfaced and drops to lane junction. **13** Turn right on lane and follow 2 miles to Cwmyoy (avoid left turn after ½ mile).

WHAT TO LOOK OUT FOR
(**a**) **Cwmyoy** Tiny village on the hill-side below Hatterrall Hill, whose jagged edge was caused by landslides. The church has become a victim of these, and the drunken angles of its walls have a quite alarming appearance (it has looked that way for centuries).

(**b**) **Llanthony** The church is a 6th-century foundation of St David; the abbey (always open) was founded by William de Lacey 500 years later. In the 1800s the poet and eccentric Walter Savage Landor bought it and had a pipe-dream of creating his own feudal domain here – he as a country magnate, and everyone else as villeins or serfs. The locals did not care for the idea and he gave it up in 1814; now the only reminder of the scheme is a ruined barn some way above the abbey.

(**c**) **View** E over the Golden Valley, with the jagged Malvern ridge beyond and the Cotswold escarpment further still; SE to the Forest of Dean and hills of the lower Wye Valley.

GWYNEDD

Capel Curig and Swallow Falls

Contributed by Geoffrey Bourne
Recommended by Brian Hathaway,
Colin Glover and Wendy Short,
Dr and Mrs B W Davies, Nils
Blythe

Scenically varied: part upland, part lowland. Takes in a series of reservoirs, then forestry and rough pasture. Gets a free view of the Swallow Falls (those who approach from A5 have to pay), from a woodland path above the Llugwy Gorge; view opens out at end over Moel Siabod and the Glyders. Not all paths across grassland are well defined; route-finding rather involved, but not difficult.

Length 13 miles (21km), 6 hours
Difficulty 3–4
Start Capel Curig, at junction of A5 and A4086, 15 miles SE of Bangor. Roadside parking. Grid reference SH 721581
OS maps 1:50,000 115; 1:25,000 Outdoor Leisure 16
Refreshments Shop and hotels (with bars) in Capel Curig; lakeside café at Llyn Crafnant reservoir; teas at Allt Isaf farm on some summer days

WALK DIRECTIONS

1 Leave Capel Curig by ladder-stile opposite the post office and by war memorial. Clear path passes through two fields, through woods, then opens out on to bracken-covered hillside, and runs parallel to main road, visible below. **2** After crossing stream by footbridge, path veers left (¾ mile from start). Path soon passes alongside fence, with flat marshy plain to left encircled by rugged hills, then leads gradually up small valley through heather and bracken with craggy ridge on the left.

3 1 mile later, fork left for steep descent to Llyn Crafnant Reservoir (right fork leads uphill). Near bottom of slope path is joined by wall on left. 50 yards later cross wall by gate, heading for farmhouse **4**. Just after farm itself, turn right on track. Here you can decide which side of the lake to follow: the N side is more pleasant (no traffic on forestry track) but there is a lakeside café on road on S side.

For northern route turn left after 30 yards on grassy path leading towards wooden bungalow. Continue forward 200 yards, then turn right in front of stone farmhouse (Hendre) by signpost, and take right-hand of two gates. 300 yards later enter woods on left by stile, then continue forward on forest track. At end of reservoir, by monument, join road running on S side of lake and turn left along it.

For southern route continue forward to join lakeside road.

5 ¼ beyond end of the lake, and opposite Forestry Commission sign for Llyn Crafnant, fork right on to forestry track. This climbs uphill through old slate quarry, at which continue forward on narrow path skirting hill, which is on your right. **6** After ¼ mile, cross fixed gate in stone wall, and 50 yards later turn right on grassy path uphill, leading to reservoir (Llyn Geironydd) **7**.

Follow path on right side of the Llyn Geironydd Reservoir through bracken and gorse (ignoring any right turns uphill), then through the plantation. Where path enters pasture by stile, bear quarter right on faint grassy path. Pass behind cottage, through gate and on to track **8**. Turn left on track alongside head of lake. Cross road at end of it, and take track beyond gate opposite and slightly to left. Follow forestry track which initially snakes uphill and after 600 yards reaches barrier/ladder-stile just before road.

Do not proceed to road but look carefully for track 50 yards before barrier and **9** turn sharp left (forest felled at time of writing) – follow this track, which climbs through wood to reach stile. Climb stile and bear half left towards disused mine workings, then turn right to stile leading into grassy pasture **10**. Follow power lines uphill to next stile, then forward to reach the end of Llyn Glandors (reservoir), at which turn right along edge of reservoir. **11** At end of the reservoir, cross ladder-stile into forest along narrow path leading to wide forest track. Turn right on track, passing cottage on left after ¾ mile.

12 Turn right just after cottage, then immediately left on narrow path

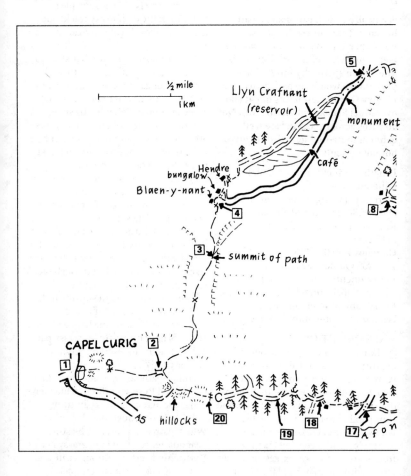

which descends past lake on right 200 yards later, and reaches road shortly after. Turn right on road for 100 yards to reach old mine workings on left **13**. In the middle of these, look for and cross ladder-stile and go forward to wall 100 yards ahead, then quarter right (signposted) to ladder-stile just to left of abandoned farmhouse. Yellow waymarking in next section, **14**.

Drop down to diagonally opposite corner of first field (ladder-stile) then turn left in second field, proceeding with fence on left. At end reach track, turn left on it soon to pass through gate. **15** 10 yards after gate turn sharp right on to narrow path, which descends through woods to reach tarmac lane. Turn right, passing over stone bridge and **16** fork left on track 50 yards later. Track passes Allt Isaf farm and 300 yards later crosses bridge and turns left downhill. Path narrows to climb along gorge above Swallow Falls, beyond which reach forestry track; continue until tarmac road **17**.

Turn right, uphill, on road. After 200 yards turn left on track opposite Forestry Commission notice. 100 yards after cottage on left, fork left. At second cottage, pass through stile ahead into woods, crossing stream and keeping left beyond, on path. Path climbs to join forestry track **18**. Continue forward on forestry track and turn right after 150 yards at first junction. 50 yards later take path half left into woods. This crosses small stream bridged by old railway sleepers after 100 yards, then climbs steeply through forest to further forestry track **19**.

Turn left on track. 300 yards later avoid right turn and follow to turning-circle at edge of forest, then forward on path leading to stile. **20** Emerge into open country and continue forward alongside wall on left (or on easier path on other side of wall), down to cross boggy area in copse, where path bends round right up to cross wire fence. Continue forward for about 300 yards, looking for second and third small hillocks on the left (third hillock is enclosed by fence). Follow grassy track down between them that joins farm track, then drops down steeply to join A5. Turn right and follow ½ mile to start.

The Mawddach Estuary and Cregennen Lakes

Contributed by G J Fox

Starts along the old railway line next to the Mawddach Estuary, with views towards the Rhinogs and good opportunities for bird-watching. Ascends on tarmac lane to lakes close by Cader Idris, then follows the Arthog waterfalls down to the bottom. Route-finding slightly involved from [9] until [11], otherwise easy.

Length 11 miles (7.5km), 5 hours
Difficulty 3
Start Morfa Mawddach station (just N of A493), 1 mile W of Arthog, 8 miles WSW of Dolgellau. Grid reference SH 628141
OS maps 1:50,000 124; 1:25,000 Outdoor Leisure 23

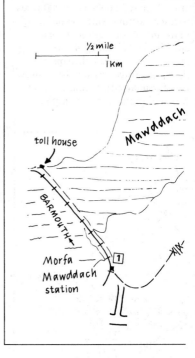

WALK DIRECTIONS

[1] From station, with railway on your right, turn left on to old railway track (**a**). [2] After 4 miles, watch out for where track crosses bridge with iron railings. ¼ mile later, immediately after next (similar) bridge, turn right (off railway track) to head down over wooden footbridge (can be wet here). Beyond footbridge continue forward towards trees [3].

At edge of woods join track; turn right on to this and follow into woods, until track bends through gate. Go through this and follow stony track across field to gate. Continue ahead on tarmac lane, and follow up to main road [4]. Left on road for 30 yards, then right on lane signed 'unsuitable for coaches', and follow for 1 mile [5]. 100 yards after passing youth hostel on your left, and where lane bends sharp right, proceed forward through gate into wood. Follow woodland path uphill for 300 yards, re-emerge on lane opposite ruined chapel, turn left.

[6] After 200 yards, when road bends sharp left, continue forward on track, and follow to gate. Beyond gate make for gate just to right of stone farmhouse which is visible ahead [7]. Beyond gate continue forward (uphill) on path which skirts base of craggy hill (**b**). [8] Near lakes, cross ladder-stile, proceed round back of old club-house to reach road (**c**). Left on road, then 150 yards after car park right on path by footpath signpost [9].

250 yards later cross stile in wall on right. Path follows close to wall on right (it leaves wall after 50 yards but returns to it at end of field). After end of field, path runs between walls for 50 yards, then where walls open out bear left down to gate/signpost; do not pass through gate but turn right on grassy track alongside wall on left. Proceed through two gates, then at signpost at wall ahead, follow track

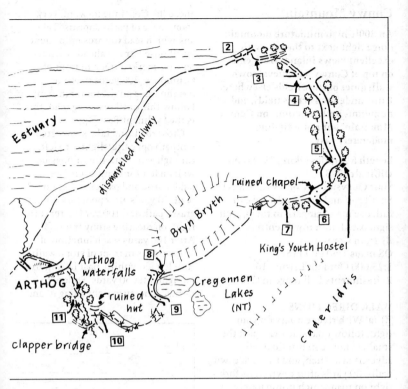

which turns off to the left.

10 50 yards later, where main track bends right, continue forward (slightly uphill) to gate ahead, and follow track. 200 yards later, as track veers left, bear down to cross clapper bridge just visible on right, then cross ladder-stile on right to follow path along stream. **11** After ½ mile, and 100 yards after ladder-stile, take narrow path on right winding down through trees towards stream. It leads past triple-spout waterfall downstream, then briefly emerges into field by stone posts before re-entering woods by waymarker, eventually arriving by gate at main road.

Turn left on road, and after 40 yards (just after end of churchyard) take signposted kissing-gate on right. Continue forward to stream, then turn left on bank of stream, soon picking up raised dyke. At tarmac lane turn right, then left on to old railway track and back to start.

WHAT TO LOOK OUT FOR
(a) The **estuary** and its immediate surroundings are an important site for wildlife. Mammals include otters, polecats and dormice. **Flora** Orchids, crowfoots, saltmarsh plants; Arthog bog is the northernmost site in Europe for St John's wort. **Birds** Geese, shelducks, curlews, snipes, lapwings, wild swans.
(b) The **Cader Idris ridge** (2,927ft) is on your left. If you have any energy left, find your way across the craggy ridge on your right (to the car park by the lakes) for good views.
(c) **View** From any of these small hillocks over the mouth of the estuary, and over Barmouth.

Conwy Mountain

An 800ft-high miniature mountain range right next to the sea, with excellent views inland. Walk ends on top of Conwy's medieval town wall; quiet pasture fields elsewhere. Paths undefined across fields, and numerous path junctions on Conwy Mountain, but route-finding moderately easy.

Length 5½ miles (9km), 2½ hours
Difficulty 2–3
Start Quayside at Conwy (Conway). Small pay-and-display car park (if full, use main car park in town, well signposted from town centre)
By train Conwy
OS maps 1:50,000 115; 1:25,000 Outdoor Leisure 16
Refreshments Full range in Conwy

WALK DIRECTIONS

1 (**a**) With river estuary on your right, follow quayside road, past the smallest house in Britain (well advertised as such) and through town walls. 30 yards after town walls fork right on road which immediately becomes tarmac path running along estuary for ½ mile. **2** At road turn sharp left and cross main road to take track opposite, leading over railway. 100 yards after railway join lane (leading to house on right), continue forward on it for 50 yards, then turn right at T-junction (signposted Mountain Road). 150 yards later fork right uphill, on track which immediately becomes narrow (but clear) path leading through bracken.

3 After ½ mile reach fork of wide paths by low stone boulder and small iron bollard. (All routes along ridge end up at same place but seaward side has the best views.) Fork right, and 50 yards later turn left at crossing of paths. 200 yards later keep right in front of crags on narrow (but clear) path leading uphill to top. Summit is not pronounced but views open up

ahead (**b**). Continue forward: very soon, maze of paths appears. Take any which lead towards prominent farmhouse ½ mile ahead. Turn left on well-marked track in front of farmhouse (300 yards to left of farmhouse is public footpath sign). Follow this until reaching road: this is the Sychnant Pass **4**.

Cross road, and take signposted footpath opposite/slightly to left, through gate. Path runs alongside wall on left for ½ mile, crosses ladder-stile and passes to right of pool. 50 yards after pool fork left on grassy path and 100 yards later turn right, on meeting stony track. **5** After 100 yards reach junction of stony tracks in front of stone wall: turn left (downhill), past farmhouse on right after 50 yards. Follow to tarmac lane, turn right along it, and

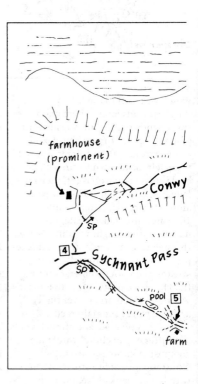

after 100 yards turn left through kissing-gate immediately before house. After short section between fences continue forward alongside fence on right to next gate. In second field bear half left to small gate.

6 In third field continue to gate 100 yards ahead, and in fourth field continue forward to corner of fence ahead, then continue forward alongside fence into fifth field 7. Continue forward, keeping close to trees on right, leaving field by gate at end, leading on to tarmac lane. Turn right on lane. 8 ¼ mile later turn right at T-junction then, after 30 yards, take small gate on left (signposted). Follow right edge of first two fields, cross third field to gate ahead and turn left along edge of fourth field to emerge by gate on to road on outskirts of Conwy 9.

Turn right on road; after ½ mile pass under town wall and take steps up on to it on other side. Turn left on top of wall and follow to quayside.

WHAT TO LOOK OUT FOR
(a) **Conwy** The castle and the virtually intact town wall, with its 21 stone turrets and three gateways, were built for Edward I between 1283 and 1292. Within the walls (if you can bear the traffic) there is much to see, including Plas Mawr, an Elizabethan town house, and a 15th-century rood screen in the church.
(b) **View** W to SE part of Anglesey, including Beaumaris Castle; N across Conwy Bay to Great Ormes Head; SSW into Snowdonia, including Tal y Fan (2,001ft); S down the Vale of Conwy; E towards the Clwydian Range (1,818ft).

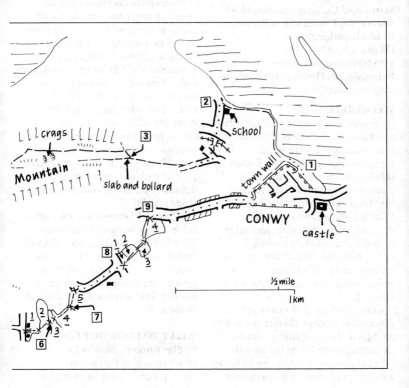

Moel Siabod

Contributed by Dr and Mrs
B W Davies
Recommended by Brian Hathaway

A pyramidal mountain on the eastern edge of Snowdonia, with particularly good views. Easy first few miles through woodland and pasture before the start of the ascent past two lakes and old quarry workings, with the formidable wall of Siabod on your right. Route to summit requires some tough scrambling, before a descent on the grassy northern slopes. Paths undefined up to summit and for much of the descent, but route-finding is quite easy in clear weather. Compass is essential, however, in case of mist. Ascent 2,250ft.

Length 7 miles (11km), 4 hours
Difficulty 5
Start Capel Curig, at junction of A5 and A4086, 15 miles SE of Bangor. Roadside parking
OS maps 1:50,000 115; 1:25,000 Outdoor Leisure 16
Refreshments Hotels (with bars) and shop in Capel Curig

WALK DIRECTIONS

1 Follow A4086 out of village. After 600 yards, immediately after Plas y Brenin outdoor centre (**a**), take signposted footpath on left. Follow this over bridge then turn left on track. ¼ mile later avoid left turns into farm but proceed into forest. **2** ¼ mile later, and 50 yards after avoiding sharp right turn, fork right on track immediately passing through barrier. This eventually leads up steps and reaches signpost shortly before bridge down on left (do not cross) **3**.

Continue forward from signpost, descending to river, then turn right along river bank, at first in woods, then entering fields by ladder-stile. **4** Leave second field by gap 30 yards away from river, then immediately turn left below cottages and follow track through gate to tarmac lane. Turn right on lane, then 50 yards later, at the cottages, turn right (signposted) on lane over cattle-grid (signed 'no cars'). After ¼ mile, at farm, continue uphill on obvious rough track to left of farm. Cross two sets of gate/ladder-stiles in next ½ mile and continue up to ladder-stile in fence: avoid ladder-stile 50 yards to right **5**.

From stile continue slightly downhill to lake, then follow right side of lake on clear path that then ascends past old slate quarries, at top of which is a dark pool, just on right of path **6**. From pool path is less clear, but continue forward, heading to lowest point of shoulder ahead, from where clear path leads to another lake.

After end of lake turn right up ridge: a rough path is marked with cairns to begin with, but make your own way, keeping close to steep slope on right, up to summit (a stiffish scramble) (**b**) **7**. From trig. point turn right along ridge, heading for lesser summit (no path). After 400 yards, just before ridge rises, bear half left down off ridge: soon lake and outdoor centre passed at start of walk are seen below – make down for right-hand end of lake. ½ mile down you should pick up path that soon becomes well defined and leads to ladder-stile in stone wall **8**.

Stony path is now obvious: follow it for ¾ mile to reach forest track. Turn left along it then, after 50 yards, find narrow path on right alongside stream. 200 yards later take clear path on left leading down through forest to bridge crossed near the start of the walk.

WHAT TO LOOK OUT FOR

(**a**) **Plas y Brenin** Built by Lord Penrhyn, one of the richest slate-quarry owners, as an inn for

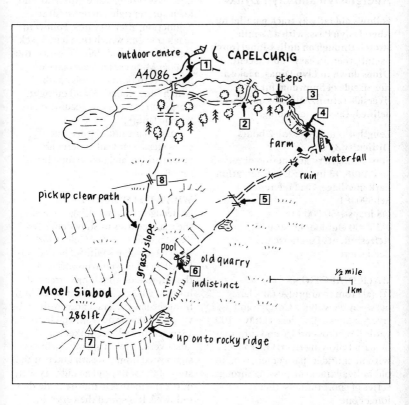

travellers. He also constructed the road along the S side of the Upper Llugwy Valley and the one along this valley. Now owned by the Central Council for Physical Recreation.

(**b**) **View** W to Snowdon (3,560ft); NW to the Glyders (3,279ft) and Tryfan (3,010ft) just to the right of them; N to Penyrhelgi-du (2,733ft), NE over the chain of lakes N of the Llugwy Valley; ENE to the Clwydian Range (1,818ft); E over Llyn Elsi Reservoir and the hills near Betws-y-coed; SE to the Arenigs (2,801ft) and Berwyn (2,712ft); SSE to Dolwyddelan Castle (immediately below); S to the Rhinogs (2,362ft).

Aberglaslyn and Llyn Dinas

Follows old railway track parallel to Aberglaslyn Pass, with a ¼-mile stretch through an unlit tunnel (torch useful), then an easy 700ft ascent. Drops down to Llyn Dinas, a lake at the SE side of Snowdon, for a riverside return. All paths quite well defined; easy route-finding.

Length 4½ miles (7km), 2 hours
Difficulty 3
Start Beddgelert, at junction of A4085 and A498, 13 miles SE of Caernarfon. Park in village. Grid reference SH 590481
OS maps 1:50,000 115; 1:25,000 Outdoor Leisure 17
Refreshments Full range in Beddgelert

WALK DIRECTIONS

1 (a) From road-bridge take lane between Llewelyn's Cottage and river, signposted Gelert's Grave. 100 yards later cross bridge and turn right on path following river. Once level with next bridge, path emerges on to old railway track (b), passing through series of short tunnels, then a longer one.

2 On emerging from tunnel turn sharp left uphill (left-hand of two paths). Path climbs steadily, and is easy to follow. After ¾ mile it follows disused mine conveyors uphill. **3** At top, view opens out suddenly (c): continue forward, descending gently towards distant lake (Llyn Dinas). Final part of descent is much steeper.

4 Turn left at lake and after 30 yards proceed beyond footpath signpost (avoid crossing bridge) to follow left side of river. **5** After ½

mile pass through gate into field, and keep quarter right (signposted) at X-junction, after 30 yards. Follow to reach track on which turn left. Track immediately bends left; 10 yards after Copper Mine car park entrance on left (d), turn right on grassy path which runs alongside wall on right. This soon reaches gate leading on to tarmac lane **6**.

Follow lane until bridge, then **7** cross steps over wall on left just before bridge, and take riverside path into Beddgelert.

WHAT TO LOOK OUT FOR

(a) **Beddgelert** Stone village, one of the main centres in Snowdonia. Its name means Grave of Gelert, for Prince Llewelyn's faithful hound was killed by its master who was under the impression that it had attacked his son, when it had in fact saved him from the jaws of a ravenous wolf. All very melodramatic stuff, and in the 18th century a local innkeeper 'discovered' Gelert's Grave (which is signposted from the path taken at the start of the walk) and he did very well out of the increased tourist trade that followed. It inspired the verse:

Pass on O tender-hearted,
Dry your eyes
Not here a greyhound
But a landlord lies.

(b) **Old railway** The former N Wales Narrow Gauge Railway, which ran from Beddgelert to Dinas Junction, S of Caernarfon.
(c) **View** N to Snowdon (3,560ft); NE to the Glyders (3,279ft); W to Moel Hebod (2,568ft); and E to the pyramid-shaped Cnicht (2,265ft).
(d) **Sygun copper mine** (open to public; fee) Mining finished in 1903.

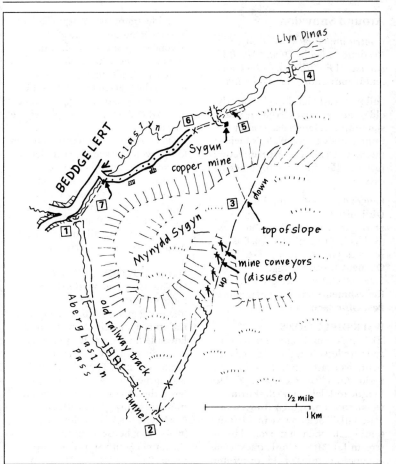

Llyn Dinas

4

Glaslyn

6

X

5

Sygun
copper mine

down

7

3

top of slope

1

Mynydd Sygyn

mine conveyors
(disused)

up

Aberglaslyn pass

old railway track

½ mile

1 Km

tunnel

2

Around Snowdon

Contributed by R W Willson
Recommended by Dr and Mrs B W
Davies, M E Williams, Colin Glover
and Wendy Short, A M Podhalicz

**Follows nearly level tracks, mostly
old tramways that served the nearby
slate-mines, along a deep valley
immediately below Wales's highest
mountain. Take care with directions
just after** 5 ; **route-finding otherwise
easy.**

Length 4 miles (6.5km), 2 hours
Difficulty 1
Start Car park at Bethania on A498
(Beddgelert to Capel Curig). Bus
services. Grid reference SH 627506
OS maps 1:50,000 115;
1:25,000 Outdoor Leisure 17
Refreshments Snacks at Bethania
Post Office and Stores

WALK DIRECTIONS

1 From car park, cross main road
and turn left on it, then immediately
right, over cattle-grid (**a**). Follow lane
beside Afon (River) Glaslyn. 2 After
¼ mile fork left on track skirting
wood, soon emerging with view of
waterfall. Track now swings left in
semi-circle, then runs parallel to
stream. 3 After ½ mile track levels
out opposite ruins of old copper-mine
buildings on other bank of stream.

4 Track crosses stream by bridge
and passes ruins of old house (**b**), and
continues past Gladstone Rock (**c**).
Carry on until waste-heaps and the
ruined buildings of the old South
Snowdon slate mine (**d**) 5 . Keep
forward, to leave Watkin Path, which
ascends right, by signpost. 100 yards
later, by ruined building (miners'
barracks), turn left, finding steep
grassy incline heading down across
footbridge over stream to old slate-
dressing sheds. Continue forward,
soon picking up track (former tramway) which doubles back on other
side of valley from Watkin Path.

Follow tramway – Watkin Path can
be seen below and to left. 6 Just
beyond the point above old mine
manager's house, turn left on track
which descends steeply to stream and
rejoins the Watkin Path. Cross the
stream using natural stepping-stones
(if you don't fancy this simply retrace
steps).

On far side of stream turn right and
follow well-marked path parallel to
stream. Pass old copper-mine
buildings and continue down hillside.
After ¼ mile path crosses bridge
(single slab of slate) just above
waterfall. Regain Watkin Path by
proceeding with wall on right directly
uphill. Retrace steps (**e**) to start.

WHAT TO LOOK OUT FOR

(**a**) The start of the **Watkin Path**, a
route up to the top of Snowdon
(requiring more climbing than any of
the other approaches), created by Sir
Edward Watkin, a railway engineer
and pioneer of an early attempt to
build a Channel Tunnel. The path
was opened in 1892 by Gladstone,
when the 83-year-old former prime
minister followed the path as far as
Gladstone Rock (see below).
(**b**) Ruins of **house** of the manager of
the former South Snowdon slate
mine. The area was used for army
training in the last war, and there are
bullet holes in the walls of the house.
(**c**) **Gladstone Rock** A plaque inserted
by Watkin himself commemorates
Gladstone's speech from this rock,
and the audience's rendition of *Land
of my Fathers*.
(**d**) **South Snowdon slate mine** One
of many disused slate mines in
Snowdonia; spoil heaps, courses of
the old tramways and ruined
outbuildings much in evidence.
(**e**) On return journey, on re-entering
woods, notice an **iron gate** on the
right. Beyond, an overgrown
driveway leads to the scant remains
of Watkin's house, The Chalet.

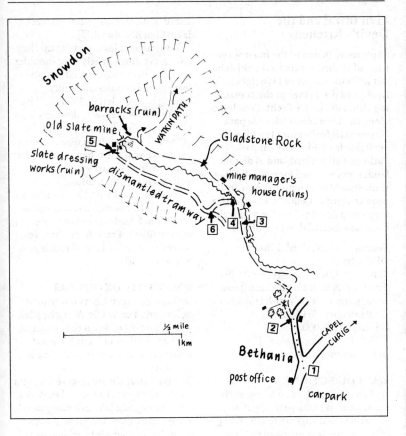

Snowdon

barracks (ruin)

old slate mine

WATKIN PATH

5

slate dressing
works (ruin)

Gladstone Rock

dismantled tramway

mine manager's
house (ruins)

6   4   3

1/2 mile

1km

2

Bethania

CAPEL
CURIG

post office

1

car park

Llyn Idwal and the Devil's Kitchen

Short route in one of the most severe parts of Wales, making a roughish but not difficult ascent to Llyn (lake) Bochlwyd (first stage of the demanding climb of Glyder Fâch). Concludes along the Llyn Idwal lakeside path. Nature trail leaflet for Llyn Idwal available from kiosk by car park. Paths not all defined, and as distant landmarks are used for route-finding, walk should be attempted only in good visibility. 1,000ft ascent, with a very steep descent into Cwm Idwal. Compass essential in case of mist.

Length 3 miles (5km), 2 hours
Difficulty 3
Start Llyn Idwal car park, on A5 5 miles WNW of Capel Curig (signed to car park, toilets, Youth Hostel). Grid reference SH 650603
OS maps 1:50,000 115; 1:25,000 Outdoor Leisure 17
Refreshments Kiosk at car park

WALK DIRECTIONS

1 Leave car park at end nearest the main road and take path opposite phone box and slightly to left. After 30 yards this is signposted to Llyn Idwal. **2** After 300 yards, at obvious right bend in path, continue forward (no path at first) heading towards prominent stony path over shoulder of ridge 400 yards in front of you, crossing boggy area to reach it. On reaching path you are joined by stream on left. At top of slope, path becomes less distinct but continue

ahead, with stream on left, to reach lake (Llyn Bochlwyd) **3**.

Turn right at lake, picking up clear path ascending slightly over shoulder (**a**). Once over top, descend steeply (path soon becomes indistinct), aiming towards left end of lake (Llyn Idwal) below. Half-way down pick up clear path. Reach stony track at the bottom (**b**), turn left on it to ascend towards Devil's Kitchen (narrow cleft at top of boulder-strewn slope). Follow clear path uphill.

4 Once level with Devil's Kitchen on your left, descend, picking up the rough track leading down other side of Llyn Idwal. Track soon improves: follow past end of lake, through gate and to car park.

WHAT TO LOOK OUT FOR

(**a**) **View** Between Llyn Ogwen (just below) and Pen yr Ole Wen (the peak immediately N), down the glaciated, U-shaped valley of Nant Ffrancon towards Bangor, and over the sea to Anglesey.

(**b**) **Llyn Idwal nature reserve** The first nature reserve to be created in Wales, a half-mile-long lake in a vast glacial cwm whose great variation of rock types has encouraged a wide range of **flora**, including high-altitude arctic/alpine types and some more common species: early purple orchid, moss campion, some saxifrages, globeflower, parsley fern, green spleenwort and others. Feral goats live high up on the slopes. Legend has it that no bird has flown over the lake since Idwal, the Prince of Wales, was hurled into it by his foster father.

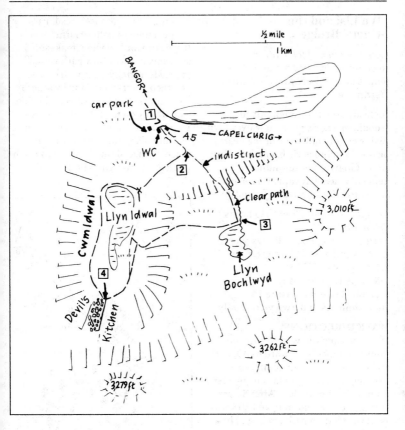

Llyn Elsi and the Miners' Bridge

Contributed by Jack Crewe
Recommended by Tom and Teru
Salusbury, Steve Newman, Martin
Herrington

A steady ascent through mixed woodland, leading to a view over Llyn Elsi reservoir and some of the nearby peaks. Concludes with a path by the River Llugwy. Route-finding generally easy, but some care needed with directions between 3 and 6.

Length 4½ miles (7km), 2½ hours
Difficulty 2–3
Start Station car park, Betws-y-coed, on A5 4 miles S of Llanrwst. Grid reference SH 795765
OS maps 1:50,000 115;
1:25,000 Outdoor Leisure 16
Refreshments In Betws-y-coed only

WALK DIRECTIONS

1 From car park, with station on your left, proceed forward to A5, turn right on A5 then immediately left just before St Mary's church and just after post office on left. After 50 yards turn right at T-junction, and 50 yards later turn left on path leading uphill into woods (immediately after bungalow on left). Path ascends steadily. 2 After ½ mile, and immediately after path crosses stream, turn right, by stone post, on path which recrosses stream by footbridge, and zigzags uphill. Beyond top of slope continue straight on (following green and purple paintmarks on rocks) at next two cross-tracks, which appear at ¼ mile intervals. Path emerges from forest shortly before reaching monument by Llyn Elsi reservoir (a) 3.

At monument, take path quarter right downhill (waymarked). Ignore turnings to left, continue to cross forestry track 300 yards later, and take path opposite. 4 After 200 yards climb ladder-stile and turn left,

heading for farmhouse ahead. Pass immediately to right of farmhouse, leave farmyard by wide (makeshift) stile ahead, and follow path which proceeds initially with wall on left and then enters woodland by stile 5. Path in woodland snakes a little: take care to stay on it, and 250 yards into wood (shortly after crossing stream by stone slab), turn left on meeting fence. Path leads out of wood to reach track 6. Turn right on track and

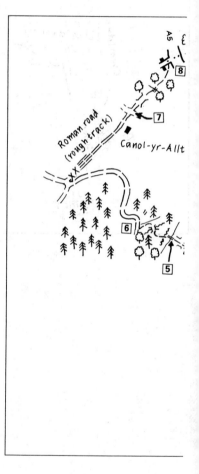

continue on it for 600 yards to reach junction of tracks. Turn sharp right, through two sets of gates, to descend on grassy track between walls. **7** Continue straight ahead at next junction of tracks (600 yards later) and follow down to A5 **8**. Cross road and take path opposite. After crossing Miners' Bridge (**b**) turn right and follow river ¾ mile back to Betws-y-coed. Cross Betws-y-coed bridge and turn left to return to station.

WHAT TO LOOK OUT FOR

(**a**) **Llyn Elsi reservoir** Fine views from this peaceful lake of the pyramidal peak of Moel Siabod (2,861ft).
(**b**) **Miners' Bridge** A wooden structure like a ship's gangway, spanning the Llugwy. The original bridge, a rough step-ladder, was part of a miners' route to the lead mines at Rhiwddolion. The river was a favourite scene for Victorian artists, notably David Cox.

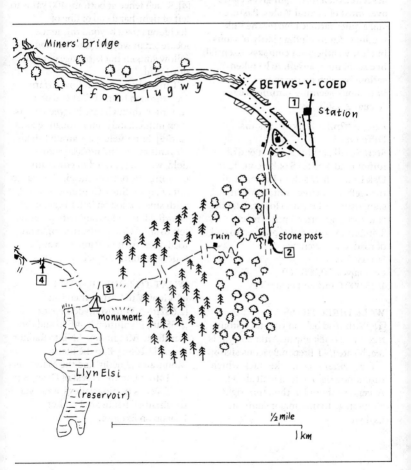

POWYS

The Brecon Beacons Horseshoe

Approaches the summit of the Beacons from their most dramatic (though not most frequented) side, with one of the best ridge walks Wales has to offer between the peaks of Cribyn and Pen y Fan. The slow descent over a turfy spur gives views over most of central Wales. Pasture and a quiet tarmac lane for the link sections. Route-finding fairly obvious in clear weather, but compass essential in case of mist; a walk to be taken seriously, even on the most innocuous-seeming summer's day. Ascent 2,350ft.

Length 6 miles (9.5km), 5 hours
Difficulty 5
Start Small parking space at end of minor road 4 miles S of Brecon. Take Usk Ridge on W side of Brecon, and turn left just before church on left, signposted St David's Hospital. Ignore side turnings; after 3 miles reach T-junction. Turn right, proceed to end of road. Grid reference SO 036235
OS maps 1:50,000 160; 1:25,000 Outdoor Leisure 11

WALK DIRECTIONS

1 With road behind you, take stony tree-lined track ahead. After 250 yards reach gate (NT Brecon Beacons sign).

For gentler ascent take track which runs along right side of wall ahead. Ascend to shoulder, then turn right along ridge to first major summit, Cribyn.

For direct ascent take grassy track up on to spur ahead and ascend to first major summit, Cribyn.

2 From Cribyn, proceed to the next major summit (Pen y Fan), descending steeply at first, then following ridge up.
3 (a) At summit (trig. point) of Pen y Fan, turn right on to grassy spur for descent. At end of spur, keep to right.
4 Reach fence at bottom; 400 yards to left of right-hand end of line of deciduous trees beyond this fence, locate small wooden gate. Beyond it, follow sunken track (or edge of field) until road.

Turn right on road, follow to farm. Pass through farmyard, at end of it, turn right through gate between barns, then immediately left through second gate **5**. Enter field, pass around sheds 20 yards away, and proceed across field, walking parallel to power lines, crossing line of trees ahead, 20 yards to left of power lines. Continue forward, with small wood on left, to gate into next field; then forward with fence on left to stile. Cross stile, turn right on road, then right at T-junction and follow to starting-place.

WHAT TO LOOK OUT FOR

(a) View W to Carmarthen Fan (2,632ft); NW to Mynydd Eppynt (1,559ft), Plynlimon (2,467ft) and the Cambrian Mountains; ENE to Radnor Forest (2,166ft); E to the Black Mountains (2,660ft) and the Malverns (1,114ft); SE to the Forest of Dean; S to the S Wales mining valleys, and over the Bristol Channel to Dunkery Beacon on Exmoor.

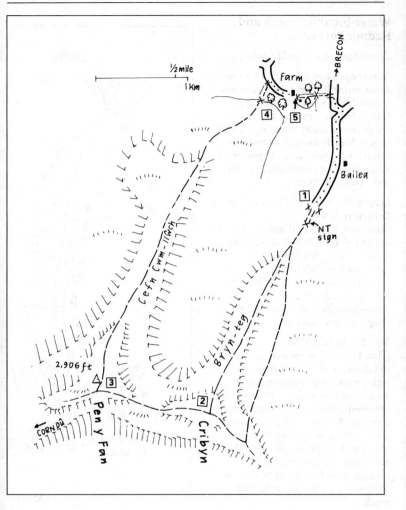

Water-break-its-neck and Radnor Forest

Contributed by Ronald Locke

Across open upland, with a section in dense forest for contrast. Takes in a romantically sited waterfall and Harley Dingle – more a dale than a dingle, enclosed by plunging 1,000ft slopes. Mostly on defined tracks but directions require care. Approach to Water-break-its-neck usually very wet. Ascent 1,300ft.

Length 8½ miles (13.5km), 4½ hours
Difficulty 3–4
Start New Radnor village centre, just off A44, 6 miles WNW of Kington. Grid reference SO 213609
OS maps 1:50,000 148; 1:25,000 SO 05/15, SO 06/16, SO 15/25 and SO 16/26
Refreshments Three pubs and two shops in New Radnor

WALK DIRECTIONS

1 (**a**) From T-junction in the centre of village, with Radnor Arms on right, walk down main street. **2** Reach main road, turn left along it for 100 yards, then cross to tarmac track opposite. Follow track past caravan site (**b**), then steeply uphill into woodland, ignoring side turns. 200 yards after passing entrance to cottage away to right, turn right at T-junction with another tarmac track.

3 Beyond gate, track ceases to be tarmacked and traverses hillside between fences (**c**). Beyond next gate avoid track to left, dropping down to farm, but keep right through second gate. Track continues along edge of field alongside fence on right; where another track diverges right, up to old quarry, keep left.

4 Track enters conifer plantation by gate; on other side, go through gate and turn immediately right, to continue along left edge of field to reach gate, beyond which track is

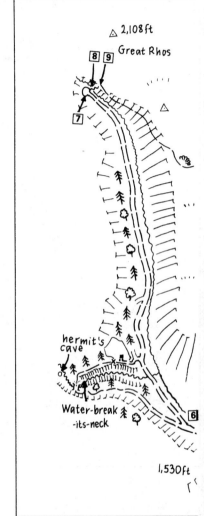

seen dropping down slope slightly to left (avoid track up on right). Track passes small quarry and continues through gates to stream at foot of hill. Cross it by footbridge and walk up rise to main road **5**. Cross road and take turning opposite and slightly to left, signposted 'by-way'.

6 After ½ mile take right fork into forest. Shortly, reach signpost

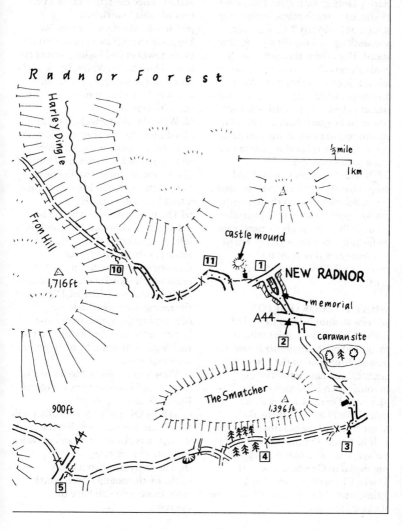

Radnor Forest

Harley Dingle

From Hill

½ mile

1 km

castle mound

11

10

1

NEW RADNOR

△
1,716 ft

memorial

A44

2

caravan site

The Smatcher

900 ft

△
1,396 ft

A44

4

3

5

pointing to Water-break-its-neck, at
which detour as indicated, to view
falls (**d**). Returning to signpost,
continue on main track, soon forking
right (**e**), and continue through the
forest, avoiding left fork, to reach end
of track at turning-circle **7**.

Keep forward to cross fence and
emerge on to moorland and, a few
yards beyond, pick up line of

trackway heading to right towards
valley and towards zigzag pathway
seen ascending hill opposite. Follow
track to where it crosses stile and
then stream by stepping-stones **8**.
On far side, path leads up bank to foot
of zigzag. Climb this (final ascent of
walk) **9**.

At top, track becomes fainter, but
continues straight ahead (**f**), soon

becoming clearer as it descends into Harley Dingle (valley) (**g**). Follow for 1½ miles to reach plank-bridge over stream at bottom **10**. Cross bridge and walk up to footpath sign on lane ahead. Turn right, through gate. 20 yards ahead take tarmac driveway on left leading to another gate. When driveway swings left, take grassy path straight ahead. This continues round side of hill to gate. Path can be seen continuing across field to next gate, beyond which it continues as grassy track between hedges.

11 Track becomes tarmac and drops downhill. When castle mound is reached on left, pass through gate marked public footpath into castle grounds (**h**). Path leads to metal gate on far side, then through two small wooden gates into New Radnor churchyard. Descend to village centre.

WHAT TO LOOK OUT FOR

(**a**) **New Radnor** Former capital of Radnorshire (now a quiet village by-passed by the main road), laid out on a gridiron plan in the 11th century, and once a flourishing borough with a Norman castle (destroyed in the Civil War and marked only by its earthworks). Some traces of the old town wall can still be found. On the way out of the village, the route passes an enormous memorial to George Cornewall Lewis, Chancellor under Lord Palmerston 1855–58 and MP for New Radnor 1855–63.

(**b**) The caravans are on the site of the **station**, once the terminus of a very unprofitable branch line.

(**c**) **View** E over the vale of the River Lugg. On the hill away to the left (SE) is the tower of Old Radnor, one of the finest churches in Wales. Below is the farmstead of Wolfpits, a reminder that this was a haunt of wolves until the 17th century.

(**d**) **Water-break-its-neck** Approached along a narrow, twisting ravine with trees growing out at implausible angles, and hidden from view until almost the last moment. Best after rain, as the waterfall is no more than a trickle in a dry season.

(**e**) The top of the waterfall can be reached by forking left here, and then left again, keeping to the left of the garden at the farmhouse and following a faint path through the grass which shortly enters the woods and becomes well defined. High up in the ravine is a cave which was occupied in the 18th century by a hermit who scratched graffiti on the rock wall. Return to the main route after exploration.

(**f**) **View** S to the Black Mountains (2,660ft); SSW the twin peaks of the Brecon Beacons (2,906ft).

(**g**) **Harley Dingle** is occasionally used for testing ammunition, but the track described is always open and provides magnificent walking.

(**h**) The short climb to the top of the **castle mound** is well worth it for those who still have the energy.

Norton and Offa's Dyke

Contributed by Ronald Locke

Easy walk through pasture and woodland, incorporating a well-preserved section of Offa's Dyke, with views further into Wales. All on farm tracks and field paths, with an unfrequented road downhill at end; route-finding quite easy.

Length 5½ miles (9km), 3 hours
Difficulty 2
Start Norton, 2 miles NNW of Presteigne on B4355 (Knighton to Presteigne). Grid reference SO 305672
OS maps 1:50,000 137 or 148; 1:25,000 SO 26/36
Refreshments Shop in Norton

WALK DIRECTIONS

1 Leave Norton by lane opposite church lych-gate, at first between modern houses, then, beyond gate, on track uphill. This shortly leads past mound of Norton Castle on right (**a**). At top of rise, pass through another gate and maintain same direction past 'no through road' sign, ignoring forks right and left. **2** Track becomes tarmac again, and leads between conifer plantation on right and field on left (**b**). Past cattle-grid, track continues through another gate to right of farmhouse, then becomes unmetalled bridleway curving to left, past track coming in from right.

At junction just short of next farm, take track going right over rise, ignoring path left into buildings. Go through gate at top, heading towards woodland. **3** 200 yards further, pass through another gate on to lesser track, leaving main track, which veers right. Track continues with woodland on right and wire fence on left, then enters wood with oaks on both sides. When wood ends, pass through gate into field, and follow path which can be seen leading to Offa's Dyke Path signpost on skyline **4**.

Proceed straight ahead in signposted direction for next ¾ mile, following acorn symbols. Beyond second stile, clearly marked stretch of Offa's Dyke is reached (**c**); continue to follow until waymarked stile in right-hand fence. Cross stile and maintain direction, with fence on left and conifer plantation on right.

5 Beyond next stile, memorial will be seen on right on top of grassy mound (**d**). Take path skirting to right of mound, leaving Offa's Dyke Path. Continue along grassy valley, to gate. Turn left at road and cross main road to driveway signed Hill House **6**. Follow driveway over cattle-grid and continue to farm **7**.

Take gate to right of farmhouse (**e**). Track descends field through gap in hedge to gate. Past gate go diagonally (no path) across field towards far right-hand corner, where house can be seen in trees. Beyond gate in corner, cross stream by footbridge on to driveway **8**. Turn left and cross second footbridge. Follow driveway steeply uphill to T-junction, at which turn right down road and continue downhill for 1 mile to meet main road at edge of Norton village. Turn left to complete walk.

WHAT TO LOOK OUT FOR

(**a**) **Norton Castle** A motte and bailey castle that belonged to the Mortimers; captured and destroyed by the Welsh under Llewelyn Griffiths in 1262.
(**b**) **View** Over the valley of the Lugg to the fine upland country between Presteigne and Knighton.
(**c**) A very clearly defined section of **Offa's Dyke**, constructed by order of Offa, King of Mercia, about AD784 to mark the boundary between his kingdom and the lands of the Welsh.

(d) The **memorial** commemorates the magnate who brought railways to Radnorshire (see inscription). He would no doubt be saddened by the loss of the lines to Presteigne and New Radnor, but at least the mid-Wales line through Knighton and Llandrindod has survived.

(e) The OS map shows the path going left of the farmhouse, but the farmer has confirmed that the line of the path is as given in our directions.

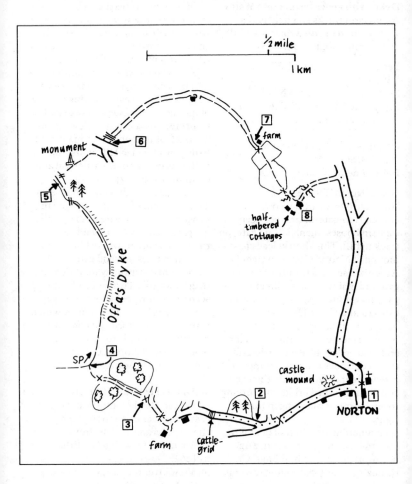

Special interest lists

Walks taking in interesting buildings and villages

9 Fishermen's cottages at Polperro

13 Dartmouth Castle (open mid-Mar to mid-Oct, 9.30 to 6.30 Mon to Sat, 9.30 to 4 Sun; early Mar and late Oct, 2 to 6.30 Sun; mid-Oct to mid-Mar, 9.30 to 4 Mon to Sat, 2 to 4 Sun)

14 Sidmouth seafront

18 Lustleigh village

19 Castle Drogo (open Apr to end Oct, 11 to 6 daily) and Drewsteignton

24 Milton Abbey, chapel and Milton Abbas

25 Corfe Castle (open Mar to end Oct, 10 to 6 daily; Nov to end Feb, 12 to 4 Sat and Sun), St Catherine's Chapel

26 Studland Church

29 Cerne Abbas

31 Selworthy village and church

34 Old Wardour Castle (open Mar to Oct, 9.30 to 6.30 Mon to Sat, 2 to 4.30 Sun; Oct to Mar, 9.30 to 4 Sat, 2 to 4 Sun)

35 King John's House

37 Breamore House (open end Mar to end Sept, 2 to 5.30), and church

38 Hale House and church

41 Solent Forts (open Easter to Oct, 11 to 5.30 daily)

42 Appuldurcombe House (open mid-Mar to mid-Oct, 9.30 to 6.30 Mon to Sat, 2 to 4.30 Sun; mid-Oct to mid-Mar, 9.30 to 4 Mon to Sat, 1 to 4 Sun)

43 Dover Castle (open mid-Mar to mid-Oct, 9.30 to 6.30 Mon to Sat, 9.30 to 4 Sun; mid-Oct to mid-Mar, 9.30 to 4 Mon to Sat, 2 to 4 Sun), Roman Lighthouse, Windmill at St Margaret's at Cliffe (open 8 to 6 daily), Walmer and Deal Castles (open times as for Dover Castle, exc Sun in summer (open 2.30 to 4) and Mon; open bank hol Mons only)

44 Saltwood Castle, Hythe church

46 Wye College

48 Quebec House (open 2 to 5 daily, exc Thur and Sat), Chartwell (open Apr to Oct, 12 to 5 Tue to Thur; 11 to 5 bank hols, Sat and Sun; Mar and Nov 11 to 4 Sat, Sun and Wed)

49 Ightham Mote (open Apr to Oct, 11 to 5 daily, exc Tue and Sat), and Knole (open Apr to Oct, 11 to 5 Wed to Sat, 2 to 4 Sun; also bank hols)

50 Hever Castle and church, Penshurst Place

51 Polesden Lacey, Ranmore Common church

52 Leith Hill Tower (open Apr to end Sept, 2 to 5 Wed, Sat, Sun and bank hol Mons)

55 Ewhurst Windmill

58 Stansted House (open 2 to 6 Mon, Tue and Sun), and Racton Monument

59 Jack and Jill windmills

60 West Dean rectory

61 Glynde Place (open June to Sept, 2 to 5 Wed and Thur; bank hols and Easter)

62 Poohsticks Bridge

63 Hastings Old Town and Net Houses

65 Scotney Castle (open Apr to 15 Nov, 11 to 6 Wed to Fri (closed Good Fri), 2 to 6 Sat, Sun and bank hols)

66 Nutley windmill

67 Burwash, Socknersh Manor, Mad Jack Fuller's Monument, Obelisk and Observatory, Bateman's (open Apr to end Oct, 11 to 6 Sat to Wed and Good Fri), watermill

68 Culham Court, temple

70 West Wycombe Park, caves, church and mausoleum (house and grounds open June, Mon to Fri 2 to 6· July and Aug 2 to 6

Sun to Fri; grounds only, Easter, May and Spring bank hols)

71 Hampden House and Chequers

72 Peckforton Castle

75 Lyme Hall (open Apr to end May, 2 to 5 Sat, 1 to 6 Sun and bank hols; June to Sept, 2 to 5 Tue to Sat, 1 to 6 Sun and bank hols; Oct, 1 to 4 Sat and Sun)

79 Edensor, Chatsworth House (open 1 Apr to 1 Nov, 11.30 to 4.30)

80 Padley Chapel

81 Peveril Castle (open mid-Mar to mid-Oct, 9.30 to 6.30 Mon to Sat, 2 to 6.30 Sun; mid-Oct to mid-Mar 9.30 to 1 Mon to Sat, 2 to 4 Sun)

85 Staunton Harold Hall, church (open Apr to end Oct, 11 to 1, 2 to 6 (or dusk) Wed to Sun, bank hols), Calke Abbey

88 Buckland church, Stanton village

91 Ledbury market hall, Church Lane, Eastnor Castle

92 Witley Court and church

93 Old Radnor church

94 Croft Castle (open May to end Sept, 2 to 6 Wed to Sun, bank hols; Apr and Oct 2 to 5 Sat, Sun, bank hols)

96 Dorchester-on-Thames and Abbey

97 Streatley

98 Alnutt's hospital, Mapledurham House (open Easter to late Sept, 2.30 to 5 Sat, Sun and bank hols), and village

105 Packwood House (open Apr to end Sept, 2 to 6 Wed to Sun; Oct, 12.30 to 4 Sat and Sun)

107 Medieval streets in Saffron Walden, Audley End House (open mid-Mar to mid-Oct, 1 to 5.30 Tue to Sun; open bank hol Mons) and estate village

108 Brocket Hall, Waterend, Shaw's Corner (open Apr to end Oct, 2 to 6 Mon to Thur, 12 to 6 Sun, bank hols; Mar and Nov, 11 to

5.30 Sun to Thur), and St Laurence's Church

109 Bridgewater Monument (open Apr to end Oct, 2 to 5 Mon to Thur, 2 to 5.30 Sat and Sun)

111 Old John's Folly, Bradgate House

115 Westgate in Louth, Raithby church

118 Holkham Hall (open July and Aug, 1.30 to 5 Sun, Mon, Wed, Thur; June and Sept 1.30 to 5 Sun, Mon, Thur), Burnham Overy watermill and windmill

120 Moot Hall at Aldeburgh (open June to end Sept, 10.30 to 12.30, 2.30 to 5 daily), the House in the Clouds

121 Badley church, Needham Market church

123 Arnside Tower

129 Dove Cottage and Rydal Mount (open 9.30 to 5 daily)

130 Townend (open Apr to end Oct, 2 to 5.30 Tue to Fri, and Sun, also bank hol Mons)

140 Cregneish Manx Museum (open May to late Sept, 10 to 1, 2 to 5 Mon to Sat, 2 to 5 Sun)

141 Peel Castle (open 10 to 5 Mon to Sun)

142 Hulne Abbey Gatehouse, Hulne Priory, Brizlee Tower, Alnwick Castle (open 2 May to 2 Oct, 1 to 5 Sun to Fri, exc bank hols)

145 Dunstanburgh Castle (open mid-Mar to mid-Oct, 9.30 to 6.30 Mon to Sat, 2 to 6 Sun; mid-Oct to mid-Mar, 9.30 to 4 Mon to Sat, 2 to 4 Sun)

146 Castle Howard (open 11 to 5 daily)

149 Bolton Abbey, Barden Tower

151 Kettlewell, Arncliffe

156 Rievaulx Terraces (open Apr to end Oct, 10.30 to 6 daily (exc Good Fri); Ionic temple closed 1 to 2), Rievaulx Abbey (open mid-Mar to mid-Oct 9.30 to 6.30 Mon to Sat, 2 to 6.30 Sun; mid-Oct to mid-Mar 9.30 to 4 Mon to Sat, 2 to 4 Sun)

162 Wallace statue, Dryburgh Abbey (open 24 Mar to 30 Sept, 9.30 to 7 Mon to Sat, 2 to 7 Sun; Oct to Mar 9.30 to 4 Mon to Sat, 2 to 4 Sun), Temple of the Muses
165 Falkland Palace (open 1 Apr to 30 Sept, 10 to 6 Mon to Sat, 2 to 6 Sun; Oct to Apr 10 to 6 Sat, 2 to 6 Sun)
177 Corra Castle
180 Inveraray village and Castle (open Apr to mid-Oct, 10 to 1, 2 to 5.30)
181 Gylen Castle
182 Craigend Castle, Mugdock Castle
183 Monzie Castle
184 Binnhill and Kinnoull Towers
185 Kenmore, Taymouth Castle
186 Blair Castle (open mid-Apr to mid-Oct, 10 to 6 Mon to Sat, 2 to 6 Sun)
190 St Govan's Chapel
194 St Illtyd's Church, Oxwich Castle
195 St Donat's Castle
198 Chepstow Castle and bridge, Tintern Abbey (open mid-Mar to mid-Oct 9.30 to 6.30 daily; mid-Oct to mid-Mar 9.30 to 4 Mon to Sat, 2.30 to 4 Sun)
199 Naval Temple
200 Clytha Castle, Bettws Newydd church
201 Llanthony Abbey
204 Conway Town Walls, Castle (open mid-Mar to mid-Oct, 9.30 to 6 daily; mid-Oct to mid-Mar, 9.30 to 4 Mon to Sat, 2.30 to 4 Sun) and Church Plas Mawr

Walks passing museums and gardens

11 Overbecks Museum (open Apr to end Oct, 11 to 1, 2 to 6, daily) and Garden
29 Minterne Magna wild shrub garden (open Apr to end Oct, 10 to 7, daily)
31 West Somerset Museum of Rural Life (open Easter to end Sept, 10.30 to 12.30, 2 to 4, Mon to Sat)
37 Countryside and Carriage Museum, Breamore (open July, 2 to 5.30, daily exc Mon and Fri; Aug, 2 to 5.30 daily)
43 Pines Garden, St Margaret's at Cliffe (open 8 to 6 daily)
53 Haslemere Museum (open Apr to Oct, 10 to 5 Tue to Sat, 2 to 5 Sun)
64 Priest's House Museum, West Hoathly (open Apr to Oct, 11 to 5.30 Mon and Wed to Sat, 2 to 5.30 Sun), Gravetye Manor (Gardens)
107 Museum (open Easter to end Sept, 11 to 6 Mon to Sat, 2 to 6 Sun and bank hols) and Bridge End Gardens, Saffron Walden
122 Dunwich Museum (open Mar to May, and Oct, 2 to 4.30, weekends; June, July, Sept, 2 to 4.30 Tue, Thur, Sat, Sun; Aug 2 to 4.30, daily)
129 Wordsworth Museum, Grasmere (open all year exc Christmas and Grasmere Sports Day, 9.30 to 5 daily)
177 New Lanark Visitor Centre (open 12 to 5, daily)
196 Afan Argoed Welsh Miners' Museum (open Apr to Oct, 10 to 6 daily; Nov to Mar, 10.30 to 5, Sat, Sun)

Walks passing archaeological sites

1 Hillfort, Dolebury Warren
3 Merry Maidens stone circle, stone crosses, Pipers standing stones
5 Chûn Castle, Chûn Quoit
17 Dartmoor clapper-bridges
29 Cerne Abbas Giant
30 Cow Castle
36 Wansdyke
37 Mizmaze

56 Bell barrows
59 Wolstonbury hillfort
61 Mount Caburn
72 Beeston Castle (open mid-Mar to mid-Oct, 9.30 to 6.30 Mon to Sat, 2 to 6.30 Sun; mid-Oct to mid-Mar, 9.30 to 4 Mon to Sat, 2 to 6 Sun)
86 Chedworth Roman villa (open Mar to end Oct 11 to 6 Tue to Sun)
91 British Camp
93 Offa's Dyke
94 Croft Ambrey
96 Dyke Hills and Castle Hill
101 Caer Caradoc
112 Burrough Hill hillfort
140 Mull stone circle
141 Tynwald Hill
157 Malo Cross, standing stones
178 Sculptured stones
179 Nether Largie linear cemetery, Kilmartin Cross and sculptured stones
187 Castell Dinas Bran
188 Gop Hill
199 King Arthur's cave
212 Offa's Dyke

Walks passing sites of industrial archaeology

4 Geevor mine, Levant and Botallack mines, Cornwall
5 Mineshafts and derelict mine buildings near Morvah
8 Treffry Viaduct, leats and aqueduct
20 Cliff railway at Lynton
30 Wheal Eliza
74 Quarry Bank Mill, Styal village
78 Lead mines in Derwent Gorge (Rutland and Masson Coverns open daily Easter to Oct, 10 to 5. High Tor open daily, 10 to dusk; Heights of Abraham open daily, 9 to dusk; cable car operates Easter to end Oct 10 to 5 daily, may be later in summer (times displayed)

82 Cressbrook Mill
89 Sapperton tunnel, Thames and Severn Canal
100 Snailbeach
110 Grand Union Canal, Wendover arm, Aylesbury arms, feeder reservoirs
113 Foxton Locks and inclined plane, Grand Union Canal
124 Whitehaven coal mines
125 Ravenglass and Eskdale Railway
126 Copper Mines Valley
132 Ullswater steamers
159 North York Moors Railway and original line
177 New Lanark
189 Vale of Rheidol Railway
196 Cymmer Argoed Welsh Miners' museum
206 North Wales Narrow Gauge Railway tunnel, Sygun copper mine (open daily Easter to Oct, 10 to 6)
207 Snowdon slate mine

Walks passing striking natural features

1 Burrington Combe
15 Vixen Tor and Pew Tors
17 Bellever and Laughter Tors
18 Hunter's Tor
20 Valley of Rocks
25 Hountstout Cliff and Chapman's Pool
26 Agglestone, Old Harry Rocks, Studland beach
27 Lulworth Cove, Fossil Forest
41 The Needles, Alum Bay
60 The Seven Sisters
78 Derwent Gorge
81 Winnat's Pass, Speedwell Cavern (open 9.30 to 5.30 daily, exc Christmas), Peak Cavern (open mid-Apr to mid-Sept, 10 to 6 daily, exc Christmas)
83 Wool Packs
84 Dove Dale
100 Stiperstones
125 Stanley Ghyll

130 Stock Ghyll waterfall
133 Bowder Stone, Lodore Falls
138 Striding Edge
140 The Chasms
141 Glen Maye
147 Hardraw Force
148 Kisdon Force, Catrake Force
149 The Strid
150 Kilnsey Crag
152 Janet's Foss, Gordale Scar, limestone pavement, Malham Cove
153 Gaping Gill, Ingleborough Cave (open Mar to end Oct, 10 to 5 daily)
155 Whitestone Cliff, Sutton Bank
157 Bridestones
159 Mallyan Spout
164 Bracklinn Falls
167 Linn of Dee
171 Rogie Falls
172 Quiraing
176 The Old Man of Hoy
177 Falls of Clyde
187 Eglysweg escarpment
188 Dyserth Falls
189 Devil's Bridge
197 Vale of Neath waterfalls
199 Near Hearkening Rock, Buckstone
202 Swallow Falls
203 Arthog waterfalls
211 Water-break-its neck

Walks notable for natural history (mostly in nature reserves)

18 Bovey Valley
20 Valley of Rocks (feral goats)
26 Godlingston Heath
30 Birch Cleavewoods
32 Horner Woods
36 Pewsey Down
41 Tennyson Down, Afton Marsh
50 Wye Down, Cuckmere Haven
56 Kingley Vale
77 Wolfscote Dale
80 River Derwent
82 Monsal Dale
96 Little Wittenham Wood

103 Roaches Estate (feral wallabies)
106 Wicken Fen
110 Marsworth Reservoir
116 Holme Bird Observatory
118 Overy marshes and Scolt Head
120 North Warren
122 Minsmere, Dunwich Heath, Westleton Heath
123 Morecambe Bay
124 St Bees Head
132 Ullswater
140 Calf of Man
144 Ross Back Sands
152 Janet's Foss, limestone pavement at Malham Cove
155 Lake Gormire
166 Morrone Birkwood
167 Cairngorms
175 Aberlady Bay, Gullane Bay
186 Diana's Grove
190 Bosherston lily ponds
191 Wooltack Point
198 Wyndcliff
203 Mawddach Estuary
208 Llyn Idwal

Walks starting from, or near, railway stations

6 St Ives
8 Luxulyan
9 Looe
13 Kingswear (for ferry to Dartmouth)
39 Brockenhurst
41 Lymington (for ferry to Yarmouth)
43 Dover
46 Wye
47 Shoreham, Otford
49 Sevenoaks
50 Cowden
51 Boxhill and Westhumble
53 Haslemere
54 Chilworth
58 Rowland's Castle
59 Hassocks
61 Lewes, Glynde
63 Hastings
68 Henley-on-Thames

71 Wendover
74 Styal
75 Disley
78 Matlock
80 Hathersage
81 Hope
83 Edale
91 Ledbury
95 Barnt Green
97 Goring and Streatley
99 Yorton
102 Church Stretton
105 Lapworth
109 Tring
110 Tring
117 Sheringham, Cromer
121 Needham Market
123 Arnside
124 Whitehaven
125 The Green (Ravenglass and
     Eskdale Railway; runs all year,
     exc 21 to 25 Dec; Mar to Easter,
     2 trips daily; Easter, 5 trips;
     mid-July to early Sept, 15 trips)
139 Marple
140 Port Erin (Isle of Man Steam
     Railway; runs end May
     to beg. Oct)
158 Great Ayton
159 Grosmont (BR, North York
     Moors Railway; runs all year)
161 Hebden Bridge
177 Lanark
182 Milngavie
184 Perth
186 Blair Atholl
189 Devil's Bridge (Vale of Rheidol
     Railway; runs Apr to Sept, 3
     times daily)
198 Chepstow
203 Morfa Mawddach
204 Conway
209 Betws-y-Coed

Walks with easy route-finding (no mountain ascents)

12, 13, 14, 19, 20, 21, 27, 34, 37, 43,
58, 70, 77, 78, 90, 96, 104, 106, 107,
108, 110, 116, 117, 118, 119, 129, 132,
140, 141, 142, 144, 145, 158, 160, 161,
163, 165, 167, 168, 169, 171, 172, 175,
177, 179, 181, 184, 185, 190, 191, 197,
198

Easy family walks (grade 1 or 2)

1, 8, 9, 12, 13, 15, 19, 20, 21, 26, 28,
34, 37, 38, 39, 40, 44, 45, 52, 54, 56,
58, 61, 63, 68, 69, 70, 72, 74, 75, 76,
77, 78, 79, 80, 85, 86, 87, 88, 89, 90,
94, 95, 98, 99, 103, 104, 105, 106, 107,
108, 110, 111, 112, 113, 116, 119, 120,
121, 125, 128, 129, 132, 142, 144, 145,
146, 147, 148, 149, 152, 156, 158, 159,
160, 161, 162, 163, 171, 175, 179, 182,
184, 185, 186, 190, 191, 194, 195, 207,
212